Place, Race, and

Ned Kaufman has been at the vanguard of historic preservation thought and activism for two decades. He has challenged preservationists to go beyond a traditional focus on beautiful buildings and become a part of a larger movement for social justice. *Place, Race, and Story* shows us the way by offering frameworks and case studies that both critique and provide inspiring examples of what a progressive preservation movement looks like.

—Max Page, Professor of Architecture and History at the University of Massachusetts and author of *The City's End: Two Centuries of Fantasies, Fears, and Premonitions of New York's Destruction*

Preservationists usually focus on the how; Ned Kaufman reminds us to ask why we are preserving. Then he thoughtfully answers, showing us how preservation can better connect us and our places through the shared stories in people's lives.

—Michael Holleran, Associate Professor and Director of the Graduate Program in Historic Preservation at the University of Texas at Austin and author of *Boston's "Changeful Times": Origins of Preservation and Planning in America*

Caught up in the day-to-day struggle to keep America's heritage intact and alive, preservationists don't often think about our movement's origins, milestones, and philosophical underpinnings. That's a mistake. Ned Kaufman's thoughtful and enormously useful book reminds us of the importance of knowing how we got here—and how the journey changed us.

—Richard Moe, President, National Trust for Historic Preservation

In *Place, Race, and Story*, author Ned Kaufman shows how central themes in the American experience shape the preservation of heritage—themes of race and diversity, progress and tradition, love of place and lust for property. Ranging from the eighteenth-century roots of preservation practice to the dilemmas facing New York today, these essays, many available for the first time, outline a re-energized, progressive preservation practice for the twenty-first century.

Through both big-picture essays considering preservation across time, and studies of specific sites, each chapter traces the themes of place, race, and story. From the African Burial Ground and the Audubon Ballroom in New York to the sugar plantation at Hanapepe, Hawai'i, *Place, Race, and Story* will inform, provoke controversy, and give the next generation of preservationists path-breaking tools for meeting the heritage challenges of the future.

Ned Kaufman is a founder of Place Matters and of Pratt Institute's graduate program in Historic Preservation. He is the author of studies ranging from Victorian Gothic to the management of public lands and historic sites.

Place, Race, and Story
Essays on the Past and Future of Historic Preservation

Ned Kaufman

Routledge
Taylor & Francis Group

NEW YORK AND LONDON

First published 2009
by Routledge
270 Madison Ave, New York NY 10016

Simultaneously published in the UK
by Routledge
2 Park Square, Milton Park, Abingdon, Oxon, OX14 4RN

Routledge is an imprint of the Taylor & Francis Group, an informa business

Transferred to Digital Printing 2011

© 2009 Taylor & Francis

Typeset in Sabon by Swales & Willis Ltd, Exeter, Devon

Library of Congress Cataloging in Publication Data
Kaufman, Ned.
Place, race, and story : essays on the past and future of historic preservation /
Ned Kaufman.
p. cm.
Includes index.
1. Historic preservation—United States. 2. Historic sites—Conservation and
restoration—United States. 3. Historic buildings—Conservation and restoration
—United States. I. Title
E159.K38 2009
363.6'9—dc22
2008053043

ISBN 10: 0-415-96539-X (hbk)
ISBN 10: 0-415-96540-3 (pbk)
ISBN 10: 0-203-87614-8 (ebk)

ISBN 13: 978-0-415-96539-2 (hbk)
ISBN 13: 978-0-415-96540-8 (pbk)
ISBN 13: 978-0-203-87614-5 (ebk)

CONTENTS

FIGURES

ACKNOWLEDGMENTS

Many people have contributed to this book. Because it took shape in pieces, and over years, some have surely forgotten how they helped. Gustavo Araoz, Susan L. Ball, Daniel Bluestone, Peg Breen, Robert Chapman, Charles Halpern, the late George L. Hersey, Emily Kaufman, the late Roger Lang, Antoinette Lee, Eric Sandeen, Joel Snyder, the late Clive Wainwright, and Anthony C. Wood have all helped to shape the book's basic ideas in one way or another. For stimulating ideas from other countries, and for much appreciated hospitality, I would like to thank: (from Argentina) Nani Arias Incollá, Jorge Bozzano, Mercedes Garzón, Fabio Grementieri, María Isabel Hernández Llosas, Irene Meninato, Federico del Pino, and Sol Rubio; (from Australia) Sharon Sullivan; (from Bolivia) Mireya Muñoz and Xavier Nogales; (from Germany) Gabi Dolff-Bonekämper; (from South Africa) Andrew Hall; (and from the UK) Karen Adams, Chris Bailey, Ruth Dass, Kevin Farmer, and Michael Hamish Glen. For Chapter 2, I am indebted to Michael Gerrard, Kathleen Howe, Dorothy Miner, and Elizabeth Savage. For Chapter 3, I benefited from the uncensored opinions of numerous respondents, many of whom are mentioned in the text, or in the appendix to that chapter. For Chapters 4 and 5 the support of Eve Blau, Phyllis Lambert, Richard Pare, Pauline Saliga, and John Zukowsky was essential; Henry Millon also provided an insightful reading. For Chapter 6, I have to thank the Municipal Art Society and the chair of its preservation committee, Charles A. Platt, for their institutional support, the J. J. Kaplan Fund for its financial support, Noela Hooper for research assistance, and Madeline Rogers for her expert editing; the members of the committee which advised on its contents are listed in the appendix to that chapter. Chapter 7 would not have been possible but for my fellow members of the African Burial Ground Coalition, William E. Davis, Jr., Joan H. Geismar, Eileen Millett, Gene A. Norman, the late Kellis Parker, and Samara Swanston. Patricia Ruggles offered expert statistical advice on Chapter 8; Felicia Mayro provided a valuable reading. For Chapter 9, Michael Gerrard, Harvey Molotch, Charles Starks, Mark Walters, and Charles Wilkinson provided helpful materials as well as searching critiques. Ruth Dass's support was essential for Chapter 10, as was Randall Mason's and Max Page's for Chapter 11. At various points along the way, the Association for Interpretation, Canadian Centre for Architecture, Centro para la Conservación del Patrimonio (Argentina), Getty

Research Institute, Harewood House, Harvard's Graduate School of Design, InterCulture, the Nathan Cummings Foundation (especially its environmental discussion group led by Charles Halpern, James Hillman, and Mark Walters), the National Park Service, Pace University's Institute for Environmental and Regional Studies, Pratt Institute, and the office of Rafael Viñoly Architects all provided congenial settings for developing or sharing ideas. They would not have come together into a book without the patient and intelligent editors at Routledge. Finally, thanks go to the librarians and archivists at the Art Institute of Chicago, British Library, Canadian Centre for Architecture, Columbia University's Avery Architectural Library, Library of Congress, Pratt Institute, the Victoria and Albert Museum, and countless other repositories, who not only help researchers but, when necessary, stand up against censorship and intimidation.

Though many people helped formulate the ideas in this book, they do not necessarily subscribe to them. And errors of fact, emphasis, or interpretation are, of course, mine alone.

How Place, Race, and Story Are Changing
Preservation Today

I

When it comes to thinking about the future of the craft, people who conserve heritage separate temperamentally into two groups. One looks inward, seeking progress in the elaboration of tighter criteria and more stringent professional standards. The other looks outward, seeking new areas to meddle in, new problems to take on. The first group gauges the success of preservation efforts by internal measures such as authenticity or technical competence. The second defines success by external measures such as social relevance or utility.

While I don't oppose criteria or standards, I am more comfortable with the second group. It is a question of choosing which risks to run, and I would rather risk occasionally confusing ourselves (and the public) about what we are doing than become irrelevant. Of what use, one might ask, are measures of professional competence if they don't correspond to some standard of social value? If preservation were fundamentally a technical discipline, then it would be appropriate to gauge its success by technical measures. But it is not: it is a social practice, part history and part planning. Its ultimate goal is not fixing or saving old things but rather creating places where people can live well and connect to meaningful narratives about history, culture, and identity.

It is in that spirit, then, that this book explores the interactions between place, race, story, and historic preservation. It has four parts. The first sets out basic issues and concepts. The second, a sort of historical parenthesis, explains how architectural historians and collectors learned to study buildings in place and, simultaneously, to remove them from places. The third focuses on New York City. The final part returns to basic concepts and to proposals for the future.

Place, race, and story are not new issues for historic preservation: they are merely unsolved. Within my own professional experience, race and place arose in New York City in the early 1990s. That was when destruction threatened both the Audubon Ballroom—site of Malcolm X's assassination—and the eighteenth-century African Burial Ground (Figures 7.1 to 7.6). The campaigns to save them, discussed in Chapter 7, brought forth unprecedented enthusiasm from the city's African American communities. They also posed difficult problems for the city's established preservation organizations, which at first were reluctant to join them. One reason was that these sites posed puzzling challenges to preservation orthodoxy, challenges having to do with story and place. The problem was that they did not meet the architectural criteria which could almost have guaranteed their protection. True, the Audubon Ballroom was a distinguished building, but it was in very poor condition. In any case, the merits of the building were easily overshadowed by interest in Malcolm X. As for the African Burial Ground, it was not a building at all. And although many other cemeteries were already protected by landmark status, their above-ground appearance (grass and headstones) was consonant with their significance and associations. By contrast, the African Burial Ground was covered with buildings which bore no relation to the story of what was underneath. And that story was the point: it was the story of all of the long-forgotten Africans and African Americans who had helped build New York. The African Burial Ground thus presented a regulatory puzzle. But the bigger puzzle was that, for both sites, history, stories, and associations counted for much more than appearance and indeed formed the basis for broad popular concern.

One response to the challenges posed by these and other sites of historical interest is represented by Chapter 6, a study carried out for and first published by the Municipal Art Society of New York in 1996. Outside New York, of course, the issues of place and race have arisen in other ways and at other times, but the important point is that they have arisen nearly everywhere. And everywhere they have prompted profound questions. How should preservationists balance the competing claims of disparate sites and divergent values recognized by culturally diverse groups? How do historical narratives, traditions, and memories define sense of place? Is the persistent whiteness of the profession a problem in a society becoming ever more diverse? These and other questions about place, race, and story deserve answers.

While these issues continue to challenge preservationists, they also produce conflicts and misunderstandings between the profession and members of communities, including communities of color. Most widespread and damaging is the utter incomprehension or distrust with which many view historic preservation, as if it were something irrelevant or even harmful. This view is partly a product of outdated notions of historic preservation as an elite curatorial practice related to the care of ornate mansions and national shrines, but it gains credence from preservation's lack of racial diversity and from its apparent inability to take on or even understand the heritage issues of communities of color: "We're tired of educating yet another Anglo," remarks Guadalupe San Miguel, a professor of history and an expert on Mexican-American heritage.[1] At times it is also fed by the apparent narrowness of preservation's conception of community and place. "I am appalled," said a Russian immigrant to the chair of New York's Landmarks Commission at a hearing a decade or so ago, "that we are not allowed to be emotional." The speaker was convinced that his feelings of attachment to the place at issue were relevant to public decisions about the buildings that defined it and therefore ought to be considered. But the chair admonished him that the law provided no room to consider residents' feelings, stories about places, or indeed anything other than the "appropriate-ness" of the proposed changes. Her understanding of the law was accurate, and therein lay the problem. People's feelings of attachment to particular places can be very strong, and, though they may appear unrelated to what preservation professionals identify as "resources," they do at some point become part of the cultural heritage of places: at times an important part. The inability or some-times unwillingness of heritage preservers to make room for them is an example of the professional standards problem: impeccable standards main-tained at the expense of broader relevance or helpfulness, and perhaps of a certain dimension of human empathy.

One of the ways people express feelings about places is by telling stories. By stories, I mean first of all anecdotes or recollections of things that happened in specific places. Place-stories may also include written histories (especially when lodged in people's minds and remembered or retold to visi-tors), traditions, rituals, and habits whose repetitive enactment brings people regularly back to specific places. These latter stories are essentially narratives which people tell by reenacting them. They range from the trivial to the sacred and may be reenacted by specific individuals, groups such as labor unions or Gaelic football teams, or categories of people such as debutantes, break dancers, or first-time visitors to New York. Some of these traditions or habits may be reenacted over generations.

Stories live in people's minds. But they also live in places: indeed specific places are often essential to their survival. And though we cannot see and touch stories in the same way as buildings, they too are part of the meaning of places and, eventually, of their heritage. Seen in this way, the cityscape becomes a *storyscape*; sites that collect interesting stories, meaningful memo-ries, or intense feelings of attachment become *story sites*. Learning to see story sites and storyscape can reveal unexpected heritage values in places, as Chapters 1, 2, and 9 explain.

This is obviously not the only way to understand places, or sense of place. A character in Jim Harrison's popular novel *Dalva* expresses an almost diamet-rically opposed view when he remarks, "'We always destroy wilderness when we make it represent something else.'" To Fred, the great challenge is to see places for what they really are, which means stripping away, rather than reveal-ing, all of the stories and memories associated with them. At the moment when we are tempted to hear "'the voices of those who lived there speaking from every petroglyph and pottery shard,'" he advises us, we "'must let the desert go back to being the desert.'"[2] According to this view, associations and symbolism are not legitimate dimensions of sense of place but rather distrac-tions. The real estate industry provides another opposing point of view, one which evaluates places in terms of tradable quanta of real property. To propo-nents of these views (and there are many others), the notion of storyscape may seem irrelevant or even annoying. Still, the ideas behind storyscape seem to correspond well with the experiences of many ordinary people.

I could have chosen terms other than story and storyscape to get at some of the same ideas. Association is one. The idea behind association is that certain ideas or images, not physically belonging to places and buildings, can nonetheless become linked to them so that the act of seeing the place or building calls up the images in the viewer's mind. The theory has a long history, going back to the eighteenth-century philosophical doctrine of the "association of ideas." John Locke invented the phrase, which soon covered a wide range of mental processes. Through association, a picture could conjure up the image of its original, the shape of a flower its aroma, a cause its effect. Association could be rich in narrative possibilities: thus landscape painters and architects exploited the ability of smoke rising from a cottage chimney to bring to the viewer's mind an image of a family comfortably seated around the hearth, as well as other images of domestic felicity. At its extreme, the idea of association could lead some aesthetic philosophers to assert that "nothing is beautiful in itself," but only by virtue of its ability to invoke the viewer's associational capacity in some pleasing way. The power of association shaped life as well as art: some asserted that the fruits of all past experience became available to the human mind as a reservoir of associative response from which to nourish imagination and insight.[3]

Preservationists in the twenty-first century continue to rely on the idea of association as a sort of catch-all for a wide range of cultural meanings which cannot be fully explained by a building's physical fabric or architectural character. Yet for many modern practitioners the word has lost most of its philosophical underpinnings. The Burra Charter, an admirable and influential preservation manifesto developed in Australia in 1988, defines association rather vaguely as "the special connections that exist between people and a place."[4]

A second useful concept, introduced in Australia, is social value. The Burra Charter lists social value as one kind of cultural significance (along with aesthetic, historic, and scientific, i.e. archaeological) and explains that it "embraces the qualities for which a place has become a focus of spiritual, political, national or other cultural sentiment to a majority or minority group."[5] Early in the 1990s, the Australian Heritage Commission began to explore social value in greater detail, in part because it was felt that existing heritage assessment methods were too narrow and failed to reflect people's "deep sense of attachment to place." Social value, then, was explicitly connected to specific places, and a study on the subject listed several kinds of places that informants believed were particularly likely to possess it. They include public places, informal meeting places, public entertainment places, and places associated with recent significant events. As the generally public nature of these places suggests, social value does not stress personal or individual feelings so much as "collective attachment to places that embody meanings important to a community."[6]

A third related concept is that of intangible cultural heritage, which refers essentially to all the aspects of culture that do not take material form. Like associational qualities, this covers a broad range. According to the 2003 UNESCO Convention for the Safeguarding of the Intangible Cultural Heritage, it includes "oral traditions and expressions including language . . .;

performing arts (such as traditional music, dance, and theatre); social practices, rituals and festive events; knowledge and practices concerning nature
and the universe; [and] traditional craftsmanship."[7] Intangible cultural
heritage is usually linked to place in a general way; examples recognized by
UNESCO include Albanian folk iso-polyphony, oxcart traditions in Costa
Rica, and the Ifa divination system of Nigeria. Some other officially recognized manifestations are more closely tied to particular places, like the carni-
vals of Oruro or Barranquilla, in Bolivia and Colombia respectively. In fact,
it is easy to find much more specific pairings of intangible heritage and
places: Indian vision quest sites, the basilica of Lourdes in France (or for that
matter Our Lady of Lourdes Grotto in Staten Island, New York), and so on.
But official thinking, at least within UNESCO, has not sought to underline
or indeed to understand the linkages between intangible heritage and place.
As a result, though the conservation of intangible heritage has added a new
range of important specializations to the field, it has not yet fulfilled its
potential to enrich our understanding of place or augment the tools available
for protecting places.

Each of these concepts has great potential to enrich heritage conservation
in the United States. Still, I shall talk here mainly about story and storyscape.
Why? Terms like association, intangible cultural heritage, and even social value
sound rather dry and theoretical. By contrast, story is concrete and mundane.
You do not need to be a trained professional to tell or appreciate stories. They
are the common coin of humanity, and life without them is nearly unimagin-
able. Listening to stories and analyzing them for what they reveal about
people and places are specific things that heritage conservers can do to get at
social value and sense of place. They are also ways of connecting with places
at a deep human level which architectural or urbanistic evaluation sometimes
frustrates. Also, because stories live at once inside people and places, they
remind us of an important truth: that the meaning of a place lies neither
wholly in its forms and materials nor wholly in the minds of the people who
use it, but arises out of the interaction of the two. Finally, stories have specific
properties that make them valuable to heritage conservation, because when
people frame their thoughts in narratives they reach into realms of feeling and
value that the profession's scientific or evaluative methods do not capture.
Some preservationists may fear that working with such subjective, unscientific
material will compromise the profession's standards. But this need not
happen: instead, preservationists can collaborate with cultural geographers,
sociologists, anthropologists, environmental psychologists, and folklorists to
develop new standards that capture the power of stories.

II

What is race? And does the topic belong in historic preservation? The answer
to the latter question is yes. The first, however, has no very good answer.
Geneticists have showed that supposed "racial" characteristics like skin color
represent an insignificant portion of the human genetic makeup, and that
more genetic similarity may exist among people of different races than of the

same. The classifications used to define race lack any logical validity, and historians have shown that, time and again, the pseudo-scientific reasoning which societies have produced to explain race-based inequalities has been circular: racial differences did not already exist in nature but were posited after the fact in order to justify slavery and other forms of racism. There is a case to be made that race does not exist.

There are other reasons not to talk about race. Some argue that class, rather than race, is the real root of inequity in our society. Others urge attention to the impact of gender roles and the continuing problem of sexism. Some who oppose discussion of race are motivated by explicitly political considerations. Conservatives have long opposed government programs and mandates like affirmative action that recognize and seek to counter racial inequality as a factor that leads to different outcomes in education, employment, and other areas of society. They deny the importance of race as a social factor. Some race-deniers seem anxious mainly to suppress the anger that destabilized society in the 1960s, and that could do so again. But other critics on the left also fault identity politics for dividing groups along racial lines when shared economic interests should bring them together.

Race Matters, asserted leading black intellectual Cornel West in a widely read book published in 1993. Yet now scientists tell us that race does not exist, pundits that it is no longer important, social reformers that it is beside the point. Should West's book be retitled *Race Mattered*? The organizers of a public forum, held in New York in 2008 to discuss the Obama candidacy, evidently thought not: they titled their event *Race Still Matters*. Why? One reason is that most of society continues to act as if it does, ignoring the scientists and the pundits. Though discredited as a scientific concept, race—or, rather, skin color—has not vanished as a social reality. The difference between being born white and being born black continues to shape the life chances of millions of Americans and to underlie deep disparities in wealth, health, and opportunity. The repercussions of race and racism also continue to shape historic preservation. To point this out is not to underestimate the impacts of class and gender discrimination. But they have affected preservation in quite different ways whose treatment goes beyond the scope of this book.

Racial disparities can be found everywhere in society. The gap in wealth is fundamental and deep and, despite decades of social and political reform, it has not disappeared. At the beginning of the twenty-first century, the median net worth of white Americans was $81,700; that of African Americans was $10,000. Non-whites were more than twice as likely as whites to lack the necessary financial reserves to cover basic household needs during short periods without income: in fact, the gap in asset poverty had actually widened slightly since 1984.[8] Racial disparities continue to affect people's earning potential in sometimes surprising ways. For example, a 2007 study found that light-skinned immigrants made more money on average than those with darker skins; researchers attributed the difference to discrimination. According to Vanderbilt University professor Joni Hersch, "being one shade lighter has about the same effect as having an additional year of education."[9]

Environmental health is another important racial indicator. In 2007, twenty years after a groundbreaking study found that communities of color were significantly more likely than whites to be exposed to toxic waste, a follow-up study found these disparities almost unchanged. "It is ironic," summed up United Church of Christ Executive Minister M. Linda Jaramillo,

> that twenty years after the original *Toxic Wastes and Race* report, many of our communities not only face the same problems they did back then, but now they face new ones because of government cutbacks in enforcement, weakening health protection, and dismantling the environmental justice regulatory apparatus.[10]

The impacts of pollution remain so racially divided in part because of the persistence of segregation. Sociologists Massey and Denton have shown how residential segregation has actually increased since the nineteenth century, in northern as well as in southern cities, and they argue that it is not decreasing now. Measuring five different dimensions of segregation, they describe a condition of hypersegregation in which African Americans are radically isolated from civic participation as well as public services, job opportunities, good education, and housing choices. According to this measure, they found that sixteen metropolitan areas were hypersegregated as of the early 1990s, including such major cities as Chicago, Dallas, Los Angeles, New York, and Philadelphia.[11] Another study by James Loewen documents the little-discussed but pervasive phenomenon of "sundown towns": towns and suburbs where African Americans were not permitted to remain after dark. He describes how, decades after the civil rights movement, zoning rules, school boards, and realtors continue to protect the whiteness of communities across the country. And he shows how historians and social commentators—including historical societies and preservation agencies which install historical markers—have suppressed public awareness of these facts.[12]

Because Part Three of this book focuses on New York, it may be appropriate to consider briefly the question of segregation there. Everyone who rides the subways or walks the streets of midtown Manhattan is impressed by what former Mayor David N. Dinkins famously called the city's "gorgeous mosaic." Yet New Yorkers go home to sleep in segregated neighborhoods. Sociologists Andrew A. Beveridge and Susan Weber use a different measure from Massey and Denton but reach a similar conclusion: New York City is hypersegregated.[13] They rely on a statistical measure called D, or the index of dissimilarity: D scores above 0.7 indicate "major levels of segregation/separation." In 2000, all five boroughs of New York scored above 0.7, with Manhattan at 0.77, Queens at 0.82, and Brooklyn at 0.86. These scores had not declined since 1980. So extreme indeed was segregation in Brooklyn that, among the 12,000 inhabitants of the eight contiguous census tracts that make up the neighborhood of Bensonhurst, the 2000 census could not find a single black resident—and this although Brooklyn was 36 percent black. It was in this neighborhood, not coincidentally, that in 1989 a group of enraged young white residents killed Yusef Hawkins, a young black man shopping for a used car. The crime was typical of the racial enforcement that characterized sundown towns and could have happened at any time during the previous century.[14]

Residential segregation perpetuates racial inequality by limiting access to education, jobs, housing, medical care, environmental health, and consumer staples like healthy food and medicine. It also shapes what people believe. Among the consequences of sundown-town segregation described by Loewen are its pervasive impacts on people's attitudes, including (for whites) negative racial stereotyping and an internalized feeling that privilege is a natural right, and (for African Americans) pessimism about social change and feelings of discomfort in many places. So it is perhaps not surprising that political attitudes also diverge sharply around race. CNN exit polls found that in the 2004 presidential election, while the Republican candidate won by a margin of 58 percent among white voters, the Democratic candidate won by an almost equal percentage among Latino and Asian voters and by an enormous 88 percent margin among African Americans.[15] No other demographic factor came close as a predictor of voting patterns.

Not surprisingly, perceptions of race relations divide particularly sharply along racial lines. In 2008, a *New York Times*/CBS poll found that 59 percent of African Americans surveyed thought that race relations were generally bad, as compared to only 34 percent of white respondents. The same poll found that 43 percent of black respondents felt that they had been stopped by the police at least once solely because of their race: only 7 percent of whites reported a similar incident.[16]

The impacts of race and racism can be seen everywhere, yet for many years the United States has lacked a constructive public discussion of race issues. Such a conversation is much to be desired and if, as some hope, the political rise of Barack Obama facilitates it, one can only hope that it will include heritage conservation. Race and racism shape what historical plaques and markers say (and what they do not say). They influence which buildings and neighborhoods preservationists choose to save and which to ignore, which causes they take up and which they reject, which constituencies they serve and which they overlook. And they have created a heritage profession which is almost as segregated as any sundown town. These are problems whose solution will require honest public discussion.

The fact is that, nearly everywhere, heritage matters are inextricably entwined with issues of race, diversity, and social justice. While fighting to end apartheid in South Africa, the African National Congress understood that very well. Though the country faced every imaginable social, economic, and political problem, the party moved quickly after it was unbanned in 1990 to develop new heritage policies. After the elections of 1994 brought the ANC to power, the party continued to list "cultural expression and identity" alongside language rights and access to land as one of the "most emotive matters," indeed one of the most serious issues, facing the new government. Five years later the National Heritage Resources Act put a new heritage framework in place. In language strikingly different from that of traditional heritage legislation, the Act emphasized that heritage educates, promotes empathy, "contributes to redressing past inequities," and "facilitates healing and material and symbolic restitution."[17]

In other countries too, advocates for racial justice have harnessed the power of heritage: in Bolivia, for example, where the empowerment of indigenous peoples involves the most pressing questions of land rights, educational reform, language, industry, religion, and politics. In 2006, Evo Morales marked his inauguration as the country's first indigenous president with a traditional ceremony conducted by native Aymara priests at the prehistoric ruins of Tiwanaku.[18] In the United States, movements for African American, American Indian, Native Hawaiian, and Hispanic rights have all included efforts to rediscover and reinterpret history and culture. And they have led to important developments in heritage conservation, such as the Native American Graves and Repatriation Act of 1990, and some of the programs described in Chapter 3.

We need not look to liberation movements to demonstrate the close ties between heritage matters and issues of rights and justice. History and culture—heritage—are implicitly present whenever Americans discuss funding for black colleges and universities, the administration of law on tribal reservations, the effects of affirmative action, Indian gambling, new immigration policies, the role of religion in politics, the status of Puerto Rico, the meaning of the First, Second, and Fourth Amendments, the extent of women's rights to birth control, zoning amendments in Chinatown, and a host of other questions. History continues to shape current options on these and other issues of rights and responsibilities, and all sides in the debate use interpretations of history to buttress their cases.

All of this means that those who conserve heritage are under constant pressure to adjust their work in order to support this or that interpretation. There are no doubt some who believe that the profession should seek to insulate itself from these pressures. But it is hard to understand how separating heritage from society's most pressing concerns can enhance the cause of conservation, or how turning away from these concerns can strengthen the work of those who seek to conserve it. In any case, it is questionable whether this kind of detachment can even be achieved. Certainly the current state of historic preservation is not one of independence but of partisanship disguised as professional objectivity. At any rate the profession opens itself to this charge when, for example, a not-for-profit organization decides to allocate its resources to protect a historic site admired by architectural historians rather than another one that is important to the local Chinese, Filipino, Mexican, African American, or Puerto Rican community—and yet that organization lacks a single board or staff member from the affected community, or even a contact within it who might be able to explain the importance of the overlooked site. Decisions are made in this way every day, in cities and towns across the country, not because of overt racism but because the system is structured to produce this result. It would be senseless to suggest that every non-profit agency should include representatives of every social faction. Yet when most preservation organizations lack representation from most of the racial or ethnic groups in the United States' diverse society, and, when they purport to establish policy or allocate resources in the interests of the entire community, then insulation has become isolation. Something has to be done.

The question is what. If insulation from the social pressures of race and equity is neither possible nor desirable, then we must consider how best to engage them. Will preservation do so with eyes closed or open? Reluctantly or constructively? With nostalgia for a non-existent past or zest for a future that it can help to construct?

Obviously vigorous public debate, and probably public pressure, will be needed to settle these questions. But there is more than one way to frame a debate over race and preservation, and the question of vocabulary is important. Among preservationists, "cultural diversity" (or the shorthand "diversity") and "multiculturalism" are popular. They have a cheerful ring: they make people feel good. In fact, many North Americans endorse cultural diversity as a positive trait of their society. Yet they do not always define it very carefully: to some it means mutual respect for other people's customs, to others the chance to enjoy Peruvian cooking on Tuesday and Malaysian on Wednesday. The problem of vagueness is not limited to the United States. A Venezuelan heritage expert defines cultural diversity as "the social capital of humanity, which, added to financial capital, scientific-technological capital, and environmental diversity, ought to allow the construction of sustainable actions in the search for greater equality in the quality of life of those who inhabit this planet."[19] Like many formulations of diversity, this fails as a prescription or policy guidepost because it does not identify the problem. If diversity is something that is desired, then what is the obstacle to achieving it? If it is something we already have, then what is wrong with the status quo?

The language of diversity leads to other confusions. Diversity of what? The word means so many different things. Cultural diversity is very popular in Argentina, as in the United States, but it means something quite different there. When North Americans express pride in diversity, they generally mean the blending of people from all over the world—Africans, Asians, Latin Americans, Europeans, and Natives. But when Argentines express similar pride, they are more likely to mean the mixture of immigrants from Italy, Spain, and Poland. The difference is understandable. In 2006, no less than 97 percent of Argentina's population was of European descent. In the United States, though census figures are not exactly comparable, at least 30 percent of the population is of African, Asian, or Native descent or, if European in origin, has arrived via Latin America. With such different factual backgrounds, it is easy for misunderstandings to arise. But sometimes the language of diversity appears to be emptied of any meaning whatsoever: thus the U.S. National Park Service's website in 2007 identified diversity as the "keynote" of the nation's forty-three presidents—that unbroken succession of white males of northern European descent who have held the office for more than two hundred years.[20]

Whatever diversity means in this context, it does not mean race. This may indeed be one reason for the word's popularity: race is a difficult topic and, while "diversity" appears to help people talk about it, it sometimes does exactly the opposite. Paeans to diversity promote avoidance of other difficult topics too. One would hardly guess from them that there is anything the matter with the way income, housing, education, or jobs are distributed. The language of diversity is not very good at acknowledging injustice, and has little to say about rights, and even less about wrongs. For these purposes, and for driving towards genuine solutions, the heritage discussion needs also to admit the harder language of race, including phrases like discrimination, inequity, and racism.

At the risk of oversimplifying, one may point to three aspects of preservation that particularly demand to be studied through this double lens: content, process, and constituency. The first concerns the narratives that preservation offers to the public. For a long time, books and classes on American history failed to give adequate recognition to the multiplicity of races and ethnic groups which produced it. They glanced over the sufferings caused by injustice as well as the achievements of marginalized groups. The resulting narrative not only diminished immigrant and minority groups but also gave a slanted picture of American history. During the past thirty years or so, a flood of scholarly and popular books has helped to correct the problem by giving Americans access to more complete historical narratives. Yet, despite notable advances, historic preservation has not kept pace. The picture of American history presented by historic sites continues to undervalue the experiences and contributions of immigrants, working people, and communities of color.

There are surely many reasons for this lag. One is the inertia built into the conservation of buildings. Raising money or organizing political support to preserve a historic site can take years. Interpretive programs, once instituted, become hard to revamp. Change to official lists such as the National Register encounters bureaucratic resistance and is at best incremental. And since all of these changes in heritage conservation draw on prior changes in both the academic and the political spheres, conservation may well lag. But another reason for the slowness of change is the absence of powerful interest groups pushing for it. And this in turn points to the second issue which needs attention: process. While many effective organizations are nurturing the cultural heritage of particular groups (a few are discussed in Chapter 3), most of these groups have at best a distant relationship with historic preservation. Some have not yet discovered it, while others have had bad experiences with it and have written it off. The preservation profession itself, as noted earlier, remains heavily dominated by white people of European descent. This is true of the staffs of non-profit agencies as well as their boards of directors, of the professoriate as well as government officialdom. It is true from the smallest local groups up to the national level. The demography of the profession, quite simply, does not remotely resemble the diversity of the country as a whole. This impairs the profession's ability to gather information, respond to new ideas, and act effectively on behalf of heritage. The process of preservation—who is hired, how information is gathered and decisions made—needs to be updated.

The third issue is constituency. Beyond what is being preserved, or who is getting the jobs, it is useful to ask who benefits from the work, and who will support it. Right now, most of the benefits are going to relatively affluent white people, who also provide both funding and political support. They form the bulk of preservation's constituency. This puts preservation in a trap. If it is to remain useful to an evolving society, and continue receiving public support, preservationists will have to figure out how to broaden the constituency: how to provide benefits to, and work on behalf of, more diverse communities.

The definition of preservation's potential constituency has changed dramatically in recent decades and is continuing to change. Moreover, it varies from region to region. In New York in the early 1990s, the emergence of grassroots campaigns for the African Burial Ground and the Audubon Ballroom demonstrated the potential for a significant African American constituency. New York also had a large and politically influential Hispanic population, mainly Puerto Rican (897,000 Puerto Ricans lived in New York in 1990). But at that time Latino groups showed no special interest in historic preservation. A preservationist working in New York during those years might therefore be forgiven for treating the question of race and preservation (as Chapters 6 and 7 do) as if it were basically a matter of black and white. Even in 1990, preservationists in other regions would have been less likely to reach this conclusion: on the West Coast, for example, the claims of Asians and Mexicans or Chicanos for inclusion would have been obvious.

Today, the possibilities for redefining preservation's constituency are more open than ever, for recent decades have brought significant population changes throughout the country, and historic preservation will have to take these into account. Most obviously, residents of Hispanic origin have now surpassed African Americans as the largest non-white group. Within New York, the Dominican population grew by 165 percent between 1980 and 1990, the Mexican population by 173 percent; large gains were registered also among Colombians and Ecuadorans, so that New York's Hispanic population is now not only larger but more diverse than ever before. There are growing Mexican communities in every part of the country: in Wichita, Kansas, Eugene, Oregon, and Green River, Wyoming, among thousands of other places. Immigrant flows also continue to be very large from other countries: from China, the Philippines, and India, for example. The landscape of race and diversity is being transformed; while this process poses significant challenges for historic preservation, it also opens up extraordinarily exciting possibilities for revitalization.

III

The campaign for New York's African Burial Ground (Figures 7.1 to 7.3) sparked the creation of an alliance between the environmental justice and historic preservation movements. It was not an obvious pairing. The environmental justice movement had arisen to prevent harms like toxic waste and effluents. The preservation movement had arisen to protect goods like beauty, craftsmanship, and symbols of patriotism. The African Burial Ground campaign dramatized the fact that, just as communities of color suffered disproportionately from environmental harms, so white communities profited disproportionately from preservation benefits. This realization opened the way to an alliance. By thinking of the heritage values represented by the African Burial Ground as environmental goods, it became possible to see them as legitimate objects of an environmental justice campaign. Moreover, argued some advocates, the fight for environmental equity need not be limited to preventing harm but could also encompass demands for a fair share of environmental goods. Did not communities of color have a right to historical and cultural sites along with clean air and water? And was this not an *environmental* right?

Unfortunately, this promising alliance did not outlast the campaign, at least in New York. But elsewhere, environmental justice movements have been fusing notions of environment and cultural heritage in ways that are highly promising for historic preservation. Many Native groups not only assert their deep historical connections to places but also point to culture, myth, and place affection, alongside ecology and health, as reasons to protect them. Moreover, they resist separating these arguments into the neat but artificial categories favored by heritage practice: archaeological versus historical significance, local versus national importance, natural versus cultural, and so forth. Typical in this regard is the Australian Aboriginal concept of *Tjurkurpa*, sometimes inadequately translated as "Aboriginal law." In 1985, the Australian government turned over ownership of Uluru–Kata Tjuta National Park to Aboriginal peoples and entered into a joint management relationship with them. A management plan drafted in 1999 sought to put the principles of Tjurkurpa into practice. According to the plan, Tjurkurpa not only explains how the landscape was formed but also unites the place's traditional residents with each other and with the place. It "embodies the principles of religion, philosophy and human behaviour that are to be observed in order to live harmoniously" there. According to Tjurkurpa, "humans and every aspect of the landscape are inextricably one." Managing the park according to Tjurkurpa imposes many specific obligations, such as learning the country well enough to find food, water, and natural medicines; burning brush and keeping waterholes clean; visiting sacred sites; teaching and learning stories; "making the country alive—for example, through stories, ceremony and song"; remembering the past; and thinking about the future.[21] Here, protecting heritage is integral to attaining environmental justice; conversely, protecting the environment is integral to conserving heritage.

In the United States, the Indigenous Environmental Network is a grassroots group established in 1990; its mission is to "protect our sacred sites, land, water, air, natural resources, health of both our people and all living things, and to build economically sustainable communities."[22] Offering a "native perspective," the Indigenous Environmental Network stresses that environmental justice goes beyond toxic and nuclear contamination to include "protection of all areas that are sacred and that are culturally and historically significant to our peoples." Similar fusions of heritage and environmental justice can be found elsewhere within the Native world. In Hawai'i, non-profit groups including Kahea and Kohanaiki 'Ohana seek to protect both heritage and the environment in their campaigns for Native Hawaiian rights (Figures 9.1 and 9.2). Kahea describes itself as an alliance of Native Hawaiian cultural practitioners and activists, together with environmentalists and people concerned with social justice; its motto is "The Land and the People Are One." Along with more conventional environmental campaigns, the group has fought to maintain public access to beaches for traditional activities like surfing, and to prevent the encroachment of additional telescopes on the summit of Mauna Kea, the tallest mountain in the Pacific and a sacred place in Hawaiian religion. Earthjustice, a non-profit public interest environmental law firm, maintains a regional office in Hawai'i: it has helped Native Hawaiian groups protect sacred and cultural sites in Oahu's Makua Valley from the U.S. Army, and gain access to them for ceremonial purposes.

Native efforts to win acknowledgment for the environment's cultural dimensions have been fueled not merely by a general desire for political legitimacy but more specifically by an effort to win back land captured or stolen by colonizers. In the absence of Western-style title deeds, a key part of these efforts is to demonstrate the Native group's deep connection with the place in question. Thus in 1990 the Wichí of northwestern Argentina, threatened by growing pressure from settlers and government-sponsored development projects, sought to buttress their land claims. They called in anthropologists to help collect their oral history and document their long association with the land. A similar process has been given legal weight in Australia. There, in 1992, the High Court affirmed in the Mabo decision that indigenous land rights had not been wiped out by the European conquest: the following year, the Australian Federal Parliament passed the Native Title Act, which created a process for adjudicating land claims. The test for proving a land claim was to demonstrate a long historical link to the place in question. As one observer explained, in "post-Mabo" Australia, local history had "a new moral and environmental edge to it. . . . Suddenly there is a real reason—politically, morally—why we need to engage in a local sense of place."[23] No longer merely interesting, the cultural heritage of particular places had become instrumental to people seeking environmental justice.

Even where land claims have not been directly involved, the senses of place articulated by Native peoples across the Western Hemisphere and the Pacific have challenged and inspired may preservationists with their emphasis on place affection, reverence, ritual, tradition, spiritual immanence, and story-telling. It is not that the physical configuration and appearance of places do not matter in these views; rather, they have been fused with both ecological and narrative dimensions. This has taken Native American and Native Hawaiian senses of place far beyond the categories of significance spelled out by the National Register of Historic Places or local preservation ordinances.[24]

Native ideas of place and story are reshaping preservation practice in concrete ways. The Australian concept of social value, discussed above, owes much to Aboriginal influence.[25] The rise of the African National Congress in South Africa shifted the emphasis from monuments to new categories of heritage such as places and objects "to which oral traditions are attached or which are associated with living heritage," graves and burial goods, sites of significance to the history of slavery, and heritage areas.[26] In the United States, Native American relationships to land, including concepts of traditionally significant and sacred places, prompted the National Register of Historic Places to develop the concept of traditional cultural properties. Hawaii's law requiring the preparation of Cultural Impact Statements, discussed in Chapter 9, is yet another example.

An important step toward redefining preservation practice may have been taken in September 2007, when the United Nations adopted the Declaration on the Rights of Indigenous Peoples. The Declaration provides a good summary of the role of cultural heritage in struggles for social and environmental justice.[27] It attributes to indigenous people rights "not to be subjected to forced assimilation or destruction of their culture"; to "practice and revitalize" cultural traditions and customs (including the protection and development of archaeological and historical sites); to maintain spiritual and religious traditions (including "religious and cultural sites"); to secure repatriation of human remains and ceremonial objects; to revitalize and transmit "histories, languages, oral traditions, philosophies, writing systems and literatures"; and to benefit from the "dignity and diversity of their cultures, traditions, histories and aspirations."

Article 31 appears to continue in the same vein but in fact introduces a new problem. It asserts the right of indigenous peoples to "maintain, control, protect and develop their cultural heritage, traditional knowledge and traditional cultural expressions." These phrases point to a grave new threat to Native rights. Backed by governments, Western and multinational corporations are seeking to profit from traditional medicines, seeds, and genetic codes, as well as traditional narratives and artistic patterns. Worse, they are asserting ownership and control over these previously unowned elements of Native culture. Native groups have responded by elaborating concepts like "traditional knowledge" (sometimes "traditional cultural knowledge") and "traditional cultural expressions" in order to give legally defensible shape to the vast reservoir of blended cultural and environmental knowledge which they have built up over centuries of living in places. It may seem fanciful to connect the current battle over intellectual property with preservationists' efforts to grasp sense of place, but the corn and rice, the legends and artistic designs are products of the place, along with the land itself. Moreover, the effort to patent and own these products of the land is but the latest episode in the West's 500-year campaign to privatize and seize the land itself. It is the most extreme attack by those who would own places on the rights of those who would merely use or inhabit them, a conflict discussed further in Chapter 1. Indeed it is the latest incarnation of the peculiarly Western idea that everything can be owned and used for profit—even the genes of indigenous individuals who did not knowingly part with them and will never profit from them. It is, in short, the new frontier in the entwined struggles for heritage rights to place and culture.

The Inuit have had the misfortune to reach a different frontier. In 2005, the Inuit Circumpolar Conference (ICC), an international organization representing over 150,000 Inuit in Alaska, Canada, Greenland, and Russia, petitioned the Inter-American Commission on Human Rights to oppose climate change caused by the United States.[28] The petition requested hearings in northern Canada and Alaska and asked the Commission to declare the United States in violation of human rights spelled out in the 1948 American Declaration of the Rights and Duties of Man, among other international agreements to which the United States adhered. It alleged that global warming was not only drastically altering the Arctic environment but also destroying Inuit property, threatening traditional culture and ways of life, and infringing on basic human rights to land, property, culture, residence, preservation of health, and means of subsistence. The catalogue of depredations was long and depressing. The melting of permafrost causes buildings and infrastructure to collapse; the thinning and unpredictable behavior of sea ice impedes the hunting of seals and sometimes kills the hunters; the disappearance of sea ice in some places exposes coastal communities to devastating storms; unprecedented weather patterns make it impossible to forecast accurately or to travel safely; declining fish and game stocks threaten traditional foodways and cause malnutrition; changes in the snow prevent the building of igloos or the teaching of this ancient skill to younger generations. The best scientific predictions are that these and other impacts of climate change will become more, rather than less, severe over time. The ICC petition proves, exhaustively and with tragic irony, the linkage between cultural heritage, the environment, and place. And it shows how the disruption of one destroys the others. As the petition claims, "Inuit culture is inseparable from the condition of their physical surroundings."[29] In such a situation, environmental rights are equally inseparable from cultural heritage rights: the fight for one must be the fight for the other.

Since filing the petition, ICC chair Sheila Watt-Cloutier has been loaded with awards and recognition, including a Nobel Peace Prize nomination. Climate scientists, including the Intergovernmental Panel on Climate Change, have amply confirmed the petition's charges. Yet the Inter-American Commission on Human Rights rejected the petition, refusing to send the case to the Inter-American Court of Human Rights. In language Watt-Cloutier called "evasive and dismissive," the Commission made the astounding claim that the 175-page petition had not provided enough information to "enable us to determine whether the alleged facts would tend to characterize a violation of rights protected by the American Declaration."[30] This did not mean that the United States was untouched by the plight of the Inuit. The following year, the U.S. Environmental Protection Agency (EPA) mounted its own effort to stem the impact of global warming on the Arctic: it solicited proposals for projects to "communicate climate change impacts on, and adaptive responses in Indian Country and Alaskan Native Villages." The idea was to develop a "communications strategy" to transmit information on the impacts of climate change to Arctic villages, tribes, policy-makers, and the public. This important work was to be accomplished for the sum of $40,000.[31] It was not entirely coincidental that, the very same month, the United States voted against the United Nations Declaration on the Rights of Indigenous Peoples. The General Assembly adopted it anyhow, by a vote of 144 in favor, 11 abstaining, and 4 opposed.[32]

IV

Within the United States, Native people have not been alone in seeking to expand the heritage profession's sense of place. Immigrant peoples have done so too. One reason is that they have generally also been communities of working people, and, though the criteria used by many landmark groups are excellent at divining value in mansions, museums, and civic buildings, they do not do so well with tenements, warehouses, docks, roadside chapels, and canneries. Many such sites are not only undistinguished as architecture but have also been poorly built, altered, and generally used hard. Like the African Burial Ground, they pose the problem of how to protect places which matter more for their stories than their material or aesthetic values. One answer is offered by New York's Lower East Side Tenement Museum, which uses its historic tenement building as a setting for interpretive programs focused on the stories of former occupants. In fact, interpretation is essential for preserving the histories of communities of color, immigrants, and working people. But its success depends on preservation, as the Lower East Side Tenement Museum demonstrates. Interpretation, then, cannot substitute for preservation: even if interpretation remains the ultimate goal, the hard preservation challenges posed by places associated with immigrant groups and communities of color must be solved.

And that means not only the public history challenge of telling good stories but also the urban or regional planning challenge of sustaining good neighborhoods. Here as well, a socially equitable practice requires an expansion of preservation's sense of place. The environmental justice movement reminds us that preservation can help correct deep inequities in the management of our cities. Indeed the potential is great. Communities of color continue to be disproportionately targeted by urban redevelopment and highway, railroad, shopping mall, and other development schemes: preservationists could get involved in more of these causes, working with community planners and neighborhood groups not merely to protect iconic sites but to sustain the living heritage of communities. The centers of dozens of American cities, as well as inner-ring suburbs, are currently suffering from a wave of economic collapse, vacancy, and abandonment. Detroit has lost half of its peak population, while cities like Buffalo, Philadelphia, Baltimore, Birmingham, Cleveland, Pittsburgh, Rochester, and Saint Louis have hundreds of thousands of abandoned properties. Worst affected are poor neighborhoods and neighborhoods of color, which are frequently located in the oldest parts of the city—the sections with the most historic architecture and cityscapes. Urban collapse is simultaneously causing environmental injustice and destroying heritage.

Though city administrations and planners have long been aware of these trends, many preservationists are only beginning to confront the heritage catastrophe they represent. For it is not only buildings which are disappearing but also a legacy of urban living, not only cityscape but also storyscape. Though a counter-current is bringing some relatively affluent young people (and empty-nesters) into "rediscovered" downtown neighborhoods, this does not appear sufficient to stop the loss of buildings, much less of community lifeways. On balance, it would not be a victory for heritage conservation if the destruction of urban neighborhoods is allowed to run its course so that well-off newcomers can lovingly restore and reinhabit their shards.

If preservationists have been slow to respond to the collapse of historic cities, that may be because the problem seems impossibly large. It has been tempting, moreover, to dismiss it as someone else's problem—urban planners, community development corporations, mayors, or what have you. Whatever the reason, historic preservation has not played a large enough role in attacking a problem that affects millions of people. Surveying the panorama of American cities, economist Mason Gaffney notes the "malignant propensity to pour the national treasure into dead monuments while their living matrices starve, rot, and crumble."[33] Preservationists may bristle at the criticism, but they could be doing more to prove Gaffney wrong.

Like other challenges that arise at the intersections of place, race, and story, preserving the heritage of collapsing cities is a big, unfamiliar, but socially important problem. It is the kind of problem a reenergized preservation movement could take on, one in which success is measured more by social impact than by technical skill or correctness. Though preservation cannot solve the nation's racial problems, cure environmental injustice, or save everyone's sacred places, it can renovate itself by addressing these challenges. There will be mistakes, failures, and "learning experiences." But practitioners will gain new skills, and eventually there will be successes too. In the process, the profession will become more useful to society.

NOTES

1. Personal conversation, May 2003. See Chapter 3.
2. Jim Harrison, *Dalva* (New York: Washington Square Press, 1988), 237–238.
3. See Walter Jackson Bate, *From Classic to Romantic: Premises of Taste in Eighteenth-Century England* (New York: Harper & Row, 1946), esp. 93–128. The quotations are from Abraham Tucker and David Hume (pp. 103, 112).
4. Burra Charter, 1988, I.15, at http:www.icomos.org/australia (consulted July 2008).
5. Australia ICOMOS, "Guidelines to the Burra Charter," 1988, 2.5, at http:www.icomos.org/australia/ (consulted July 2008).
6. Chris Johnson, *What Is Social Value? A Discussion Paper* (Canberra: Australian Government Publishing Service, 1992), 4, 7–9, 10. For a more recent development of these ideas, see Denis Byrne, Helen Brayshaw, and Tracy Ireland, *Social Significance: A Discussion Paper*, 2nd ed. (Hurstville, NSW: New South Wales National Parks and Wildlife Service, 2003).

7. UNESCO: Intangible Cultural Heritage website, at http:www.unesco.org/culture/ich/index.php?pg=00002 (consulted July 2008).

8. Edward N. Wolff, "Recent Trends in Wealth Ownership, 1983–1998," *Jerome Levy Economics Institute Working Paper No. 300* (May 2000), see e.g. Table 7; and Asena Caner and Edward N. Wolff, "Asset Poverty in the United States, 1984–99: Evidence from the Panel Study of Income Dynamics," *Review of Income and Wealth*, Series 50, No. 4 (December 2004): 493–518, see esp. pp. 500ff. and Table 3.

9. Associated Press, "Study of Immigrants Links Lighter Skin and Higher Income," *New York Times* (January 27, 2007).

10. Robert D. Bullard et al., "Toxic Wastes and Race at Twenty, 1987–2007: A Report Prepared for the United Church of Christ Justice and Witness Ministries" (United Church of Christ, March 2007), x, vii. According to the new study, people of color on average formed 56 percent of the population of neighborhoods hosting commercial hazardous waste facilities, versus only 30 percent of neighborhoods that lacked such facilities. Poverty rates were 1.5 times higher in host areas than in non-host areas, but concentrations of African Americans and Hispanic/Latinos were 1.7 and 2.3 times higher.

11. Douglas S. Massey and Nancy A. Denton, *American Apartheid: Segregation and the Making of the Underclass* (Cambridge, MA, and London: Harvard University Press, 1993), esp. 74ff.

12. James Loewen, *Sundown Towns: A Hidden Dimension of American Racism* (New York and London: New Press, 2005).

13. Andrew A. Beveridge and Susan Weber, "Race and Class in the Developing New York and Los Angeles Metropolises, 1940–2000," in David Halle (ed.), *New York and Los Angeles: Politics, Society, and Culture* (Chicago and London: University of Chicago Press, 2003), 63.

14. David Halle, Robert Gedeon, and Andrew A. Beveridge, "Residential Segregation, Racial and Latino Identity, and the Racial Composition of Each City," in Halle (ed.), ibid., 157, 166, 169–170.

15. CNN.com Election Results, at http:www.cnn.com/ELECTION/2004/pages/results/states/US/P/00/epolls.0.html (consulted July 2008).

16. http:www.nytimes.com/ref/us/polls_index.html. Other examples of racial disparities are too numerous and varied to cite. Crime statistics provide one more instance. According to the U.S. Department of Justice, although the rates at which both blacks and whites were victimized by serious violent crime dropped dramatically between 1973 and 2005, the gap between the victimization rates for black and white people actually increased: the black rate was almost 1.9 times the white rate in 1973 but more than twice the white rate in 2005 (U.S. Department of Justice, Office of Justice Programs, Bureau of Justice Statistics, at http:www.ojp.usdoj.gov/bjs/cvict_v.htm#race, consulted July 2008).

17. South Africa, Department of Arts, Culture, Science and Technology, "White Paper on Arts, Culture and Heritage," June 4, 1996, n.p.; and National Heritage Resources Act of 1999, in Republic of South Africa, *Government Gazette*, Vol. 406, No. 19974 (April 28, 1999), Preamble. See also Andrew Hall, "Rethinking Heritage Conservation in South Africa in the Post-Apartheid Era: Innovation in Policies and Legislation Since 1994," in *La Dimensión Social del Patrimonio: VIII Congreso Internacional de Rehabilitación del Patrimonio Arquitetónico y Edificación*, vol. "Memoria/Identidad . . ." (Buenos Aires: Centro Internacional para la Conservación del Patrimonio, Argentina, 2006), 31–35.

18. See Mireya Muñoz, "The Case of Bolivia: Diversity and Interpretation of its Cultural Heritage," in *Interpreting the Past: Who Owns the Past? Heritage Rights and Responsibilities in a Multicultural World*, Proceedings of the Second Annual Ename International Colloquium (Brussels: Flemish Heritage Institute, Province of East-Flanders, and Ename Center for Public Archaeology and Heritage Presentation, 2007), 225–228.

19. Ciro Caraballo Perichi, "El patrimonio cultural: capital social o capitalización de los bienes?," in *La Dimensión Social del Patrimonio*, op. cit., vol. "Gestión/Planes. . .", 13.

20. http:www.nps.gov/history/history/online_books/presidents/bio.htm (consulted September 2007).

21. "Uluru–Kata Tjuta National Park Draft Plan of Management" (February 1999), *Australian Indigenous Law Reporter* 4 (December 1999), at http:www.austlii.edu.au/au/journals/AILR/1999/47.html (consulted September 2008).

22. http:www.ienearth.org/iensub.html (consulted July 2008).

23. Tom Griffiths, quoted in Denis Byrne, Helen Brayshaw, and Tracy Ireland, *Social Significance: A Discussion Paper* (Hurstville, NSW: New South Wales National Parks and Wildlife Service, 2003), 68.

24. As an example, see Keith Basso, *Wisdom Sits in Places: Landscape and Language Among the Western Apache* (Albuquerque: University of New Mexico Press, 1996). See also Andrew Gulliford, *Sacred Objects and Sacred Places: Preserving Tribal Traditions* (Boulder: University Press of Colorado, 2000); and Clara Bonsack Kelly and Harris Francis, *Navajo Sacred Places* (Bloomington and Indianapolis: Indiana University Press, 1994).

25. For other dimensions of Aboriginal influence on Australian conservation practice, see, for example, Anthony English, *The Sea and the Rock Gives Us a Feed: Mapping and Managing Gumbaingirr Wild Resource Use Places* (Hurstville, NSW: New South Wales National Parks and Wildlife Service, 2002); and Denis Byrne and Maria Nugent, *Mapping Attachment: A Spatial Approach to Aboriginal Post-Contact Heritage* (Sydney: New South Wales Department of Environment and Conservation, 2004).

26. South Africa National Heritage Resources Act of 1999, op. cit., Chapter I, 1.3.(2)(b), (g), (h), and (i)(i).

27. At http:www.un.org/esa/socdev/unpfii/documents/DRIPS_en.pdf (consulted July 2008). The phrases quoted are from Articles 8, 11, 12, 13, 15.

28. "Petition to the Inter-American Commission on Human Rights Seeking Relief from Violations Resulting from Global Warming Caused by Acts and Omissions of the United States," submitted by Sheila Watt-Cloutier, with the Support of the Inuit Circumpolar Conference, December 7, 2005, at http:www.inuitcircumpolar.com/files/uploads/icc-files/FINALPetitionICC.pdf (consulted July 2008).

29. Ibid, p. 5.

30. Jane George, "ICC Climate Change Petition Rejected," *Nunatsiaq News*, December 15, 2006, at http:www.nunatsiaq.com/archives/61215/news/nunavut/61215_02.html (consulted July 2008).

31. EPA website, at http:www.epa.gov/air/grants/07-13.pdf (consulted September 2007).

32. The opposing votes, in addition to the United States, were Canada, New Zealand, and Australia.

33. Mason Gaffney, "The Role of Ground Rent in Urban Decay and Revival: How to Revitalize a Failing City," in Clifford Cobb and Joseph Giacalone (eds.), *The Path to Justice* (Malden, MA and Oxford: Blackwell, 2001), 58.

PART I

Place, Race, and Story: Basic Issues

INTRODUCTION: NEEDS AND OPPORTUNITIES

The following chapters were originally drafted at the request of organizations representing three distinct groups of professionals—academics, lawyers, and government officials—but they should be perfectly accessible to general readers interested in preservation. They introduce the basic themes of this book.

Chapter 1 is about the concept of place. More and more preservationists are appreciating the importance of place, and practitioners as well as scholars are seeking to understand what factors are most important in defining places. But the research remains compartmentalized among a dozen different fields: environmental psychology, sociology, anthropology, economics, political science, folklore, cultural geography, public health, landscape architecture, urban planning, transportation planning, community planning, and so on. Here, claims are made for the economic services provided by places; there, for their affective qualities. Some researchers stress the formative influence of places in early childhood, others their organization as markets. What we lack is a comprehensive description of what place *is*. Even more fundamentally, we lack a broadly accepted language of place: a persuasive and flexible vocabulary to describe the characteristics of places, explain why they are important to people, and argue for their protection. An interesting example of this absence was noted some years ago by the sociologist E. V. Walter, who pointed out that the English language does not even have an adjective corresponding to the noun "place." The word "spatial" emerged from "space" in the nineteenth century, but, seeing no future in the word "platial," Walter instead proposed "topistic," from the Greek *topos*, together with the noun "topistics" for the study of what he called placeways.[1] These coinages have not caught on. In any case, until we have a language of place and know how to use it, we will not have a public policy consensus in favor of sustaining places.

The need for a language of place is not merely academic: it is made urgent by the wrenching changes made to places across the country every day. Chapter 1 suggests that the social value of stability in places remains underestimated, even by preservationists. But it also argues that people need and deserve more control over the future of their own places, whether the result be to promote, in some cases, stability or, in others, change. The right to choose between these two options is an important dimension of environmental equity, and one that is very unfairly distributed. Sharing it more equitably will help people preserve their places and their heritage; some ways of doing this are discussed in Chapter 9.

Chapter 2 introduces the idea of storyscape to the discussion of place. It is a simple idea, which starts with the concept of story sites. A story site is a place that supports the perpetuation of socially useful or meaningful narratives. It may provide space for carrying them out or simply call them to people's mind when they visit or use it. The stories may be about history, tradition, or shared memories. They may be recollected or passed on to other people: if passed on, they may be either told or reenacted—the difference is between going to a diner with friends every Sunday morning and telling someone, "That's where I used to go for brunch on Sundays." Story sites include all really successful historic sites, but they also include many places that preservationists and planners overlook. In general, their value to people—and specifically their heritage value—cannot be estimated simply by looking at them: one has to talk to people and observe how they behave. By putting together all of the story sites in a neighborhood, city, or region, one arrives at a storyscape, which is simply a landscape or cityscape seen through the lens of stories, memories, and traditions. In Chapter 2 I explain the ways in which story sites and storyscape are valuable to society, as well as the reasons why preservationists should identify and protect them. I also discuss some of the legal mechanisms available for safeguarding them. But those mechanisms are severely inadequate. Historic preservation law does not really recognize story sites: environmental law, surprisingly, does somewhat better. But a new framework is needed to recognize and protect storyscape.

With Chapter 3 I turn to race. What is the diversity deficit? It is the gap between the nation's racial and ethnic diversity and the preservation profession's lack of diversity. Just as diversity characterizes both the nation's past and its present, so the absence of diversity affects both how preservation portrays the past and how it organizes itself professionally in the present. This admittedly broad statement, to which there are of course exceptions, is based on reviewing actual preservation programs and on interviewing many heritage experts outside the profession's white mainstream. Chapter 3 helps readers see the current state of historic preservation as these experts see it and introduces readers to some of what they have been accomplishing outside its mainstream. This chapter also proposes specific steps that can be taken to close the diversity deficit. While this represents a challenge, it also offers a tremendous opportunity to carry out important preservation work, creating new partnerships, launching projects that will expand the nation's stock of heritage, and engaging in intellectual exchanges that can revitalize the profession.

NOTE

1. Eugene Victor Walter, *Placeways: A Theory of the Human Environment* (Chapel Hill and London: University of North Carolina Press, 1988), 20–21.

CHAPTER 1

Placing Preservation

The following chapter originated as the keynote address for a symposium called "Senses of Places: Urban Narratives as Public Secrets," and held at Pace University's Institute for Environmental and Regional Studies in New York City in 2004.

In pondering the phrase "urban narratives as public secrets," it occurred to me that the greatest public secret of all is place itself. We live in place: it is as fundamental an aspect of our environment as air, water, or the ground. We talk about place all the time. We can distinguish between different kinds of places—urban, suburban, and so forth. Yet we don't really know what place *is*. It is as if we could distinguish among different kinds of fruit—grapefruit, peach, or banana—without having a clear concept of "fruit" itself. Perhaps place is not a thing at all. Maybe it is just a quality—*placeness*, as one might say, or *place-itude*. That would explain why we are not always certain when we have left one place and entered another—a sort of confusion that never occurs with a fruit. We are in no doubt about when we have stopped eating a kumquat and bitten into a grape. And yet, when we have crossed City Hall Park, we may not be certain whether we are still in the same place or in a different place. And if we are still in the same place, then what happens when we cross Canal Street? How about Houston Street? For that matter, what happens when we go home at night? At what point do we enter the place of home? Is the neighborhood a place? The house or apartment? The dining room? A chair? These questions may seem trivial. But all sorts of public policy decisions hinge on how we answer them. And these decisions are not trivial at all.

The fact is, we live in place and depend upon place, yet for the most part we take our places for granted and do not think much about how they got there, what we owe to them, or what is required to maintain them in the way we like. This would not be a problem if powerful actors in our society were not also operating almost constantly on place, shaping and reshaping it in profound ways. They build and tear down buildings, construct highways, install sodium-vapor lights, erect fences and gates, extend runways, move bus stops, restore fire towers, clear paths, and fortify streams with riprap and beaches with jetties. They adopt rules that preserve this building while allowing that one to be demolished, that encourage the development of thirty-story buildings but prohibit forty-story buildings, that steer invest-ment in this direction but not in that. They create and approve plans to turn thousands of acres of field and forest into spreading suburbs. They declare other land to be wilderness, or they permit the construction of roads so that it cannot be declared wilderness. Our places are being dramatically transformed—often not for the better—and all of this with hardly a thought, much less a consensus, about what place really *is*, what it does for us, or what we need from it.

I recently had occasion to confront my own ignorance on this subject, thanks to my colleagues at Pace University, where I had the opportunity to serve as visiting scholar in environmental studies. To my seminars I brought some proposals about law, policy, land use, and concepts of property. I wanted to explore these concepts with students and faculty and thought I would begin by simply laying down a few basic concepts about place—about what place *is*—before getting to the meat of the issue. But the participants' persistent questions soon made me realize that I myself had taken too many things for granted. Just what *was* this thing I called place? And how did I know? I quickly realized how little, in fact, I knew.

I also realized how much work still needs to be done in findings ways to talk about place—ways that people will understand and recognize as true. Given the rapid pace at which the places of North America are being trans-formed, this kind of study may seem to be an unaffordable luxury. Yet before the national policy debate about places can be reoriented—before we can even *have* a meaningful debate—we will need better arguments with which to oppose such conventional wisdom as: change is the inevitable price of progress, which is always good; those who seek to preserve (fill in the blank) are simply standing in the way of progress; and democracy depends upon the unhindered operation of markets, whose decisions are always right. I am not suggesting that the defenders of places, whether they call themselves environ-mentalists, historic preservationists, or community advocates, should walk away from the struggle because their tools leave something to be desired. I am calling upon the ranks of intellectuals to help them out, to work with them to create the conceptual underpinnings of a new and persuasive argument on behalf of places. This is the only way we will ever turn the tide.

Where to start? Perhaps by putting up two views of place that usefully bracket much of what we might want to say about this most basic of concepts. First, a passage from Tony Hiss's *The Experience of Place*, a book that electrified some New Yorkers when it appeared in 1990. The author is describing a stroll through New York's Grand Central Terminal:

> I came out of the East Side IRT subway into the more southerly of the two
> straightaways and immediately found myself part of a stream of people, four
> and five abreast, all of them looking straight ahead and moving at a fast New
> York clip toward the concourse along the right-hand side of a tunnel only
> twice the width of the stream itself. Toward me along the left-hand side of the

corridor . . . came a second stream of people. . . . I felt hurried along. My breathing was shallow and slightly constricted; my neck and shoulders were tight. . . . Then these two streams of people crossed a second pair of streams, running at a right angle to them. The stream I was in entered a space with a slightly higher, cross-vaulted ceiling, and I had a moment to feel alarmed in retrospect, wondering why no one had bumped into anyone else during the crossing. . . . In another step, I was in the concourse. I knew this first not by sight but by body sensation, sounds, the absence of a smell, and breathing. I felt as if some small weight suspended several feet above my head that I had not till then even been aware of, had just shot fifteen stories into the air. I straightened up, my breathing slowed down, and I noticed that the scentless air around me was warm. . . . All the sounds that reached me seemed to have been fused into a single sound. Vast and quiet, it seemed to be evenly distributed throughout the great room. This sound, pleasant in all its parts, regular in all its rhythms, and humorous and good-natured, seemed also to have buttoned me into some small, silent bubble of space. I felt that I wasn't quite walking but was paddling—or somehow propelling—this bubble across the floor.[1]

Next, a passage from A. B. Guthrie's *The Big Sky*. Published in 1947, this was one of the first great western novels. It established the Montana school of writing and became a formative influence on how people have written about western places:

> When they were going again his thoughts went back. As a man got older
> he felt different about things in other ways. He liked rendezvous still and
> to see the hills and travel the streams and all, but half the pleasure was in the
> remembering mind. A place didn't stand alone after a man had been there
> once. It stood along with the times he had had, with the thoughts he had
> thought, with the men he had played and fought and drunk with, so when he
> got there again he was always asking whatever became of so-and-so, asking if
> the others minded a certain time. It stood with the young him and the former
> feelings. A river wasn't the same once a man had camped by it. The tree he saw
> again wasn't the same tree if he had only so much as pissed against it. There
> was the first time and the place alone, and afterwards there was the place and
> the time and the man he used to be, all mixed up, one with the other.[2]

These two experiences of place could hardly be more different. Hiss is all about sensory perception. Guthrie is all about memory. Is one more right than the other? Not necessarily. I myself have moved from a Hiss position to one more like Guthrie's. I remember how, many years ago, I took a group of fourteen-year-olds from small towns and suburbs in the Poconos to St. Paul's Cathedral in London. None of these children had ever been in a building remotely like this magnificent stone cathedral, with its spacious vaults and, soaring overhead, the great dome. I wanted them to sense the reverberant volume of air above their heads, to take in the sound that distant footfalls made on stone floors under that echoing vault. My understanding of place, in short, was much like Hiss's.

After we had spent some time in the church, I took them up into the dome, and we walked around the base of the lantern and looked out over all of London. We talked about how different it felt up there from inside the church. After I returned, the group leader seemed perturbed. She asked again and again if everyone was all right—an odd question, I thought, since it was evident that all the boys had enjoyed the experience. I learned later that one of my adolescent charges had a history of suicide attempts; no one had thought to tell me this before the outing.

Had I been more perceptive, I would have taken from this episode the realization that places can mean very different things to different people: that what looks to one person like a grand place to climb up to might strike someone else as the perfect spot from which to jump off. The difference lies in what each brings to the encounter, and in this sense Guthrie is clearly right: the place doesn't stand alone, even if a man has *never* been there. Yet it was only later that I began to appreciate the importance of story—memory, tradition, legend, association, inner narrative—in place. I do not want to jettison the sensory or the aesthetic, but I now find it necessary to emphasize what I shall call the Guthrie point of view, partly because it has been so little acknowledged in the public debate—and because its acceptance can so dramatically deepen our appreciation of place.

Beyond sensory perception and memory, there is a third way of looking at place. This third way holds Hiss and Guthrie together the way a single pair of manacles might hold two prisoners. Here is how John Logan and Harvey Molotch explain this third way:

> Any given piece of real estate has both a use value and an exchange value. An apartment building, for example, provides a "home" for residents (use value) while at the same time generating rent for the owners (exchange value). Individuals and groups differ on which aspect (use or exchange) is most crucial to their own lives. For some, places represent residence or production site; for others, places represent a commodity for buying, selling, or renting to somebody else. The sharpest contrast . . . is between residents, who use place to satisfy essential needs of life, and entrepreneurs, who strive for financial return, ordinarily achieved by intensifying the use to which their property is put.[3]

A bit dense, perhaps. And hard-edged, in contrast to the warm humanity of Hiss or Guthrie. Worse, Logan and Molotch go on to explain that efforts to maximize use and exchange values are inherently in conflict, that the system pretty consistently favors those who trade in places over those who wish to live in or enjoy them, and that in the end exchange values too often trump other dimensions of use or pleasure.

We cannot afford to ignore the insights of Logan and Molotch, because in our aggressively capitalistic society many of the values Hiss and Guthrie see in places are constantly imperiled by a marketplace which recognizes only the value of exchange, and by a political culture which turns to that same marketplace as the final arbiter of value. Humanists may disdain or profess a lack of interest in the marketplace, but they should get involved in the civic machinery that Logan and Molotch describe, not only to influence the outcomes it produces but also to understand them better. It is extraordinarily enlightening to see how the process actually works, and no amount of theory can replace the insights gained from participating in it. As you continue to study place, to elaborate a language of place, these insights will be particularly fruitful. Indeed they are essential, if this knowledge and this way of speaking are to lead to an improvement in the places we inhabit, rather than to mere discourse.

I want now to suggest a few specific directions in which it might be most helpful to pursue this research. Recently, at a street fair in Manhattan, I stopped in front of a booth that was selling marionettes. They were simple, cheap things that resembled fantastic animals made of bright-colored fake fur. They reminded me of marionettes I had seen in street fairs in Leningrad (as it then was), and they prompted me to think about marionettes and puppets. I could visualize the delight of children playing with puppets, whether in St. Petersburg or in New York. I recalled that, at one time, adults had delighted in puppets too. Many still do. I began to think about the passing of time, because puppets, after all, have been with us for thousands of years. I wondered how the world might have been different if, after the first puppets had been invented, there had been no more. What if a great many people enjoyed these new inventions, but then, when the inventor died, there was no one, and no way, to carry them on? What if, instead of being transmitted from person to person and generation to generation, the idea had simply stopped? What if the entire world was like this—a world in which everyone had to reinvent and rediscover everything from scratch— food, games, clothing, religious beliefs . . . *everything*? A world in which, whenever someone died, *all* of that person's knowledge disappeared?

Trying to envision this unthinkable situation helped focus my mind on certain things whose existence we take for granted, things like culture, tradition, and memory. All of these phenomena point away from the nightmare scenario described above and encourage us instead to visualize one in which knowledge is easily conferred and leaps gracefully from person to person, and from moment to moment. But the words we use to name these dimensions of our social existence don't really illuminate the issue. Memory, in particular, is problematic. Despite a good deal of loose talk about cultural memory, community memory, and so forth, memory is fundamentally something that exists within an individual's mind. To say "I remember" is to connect with something in your own experience. You can conserve this recollection in your memory whether or not you tell anyone else about it. Conversely, if an acquaintance tells you something that *she* remembers—a story about unexpectedly meeting a friend, for example—you will not later say that you remember this incident, though you may of course say that you remember being told about it. The distinction, between events that are directly experienced and others that are described to you, is well understood by the courts, which demote the latter to the class of hearsay evidence. But phrases like cultural memory obscure this distinction. In the nightmare case of the marionettes, what has been lost is not people's ability to remember but rather their ability to transmit or receive information. Without countless acts of transmission, there probably would have been no marionettes that morning in New York.

But now, my thoughts moved to a second nightmare scenario. They moved from marionettes to places. What if *places* had to be created anew for each generation, each person? What if churches, restaurants, bookstores, parks, and gas stations simply ceased to exist with each generation? Not *some* churches, restaurants, and so forth, but *all* of them? What if each person took his or her home away with them when they died or moved? What if every thing in every place had to be constantly reinvented?

Like the case of the marionettes, this scenario is literally unthinkable. But one should not be lulled into taking the continuation of things and places for granted. Powerful phenomena are involved in making it possible, and trying to imagine a world without these phenomena helps one appreciate their magnitude. Some of them are physical. Rocks and trees possess properties which allow them to last many times the length of a human life. Even many buildings, being composed of natural substances like stone and wood, have the capacity to outlive the people who built them. Yet this capacity is not unlimited. Most buildings that continue to exist for more than a short time do so because humans are determined to keep them standing. In fact, the amount of human energy devoted to ensuring that buildings survive is truly remarkable. I don't mean simply the preservation campaigns that are sometimes mounted to save much-loved buildings from demolition. I mean something more basic. Anyone who has ever owned a house will understand this: forces of entropy are steadily, remorselessly reducing everything to ruin, and ceaseless effort is required to stave them off. Twigs clog gutters, water freezes in mortar joints, paint flakes, wood rots, the ground heaves up concrete footings, and so on and so forth. There is hardly a minute of the day when some process is not working to bring buildings down. So when the homeowner is not fixing the roof, he is replacing the downspout; when she is not waterproofing the foundation, she is painting the sills. And so on and so forth.

Some apartment-dwelling urbanites may be tempted to dismiss such ceaseless activity as merely the misguided obsession of house-proud suburbanites. But the ceaseless efforts that people make—and not merely suburban homeowners but also the owners of New York's skyscrapers and Europe's cathedrals—to keep buildings standing cannot be so easily dismissed. To the contrary, this frantic effort to hold onto things, this spectacle of people struggling to preserve a kind of stasis, constitutes a social phenomenon of great importance. It is, in effect, a process of cultural transmission at work.

Let us look a little more closely at the forces of destruction which call forth such superhuman efforts to preserve things. For these are not limited to the natural forces of entropy but are cultural as well. We recognize them readily: war, real estate development, suburban sprawl, pollution, highway construction, disinvestment. Not only do we recognize them, but we have no difficulty naming and discussing them, for, in contrast to the forces of stability, we are constantly alert to those of destruction and readily acknowledge them as real and interesting phenomena. Whether or not we like them, we respect their existence, whereas, regrettably, we tend to take the forces of stability for granted and lack even a language to talk about them. Admittedly we have a few labels, like memory and tradition, that get tossed around in public debates. But they tell little and obscure much. Memory obscures the all-important act of transmission which makes tradition possible. As for tradition, it sounds dead, like something that *happens* to people or objects, whereas as we have seen—and as homeowners well understand—preserving places and things is always a form of action. It requires energy and purpose. It is something people do.

Right now, our public debate about places is a little like one side of a telephone conversation. The discourse of change is dinned into our ears, the response of stability barely audible. We do hear some contemptuous accusations leveled at stability ("standing in the way of progress") and some shorthand labels (tradition, culture, memory). We do not hear explanations of how places nurture people and communities, and why their persistence is valuable. Many people do instinctively understand that places nurture people, yet such instinctive understanding is not enough. The debate over the future of our places is going on loudly every day, all around the country; it is going on in the halls of government, in boardrooms and newsrooms; it is carried out in the hard-edged language of public policy, often reduced to slogans; and its stakes are high. To be heard amidst the cacophony of public debate, the case for the persistence and preservation of places must be made more forcefully—not just louder but also smarter. And for this we need a better language to appreciate places and to assign social value to their durability, their capacity for remaining recognizably the same. We need a language to describe, understand, and appreciate the humans who invest energy in keeping them that way. We need these things not in order to have an interesting discussion but to guide action and decision-making: to save places that matter to people.

Let us focus for another moment on change and stability. Strictly speaking, nothing stays the same, nor can it. The laws of physics are against it. Even the mountain that seems the very emblem of permanence is changing. Among people it is much the same. The young become old, the thin fat. Beginners become experts, friends lovers, lovers indifferent. In a dynamic society, social institutions are just as changeful, and there is nothing so calculated to destroy an energetic organization (or an art form) as determined efforts to keep it the same. Yet for all this, stability and the forces that produce it are essential and are generally underrated. The mountain lasts a very long time; people remain friends for years; an organization cannot grow if it is not nurtured; puppetry, music, and language cannot become more expressive if they stop being taught, practiced, and passed on from generation to generation. The same is true of places. It is easy to chide misguided attempts to resist changes to the places which we inhabit and love. But it is easier to undervalue people's affection for them as they are, and the effort they put into nurturing them and assuring their permanence amidst the constant flux of change.

We should also take into account that our adulation of change goes far beyond what is justified by the laws of physics, or for that matter of society. The oft-repeated accusation that ours is a throw-away society gets at part of our addiction to change—and incidentally says much about how American society treats places. But our attitudes to change are in fact deep-seated. Let us briefly review some of their sources. First is the eighteenth-century notion of progress, the idea that society moves constantly towards a better condition (a theory sometimes perversely and illogically inverted into the belief that all change must necessarily be positive). Next comes the nineteenth-century notion of capital as the supreme lever of beneficial change, together with the acceptance of disruption as the necessary price for using it. And finally, from the twentieth and twenty-first centuries, the image of globalization and electronic communication as ways of making change instantaneous and constant—and incidentally of dissolving the very notion of *place* in a solvent of global ubiquity.

Most of us have unconsciously adopted some if not all of this set of beliefs. We accept constant change as normal, frequently beneficial, and if not beneficial then at any rate inevitable. Specifically, we accept the ceaseless disruption and destruction of places as natural. But is it? If the constant rearrangement of places were a natural force, like wind, rain, or ageing, we might expect to find that it affects everyone more or less equally. If it were a natural condition, we might expect to find that both its costs and its benefits are more or less equally distributed. Yet this is not the case. The destruction of places affects people very unequally: it is not at all fair. One reason is that the power to change places is very unequally, and very unfairly, distributed. A few people have enormous power to change both their own and other people's places, while the rest of us have almost no such power. Donald Trump and Donald Rumsfeld may have little in common, but they do share an awesome power to change other people's places, whether by development or by bombs, and they do not ask permission first. As for the rest of us, we can change other people's places only in the most trivial ways: we cannot even keep our own places the same if Mr. Trump or Mr. Rumsfeld decrees that they shall be otherwise.

Let us look more closely at some of those who largely lack the power to determine the fate of their own places. Certain examples are well known, such as the African American towns which line the part of the Mississippi River known as Cancer Alley. Their fate is pretty much determined by large corporations located far away. Residents of places like these are aware of their powerlessness because it is regularly underlined by decisions which they did not make yet which powerfully affect them: to open or close a plant, clean up toxic waste or keep polluting, and so forth. A similar awareness is widespread among residents of large areas of the west where natural gas companies own the right to drill wells, install tanks and compressors, and build roads pretty much wherever they want. People in these conditions adapt to living with the knowledge that they have little power over their own places, because this fact forms part of their daily reality.

Yet I suspect that most of us go through life accepting places pretty much as they are and rarely thinking about what might happen to them, or who has the power to decide. As long as nothing goes terribly wrong, we can maintain the comfortable illusion that we are in control and that everything is all right. But to test just how thin the ice is, try an experiment. Make a mental list of all the places you appreciate or depend upon: your home, the public library, the subway station, the park, bakery, synagogue, pharmacy, office or factory, schoolyard, pizzeria, community garden, crosswalk. The flowering crabapple tree on the next block. The view across the river. The path across the field. Now make a second list of the places you actually control. If you are a homeowner, you will probably include your own house on this second list. You may even include your front yard (though your control over this may in fact be tenuous). And that is about as far as it goes. If you live in an apartment, you probably do not control the front of your own building: you may not even control the interior. Most people, then, will draw the line of control somewhere between the inside and the outside of their own dwellings. As for the rest of the places which we love and on which our lives depend, we can do little more than hope they will be there tomorrow and the next day.

My aim in pointing this out is not to incite paranoia but rather to underline an important yet often overlooked truth. The issue about places is not simply whether change or stability is better, though that is how the media and politicians generally cast it (in the process usually slighting the arguments for stability). Rather, it is fundamentally a question of power and equity: of who gets to choose. In a perfect world, everyone would be able to choose stability or change in their environment. In reality, most people have little control over the fate of places they care about, whereas, by contrast, a few people—all too often outsiders—have the power to disrupt everything, sometimes ordering unwanted change, sometimes blocking desired improvement. The situation is manifestly unfair, and it suits the interests of the powerful few to downplay the value of place affection and stewardship.

In calling attention to this fact, I should make it clear that I do not oppose change. On the contrary, I am in favor of change. Things that are broken should be fixed. Wrongs should be righted. And the imbalance of power over places, an imbalance which harms so many people and disrupts so many places, is one of the wrongs that should be righted.

The solution does not lie in extending individual control over more places. The fact is, as long as we are a society, rather than merely a collection of individuals, we will continue to share most spaces with others, and so we will have to negotiate ways of sharing control over them. But the situation we have now is not generally one of communitarian sharing but of grossly unequal power. A relatively small number of people have enormous power to determine the future of our places, while the rest of us have almost none.

One might liken the situation to a sort of imperialism, practiced not abroad but within our own communities.

The point is not merely rhetorical. As I travel around the country, I find that people everywhere share a feeling of helplessness as they see cherished places—places they regard as *theirs*—changed out of all recognition by forces they cannot really comprehend, much less control. It is a great source of social unhappiness in communities of all kinds, from inner-city ghettos to gated suburbs and outwards into the as-yet undeveloped countryside.

What people are finding in all of these places is that laws, procedures, and social codes are not helping them as much as they should to control the forces reshaping the places they live. Let us consider a few of those laws and procedures. One is zoning. Though many people trust zoning to protect their neighborhoods, the fact is that most zoning codes provide blueprints for *changing* places, not for keeping them the same. Zoning regulations can actually make it impossible to preserve places. Another is historic preservation. Surely, many people assume, preservation laws will take care of the problem. But they usually don't. Quite apart from the political weakness which characterizes most preservation agencies, their scope is severely limited by legal criteria of significance, integrity, and so forth. If a building meets all of the criteria, the law *might* save it. But many preservation laws are toothless. In any case, many or perhaps most of the cherished places that are being threatened do not fall within the narrow scope of historic preservation criteria because they are not sufficiently old, attractive, or historically important. And so the preservation laws never come into play. Another tool is provided by our environmental laws: valuable but, again, loaded with criteria and conditions, not to mention loopholes. What about right-to-farm laws? These were passed in some states to help protect family farms. Instead, outraged citizens have found them used to protect vast and stinking hog factories, so-called farms that have radically changed the places around them, sometimes making them virtually uninhabitable—always, of course, without asking permission.

The laws, in short, turn out to be less helpful in protecting places than one might hope, a problem discussed further in Chapter 9. People are also finding that the civic and non-profit machinery of their communities lacks power to avert the disruption of places. We have historic preservation and environmental organizations on every scale from the National Trust for Historic Preservation or the Sierra Club down through the Greater Yellowstone Coalition and on down to Manhattan's Greenwich Village Society for Historic Preservation or Houston's Tejano Association for Historic Preservation. Most of these groups are simply overwhelmed. They pick their battles from among dozens if not hundreds of worthy candidates. They spend much of their time raising funds to stay in business. Though they sometimes win their causes, many are essentially fighting a tactical retreat, trying to save bits and pieces from a front which moves ever forward.

What about land trusts? Land trusts are becoming deservedly popular around the country as a way to ensure the preservation of open spaces. But looking to land trusts to solve the problem can be as disappointing as looking to zoning. A couple of years ago I participated in a planning exercise in Chester County, PA. We talked to numerous citizens, both in the countryside and in the local town center of Kennett Square. We found that many people shared two deeply felt concerns which represented opposite sides of the same coin: the decay of historic town centers and the loss of open spaces. Both problems were byproducts of suburbanization. Farms and woodland were being eaten up for suburban and exurban development. Fortunately, said some residents, we have land trusts. However, when we started looking at maps, we realized that the amount of land that the trusts will ever be able to save is a fraction of what is up for grabs. Thousands of acres are being developed; tens or hundreds of acres are being donated to land trusts. On a return visit in 2007, and despite this pessimism, I was impressed by the extent to which land trusts seem to be succeeding in protecting parts of the landscape, including some particularly beautiful vistas. But still, the question remains whether relying on donations to land trusts can provide an effective strategy for preserving a larger sense of place, the character and feeling of an overall landscape, against the pressures of suburbanization and rising land values.

We need more and better tools, and we need them fast. But first we need a more persuasive language of place, for without that we will not be able to explain why we must have the tools. We need more powerful and nuanced words for explaining why the stability of cherished places is useful to people, communities, and society in general. We need more confident arguments with which to oppose the normative language of development, change, progress, capitalism, and property.

If there is urgency here, it arises not only out of threat, but also out of opportunities that should not be missed. A promising convergence has been occurring among those who care about preserving place. In general, the historic preservation and environmental movements have had surprisingly little to say to each other about the protection of places. Each has tended to reduce the characteristics of specific places to technical concepts specific to the discipline: architectural quality, historical significance, biotic diversity, clean air or water. Neither has adequately appreciated how people and communities relate to particular places, how people's affection contributes to the historical and environmental content of places, and how changes in those places affect communities. Yet now, some leaders on both sides are beginning to agree on a shared notion of place as a new foundation for their work.

As an example, consider how the controversy over a historic house called Camp Santanoni, which once roiled the Adirondacks, was resolved. The problem was, Camp Santanoni was located on land that had become part of New York State's forest preserve, and the state constitution declared that the forest preserve should be kept "forever wild." To environmentalists, this meant that the historic house should be removed, or at least allowed to deteriorate so that it would eventually disappear. Preservationists of course wished to protect it as a valuable work of architecture and a significant marker of the Adirondacks' history. Eventually, a solution was found. The house will stay. But its presence within the wild forest around it will be minimized as far as possible.

Today, many environmentalists are more willing than in the past to recognize the cultural values of place, even of a "wilderness." One can see this too in the often bitter debate over western ranching. While some environmentalists remain dead set against cows, others are willing to work with ranchers. They think the action of bovine hoofs, if properly managed, may be a valuable part of grassland ecology—a substitute for the buffalo. They also recognize that they and the ranchers share a common enemy, suburban development, and they would rather preserve the open space with cows, and ranching traditions, than lose it entirely.

This compromise represents more than pragmatism. Many environmentalists have found new interest in the cultural dimensions of the environment, the factors that transform pieces of the earth's surface into *places*. Some years ago, the Nathan Cummings Foundation, a small foundation that saw itself as a bellwether for bigger trends, focused one of its environmental programs on Native Hawaiian culture. Why? Not merely because the Hawaiian islands harbored thousands of endangered species, but also because Native Hawaiian culture embodied a sense of place that was crucial to understanding that particular environment—that was indeed part of that environment and that was as endangered as any bird or flower. Here at Pace University, both the Institute for Environmental and Regional Studies and the Environmental Studies Program promote a similar fusion of nature and culture.

This interest in the cultural dimensions of the environment can lead in surprising directions. Recently a historic preservationist, Daniel Bluestone of the University of Virginia, was invited to speak at an environmental conference on the remediation of superfund sites. Bluestone questioned whether capping and covering, or hogging and hauling, were always the best solutions for every site. Perhaps, he wondered, erasing the troubling past of these sites was not always the smartest thing to do. Did they not have important lessons to teach? How could people learn them if the sites were all remediated, their history erased? What was surprising was not so much the argument itself as the fact that the environmentalists did not dismiss it out of hand. Somehow, while remediating these terrible places, they would have to find a way to preserve their cultural content, which lay—challengingly—in their very badness. I doubt whether such a conversation could have taken place fifteen or twenty years ago.

As this example suggests, the convergence has two sides. Just as some environmentalists are becoming increasingly open to the stuff of everyday life and everyday places—stories, traditions, local customs and beliefs, folklore, oral history—so are some historic preservationists. In 2003, I presided over a panel discussion at Pratt Institute on the future of historic preservation. One speaker argued for the importance of stories and local traditions. A distinguished elderly architect responded. Gene Norman had been the chair of New York City's Landmarks Preservation Commission some years earlier. He agreed, he said, yet hoped that this new focus would not push the buildings themselves out of the picture. Conceding that architectural values had been over-emphasized in the past, he pointed out that buildings *were*, after all, the three-dimensional definers of our urban habitat, and he argued that it would be a mistake to throw them overboard. Instead of replacing one part of the solution with another, he urged, we should create a broadly inclusive way of understanding place, one with room for all of the elements that contribute to it and all of the ways in which people relate to and depend upon it. Such a concept of place would give us building *and* story, history *and* place, aesthetics *and* association. It was an important piece of advice.

These convergences, of natural and cultural conservation, of the tangible and intangible dimensions of places, hold out hope that the stewards of places may be able to agree on a common language of *place* before it is too late, one that helps them fight for the protection of places in their fullness of meaning. And new possibilities are emerging to support this trend. Internationally, as noted in the Prologue and the Introduction to Part IV, organizations ranging from the Inuit Circumpolar Conference through the city government of Buenos Aires to UNESCO's World Heritage Committee are working towards more holistic models for conserving places. Moreover, some of these organizations are resisting the destruction of places as not merely a misfortune but a violation of human rights. In the United States, meanwhile, possibilities of political and cultural change have arisen that were hardly imaginable even a few years ago. Yet new difficulties are also emerging. The elevation of global warming to the forefront of the public agenda is an enormously positive development, yet one which also threatens to suppress recognition of the cultural dimensions of the environment, including historic buildings, just when hope was growing for their greater recognition. Some professionals and advocates are beginning to focus on understanding how respecting both historic buildings and intangible dimensions of the environment like tradition and place attachment can actually support efforts to ward off catastrophic climate change, but it promises to be a difficult fight.

All of these factors, both threats and opportunities, underline the urgent need for a robust discussion of why the persistence of places is valuable to people and communities—a discussion that can help environmentalists and preservationists find common ground and move forward together.

As we seek to answer this question, it will quickly become clear that we do not yet know as much as we should. Yet we may already know more than we think. We can make quite a few useful statements. We can say that certain places anchor people's individual memories: that the persistence of, say, the lions in front of the New York Public Library, or a pool hall in Bensonhurst, helps people stay connected to their own biographies. We can say that the persistence of a place like Steinway Hall in New York helps preserve a strand of culture—playing the piano—and that many other places play similar roles for other cultural strands. To fly a kite, one needs a place to fly it. A muezzin needs a minaret. We can say that, in neighborhoods throughout the country, the persistence of local diners, bookstores, schools, churches, and other gathering places helps conserve social capital by providing settings for people to work, recreate, and organize together. We can say that the presence of local landmarks instills pride among neighborhood residents. We can say that the persistence of all kinds of storied places, from Mount Vernon to the local superfund site, transmits important lessons about history and community. We can say that efforts to ensure the persistence of places, be they the nearby wetland or the local drive-in, provide opportunities for people to exercise citizenship. And we can say with certainty that the potential for place-based education has barely been tapped: that we have barely scratched the surface of what places can do as subjects of study for our schools—and not for children only, but also for the lifelong learning that is becoming so important a part of our future.

All of these are useful statements. But they are not enough. Those who want to continue treating places as commodities will dismiss every statement about a particular place as an exception to the general rule that places are fundamentally blank pages on which to inscribe market calculations. The case for places and their persistence must be made more broadly and deeply. Obvious questions must be extrapolated: if society needs certain places to persist as a matter of community and individual health, then *what should we be doing to protect them*? And if communities deserve greater power over their places as a matter of social equity, then *how can we best give communities that power*? These are practical questions to which opinion-shapers and decision-makers need answers. It is up to citizens to provide them, but those who study place can help by offering essential insights and information.

As I look around today, I sense that society is ready for change. It may not happen. Or it may be the wrong kind of change. But there is at least the possibility of revitalization, of new social contracts and laws that could lift us above the exploitation of people and places that we have come to accept as normal. To secure this future is the challenge and the opportunity I see ahead. It may seem romantic or visionary. But it can become entirely practical if citizens and activists, decision-makers and scholars, roll up their sleeves and work together to uncover the secrets of place.

NOTES

1. Tony Hiss, *The Experience of Place* (New York: Vintage Books, 1990), 5–6.
2. A. B. Guthrie, Jr., *The Big Sky* (New York: Time-Life Books, [1947] 1964), 191.
3. John R. Logan and Harvey L. Molotch, *Urban Fortunes: The Political Economy of Place* (Berkeley, Los Angeles, and London: University of California Press, 1987), 1–2.

CHAPTER 2

Protecting Storyscape

This chapter was written at the request of Environmental Law in New York *and first published there in 2001. Thus while the concepts it outlines, especially the notion of storyscape and story sites, are applicable everywhere, the examples are drawn from New York City, and the legal tools discussed in the last section are oriented towards New York State and may have to be modified elsewhere.*

INTRODUCTION

There is a gap in the legal system of protection afforded to socially valuable resources. Environmental conservation laws and policies provide some protection for water, air, forest, farmland, and scenic resources; they also help prevent harm from pollution of land, air, and water. Historic preservation protects man-made aspects of the cityscape, especially architecturally significant buildings. Largely unprotected are resources that are valuable for their ability to convey history, support community memory, and nurture people's attachment to place. There is not even a generally accepted term for this category of resource, some of which could be called historical landmarks, others cultural or social landmarks. In Australia, the term "social value" has been used to denote places that:

> provide a spiritual or traditional connection between past and present; tie the past affectionately to the present; help give a disempowered group back its history; provide an essential reference point in a community's identity or sense of itself . . .; loom large in the daily comings and goings of life; provide an essential community function that over time develops into a deeper attachment that is more than utility value . . .; have shaped some aspect of community behaviour or attitudes; are distinctive . . . features that lift a place above the crowd, making it likely that special meanings have been attached to that place; are accessible to the public and offer the possibility of repeated use to build up associations and value to the community of users; and [are] places where people gather and act as a community, for example places of public ritual, public meetings or congregation, and informal gathering places.[1]

I propose the term "story sites" as broadly inclusive of historical sites, cultural sites, and sites of social value. All act as mnemonics, bringing socially valuable stories to mind: stories of history, tradition, and shared memory. The term "storyscape" might then be used to refer to the full panorama of such sites.[2]

Though difficult to label, story sites can be identified, described, mapped, and evaluated. They can even be protected, though available mechanisms are imperfect and further work needs to be done to understand precisely how and where they should be applied.

This chapter sets forth the concept of story sites and their value to society, provides guidelines for identifying, assessing, and applying legal mechanisms for protecting them, and finally offers some suggestions for improving those mechanisms.

STORYSCAPES AND STORY SITES

The Brooklyn Bridge, the lions at the New York Public Library, Twin's Pizza in downtown Brooklyn, the African Burial Ground just north of City Hall, Brooklyn's Old Stone House, and many of New York City's public schools are story sites. They differ in almost every way, ranging from a monumental work of *beaux arts* architecture to a nondescript taxpayer; one is not even a building at all. Yet each has a capacity to trigger the retelling and reliving of important stories. Some of these stories fall into the range we are accustomed to call history, while others approximate folklore, but this distinction does not match the way people think about sites and stories. The important point is that all of the stories describe some aspect of a shared past, and each story is felt by the tellers to have some bearing on the character of their neighborhood, village, city, or region, and its citizens today.

Though a few of these sites are well known, it may be helpful to describe each of them. The African Burial Ground, rediscovered in the early 1990s as the federal government began excavating it for a new office tower, was the site of the city's largest burying ground for Africans and African Americans throughout the eighteenth century (Figures 7.1 to 7.3). Some estimates are that as many as 20,000 were buried there; perhaps 400 human remains were still in the ground when excavation started, of which some 200 or more are estimated to remain today. The discovery of the Burial Ground and the furious battle to preserve it (about which more is said in Chapters 6 and 7) led to an outpouring of research, writing, and rediscovery of the history of black people in New York. Indeed it wrote African American into the city's history in new and important ways, triggering a permanent change of consciousness that continues to be nurtured by research, discussion, and educational and spiritual activities at the site. Even before its "discovery" a few people had always known about the African Burial Ground. And before the excavation began the burials and artifacts were, of course, more complete than they are now. So the Burial Ground was always a story site, but it was a latent story site. The threat and the response to it activated the site, making it one of New York's most powerfully evocative story sites.

Brooklyn's Old Stone House, located in J. J. Byrne Park just off Fifth Avenue near the Gowanus Canal, is not the original house built by Dutch settlers around 1700: it is a twentieth-century recreation. In August of 1776 the original house had witnessed key episodes of the Battle of Brooklyn, the first and one of the most important battles of the Revolutionary War, as British and American troops took and retook the building (and as the core of Washington's troops managed to escape to Manhattan). Even though it is a fabrication, the Old Stone House provides a tangible, on-the-spot reminder of events that were pivotal to America's victory in the war, and it has become the home of a small museum that tells the story through exhibits and educational programs. Though not an original artifact, and from an architectural perspective of dubious value, it is an active and useful story site. There are other Revolutionary War story sites in Brooklyn. The Prison Ship Martyrs Monument is a prominent one, a splendid Doric column designed by McKim, Mead & White in 1908 and rising above an eminence in Fort Greene Park. Not far away, in the neighborhood of Vinegar Hill, the remains of the martyrs—the literally thousands of Americans who died aboard British ships in Wallabout Bay—were buried and remained buried until most were reinterred at the monument. But the unmarked spot, thought to contain remnants of the original vault and perhaps even of human remains, was locked away in a vacant lot behind a chain-link fence. It remained a latent story site, awaiting activation through marking, protection, and ritual observance, until a developer filed plans to build there in 2003. Then the city's Landmarks Preservation Commission ordered an excavation. The results were somewhat disappointing: the diggers found remnants of the original structure but no human bones. Still, the process was not without results. Calling Vinegar Hill a "dead-end neighborhood" because of its out-of-the-way location, local resident and artist Nicholas Evans-Cato remarked that the site and its history "make us look at it in a different way. It's not a dead end anymore. It's meaningful."[3]

The Brooklyn Bridge symbolizes America's, and specifically New York's, daring in engineering and architecture. It tells other, equally important, stories. For while many people use the bridge simply as a means of transportation, others turn the trip over its walkway, on foot or by bicycle or roller-blades, into a form of recreation, even of spiritual renewal. Some walk the bridge regularly—the encounters with its stunning views of the Manhattan skyline, the harbor, the great sweep of sky, the liberating awareness of air and light, as well as with throngs of people, are cherished episodes and part of what defines their lives as New Yorkers. For others, particularly visitors to the city, a walk over the bridge may be an eagerly anticipated and long-remembered experience: for them, too, it will define the experience of being in New York. Each of these bridge crossings is not so much a retelling as a reliving of a story, and that story has a fourth dimension, for people have been crossing the Brooklyn Bridge, and experiencing it in more or less this way, for over a century. Each time a person crosses the bridge, he or she reenacts a tradition, forging a link to both past and future generations of bridge-crossers. One might say that this episode of crossing the Brooklyn Bridge is important not only within the individual life stories of those who do it but also within the life story of New York.

Similar remarks could be made of the lions that proudly survey Fifth Avenue from their pedestals in front of the New York Public Library. How many generations of New Yorkers have met at the feet of these honored beasts? "Meet me at the lions" may signify the start of a shopping expedition, a lunch date, or a romantic tryst. For us, the lions clarify how understanding a site's narrative content can add an important dimension to even the greatest work of architecture. Architecturally, the lions, though imposing, are no more prominent than several other features that lend majesty to the procession towards the front door: fountains, balustrades, terraces, the steps themselves. They are well-placed grace notes in a symphony of classical grandeur. Yet the many New Yorkers and visitors who continue to enact the ritual of meeting at the lions have given them a special significance that is not apparent to the eye. Were design changes to the Library's facade contemplated, the lions' value as storyscape elements would require careful consideration.

Less famous sites may also have storyscape value that equals or surpasses their aesthetic, architectural, or environmental value. Twin's Pizza on Nevins Street in downtown Brooklyn (Figure 2.1) was once the Wigwam, a bar that served as a center of communal life for the Mohawk Indians who lived in the neighborhood during the mid-twentieth century. The men were mostly ironworkers who built the Verrazano Bridge and many of New York's great skyscrapers. At the Wigwam they drank, of course, but also weddings and community get-togethers happened there. News was exchanged. "It was a lot more than just a bar," recalled a former bartender in 1996; "it was like Grand Central for the Mohawk Indians who came here," she said. "People sometimes picked their mail up there. They got rides back to the reservation there. They found out about jobs there. They met there. I saw everybody."[4] For those who remember the Wigwam, or have been told about it, its site is powerfully evocative. Even though Twin's Pizza has no architectural distinction and no visual clues to its history, those who know its story are inclined to remember or, if possible, tell it to someone else whenever they pass it.

Figure 2.1   Story sites with new uses. Twin's Pizza (right), in downtown Brooklyn, was once the Wigwam, gathering spot for New York's Mohawk Indians. The Langston Hughes Public Library (left) in Corona, Queens, was once a Woolworth's store: older residents remember it for an important demonstration against racist hiring.

New York has many other sites that continue to recall important stories even though their functions have changed and they are quite lacking in architectural distinction. The Stonewall Inn, launching point for the gay pride movement, later became a leather and souvenir shop and, as of 2001, was a restaurant. A Woolworth's store in Corona, Queens, the site of an important demonstration against racial prejudice in hiring, is now a branch library (Figure 2.1). Unlike the other examples, however, its exterior still looks pretty much as it did, though without the Woolworth's sign.

Some of New York's least appreciated story sites are its public schools. These figure in public discourse largely as sites of contention, as politicians vie with each other to criticize the state of schooling and gain public favor with their proposed solutions. Meanwhile many schools continue to provide a good education to students year after year. They also continue to anchor community memories. In many neighborhoods the public schools have been strong unifying forces: older people remember their schools, often with fondness and usually as extremely important places in their lives. They are important places for students today, who reenact their predecessors' stories and will pass their own stories on to their children.

Finally, and perhaps even less recognized as story sites, there are the candy store where children stop on the way home from school, the pizzeria where teenagers hang out, the bakery with "the best" challah or cannoli, the cherry tree that for a few weeks each spring beautifies an otherwise ordinary block, the corner where you can suddenly see the Statue of Liberty or the Hellgate Bridge, and the park bench where there is conversation among old friends. Every neighborhood has places like these. Outsiders may completely miss them because they do not stand out to the eye: it is their stories that make them important. Insiders know and live those stories. They reenact meaningful details of daily life at these sites. For them, these places define what it is to live in that neighborhood, and indeed in New York.

While these examples are all drawn from New York City, every village, town, and rural area has story sites that give meaning to life there. Because their value is based in their stories, there can be no simple key by which to identify them at sight. A spot on a river bank may hardly look different from any number of other spots, yet it is here, rather than there, that people swim, fish, or enjoy picnics.

THE MANY VALUES OF STORY SITES TO SOCIETY

Story sites represent a social investment made and tended by many people over many years, an investment that continues year after year to pay substantial dividends. Some of the social values represented by story sites are described below.

Story Sites Anchor Individual Life Stories

Everyone has a personal storyscape. The sites within it are associated with important events or episodes: the place where one went roller-skating, met friends, celebrated after passing the bar exam, last saw a loved one, habitually goes for brunch after church, and so forth. Personal storyscapes may include buildings of recognized architectural value but will almost certainly include sites whose importance is not obvious to others and that indeed may hardly seem to be "sites" at all—a street corner or a park bench, for example, or even a flower-box. Restaurants and bars tend to figure in people's personal storyscapes. So do community gardens, neighborhood stores, coffee shops, laundromats, barber shops (Figure 6.1), basketball and handball courts, health clubs, and so forth. Even a parking lot may support important activities or memories.

Each of the sites that make up one's personal storyscape supports a memory or pattern that in turn represents an important dimension of one's life. Together, they uphold one's sense of oneself as an individual with a specific set of experiences, habits, and preferences. Some story sites may be easily replaceable—one coffee shop may do as well as another for reading the Sunday paper. Yet for others there is no substitute: their loss would cause an irreparable gap or disruption.

It is not clear to what extent society is responsible for places that are important to its individual members. In the purely imaginary and absurd extreme case, a society that undertook to protect *everybody's* individual storyscapes would quickly reach deadlock or irresolvable conflict. But what if certain sites represented the memories and traditions of not one but *many* individuals? Simple arithmetic might then raise individual story sites to the level of legitimate social concern. Such a case might be made for Coney Island, H. Kauffman & Sons (purveyors of riding equipment since 1875), Frank Music Company ("classical music of all publishers"), Gleason's Boxing Gym, Junior's Restaurant ("Most Fabulous Cheesecake and Desserts"), or many neighborhood parks and schools. The social value of these and other story sites does encompass the experiences of many individuals. But it also goes beyond individual experience, however extravagantly multiplied, to include the connections *between* people.

We next consider the ways in which story sites symbolize and cement the bonds among society's individual members.

Story Sites Preserve Social Capital

Social capital is a form of wealth that is distinct from financial capital but equally important, indeed arguably even more so. The term refers to "connections among individuals—social networks and the norms of reciprocity and trustworthiness that arise from them."[5] Social capital includes belonging to clubs, voting, socializing with friends at home or in restaurants, attending church, mosque, or synagogue, volunteering, chatting with neighbors, and performing community service. Some forms of social capital create close bonds among people, while others support looser, more distant relationships.

The phrase "social capital" has the ring of metaphor, yet its value to society is real. Social capital "allows citizens to resolve collective problems more easily, . . . greases the wheels that allow communities to advance smoothly, . . . widen[s] our awareness of the many ways in which our fates are linked, . . . serve[s] as conduits for the flow of helpful information that facilitates achieving our goals," and also helps people "cope better with traumas and fight illness more effectively."[6] And these factors show up in social statistics. Evidence also suggests that states with ample social capital enjoy better schools and greater gender and racial equality, while states with a dearth of social capital rank high in violence and tax evasion.[7]

Unfortunately, some observers, led by sociologist Robert Putnam,[8] argue that social capital is diminishing. Activities from voting to league bowling, from club membership to dining with friends, are on the decline. The reasons for this decline, if indeed it is occurring, are complex, taking in large-scale trends such as increasing job pressures, lengthening commutes, television, and generational shifts. Compared with social forces of this magnitude, the influence of story sites, or the impact of their loss, probably has at most a secondary importance. Nevertheless, it is striking that many "social capital" activities depend on appropriate spatial frames or settings—places that are conducive to them—and many of these, in turn, are outside the home, ranging from churches through coffee shops and bars to street corners, undeveloped lots, and park benches. Within specific communities, activities need specific places, and the loss of these quite particular places could therefore have a local impact. The closing of a diner may doom the Tuesday morning breakfast-and-politics group; the disappearance of a newsstand, laundromat, or community garden (or the loss of a playground to drug dealers) may bring long traditions of neighborhood sociability to an end. When an empty lot is developed, children may lose the opportunity for informal group play. Out on the strip, rigorous policing may deprive teenagers of a parking lot used as a much-needed nighttime hang-out spot. Each of these places could *in theory* be replaced, but the conditions (location, catchment area, traffic patterns, scale, ambience, price, sense of being welcome, and so forth) are rigorous and may in practice be difficult if not impossible to meet. Even a close functional match at the same location may fail to replace traditional social-capital activities: a fast-food donut store, or a themed western restaurant serving tourists, does not have the same social-capital value as the old-fashioned coffee shop it replaces (Figure 2.2). Nor can these losses of *place* necessarily be made good through the sort of urban design remedies often applied to situations of unwanted change: however handsome a new building may be, it is no replacement for a garden, a tricycle course, or a hang-out spot. And some fishermen may find the award-winning esplanade less inviting than the neglected and very undesigned shoreline it replaced. The point is simply that neither function nor design is a very good proxy for the social value of story sites. This we must identify by learning the stories, and protect by identifying the elements that support them.

Story Sites Nurture Cultural Capital

Cultural capital is related to social capital but is not the same thing. Cultural capital denotes society's stock of traditions, lifeways, beliefs, and modes of thought and expression. Global cities like New York or Los Angeles are almost unbelievably rich in cultural capital, but every city, town, suburb, or region has

Figure 2.2   The Coffee Pot in Walden, CO, with its owner and chief waitperson. Until it was closed and replaced by a western-themed restaurant serving tourists, the Coffee Pot was typical of unpretentious restaurants which serve as traditional gathering spots in many western towns.

its own stock. Much of this is often referred to loosely as cultural diversity, but it is really a centuries-deep and growing accumulation of cultural abilities: fluency in languages; aptitude in religious and family rituals; knowledge of traditional gardening techniques and herbal medicines from around the world; ability to tie a necktie or fold a sari; easy familiarity with games from dominoes to kite-flying; mastery of musical instruments and singing styles from salsa to the Jewish traditions of Bukhara or the throat-singing of Tuva; deep grounding in performance traditions from Tchaikovsky ballets to Chinese opera; access to storehouses bulging with memories and tales (some heard, some read, some learned in school) of life on a Mohawk reservation, the high plateaus of Tibet, a village in Ireland or Russia, or a South American metropolis; and, of course, mastery of a bewildering variety of cuisines.

Framing cultural capital in terms of "cultural diversity" encourages one to focus on ethnic differences. By refocusing on cultural capital we acknowledge that *all* cultural abilities represent a quantum of tradition, training, and mastery that contributes to society's stock and has some claim to be nurtured. Playing the didgeridoo embodies social capital but so does mixing an elegant martini; looking comfortable in a guayabera qualifies but so does looking good in penny-loafers or deck shoes.

Though cultural capital is located in people, it is expressed and nurtured by places. Casitas, the home-made wooden structures erected by Puerto Rican groups on vacant lots and used as social clubs, are an obvious example. (Of course they also nurture social capital.) Other clubhouses are important too, from the Century to the Dominican social clubs of Washington Heights. Community gardens offer another example. Religious buildings are almost too obvious to require discussion, as are a dizzying array of specialty shops such as botanicas, butchers offering live poultry, purveyors of riding crops and ballet shoes, record stores specializing in Latin jazz, Kosher delis, or music stores that can quickly supply the string parts for a Mozart symphony. The existence of these and innumerable other establishments reflects the presence of specific cultural groups; some serve, and are known to, the general public, but others are almost invisible to those outside the community that depends on them. Sometimes indeed they are invisible even to those who do depend on them. How much thought does the typical Broadway theatergoer spare for those shops, clustered in the neighborhood's side streets, where a saxophone key can be repaired in time for the evening's performance or a didgeridoo rented in a hurry? At other times, low visibility is cultivated by habitués, making it even easier for planners and developers to harm important places unknowingly. Visible or not, each of these places helps to support certain traditions and rituals, and the loss of an important support place may hit a community's cultural capital hard.

Cultural capital is a fluctuating thing. Cultural practices come in, grow, and die out or decamp. They also change. Catholics no longer worship as they did a hundred years ago, and they have reorganized their churches to reflect that. Who knows, perhaps New York's Chinese will someday cease to cook in woks. Sites that support the evolving stories associated with cultural capital must be able to change with it. We must be resigned to see some stories leave long-established sites behind, except perhaps as memories.

Nothing, of course, is more basic to cultural capital than memory. An awareness of history and a desire to maintain continuity with it are fundamental to many cultural practices. A particular kind of memory, the commemoration of cultural points of origin, has become important to many groups throughout America. The gay and lesbian liberation movement began, at least symbolically, in a police raid and riot at the Stonewall Inn in Greenwich Village; though gays no longer drank there by the 1990s (the building had been given over to other uses, such as a leather and souvenir store), many continued to treasure the site of the Stonewall Inn as a point of cultural origin. For them, it was important to be able to visit the spot and say "this happened here." Indeed commemorative attention increased during the 1990s, culminating in 2007 with the site's designation as a National

Historic Landmark; as of 2007 the building was once again a club catering to a gay clientele and called the Stonewall. While it is perfectly possible to visit and commemorate sites even though their appearance has been altered, generally people prize stability over flexibility in their commemoration places: sites that haven't been altered offer the strongest reminders of important stories. New York has plenty of examples. For many immigrants, Ellis Island is a preeminent cultural-commemoration site. For black Americans, the African Burial Ground is another. For labor activists, the site of the Triangle Shirtwaist fire is yet another. Each is commemorated with public observances as well as the private observances of many respectful visitors.

Places like these are often loosely called "historic sites," and they are certainly historical. But they should also be seen as supports to cultural capital. Though none is actively used by its respective community—at least not for its original purpose—each helps to anchor the community's cultural identity by attaching historical memory to place. Each reminds the community of a foundation story. A final example makes the point: in the stairhall of a West Side prep school is a plaque listing its headmasters since the 1630s (and noting modestly that the school's operations were interrupted by the Revolutionary War). The school's buildings were designed at the end of the nineteenth century in the Dutch style of its founders. There may be little genuine history here but there is certainly a stiff reinforcement of cultural capital.

Story Sites Anchor Neighborhood Identity

Neighborhoods are fundamental units of community, particularly in a large city. People who are happy with their neighborhood find that it enhances their sense of individual identity—the Upper East Side, Greenwich Village, Dyker Heights, Hamilton Heights, Todt Hill, and the Grand Concourse all do this for many of their residents. Neighborhoods are where working adults come home; they support the important activities of full-time homemakers, school children, and many laborers and professionals, offering opportunities for necessary shopping, entertaining, socializing, worship, and the mutual ties of support and caring that come from having good neighbors. Beyond all these important and specific benefactions, neighborhoods are the extended living rooms of every house or apartment, in that a certain amount of hard-to-define living takes place there. A neighborhood's look and feel, its sense of comfort and safety, its decor, can indelibly color one's sense of self and home.

Story sites contribute powerfully to the richness of life that neighborhoods offer their residents, offering a sense of identity, an anchor in tradition, convenient places for essential activities, and even a dimension of joy in daily rounds and rituals. People who are old or young, single or married, men or women, richer or poorer, Catholic, Jewish, or atheist will of course see different storyscapes within the same neighborhood. For example, for boys growing up in Brooklyn Heights in the 1950s, neighborhood life revolved around a clutch of stoops that were conducive to the playing of stoop ball; a cul-de-sac where children could ride bicycles without fear of traffic was another important spot, as was a playground at which the Good

Humor truck stopped (and continues to stop) on summer afternoons. These were sites that made essential activities possible: a particular pizzeria became an important stopover between school and home, as did a small shop where one could buy inexpensive candy and Spaldings. Much later, in a different neighborhood, different kinds of sites become important to a grown-up child of that era. Meanwhile, in another part of Brooklyn, teenagers create their own list of neighborhood story sites that characterize life in Bensonhurst for them: it includes basketball courts, a fitness club, a neighborhood shopping street, and their schools.[9]

Neighborhood storyscapes are not purely a matter of individual creation and experience. Neighborhoods have histories that are represented by places: the pleasant suburban house where Gus Hall (long-time Communist Party leader) used to live, a factory building once famous for its carpets, a mural, an exceptionally odd or distinguished building. Sites like these help to create a publicly shared sense of neighborhood identity. Long-time residents will make sure that newcomers understand and respect them. Many newcomers in turn are quite happy to be inducted into this knowledge and will in time pass it on.

Some neighborhood story sites can be replaced. Others cannot. Story sites vary enormously in their robustness to change. This can be assessed on two separate scales: character and location. A church or school might continue to serve its neighborhood from a new building a few blocks away: its institutional power compels a high level of allegiance. But the stoop-ball stoops on (let us say) Willow Street could not be replaced by new stoops a few blocks away: children's limited range of mobility would put them out of reach. What if their owners decided to replace the stoop-ball stoops with new ones? New stoops at the same location might adequately take the place of the old ones, but only if the owners precisely replicated the curvature and projection of the stair nosings. This is a detail that might not seem crucial to the architect, who will more likely concentrate on assuring the proper width, a good surface finish, and an elegant balustrade—all details of no importance whatsoever to the conduct of stoop ball. The point is that, if we aim through our planning and developing to respect neighborhood stories, we need to understand the stories, situate them in the lives of their owners, and learn how they are grounded in the physical environment. Otherwise, we will find that the most elegant planning and design solutions have missed the mark.

Story Sites Are the Lighthouses of Historical Awareness

Story sites have an obvious historical value to neighborhoods, and residents will likely care about them, either because they record an important stage in the neighborhood's formation or because they demonstrate that the neighborhood was once quite different from today. What we must now also recognize is the historical value of story sites to the general public, even to people who feel no particular connection to the place in question.

What is history? This is not an easy question to answer. History, folklore, tradition, and personal and communal memory are all closely entangled, and sometimes are best left so. But for clarity, we can say that the special contribution of history is the recounting of the past as it extends beyond the reach of individual memory. "History" is a story that has shaped each one of us in profound ways. Yet because it is much bigger even than all of the individual memories of everyone alive, it must be constructed, told, and retold in order to exist at all. Without this continual retelling, we would see only the most recent effects of history, never their causes, conditions, or connections. History only exists in the telling.

There are many ways of telling history. Our culture relies largely on the printed word, heavily supplemented, on the one hand, with broadcast and electronic media and, on the other, by the most traditional medium of all, oral transmission: talking, gossip, telling stories. In fact, twentieth-century media like film, radio, television, and video may actually have enhanced the importance of talking; so in a different way have telephones and, most recently, cellphones. But places are also important in telling history. While places rarely "speak for themselves," they are remarkably adept at prompting others to speak about them. They are superb fodder for tour guides and provide material for all kinds of publication—print, electronic, and broadcast—relating to travel. They prompt people to write guidebooks, travel narratives, historical accounts, and memoirs, to photograph, film, paint, draw, and map them, to visit them and, of course, to talk about them. They even provoke people to spend large sums of money and create elaborate institutional structures to preserve and manage them. In short, historical story sites act both as mnemonic devices and as touchstones, provocations to tell history.

This is not a new role for buildings or places. In the middle ages, the storied windows and sculptured portals of the great cathedrals provided opportunities for pilgrims and congregants to remember and retell the sacred stories (perhaps helped along by tour guides). For Native Americans, special places have long provided stimuli for recounting foundation stories and ethical exemplars. Historical sites provide this kind of stimulus for contemporary Americans, in a variety of sometimes contradictory ways whose complexity mirrors that of society itself. The explosions of print and most recently of electronic media have not destroyed the power of places to keep history alive.

The acute ethnic and racial consciousness of contemporary American society has led to the wide adoption of constructs like "African American history," "Irish American history," or "women's history." While useful in themselves and in correcting the errors and omissions of larger "American history," such segmented narratives should not trick us into forgetting that, for better or worse, we are part of each other's histories. When New York's eighteenth-century African Burial Ground was simultaneously rediscovered and violated, the resulting whirlwind of talking, reporting, speechmaking, and research eventually reshaped the history of *all* New Yorkers. African Americans are prominent visitors to the site, but white people go there too, just as non-garment workers visit the Triangle Shirtwaist Factory, non-writers visit the White Horse Tavern (frequented by Dylan Thomas), and non-Dutch New Yorkers ponder the excavated foundations of early build-ings on Pearl Street downtown. When the Audubon Ballroom, site of Malcolm X's assassination (Figures 7.4 to 7.6), was threatened with demoli-tion, a rather conservative middle-aged white gentleman remarked to me, "Malcolm X was *my* heritage too," and he meant it. Historical places bring people together across many kinds of barriers because their stories reach across those barriers: we do not have to be the heroes in a story to recognize that we are somehow implicated in it. No matter how seemingly parochial, sites associated with ethnic, racial, gender, or class narratives have for this reason a tremendous potential to stimulate constructive discussion across the lines represented by those distinctions.

Historical sites associated with seemingly narrow geographical regions also have surprising value to the broader public, and to the larger social project of keeping our history alive. There is no such thing as an exclusively local history: every local event relates to a bigger historical narrative. It is therefore quite feasible to keep history alive through places that are intimately connected to our neighborhoods, though perhaps hardly visible outside them. In the neighborhood of Park Hill, in Yonkers, NY, for example, some ruins in a local park frequently prompt the retelling of a story that runs something like this: There was once a great hotel here, with a railroad to it, but it burned down on opening night and was never rebuilt. This simple story draws on larger narratives of urban expansion, upper-middle-class leisure, changing land use, and eventually urban decay. In Corona, Queens, patrons of a branch library gain access to the larger narrative of the civil rights movement when they are informed that the building, formerly a Woolworth's department store, was in the 1930s the site of demonstrations that made it possible for black residents of the neighborhoods to get jobs (Figure 2.1). Though our formal exposure to the story of American history may have taken place only once, in fourth grade, and have lasted no more than a hundred hours or so, our propensity to learn stays with us through life and is fed by places and the stories associated with them. As a potential teacher of history no historical place, however seemingly local in relevance, can be dismissed.

Story Sites Foster Citizenship

Amidst the globalized placelessness of modernity, represented by the world-wide web and the chain store, free trade and multinational corporations, are contrary strands of thinking, strands that lead back to the idea that being firmly rooted in a particular place is the best basis for civic culture. Interest in people's propensity to become attached to places is not new.[10] What seems rela-tively novel is a shift from descriptive scholarship to prescriptive reformism: to the idea that place attachment not only exists but should be fostered as the necessary way to preserve citizenship and the life of the community in the twenty-first century. Common Ground, an English organization, advances the notion of "local distinctiveness," defined as "the sum of the points of connection between the place and the person"—an "environmental question" but also a "psychological" one:[11]

Local distinctiveness is essentially about places and our relationship with them. It is as much about the commonplace as about the rare, about the everyday as much as the endangered, and about the ordinary as much as the spectacular. In other cultures it might be about people's deep relationship with the land. Here discontinuities have left us with vestiges of appreciation but few ways of expressing the power which places can have over us. But many of us have strong allegiances to places, complex and compound appreciation of them, and we recognize that nature, identity and place have strong bonds.[12]

In the United States, Daniel Kemmis argues that "no real public life is possible except among people who are engaged in the project of inhabiting a place."[13] He quotes sociologist Robert N. Bellah to explain how community stories help install "practices of commitment" that foster community:

> People growing up in communities of memory not only hear the stories that tell how the community came to be, what its hopes and fears are, and how its ideals are exemplified in outstanding men and women; they also participate in the practices—ritual, aesthetic, ethical—that define the community as a way of life. We call these "practices of commitment" for they define the patterns of loyalty and obligation that keep the community alive.[14]

Scholarship has hardly begun to address the question of how storyscape and story sites contribute to the place attachment that fosters citizenship. But it is clear that people's understanding of place is more than a sensory thing, that it has a narrative dimension encompassing legend, memory, gossip, tradition, and habit. The strength of these narrative attachments has been well documented among Native American cultures, and among other indigenous peoples.[15] Among European and European American cultures ongoing research is revealing deeper-than-expected connections. For Common Ground, places are "process and story as well as artefact, layer upon layer of our continuing history and nature's history intertwined."[16]

Within a modern context, storyscape may in fact be working on two levels. On the first level, citizens of New York City (for example) are unconsciously molded by certain frequently told stories about the city and its residents: "If you can make it in New York you can make it anywhere"; we're smart, tough, enterprising, sophisticated; "the city that never sleeps"; the "melting pot"; and so forth. Actually, these stories are quite banal. Yet the iconic places and images that represent and trigger them—the skyline, the Statue of Liberty, Ellis Island, the prototypical pushcart, Tavern on the Green—are not. They are powerful symbols of what we think (or assume without thinking) it means to be a member of the community of New Yorkers, touchstones and teachers of citizenship.

One reason stories like these seem banal is that they are quite impersonal. That indeed may be why they can be publicly traded as widely as they are. It is questionable, though, whether their value as currency would be so widely accepted were there not also a broad layer of more private, more local, stories. These stories form the second level, and it too has its representative places:

they are the story sites of personal memory, neighborhood tradition, local history, community identity, and social and cultural capital. Perhaps then the publicly traded stories of place work because they serve as proxies for the more private and local attachments of its citizens. In any case, anyone who lives deeply in a place is likely to become attached to it through these local and personal stories and sites. And if being attached to place, if being aware of and dedicated to inhabiting a particular place, can bolster citizenship in the twenty-first century, then cultivating a rich storyscape will be an enterprise of the greatest social value.

IDENTIFYING AND EVALUATING STORY SITES

Given the wide range of values that they provide to the public, one might think that story sites would be zealously protected. Yet this is not the case. The vast majority are unrecognized: all too often their importance will be discussed only in the face of imminent destruction. (And, then, the structure of public debate may provide little room for discussion.) Even many widely recognized sites lack adequate protection. In some cases this is because the existing conservation and preservation laws are not well adapted to the special qualities of story sites: new legal mechanisms, or at least new standards and guidelines, deserve discussion. Yet in other cases, lack of protection reflects failure to recognize and harness the potential of the existing law. The remainder of this chapter focuses on how to use the tools that are currently available, considering the questions first of identifying story sites, then of assessing their significance, and finally of applying the existing laws to their protection.

Surveying and Identifying Story Sites

To identify every significant story site within a state, region, or city would be such a formidable task that no public or private agency is equipped to carry it out within a reasonable period of time. However, more limited surveys are not only practical but likely to be useful in many situations. One occurs whenever communities find themselves suddenly threatened by environmentally harmful proposals. Typically, communities in this situation are thrown into emergency-response mode: it is too late, and resources are stretched too thin, to begin identifying and documenting story sites. By contrast, surveys carried out in a timely manner can provide communities with valuable information and establish a record for when it is needed.

Absent the threat of an emergency, there are many other reasons why a community might find a survey useful. A preservation agency or civic group may wish to identify sites that relate to a theme of importance to the community, such as Scandinavian folk traditions or the experiences of working women. Planners concerned with zoning, community-based plans, tourism development, special districts such as national or state heritage areas, empowerment zones, or coastal management zones may find opportunities for economic and cultural development in storyscape surveys. So may the administrators of history museums, historic houses, and community-based or ethnically specific cultural institutions. For schools and colleges, storyscape surveys may contribute to curriculum as well as to community relations. Those responsible for siting facilities from waste-transfer stations to cellular towers may save time and money by identifying story sites in an early planning stage. And environmental justice advocates will surely want to understand the cultural dimensions of their community's environment. Fortunately, storyscape surveys are eminently "do-able," requiring modest resources of money, time, professional expertise, and community involvement, and leading to results on which sound protection decisions can be based.

Though each of the laws available to protect story sites imposes its own eligibility requirements (discussed below), the basic principles of storyscape survey can be easily summarized. They are quite simple: to discover the stories, situate them within the life and beliefs of the community, demonstrate their connection to specific places, and document the ways in which those places' form or appearance supports the retelling or reliving of the stories.

To understand how these principles can be applied in practice it helps to contrast a storyscape survey with an architectural survey, one of the standard forms of landmark survey. In an architectural survey the first goal is to identify visually distinctive buildings or groups of buildings. The major work is done by eye, often from a moving car. Research in printed sources shores up the findings of this visual survey but will frequently focus on identifying architects, dating buildings, and naming styles. Architectural surveys may also include research into the neighborhood's history, but this is likely to be considered background information. In a story-site survey, by contrast, the major work will be in prizing out the stories and linking them to particular places. This is largely a matter of research in printed sources and of talking and listening to people: the balance between written and oral sources will depend on the nature of the particular survey. Either way, visual documentation will follow, rather than precede, research into the stories, and identification of architects, styles, and building dates may be quite unimportant.

In practice, story-site surveys are likely to fall into one of two types: place-centered and theme-centered. In the former, the goal is to identify and document the full scope of story sites within a community; in the latter, to identify sites related to a particular theme, perhaps taking in a broader geographic radius. The difference is a matter of emphasis. Even a tightly focused thematic survey will be alert to the nuances of place, while a wide survey of places will likely use themes to organize its stories. Either way, the basic principles are the same.

A successful story-site survey requires a different array of professionals from an architectural or environmental survey: historians, specialists in oral history, folklorists, geographers, anthropologists, and archaeologists all have roles to play. A successful survey also requires extensive community participation because, where living traditions are concerned, community members are critically important sources of information on stories and sites: indeed their views may be definitive, as explained below. For Native Americans, of course, history is a living tradition too, no matter how long ago the events may have taken place. There is a useful lesson here for European Americans: even where a survey concentrates on the sort of historical stories for which written sources are usually favored, it is well worth collecting related oral traditions because they will reveal the site's contribution to the place's culture and sense of identity.

There are many ways to gather this information, but all are based on talking and listening. Public meetings, informal discussion groups, individual interviews, and questionnaires can all be effective tools. Each may reach a different segment of the public, and in constructing the survey it is important to ensure that the right kind and number of events are scheduled, in the right locations, to reach a representative sample of the community.

A word on architecture is necessary. While the traditional documentation of landmark surveys, and the judgments of architectural quality that they typically make, may be largely irrelevant, architecture in its broadest meaning, as the physical shaping of space and place, is extremely important. Architecture in this sense, and more broadly the physical environment, is both the container of stories and their embodiment. It is also that which the law may be invoked to protect. Thus it is essential to document the shape, layout, and appearance of story sites, and to do so without prejudice as to the aesthetic merits of certain styles, periods, building types, architects, materials, or forms. Where possible, it is a good idea to visit the sites with local informants, and to document them in use (though with certain kinds of places, like Indian sacred sites, this is clearly inappropriate).

Assessing the Relative Importance of Story Sites

For many preservationists, the challenge of assessment looms over the entire storyscape enterprise like a wall that cannot be scaled: how to distinguish the really important sites from the less important or even unimportant ones? The difficulty has been exaggerated to the point where it inhibits valuable survey work and creative thinking about story sites in general. The fear is of the act of assessment in the abstract, of the impossibility of ranking hundreds or thousands of sites competitively against each other. But there is rarely any need to do so. In many cases, it will be valuable simply to identify, document, and publicize the sites. And when the need for assessment does arise, it generally does so within the context of a particular law or procedure. Each of these has its own criteria which, though not always helpful to story sites in general (or to specific kinds of story sites), are not particularly difficult to understand or apply. Nor do they generally turn on comparative claims that, for example, a site is "the most important," or "the last remaining," or "more significant than x or y." In general, the case for a site should be based on positive assertions about the stories associated with it, its contribution to community life and tradition, its value as a historical marker, and the consequences that its loss would have for the local or wider community.

Some further remarks on the problem of assessment may be useful, if only to clear away certain misconceptions. One is that architectural assessment, that is, the traditional form of landmark assessment, is "objective," while story-site assessment is "subjective." In fact, both forms of judgment can be equally objective. Conversely, both are equally rooted in changing professional standards and an evolving social consensus. In 1965, when the New York City Landmarks Law was passed, sober architectural historians did not consider the Chrysler Building landmark material; now its landmark quality seems self-evident. The law has been successful in part because it has been able to respond to changing views and changing citizen needs. Like architectural judgments, concepts of history have evolved, from a focus on national narratives, the founding fathers, and important individuals (generally white and male) to a broader appreciation of the experiences and contributions of ordinary people of all kinds. But this does not mean that judgments of significance are based on mere whim or personal preference. The objectivity that should be expected of the case for a story site is the same as for an architectural landmark: the analysis should reflect high standards of professional expertise and the soundest judgment available at the time and place.

A second misconception is that admitting an interest in story sites will lead agencies and the public into a morass of invidious racial or ethnic distinctions: is an Irish site more important than a Dominican site, a women's site more worthy than a dock workers'? In point of fact, arguments like these should be avoided at all costs, and responsible leaders will surely help to do so. But if the work of assessment is honestly and well done, there is no reason to dread this outcome. Deeply divided though our society may be, story sites are more likely to provide a focus for constructive public discussion than for strife.

One reason for the fear of strife is, again, the suspicion that there are simply no standards of significance for history and culture: every person, every group, every locality has a history, and who is to judge among them? But historians and others who deal with culture have developed standards with which to sift the superfluity of information. The choice of themes and subjects presented in a college-level textbook of American history, for example, reflects the application of such standards. The National Register of Historic Places has turned such standards into a practical policy device by setting forth an array of broad historical themes and requiring that nominations based on historic significance relate to one or more of them. The list, of course, is not closed: it can evolve over time.

Relating sites to themes of recognized importance, then, provides one basis for evaluation. It also helps solve another problem, that of scale. How can a locally significant site be measured against one of national importance? Under what conditions should a national, state, or municipal law recognize a site whose direct value is limited to its immediate locality? A good answer can be reached by relating the site to a larger theme. If a site's story gives access to a larger narrative or theme, if it grounds that narrative in place, then the site is significant within the larger municipal, state, or national community—even if its particular story is of largely local interest.

According to this standard the former Woolworth's store in Corona (Figure 2.1) deserves recognition under city, state, or national laws: though the direct effects of the events that took place there were limited to the immediate neighborhood, they relate to a much larger theme of undisputed national significance, the story of race relations and civil rights.

Within any given city or state, there may be dozens of local sites that relate to the same theme, and another frequent worry is how to assess their relative merit. It must be repeated that such an assessment is not required by any environmental or historic preservation law. If it arises at all it is only in the context of an arbitrary administrative decision, for example to add twenty (but no more than twenty) civil rights sites to the State Register, or to designate five (not six) sites as local landmarks. When it is necessary to compare sites from different localities, two standards can be used. First, some sites may clearly have a stronger connection to a larger theme than others. Equally important is the site's local effectiveness at telling a story, and this must be judged by setting the site within its local context. Those making the case should therefore clearly establish the strength of the site's connection to broad themes *and* its value within the community.

A final point concerns sources. For most historical topics, the strongest sources are written records. Conservation professionals are usually comfortable with these. However, where a site's story relates to the ongoing life or beliefs of a community, oral testimony is critically important. And where community members speak of a site's significance to them, their words must be regarded not as opinions but as statements of fact: they are the authorities on this question and their testimony must be accepted as authoritative. This does not mean that outsiders or decision-makers must accept what they say uncritically: like written statements (including ones hundreds of years old), oral statements should be sifted for signs of conflict of interest, special pleading, or insincerity. And of course one should expect differences of opinion within a community. But once the sincerity of a statement of community significance is established, its authority must be accepted. This principle has been recognized within a Native American context by Executive Order 13007, which entrusts the authority for identifying Indian sacred sites unrestrictedly to "an Indian tribe, or Indian individual determined to be an appropriately authoritative representative of an Indian religion."[17]

LEGAL TOOLS FOR PROTECTING STORY SITES

The legal protection available for story sites, as already stated, is inadequate. No law addresses them as a category. Nevertheless, many sites do meet the standards established by local, state, and federal historic preservation and environmental laws. And these laws offer some protection for the physical elements of story sites—buildings, landscape settings, and so forth. It is worth considering how they can be used to the benefit of storyscape.

It is also important to consider the ways in which they are inadequate. There are three. First, only the local laws (and not all of them) offer real protection against demolition or inappropriate alteration: most relevant state and federal preservation and environmental laws are essentially disclosure requirements that can help to ensure that the fate of an important site is publicly aired but can rarely preserve it. Moreover, such limited protective power as the state and federal laws do have is directed narrowly at actions sponsored, funded, or permitted by state and federal governments. (These shortcomings, of course, apply equally to all categories of resources and do not particularly disadvantage story sites.)

A second shortcoming, felt particularly by story sites, is that, even where protection is effectively exercised, it extends only to the physical aspects of the site, whereas the heart of a story site often seems to lie in another dimension. It is the sociability and the service provided by coffee shops, laundromats, candy stores, and beer gardens (and sometimes even churches, synagogues, and mosques), rather than their architectural form, that makes them cherished sites. Saving buildings like these won't necessarily save the activities that make them valuable, and for these activities the law offers even fewer protective measures than for their outward forms, a problem taken up in more detail in Chapters 2 and 9. Zoning may help protect a use; so may the investment tax benefits available to commercial properties through National Register listing (but they may also encourage its replacement);[18] neighborhood planning may help create supportive conditions for it; but none of these can assure the continuation of a site's traditional use. Where farms and open space constitute story sites, perhaps by virtue of their vistas or informal but long-established community use, land trusts, tax assessment policies, transfers of development rights, and other related planning tools may help assure the preservation of use along with form. But generally uses remain beyond reach. This has led some preservationists to question the value of protecting story sites and buildings at all. There is, however, a case to be made on the other side. Physical artifacts are at the heart of many story sites—despite some examples to the contrary—and protecting them is very much to the point. Moreover, even where a site's physical form is of secondary importance, the ability to protect it may increase the chances of its use or associations surviving as well. Incomplete though it may be, the physical protection afforded by law is still worth invoking.

The third shortcoming is the difficulty of getting story sites listed, designated, or recognized as environmentally significant for the purposes of protective legislation. This is very much a problem specific to story sites. It is not that story sites fall outside the laws' scope—many fall squarely within it—but rather that interest in protecting them is relatively new, communities inexperienced, procedures untested, and agencies cautious. The remainder of this chapter therefore focuses on the challenge of crossing the legal threshold: meeting the substantive standards for listing, designation, or a showing of environmental significance.

Before proceeding, it should be noted that, in addition to the preservation and environmental laws of general applicability, a separate set of laws applies to Indian sites: the Archaeological Resources Protection Act, Reservoir Salvage and Archaeological Protection Act, Native American Graves and Repatriation Act, American Indian Religious Freedom Act, and Executive Order 13007. State statutes may apply as well: in New York, these include Section 12-a of the New York State Indian Law and the "Standards for Cultural Resource Investigations and the Curation of Archaeological Collections in New York State," adopted by the New York Archaeological Council.[19] Yet other state laws apply to certain story sites whether or not they are Native American: in New York, for example, properties affected by major utility transmission facilities will be subject to the environmental provisions of the Public Service Law, while those located in the Adirondack Park are covered by the Adirondack Park Agency Act.[20] Finally, the law of environmental justice may be applicable to storyscape in some instances.[21] All of these areas deserve further exploration. This article focuses on the laws of general applicability, and by way of example, specifically on those of New York State and City.

Local Landmarks Protection: The New York City Landmarks Law

The New York City Landmarks Law envisions the protection of many kinds of story sites. Its public purposes are (*inter alia*) to protect improvements, landscape features, and districts which "represent or reflect elements of the city's cultural, social, economic, political and architectural history" and to "safeguard the city's historic, aesthetic and cultural heritage, as embodied and reflected" in such places.[22] These terms seem to encompass the protection of significant story sites. Nevertheless, there has been considerable debate about how the Landmarks Preservation Commission should achieve these goals.

In recent years, this debate has often been framed in terms of a stark question: what is the Commission's responsibility for protecting sites that lack architectural merit (but have historical significance)? This is not a very helpful way to approach the issue. While it accurately reflects the Commission's tradition of giving priority to architectural excellence as a criterion for designation, it does not correspond very closely to the real world, which contains many story sites with architectural interest, as well as fine buildings with significant stories. Through its designations, in any case, the Landmarks Commission has clearly established the principle that architectural distinction is not required for landmark designation. The Louis Armstrong house (Figure 2.3) is an utterly ordinary product of a twentieth-century builder; the Lewis Latimer house has not only been altered from its modest Victorian origins but also moved; the African Burial Ground's historic resources are underground and cannot be seen at all (Figures 7.1 to 7.3). Beyond sites like these, the Commission has relied largely on historical arguments to designate many sites that, as a secondary matter, also possess architectural interest, for example a group of historic Broadway theater interiors and (when it was under New York's jurisdiction) Ellis Island.

The Commission has never promulgated explicit or detailed criteria for story sites or, for that matter, for architecturally significant buildings. Apart

Figure 2.3 A "Custom Architectural Replica" sold at Louis Armstrong's house (Corona, Queens: left) suggests the house's lack of architectural distinction. A world-famous musician, Armstrong was a beloved figure in the neighborhood. His widow willed the house to the city on condition that it receive landmark status. Later, local groups agitated to have it opened as a museum and to keep the collections in the neighborhood. In 2003, Queens College opened the house and in 2008 announced construction of a visitor center and archive across the street. A nearby house which has received no recognition is the bungalow on 97th Street where Malcolm X lived at the time of his assassination at the Audubon Ballroom (right; see also Figures 7.4 to 7.6).

from its general references to history and culture, cited above, the law states only that a landmark must have "a special character or special historical or aesthetic interest or value as part of the development, heritage or cultural characteristics of the city, state or nation."[23] It is important to note that the law does not require a landmark to be the first, biggest, best, only, or only surviving example of its type: merely that it have a "special character" or "special historical or aesthetic interest." It, or any part of it, must also be at least thirty years old.[24]

The thirty-year rule does not apply to buildings within historic districts. The definition of historic district (discussed in more detail below) does, however, introduce another standard which may be relevant. The law requires a historic district (among other conditions) to "represent one or more periods or styles of architecture typical of one or more eras in the history of the city."[25] Importantly the standard is "typical," not "exceptional," "remarkable," or "best," and the district need do no more than "represent" those typical periods or styles. The criterion applies specifically to architectural styles, yet the concept of typicality seems to have broader applicability. Certain early farmhouses are landmarks not because of their architectural distinction but because they are typical of their time (and are now rare); a great many nineteenth-century rowhouses, protected as landmarks or within historic districts, are typical, rather than exceptional, and they are not rare at all. "Typical" is certainly a useful standard for many story sites. The lives of millions of immigrants and working people can be represented through tenements, factories, and other buildings that are typical of their kinds, just as the stories of those who lived or worked in them are likely to be typical of many others like them. Again, a dock or factory might be more valuable as a typical exemplar of New York's broad heritage (for example as a global trade center) than for the particular history of the company that built or used it. A good practical rule for regulators and advocates is that, the more a site's significance is argued on the basis of typicality, the more important it is to establish the broad scope and significance of the bigger story which is being typified, and to draw the connections between it and the site.

Questions sometimes arise about what level of geographical significance a site needs to attain. The law requires that a landmark "represent or reflect elements" of the city's history or heritage, and that it be "part" of the "development, heritage or cultural characteristics of the city, state or nation." This is not the same as requiring that it measure up to some general standard of "city-wide" (or broader) significance to which the entire city, or even a broad consensus of the entire city, might subscribe. The criterion leaves plenty of room for stories that do not claim to include all, or even a majority of, New Yorkers— ethnic and racial stories, neighborhood stories, stories of particular classes, affinity groups, professions, or pastimes, stories of dock work and high finance, Puerto Rican cigar-making and ballet dancing, life in tenements or mansions. All of these and many more are "part" of the city's (and state's and nation's) heritage and culture. So are the sites that represent them.

The law's thirty-year age requirement has an obvious filtering effect on story sites.[26] It is intended to ensure that sites do not become landmarks before their significance has been soberly weighed with the benefit of historical perspective (or hindsight). Unfortunately, this makes it hard to protect sites which are important as focal points of ongoing neighborhood traditions. Still, it should be noted that the law does not require a landmark's *significance* to date back further than thirty years, but only some part of its physical fabric. Could an architecturally undistinguished old building be designated a landmark because of important community traditions or associations that were less than thirty years old? In theory, yes, though this has never been proposed. The thirty-year rule has another unexpected consequence: to protect the site of a truly ancient tradition, advocates must show that some part of the physical fabric is also older than thirty years: the site of a long-established procession or observance could fail the test if the building that housed it had been replaced less than thirty years ago.

These concerns are somewhat theoretical. In practice, advocates and decision-makers should keep in mind that information concerning ongoing traditions or ways of life can at the very least contribute to the rationale for designating a landmark and that, to the extent that it can be shown that these ways of life are older than thirty years, the case is surely strengthened. It is also important to note that the thirty-year rule does not apply to buildings within historic districts, so that a story site of even quite recent vintage, located within a historic district, would fall solidly within the Landmarks Commission's regulatory jurisdiction—even if the site's story was not part of the rationale for designating the district and is not reflected in the designation report.

The standard for historic districts is subtly different from that for landmarks in other ways. Districts must contain improvements that, like individual landmarks, have "a special character or special historical or aesthetic interest or value." These improvements must also (as noted above) represent a period or style of architecture. Finally, by virtue of these factors, they must "constitute a distinct section of the city."[27] Historic districts range in size from small clusters of buildings to neighborhoods spanning many blocks. To each, the Commission has applied the "distinct section" criterion, essentially by requiring that a historic district possess a distinct "sense of place."

Can the required sense of place be created by factors other than architectural appearance? Can a story or set of stories constitute a "distinct section"? The Landmarks Commission has set a positive precedent in answer to these questions. The buildings on the surface of the African Burial Ground are a mixed company that does not coalesce visually into a sense of place and would not, on its own, constitute a "distinct section" (Figures 7.1 to 7.3). Rather, the sense of place is powerfully created by the site's history as a burying ground—even though the burials that still exist are underground and intended to remain hidden, while those that have been removed are no longer part of the site at all.

More recently, when Ellis Island was within New York's jurisdiction, the Landmarks Commission designated the island's complex of buildings as a historic district. Here the sense of a place with a special purpose and history was visually embodied in the buildings, but there was no question that the primary rationale for the designation was historical.

Beyond powerful examples like these, storyscape's role in creating historic districts remains undefined, but there seems no reason why a story, or set of stories, could not provide the rationale for a historic district, as long as those stories give the proposed district a distinctive sense of place. It seems too that these stories need not be all-pervasive to meet this standard. The law does not require that every building in a historic district contribute to its sense of place, only that the district contain improvements that constitute a "distinct section." In practice, most historic districts contain some jarring buildings as well as vacant lots. The African Burial Ground once again represents the extreme case of a district not one of whose buildings contributes to its historically derived sense of place. Elsewhere, the question of how many historically out-of-character or non-contributing buildings a district may contain before it loses its sense of place will require an exercise of judgment comparable to those that commissioners routinely perform with regard to architecturally non-contributing buildings or vacant lots.

Beyond providing a sole or primary rationale for historic districts, stories may figure constructively in establishing or revising the boundaries of districts that have been designated mainly for other reasons. An area characterized, for example, by rowhouses might have strong historical ties to a nearby canal, waterfront, industrial area, shopping street, school, or vista, or to an adjoining area of tenements or apartment buildings. These adjoining areas might be visually quite distinct. Yet an understanding of the stories that link them could provide a strong rationale for joining them in a single historic district.

Designation as either a landmark or a historic district requires meeting another criterion which, though not spelled out, can be inferred. The law is essentially a regulatory device, and the commission's main activity is to regulate the treatment of designated "improvements" or "landscape features." The law's use of these terms ensures that what is designated will have a physical dimension capable of being regulated. But practice has added a further expectation, that a landmark's physical qualities—its regulable aspect—will display a close connection to the aspect of the city's heritage that its protection is intended to safeguard. In other words, there is no point regulating a landmark's physical characteristics if this does not help to safeguard the heritage associated with it. With respect to architecturally significant landmarks, this has meant an expectation that the building be in a good state of preservation: that it retain all or most of the architectural features that make it significant. With regard to story sites, the expectation has been a little less clear. In effect, it is that the landmark's current appearance should be reasonably close to the appearance it had at the time of the historical events, persons, or cultural activities for which it is being designated (though some staff and commissioners find it difficult to relinquish the requirement's more architectural expression). It is important to note, once again, that this standard does not require the landmark to be aesthetically distinguished but only reasonably unchanged: the Louis Armstrong house (Figure 2.3) perfectly exemplifies this. Still, how unchanged has never been precisely decided. Apartment buildings on Edgecombe Avenue, home to many important figures from the Harlem Renaissance, had suffered alterations to windows and other ornamental features (alterations that might have counted against them had their rationale for designation been architectural); the Lewis Latimer house, altered and moved from its original location, stretched the connection between historical and current condition even further.

These landmarks are associated with particular people who lived within a precisely defined span of years. What about potential landmarks associated with traditions or cultural activities that span long periods, perhaps extending to the present time, and whose link to the site depends only loosely on specific physical attributes? Fishing may require a pier but be indifferent to the shape or material of the pilings. An annual procession may require a street or square, may be aided by the presence of low-rise, traditional-style buildings (as opposed, say, to parking lots, gas stations, a prison, or steel-and-glass office buildings), yet be indifferent to the details of cornices along the route. These are not regulatory questions which the commission is used to addressing, for the law and the people who administer it remain more receptive to sites associated with significant individuals or historical events than with traditions or ways of living. A case in point occurred when Spanish Camp, a bungalow colony on Staten Island, was sold to a developer. The colony had been founded in 1923 by immigrants from Spain: many of the bungalows were still occupied by descendants of the original owners, and the community represented a distinctive and cherished traditional way of life. One house in particular interested preservationists because it had been the home of Dorothy Day, the inspirational leader of the Catholic Worker movement. As demolition loomed ever closer, the city's Landmarks Commission considered declaring the Dorothy Day cottage a landmark. But it never considered protecting the entire colony. (In the end, all of the houses were bulldozed.)[28]

In the absence of established standards for regulating sites of tradition or cultural association, a reasonable working standard would be to require that a demonstrable connection exist between the story and some physical aspect of the site that falls within the Landmarks Commission's regulatory jurisdiction.

The National and State Registers of Historic Places

The National and State Registers form the basis for protection under federal and state preservation law. Their standards and procedures are substantially similar; the main difference is that one offers protection from federally funded, sponsored, or permitted actions, the other from comparable state actions. As between the Registers and local laws such as New York City's, there are three major differences. First, the Registers provide no protection against the actions of private landowners. Second, in some circumstances they do provide access to state and federal tax benefits.[29] Third, whereas designation reports (at least in New York City) are prepared by agency staff (or at least under its guidance), Register nominations and research are typically provided to the agency by citizens.

Like the New York City Landmarks Law, the Registers take a broad view of what factors make a site eligible for listing. However, the Registers' recognition of historical value is both more explicit and more codified. Register-listed or eligible properties must possess "significance," which is defined as stemming from architectural value or from one of three explicit historical criteria: association with "events that have made a significant contribution to the broad patterns of our history," association with "the lives of persons significant in our past," or the capacity (proven or potential) to yield "information important in prehistory or history."[30] These standards clearly embrace a broad range of story sites, though that range is somewhat narrowed by special considerations regarding particular classes of property (cemeteries, commemorative structures, birthplaces, graves, religious properties, and structures that have been moved are typically excluded). It is more substantially narrowed by two further requirements: first, that properties possess "integrity of location, design, setting, materials, workmanship, feeling, and association" (discussed in more detail below); and, second, that they "achieved significance" more than fifty years ago (unless they are of "exceptional importance").[31] Beyond setting forth these criteria, the National Park Service has published an extensive series of bulletins explaining how to apply them to particular contexts, building types, and so forth.[32]

In practice, the Registers, at least in New York State, have been more receptive to arguments based on historical significance than the New York City landmarks law, and in establishing the boundaries of districts their recognition of historical factors has often been expansive, whether in large urban districts such as the National Register's Sunset Park district in Brooklyn, or much larger rural ones such as Montana's Sweetgrass Hills. In the area of rural historical landscapes, for example, the National Register's guidelines admit of a very broad consideration of historical and cultural factors and encourage nominators to consider the relationship between small intact properties and larger assemblages that could be listed as "large and cohesive historic districts."[33] The Registers have on occasion used elevation contour lines rather than property lines to establish district boundaries, thus encompassing large swaths of countryside and scattered groups of buildings. In addition to historic districts, the Register offers another useful tool for recognizing stories that pervade a landscape or neighborhood, the multiple property submission. Essentially a group of individual nominations bundled under the heading of a place or historical theme or themes, the multiple property nomination provides a way to develop a set of neighborhood or regional stories that go beyond a single site, and to gain recognition for all of the contributing sites at once.[34]

Despite these encouragements to storyscape, the Registers present impediments too. The fifty-year rule is one: it could disqualify many sites whose association with traditional practices or community customs cannot be shown to have achieved significance more than fifty years ago (a genuine concern in large and dynamically changing cities). The integrity criterion is another. The law does not define integrity beyond the requirement quoted above. But various National Register publications offer guidance on interpreting it. With regard to rural historic landscapes, for example, the property's appearance and condition during one or more identified "periods of significance" furnish a "benchmark" for a professional judgment as to "whether a property today reflects the spatial organization, physical components, and historic associations that it attained during the period of significance." More specifically, historical integrity requires that "the various characteristics that shaped the land during the historic period be present today in much the same way they were historically."[35] Informally the question is often asked with regard to Register nominations of various kinds: would a visitor from the property's period of significance recognize it in its current condition?

While not inflexible, the integrity criterion obviously favors sites with a precisely definable and datable historical significance—where x happened, or y lived—over sites of broader association with community culture or tradition. It also prizes continuity of material and design over continuity of use or association. A building of substantially original form and materials that had lost its popular associations would likely meet the integrity criterion whereas one with powerful association appeal and importance to tradition whose form or materials had been altered since its "period of significance" would have difficulty qualifying. Part of the problem, of course, is that the fifty-year requirement rules out the present or even the recent past as a potential period of significance. Thus the integrity criterion tends to work against story sites whose importance is based in current use or association, or even in continuous use over an extended period of significance. Industrial buildings, for example, are prone to frequent and sometimes dramatic alteration: this might well disqualify a factory, warehouse, or dock even if its main significance lay in the very history of long-continued use that prompted the alterations. The same problem threatens to disqualify clubs, commercial establishments, and other places of public assembly whose social value tends to survive occasional alteration (and may indeed be extended by well-considered alteration), as well as structures whose materials are prone to frequent replacement, such as piers.

Fortunately the National Park Service has pioneered a route that may at least help some properties maneuver around these obstacles. The Register-sanctioned concept of "traditional cultural property," discussed in detail in one of the Register's bulletins,[36] was developed in response to the challenges of Native American sites. Native Americans did not apply the same sense of time to historic sites as European Americans; indeed they did not make the same distinction between historical and present time. Nor did they distinguish between oral history or tradition and the kinds of sources that European Americans typically regard as historical (primarily written accounts produced at a precise date). Yet their attachment to places was very strong: their stories endowed these places with an extraordinary richness of cultural association, and the continuity of their traditions was deep. Clearly there were many important Native American sites that met the broad intent of the National Register program. Some had already been listed or determined eligible. But clearly others would face shipwreck were an attempt made to pilot them through the Register's criteria for evaluation. The concept of traditional cultural properties was elaborated to provide an appropriate framework within which Native American sites could be assessed and listed on the Register.

While much about the traditional cultural property (TCP) concept is specifically relevant to Native American sites, there is nothing in the concept itself, or in the Register's regulations, to prevent its extension to other contexts and types of property.[37] In 2000, two sites in New York City were entered into the State and National Registers as traditional cultural properties: a beer garden (Figure 2.4) and a religious grotto.[38] Yet extension of the concept beyond Indian sites has been slow and tentative: attempts to list Gaelic Park and the Casa Amadeo (a record shop), both in the Bronx, and Stiltsville, a community of fishing cottages in Florida, as traditional cultural properties failed (though the Casa Amadeo was admitted to the Register under the "exceptional significance" condition[39]).

The National Register defines "traditional," in the context of "TCPs," as referring to those "beliefs, customs, and practices of a living community of people that have been passed down through the generations, usually orally or through practice." Traditional cultural significance is based on "the role the

Figure 2.4 Bohemian Hall in Astoria, Queens. The city's last central-European-style beer garden was listed on the National Register of Historic Places as a traditional cultural property in 2000.

property plays in a community's historically rooted beliefs, customs, and practices."[40] These definitions have prompted some fine-tuning of the Register criteria for eligibility: where they refer to events that have contributed to "our history," or to persons significant in "our past," it has been determined that the word "our" may be taken to refer to the specific group associated with the TCP (rather than to the state or nation as a whole); also, a place's association with "persons" may include relations with gods and demigods who figure in the group's traditions. The integrity criterion has also been interpreted with regard to TCPs: the property must have "an integral relationship to traditional cultural practices or beliefs" and exist in a condition "such that the relevant relationships survive."[41] These standards lift the Register's heavy emphasis on unchanged physical condition and place it where it should be: on the ability of the place to sustain tradition or belief. Finally, in order to recognize the nature of traditional cultural properties as continuing expressions of traditional culture or belief, the Register has recognized that the period of significance must be allowed to extend to the present. Unfortunately, the fifty-year rule remains largely in effect. Generally accepted views of Indians as living in a world of deep, almost timeless traditions give sanction to the statement that "a significance ascribed to a property only in the last 50 years cannot be considered traditional"[42]—a questionable assertion with regard to modern urban civilization.

It is useful to consider some of the concerns that Register staff have raised in response to attempts to list non-Native sites as TCPs. Perhaps the most serious involves the definition of traditional culture. A site could be associated with a culture, yet the culture might not be traditional. Reliance on oral tradition (as for example characterizes some African American communities) would certainly strengthen the case. So might a distinct ethnic association. Even with such an association, however, the culture might be judged to have been displaced from its point of origin and to have been sufficiently changed in the displacement no longer to be traditional (the Latin jazz whose development was associated with the Casa Amadeo, for example, was not the same as the Latin jazz of Cuba or Puerto Rico: it was a new form of music developed in New York). Then too the traditional culture must qualify as a culture. A site might, for example, be profoundly important to a particular religious denomination, profession, or group of hobbyists yet fail as a TCP if it were judged that the practices of the group did not constitute a distinct culture. Finally, the cultural association must continue to the present: the community of Stiltsville, while once a fishing village, failed because it had become largely a weekend community for relatively affluent people. Clearly the door to TCP listing is hard to get through. Yet Register staff and advocates agree that, as thoughtful and well-documented TCP nominations are brought forward, it may open wider.

As for Native American TCPs, the picture is somewhat different. Long before Bulletin 38 was published, New York's State Historic Preservation Office (SHPO) understood that Native American burial sites were significant and was able to list them or find them eligible. As of 2001, no non-burial sites had been listed as TCPs in New York State. But this does not mean that the concept has been useless. A proposal to build cell towers on a site in western New York that encompassed two hills mentioned in the Seneca origin myth was withdrawn before Register listing was formally considered. Yet Register staff credit the TCP rubric with helping to save the site by providing a convincing framework in which to explain its significance. Invoked in conversation and negotiation, the traditional cultural property concept has helped to change the way in which both federal and state agencies understand Indian sites and has increased dialogue between federal agencies, the SHPO, and the tribes.[43]

Federal and State Environmental Law

Though the leap from storyscape to environmental law may seem a difficult one, environmental law in fact offers some of the best opportunities to protect story sites, starting at the federal level with the National Environmental Policy Act, or NEPA.

NEPA defines the environment in a way that is broadly inclusive of storyscape, making it federal policy to "preserve important historic, cultural, and natural aspects of our national heritage."[44] NEPA requires federal agencies to carry out environmental impact statements (EISs) whenever they propose major federal actions "significantly affecting the quality of the human environment."[45] The Supreme Court has interpreted this to mean that, for an EIS to be required, the action in question must change the physical environment—aerial, aquatic, and terrestrial (including urban environments, and including historical and cultural resources).[46] But the EIS may document harms that go beyond the physical changes themselves to include physical and psychological health, social welfare, and aesthetic values.[47]

NEPA's approach is supportive of storyscape in several ways. Where federal and state preservation law are narrowly focused on sites that meet certain criteria of age, integrity, and so forth, NEPA encourages a more humanistic understanding of the ways in which communal life, beliefs, and customs interact with the physical environment. And where preservation law favors sites with a definable period of significance, preferably in the historical past, environmental law may be more willing to recognize the importance that story sites have in a community's ongoing life and character: NEPA's "period of significance" is, after all, the present and future. Also, NEPA encourages what the federal Council on Environmental Quality calls an "interdisciplinary, place-based approach to decision-making."[48] Although in practice this has largely meant the synthesis of environmental or ecological considerations into economically or politically driven decision-making, and although this approach has often been put into practice in the context of large watersheds or other regions, the approach could also prove supportive of a methodology that recognizes the ways in which culture and tradition inform the meaning of neighborhoods, towns, sections of cities, riverbanks, valleys, plateaus, or watersheds—in short, an approach informed by storyscape.

New York State's State Environmental Quality Review Act (SEQRA) provides New Yorkers with legal tools that may prove valuable in protecting storyscape,[49] though, like the State and National Register programs, it is largely a disclosure requirement and provides little actual protection. The legislature's intent, according to SEQRA, is to give the "protection and enhancement of the environment, human and community resources . . . appropriate weight with social and economic considerations in determining public policy."[50] SEQRA's definition of the environment, like NEPA's, is broadly inclusive of cultural dimensions, including "resources of agricultural, archaeological, historic or aesthetic significance, existing patterns of population concentration, distribution or growth, [and] existing community or neighborhood character."[51] SEQRA requires the preparation of an environmental impact statement for a wide range of state or municipally sponsored, funded, or permitted projects if the action "may include the potential for at least one significant adverse environmental impact."[52] Of the criteria that SEQRA sets forth for determining whether an adverse impact is "significant," three call for close attention:

(iii) the impairment of the environmental characteristics of a Critical Environmental Area . . .;

(iv) the creation of a material conflict with a community's current plans or goals as officially approved or adopted;

(v) the impairment of the character or quality of important historical, archaeological, architectural, or aesthetic resources or of existing community or neighborhood character.[53]

Of these three the last offers the strongest substantive handholds, and so we consider it first.

SEQRA's concern with the impairment of character or quality brings together two subtly different kinds of resources. First are those that are clearly physical in nature, the archaeological and architectural resources (and perhaps the aesthetic and historical ones): these are artifacts and sites. Here SEQRA appears to overlap with state and federal historical preservation laws. But unlike the State and National Registers, SEQRA does not impose specific requirements, criteria, and considerations for listing. While SEQRA does grant higher recognition to Register sites, in that actions occurring within or "substantially contiguous" to them automatically become "Type I" and are therefore more likely to trigger an EIS, a site *need not* be Register-listed to qualify as a protected environmental resource.

SEQRA's willingness to consider cultural significance in broad terms is further demonstrated by its protection of "community or neighborhood character." Many story sites whose purely architectural or historic value would be hard to demonstrate clearly contribute to community or neighborhood character: favorite trees or park benches, and public gathering places of all kinds, from handball courts to coffee shops, social halls to street corners. In addition, consideration of community character can strengthen the case for the value of locally significant historical or aesthetic resources: the place where longshoremen used to seek day work, a favorite vista.

"Existing community or neighborhood character" has a further significance in that it seems to go beyond the purely physical dimensions of the environment, to engage other non-physical dimensions (as arguably may historical resources). SEQRA permits the consideration of non-physical concerns as long as they are grounded in some aspect of the physical environment. "Community or neighborhood character" has been interpreted to encompass ethnicity, economic profile, population density, rising housing costs, secondary displacement, school crowding, the aesthetic impact of a mall, and even psychological concerns like the fears that a new homeless shelter might trigger among community members.[54] The boundaries are not clearly drawn, but they seem open to the inclusion of places that, by virtue of association, tradition, shared memory, or habitual use, contribute to residents' perceptions of the community's character or amenity.

SEQRA's anxiety to avoid conflicts with a community's "plans and goals" opens another door for story sites. New York City, for example, has a procedural vehicle for creating community-initiated plans that qualify under SEQRA. Called 197(a) plans, these can cover a small neighborhood, a community planning board, or a larger area such as a broad swath of waterfront. They may be comprehensive in scope or focused on a particular aspect or problem. Once approved by the City Planning Commission, they are official city documents. Though 197(a) plans do need to earn approval, communities writing them are effectively unlimited in the spectrum of techniques and criteria they can apply in identifying and planning for story sites. Once a 197(a) plan is approved, its protective goals with regard to storyscape, local tradition, or community character are officially recognized by SEQRA, and actions causing conflict with them will trigger an environmental impact statement. This provision gives communities a valuable tool, and, if communities have not rushed to take it, that may be due more to unfamiliarity than lack of interest.

SEQRA's recognition of critical environmental areas (CEAs) opens yet another door to community protection of storyscape. A critical environmental area is "a specific geographic area designated by a state or local agency, having exceptional or unique environmental characteristics."[55] To qualify, an area must have "an exceptional or unique character" covering at least one of four specific areas. One of these is "agricultural, social, cultural, historic, archaeological, recreational, or educational values"[56]—values which broadly encompass those of story sites. Though no critical environmental areas have thus far been designated for purely cultural or historical character, the possibility exists. And, importantly, the power to designate CEAs rests with local agencies.[57]

SEQRA applies only within New York State. But other states' environmental laws also contain provisions helpful to communities seeking to protect their storyscapes. Hawai'i, as explained in Chapter 9, now requires all environmental impact statements to consider the impacts of proposed developments on "cultural practices" as well as economic and social welfare; in 2007 the state legislature considered extending this broad recognition of culture by amending the historic preservation law to require the state's historic preservation division to carry out a "comprehensive cultural impact study" whenever an environmental impact statement is required.[58] Sometimes even state constitutions may be helpful. Hawaii's 1978 constitution bound the state to protect the rights of descendants of Native Hawaiians to continue using traditional lands for "subsistence, cultural and religious purposes." The 1995 constitution similarly guaranteed that the law would "not infringe upon the right of the Kanaka Maoli Nationals to preserve their traditional culture."[59] The state constitution of Louisiana enumerates the right to hunt, fish, and trap as a fundamental protected right, "a valued natural heritage that shall be forever preserved for the people." The point is that historic preservation law furnishes only one, and not necessarily the best, of many tools available for protecting storyscape. Advocates in each state will do well to look to other sources of authority.

SUMMARY AND CONCLUSIONS

Storyscape—the imprint of personal and communal stories on the environment—encompasses sites associated with history, tradition, and memory. It has great social value, helping to ground people's sense of identity, preserve social and cultural capital, anchor neighborhood identity, convey historical messages, and support the development of citizenship. Yet as a dimension of the environment, storyscape has received little attention or protection. In most communities, knowledge of significant story sites is informally held by residents but has never been codified or publicly recorded, so that when faced with environmental threats communities are unable to act effectively to protect them. By carrying out storyscape surveys, communities, government agencies, and developers can create a basis of sound factual information before emergency strikes. Many kinds of cultural organizations and planners will also be able to use story sites to identify economic and cultural opportunities.

Storyscape surveys can be locally or thematically focused. They require willing and often extensive community participation as well as the contribution of experts in fields such as history, folklore, anthropology, geography, oral history, and archaeology. While goals and methods should be adapted to particular circumstances, the principles of storyscape survey remain constant: to identify important stories, situate them within the life and beliefs of the community, describe their connection to specific places, and document the ways in which the form and appearance of those places support the retelling or reliving of the stories.

Currently three different kinds of law provide some protection for story sites: local historic preservation law, state and federal preservation law, and state and federal environmental law. Each legal umbrella, so to speak, casts a patch of protective shadow: the patches overlap but also leave some areas exposed. The New York City landmarks law recognizes story sites in principle and has protected a number of sites associated with well-known individuals, important historical developments, and widely recognized cultural contributions. It is harder, however, to gain protection for sites associated with community traditions. State and federal preservation law, exemplified by the National and State Registers of Historic Places, recognizes historical and cultural sites in ways that are both more explicit and more codified than the city's landmarks law. But again, these laws are not very welcoming to sites associated with ongoing activities. Environmental law, especially the New York State Environmental Quality Review Act, recognizes the cultural dimensions of the environment, including the importance of community character, without imposing the conditions that tend to limit landmark and Register protection to story sites of a narrowly historical nature. It therefore currently provides the most promising avenue towards formal recognition for story sites that contribute to the cultural identity, practices, and beliefs of communities now.

Many story sites that could be protected lack protection simply because they have not been identified and listed in the appropriate place. This is why it is important to carry out well-documented surveys. What is more, as such surveys are completed and as more sites are listed or designated, it is likely that public agencies and the courts will reinterpret established standards and definitions to better protect story sites. These will be positive developments. But it is unlikely that reinterpretation alone will ever lead to an adequate level of protection for story sites. Given the importance of storyscape to individuals, communities, and society at large, the problem of protecting it deserves a fresh look and a fresh legal approach.

NOTES

1. Chris Johnson, *What Is Social Value? A Discussion Paper* (Canberra: Australian Government Publishing Service, 1992), 1.

2. I am indebted to Richard Rabinowitz, who first used the term "storyscape" to describe sites important to his memories of growing up in Brooklyn. (See the Epilogue to Chapter 6.)

3. Jim O'Grady, "What Remains of the Day; in Vinegar Hill, a Last Look at a Revolutionary War Grave Site," *New York Times* (December 13, 2003).

4. Verlain White, as quoted in Randy Kennedy, "An Indian Community Flourished and Faded in a Section of Brooklyn," *New York Times* (August 31, 2008).

5. Robert D. Putnam, *Bowling Alone: The Collapse and Revival of American Community* (New York: Simon & Schuster, 2000), 19.

6. Ibid., 288–289.

7. Ibid., 290ff.

8. Ibid.

9. These identifications were made by a group of Russian immigrant teenagers during a semester-long neighborhood-discovery program conducted by the author at the Jewish Community House of Bensonhurst.

10. See, for example, Yi-Fu Tuan, *Topophilia: A Study of Environmental Perception, Attitudes, and Values* (Englewood Cliffs, NJ: Prentice-Hall, 1974); and Irwin Altman and Setha M. Low (eds.), *Place Attachment* (New York and London: Plenum Press, 1992).

11. Roger Deakin, "A Local Habitation and a Name," in Sue Clifford and Angela King (eds.), *Local Distinctiveness: Place, Particularity and Identity* (London: Common Ground, 1993), 1.

12. Sue Clifford and Angela King, "Losing Your Place," in Clifford and King (eds.), op. cit., 7.

13. Daniel Kemmis, *Community and the Politics of Place* (Norman: University of Oklahoma Press, 1990), 79–80.

14. Robert N. Bellah, Richard Madsen, William M. Sullivan, Ann Swidler, and Steven M. Tipton, *Habits of the Heart* (Berkeley: University of California Press, 1985), 20–21 (quoted in Kemmis, op. cit., 81).

15. See especially Keith H. Basso, *Wisdom Sites in Places: Landscape and Language Among the Western Apache* (Albuquerque: University of New Mexico Press, 1996). For the ways in which sacred places are informed by stories, see also Andrew Gulliford, *Sacred Objects and Sacred Places: Preserving Tribal Traditions* (Boulder: University Press of Colorado, 2000). For examples of indigenous traditions of place narratives from Australia, see Anthony English, *The Sea and the Rock Gives Us a Feed: Mapping and Managing Gumbaingirr Wild Resource Use Places* (Hurstville, NSW: New South Wales National Parks and Wildlife Service, 2002).

16. Clifford and King, "Losing Your Place," in Clifford and King (eds.), op. cit., 8.

17. Executive Order 13007, May 24, 1996, 1(b)(iii).

18. For tax credits, see *infra*, note 27.

19. See Christopher A. Amato, "Protection of Native American Burial Sites: Opportunities for State/Tribal Cooperation," *Environmental Law in New York* 12 (2001): 65, 76–82. For a detailed analysis of the attributes of Indian sacred sites, which are protected under Executive Order 13007, see Gulliford, op. cit.

20. See Michael B. Gerrard, Daniel A. Ruzow, and Philip Weinberg, *Environmental Impact Review in New York* (Albany, NY: Matthew Bender, 1990), §8.18[1–2].

21. For example, the Clean Water Act protects "existing uses" as of 1975, and it has been argued that, "to the extent that minority or low-income populations are, or at any time since 1975 have been, using the waters for recreational or subsistence fishing, EPA could reinterpret the current regulations to require that such uses, if actually attained, must be maintained and protected." (Memorandum, "EPA Statutory and Regulatory Authorities Under Which Environmental Justice Issues May Be Addressed in Permitting," from Gary S. Guzy, General Counsel to the Environmental Protection Agency, December 1, 2000. Here an environmental justice interpretation of the law suggests that not only a physical resource but also habitual ways in which a community has used that resource could be protected. See, generally, Michael B. Gerrard (ed.), *The Law of Environmental Justice* (Chicago: American Bar Association, 1999).

22. New York City Administrative Code, §25–301(b).

23. Ibid., §25–302(n).

24. Ibid.

25. Ibid., §25–302(h)(1)(b).

26. I am grateful to Dorothy Miner, former counsel to the New York City Landmarks Preservation Commission, for information on the application of the thirty-year rule.

27. New York City Administrative Code §25–302(h)(1)(a–c).

28. The story is summarized and the place's significance discussed in articles in the newsletter of the Preservation League of Staten Island in September 1997 and April 2001.

29. While properties are entitled to receive the protective measures of federal or state preservation laws upon a determination of eligibility for Register listing, a relatively quick and simple process that does not require owner consent, access to tax benefits is restricted to properties that have been listed in the Register, a longer process that requires owner consent as well as a fully developed nomination. Current information on the federal preservation tax incentives program, including all applicable IRS regulations, is available through the National Park Service's website at www.nps.gov/history/tax (last consulted 2009).

30. 36 CFR §60.4.

31. Ibid.

32. National Register Bulletins include numbers on types of properties such as archaeological sites, aviation properties, historic battlefields, cemeteries, rural historic landscapes, mining sites, properties associated with significant persons, traditional cultural properties, and shipwrecks, as well as general guides on carrying out local surveys, applying the criteria for evaluation, submitting multiple property nominations, and so forth. A complete list is available through the National Park Service's website at www.cr.nps.gov/nr/publications/bulletins/puborder.htm (last consulted May 2008).

33. Linda Flint McClelland, J. Timothy Keller, Genevieve P. Keller, and Robert Z. Melnick, *Guidelines for Evaluating and Documenting Rural Historic Landscapes*, National Register Bulletin (Washington, DC: National Park Service, 1989, rev. 1999), 25.

34. 36 CFR §60.3(g) and *How to Complete the National Register Multiple Property Documentation Form*, National Register Bulletin 16B (Washington, DC: National Park Service, 1991). Multiple property submissions in New York State have included Broome County Carousels, Civil War Era National Cemeteries, Harriet Tubman in Auburn, Sidewalk Clocks of New York City, Women's Rights Historic Sites, as well as many that cover specific villages or towns. The National Park Service has sponsored national themes studies on racial desegregation in public education and on the Underground Railroad. (A full list is available on the National Register's website at www.cr.nps.gov/nr/research/mpslist.htm [last consulted May 2008].)

35. McClelland et al., op. cit., 21.

36. Patricia F. Parker and Thomas F. King, *Guidelines for Evaluating and Documenting Traditional Cultural Properties*, National Register Bulletin 38 (Washington, DC: National Park Service, 1982).

37. I am indebted to Elizabeth Savage, of the National Register staff, and Kathleen Howe, of the New York State Office of Parks, Recreation and Historic Preservation, for insights into agency handling of traditional cultural property nominations for non-Indian sites, and to Robert D. Kuhn, of the New York State Office of Parks, Recreation and Historic Preservation, for information on the status of Indian traditional cultural properties.

38. Bohemian Hall and Park, Astoria, Queens, and Our Lady of Mount Carmel Grotto, Staten Island.

39. With regard to "exceptional significance," the condition under which the fifty-year rule may be waived, it is important to note that the significance need not be national: a site's significance could be judged to be exceptional within a local context.

40. Parker and King, op. cit., 1.

41. Ibid., 11, 10.

42. Ibid., 15.

43. I am grateful to Robert D. Kuhn of the New York State Office of Parks, Recreation and Historic Preservation for information on the use of the traditional cultural property rubric for Native American sites in New York State, and to Fred Chapman of the Wyoming State Historic Preservation Office for perspectives on its application elsewhere.

44. 42 USC §4331[b]4.

45. 42 USC §4332[c].

46. Valerie M. Fogleman, "Environmental Impact Statements," in Michael B. Gerrard (ed.), *Environmental Law Practice Guide: State and Federal Law* (Newark, NJ: Lexis, 2000), §1.04[2].

47. Ibid., §1.04[2][e].

48. *The National Environmental Policy Act: A Study of its Effectiveness after Twenty-five Years* (Washington, DC: Council on Environmental Quality, Executive Office of the President, January 1997), 25.

49. For the contents of environmental impact statements under SEQRA, see Gerrard, Ruzow, and Weinberg, op. cit., esp. §5.12; for actions affecting historic structures, §4.20; for SEQRA's interaction with historic preservation laws, §8.12; and for New York City's implementation of SEQRA through the City Environmental Quality Review procedure (CEQR), as well as CEQR's interactions with the New York City Uniform Land Use Review Procedure, landmarks law, fair share process, and other city laws, §8A.

50. 6 N.Y.C.R.R. §617.1(d).

51. 6 N.Y.C.R.R. §617.2(l).

52. 6 N.Y.C.R.R. §617.7(a)(1).

53. 6 N.Y.C.R.R. §617.7(c)(1)(iii–v). Other criteria may also be helpful in protecting story sites, for example substantial increase in traffic or noise levels, "removal or destruction of large quantities of vegetation or fauna" or interference with wildlife movement or habitat, creation of hazards to human health, "substantial change in the use, or intensity of use, of land including agricultural, open space or recreational resources, or in its capacity to support existing uses," and of course "creation of a material demand for other actions that would result in one of the above consequences." Ibid. (i, ii, vii, viii, x). Certain impositions of non-agricultural uses in agricultural districts and actions within or "substantially contiguous" to sites listed or proposed for the National or State Registers or to "publicly owned or operated parkland, recreation area or designated open space" are also specifically called out as significant. Ibid., 617.4(8–10). In addition, EISs must document "any growth-inducing aspects of the proposed action." Ibid., 617.9(b)(5)(iii)(d).

54. Gerrard, Ruzow, and Weinberg, op. cit., §5.12[12].

55. 6 N.Y.C.R.R. §617.2(i).

56. 6 N.Y.C.R.R. §617.14(g)(1)(iii).

57. 6 N.Y.C.R.R. §617.14(g).

58. State of Hawaii, House of Representatives, Twentieth Legislature, 2000, H.B. No. 2895 (A Bill for an Act Relating to Environmental Impact Statements), Sec. 1, 2. See Hawaii Revised Statutes, Chap. 343–2. For the 2007 amendment, see 24th Legislature, 2007, H.B. No. 610, Sec. 1.

59. Hawai'i Constitution (1978), art. 12, sec. 7 (as quoted in Public Access Shoreline Hawai'i vs. Hawai'i County Planning Commission, 79 Hawai'i, 903 P.2d, Sec. IV.B); Hawai'i Constitution (1995), art. 16, sec. 5; Louisiana Constitution (1974), art. 1, sec. 27.

CHAPTER 3

Eliminating the Diversity Deficit

The following chapter originated as a policy study carried out for the Cultural Resources Division of the National Park Service (NPS) in 2002–3. Though best known as the manager of great wilderness parks, the NPS is also the nation's chief preservation agency, responsible for the National Register of Historic Places, the National Historic Landmarks program, the rehabilitation tax credit program, and many other programs related to historic preservation. The study was intended to provide a baseline of infor-mation as well as recommendations to help the agency better preserve a multi-racial past and serve a multi-racial public. Portions were rewritten and published in CRM: The Journal of Heritage Stewardship *in 2004. This chapter incorporates material from both versions, recast to reflect the fact that it is no longer a government document.*

I. BACKGROUND

The National Park Service's Cultural Heritage Needs Assessment: What and Why?

The United States has always been racially diverse. Now it is more so than ever. Yet historic preservation has not done enough to address this reality. Between the nation's history as presented at its historic sites and as lived by its people lies a significant diversity gap. How should historic preservation present racially, ethnically, and culturally diverse historical experiences? How should it serve diverse constituencies? In 2002, the National Park Service commissioned a cultural heritage needs assessment to answer these questions by gaining—as the agency's official project statement put it—a "better understanding of what aspects of cultural heritage are important to minority cultures and what the federal government's cultural programs could do to better address these aspects of heritage."[1] Since an ambitious study of Native American preservation issues, called *Keepers of the Treasures*, had recently been carried out,[2] "minority cultures" in the context of the assess-ment meant African, Hispanic, and Asian Americans. The study's findings and recommendations are presented here. While designed to assist the federal government, they are relevant to preservation programs at every level. Readers seeking to close the diversity gap within their local preservation organization or historical society, statewide non-profit, or municipal or state agency will be able to adapt many of the suggestions below to their particular circumstances.

That the United States is, has always been, and will continue to be a country of many cultures needs no demonstration. The concern behind this study was that the nation's official heritage preservation programs had not measured up either to the promise or to the demands presented by this fact. Minority participation in heritage programs has been limited, and the picture of American history presented by officially designated sites understates the diversity of the nation's actual history. Though this is admittedly difficult to measure, the National Register of Historic Places provides one yardstick. National Park Service policy states that the NPS will "present factual and balanced presentations of the many American cultures, heritages, and histories."[3] Yet out of over 77,000 listings included in the National Register of Historic Places in 2004, only about 1,300 were explicitly associated with African American heritage, 90 with Hispanic, and 67 with Asian.[4] The nation's preservation programs are not keeping up with the reality of racial and cultural diversity, now or in the past.

Unlike some studies which are aimed at broadening program participation, this one did not start by asking how the National Park Service could interest more people in the programs it already offers. Nor did it ask what the NPS is doing wrong. Instead, it asked simply: What do people value? What would they like to conserve? How do they understand their heritage? What services do they want from government?

These are open-ended questions, and the assessment was not expected to provide complete answers. It *was* expected to lay a foundation for new or redesigned programs, mainly by interviewing heritage experts and amateurs within each of the subject communities, and by presenting their views in a format useful to policy-makers and program officials. It was also expected to make some specific recommendations to the National Park Service on the basis of these findings. How information was collected, and how recommendations were framed, requires a note of explanation.[5]

A Note on Methodology

Behind the decision to carry out the cultural heritage needs assessment lay the example of the 1990 report *Keepers of the Treasures*, which presented a powerful statement of tribal preservation needs and led to significant advances in federal programs for Native Americans. However, there were important differences. Unlike tribes, African, Asian, and Hispanic Americans are not officially recognized entities, and they cannot be treated according to a government-to-government model. Furthermore, while the major constituency for tribal preservation programs could be assumed to be future tribal members, similar assumptions could not be made about the groups now being considered.

Another difference was that, unlike many tribes, African, Asian, or Hispanic American communities do not have officially recognized heritage spokespersons. The Cultural Heritage Needs Assessment did not consult with spokespersons, but rather with dedicated experts and amateurs, representing various points of view, who were willing to talk. Most of the study's respondents were professionals in some aspect of heritage conservation; some were citizen leaders. Respondents included first-generation immigrants as well as the descendants of Spanish landowners, teachers, architects, poets, artists, archivists, museum professionals, students, dentists, heritage tourism operators, government officials, activists, film makers, anthropologists, historians, literary scholars, and professional preservationists. Respondents covered a wide age range; and they lived in California, the District of Columbia, Florida, Georgia, Hawaii, Louisiana, Massachusetts, Michigan, New Mexico, New York, Texas, Virginia, Washington, and the Philippines.

The limited resources of time and money available for the assessment prompted other pragmatic decisions. To present the heritage preservation needs of the "Latino community" or the "Asian American community" would have been not only impossible but presumptuous. "There is no real 'Latino community,'" writes Miguel Vasquez: "Instead, there are many."[6] Focusing on one of them—and on one of the equally numerous Asian communities—offered a way to avoid over-generalizations, and so it was decided to focus on Mexican American and Filipino American heritage issues. Still, even national labels turn out to mask great complexity. "Filipinos are so diverse," sighs Angel Velasco Shaw, one of the study's respondents: "our histories are so complicated."[7] Many Filipino immigrants experienced life in this country as farm workers, but others were nurses, doctors, and cooks; still others were artists, writers, and architects. Life in New York City was different from that of the west coast. Migrants from different parts of the Philippine archipelago brought different cultures with them. Those who migrated immediately after World War II may have a different outlook on Filipino history than those who migrated during the Marcos dictatorship.

The label "African American" presents its own problems. It is generally taken to refer to a sector of the population whose ancestors arrived in North America between the beginnings of colonial times and the nineteenth century, largely through the slave trade. But it can also include recent immigrants from Africa or even the Caribbean. In considering African American music, advises another respondent, John W. Franklin, one is practically "*forced* to look at international dynamics," and he argues that placing (for example) "the Maryland experience" in the larger picture of African history, culture, and migration adds greatly to understanding that experience. This, however, was beyond the scope of the assessment. Another pragmatic decision was made to exclude the impact of recent African and Caribbean immigration from the scope of this study.

Readers may ask how far it is safe to generalize information about Mexican American or Filipino American heritage to (say) Dominican or Chinese issues. The answer is, first, that the subjects chosen for study, and the experts interviewed, were not expected to be representative of others and, second, that great care is needed in generalizing. Obviously there are issues that are specific to different groups: the question of Mexican land grants in the southwest is one example. Ideally, the specific needs and goals of every group and sub-group would be known and expressed in discussions over policy and programs. On the other hand, the consistency with which respondents expressed certain views, such as the nature of history and its relationship to community development, suggests that a broader consensus on many important points may in fact exist. The danger of generalizing is obvious. The danger of *not* generalizing—of refusing to draw conclusions and always demanding more information as a precondition for action—is perhaps greater. Enough information already exists for preservation programs at every level from federal agencies to neighborhood non-profits to take significant steps towards reducing the diversity deficit. This is one of the points on which respondents broadly agreed.

While the selection of study topics was on one level pragmatic, the three groups chosen—African, Mexican, and Filipino Americans—have played unusually important roles in American history. All three were among the earliest immigrants to what is now the United States. Africans arrived in the Americas with the Spanish and Portuguese in the sixteenth century, and with the English early in the seventeenth century: the work they did, generally as slaves, played a determining role in shaping the country's economy and history, while their cultural influence has been profound. The Mexican role is also deep. To Spanish colonists in Mexico, what later became the United States' southwest was their far north, a provincial extension of the Spanish empire. Spanish settlement extended from California to Florida; before becoming part of the United States, an area equivalent to twenty states had had contact with Spain, and six took their names from Spanish. When English-speaking colonists moved westward into these territories, they encountered not wilderness but missions, presidios, and pueblos numbering close to 100,000 people.[8] Chicana artist Judith Baca, one of the study's respondents, points out, "We didn't cross the border; the border crossed *us*"; Baca's grandmother habitually called California, where she lived, "El Mexico del Norte." As for Filipinos, they first reached North America during the sixteenth century as sailors aboard Spanish ships—the so-called Manila galleons—and some certainly reached California. The first permanent Filipino settlement seems to have been made during the eighteenth century near New Orleans. The ending of the Spanish–American War in 1898 brought the United States into a closer relationship with the Philippines which, after a bloody struggle, became an American colony.

The relationships between the United States and these three groups have been long, close, and often troubled. Episodes like the slave trade, the Mexican–American War, or the Philippine–American War have not been forgotten. Of course there have been positive episodes too. The point is that each region and its people are intricately braided into American society and have been part of its history for centuries.

II. CONTEXT

Immigration

An important component of the United States' relationships with Mexico, the Philippines, and Africa has been immigration, and this has always been more complex than simply the movement of people from one place to another. African immigration to the U.S. was largely coerced. Filipino immigration was conditioned by what is often called the islands' "special relationship" with the U.S., deriving from colonial status following the Philippine–American War but also from the bravery of many Filipino soldiers who fought for the U.S. in World War II. As for Mexico, U.S. expansion repeatedly pushed the border southward and westward, making U.S. residents of many Mexicans who had not moved an inch.

Today, immigration is changing the United States in important ways and is affecting the position of these groups within American society as well. According to the 2000 Census, more U.S. residents (almost 1.4 million) were born in the Philippines than in any other Asian country, a fact that surprises many white Americans. Mexicans are the largest immigrant group, period, and the largest component of a broad Hispanic influx that may dramatically reshape American culture. "The United States is undergoing a Latinization," writes well-known television anchor newsman Jorge Ramos, "and there is no turning back. It is an overwhelming, definitive, and irreversible phenomenon that is changing the face of America."[9] While some may regret and others may welcome this change, the data suggest that important changes are indeed taking place. Of the roughly 40 million foreign-born residents estimated in the Census Bureau's 2006 American Community Survey, about 20 million, or fully half, were born in Latin America (the next largest number, 10 million, came from Asia). A historical atlas shows that virtually every part of the country has seen substantial recent percentage increases in Hispanic population.[10] In California, where Judith Baca has observed dramatic changes since 1990, "the Mexicanization of Los Angeles has completely transformed the city." Nationally, Hispanics have now replaced African Americans as the largest minority group: in 2007, according to the U.S. Census, Hispanic Americans topped 15 percent of the national population for the first time. Together, they sent almost $46 billion in remittances to family members throughout Latin America, suggesting the strength of international ties.[11] As Ramos notes, the purchasing power of Hispanics nearly doubled during the 1990s, to almost $400 billion in 2000, or more than the gross domestic product of Mexico. The radio stations in Los Angeles with the largest audiences broadcast in Spanish and, "in the United States, more tortillas are sold than bagels, and more hot salsa than ketchup."[12]

It is important to understand what these statistics say and what they do not say. The proportion of foreign-born residents has been higher in the past: in 1870, 14 percent; in 1910, 14.7 percent. Today it is a little less than 11 percent. But as recently as 1970 the figure stood at a mere 4.7 percent,[13] so the change has been rapid and the perception of it vivid. It has also been different from the wave of a hundred years ago. Where ninety of every hundred immigrants came from Europe around 1900, a hundred years later forty-five come from Latin America, twenty-six from Asia, twenty-three from Europe, and the remaining six from other regions.[14] Of the 40 million foreign-born Americans estimated in 2006, the Census Bureau found that only about 5 million, or about one-eighth, came from Europe. The United States has always been a nation of immigrants, but they have not come from as many parts of the globe as now. And the new flows are upsetting traditional orders. Not only are Hispanics (not African Americans) now the largest minority group, but, even within the Hispanic world, traditional balances are shifting. At the beginning of the millennium roughly 800,000 Puerto Ricans lived in New York: they remained the city's largest Hispanic group. But whereas in 1950 Puerto Ricans had totaled 79 percent of New York's Latino population, by 2000 they accounted for only 37 percent: if Puerto Ricans were down, Dominicans and Mexicans were dramatically up.[15]

Most significant are the totals. More than one-third of Americans now belong to racial or ethnic minorities. The percentage is growing, and it is growing fastest among the young. In fact, the U.S. Census reports that in twelve states a majority of children under the age of five now belong to minority groups; these states include giants like California, Texas, Florida, and New York. According to some projections, "minorities" will become a majority of the national population by 2050.[16] Obviously notions like "majority" and "mainstream" will have to adjust to changing realities.

It is difficult to generalize about education and income levels among immigrants, except to say that stereotypes are often wrong. While many immigrants come to the United States (as they always have) with little education and no money, the household income of immigrants from India in 1980 substantially exceeded the U.S. national median. Even among undocumented Mexican immigrants in 1990, estimates place illiteracy at between 3 and 10 percent, versus 22 percent for Mexico as a whole. Similarly, in contrast to the stereotype of undocumented Mexican immigrants as "impoverished peasants," almost half originated in cities, while "white-collar and urban skilled and semi-skilled occupations employed between 35 and 60 percent," as opposed to about 30 percent of the Mexican population as a whole.[17]

These figures, and the complex changes they suggest, are relevant to heritage conservation in several ways. First, they frame the experience of our times, which will become the heritage that future conservationists seek to understand and preserve. Second, they tell us something about the constituency for heritage conservation, both now and especially in the future. Whose needs will heritage programs serve? To whom will heritage professionals turn for support? Increasingly, if recent trends continue, the answers are: members of "minority" groups.

This, however, is only part of the answer to the all-important constituency question. Who will the future members of the nation's majority-minority groups be? Immigration statistics are illuminating, but they also present puzzles. For immigration itself is changing, and with it notions of residence and even citizenship. Scholars have coined the word "transnationalism" to refer to some of these complex and still only partially understood changes.

Transnationalism

Judith Baca, a well-known Chicana artist, has worked with Los Angeles's Mexican communities for over thirty years. In recent years she has noted a change. Mexicanos now outnumber Chicanos, two to six; whereas Chicanos have put down strong roots in Los Angeles, Mexicanos, recent immigrants, maintain networks of relationships with Mexico and have not developed such strong local roots.

This is one aspect of transnationalism: the establishment of communities based on "sustained ties of persons, networks and organizations across the borders across multiple nation-states."[18] Whereas traditional options for immigrants were pretty much limited to settling into the new place or going back to the old, migrants now can also choose to continue making regular visits to their places of origin, sending remittances, keeping in touch through phone calls and emails, carrying on cross-border business and financial dealings, and even maintaining civic and political engagements in their old communities. All of these are happening among today's migrants, and they are creating new cultural situations on both sides of the border. John Silva points out that half of all tourism to the Philippines is Filipino immigrants to the United States—about a million of them each year. "In Mexico," remarks Carlos Monsiváis, "the border with the United States is everywhere, and economically and culturally speaking, all of us Mexicans live along that border." Might Mexico one day become a nation of Chicanos?, he asks.[19] Our concern of course is with developments on the U.S. side of the border.

But where is the border, if people live significant parts of their lives and maintain thick economic and cultural relationships on both sides of it? And what will Mexican American (or Filipino American) cultural heritage look like, fifty years hence, on "our" side of it? Along with challenging traditional notions of migration, transnationalization is also challenging established understandings of ethnic heritage. Until recently, concepts of how ethnic culture develops have tended to follow one of two idealized models. One is assimilation: immigrants gradually blend into the mainstream until their cultural identity is submerged, perhaps to resurface in symbolic representations of ethnicity (St. Patrick's Day parade) by later generations. The other is cultural pluralism: ethnic groups will retain the cultural characteristics of their countries of origins to a significant degree, coexisting as culturally distinct groups within the national borders of their new country. Transnationalization adds a third possibility, that new cultural practices, derived from the mixture of languages, customs, and identities, might emerge out of the experience of straddling a border.[20]

Most perplexingly, transnationalization is challenging accepted notions of national identity and even citizenship. National identity has been a sort of umbrella, big enough to shelter most aspects of a citizen's life—economic transactions, cultural identity, family, social, and political commitments. But the lives of transnational migrants do not fit under a single umbrella. Would two national-identity umbrellas, side by side, encompass them? Or should the two umbrellas become one? Should people be able to shelter under one umbrella for certain aspects of life, under another for others? Whatever the answer, it seems at least possible that national labels may be less compelling as descriptions of identity for many transnational migrants than they have historically been for most residents. And this raises a further question: if *national* identity loses some of its force, will *regional* identity gain? Will some residents come to feel a stronger sense of affiliation to the hyphenated culture of their city or region—Los Angeles, Denver, or New York, for example—than to the more distant abstraction of the nation-state?

It is not only low-income migrants who are stretching the bounds of national identity. A well-to-do Manhattanite might well choose to see a travelling exhibition in Amsterdam rather than take the subway to Brooklyn, and the international art venues frequented by cultural elites form a network of sites that have more in common with each other than with their own cities or regions. Internationalism at the top holds out the promise of enriching heritage practice through a rich network of professional contacts across borders. To gauge the potential contribution to heritage conservation of internationalism across the rest of the spectrum, transnational migration needs to be better understood.

If immigration experts lack definite answers to these questions, historic preservation professionals have hardly begun to ask them. Yet they need to be asked. The answers can enrich the future of heritage work. They may also reshape it. For without venturing too far into the unknown, we can guess that in the future many constituents will maintain active ties to their homelands, and that federal programs will do well to develop new ways to engage their interest and serve their needs.

III. HERITAGE AND CONSERVATION

What Is Heritage?

Describe your symptoms to a group of medical specialists: the pharmacist will prescribe a pill, the surgeon an operation, and the psychiatrist counseling sessions. Something similar happens when you ask heritage specialists what is the highest conservation priority: the literary expert prescribes the written record, the preservationist historic sites, the head of a cultural tourism agency cultural tourism promotion . . . and so forth. The information contained in this report reflects the perspectives of respondents (who were not chosen scientifically) as well as the way questions were asked. Rather than structure interviews around a definition of heritage, we left it open for respondents to interpret the concept in their own ways. "Heritage," after all, has no exact meaning: it might refer to buildings, historic sites and places; collectable things such as books, manuscripts, photographs, artwork, and domestic artifacts; intangible goods such as music, dance, cuisine, stories, and traditions or folkways either old or young; recordings and other productions that lie somewhere between the solid and the insubstantial; and finally, the most elusive, history—the created record of the past.

As to what makes heritage ethnic, a basic premise of this study was that ethnic heritage is not just what immigrants bring with them but also how groups adapt to new conditions in the United States. Dell Upton makes a useful distinction between the "architecture of memory"—features that derive from the country of origin—and "landscapes of experience"—features that register the experiences of an ethnic community in the United States. He argues that landscapes of experience are not only the more widespread but also the more important of the two.[21] Nevertheless, much thinking about ethnic heritage has concentrated on visually striking manifestations of ethnicity, such as Chinese pagodas or German bank barns, which largely belong to the architecture of memory. Moreover, such studies have frequently ignored urban contexts and given short shrift to non-European immigrant groups. Recent studies have begun to break the mold. Turning to urban settings, one study identifies retail signs, food shops, and recreational structures such as Italian social clubs and German beer gardens as markers of ethnic heritage.[22] Outside the European American ambit, an entire book has been devoted to Filipino American design issues.[23] And a particularly vibrant area of study—one with a long scholarly tradition all its own—has been the identification of Africanisms in American architecture and design.[24]

These investigations were helpful to the current study. But it was important to define heritage in ways that reflected as directly as possible respondents' own priorities, and, with the exception of Africanisms, visible manifestations of ethnicity were not generally high on the list of cultural productions identified by respondents as critically important.

Insight into how heritage is perceived can be derived from the biographies of some of the field's leaders. Chicana artist Judith Baca, founder and director of Los Angeles's Social and Public Art Resources Council, recalls that she started as a "cultural worker" within the social justice movement of the 1960s and 1970s. While painting murals with youths in the barrios she was also negotiating gang treaties. Nicolás Kanellos, founder of Arte Público Press and of the Recovery Project (whose full name is "Recovering the U.S. Hispanic Literary Heritage") recalls that the press was born "on the artistic fringe during the Hispanic Civil Rights Movement." Frustrated that mainstream presses were not publishing Hispanic writers, Kanellos launched the Revista Chicana-Riqueña in 1972, which led in 1979 to the establishment of Arte Público Press as a national outlet for Hispanic literature;[25] the name, says Kanellos, was intended to place the enterprise within the context of the public art movement that was producing important community expressions such as Judith Baca's murals. Dorothy Cordova, founder of the Filipino American National Historical Society, also became involved with heritage during the 1970s, collecting Filipino American oral histories. She had already founded Filipino Youth Activities and would then found the Democracy Project for Asian Americans. During the same years Joan Maynard was founding

Brooklyn's Weeksville Society to preserve the neighborhood's surviving African American sites; she saw a knowledge of history as essential to the ability of African American youths to survive in a troubled neighborhood. Stanley Lowe, a leading figure in the African American preservation movement and now a senior official at the National Trust for Historic Preservation, got his start in historic preservation by dumping garbage on the desk of Pittsburgh's mayor: he was protesting the deterioration of the African American Manchester neighborhood. For Lowe, preserving Pittsburgh's African American heritage was inseparable from the efforts of the city's African Americans to secure decent homes and neighborhoods. For Baca, Kanellos, Cordova, Maynard, and Lowe, a firm belief in the importance of heritage was rooted in a passionate dedication to social improvement for their communities.

These linkages between heritage and social activism may reflect the generational experience of having participated in the social movements of the 1960s. Yet they have been far less obvious among white preservation leaders of the same generation, while many younger African American respondents continue to emphasize community development in ways atypical of white preservationists. Lynn Pono exemplifies a similar blending of cultural and social activism. The daughter of Filipino immigrants, Pono describes her sense of Filipino identity as a "learned heritage," something she picked up from family and from other Filipino Americans in Skokie, Illinois, where she grew up. But the most important experience was joining a college study group that "did a really great job" teaching Filipino history. Since then she has sought outlets for both cultural and political expression, first in the Chicago area and then around New York, including joining Alianza Latina and working with both Cambodian and Filipino immigrants. Now she works as an arts professional in New York and is actively involved with two Filipino cultural groups.

Pono says she is not interested in issues of representation, by which she means the expectation that she should represent herself as a "Filipino artist" and, through her identity and work, exemplify some sort of Filipino-ness. Though informed by one's identity, she believes, one should not be bound by it. Yet, like many Filipino respondents, she is "always questioning Filipino identity and what it means": "it should be changing," she believes, but, whatever it is, it absorbs a good deal of attention. So does the bigger question, which interests her very much, of "how Filipinos fit into the large thing called American heritage . . . what does it mean to be a Filipino in American society?" Questions like these do not absorb mainstream conservationists to nearly the same degree; to the contrary, they reflect a point of view which is consciously outside the mainstream. In fact, Pono believes her Filipino American perspective, rooted in the Philippines' tangled, messy, multicultural, and multi-colonial history, gives her a distinctively valuable vantage point on American society. She sees a potential for the Filipino community to be at the forefront of thinking about American identity. "The United States is basically a big experiment," she says; thinking about cultural issues related to Filipino identity can "inform what American identity will become."

Pono is uncomfortable with the word heritage. It is too "subjective," and she prefers words like identity and history. Best, however, is culture: "how do people live? The things that people think are important—their values, beliefs . . . art too." She is more interested in this living culture than in "memorializing history," though she concedes that there is considerable value in marking historical events—and it was through the study group on Filipino history that her commitment to cultural issues was aroused.

The Centrality of History

"History is important," says Filipino American Alan Bergano, "because it is the foundation of a people." Like Bergano, many respondents feel that they cannot take history for granted, because history shapes identity and describes relationships with the majority culture that, in turn, define life in crucial ways. History requires constant attention. Evidence of achievement must be unearthed, underlined, spotlit. Memories of discrimination and suffering must be maintained. And sometimes evidence of existence, of presence within the larger story, must be discovered and defended. This is because much of history lies forgotten or buried. Before becoming part of *heritage*, history must be rediscovered.

For a long time the experience of slavery was glossed over with little explanation, even excused as essentially benign or unimportant. Putting slavery back into the story required energy and persistence. Today some Filipinos are intent on restoring historical awareness of the Philippine–American War, and others on rediscovering the historical experiences of immigrants from the Marcos era, while some African Americans are bringing back to light the history of urban churches and their pastors. Arte Público Press, based at the University of Houston, has launched an ambitious project, "Recovering the U.S. Hispanic Literary Heritage," to rediscover, catalogue, and publish the rich and largely forgotten literary heritage of Hispanic Americans, including not only novels and poetry but also community newspapers and unpublished letters.

Within the mainstream preservation movement, history is hardly ever given the critical importance which many respondents ascribe to it. Preservation professionals diligently and thoroughly research it; civic advocates point to it with pride. Yet history is generally treated either as a subject for academic research or as a sort of luxury good, an adornment of civilized life. Rarely does it have the kind of intense bearing on community self-image that many respondents perceive. For these respondents, history has little in common with the appreciation of the "finer things" that the word heritage frequently connotes, or with the "souvenir history" that Puerto Rican poet Martin Espada derides—the superficial and congratulatory commemoration of symbolic highlights.[26] History does not paint the past as "simpler times": it is instead a relentless struggle to discover, uncover, rediscover, and recover facts about the national past that have been swept from public consciousness either because they are uncomfortable or because the evidence is ephemeral. For many respondents, history is what Antonia Castañeda calls "oppositional history": history of groups that have had to fight for rights or recognition, and history in opposition to stereotypes and social amnesia—history opposed to forgetting.

John Kuo Wei Tchen, a leading Chinese American historian, stresses nonetheless that the goal of this kind of history is not opposition but, rather, reconciliation, specifically *racial* reconciliation. Referring to lawyer and scholar Eric Yamamoto's study of the subject,[27] he underlines the importance of three steps toward reconciliation: recognition, redress, and finally reconciliation itself. The process can best be described backwards. *Reconciliation* is achieved when people of different races and ethnicities accept one another as equals, forgive past wrongs, and withdraw barriers to equal participation in society. This requires *redress*: acknowledgment of wrongs and a commitment to right them. Redress rests on *recognition*, and the key to this essential first step, in Tchen's view, is to educate Americans about the history of intergroup relationships. "In many places," he remarks, "Asian Americans were literally run out of town, so they become to all appearances white places. These things need to be redressed and reconciled . . . it's not enough to just sing praises of this country." If these comments sound adversarial, it is important to note again that his goal is to move beyond hostility, which requires dislodging people from fixed positions and stereotypes with an honest appraisal of the facts. In 1980, Tchen and others founded the Chinatown History Project in New York, later renamed the Museum of Chinese in the Americas; he explains that the project's central goal was to achieve "recognition," because, "once you've established that, people are willing to be less dogmatically nationalist"—on either side of the question.

Sometimes confronting the painful history of intergroup relationships causes discomfort, and not only among white people. A sense of shame, says Angel Shaw, keeps many Filipinos from knowing their own history. Referring to slavery, Jeanne Cyriaque, who coordinates African American programs for Georgia's State Historic Preservation Division, notes that "some African Americans feel it's a part of the past that they want to forget": they want to get past the slave cabins. William E. Davis, an African American architect in New York who participated in the campaign to save the African Burial Ground (Figures 7.1 to 7.3), notes the case of a southern town where black legislators blocked, as too divisive, a citizen-led initiative to commemorate the arrest in the 1960s of a couple for marrying across racial lines. "Sometimes," Davis concludes, "history may still be too painful or controversial for people to want to commemorate." Certainly talking about difficult episodes requires tact as well as honesty. Yet Tchen believes it is an essential step towards reconciliation and increased social harmony. So does Davis, who looks to South Africa's great experiment in truth and reconciliation as a source of inspiration for Americans.

Historical Themes

The themes of African, Mexican, and Filipino American history are richly diverse. Yet a few appear with significant persistence across all three. Manual labor—hard, low-paid work—is one that takes in the experience of enslaved people as well as farm and cannery workers, nurses, cooks, and domestic workers. Episodes of persecution, prejudice, and exclusion are also prominent. While the legacy of slavery and violence towards African Americans is well known, the ubiquity of discrimination against Asian and Hispanic Americans is less so. A Filipino describes encountering a covenant, written in 1941, as part of the final sale packet for a house in Vallejo, California, purchased in 1994: "No person not entirely of the Caucasian race shall use or occupy the said land or any part thereof, except that persons of other races may act as servants to personnel of the Caucasian race actually occupying said land."[28] Many Mexican Americans remember signs proclaiming, "No dogs, no Mexicans." Despite these impediments, many Filipinos, Mexicans, and African Americans managed to do extraordinary things—found churches and businesses, lead unions, write books, be elected mayor or governor, defend America (or New York or Texas or Hawaii or the Philippines)—and these stories form a third prominent theme. A fourth, closely related both to achievement and to exclusion, is the experience of struggle, often expressed in movements for justice that continue to inspire Americans, such as the civil rights movement and the United Farm Workers' struggle for decent wages and working conditions. Finally, many people managed simply to survive, perhaps to marry, raise families, maintain friendships, cook, sing, wash clothes, pick asparagus or cotton, change bed pans or tend sleeping cars. It is important to remember and understand their stories too, and to honor their experience.

These themes—manual labor, persecution, exclusion, struggles for justice, achievement, contribution to society, and sheer survival—recur frequently in respondents' views of history. So does one further theme: invisibility.

Invisible Man

"I am an invisible man," announces the black protagonist of Ralph Ellison's famous novel of 1952: "I am invisible, understand, simply because people refuse to see me."[29] *Invisible Man* explores the sensation of being unrecognized by a white majority. Many respondents identified invisibility as a defining part of their community's historical experience. In Los Angeles, the historic Merced Theater still stands (Figure 3.1), but guides fail to mention that it was a Spanish-language theater in the 1850s. "They erased that history," comments Nicolás Kanellos. Traveling through California, Angel Shaw knows that Filipino migrant laborers once cultivated the fields around her, yet sees no trace of them in the landscape: their history has become invisible (Figure 3.2). Shaw wants this heritage to be revealed, perhaps by putting up plaques, or by teaching about it in schools—some means that would proclaim: "There were labor camps. *Right here*."

Many Filipino Americans feel that the problem of invisibility is particularly fraught for them. While John Kuo Wei Tchen regards all Asian Americans as basically invisible, many Filipinos refer to themselves as the "invisible Asians," and with some justification: an informal survey conducted in 2004 among the author's neighbors found that not one knew that Filipinos are the largest Asian

Figure 3.1   The two faces of forgetting and remembering. The Merced Theater in Los Angeles (left), whose history as a Spanish-language theater has largely been erased. The Edmund Pettus Bridge in Selma, Alabama (right), an inspiration to many for the bravery of civil rights marchers who strode unflinchingly towards troopers waiting to meet them with clubs and tear gas.

Figure 3.2   Photographer Ricardo Alvarado documented Filipino American life in California at mid-century, as in this harvest scene. Today, the presence of generations of Filipino American farm workers in these fields has become virtually invisible.

immigrant group. The fact, moreover, appeared to mystify them, because they lacked a clear image of Filipinos or the Philippines. As Angel Velasco Shaw put it, "They don't know what to do with Filipinos, where to place us." That may be in part because, as Shaw points out, Filipinos are "among the most under-represented groups" in museum collections, monuments, sites, or other publicly visible acknowledgments of presence. Filipino American respondents are seeking greater public recognition. Yet for many Filipino Americans, proclaiming one's presence entails a certain anxiety. "Filipinos themselves don't know their own histories," comments Shaw, "and part of it is shame." Roz Li speaks of an "identity crisis. . . . Are we Asians or Americans?" Unlike, say, neighboring Thailand, the Philippines do not have a "pure culture. Ours," she says, is "more like a 'mutt' culture," the result of cycles of Chinese, Spanish, and American domination that have left many Filipinos asking: "Do we have our own heritage?" And, if so, what is it? Because of this "identity crisis," she says, and "because the Philippines have been under America so long, Filipinos think they're very western. Then they come here and find out they're not . . . they're eastern." Li's entire experience has been defined by the tug of east and west, and that, she says, is typical. It can be extraordinarily tough on people. Other Asian groups, she thinks, have more realistic expectations. But "many Filipinos think they're going to come over and instantly be part of the mainstream. Then when it doesn't happen, they get disillusioned and bitter. . . ." Moreover, as Angel Shaw points out, the culture that immigrants bring with them is extraordinarily diverse, divided according to place of origin, date of arrival, class, form of work, place of settlement, politics, and so forth. And so the desire to be recognized brings unresolved questions about identity to the foreground.

Cultural identity is fluid and is always in the process of being defined. Heritage is central to that process, and so the desire to become more visible within society provides a powerful impetus to conserve heritage—and to make it more visible. When this happens, the results can be striking. In 1991, intact eighteenth-century African burials were found on a site being excavated for a new federal office building near City Hall in Lower Manhattan (Figures 7.1 to 7.3). Though the ensuing public campaign failed to save the entirety of New York City's African Burial Ground, it succeeded brilliantly at making African Americans visible protagonists within New York's history. Through newspaper articles, documentary films, and scholarly studies, white as well as black New Yorkers developed an entirely new awareness of African Americans in early New York: they had become decisively present in New York's history. Today, more than a decade later, thousands of visitors from all over the world participate in educational programs and commemorative observances at the site,[30] which continues to provide visible proof of African Americans' presence in the history of New York.

Mexican and Filipino heritage advocates understand the value of sites like the African Burial Ground—or the Edmund Pettus Bridge in Selma, Alabama, a National Historic Landmark (NHL) that was the site of a pivotal confrontation of the civil rights movement (Figure 3.1). Would it not be wonderful, asks Refugio Rochin, if the sites of Mexican American struggles were marked in a similar way? "To be able to go to Selma and say I've crossed the bridge. . . . We need opportunities for reflection like that."

IV. EFFORTS, ACHIEVEMENTS, RECOGNITION

While African, Mexican, and Filipino Americans have all launched major heritage conservation programs, public and official responses to these initiatives have been unequal. African American issues have earned significant official interest and support, as can be seen by browsing the web pages of the National Park Service. This is not true of Mexican or Filipino heritage, which remains more invisible to society at large. That is not to say that African American heritage has been "done": even in Washington, DC, notes John W. Franklin, important African American sites continue to be ignored or bulldozed. And as NPS consultant historian Michele Gates Moresi observes, "African Americans are not fully integrated into the professional field, not 'mainstreamed,' if you will." On the one hand, then, the existence of programs does not prove that the problem has been solved. On the other, there have been significant successes in conserving African American heritage.

African American Heritage

The growth of interest in African American heritage demonstrates how social militancy, political pressure, scholarly and professional interest, and official action can combine to produce impressive results. As early as 1941, Melville J. Herskovits's *Myth of the Negro Past* set out to document the African past that was embedded in African American culture. During the 1950s, the civil rights movement encouraged growing interest among scholars and sparked new efforts to grapple with the issue of slavery. During the 1960s militant protests were directed at both universities and museums, and by the end of the decade Afro-American studies were entering the curriculum, while a few major museums were beginning to address African American topics and audiences. Community museums were also opening: the Smithsonian's Anacostia Museum in 1967, Brooklyn's Weeksville Society in 1971. Scholarly and popular interest seemed to spur each other on: the life story of a black sharecropper, *All God's Dangers: The Life of Nate Shaw*, became a national bestseller in 1974; Alex Haley's fantastically successful *Roots* appeared two years later.[31] Meanwhile, the academic field of material culture studies was opening up new approaches to African American heritage, particularly architecture and crafts, and by the 1990s readers could consult studies in which the full range of material production, from plantation houses to walking sticks, was analyzed in the context of social conditions, folklife, race relations, and the survival and evolution of cultural traditions.[32]

By the 1980s, some preservation agencies and organizations were making serious efforts to incorporate African American heritage into mainstream preservation work. This was especially true in the south, where several states launched official programs, including the Black Heritage

Council of the Alabama Historical Commission, the Georgia Minority Heritage Coalition, and groups in Kentucky, Florida, South Carolina, and Louisiana.[33] In 1984, Georgia's State Historic Preservation Office published an important guide to historic black resources,[34] and by the early 1990s guidebooks to African American heritage sites and newsletters on African American heritage preservation were available in Alabama, Tennessee, Florida, Georgia, and Kentucky. Meanwhile, historic houses and sites like Colonial Williamsburg began to put African Americans back into the historical picture and to deal with subjects like slavery in a forthright way.[35] Today, although many plantations continue to portray a false history from which slavery has been erased, others (like the Cane River Creole National Historical Park [NHP] and Evergreen Plantation, both in Louisiana: Figure 10.2) depict the facts of slavery forthrightly and with concrete details that teach and indeed fascinate visitors.

Progress was taking place in the north as well. The Weeksville Society was launched in Brooklyn in 1971. By the 1980s, Sturbridge Village was developing living history techniques related to African American history. New York's State Historic Preservation Office released an excellent handbook on identifying African American historic resources.[36] The campaigns to save New York City's African Burial Ground and Audubon Ballroom (site of Malcolm X's assassination: Figures 7.1 to 7.6) generated enormous public involvement, moving African American heritage issues to the foreground. Meanwhile, African American preservation movements developed in Pittsburgh, Indianapolis, and elsewhere.

Nationally, the issue of diversity reached a new level of recognition within the field in 1992, when the National Trust for Historic Preservation organized its annual conference around the theme of diversity and launched scholarship and training programs to nurture preservation leaders from minority communities. Today, a department of the National Trust focuses on diversity initiatives, while the National Register of Historic Places lists over 800 properties associated with African American history. National Historic Landmark Theme Studies have been carried out or authorized on Black Americans in United States History (1974), Racial Desegregation in Public Education (1998), and Civil Rights (2000). The U.S. Congress has authorized the NPS to carry out other major projects focused on African American heritage. For example, the Lower Mississippi Delta Development Commission (1988) led to plans for a Delta Region African American heritage corridor, cultural center, and music heritage program emphasizing the blues (1994).[37] A preservation and interpretation study of the Underground Railroad (1990) resulted in a travel itinerary of fifty-nine National Register properties in twenty-one states, a number of National Historic Landmark designations, and a published interpretation guide for historians and site administrators.[38] The Cane River National Heritage Area, Cane River Creole National Historical Park, Jean Lafitte NHP, and New Orleans Jazz NHP interpret aspects of the history of Louisiana's Creoles of color. The NPS has studied the Gullah–Geechee heritage of the Georgia and

Florida coasts and has prepared a travel itinerary of National Register properties connected with the civil rights movement. And in addition to the material available on its other websites, the NPS maintains an informative website specifically about African American heritage.[39] Since 1995, grants have been made from the Historic Preservation Fund to the historically black colleges and universities for preserving historically significant buildings. In addition, the National Trust for Historic Preservation regularly highlights cultural diversity in its conferences—especially African American themes—and offers scholarships to attend them. Two states, Georgia and Alabama, have full-time African American heritage programs. State and national guides to African American historic sites are widely available. There are regular conferences on African American heritage topics. And according to architect Richard Dozier, most of the eight architecture schools among the historically black colleges and universities offer courses in historic preservation.

John W. Franklin offers a sharp corrective to anyone who might think that these achievements mean that the problem has been solved. In cities like Baltimore, Annapolis, or even Washington, DC, he says, there is still "great resistance to telling the story." Meanwhile, all over the country, African American communities continue to be destroyed by transit schemes and other forms of development. Geraldine Hobdy, former Louisiana State Historic Preservation Officer (SHPO)—the state's first black SHPO and the nation's second—offers another caveat to the picture of bustling achievement. "There has sometimes been a need," she says, "to create the *appearance* of helping a segment of the population for political reasons, or for reasons driven by tourism." A state might "create some materials—beautiful posters—but it doesn't necessarily go beyond that"; you might find "beautiful publications but no archives." In Georgia, Hobdy credits SHPO Elizabeth Lyon with making sure "there were real programs, even if they were not always obvious to the general public." But, she warns, you have to look beyond appearances to see whether genuine programs of lasting value are being created.

Mexican and Filipino Heritage

Neither Mexican nor Filipino American heritage has yet become visible to the general public, or been recognized by the historic preservation profession, in the way African American heritage has. True, public acknowledgment has not been completely lacking. In the winter of 2003, two exhibitions could be seen simultaneously in Washington. One, at the Smithsonian's National Museum of American History, depicted Filipino American life in California during the 1940s and 1950s (Figure 3.2); the other, across the Mall at the Smithsonian's Arts and Industries Building, life in the traditionally Mexican American region of the Rio Grande Valley.[40] In May 2003, the National Trust for Historic Preservation named Little Manila, Stockton's historic Filipino American neighborhood, in its annual list of Eleven Most Endangered Historic Places—an unfortunate way to recognize a "cherished local landmark" that, in President Richard Moe's words, provides "one of the few remaining sites that reminds us of the important role played by Filipino Americans in shaping our nation."[41] (In 2007, the California Preservation Foundation honored the Little Manila Foundation, a group based in the Filipino American community, for its efforts to save the district.) The Trust has also named a 200-mile stretch of the Lower Rio Grande, associated with Mexican American heritage, in its Eleven Most Endangered List.[42] Yet such marks of recognition are unusual. Out of over 77,000 properties listed on the National Register of Historic Places in 2004, only thirty-five were listed as relating to Asian American heritage and thirteen to Hispanic heritage; of the Asian American sites only one related directly to Filipino history. In 2003, the keyword "Mexican" brought up only twenty-eight entries on the National Trust's website, "Filipino" seven (almost all relating to Stockton's Little Manila neighborhood).[43] Out of approximately sixty National Historic Landmark Theme Studies, only two have ever been undertaken on Asian or Hispanic American themes: Spanish Exploration and Settlement (1959) and Japanese Americans in World War II (1991). Of twenty-three authorized National Heritage Areas, only one is located in the Spanish southwest and none directly relates to Hispanic or Filipino American heritage.[44]

This review makes it clear that, despite some significant achievements, much remains to be done. It also highlights the existence of not one but two diversity gaps. While recognition of the heritage and heritage needs of communities of color in general lags behind that of the white mainstream, recognition of Asian American and Latino heritage lags further behind that of African American. One reason for this second gap may be political. Effective heritage preservation depends on political leverage, and indeed Geraldine Hobdy attributes the success of many black heritage initiatives to the political power of African American constituents. Where other minority groups wield significant political power, a similar pattern can sometimes be seen. For example, in 1994 Florida's state legislature recognized an important political constituency by creating a Cuban heritage trail; it later added Jewish and women's heritage trails, thereby paying homage to two more major voting blocs.[45]

In general, Asian and Hispanic groups have lacked the sustained leverage of African Americans—or of Cubans in Florida. But that may change. Growing Latino political power may already be laying the groundwork for greater recognition of Mexican American and other Hispanic heritage. Whether this happens will depend on whether Latino politicians and their constituents choose to use their leverage for this purpose. Given rapidly growing Asian American populations, similar leverage may become available to proponents of Chinese, Indian, and Filipino heritage.

In the meantime, the lack of official recognition or support has not stopped Mexican and Filipino American groups from creating impressive heritage conservation projects within their communities. A few are described below: they provide insight into the heritage priorities expressed by respondents as well as the community-based approaches which have been developed to achieve them.

V. PRIORITIES AND STRATEGIES

Filipino American Heritage, FANHS, and the
National Pinoy Archive

The Filipino American National Historical Society (FANHS),[46] founded in 1982, has encouraged and organized much of the energy that Filipino Americans have devoted to heritage conservation. Based in Seattle, FANHS has twenty chapters around the country, including Alaska, Oregon, Virginia, New York, the Midwest, New England, and New Mexico; there are seven chapters in California. Active members include both professional and amateur historians. FANHS trustees meet regularly to exchange information and strategize, and the organization hosts a national conference every other year. Within the last few years, some younger scholars have begun to challenge some of the assumptions about Filipino American history (and ethnic heritage in general) on which FANHS was built. Yet even they continue to hold FANHS in high esteem for having sustained a sense of community and purpose among heritage advocates, nurtured the work of historians both professional and amateur, and overcome severe obstacles to create scholarly resources of irreplaceable value.

Many Filipino heritage advocates also hold its founders and leading spirits, Dorothy and Fred Cordova, in great affection. John Kuo Wei Tchen, a respected scholar of Asian American history who has mentored many younger Filipino scholars, calls the Cordovas the "grandparents or godparents" of those younger scholars—some of whom continue to refer to them in Filipino fashion as Auntie Dorothy and Uncle Fred. Their moral authority stems from a combination of sources: an unshakeable belief in the importance of Filipino American heritage, an indomitable will to protect it, personal warmth and generosity of spirit, and authenticity of experience. The Cordovas have *lived* Filipino American heritage. Dorothy Cordova's father was a salmon cannery contractor; Fred Cordova grew up in a family of migrant farm workers in Stockton, California, before moving to Seattle in 1946. And their dedication to heritage conservation is legendary, reaching back more than thirty years.

In 1987, FANHS established the National Pinoy Archive in Seattle, and under Fred Cordova's leadership this repository has become an indispensable resource for the Filipino American history. "It's amazing what this man has achieved," says scholar Angel Velasco Shaw. As John Silva sees it, FANHS went "hog-wild" to collect absolutely everything: documents, letters, diaries, newspaper clippings, oral histories, photographs. Indeed, Shaw asserts, many Filipino American leaders "will want everything preserved"—and, she adds, "I would agree with that."

Dorothy Fujita-Rony distinguishes between two kinds of objects that can be collected: first, things that reflect old-country traditions and accepted values; second, those that reflect the community's experience here. These latter—oral histories, photographs, letters, posters, work tools, diaries—are especially fragile and ephemeral. They also represent a contested terrain.

Fujita-Rony says that, in any marginalized or immigrant community, people will try to collect these things, and keeping them in the community will become politically important. Conversely, external organizations interested in collecting the same things may be perceived not as allies but as outsiders eager to "come in and take" things.

Many Filipino American respondents believe the core of heritage lies in the life experience of Filipino immigrants. "You have to have lived that life," says Shaw, to fully understand what abstractions like farm work or racism really meant: most people simply would not believe what it was actually like. Alan Bergano says that "Filipino American history starts at home," with efforts to understand the experiences of one's parents. Another testimonial to the historical value of information possessed by family elders comes from Aimy Ko, a recent university graduate and first-generation immigrant. She remembers that when she undertook a historical research project on her grandfather Maximo Manzón, who graduated from NYU Law School (but was not allowed to practice law in this country), she was able to go to her uncle for family stories. Where, she asks, will future generations of students turn? And how will they place their family stories within the larger historical narrative? "It's important," she urges, "to have the documents available to students or to anyone who's trying to locate themselves relative to their families and the past." That is what the National Pinoy Archive is trying to do.

Luis Francia emphasizes the centrality of one particular kind of document: community-based newspapers. These provided the "ways in which Filipinos and Filipino Americans communicated with each other," and today they are indispensable both as cultural products of the Filipino community and as records of its experiences. As Rick Bonus puts it, community newspapers are "fixtures" in Filipino American stores, beauty salons, and other community spaces.[47] The newspapers are numerous and varied, and stem from many parts of the country: one published in New York, for instance, served as an outlet for immigrants opposed to the imposition of martial law in the 1970s. "It would be great," says Francia, "if there were a whole set somewhere"—for example, at the Library of Congress. But not only there: another set should be lodged within a leading Filipino community-based organization.

The National Pinoy Archive deserves and needs financial support. FANHS board members place a high priority on securing the Archive's future. Angel Shaw agrees: "Someone should give Fred Cordova money to preserve the archive," she says. The tasks of collecting and conserving are simply outgrowing the resources of a community-based non-profit. So is the collection's national importance. But cultural politics have to be considered too. While many Filipino American respondents would appreciate both the financial support and the professional expertise that federal agencies like the Library of Congress could bring, they want the collection to remain within the community, and they want Filipino American sensibilities to continue directing its evolution.

Important as FANHS is, Filipino American heritage studies are expanding in new directions. Whereas FANHS has emphasized the west coast experience, especially that of agricultural and fishery workers, some New York respondents believe that the experiences of Filipino immigrants there, including those of professionals, artists, and intellectuals, also deserve exploration. Moreover, a new generation of well-trained and highly motivated young scholars is emerging. Their books and teaching are creating the kind of intellectual heft that has so effectively sustained African American heritage conservation efforts—though the gains in political influence and militancy that accompanied the development of Black Studies are so far lacking.[48]

Hispanic Heritage and the Recovery Project

Like Filipino respondents, many Mexican American respondents stressed the importance of written records for uncovering, preserving, and teaching history. And here again, amateur historians and genealogists have done essential work. Indeed, Nicolás Kanellos credits them with being "way ahead of the scholars" in finding important historical materials. And "there are thousands of them out there," piecing together early land claims, genealogies, settlement records, stories, and local traditions. They meet nationally and are most numerous and active in the formerly Mexican southwest, including California and Texas. There are also local preservation societies like Houston's Tejano Association for Historical Preservation. And there are amateur journals of history and genealogy, like *El Mesteño* in south Texas and *La Herencia* in New Mexico.

Meanwhile, Kanellos's own Recovery Project, based at the University of Houston, has established itself as an academic powerhouse, discovering, inventorying, and publishing important but long-forgotten Hispanic American texts. Known formally as "Recovering the U.S. Hispanic Literary Heritage," the Recovery Project has made major steps towards preserving and making accessible a literary heritage that includes not only the "conventional literary genres" but also letters, diaries, oral lore and popular culture stemming from Cuban, Mexican, Puerto Rican, Spanish, and other Hispanic Americans. Kanellos launched the Recovery Project in 1992 as an outgrowth of Arte Público Press, which he had founded in 1979 as a national non-profit publisher of Hispanic literature, and which he had moved to the University of Houston the following year. In 2004, the Recovery Project's on-line catalogue listed twenty-five volumes of poetry, stories, letters, novels, and other accounts, in addition to scholarly works on Hispanic literature, including a history of early Hispanic periodicals in the United States.[49] But these publications offer a mere glimpse into the vast database on Hispanic writing that Arte Público is compiling and digitizing for internet use. Calling newspapers and other periodicals the "primary cultural repository of Hispanic written thought,"[50] Kanellos notes that the Recovery Project has already assembled bibliographic information on 1,700 Spanish-language periodicals before 1960 and digitized 350,000 articles; eventually it plans to digitize 700 books and 900 newspapers.

Gerald Poyo, a professor of history at St. Mary's University in San Antonio, thinks the Recovery Project is having a major impact in redefining Hispanic history and culture, and he credits the project with bringing scholars together, nurturing their work, and enhancing their consciousness of an evolving field. Literary scholar Rosaura Sanchez believes the Recovery Project's value extends beyond the universities. Before the Recovery Project, students and general readers had "only what scholars have written" about these priceless literary sources, and this remains largely true: "Why," she asks, "should only the few be able to read those texts?" Making them available enriches and changes the public culture and makes it possible for teachers to tackle previously inaccessible historical subjects. After the Recovery Project published María Amparo Ruiz de Burton's long-unavailable novel of 1885, *The Squatter and the Don*, Sanchez notes, teachers began to use it in classes. Now it is "part of the Chicano canon." Sanchez has a vision: someday, the diaries, novels, and newspapers of Hispanic North America will be so widely available "that anybody wanting to study this, all they have to do is go to their library and read it themselves."

Kanellos too would like the Recovery Project's books to be more widely available. The bookshops of museums and historic sites—including those of the Smithsonian and the National Park Service—would make ideal distribution points. Yet Kanellos is frustrated that so few have taken advantage of the opportunity, even where the press's titles are directly relevant. Of course other presses also offer titles that would expand visitors' perspective on American history. Stocking them would be a relatively simple step that many historic site managers could take to help close the diversity deficit.

Museums

Many respondents believe museums are important tools for heritage conservation. One reason is that they offer a route towards what John Kuo Wei Tchen calls recognition. They also provide centralized collection and display points for artifacts advocates consider it important to preserve. And of course they present opportunities to educate. Yet both the politics and the economics of museums are complex.

Some Filipino respondents identified the establishment of a major national Filipino-American museum and library as a high priority. Respondents in New York take inspiration from the Smithsonian Museum of the American Indian and its George Gustav Heye Center in New York, as well as from the city's Museum of Chinese in the Americas. "We don't have that," comments Angel Shaw: "Filipinos are the last nationality without a museum." In fact, certain FANHS chapters have undertaken to raise funds for a museum in Stockton, California. But the project is not without controversy. Some respondents wonder whether it will adequately present the experiences of east-coast Filipino American communities, how it will relate to the National Pinoy Archive in Seattle, and whether the community can sustain a top-notch museum. These respondents feel there is a need for "someone of the caliber of the Smithsonian" to manage a museum and establish the most up-to-date "professional ways to preserve and document artifacts." On the other hand, they recognize that a proposal to surrender community control to a federal agency would be highly controversial and, indeed, problematic since it might deprive Filipinos of the very voice they had worked so hard to gain. They admire the way tribal voices and interpretations come through at the American Indian museum. That of course owes something to the governmental standing of Indian tribes. Lacking this, ethnic or national immigrant groups might have more difficulty achieving this balance in a partnership with the federal government. But the question is worth posing: could a similar result be attained through some sort of partnership arrangement in which, perhaps, local collecting projects could "link up with the Smithsonian"? One way or another, a highly professional, national-scale repository for art, artifacts, documents, and oral histories is needed.

As an interim step, Luis Francia asks, "would the Smithsonian be willing to do an oral history project" on a national scale? Such a venture, as Francia sees it, would include interviews to illuminate "all different aspects of Filipino American experience" across the country and across generations. It would build on existing work but add to it and, as it were, fill in the gaps. Such a project could become "a seed bed for what a museum could be."

Some Mexican American respondents identified museums as important components of heritage conservation, frequently in conjunction with historic sites. Both Nicolás Kanellos and Rosaura Sanchez emphasize the tremendous value of the archives and collections held by missions, presidios and other historic sites. All too often the potential of these collections is frustrated by inadequate funds for cataloguing, research, and conservation, sometimes putting fragile objects at great risk. Professional expertise may be in short supply as well. A further problem is that the interpretation of collections is frequently controlled by institutions outside the community. As a result, they sometimes aim more at gratifying Anglo tourists than at presenting history in what respondents believe is an objective way.

Clearly, the politics of culture and community are complex, and Hispanic, like Filipino American, respondents, expressed uncertainty about how to balance community and external forces. For example, Kanellos points out the value that a major national repository like the Library of Congress could bring to a partnership. Major collections of documents, he says, should be lodged either there or at their sites of origin: if the former, then the sites must have facsimiles, for such collections are invaluable teaching tools for historic sites.

Despite some uncertainties, what is clear is that Mexican and Filipino American heritage groups are performing a national service of inestimable value by assembling the historical evidence of their participation in American history: books, manuscripts, letters, diaries, newspapers, restaurant menus, news clippings, photographs, land deeds, genealogies, oral histories, and so forth. Public agencies could help close the diversity gap by supporting their work through technical assistance and grants.

"I Don't Like Turkeys": Folkways, Ethnography, and Historic Preservation

A particular question for the assessment was whether federal agencies should do more to protect or interpret folkways and traditions. No clear answer emerged. However, the comments of respondents do suggest several constructive lines of action.

Many respondents include folkways within their concepts of heritage. Jeanne Cyriaque notes that music provides an effective way to preserve an elusive "spirit of place," particularly when significant buildings no longer exist: she appreciates groups like the Georgia Sea Island Singers and the McIntosh County Shouters who continue to maintain traditional forms of music. Traditional ways of transmitting community experience from generation to generation are also valued. "Filipino American history starts at home," says Alan Bergano: it is very family-oriented. However, beyond generalities like these, the picture becomes less clear. The question of language, a central feature of culture, is symptomatic. Here is Moses Spear Chief, of the Blackfeet Reservation, on the subject: "If it's gone then their culture is gone. . . . Without the language, values are lost, your sense of belonging is gone."[51] This is a classic statement of the centrality of language to culture. Yet if the role and survival of languages are a key issue for many tribes, the issue was less clear cut to respondents to this study. Some Filipino Americans regret the loss of language ability within the community. Roz Li says that second-generation Filipino Americans typically lose their native language: "hardly any of the kids know how to speak it. . . . They're so afraid of being stigmatized. . . . I think it's very sad." Jorge Ramos agrees with the premise that the "link between language and identity" is important: Latinos' sense of identity, he asserts, "is intrinsically linked to where we came from and what language we speak."[52] But Spanish appears to be in no danger of disappearing. Quite the contrary, "Spanish is more alive than ever in the United States." Nine out of ten Hispanics, according to Ramos, speak Spanish at home; the Spanish-language media flourish in a way that previous immigrant presses never did. And, in contrast to earlier immigrant groups, "Hispanics have not had to lose their language or their culture in order to feel as if they have assimilated; in fact, many have taken a stand in defense of that culture."[53]

Judith Baca agrees that "cultural retention is something the Mexican American community itself is quite committed to." In contrast with the African or Filipino American diasporas, she points out, Mexican Americans are able to continually refresh not only their language but also their historical awareness and cultural production by movement across the border—that same border that had originally crossed them. Throughout the southwest they also draw on what Baca calls "land-based memory": deep roots in places where Mexicans have lived continuously for as much as 500 years. And many remain acutely aware of their ancestors' loss of land following the Treaty of Guadalupe Hidalgo, no mere historical curiosity but an obstacle to Mexican Americans seeking to maintain old ties to the land. Here is an area where traditions and folkways are clearly important, yet government's role in protecting them is neither obvious nor simple.

And transnationalism is making everything still more complex. An anecdote told by Jorge Ramos reminds us that immigrants do not simply bring their traditions with them. A Mexican immigrant, Amelia, was preparing to celebrate Thanksgiving Day:

> She had just arrived in the United States, but she was very interested in the upcoming holiday and wanted to know what I was planning to do for San Guivi.
> "San Guivi?" I asked, puzzled.
> "Yes, San Guivi, that saint that they pay tribute to here," she replied.
> Amelia had assimilated this new holiday into the Catholic traditions that were familiar to her. In this context, she had interpreted Thanksgiving phonetically as San Guivi.[54]

A website, www.filipinoamericans.net, calls itself "A One-Stop Site for Filipino American History and Culture" and manages an on-line community forum called "The Filipino Forum."[55] This a good place to sample the concerns that some Filipino Americans express about retaining their cultural heritage: it too suggests the flavor of transnationalism, of improvisation, of traditions that are not so much maintained as learned and, sometimes, reinvented.

Arranging weddings in the Philippines prompts many questions in the Filipino Forum. One man writes: "I'm also getting married next year and wanted to have a somewhat traditional Filipino wedding. So I'm interested to know what a Filipina gown looks like? And what is the groom (me) supposed to wear? A Barong?" One helpful response refers the questioner to a website, mybarong.com, which "provides pictures of barong tagalog, Filipina gowns, wedding rituals, wedding accessories and other Filipino wedding traditions." Clearly not all Filipino Americans know the traditional customs, but some want to learn and follow them. This is shown even more clearly in a posting concerning another important ritual:

> Traditionally or maybe a religious calling, we Filipinos celebrate? (sorry, don't know what the proper word to use) the one year death of a family member. Am I right so far? Anyway, that's the reason I am writing. . . . I will be assisting my deceased brother's wife in preparation for this "babang luksa" and I don't have a clue on what are we suppose to do or what to present to our guests? I have not attended this type of event and I don't know what goes on except prayers. I appreciate any advice on what needs to be done for this occasion. BTW, we are Tagalogs if this matters at all. I am thinking maybe each region have different ways to doing it?

How to celebrate American holidays like Thanksgiving prompts further questions. One writer remembers:

> in my neck of the woods . . . here in Little Manila town, my family had roast pork (from the oven) not the lechon kind. Never really developed the acquired taste for turkey . . . maybe next year, it'll be lechon manok. Remember those, guys?? Thanksgiving never really became a family tradition, only a tradition of four-day weekends which we all enjoy."

To which another responds: "Never had lechon manok. How do you prepare and cook it? It will be a good sub for a turkey. I don't like turkeys." And a third:

My family is not really much of a turkey eater either but we have it for the Caucasian members of the family. What interesting though that my mother did this year was to take a whole turkey to the Chinese Deli/Restaurant nearby and have the Chinese cook there roast it for us. . . . We almost always have the Honey Baked Ham. . . . yummm yummmm and the rest of the food on the table are Filipino dishes. We look forward to this holiday to get everybody together and catch up on everyone's lives.[56]

Anyone who thinks tradition is static might ponder these passages, as might those considering government's role in protecting folkways. Neither Mexican nor Filipino respondents asked for or saw a clear role for government in helping to protect traditions that their communities are actively managing. Two respondents even cautioned against misdirected government efforts. Guadalupe San Miguel, a historian with a wide knowledge of Mexican American musical traditions, noted that the Smithsonian has "done wonderful work with some of the schools" in South Texas but questioned whether the Institution's efforts to preserve the *conjunto* music of that region were too narrowly focused on preserving a particular stage in its evolution, one popular in the 1950s. In fact, San Miguel explains, *conjunto* continues to evolve, like other aspects of a living culture. Was the Smithsonian promoting an image of a "static culture," creating "a stereotype of what Tejano music is?" Dorothy Fujita-Rony cautions that Filipinos themselves are divided on what counts as authentic Filipino folklore. Pilipino Cultural Nights emerged as major community events during the 1970s and 1980s, involving hundreds of students in dances, skits, and political commentary. They were "major avenues of cultural reclamation." But, she says, some Filipinos argue that folk dances actually reflect 1950s-era government cultural policies more than they do genuine Filipino folk culture. And Filipinos differ on whether folklore should properly be about the home country or about the community's experiences here.

While it may be difficult for government programs to support folkways, it is all too easy for government actions to harm them. Regulations that outlaw cockfighting, restrict the selling of live chickens, or ban fishing or hunting may interfere with traditional activities. The condemnation and redevelopment of downtown properties may displace traditional communities. Even *laissez-faire* decisions to let the real estate market take its course may lead to displacement and to the transfer of land, water, and other resources from traditional communities to new owners. Some (but by no means all) of these government actions are taken in pursuit of broad social objectives that policy-makers believe transcend the value of imperiled traditions. But the social value of these traditions is not always considered in the political process, and few tools exist to help decision-makers assess it even if they wanted to.

A good first step towards rethinking government's responsibilities to living cultural heritage would be to institute a broad review of government's impact on the ability of communities to maintain their folkways. A second would be to develop legal and policy tools with which decision-makers and the public could assess the impact of proposed actions on traditions and values that are at stake. A third might be to inventory traditions that require buildings or other kinds of sites or spaces for their continued performance: that is, traditions that are rooted in places and cannot survive without them. These are the kinds of traditions discussed elsewhere in this volume as *placeways* or *storyscape*; further suggestions are offered in the last section of this chapter.

If government's role in protecting folkways remains somewhat murky, it is clear that folklore can enrich the nation's historic preservation programs. In Florida, historic preservation and folklife programs have been placed together within the state's Bureau of Historic Preservation and, according to Deputy State Historic Preservation Officer Barbara Mattick, the merger has made preservation staff "more aware of what are the cultural aspects—not just the architecture." Eatonville exemplifies how the "challenge to think folk life in things" can enhance historic preservation. Eatonville is the oldest and most intact example of a black town established during the Reconstruction period. It was also the home of renowned folklorist and author Zora Neale Hurston, and now of the annual Zora Neale Hurston Festival of the Arts and Humanities, a community-launched event that has made the town a magnet for heritage tourism. State preservationists had struggled for a decade or more to figure out how to successfully nominate Eatonville, a place of unquestioned historical importance, to the National Register of Historic Places. The problem was that few historic buildings survived. Thanks to a government grant, a folklorist was able to visit Eatonville and document "games, food, religious practices," and other non-architectural aspects of what made Eatonville significant. That work is still going on; meanwhile, the town has been listed on the National Register for its historical and architectural importance—thanks, in part, to the boost given by the folklife documentation.

The State of Florida has also worked with local groups to carry out a historic marker program in Eatonville. Here again, standard approaches to preservation would have been unsatisfactory. The problem, according to Mattick, was that "everything you'd want to talk about is no longer there." Documenting folk life—including a map of traditional pathways through the town—helped the project's designers to create ten wayside markers and a brochure that tell a satisfying story.[57]

Folklorists may differ on what is the best administrative arrangement for their discipline. But, from Mattick's point of view, having folklife in the department "adds substance" to historic preservation. Descriptions of folkways provide a "reflection of the place" that goes beyond its architecture—an approach, she believes, that has been particularly valuable to "the way we look at cemeteries, schools, and churches"—all important places of community memory.

Florida's folklife program has involved Greeks, Seminoles, Polynesians, Hawaiians, Ukrainians, Japanese and Chinese, Haitians, and Cubans. They have created an impressive public representation of a truly diverse culture, one which encompasses Palestinian needlework, Hungarian embroidery, and African American quilts—not to mention Seminole canoes, Caribbean music, and a host of traditional skills that are not necessarily ethnic, from surf-boarding to fly-tying. They have worked hard to perpetuate some of these same skills.[58] Yet, according to Mattick, "African American is probably *the* area where there's been this merging of historic preservation and folklife." Why? In part because African Americans are Florida's largest minority, "African American has been a major focus" of state historic preservation work, and the department has launched particularly vigorous efforts to reach out to and include African Americans in its work.

Including folklife as an integral part of a community's history is another constructive role that government preservation programs can play. Emily Lawsin, a FANHS trustee from Michigan, urges the National Park Service to publish a brochure of important Filipino historical sites across the country; hers would be a *different* kind of brochure, because along with standard historical information it would feature oral histories about the sites. Many Mexican and Filipino American respondents place a strong emphasis on understanding the life experiences of ordinary people in the past, and conservation groups are already collecting newspapers, memorabilia, photographs, oral histories, and other sources with which to document those experiences. But documenting the historically evolving folkways of their respective communities may exceed the capacity of community-based (or even university-based) non-profit groups such as those that currently exist. The difficulty is not so much history's breadth as the kind of documentation that would be required. To photograph and catalogue domestic interiors, create high-quality musical sound recordings, or identify and document community businesses—whether "third places" (see pp. 127–128) or simply examples of successful entrepreneurship—will demand substantial resources of money, equipment, technical skill, and organization. Federal and state agencies could provide these in ways that richly supplement and support the work of heritage conservationists and help to create invaluable historical resources for the future.

Site-Seeing: A Cure for Public Blindness

One of the assessment's most striking findings was a tremendous unmet demand for historic sites, in the sense of formally recognized places that represent the stories of minority communities candidly and engagingly. Since historic sites are one of preservation's oldest tools, this finding surprised some of the study's organizers, who had anticipated that respondents, in demanding new programs and content from preservation, would also demand new techniques. Still, respondents' demands for more historic sites are far from being an endorsement of the status quo. Their expectations of historic sites are very specific and very high. They are by no means inconsistent with standard practice, yet, if widely adopted, they would push that –practice to new levels of relevance and excitement.

Explaining why historic sites are important, African American historian James Horton remarks that "it is easier to understand the people of history when you can be in the spaces that they occupied, the spaces where they lived their lives."[59] For Luis Francia, a Filipino American poet and journalist, "it's important to have visible artifacts": the artifact may be a site, monument, or marker, but, whatever it is, "it reminds people that at a certain time, and at this place, there were people who lived here, achieved something, and contributed to society." Fred Cordova agrees: historic sites are a high priority for FANHS.

John Kuo Wei Tchen takes the argument further: gaining public recognition for historic sites helps make invisible communities visible; it also helps educate other Americans about them. In fact, one reason why historic sites are so important is that they are so public and, very often, official. Designating one frequently involves some kind of formal recognition, whether it be listing on the State or National Register of Historic Places or, more substantially, acquisition and management by a public agency. To designate a historic site, then, is not only to preserve but also to confer public recognition on heritage.

Although few heritage groups within communities of color are heavily involved with historic sites in the way of many preservation groups within white or largely white communities, they do campaign at times to save them from destruction. This happens with tragic frequency, for many important sites are threatened by redevelopment or disinvestment. Historic African American neighborhoods in cities around the country have been destroyed by the combined forces of disinvestment, highway or rail construction, and urban renewal. With virtually all of the historic Manila towns razed, urges Tchen, it becomes crucially important to preserve *any* surviving remnants of Asian American historical presence. In fact, in 1999 the Stockton chapter of FANHS organized the Little Manila Foundation to preserve the remnants of Stockton's Little Manila neighborhood from a typically toxic combination of urban renewal, disinvestment, and highway construction, followed by the *coup de grâce*: strip-mall development. The case of Stockton has received some public attention, as well as the support of the National Trust for Historic Preservation, but all too often public ignorance of Mexican, African, or Filipino heritage causes important sites to be threatened or even casually swept away before their significance can even be recognized. Though Rolando Romo can easily point out the center of Houston's first Mexican community, that important spot now lies under the parked cars outside Minutemaid (formerly Enron) Stadium. Buildings associated with the history of migrant farm workers have also succumbed to demolition, as have the gravesites of important Mexican Americans like Lorenzo de Zavala. When powerful economic and political actors—politicians, developers, civic leaders—combine forces to demolish a historic site, it is hard enough even for politically well-connected and well-funded groups within the majority community to prevail: African, Mexican, and Filipino American advocates find it even harder.

There are probably many reasons for the relative rarity of preservation organizations—that is, not-for-profit organizations which focus specifically on identifying, preserving, and managing historic sites—within communities of color. One is that the barriers to entry are relatively high. Acquiring historic sites costs money; operating them costs more. As for listing programs such as the National Register, the rules are somewhat arcane and are not widely understood. Many respondents, even sophisticated ones, did not know how to use them; some did not know they existed. (Neither, it should be noted, do most citizens of European descent.)

It is unreasonable to expect the same degree of success with historic sites that non-profit organizations based in communities of color have achieved in other areas of heritage conservation—unless, that is, established preservation groups become true partners in the effort. Success requires a broad array of resources which heritage groups based in communities of color do not typically have in sufficient quantities, including money, political leverage, and technical expertise of a very particular kind. Established preservation groups have them and can put them to use right now. The opportunities for partnership are substantial, as are the benefits to both partners.

A Typology of Sites

If heritage organizations based in communities of color cannot do the job alone, neither can mainstream preservation organizations. Though rich in technical expertise, most are very poorly informed on the heritage of communities of color. Partnerships offer one solution to the problem; diversifying the staff and leadership of mainstream organizations offers another. Meanwhile, although the assessment did not attempt to carry out a survey of potential historic sites,[60] the comments of respondents did suggest a rough typology which may be helpful to preservation advocates and agencies. The nine categories which it includes do not refer to architectural form, style, or building type, but rather to the historical experiences that make the sites important.

Places of Entry

The places where immigrant groups entered the country have special resonance for many respondents. For Bradford Grant, Jamestown, Virginia, is "incredible—very rich historically: as one of the first sites where Africans were enslaved and brought to this country, the site is as significant for African Americans as for European Americans." For Filipinos, San Diego was an important point of origin: Ronald Buenaventura calls it the "gateway to Filipino American immigration." Did Filipinos establish a permanent settlement near New Orleans in the mid-eighteenth century? Many scholars believe so, but Tchen regards the question as not quite settled. Resolving it, he says, "would be a major accomplishment" that "would have huge implications for the history of the U.S." Mexican Americans have their own list of gateways: Judith Baca calls El Paso the "Ellis Island of the Southwest." But for Mexicans, who settled the southwest long before the "norteamericanos" arrived, the question of origin-points has other dimensions. Baca, whose lineage is Tejano, believes that marking and interpreting the early Spanish land grants, which predated the arrival of Anglos, is crucially important. Rosaura Sanchez agrees: she would like to see the evidence of Mexican landholdings around San Diego publicly identified. Imagine how instructive a drive up Interstate 5 would be, "when you see that and you see what's happened."

Interest in early experiences within the United States is not limited to points of arrival. Isaac Johnson comments, "We are dealing with African Americans, but we're leaving out some important factors because we're not looking back at the beginnings, the 1700s"; he urges greater attention to southern cities, to free blacks, and to those early ministers whose "names were not as well-known as George Washington" but who played a crucial role in the early history of African Americans.

Places of Dispersion

How immigrant groups moved beyond their points of entry into the country, the places they settled, and the routes they travelled across the country are an important part of their experience. Judith Baca would like to see the "major movements of the Mexican diaspora" presented. "How did Filipinos end up where they ended up?", asked several respondents. Inspired by Boston's Freedom Trail and Black Heritage Trail, Joan May Cordova imagines a map showing Filipino migration routes across the United States. Adélamar Alcántara would like to trace these migrations back to their origins in the Philippines. John W. Franklin notes that recent research in Louisiana allows the National Park Service to tell visitors where the state's African American families came from.

Places of dispersion do not have to be specific locations. They can be routes, or even patterns of movement. Adélamar Alcántara notes that Filipino workers followed crops around the country: those seasonal migrations were an important aspect of the Filipino experience and deserve to be marked. Many routes have great emotional power because they led toward enslavement (African diaspora), or toward freedom and opportunity (Underground Railroad), or because they represent struggles for justice (civil rights or United Farm Workers marches). Such routes have the power to convey compelling narratives. Moreover, they have the practical advantage that they lend themselves to being followed: they fit comfortably, that is, into many people's idea of how to spend a vacation.

Places of Experience

These are places which represent the daily experiences of large numbers of people. Asparagus fields in California, cotton fields in the south, salmon canneries in Alaska, sugar plantations in Hawaii, hospitals, military bases, tenements almost everywhere, downtown neighborhoods in many American cities, dance halls and union halls, Spanish land grants, a carrot warehouse in Grants, New Mexico—all are places where Filipinos, Mexicans, and African Americans lived and worked in significant numbers (Figures 3.2 and 3.3). Each advocate has a personal list of important sites that convey the experience of ordinary immigrants. John Silva's includes Filipino labor camps (Stockton, California), restaurants and hotels, military installations (the

Figure 3.3   Houston's Casino Hall was built by the Sociedad Mutualista Benito Juarez, a Mexican American mutual aid society, in 1928 and hosted plays, concerts, dances, and public meetings. Also known by the name of a hero of Mexico's liberal revolution, the Salon Benito Juarez has been called the first purpose-built, non-religious institution built by and for Houston's Mexican community. Its survival is in doubt.

Presidio), Chinatowns (Los Angeles, San Francisco; see also Figure 6.1), and pineapple plantations (Hawaii). For Angel Shaw, "going to the plantations is a very sad thing." While Japanese plantation workers had families and slept in beds, Filipinos were bachelors and were housed in straw cots. Yet it is "very hard to get information on Filipino life at the plantations in Hawaii." And the situation may be worsening: Linda Revilla, a FANHS trustee with roots in Hawaii, warns that Hawaii's plantation heritage, so important to Filipinos, is rapidly disappearing. Judith Baca's list of important places of experience *would* have included the ghetto on the other side of the tracks in La Junta, Colorado, had it not been torn down. Mexicans, she says, were forced to live there: they included service workers and military personnel. She laments "a place like that going unrecognized and unacknowledged." Refugio Rochin emphasizes the importance of the *barrios*: "they're eye-opening," he comments—to see them, to understand how many people lived there, to absorb the details of life (the outhouse, the cactus, the animals). "That kind of stuff is not being preserved as a walk-through exhibit," he says; but it should be, and if it is not done soon the opportunity will vanish. Rochin also notes markets and plazas (including "quite a few" in the southern parts of Colorado), and of course the missions and presidios. Guadalupe San Miguel, an expert on the history of Latino music, emphasizes the dance halls of South Texas. Fred Cordova's list includes churches and lodges; he would also like to see tours of Filipino businesses. Terri Torres, a FANHS trustee from Stockton, California, wants to mark the asparagus fields there with something that says, "this area, this field . . . Filipino farm workers were here, and they made possible the biggest industry out of Stockton." Adélamar Alcántara wants to preserve the bunkhouses for Filipino farm workers in Grants, New Mexico, carrot capital of the U.S.

Places like these offer extraordinary opportunities, in James Horton's words, to "understand the people of history." Because few decision-makers have recognized them as important historic sites, many of the buildings have been demolished. That makes telling the story harder—and preserving the remaining ones that much more important. But even without the buildings, the places are evocative and instructive.

Places of Suffering and Struggle

Certain places are sanctified by suffering, or by people's struggle to achieve justice: they have important stories to tell. Historic sites associated with slavery provide an example (Figures 6.3 and 10.2). Many are interpreted far better now than ten or twenty years ago, and this is helping the American public to accept and understand slavery as an episode of national history. Places connected with the Underground Railroad and the civil rights movement have become popular historic sites. Places of Mexican and Filipino suffering and struggle, however, remain largely ignored. "We should be marking the hell out of places where Cesar Chavez worked," says Judith Baca: starting with his home at Salsipuedes and the site of the famous United Farm Workers demonstration at Delano, California. Refugio Rochin agrees, adding the 350-mile route of Chavez's march from Delano to the state capital at Sacramento (Figure 3.4), as well as the sites of other demonstrations and speeches, like one at Crystal City, Texas. Rolando Romo, founder and past president of Houston's Tejano Association for Historical Preservation, also agrees, and he has organized a number of events commemorating Chavez, including a Cesar Chavez Hispanic Pride Parade and Celebration. Because Filipino and Mexican farm workers united behind Chavez, he has great importance to Filipinos as well. There were other demonstrations too: John Silva notes the important strike at Hanapepe in Hawaii, where twenty-five Filipinos were killed.

Places of Achievement

These are places where individuals or groups rose above the hardships of life to achieve notable successes or contribute to American society in significant ways (Figure 3.5). How many visitors know that the White House cooks and stewards were traditionally Filipino? That represents an achievement in which John Silva takes pride. Guadalupe San Miguel wants to preserve and mark Ideal Records in Alice, Texas, a recording studio and dance hall that played an important role in the development of Tejano music in the 1940s. He is also working to commemorate the birthplace of General Zaragoza. Rolando Romo was moved to found the Tejano Association for Historical Preservation

Figure 3.4   Mexican and Filipino Americans joined together behind United Farm Workers leader Cesar Chavez. Here, as one of the UFW's protest marches nears the state capital of Sacramento in 1966, the numbers swell. Flags include those of the United States and Mexico as well as brilliant red Huelga or strike flags adorned with Aztec eagles.

by the destruction of the house and graves of Lorenzo de Zavala, a pivotal figure in the formation of the Republic of Texas.[61] Refugio Rochin notes the homes of Leo Carillo, a rancher who owned most of the land which became Santa Monica, and of California's first and last Mexican governors (in Sonoma and Whittier). Fred Cordova would like to see a directory showing where the "Filipino illustrious" are buried.

In recent decades, historians have emphasized the importance of documenting the lives of ordinary people. Many have sought to go beyond chronicling the contributions of individuals. Yet many respondents continue to feel that it is important to celebrate the contributions and the achievements of both the famous and the unknown. Judith Baca says that making known the "contributions made to the United States by this group [Mexican Americans] would be a profound statement. . . . To have this information publicly available would be a critically important acknowledgement of how much has been given to this country." The website of the Tejano Association for Historical Preservation has a page listing eighty-two "Famous Tejanos & Tejanas in Texas History,"[62] while the home page of Filipino Americans.net assures readers that "Filipino Americans quietly have made their indelible marks on America as politicians, doctors, judges, entrepreneurs, singers, professors, movie and television stars, etc. You name it, and there are many Filipino American achievers in every field of dream." However ambivalent many academic historians and preservationists may feel about them, sites of individual achievement remain important for respondents.

Figure 3.5   The bandstand in Houston's Hidalgo Park (formerly known also as Mexican Park) recalls those in every Latin American city park. The city's Mexican community organized in the 1920s to create the park and build the bandstand; both remain a source of pride, symbolizing Mexican Americans' contributions to Houston. Thus when the structure was restored in the 1990s it was important to recarve its inscription—"Houston Mexicans to their City—V. Lozano." Despite this, most tourism and city information websites fail to credit the park to the Mexican American community, referring simply to "neighborhood residents."

Places of Racial or Ethnic Interaction

"Communities are typically studied in isolation," says Dorothy Fujita-Rony, "but it's the interactions that produce some of the most interesting things in American culture." John Kuo Wei Tchen agrees. And these interactions have been far more pervasive than the general public realizes. They have taken many forms. One is intermarriage. The first Asian war brides in the U.S., she says, were Filipino women who married African American "Buffalo soldiers" posted to the western states. Refugio Rochin notes the frequency of inter-marriage between Filipinos and Mexican Americans, which was partly a product of working side by side in the fields and partly of miscegenation laws which prevented either group from marrying whites. Other respondents point to marriages between Filipinos and Native Americans in the northwest, Filipinos and Alaskan Natives in Alaska, and Mexicans and Native Americans in the southwest.

Shared cultures, life experiences, and struggles created other bonds. Black Americans fought alongside Filipinos in World War II. Filipinos united with Mexican farm workers behind Cesar Chavez and the United Farm Workers. Filipinos and Mexicans "have been pitted against each other" so often, laments Angel Shaw, but the reality was different. Their "complex and intertwining" cultural histories should be presented: telling the story of Chavez and the Delano march correctly would build bridges between the two groups.

Many of the nation's leading cities offer exceptional opportunities for interpreting interactions: Fujita-Rony nominates New York City as a naval center and Chicago as a railroad hub. In Seattle, Filipinos shared a neighborhood with African Americans. The markets and plazas of southwestern towns, suggests Refugio Rochin, offer opportunities to understand the blending of Hispanic and Native American cultures.

Sometimes, of course, interactions were neither consensual nor collegial. Rosaura Sanchez emphasizes the blending of languages, religions, and customs that took place between Hispanic and Indian, but she is also acutely aware of the suffering that Indians endured in the Spanish missions and presidios. And she wants this story told, fully and honestly, at the sites.

Fujita-Rony notes growing interest in Asian–Latino interactions. Rochin emphasizes the importance of understanding Latino–African American relations. Alcántara notes that saving the Filipino bunkhouses at Grants means collaborating with Mexican Americans and Navajo. Sites of interaction offer special opportunities for projects that build understanding among groups and that expand consciousness of American history and culture.

Places of Spiritual Observance

The importance of churches in African American history and community life is often noted. For Mexican Americans, Refugio Rochin emphasizes the importance of cemeteries. Because Anglo cemeteries were exclusive, Mexican graveyards were often as segregated as the *barrios* in which they lived. Many people, he comments, do not know this: the cemeteries have an important story to tell. Yet cemeteries like those in Tempe and Tucson are also "colorful, beautiful, and they're visited by a lot of people." Olivia Cadaval adds that they are "living spaces," in which the stories of people and families who are connected continue to be played out; by preserving them, one would be "preserving the living connection."

Places of International Contact

These places stand for important episodes in the international relations between the United States and immigrants' countries of origin. John Kuo Wei Tchen would like to mark Angel Island and the Presidio in San Francisco, California, launching points for the Spanish–American War and the subsequent Philippine–American War, as historic places. Judith Baca nominates the shifting borders between the United States and Mexico and (in Mexico itself) the site where the Treaty of Guadalupe Hidalgo was signed. For Filipino or Mexican Americans, each of these represents a milestone in the relationships between the United States and their country of origin. Typically, the general public is much less aware of these milestones than members of the groups themselves; recognizing and interpreting them as historic sites would not only have didactic value but encourage dialogue.

Places of Presentation

Respondents identify two roles of historic sites. One is to educate. "Americans are just ignorant" of Asian American history, remarks Tchen, "so we need to claim these sites." The other is to present the group publicly, both to group members themselves and to other Americans. All of the sites discussed above educate: some, like the White House or New York's African Burial Ground, also present.

Filipino respondents were most explicit in emphasizing the need for presentational places. These need not commemorate specific events; but they should occupy symbolically prominent positions. Eric Gamalinda asks, "Why is there is no José Rizal statue in the United States, outside Hawaii?" Rizal was a leader of the Philippine independence movement until he was executed by the Spanish in 1896. Describing him as "one of the few unifying factors that our fractious people have," Gamalinda notes that Rizal visited New York, and that there had once been a plaque on the hotel near Madison Square where he stayed. Now Gamalinda proposes a statue: in Central Park, where so many heroes from other nations are commemorated, yet none from the Philippines. Angel Shaw agrees that a statue in a public place like Central Park would go farther than a plaque; it is the kind of thing, she says, that "makes us visible."

Lynn Pono also sees value in memorials. "It's a corny thing to want a monument," she says, "but it's such a part of America . . . even vacations are organized around visiting them." Though a traditional memorial might be "too commemorative," she would like to bring in artists "to create something that talks about the role of Filipinos in American history." The monument she admires most is the Vietnam War Memorial on Washington's Mall. "Why," she asks, "can't memorials be more like that?"—moving in a sincere way, rather than "creating a false sense of national pride."

Museums can also fulfill the presentational role of monuments and statues, and some respondents see the Museum of the Chinese in the Americas as doing this for the Chinese community, the Museum of the American Indian for Native peoples. FANHS is planning a national museum of Filipino American history in Stockton, California.

Historic Sites: Community, Place, and Culture

As the above examples make clear, and as many respondents emphasized, the value of historic sites comes not only from their appearance but also from the meanings attached to them. Most of these meanings cannot be seen: they lie beneath the site's visible surface, and in this sense the most successful historic sites are like icebergs. The word "association" is often used to denote ideas associated with artifacts but not directly visible in them, which may include historical narratives, moral examples, mental images, recollected sights, sounds, values, or abstractions that the site may bring into the visitor's mind. For Jeanne Cyriaque, the Rosenwald schools are a good example. Built by a Jewish philanthropist for African American children in the rural south, the schools are architecturally modest and often badly deteriorated, yet each tells a larger story of African American striving and of community experience during the period after emancipation.[63] A recent initiative to document and preserve the Rosenwald schools gains significance because of these stories. Associations are important to many if not all of the sites discussed in this chapter. Yet the meanings ascribed to historic sites by respondents frequently go beyond what preservationists usually think of as associational significance. And even though a site's original form or appearance may be severely impaired, its original buildings altered beyond recognition or even demolished, these meanings may help it continue resonating with scarcely diminished power.

One reason historical awareness can become detached from highly visible physical elements is that a place's importance lies in people's knowledge of the *place* itself. Judith Baca refers to this as land-based memory, or "la memoria de nuestra tierra," the title she chose for a major mural at Denver's International Airport. Mexican Americans' "depth of presence" in the land, she points out, is unrivalled except by Native Americans, extending in places to as much as 500 years. And "people believe that memory resides in the land." Antonia Castañeda emphasizes the extent to which long-established Hispanic communities incorporated indigenous Native American cultural attributes, and Baca notes the frequency of intermarriage with Native Americans. The longevity of Mexican communities has meant not only a strong southwestern culture but distinctive local cultures as well— traditions, stories, memories, music, and ways of making a living like farming, ranching, or cutting railroad ties. Throughout the area, she says, there are "amazing stories of regional land memory."

Land memory has practical dimensions too. By and large, the United States failed to honor its treaty commitments to respect existing Spanish land grants in the territories it conquered through the Mexican–American War, and much land left Spanish ownership through force, trickery, or the courts' refusal to recognize prior Spanish land claims. Much of that land had been communal; descendants of the communities continue to live on or near their ancestors' land, and they have not forgotten history. Even now, says Baca, more than a century and a half after the 1848 Treaty of Guadalupe Hidalgo, "people live with this every day." Olivia Cadaval remarks that, in parts of the southwest, heritage issues revolve not around cultural identity but around land grants. Baca, Cadaval, and Rosaura Sanchez all agree that the land grants should be marked, along with historic sites like the missions, presidios, and trails. That would help to maintain the memory of deep presence in the land; it might also signify hope that ancient wrongs might someday be righted.

Historical awareness can also spread out from buildings to the communities in which they are situated. Architect Richard Dozier explains. "Individual sites are important," he says, but some of the most significant speak to issues outside themselves. He recalls the founding of Brooklyn's Weeksville Society in the 1970s: had Joan Maynard merely wanted to preserve some houses which had survived from a nineteenth-century free black community, her task would have been relatively simple. What made it harder, and has made the rewards greater, was her vision of how the houses could tell a broader story, and how that story could become valuable to Weeksville's modern-day African American community.

Some of Dozier's larger issues relate to the experience of community. Pervasive segregation, he explains, made the historically black colleges and universities anchors for neighborhoods where African Americans could find housing, business services, and nightlife. Later, as the barriers of segregation weakened, African Americans "found they could get their photocopying done downtown . . . they could even live across town." The tightly knit, campus-centered communities broke apart, leaving little trace on the cityscape. Today, the campus buildings are not only important historic sites in their own right but also valuable clues to a different way of life. Dozier challenges historic preservation to go beyond preserving the campus build-ings to conveying their social context—to presenting something "more repre-sentative of the history."

For Jeanne Cyriaque, maintaining historical awareness of community life is an important preservation goal, not only in famous black communities like Harlem or Chicago's Bronzeville but also in less prominent places. She lists a range of building types—churches, schools, meeting places, downtown busi-ness rows—that typically serve as "community landmarks" and that it is important to protect. But what should preservationists do if they no longer survive? "Where there are no built resources," she says, "we have to capture the *spirit of place*"—meaning the consciousness that a vibrant community was once present at that spot. At Springfield Baptist Church in Augusta, Georgia, for example, a community-based group erected a thirty-five-foot-high "Tower of Aspiration" to "signify the many people who lived in the community."

The problem of maintaining "spirit of place" without built resources is pressing, because powerful forces of destruction have long been directed at African American neighborhoods: railroads, interstate highways, mortgage redlining, abandonment of property, urban renewal.[64] John W. Franklin would like to organize an exhibition on "all of the African American commu-nities destroyed by highways . . . and now by metros." Today the depredations continue, as new forces of commercial development and gentrification are added to the older threats. "There are so many African American communi-ties that are endangered by development," says Jeanne Cyriaque. Sometimes a Wal-mart is put "right there in the community." Or it might be a "business expansion" or a "transportation issue—roads or a new train station—or a parking lot or a super-store dropped right into the community." A particular problem concerns the Georgia and South Carolina coasts, home to histori-cally important African American communities that in some cases have nurtured a sense of cultural continuity for almost two centuries. Now their beachfront location has exposed settlements like St. Simon's to the physical destruction of resort development for the affluent, coupled with the social disintegration brought by steeply rising land values. "When you build a $500,000 house next to a $50,000 house . . . well, you know what happens," shrugs Cyriaque. The situation at American Beach, Florida, a resort community developed by and for African Americans during the 1920s (when blacks were excluded from other beaches), is similar.

The most pervasive threats are directed at urban neighborhoods. One reason is the rediscovery of downtown living by white professionals, which has made long-established African American communities targets of gentrification and displacement: they are "at the center of the city," notes Cyriaque, "and now everyone wants to live there." Within her state of Georgia, examples of this process include not only Atlanta but also smaller cities like Macon, Savannah, and Columbus. Other forms of redevelopment also threaten urban black neighborhoods. Karl Webster Barnes, chairman of Georgia's African American Historic Preservation Network, describes the situation in Atlanta's West End neighborhood as typical of many threatened neighborhoods throughout the state.[65] After decades of threats from road construction, public housing projects (whites-only), disinvestment, and suburban flight, the West End is now threatened by poor-quality residential and commercial development. Part of the neighborhood was designated as the West End Historic District in 1991, and it is listed on both State and National Registers. Yet the erosion of neighborhood character continues.

White neighborhoods experience similar problems. But whereas white preservationists typically describe the problem as a loss of neighborhood amenity or architectural quality, Barnes frames it quite differently. For him, it is an issue of culture and history:

> All across Atlanta and Georgia, we are seeing a significant case of *removal of cultural memory*. Traditional African American neighborhoods are being systematically moved or removed from their historical locations adjacent to town centers. Historical African American neighborhoods are being *marginalized* and removed from their historical locations at a time when the region is developing strategies to increase heritage tourism. As preservationists, we can and must make a difference in our neighborhoods and stop the *marginalization* of African American memory from our cultural landscape.[66]

The problem described by Cyriaque, Dozier, and Barnes seems to call either for community commemoration or for community planning. Whereas the first accepts the loss of historic resources, the second aims to prevent it. Dozier holds that preservation should attempt at least to "neutralize" the effects of gentrification on the community fabric of historic black neighborhoods. New York architect John Reddick argues that this community fabric is as valuable a historic resource as the buildings themselves. In place of market-driven gentrification, in which architecturally distinguished buildings are restored but community fabric is torn apart, he would like to see an alliance between historic preservation and community planning, in which historic housing stock is improved for the benefit of the existing community.[67] Such efforts to make reinvestment in historic buildings an ally, rather than an enemy, of community conservation, have been tried in cities including Pittsburgh (PA), Savannah (GA), and Jackson (MI). They are consistent with the attempts of African American preservation advocates like Joan Maynard and Stanley Lowe to root historic preservation within the larger struggle to maintain community in the face of social, political, and economic pressures—in short, within what architect William Davis calls community development, "which for black folk, especially in urban areas, is key."

Historic sites, then, are most meaningful where the connections are strongest to their community context. Again, two approaches seem to present themselves, one focusing on preservation and the other on interpretation. The first seeks to identify and protect not only major landmarks but also a network of "community landmarks" and even the fabric of the community. The second seeks to equip historic sites not only to tell their own history but also to show how they related to a community context, and even how life within that community was shaped by larger historical forces. Either way, the important point is for historic sites to represent more than simply themselves. Embedded in cultural contexts, they must somehow explain those contexts, make them present for the visitor: never do sites "speak for themselves," in any sense of the phrase.

Preservationists have some basic tools that make it possible for historic sites to represent things and concepts beyond themselves. Jeanne Cyriaque ticks off a few: historical markers, commemorative plaques, public artworks. Beyond helping historic building to speak, each of these may be called upon to speak in the absence of a historic building or artifact. Cyriaque describes an interesting example. Many locations along inlets or rivers on the Georgia coast were once used as baptismal sites. Today, though "you have the oral history about it," many sites lack physical evidence of this tradition. At Sandfly, by erecting a commemorative sculpture out of bricks taken from downtown Savannah (another place important to the black diaspora), community members were able to give physical presence to an important cultural experience preserved only in oral tradition.

Despite some successful examples, the standard tools leave something to be desired. At best, they offer limited scope for expression: they are ripe for renewal. John Kuo Wei Tchen has a suggestion: community cultural development. While it is difficult to define in a sentence or two, experts Don Adams and Arlene Goldbard describe community cultural development as follows:

> In community cultural development work, community artists, singly or in teams, place their artistic and organizing skills at the service of the emancipation and development of an identified community. . . . While there is great potential for individual learning and development within the scope of this work, it is community focused, aimed at groups rather than individuals, so that issues affecting individuals are always considered in relation to group awareness and group interests.[68]

If readers are unfamiliar with this kind of work, that may be because, as Adams and Goldbard explain, it is "nearly invisible as a phenomenon" in the United States.[69] Nevertheless, it is globally important. In French-speaking countries it is known as *animation socio-culturelle*, and community artists are called *animateurs*—a good word that suggests the kind of impact artists can have involving community members in expressive work to address their history and shared experience. The nature of that work can cover a wide range, including visual arts such as murals (Judith Baca's work with SPARC—the Social and Public Art Resources Council in Los Angeles—is an excellent example), radio, music, and theatrical performance, which may take place on streetcorners or buses as well as in theaters.

For Tchen, community cultural development offers an important vehicle for immigrant or marginalized ethnic groups. With it, they can create and express a cultural identity that draws on historical experience while also engaging current community issues. It can provide an activist context in which to project historical awareness, using elements such as oral history and traditional crafts or activities. It could become a valuable tool for heritage conservation, not only strengthening community bonds but also maintaining historical awareness of a community's past, and specifically sustaining Cyriaque's elusive "spirit of place."

"The Past Has to Be a Performance": Teaching with Historic Sites

To serve communities, historic sites must do more than merely exist: they must also teach. Respondents emphasized this in many ways. Like others, Filipino American poet Luis Francia stresses the value of "visible artifacts" but wants them to be "tied into the larger representation of Filipino heritage and culture." Angel Shaw agrees that, as "representations of actual people and events," sites should have plaques or other informational tools that build out the story. But for these and other respondents, representation means more than plaques. For Francia, it means preserving collections, documents, and oral histories. For Tchen, it means public education, the "real redress" to years of misinformation and social exclusion.

Many respondents want historic places to teach history: better history and more of it. Where minority groups are concerned, however, the struggle to get misinformation corrected, to ensure that historic sites present a full and fair interpretation, can be exhausting. Two decades ago, as part of an important study for the State of California, Antonia Castañeda identified a number of important Mexican American historic sites and proposed improvements in the state's official site markers. Although the work was published in an impressive volume,[70] her impression is that little has changed. Gerald Poyo notes that scholarly progress in research does not ensure that errors are corrected, or that vital new information is disseminated to the public. Since the 1980s, he explains, a new school of historical research has been "slowly transforming" the study of Texas history. Not long ago the diary of a Mexican soldier at the battle of the Alamo was discovered. If the author's claims are honest, it provides the only eyewitness account of Davy Crockett's death, and it flatly contradicts the legend of his heroic self-sacrifice. But questions about the "Alamo myth" do not easily get into textbooks that must be approved by Texas's state legislature. Changing the history told at sites can be just as difficult.

Luis Francia provides another example of a historical error which is gradually being corrected, at least in some locales. He remarks that one could visit a great many monuments to the Spanish–American War without ever learning anything about the long war for control of the Philippines which the U.S. waged as the last phase of the war in the Pacific. Though the dates inscribed on the tablets bracket the entire conflict, the inscriptions rarely mention this second phase, a long and bloody engagement in which American soldiers fought to subdue the Filipinos they had promised to liberate. Where it is mentioned, it is named the Philippine Insurrection. The point is not trivial: "Americans don't want to acknowledge that the Philippines were colonies," points out Angel Shaw, and she and other Filipino American scholars have devoted considerable attention to understanding the conflict and its aftermath.[71] Correcting this omission would be more than symbolic: it would make it possible for all Americans to understand better the Filipino American historical experience and Filipino contributions to the United States. Fortunately, there has been some progress. In 1999, the U.S. Library of Congress reclassified the Philippine Insurrection as the Philippine–American War. Shaw also praises the Smithsonian Institution for a similar relabeling.

An archaeologist once observed that the greatest hope for discovering unknown masterpieces of ancient Urartu culture lay not in the mountains of eastern Turkey but in the basements of museums, where many magnificent artworks awaited proper identification. Like archaeologists, those who seek to preserve the heritage of communities of color must sometimes reclaim misidentified objects. During a recent visit to a well-known museum of folk art, for example, this author watched as a delegation from the Filipino American National Historical Society was able to identify several wood carvings, which the museum had assigned to Latin America, as rare Filipino artifacts. The delegation also explained the provenance and use of other Filipino objects that had puzzled curators. Sometimes the objects in question are historic sites: indeed some of the best prospects for "new" Mexican, African, or Filipino American historic sites lie in existing sites, which need only to be correctly identified in order to fulfill their potential for teaching history. When Nicolás Kanellos notes that Spanish drama was presented at the Merced Theater in Los Angeles (Figure 3.1) during the 1850s, he identifies the Merced as a Mexican American site: tour guides can now present it as such. When John Silva points out that early Filipino sailors left statues or tabernacles at some California missions, he identifies them as Filipino sites: even if the artifacts have disappeared, curators can now interpret the Filipino presence there. Incorrect identification and erasure, however, are not the only obstacles to interpretation. Sometimes a false or sanitized picture can be just as difficult to correct. Rosaura Sanchez regards the missions of the southwest as a case in point. While many are preserved and celebrated, she notes, and some even have small museums, they are "mostly for tourists" and present a "quaint," sanitized view of the past. San Diego's Old Town is another example of how an emphasis on tourism can distort a site's meaning: here, the significance of a genuinely important early Hispanic settlement disappears behind scented candles, "olde time" handcrafts, and expensive restaurant meals. A valuable opportunity for teaching is lost.

Like the Urartu artifacts, existing historic sites represent a hidden cache of teaching opportunities. Indeed one of the quickest ways to create "new" Mexican, Filipino, or African American historic sites is to acknowledge and interpret these groups' role at existing sites. Filipino presence at the White House has already been mentioned. About 1.3 million visitors tour the White House every year, so the teaching potential is significant and, as John Silva points out, even a mere tidbit of information about the tradition of Filipino cooks would put America's "invisible Asians" in a new light for most visitors. Some might be encouraged to ask about the reasons for this tradition: the answers could open a window into the role of Filipinos in the nation's military, its hospitals, and the kitchens of its ocean liners and naval ships. In Philadelphia, the National Park Service plans to revise its interpretation of Independence Hall and the Liberty Bell, seen by some 1.6 million visitors each year, to acknowledge the existence of slave quarters on the site—an excellent opportunity to discuss changing concepts of liberty in American history. The story could be further enriched if it also included the Latin American revolutionary leaders and intellectuals who flocked to Philadelphia during the early nineteenth century, inspired by the city's contribution to the cause of liberty. FANHS trustee Joan May Cordova points out that the Revolutionary War history of Faneuil Hall, one of Boston's most popular tourist attractions, could be similarly enriched if visitors were told about the anti-imperialist demonstrations against the Spanish–American War that were held there.

If icons of American history like Faneuil Hall, Independence Hall, and the White House can readily divulge such unexpected and important stories, how many other stories are awaiting rediscovery at historic sites across the country?

Nicolás Kanellos cautions, however, that historic sites must do more than tell a good story: "You have to have something for people to *see*," an array of things to grab visitors' attention, spin the story out, and create a memory. The best history museums are sophisticated at presenting complex stories, and historic sites can often enrich their interpretations by presenting artifacts and documents more engagingly. Bookshops, too, allow site managers to put knowledge into the hands of visitors whose curiosity has been engaged. Yet Kanellos reports that, in museums and historic-site bookshops across the country, "Hispanic presence is nil." Houston's San Jacinto Battleground State Historical Park provides an example (Figure 10.3). A monument commemorates the site of the Mexican–American War's culminating battle, while a museum interprets the conflict. Although the museum has made a significant effort to recognize Mexican perspectives on the war, the bookshop does little to present the Mexican experience—and this even though many of its visitors speak Spanish.

Rosaura Sanchez would like historic sites to go beyond the printed word. "Make the past real," she urges, "so it's not just something you read or something you touch . . . the past has to be a performance"—and not a "bland, American" performance but one that conveys the true complexity of the past, the anguish as well as the triumphs of history. "Have students play parts," Sanchez suggests; have an Indian "talk frankly about what happened to us here." Put it all on a compact disk or video for visitors to take home.

Sites, in short, live through public awareness of them. Rediscovering the roles played by communities of color, correctly identifying art objects and documents, interpreting them honestly and engagingly, and marketing them to diverse audiences are all ways of bringing them to life. It is important, too, to consider the contexts in which visitors encounter historic sites. Heritage tourism is one important context, and it is becoming more important. In particular, African American heritage tourism has been growing.[72] When Geraldine Hobdy took over as Louisiana's first African American SHPO, she worked with the state tourism office to develop an inventory of sites of interest to African Americans and to publicize them. Where there had been no market for African American heritage tourism, Thomas Eubanks, the state's archaeologist, reports that Louisiana now leads the nation.

"Preservation in a lot of ways drives economic development, and community development too," says Thomas Williams, an African American heritage leader from Georgia. Pointing specifically to heritage tourism, he recalls how he and others worked to install a market in Cairo, Georgia, birthplace of Jackie Robinson. Now, he says, "if you're going to Tallahassee, sometimes you'll detour to see the marker and the birthplace of Jackie Robinson, and while you're there you'll probably fill up on gas, buy some hamburgers." African Americans, he remarks, can "tap into the history and use it as an economic development tool." Sometimes those commemorated are less famous than Jackie Robinson, but the sites can still be important to local communities and meaningful to visitors. Thomasville, Georgia, is birthplace and burial place of Henry Flipper, West Point's first black graduate (in 1877). "A lot of people come to Thomasville to study the Flipper family," says Williams.

Printed and internet guidebooks, itineraries, and trails have helped disseminate information about many African American sites; the NPS has made a substantial effort to market its programs to African American audiences.[73] Comparable resources hardly exist for Hispanic sites and are nonexistent for Filipino sites, and respondents pointed out that awareness of sites and collections is often low. John Silva, a museum consultant based in the Philippines, thinks many Filipino Americans would like to see the Metropolitan Museum's early Philippine grave markers or its statue of a rice god, or the early Philippine flag at the New York Public Library. But they do not know they are there, nor has either institution made any special efforts to tell them. If Silva is right, many historic sites and museums could expand their public by identifying and marketing themes of special interest to diverse communities. Preservation programs like the National and State Registers of Historic Places and the National Historic Landmarks program could similarly expand their constituencies. Virgilio Pilapil would like the National

Park Service to publish a list and map of sites with particular relevance to Filipino Americans. There are opportunities for many other federal and state agencies, as well as authors and publishers, to distribute printed and internet guidebooks, itineraries, and trails that direct travelers to African American, Hispanic, and Filipino historic places. Substantial gains can be made quickly and economically by disseminating information about existing resources.

Let us for a moment imagine a future in which every historic site not only presents a correct, complete, and engaging story but also markets it energetically, and that heritage trails and guidebooks are abundant and widely publicized. Even in this ideal world, Rosaura Sanchez reminds us, many people will never see the sites, and no amount of publicity or outreach will ever change this. In San Diego, she points out, "there are kids in the *barrios* who have never even been *downtown*": how, she asks, are you going to get them to a National Park Service site? The answer is that, if the mountain won't go to Mohammed, Mohammed will have to go to the mountain: Sanchez urges the Park Service and other cultural agencies to bring their riches to the schools, with traveling displays and even dramatic reenactments that teachers can perform with their students. Joan May Cordova is excited about the curricular possibilities of teaching with sites. To her goes the last word on the subject: sites, she says, are "curriculum-*so*-friendly."[74]

VI. WHAT IS TO BE DONE?

The preceding sections have shown that a wide gap remains between what mainstream preservation institutions are doing and what needs to be done to preserve a complete and balanced picture of the American experience. The question is, "What next?" The remainder of this chapter presents some proposals for closing the diversity gap. But closing the gap is only the first step in what preservation agencies should be doing to position themselves for the future. For the nation is changing. Communities of color are simultaneously becoming older and newer, more "mainstream" and more diverse, more rooted in the community and more international in outlook. And they are becoming more populous. In 2007, the U.S. Census reported that nearly one in ten counties had a population that was more than half minority. What about trends for the future? In twelve states, the Census reported that year, a majority of children under the age of five now belong to minority groups: these states include California, Texas, Florida, and New York. In 2008, the Census Bureau released a projection that minorities would constitute more than half of all children by 2023 and would become the majority of the U.S. population in 2042.[75] Facts and predictions like these point to a future which is more, not less, diverse. For heritage professionals, they underscore the importance not only of closing the diversity gap but also of positioning the field to better serve a changing constituency.

All of this will require concentrated effort and cooperation. The necessary changes will not be accomplished all at once. But there is something which the federal government, and specifically the National Park Service, should do right away, and that is: *something*. This is also the single most important demand voiced by respondents, who are saying, *enough talk—now we want action.*

"Por Dinero Baile El Perro"

The National Park Service wins high marks from African American respondents for convening knowledgeable people to exchange ideas about African American heritage. Architect Richard Dozier particularly praises its 2001 conference on "African Reflections on the American Landscape."[76] Yet pleased as they are with the talking, Dozier and William Davis are frustrated by the slow pace at which the National Park Service advances to the next step: involving significant numbers of African Americans as professionals in the Service's preservation work. Some respondents indeed criticized this research project because its author was less knowledgeable about African American preservation issues than many African American professionals in the field. "Why don't they use people out here with experience?," asked Dozier, frustrated with this project and with the slowness of the preservation machinery to absorb well-trained African Americans. He points out that there are eight schools of architecture among the historically black colleges and universities, several of which (Tuskeegee, for example) teach historic preservation and regularly graduate architects and historians qualified to work for the National Register, the Historic American Buildings Survey (HABS), or other branches of the Park Service. Though the Service's Cultural Diversity Internship Program wins praise for bringing young people into the field, Dozier points out that it is no substitute for hiring well-trained African American professionals. In his view, there are two reasons why the NPS should do so. First, African American professionals have earned the right to jobs and money. And second, the Park Service needs their expertise for its African American heritage efforts to succeed. Conversely, by not doing so, the Park Service isolates itself from the lively discourse of African American professionals. Dozier and other respondents are tired of being asked their opinion. "There is a lot of frustration out here," he concludes, "because the money just doesn't come" and, as a result, "the projects fail."

Disillusionment with well-intentioned government fact-finding is widespread, and not only among African American respondents. Nicolás Kanellos asks, "When do we begin to feel that the institution is ready to reform itself? . . . It keeps asking us to do these things. . . . Everyone in this group"— he gestures towards a room full of seasoned Latino scholars and activists— "has had experiences with national, state, or local government—and they've been unsatisfactory." Gerald Poyo agrees: "We're tired of being asked again and again," when few results seem to come from the seemingly endless consultations. Guadalupe San Miguel too is disillusioned with government consultations, and "tired of educating yet another Anglo." Antonia Castañeda asks succinctly, "What is the NPS doing to educate itself?" (Parenthetically, it might be noted that this author did not encounter similar frustrations among Filipino American respondents. Why? "Perhaps we haven't been studied to death," ventures Lynn Pono.)

Many of these seasoned activists have had little contact with the National Park Service, and they do not blame the agency for their experiences with other branches of government. They are open-minded about what the Service might accomplish and eager to work with it. Yet, Poyo warns, the Park Service could "do more damage than good" if, like other agencies, it raises expectations and then fails to deliver on them. To overcome the burden of history, he advises, the NPS will have to demonstrate that it means to do more than talk. It will have to *do something*. That does not mean the agency should stop listening to outside experts (indeed Judith Baca believes it would be "really wonderful to put a think-tank together of great scholars" to advise on Hispanic issues). But before convening more experts and advisory committees, Poyo urges, the agency should put some money on the table, money with which to *do something*. As the proverb says, "por dinero baile el perro": the dog dances for money.

An Initiative to Close the Diversity Gap

What kind of federal initiative would meet the demands of respondents, advance national preservation goals, and shrink the diversity gap? The federal government, led by the National Park Service, should undertake a nation-wide initiative to identify, protect, and interpret places vital to the nation's diverse history. Putting money on the table, the bureau should quickly convene a diverse team of experts outside of government, including historians and community leaders. No mere review committee, this group should work directly with the federal government in shaping and carrying out the project.

To provide a thematic focus, the NPS and its steering committee should consider organizing the initiative around places that reflect the interactions among (and within) ethnic or racial groups in American history. Many respondents emphasized the importance of this theme, which would have wide relevance as well as public appeal and would help to break down the intellectual silos which keep the histories of minority and majority groups—however well told—from coalescing into a new *national* history.

Two existing NPS programs offer potential vehicles for an initiative of this kind. The National Register for Historic Places, because of its breadth and prestige, is the logical choice. A bureaucratic hurdle must however be overcome. The National Register program itself is not generally authorized to nominate places to itself. That work is largely carried out by states acting under a federal mandate: that is, state agency staffs or citizens prepare nominations, which are then forwarded upward from State Historic Preservation Offices to the National Park Service in Washington.[77] The challenge, then, is how to catalyze and coordinate a multi-state National Register initiative.

An alternative vehicle is offered by the National Historic Landmarks program. NHLs, though far less numerous than National Register sites, have the advantage that they are normally identified through theme studies which may be initiated directly by the NPS or even mandated by Congress. Moreover, these theme studies are often carried out in partnership with citizen groups and universities. As of 2004, not a single NHL study on a Hispanic theme—and only one on an Asian subject—had been carried out since 1959.[78] The time is ripe for one or more ambitious theme studies exploring the nation's diverse history.

Whatever the vehicle, it is important to ensure that identifying and listing historic sites does not become the only goal of this initiative. There is much more that the federal government can do as part of this initiative to realize the educational value of historic places. The National Endowments for the Arts and the Humanities, the Library of Congress, and the Smithsonian Institution have done important work in documenting and preserving the history of diverse communities. They have much to contribute to this initiative, as do the Institute for Museum and Library Services, State Historic Preservation Offices, and state and regional arts and humanities councils. These agencies have or can create archives or databases of historical and ethnographic materials related to the sites; fund curricular materials, publications, websites, public art, or markers to increase public understanding of the sites and stories; and assist in cataloguing and conserving priceless archival and museum collections. In addition to listing places, the National Park Service itself can update exhibits, interpretation, and bookstore offerings at national parks. Whatever its precise components, the initiative should combine deep respect for the spirit of place, a rigorous commitment to history, and a passion for teaching. It should identify the places *and* tell the stories; promote bricks *and* books; preserve *and* interpret; inspire *and* educate.

The proposed initiative could culminate with the publication of "how-to" guides that citizens' groups throughout the country will be able to use for years to come. These handbooks can be modeled on the excellent guides that already exist for identifying African American historic places, but they should also include guidelines for plaques, public art, guidebooks, curricular materials, and local preservation campaigns.

An initiative like this will accomplish many goals at once. It will give balance to the National Register, create multi-disciplinary models for heritage conservation, and enhance the capacity of both the public and the private sectors to preserve multi-racial heritage. But it will not, by itself, close the diversity deficit. For that, sustained effort is needed. The critical question is how to build capacity and create long-range, structural change. A few suggestions follow.

Jobs

Heritage agencies wishing to make significant progress in closing the diversity gap will need to hire more black, Latino, and Asian American staff. Not-for-profit agencies will also have to diversify their boards of directors.[79] As Guadalupe San Miguel explains, it can take a very long time to educate a non-Hispanic professional about cultural issues that members of the Mexican American community have imbibed from birth. If an agency is serious about preserving Mexican heritage, it makes sense to hire a Mexican American who "knows the issues and has the contacts."

Why would a Mexican or Filipino American heritage expert work for government? Geraldine Hobdy points out that government jobs offer important opportunities to advocates for a culturally broader heritage practice, because "you have to be in the bureaucracy" to effect significant change in how it works. She reviews her own career as Louisiana's first African American State Historic Preservation Officer. Her predecessor had been hostile to African American conservation issues, even to actions as simple as listing properties associated with African American history on the National Register. When Hobdy took over, there was an "explosion" of pent-up activity: listing National Register properties, appointing the first person of color to the state review board, incorporating archaeology into heritage programs (which benefited Asians and Cajuns as well), hosting partnerships with non-profits, working with the state's tourism agency to build and serve a market for African American heritage tourism, and then addressing a growing market for Latino heritage tourism. Hobdy had brought about significant changes by "being in the bureaucracy."

The lack of diversity within the profession has long troubled well-intentioned practitioners. Many, however, contend that top-quality candidates are simply not available. It is true that professional training programs in historic preservation are not producing them. However, there is no dearth of brilliant, well-trained heritage experts who are also people of color. Instead of historic preservation, they have degrees in history, literature, anthropology, urban planning, or other fields. By overlooking them, the historic preservation field closes the door not only on racial but also on intellectual diversity. Conversely, partnering with well-trained professionals in related disciplines offers one of the fastest and best ways to diversify the profession, while also bringing in stimulating new ideas.

At the entry level, the NPS has created pathways into the field, especially the agency's Cultural Resources Diversity Internship Program, which served sixty-five students between 1999 and 2003.[80] The National Trust for Historic Preservation has also created valuable pathways into the field, most notably through its Mildred Colodny Scholarship for graduate study and its Diversity Scholarship Program, which helps send about sixty community leaders to the organization's national conference each year. All such efforts are commendable. But they do not address the need, which Richard Dozier emphasizes, to create professional opportunities for experienced practitioners who continue to be overlooked when paid positions and contracts are awarded. He is thinking mainly of architects. But, as we have seen, opportunities exist in many fields to diversify the profession rather quickly: the key is to start at the top, not at the bottom.

New Preservation Approaches

Updating some basic components of the United States' conservation system will make it easier for preservationists to create a genuinely diverse national heritage. At the top of the list are the standards governing inclusion in the National Register of Historic Places. While these have proven both durable and flexible, they contain unintentional biases against diversity. A thorough audit would help to identify and correct them—starting with the integrity standard, the rule requiring that listed sites survive substantially unaltered from their "period of significance." The difficulty is that many important historical experiences did not take place in buildings that have survived intact but, rather, in open fields, *barrios*, labor camps, union halls, social clubs, street-front churches, bunkhouses, tenements, cabins, factories, and docks. As building types, all of these have been highly susceptible to alteration and demolition. Where they survive, respondents argue that safeguarding them—even if much altered—is essential for preserving immigrant and working-class history. Where they have not survived, many respondents nonetheless report feeling a strong sense of connection to the places where people lived and struggled. Jeanne Cyriaque's "spirit of place" typifies the sense expressed by many respondents that these places are hallowed by the presence of their predecessors. National Register standards that emphasize the physical integrity of historic properties frustrate their efforts and make it more difficult to honor their consciousness of place and history.

The National Register standards exist for a purpose, which is to enable the Register to serve broad national policy goals—such as the National Park Service's commitment to provide "factual and balanced presentations of the many American cultures, heritages, and histories."[81] Right now, the Register standards do not always support that goal. But they can be amended, as they have been in the past. In 1992, the agency responded to a mismatch with Native American sites by issuing new guidelines which set forth an important new concept, the traditional cultural property. Beyond fixing the obvious problem with the integrity criterion, the comments of respondents suggest that what is needed now is better ways of recognizing *place*. Without underestimating the value of buildings and other physical artifacts, a shift in emphasis is called for, from "objectness" to "placefulness."[82]

The role of intangible heritage, including folklore, within preservation practice is another area which calls for rethinking. Many respondents emphasized the importance of living heritage to their communities. Internationally, as noted below in the introduction to Part IV, greater recognition is being accorded to cultural expressions such as music, language, dance, and civic performance, as elements of heritage deserving protection. This means also that conservation practice is beginning to grant more recognition to expressions of living heritage, instead of limiting itself to purely historical phenomena. There are good reasons, then, for preservation professionals to consider how to incorporate living culture, traditions, or folkways into each aspect of their work, from identifying historic sites through planning and conservation to interpretation.

What the preservation field should *not* do is walk away from the core activities of preserving historic sites. Respondents repeatedly emphasized the importance of historic sites and made it clear that they did not want preservation agencies to abandon them in favor of folklife. Jeanne Cyriaque (who works for a State Historic Preservation Office) supports the integration of folkways into historic preservation *as long as this does not drain resources away from core preservation programs*. Franklin Odo, of the Smithsonian Institution, agrees: while it is good to think about intangibles, "for the NPS to not put full effort into identifying sites where things happened" would be a mistake.

There are several ways in which preservationists can help protect living or intangible heritage without cutting the already small preservation pie into even more minute slices. The first is to coordinate better with existing programs so as to realize the benefits of synergy. One such program is the National Park Service's ethnography program. The NPS has a policy mandate to consult with "traditionally associated peoples"—neighbors of National Park system units plus "ethnic or occupational communities" with a longstanding interest in them—regarding the treatment of places or physical features with "traditional significance."[83] The Ethnography Program helps the NPS meet this goal by "conducting ethnographic assessments, cultural affiliation studies, traditional resource use studies, ethnographic resources inventories, and other research efforts designed to provide managers with a baseline of information about cultural values attached to park lands and resources."[84] So far over 160 such studies have been completed or launched.[85] NPS ethnographer Alexa Roberts sums it up thus: "It's about the connections between people and their places, and making management decisions based on these connections."

The concept of ethnographic resources and the practice of consultation have been widely applied to Native peoples, less often to other groups. Laura Gates, superintendent of the Cane River Creole National Historical Park, describes how a painstaking process of community consultation with African Americans and Creoles of color deepened the staff's interpretation of the site while acknowledging the local communities' strong feelings about it.[86] The potential for extending the ethnography program to non-Native groups may be considerable. Alexa Roberts points out that the NPS is the only federal land-management agency with a cultural anthropology program: "Take advantage of it!," she urges her colleagues. "If we're going to talk about diversity, if we're going to talk about partnerships, then we just need to bite the bullet." While no respondents actually asked for applied ethnographic studies, Roberts has a plausible explanation: people don't often say they want to be studied. Then, too, few if any respondents were aware of this aspect of the NPS's work. Roberts sums up:

> It's up to the NPS to recognize that we have a rigorous way to find out who are the traditionally associated peoples, what their relationship to the park is, and how do their cultural values about park lands and resources translate into decisions that we can take to manage those resources in a culturally appropriate way.

A second strategy for protecting living or intangible heritage is to focus on the places which are most important for its survival. Sociologist Ray Oldenburg has already identified one important type of space, which he calls "third places," places that are neither home nor work yet provide an invaluable setting for public socializing. Oldenburg's third places can be restaurants, bars, retail shops, service establishments, or community centers, but, to qualify, they must provide not merely service but also a sense of place that nurtures community bonds.[87] Most communities, perhaps all communities, have third places. A study of Filipino communities by Rick Bonus[88] identifies three types of places where Filipino Americans typically articulate community identity in a public setting: the so-called Oriental stores, community centers, and sites of media, especially local newspaper offices. Shoppers at an Oriental store, for example, told Bonus that such stores offer not only products but also "story-telling and gossip": they are places, they said, "'where you can be comfortable, where you can be your own self, buy the best goods, find the kinds of things you cannot find anywhere else . . . where you can feel okay because you not only buy goods that you know, but you buy them with people you know.'"[89]

In Oldenburg's terms, Oriental stores are third places. As discussed elsewhere in this book, they could also be labeled "story sites": that is, places that support local traditions and memories. So could many other community gathering spots. The previous chapter described some of the ways communities can identify and protect such story sites, and it would be useful to apply this line of thinking to the particular cultural traditions of African American, Filipino, Mexican, and other diverse communities. To do so, preservation groups could work with community cultural or planning groups to carry out surveys of places important for community traditions, to nominate them to the Register as traditional cultural places, to incorporate them in urban or environmental plans, and to ensure that they are considered when environmental impact assessments are prepared. Beyond that, preservationists could advocate for changes to the law that would make it easier to protect these places. Updating the National Register standards would be one such change. Amending state environmental laws to require the preparation of cultural impact statements, as done in Hawaii (see Chapter 9), would be another.[90]

Not every preservation problem can be fixed with a preservation solution. Indeed, where the problems are caused by massive social and economic forces, preservation programs may be little more than bandaids. The third strategy for protecting living or intangible heritage acknowledges this by calling upon preservationists to confront the larger forces which alter or even destroy communities, a subject also taken up in Chapter 9. A good way to start would be to perform a comprehensive audit of the impact of government programs, as well as the private real estate market, on the lifeways of low-income and minority communities. The disastrous impacts of programs like urban renewal, highway construction, and public housing are well known; some respondents also spoke of disinvestment and gentrification as processes that disrupt communities of color. Many other government actions, ranging from the enforcement of housing and public health codes to the construction of new transit lines, also affect folkways: their operation, interaction, and effects have never been fully studied. Such a study could point to constructive policy responses which would actually enlarge the preservation pie rather than forcing preservationists to squeeze yet more slices out of it.

Support for Citizen Initiatives

Another way to stretch public preservation resources is to support private initiatives. There are good reasons why much preservation work should remain in the hands of communities rather than the federal government. Frequently the expertise lies in communities. Often political realities also favor local control. This does not mean that federal goals are not being served or that there is no role for the federal government. The challenge is to find the right balance between supporting and taking over projects.

What is the "best way to maximize partnership with the federal government?" asks Geraldine Hobdy. Sometimes, she warns, federal agencies want to take over projects, rather than support them, and, when that happens, citizen initiatives can suffer. Yet community-based heritage projects are often strapped for funds,[91] even when they are pursuing goals of national importance. The problem is that important conservation projects, like the creation of archives and museums, frequently require resources beyond what citizen-based groups can raise. In such cases, providing financial and technical support to local groups may be not only one of the best but one of the most efficient ways of meeting federal heritage goals.

Respondents noted a wide range of endeavors in which federal support would be appreciated. Assistance in acquiring, cataloguing, conserving, and providing electronic access to collections (including archives, libraries, and museums) would be a sound federal investment in the nation's history that could continue to pay dividends literally for centuries. Aid to documentation and publication projects, local historic and preservation societies, documentary films, historical research, folklore and oral history projects, and community cultural development efforts also promise large rewards.

Here the NPS need not bear the entire burden. The National Endowment for the Arts, National Endowment for the Humanities, Institute for Museum and Library Services, Smithsonian Institution, and Library of Congress, as well as state preservation offices, historical societies, and arts and humanities councils all have important roles to play. What the NPS can do is set a policy direction towards the preservation of minority heritage and take the lead in creating programmatic vehicles for collaboration, both among funding agencies and with citizen-based groups.

Building a Transnational Preservation Practice

The phenomenon of transnational migration—people regularly crossing and recrossing national borders—poses challenges for national heritage programs for two reasons: first, because it is difficult for these programs to fully serve the heritage needs of transnational migrants; and, second, because it will be difficult for them to fully capture the cultural heritage these migrants are creating for the future. To meet these concerns, we will be best served by transnational heritage programs: programs that cross borders as comfortably as people, money, goods, and information. That means creating international partnerships among agencies or not-for-profit organizations. While many countries present opportunities, the most obvious places to start are in Latin America, especially Mexico. Whether or not the federal government is the best choice for initiating such partnerships is, however, open to question. Many migrants bring a fear of government authorities, which could frustrate the well-meaning efforts of a bureau such as the National Park Service to help. Also, partnerships organized at a local or regional level may have substantive advantages: while the concept of migration between countries is both inclusive and politically relevant, migrants also establish ties between specific towns or regions: between Mexico City and Los Angeles, for example, or Oaxaca and Yonkers. Such linked localities could work together to support, preserve, and document the history and culture of migrants as part of both regions' heritage. The Department of the Interior's International Technical Assistance Program could help by coordinating and supporting such efforts.

A Federal Role for the Future

Does transnationalism obviate the need for creative federal involvement in heritage preservation? Not at all. One question that needs to be asked in planning for an effective federal role is how the constituency for heritage programs is changing. Another is posed by Geraldine Hobdy: "What are the large projects, the effective policies, that will change values?" To answer this question, it may help to pose three smaller and more focused questions:

What are people asking for? Respondents most frequently asked government to act as a foundation, supporting citizen initiatives with grants of money or technical expertise. Such requests speak to genuine needs, but they also hint at a lack of conviction that government can or will take bolder initiatives. "Our communities have been accustomed to going for project money and not looking beyond that," comments Geraldine Hobdy. They underestimate government's legitimate interest in the question, as well as its powers.

What is government's stake in the matter? The National Historic Preservation Act of 1966 states that "the spirit and direction of the Nation are founded upon and reflected in its historic heritage" and that "the preservation of this irreplaceable heritage is in the public interest so that its vital legacy of cultural, educational, aesthetic, inspirational, economic, and energy benefits will be maintained and enriched for future generations of Americans."92 The fact is that creating an honest, balanced, and inclusive representation of the national heritage is not a trivial or arcane matter: it is one in which the nation has a powerful stake. Even if citizens were not calling upon government to help preserve their heritage, government would have a compelling interest in doing so.

What can government do better than anyone else? Government agencies such as the National Endowments are very good at giving money. Their increased support, as noted above, would be valuable. But what national government can do that no one else can do is to carry out official heritage programs on a national scale. This may seem too obvious to mention. But it is the crux of the matter. Federal agencies such as the National Park Service, Library of Congress, or Smithsonian may form regional or local partnerships to carry out this work. But, when it comes to historic preservation, only the National Park Service can send a national message that closing the diversity gap is a national priority. This is what we should now look for from the National Park Service.

APPENDIX: LIST OF RESPONDENTS TO THE STUDY
The author would like to thank the following individuals, who gave generously of their time and expertise. Affiliations are for identification purposes only and are given as of 2003–4.

Adélamar Alcántara (Senior Demographer, Bureau of Business and Economic Research, University of New Mexico, and FANHS Trustee)
Judith F. Baca (Founder and Artistic Director, Social and Public Art Resource Center (SPARC), Los Angeles, and Professor, Cesar E. Chavez Center for Chicana/o Studies, University of California at Los Angeles)
Alan Bergano (FANHS Trustee, Virginia Beach, VA)
Ronald Buenaventura (FANHS Trustee, Lakewood, CA)
Olivia Cadaval (Chair, Research and Education, Center for Folklife and Cultural Heritage, Smithsonian Institution)
Antonia Castañeda (Professor of History, St. Mary's University, San Antonio)
Stephanie Castillo (Documentary Film Maker and FANHS Trustee, Honolulu, HA)
Dorothy Laigo Cordova (Founder and Executive Director, FANHS, Seattle, WA)
Fred Cordova (Founding President Emeritus, FANHS, Seattle, WA)
Joan May Cordova (Teacher and FANHS Trustee, Cambridge, MA)
Jeanne Cyriaque (African American Programs Coordinator, Georgia State Historic Preservation Office, Atlanta, GA)
Ruth Dass (Director, InterCulture, Huddersfield, UK)
William E. Davis (Principal, Davis Architects and Construction Managers, New York, Past Trustee, New York State Preservation League, and Past Member, New York City Landmarks Preservation Commission)
Richard Dozier (Professor, Florida A&M University, School of Architecture, Tallahassee, FL)
Paul Espinosa (Producer–Writer–Director, Espinosa Productions, San Diego, CA)
Thomas Hales Eubanks (State Archaeologist and Director, Louisiana Division of Archaeology, Baton Rouge, LA)
Luis H. Francia (Poet and Author, Adjunct Professor, Asian/Pacific/American Studies Program and Institute, New York University, NY)
John W. Franklin (Program Manager, Center for Folklife and Cultural Heritage, Smithsonian Institution)

Dorothy Fujita-Rony (Professor, Department of Asian American Studies, University of California at Irvine)

Eric Gamalinda (Author and Journalist, Visiting Professor, Asian/Pacific/American Studies Program and Institute, New York University)

Laura Gates (Superintendent, Cane River Creole National Historical Park, National Park Service, Natchitoches, LA)

Bradford C. Grant (Chairperson, Department of Architecture, Hampton University, School of Architecture, Hampton, VA)

John R. Gupman (Park Ranger, Interpretation, Cane River Creole National Historical Park, National Park Service, Natchitoches, LA)

Felicity Heywood (*Museums Journal*, London, UK)

Boris A. Hidalgo (Partner, Thompson & Knight, LLP, Attorneys and Counselors, Houston, TX, and Chair, Board of Trustees, Arte Público Press, Houston, TX)

Gerri Hobdy (Former Louisiana State Historic Preservation Officer, Baton Rouge, LA)

Isaac Johnson (Springfield Village Park Foundation, Augusta, GA)

Nicolás Kanellos (Founder and Director, Arte Público Press, and Professor, Department of Modern and Classical Languages, University of Houston, Houston, TX)

Aimy Manzón Ko (Alumna, Asian/Pacific/American Studies Program and Institute, New York University, New York, NY)

Emily P. Lawsin (Lecturer, University of Michigan, Program in American Culture, and FANHS Trustee, Detroit, MI)

Roz Li (Principal, Li/Saltzman Architects, New York)

Barbara Mattick (Deputy Florida State Historic Preservation Officer, Tallahassee, FL)

Michèle Gates Moresi (Consultant Historian, National Park Service, Diversity and Special Projects, National Center for Cultural Resources, Washington, DC)

Franklin Odo (Director, Asian Pacific American Studies Program, Smithsonian Institution)

Dr. Virgilio R. Pilapil (Retired Physician, Past President and FANHS Trustee, Springfield, IL)

Lynn Pono (Coordinator of Youth and Family Programs, Bronx Museum of the Arts, New York)

Gerald E. Poyo (Associate Professor of History and Graduate Program Director, St. Mary's University, San Antonio)

John T. Reddick (Architect and President, The Cityscape Institute, New York, NY)

Linda Revilla (Educational Consultant, Lecturer, California State University at Sacramento, and FANHS Trustee, Sacramento, CA)

Alexa Roberts (Superintendent, Sand Creek Massacre National Historic Site, National Park Service)

Refugio I. Rochin (Associate Director, Inter-University Program for Latino Research, University of Notre Dame)

Rolando M. Romo (Manager, Houston Metropolitan Research Center, and Founder and Past President, Tejano Association for Historical Preservation, Houston, TX)

Rosaura Sanchez (Professor, Department of Literature, University of California at San Diego)

Guadalupe San Miguel (Professor of History, University of Houston, Houston, TX)

Angel Velasco Shaw (Professor, Asian/Pacific/American Studies Program and Institute, New York University, Documentary Film and Video Artist, and Community Activist)

John L. Silva (Consultant to the National Museum of the Philippines and Founder/Director, Heritage Conservation Society, Manila, Philippines)

John Kuo Wei Tchen (Professor and Founding Director, Asian/Pacific/American Studies Program and Institute, New York University, and Founder of Museum of Chinese in the Americas)

Maria T. Torres (Home Teacher and President, Stockton FANHS chapter, Stockton, CA)

Lynn Wilder (Cajun Pride Tours, New Orleans)

Thomas Williams (Kennesaw, GA)

Sherrill D. Wilson (Director, Office of Public Education and Interpretation of the African Burial Ground, New York, NY)

NOTES

1. Project statement, "Cultural Heritage Needs Assessment Project: Phase I," 2002. The Assessment was sponsored by the National Park Service's National Center for Cultural Resources, with advice from the Smithsonian Institution's Center for Folklife and Cultural Heritage and the Library of Congress's American Folklife Center. Antoinette Lee was the project manager.

2. *Keepers of the Treasures: Protecting Historic Properties and Cultural Traditions on Indian Lands. A Report on Tribal Preservation Funding Needs Submitted to Congress by the National Park Service, United States Department of the Interior* (Washington, DC: National Park Service, 1990).

3. *National Park Service Policies 2001*, sec. 7.5.5. Quoted from Emogene Bevitt (comp.), *National Park Service Policies Regarding Native Americans, Park-Associated Communities, Public Participation, and Community Relations* (Washington, DC: National Park Service, Native American Liaison Office, 2003).

4. These figures were provided by the Keeper of the National Register of Historic Places, as of April 20, 2004. They should be approached with caution. In providing them, the Keeper also stated in a written communication to the author that "Most properties are not listed by virtue of their association with a particular ethnic group—only 3,000 of the over 77,000 listings include reference to one of the seven groups for which statistics are maintained." These groups include Asian, Black, European, Hispanic, Native American, Pacific Islander, and Other. The Keeper also observed that "The National Historic Preservation Act compliance process is a major driver for identifying properties and yet does not necessarily result in listing in the National Register of Historic Places. Thousands of properties are listed on state inventories and hidden away in the grey literature of National Historic Preservation Act compliance documentation that are associated with various ethnic groups." Thus National Register numbers are at best an impressionistic measure. Even more so (though slightly more encouraging) is the project list of Save America's Treasures, a national program founded by the White House Millennium Council and the National Trust for Historic Preservation in 1998 "to focus public attention on the importance of our national heritage and the need to save our treasures at risk." Out of over 500 projects listed in November 2002, approximately thirty-five

could be identified as bearing specifically and primarily on some aspect of cultural heritage distinct from the mainstream (of course many other projects touch on one aspect or another of diverse heritage). Of these, about seventeen relate to African American heritage, thirteen to Hispanic American, and two to Asian American. One can further characterize the sites. Of the African American sites, many relate to plantation slavery: they are, of course, in the South. In addition, there are sites relating to famous African Americans (Paul Lawrence Dunbar, Paul Robeson, Louis Armstrong [Figure 2.3], Harriet Tubman). There are a few civil rights movement sites. And there are at least two African American neighborhoods or clusters of buildings associated with urban community life: the Jackson Ward NHL in Richmond, VA, and the Weeksville Society in Brooklyn, NY. Of the Hispanic American sites, many relate to the Spanish colonization of California and the southwest, though there are also the "Hispanic Cultural Landscape of the Purgatoire and Apishapa" in Colorado and Ybor City (founded by a Cuban immigrant) in Florida. Both of the Asian American sites are Japanese World War II internment camps. See the National Trust for Historic Preservation's website, at www.nthp.org/save%20america's%20treasures/projall2.htm (consulted November 2002).

5. Respondents consulted for this study are listed in the appendix to this chapter. All interviews were carried out by person or by telephone between July 2003 and May 2004.

6. Miguel Vasquez, "Latinos—Viva La Diferencia!," *CRM* 24/5 (2001): 22.

7. In the remainder of this chapter, sources for statements without footnotes are respondents to the study.

8. David Hornbeck, "Spanish Legacy in the Borderlands," in Michael P. Conzen (ed.), *The Making of the American Landscape* (New York and London: Routledge, 1994; first published 1990), 51–62.

9. Jorge Ramos, *The Other Face of America* (New York: HarperCollins, 2002), xvii.

10. Cynthia A. Brewer and Trudy A. Suchan, *Mapping Census 2000: The Geography of U.S. Diversity* (Redlands, CA: ESRI Press, 2001). For statistics, see also Ramos, op. cit., xviii.

11. Julia Preston, "Fewer Latinos in U.S. Sending Money Home," *New York Times*, May 1, 2008.

12. Ramos, op. cit., 156.

13. Ibid., xix–xx.

14. Ibid., 110.

15. Ibid., 126.

16. Sam Roberts, "Rise in Minorities Is Led by Children, Census Finds," *New York Times*, May 1, 2008.

17. Alejandro Portes and Rubén G. Rumbaut, *Immigrant America: A Portrait* (Berkeley: University of California Press, 1990), 11, 19.

18. Thomas Faist, "Transnationalization in International Migration: Implications for the Study of Citizenship and Culture," *Ethnic and Racial Studies* 23/2 (March 2000): 189.

19. Carlos Monsiváis, "Dreaming of Utopia," *NACLA Report on the Americas* 29/3 (November/December 1995): 40–41.

20. Faist, op. cit., 211.

21. Dell Upton (ed.), *America's Architectural Roots: Ethnic Groups That Built America* (Washington, DC: Preservation Press, 1986), 10.

22. Michael P. Conzen, "Ethnicity on the Land," in Conzen (ed.), op. cit., 221–248.

23. Anatalio Ubalde (ed.), *Filipino American Architecture, Design and Planning Issues* (Los Angeles: Flipside Press, 1996).

24. See Brian D. Joyner, *African Reflections on the American Landscape: Identifying and Interpreting Africanisms* (Washington, DC: National Park Service, 2003): with extensive bibliography.

25. From Arte Público's website: http:benito.arte.uh.edu/Arte_Publico_Press/about_app/aboutapp_app.htm.

26. "Poetry and the Burden of History: An Interview with Martin Espada," published on the website of the University of Illinois's Department of English at: http:www.english.uiuc.edu/maps/poets/a_f/espada/interview.htm. I am grateful to my daughter Emily Kaufman for this reference.

27. See Eric Yamamoto, *Interracial Justice: Conflict and Reconciliation in Post-Civil-Rights America* (New York: NYU Press, 1999). Yamamoto outlines four steps to reconciliation: recognition, responsibility, reconstruction, and reparation.

28. Mel Orpilla, "Segregation and Identity," in Ubalde, op. cit., 169.

29. Ralph Ellison, *Invisible Man* (New York: Vintage International, 1999), 3.

30. Information on the African Burial Ground can (as of 2008) be obtained from the Interpretive Center at the African Burial Ground National Monument or through the National Park Service's websites, www.nps.gov/afbg and www.africanburialground.gov.

31. Theodore Rosengarten, *All God's Dangers: The Life of Nate Shaw* (New York: Knopf, 1974); Alex Haley, *Roots: The Saga of an American Family* (New York: Vanguard Press, 1976).

32. Anthropologist James Deetz has defined material culture as "that segment of man's physical environment which is purposely shaped by him according to culturally dictated plans." Quoted in Thomas J. Schlereth, "History Museums and Material Culture," in Warren Leon and Roy Rosenzweig (eds.), *History Museums in the United States: A Critical Assessment* (Urbana and Chicago: University of Illinois Press, 1989), 294. Early African American material culture studies include Robert Farris Thompson's "African Influence on the Art of the United States" (1969), James Newton's "Slave Artisans and Craftsmen" (1977), John Michael Vlach's *The Afro-American Tradition in Decorative Arts* (the catalogue to a major exhibition of the Cleveland Museum of Art, 1978), and the same author's *Back of the Big House: The Architecture of Plantation Slavery* (1993).

33. See Susan Wal and Susan Kidd, "Cultural Diversity: A Movement of Statewide Efforts in the South: Documenting and Promoting the Region's History," in *National Trust for Historic Preservation Forum* 7/5 (September/October 1993), 1.

34. Carole Merritt, *Historic Black Resources: A Handbook for the Identification, Documentation, and Evaluation of Historic African-American Properties in Georgia* (Atlanta: Historic Preservation Section, Georgia Department of Natural Resources, 1984).

35. For museums' responses to African American issues, see James Oliver Horton and Spencer R. Crew, "Afro-Americans and Museums: Towards a Policy of Inclusion," in Leon and Rosenzweig (eds.), op. cit.

36. Albany, New York State Office of Parks, Recreation and Historic Preservation, "Guide to the Survey of Historic Resources Associated with African-Americans." The author consulted an undated draft typescript from approximately 1994.

37. See http:www.cr.nps.gov/delta/home.htm (consulted July 2003).

38. See http:www.nps.gov/undergroundrr/contents.htm; http:www.cr.nps.gov/NR/travel/underground/; and http:www.cr.nps.gov/history/online_books/ugrr/exugrr1.htm (consulted July 2003).

39. "Our Shared History: Celebrating African American History and Culture," http:www.cr.nps.gov/aahistory/bhm-intro.htm (consulted July 2003).

40. The first was "Through My Father's Eyes: The Filipino American Photographs of Ricardo Ocreto Alvarado (1914–1976)." There was no catalogue; however, as of this writing, the exhibit can still be seen online at http:apa.si.edu. The second was "El Rio." See Olivia Cadaval and Cynthia Vidaurri, *El Rio* (Washington, DC: Smithsonian Institution, Center for Folklife and Cultural Heritage, 2003).

41. National Trust for Historic Preservation website: http:www.nationaltrust.org/news/docs/20030529_11most_littlemanila.html (consulted July 2003). See also the newsletter of the National Trust's western office, at http:www.nationaltrust.org/about_the_trust/newsletters/wro/wro-0703.pdf.

42. "Los Caminos del Rio": see the National Trust's website, http:www.nationaltrust.org/11most/2001/loscaminos.htm (consulted July 2003). The area identified stretches from Laredo to Brownsville. Earlier, in 1999, First Lady Hillary Rodham Clinton had led a trip to the southwest, organized by Save America's Treasures, a partnership between the National Trust and the White House Millennium Council, whose purpose had been to draw public attention to the plight of historically and culturally important sites in Arizona, New Mexico, and Colorado. See http:saveamericastreasures.org/release051399.htm (consulted July 2003).

43. http:www.nationaltrust.org/search/sitesearch.asp (consulted July 2003).

44. See the National Park Service's Heritage Areas website: http:www.cr.nps.gov/heritageareas/ (consulted July 2003). See also "Regional Heritage Areas: Connecting People to Places and History," a special issue of *National Trust for Historic Preservation Forum* 17/4 (summer 2003).

45. Florida Department of State, *Florida Cuban Heritage Trail* (n.d.); *Florida Jewish Heritage Trail* (2000); *Florida Women's Heritage Trail* (2001).

46. The FANHS website is at www.fanhs-national.org. Many of the individual chapters have their own websites.

47. Rick Bonus, "Cartographies of Filipino American Ethnicity," in Ubalde (ed.), op. cit., 179. Bonus discusses the importance of community newspapers, and of the places where they are published, at some length.

48. Young scholars who are producing important new work include Angel Velasco Shaw (New York University), Dorothy Fujita-Rony (University of California at Irvine), and Cathy Choy (University of Minnesota).

49. See Arte Público's website: http:benito.arte.uh.edu/Recovery/recovery.html.

50. See also Nicolás Kanellos with Helvetia Martell, *Hispanic Periodicals in the United States, Origins to 1960: A Brief History and Comprehensive Bibliography* (Houston, TX: Arte Público Press, 2000).

51. Quoted in Karen Ivanova, "Revitalizing Native Tongues," *Great Falls Tribune Online*, April 14, 2002.

52. Ramos, op. cit., xxii.

53. Ibid., xxi–xxii.

54. Ibid., 17.

55. www.filipinoamericans.net.

56. Ibid. All quotations are verbatim.

57. Florida Department of State and Preserve Eatonville Community, Inc., *A Walking Tour of Eatonville, Florida* (1999).

58. Florida's folklife programs are described on the Department of State's website, http:dhr.dos.state.fl.us/folklife. See also Historical Museum of Southern Florida, *Florida Folklife: Traditional Arts in Contemporary Communities*, exhibit catalogue, 1998–2000.

59. James Oliver Horton, "On-Site Learning: The Power of Historic Places," *CRM* 23/8 (2000): 4.

60. Several valuable regional surveys already exist. See *Five Views: An Ethnic Sites Survey for California* (Sacramento: State of California, Department of Parks and Recreation, 1988), which contains (*inter alia*) studies on Mexican Americans (by José Pitti, Antonia Castañeda, and Carlos Cortes) and African Americans in California (by Eleanor M. Ramsey and Janice S. Lewis). See also Monroe Fordham (ed.), *The African American Presence in New York State: Four Regional History Surveys, With a Selected List of African American Historic Sites for Each Region*, Document #90-3 (Albany: State University of New York, New York African American Institute, 1990).

61. Rolando M. Romo, "The Founding of the Tejano Association for Historical Preservation," unpublished paper, copy provided by the author.

62. www.tejanoahp.org (consulted July 2003).

63. For the Rosenwald schools, see Tom Hanchett, "Saving the South's Rosenwald Schools," *National Trust for Historic Preservation Forum* 17/3 (Spring 2003): 50–55; and Diane Granat, "More Than Blue Skies," *Preservation* 55/4 (July/August 2003): 34–37.

64. For an exploration of how urban renewal has affected the place attachment and place memories of neighborhood residents, see Mindy Thompson Fullilove, *Root Shock: How Tearing Up City Neighborhoods Hurts America, and What We Can Do About It* (New York: Ballantine Books, 2004).

65. Karl Webster Barnes, "Your Vision, Your Memory, Your Challenge: Preservation Is Good for Your African American Neighborhood Revitalization," in Georgia Department of Natural Resources, Historic Preservation Division, *Reflections* 2/4 (September 2002): 4–6.

66. Ibid., 6. Italics in original.

67. See Ned Kaufman, "Sugar Hill: Thoughts on Cultural Conservation," *Heritage Matters* (June 2002): 14–15, for a description of a panel discussion in which Reddick debated this position with Michael Henry Adams, another Harlem preservationist, who argued in favor of restoring historic housing stock even at the cost of displacing long-time community residents.

68. Don Adams and Arlene Goldbard, *Creative Community: The Art of Cultural Development* (New York: Rockefeller Foundation, 2001), 61. This is a basic text for community cultural development that includes further bibliography. See also Art in the Public Interest's website: www.apionline.org.

69. Adams and Goldbard, op. cit., 4.

70. See *Five Views*, op. cit.

71. See Angel Velasco Shaw and Luis H. Francia (eds.), *Vestiges of War: The Philippine–American War and the Aftermath of an Imperial Dream 1899–1999* (New York: New York University Press, 2002).

72. See Elizabeth Smolcic and Carol Mansfield (eds.), *Black Heritage Tourism: Exploitation or Education* (Washington, DC: Partners for Livable Places and African American Museums Associations, 1989).

73. See, for example, Beth Savage, *African American Historic Places* (New York: John Wiley & Sons, 1995); Calder Loth (ed.), *Virginia Landmarks of Black History: Sites on the Virginia Landmarks Register and the National Register* (Charlottesville: University of Virginia Press, 1995); Lenwood Davis, *A Travel Guide to Black Historical Sites and Landmarks in North Carolina* (Winston-Salem, NC: Bandit Books, 1995); Nancy C. Curtis, *Black Heritage Sites: The South* (New York: New Press, 1996); Nancy C. Curtis, *Black Heritage Sites: The North* (New York: New Press, 1996); Kevin M. McCarthy, *African American Sites in Florida* (Sarasota, FL: Pineapple Press, 2007); *Alabama's Black Heritage* (Montgomery: Alabama Bureau of Tourism and Travel, n.d.).

74. There is a growing literature on teaching with historic places. The National Register of Historic Places (National Park Service) maintains a list of publications on the subject. See also, *inter alia*, Charles S. White and Kathleen Hunter, *Teaching With Historic Places: A Curriculum Framework for Professional Training and Development of Teachers, Preservationists, and Museum and Site Interpreters* (Washington, DC: National Trust for Historic Preservation, 1995); and *Creative Teaching With Historic Places*, a special issue of *CRM*, 23/8 (2000, published by the National Park Service). Those interested in the subject may also find it useful to consult the even more substantial literature on environmental or place-based education.

75. U.S. Census Bureau News, "More Than 300 Counties Now 'Majority-Minority,'" press release, August 9, 2007; Sam Roberts, "Rise in Minorities Is Led by Children, Census Finds," *New York Times*, May 1, 2008; U.S. Census Bureau, "An Older and More Diverse Nation by Midcentury," released August 14, 2008.

76. National Park Service, *Places of Cultural Memory: African Reflections on the American Landscape*, Conference proceedings, May 9–12, 2001, Atlanta, Georgia (Washington, DC: National Park Service, n.d.).

77. 36 CFR 60.1(b); see also 36 CFR 60.6.

78. The last Hispanic theme, in 1959, focused on Spanish Exploration and Settlement. The Asian theme was Japanese Americans in World War II. See the web page of the National Historic Landmarks program at www.nps.gov/nhl/themes. A Labor History Theme Study, authorized in 1991, also has some relevance. There have been a few theme studies focusing on African American topics, including the Underground Railroad, Racial Desegregation in Public Education, and Civil Rights in America.

79. The National Trust for Historic Preservation has taken the brave step of not only tracking but also publishing statistics on the diversity of its various boards and staff categories. By 2008 it could report that minority representation on its Board of Trustees and Board of Advisors had risen to 25 percent. Professional staff, however, remained at only 16 percent. (Information from "State of Preservation Report, Working Draft," courtesy of Lisa Schamess.)

80. Cultural Resources Diversity Internship Program document "Where Are They Now?" (updated June 6, 2003). See also the NPS's website: www.cr.nps.gov/crdi (consulted August 2003).

81. *National Park Service Policies 2001*, sec. 7.5.5. Quoted from Bevitt (comp.), op. cit.

82. For a sampling of some of the building types associated with outsider ethnic groups, see *Five Views*, op. cit. For further discussion of the integrity criterion, particularly as it relates to industrial buildings, see Chapter 6 in this volume. For traditional cultural properties, see Patricia F. Parker and Thomas F. King, *Guidelines for Evaluating and Documenting Traditional Cultural Properties*, National Register Bulletin 38 (Washington, DC: National Park Service, 1992). For a discussion of TCPs within the general context of preserving sites associated with tradition, see also Chapter 2 in this volume.

83. See Emogene Bevitt (comp.), *National Park Service Policies Regarding Native Americans, Park-Associated Communities, Public Participation, and Community Relations* (Washington, DC: National Park Service, Native American Liaison Office, 2003), a useful compilation of relevant policies from *National Park Service Management Policies 2001*. The major legislative sources of the NPS's responsibilities to traditionally associated peoples are set forth in sec. 5.3.5.3. Quotations are from sec. 5.3.5.3, 5.1.5.1, and 5.2.1–2.

84. Michael J. Evans, Alexa Roberts, and Peggy Nelson, "Ethnographic Landscapes," *CRM* 24/5 (2001): 55. For the role of ethnography within the NPS, readers should consult this entire issue of *CRM*, subtitled "People and Places: The Ethnographic Connection." See also the NPS's Archaeology and Ethnography Program website, atwww.cr.nps.gov/aad.

85. Ibid. See also Muriel (Miki) Crespi (comp.), "National Park Service Applied Ethnography: Projects Completed and In Progress FY 2003," document available from NPS Technical Information Center, Denver, CO.

86. See also Muriel (Miki) Crespi, "Raising Muted Voices and Identifying Invisible Resources," *CRM* 24/5 (2001): 4–6. Another example of ethnography used in an African American and Creole context is discussed in Allison H. Peña, "Fazendeville—Highlighting Invisible Pasts and Dignifying Present Identities," ibid., 24–26.

87. See Ray Oldenburg, *The Great Good Place: Cafés, Coffee Shops, Bars, Bookstores, Hair Salons, and Other Hangouts at the Heart of a Community* (New York: Marlowe, 1999); and Ray Oldenburg (ed. and intro.), *Celebrating the Third Place: Inspiring Stories about the "Great Good Places" at the Heart of Our Communities* (New York: Marlowe, 2001).

88. Bonus, op. cit., 171–195.

89. Ibid., 177.

90. For the cultural impact statement, see Chapter 9 and the State of Hawaii's website: www.capitol.hawaii.gov/session2000/acts/Act050_HB2895_HD1.htm (consulted November 2003). Some background to the legislation can be found on the website of Kohanaiki 'Ohana, a non-profit organization dedicated to preserving Native Hawaiian culture: see www.kohanaiki.org.

91. See Adams and Goldbard, op. cit., for a discussion of funding needs for community cultural development.

92. National Historic Preservation Act (16 U.S.C. 470 et seq.), Sec. 1(b)(1, 2, 4), available at http:www2.cr.nps.gov/laws/NHPA1966.htm (consulted July 2003). A similar interest is stated in the Historic Sites Act of 1935. The National Environmental Policy Act of 1969 expresses a public interest in cultural as well as natural aspects of the environment.

PART II

Architecture In and Out of Place: Historical Perspectives

INTRODUCTION: VISITING, COLLECTING, AND PRESERVING ARCHITECTURE

Interest is growing in the history of preservation, and a recognized academic discipline may some day emerge. The following chapters, which consider the history of architectural history and museums, also shed light on the early history of preservation. Chapter 4 explores the origins of architectural travel and its role in the nascent discipline of architectural history during the eighteenth and early nineteenth century. Chapter 5 presents an overview of architectural museums and collecting, from the earliest collections of fragments and plaster casts, through the celebrated museums of Sir John Soane in London and Alexandre Lenoir in Paris, the international exhibitions of the later nineteenth century, and onward to the period rooms and restoration villages of the twentieth century. These chapters are purely historical, and readers whose sole interest is in current preservation problems may wish to skip over them. However, the issues they cover continue to resonate in preservation practice: the attitudes to architectural history, place, and the relationship between people and buildings whose origins they chronicle are still very much with us.

The relationship between collecting and preserving architecture has always been complex. The removal of friezes and other sculptural elements from the Parthenon by Lord Elgin in 1801 and their subsequent installation in London's British Museum were controversial at the time. Today, disputes over the ownership, removal, and display of cultural patrimony are sharper than ever, and not only architectural components but also grave goods, ritual artifacts, and human remains are increasingly covered by both domestic and international law.[1] The emergence of an organized preservation profession may have contributed to this process by highlighting a key difference between preserving and collecting: historic preservation generally seeks to preserve things where they are, while museums assemble them in new places for the convenience of viewers.

Despite this difference, museum practice and preservation practice share plenty of common ground. This is suggested by the title of a well-known book by a leading preservation expert, James Marston Fitch: *Curatorial Management of the Built Environment*. Despite lively debates over how far they should be carried, basic museum activities like curation, conservation, and documentation remain essential for historic preservation. The overlap creates room for sites with a dual or ambiguous identity. A classic example is Williamsburg, Virginia, the colonial city whose restoration was launched by John D. Rockefeller, Jr., in the 1920s: Colonial Williamsburg is both a historic site (indeed one of the most visited in the United States) and a museum. Other outdoor museums of the same period, like Henry Ford's Greenfield Village or the Shelburne Museum in Vermont, seem more museum-like and less preservation-like: they are not preserved villages but rather collections of buildings brought from other places and arranged to resemble historic towns. Even so, the conservation techniques employed on the buildings are the same as those used in historic preservation. An even more ambiguous example is the neighborhood in Indianapolis, battered by urban renewal and disinvestment, whose few surviving buildings were reassembled by the National Association for African American Historic Preservation into a compact grouping which preserved the spirit of the original neighborhood better than its actual remnants.

Colonial Williamsburg represents a relatively recent phase in architectural collecting. As chronicled in Chapter 5, the habit of collecting and displaying entire buildings in village-like groups emerged from the international exhibitions of the late nineteenth century. Earlier museums had collected fragments of buildings, along with plaster casts and drawings. Even today, preservation practice continues to draw on this older tradition. Two important preservation institutions, the Historic American Buildings Survey (HABS) and the History American Engineering Record (HAER), exist to document buildings and other structures in measured drawings, which are kept by the Library of Congress; founded in 1933 and 1969, HABS and HAER were joined in 2000 by the Historic American Landscapes Survey. Though many preservationists do not think that drawings and photographs constitute a legitimate form of preservation, the National Historic Preservation Act treats them as such when demolition cannot be prevented. Another echo of early collecting habits can be found in the salvage warehouses managed by some preservation agencies and not-for-profits, where fragments of demolished buildings—fireplaces, newel posts, stained glass windows, even old bathtubs—are presented to potential buyers in displays strikingly similar to those of the earliest cast and fragment museums.

A notable property of such collections is the propensity of fragments to arrange themselves into unexpected new narratives when brought together with other fragments. A project underway in Vancouver, Canada, as of 2008 promises to exploit this venerable poetry of fragments. The project, to redevelop the old Woodward's Department Store in Vancouver's Downtown East Side, will include market-rate housing, office space for not-for-profit groups, an art school, retail spaces, and several hundred units of subsidized housing for neighborhood residents. Only one of the old buildings on the site will be retained, but the architects will salvage and incorporate fragments from the others into the new development. These will be augmented by narrative fragments presented through video monitors, interpretive signage, public art, and even performance pieces; together, this multi-media collage will weave a narrative encompassing not merely the history of the department store but also that of the neighborhood, former employees, and neighborhood residents.

Chapter 4 focuses on the institution of architectural travel, which has been closely related to the history of architectural collecting. Starting in the eighteenth century, English and north European architects and amateurs fanned out across the continent with their sketchbooks (and sometimes with retinues of draftsmen) in search of the long-forgotten architecture that had filled the epochs before the Italian Renaissance had spread over Europe. Arriving at the ancient ruins of Palmyra, or at a neglected Gothic church in Normandy, they would create sets of measured drawings which they would later bring home, publish, and sometimes seek to recreate. It was through their travel accounts that the architectural forms of ancient Greece and medieval Europe were rediscovered and popularized, that the raw material of the Greek and Gothic revivals was assembled, and that the literature and the practices of architectural history were developed.

Like museums, architectural travel has left a complex legacy. The early travelers fed a growing interest in the past, helping to shape an awareness of the history of architecture as well as practices for studying and adopting its forms. This awareness and many of the practices are still with us. Yet we confront the pioneers of architectural history as if across a canyon. That canyon was the discovery of time. Today we take it for granted that time and chronologies are the backbone of history. But this was not obvious to the early traveler-historians. For them, the history of architecture was fundamentally a geographical subject, a matter not of timelines but of maps and itineraries, and it was only during the nineteenth century that buildings were gradually decoupled from place and attached to time. This was no coincidence: during the nineteenth century, rapid advances in geology, paleontology, and evolution revealed previously unimagined vistas of time. Scientists began arranging fossils, skeletons, and rock strata into timelines that could guide one securely backward into the past, through thousands and even millions of years. The architectural corollary was clear, for one could arrange Gothic moldings or tracery patterns into the same kinds of temporal sequences as rocks and fossils. Architectural history thus became a chronological subject, a narrative about the temporal evolution of forms and types. No longer was it mainly an account of places: in fact, place—the spatial relationships among buildings and their contextual relationships to their settings—played an ever smaller role.

As architectural scholars were extracting buildings from their matrix of place and local culture, a second process was underway: the consequences of their conjunction would be ironic. This second process was the growth of folklore and folklife studies. Focusing on just the kind of local customs which architectural historians were rejecting as irrelevant, the practitioners of these new disciplines created their own place-based pictures of culture. The two narratives diverged. Today's architectural history profession inherited the former, while folklorists, ethnographers, and anthropologists took up the latter. The consequences of this split for the conservation of cultural heritage have been significant. The historic preservation profession has largely sided with the historians, teaching and learning architectural history as a fundamental skill while generally ignoring the place-based disciplines. As a result, not only do the narratives remain largely separate, but so do the conservation professions: each has its own specializations, organizations, bureaucracies, laws, international agreements, and teaching programs. Though some practitioners on both sides are working towards a rapprochement that could bring the different branches of heritage conservation closer together, the structural obstacles are substantial.

To encounter the early traveler-historians is useful because it returns us to a mode of thought which predated the ascendancy of time and the split between history and folklife. Though these travelers did not think critically (as today one might wish to do) about how local culture and architecture shaped each other, or about how their own experiences as travelers shaped their perceptions, there is nonetheless something to learn from them. They savored the experience of being in places and let it show in their writings. And unlike later architectural historians, they never made the mistake of thinking that where buildings were was unimportant.

Still, the solution to our current dilemma is not to return to their ideas: on the contrary, studying them helps us recognize and reject some of the most problematic. Though the early architectural travelers relished the experience of places, it was always as travelers, outsiders passing through: they never really tried to understand places from the perspective of residents. Architects and academics inherited this attitude, which even today shows up in unconscious ways. Consider the case, which I have witnessed more than once, of an architectural student presenting a design for a house to a jury: "You enter the front door here," the student begins, "then you see the living room to the right, you ascend the stairway here [pointing], and then you go either right or left, glimpsing the view to the distant hill here," and so forth. In becoming a tour guide, the young architect has unconsciously adopted a form of exposition introduced into architectural writing by the architect-travelers of the eighteenth century, who borrowed it from the great explorers. This in itself would not be especially notable if the project being presented were intended mainly for tourists. But it is for a *home*—the building type above all others where long-time residents should take precedence over travelers. The influence of the traveling habit is deep indeed.

This influence is sometimes conscious and purposeful. Academics travel regularly to attend conferences, give lectures, and carry out field work; they may well find their richest intellectual networks sustained through these means rather than through contacts at home; many also enjoy vacations traveling. Architects ambitious for success and fame similarly travel around the world to client meetings and job sites. The structures of the professions strongly encourage these patterns. Architecture schools offer travel fellowships, semesters abroad, and summer study trips. Academic departments support professional travel with money and recognition; conversely, they offer little recognition for local engagements such as service on planning or landmark boards.

If there is a problem with these habits, it is not the love of travel. There are good reasons why architects and academics like to travel: education, enjoyment, and profit among others. The problem is rather the confusion that arises between knowing places as residents and knowing them as travelers. "Every place is both local and foreign," writes art critic Lucy Lippard: "The same place is the site of two very different experiences."[2] Visitors often notice things that have become invisible to residents. Yet it is the perspective of residents that must ultimately become the touchstone for understanding and acting upon places. Residents know things about places that can only be learned by living through the cycles of time and seasons, using the place's public services as well as its private spaces, patiently observing patterns of stability and change. Besides, residents depend on places for their lives, whereas travelers can simply leave.

Today's institutional structures provide little support for understanding places from inside—except for historic preservation, which has remained resolutely local in outlook. Unlike architects and historians, preservationists typically find their thickest professional networks close to home, linked not to international organizations and conferences but to neighborhood associations and town councils. Speaking engagements are more likely to be at local zoning boards than foreign universities. And despite its debt to architectural history, preservation still puts a high value on local knowledge: preservationists frequently know the neighborhood in ways that architects and architectural historians miss. They could know it even better if the rift between the architecture and folklife narratives—the time-based and place-based world views—were healed.

There are drawbacks to preservation's localism. At a time when information is shared globally, localism should not be allowed to become provincial isolation. In 2008, I reviewed a number of research proposals which the firm of Rafael Viñoly Architects had solicited. The variety of international partnerships was truly astounding. One proposal came from a New Zealand architect working in Auckland and a Chinese engineer in Chengdu. Another team included a Palestinian/Italian architect working for the United Nations agency for refugees, an Italian architect teaching in Ramallah, and an Israeli-born architect with a practice in London. A third was made up of an urban designer from Brazil, an American architect who had carried out research in Mexico, India, and Europe, and a Chinese consultant who had researched New York City for the World Bank. Two young professors at the University of Utah and the Universidad Nacional del Litoral in Santa Fe, Argentina, had joined forces. Italian architects based in Rome and in Melbourne, Australia, were collaborating in Ouagadougou, the capital of Burkina Faso.

Such collaborations are exhilarating, and the exchanges of knowledge and ideas they promote are essential for the future of preservation in the United States. But they too have their drawbacks, especially the risk of knowing too little about too many places. The challenge for preservationists is to extract what is most valuable from this intellectual globalism while making themselves the best localists they can be.

NOTES

1. For some recent treatments of these questions, see various essays in Barbara T. Hoffman (ed.), *Art and Cultural Heritage: Law, Policy, and Practice* (Cambridge: Cambridge University Press, 2006); Kate Fitz Gibbon (ed.), *Who Owns the Past? Cultural Policy, Cultural Property, and the Law* (New Brunswick, NJ and London: Rutgers University Press, 2005); and Neil Silberman and Claudia Liuzza (eds.), *Interpreting the Past*, Vol. V, Part 1: *The Future of Heritage: Changing Visions, Attitudes and Contexts in the 21st Century. Selected Papers from the Third Annual Ename International Colloquium* (Brussels: Province of East-Flanders, Flemish Heritage Institute, Ename Center for Public Archaeology and Heritage Presentation, 2007).

2. Lucy R. Lippard, *On the Beaten Track: Tourism, Art, and Place* (New York: New Press, 1999), 2.

CHAPTER 4

History, Design, and the Rise of Architectural Travel

The following chapter was written for the inaugural exhibition of the Canadian Centre for Architecture in Montreal in 1989 and is reprinted here in a slightly abridged form, without some of the original illustrations and catalogue notes.

> Egyptian architecture, I went to investigate on the banks of the Nile; Grecian, on the shores of Ionia, Sicily, Attica, and the Pelopon[n]esus. Four different times I visited Italy, to render familiar to me all the shades of the infinitely varied styles of building, peculiar to that interesting country.. .. Moorish edifices I examined on the coast of Africa, and among the ruins of Grenada, of Seville, and of Cordova; the principle of the Tartar and Persian constructions I studied in Turkey and in Syria; finally, the youngest branch of the oldest of arts, that erroneously called Gothic, I investigated the most approved specimens of throughout England, and most of the provinces of France, Germany, Spain, and Portugal.
>
> (Thomas Hope, "Observations on the Plans and Elevations designed by James Wyatt for Downing College," 1804)

Nowadays, architects and architectural historians travel voraciously. It is expected of them. It is useful: the knowledge they bring home is not only the stock for a highly competitive trade in anecdote but also a source of ideas for research, writings, and buildings. Travel is also considered to be among the great pleasures of professions that are not, in general, highly remunerated. No one, in short, questions the value of travel.

The roots of this authorized passion can be traced to the nineteenth century. It is then that architects began routinely taking summer sketching trips, and then, too, that they began spending a great deal of time in transit between far-flung building sites. But the ascendancy of architectural travel really began about the middle of the eighteenth century, at least in England, and was, at least in one very particular sense, at its peak for approximately a century thereafter. During the hundred years from about 1750 to about 1850, most of the significant shapers of architectural taste and knowledge were travelers, and their outlook was fundamentally shaped by travel. To be sure, earlier architects had traveled in search of ideas, inspirations, and professional advancement. But, in the eighteenth century, the idea of travel was institutionalized as part of the architect's professional competence, added to the classical stock of his accomplishments. Thus the Italian theorist Carlo Lodoli held "that if Vitruvius had had a more lively and wide-ranging intelligence, he would have recognized that to compose his architectural history it would be essential to leave his retreat and visit . . . ancient Etruria, the realms of Naples and Sicily, no less than Egypt and Greece."[1] He would, in short, have been more like Thomas Hope, the author of our epigraph.

The process by which travel came to be instituted in architectural training through a whole apparatus of competitions, fellowships, and *envois* is reasonably well known.[2] But I want to consider the question of architectural travel in the context of a significant reorientation in the nature of architectural knowledge that began to take place around the middle of the eighteenth century. It was at this time that a wide range of architecture outside the Roman-Renaissance tradition first came to be known and to have a substantial impact on the practice and theory of architecture.

This knowledge was largely acquired through travel. But what exactly was it? Since the middle of the nineteenth century, knowledge of past architecture has been historically formulated: information is accordingly fed into a model of the world that emphasizes temporal succession and change—a model that tends, in other words, to order things in relation to a timeline. This view sees architecture as gradually evolving, changing, developing, at different rates in different places but always with a sense of underlying connection. Viollet-le-Duc wished to "analyze the past . . . by following step by step the march, the progress, the successive phases of humanity."[3] For William Morris, history was the story of an "inchoate order" ever "moving forward," changing, reshaping itself.[4] A little later, the Viennese art historian and theorist Alois Riegl summarized this view with exemplary clarity:

> Everything that has been constitutes an irreplaceable and irremovable link in a
> chain of development. In other words: each successive step implies its
> predecessor and could not have happened as it did without that earlier step.
> The essence of every modern perception of history is the idea of development.[5]

But, from the standpoint of the late eighteenth century, the world of the past did not look this way. True, scholars made staggering progress in establishing dates and identifying styles. But their work does not show the consistent attention to development, to historical change, that we find in more recent works; the probing of time seems quite incidental. Instead, their investigations were founded upon the exploration of place. The titles of the books they published are suggestive: *The Antiquities of Athens* (or of Normandy, or of Great Britain); *The Ruins of Palmyra* (or of Baalbek); *The Erechtheion at Athens; Fragmenta Vetusta, or the Remains of Ancient Buildings in York*— none expresses the passage of time, except insofar as it has turned certain objects into "antiquities." Each specifies a physical object or group of objects at a particular location; the place seems to own the objects. Other titles indicate movement to or through places: *Anglo-Norman Antiquities, Considered in a Tour through Part of Normandy; An Architectural Tour in Normandy;*

and *Voyages pittoresques et romantiques dans l'ancienne France*. We might pay heed to John Britton, one of the period's most influential Gothic scholars, who suggested that it was the spirit not of historical but of *topographical* enquiry that had led English scholars "to explore and illustrate the vast and varied antiquities of Egypt, of central America, of Asia Minor, and of other districts, which had previously been unknown."[6]

One thinks of the age of Vasco da Gama, Columbus, and Magellan, as the great age of European exploration; but the spirit of topographical enquiry manifested itself almost as vigorously in the century or so following 1750. At that date, *terra incognita* was still a substantial portion of the globe; by the end of the nineteenth century, exploration had reduced it to a few corners. Meanwhile, ambitious ventures in cartography, like the Cassini map of France or Britain's Ordnance Survey, imposed structure and control over the earth's surface. This spirit of topographical enquiry did not serve geographical interests alone: ethnography and ultimately anthropology benefited, as did the natural sciences, through a host of voyages, of which Darwin's on the *Beagle* was merely the most famous. Those who wished to understand their own society better also resorted to travel as a means of research—men like John Howard (prisons), Arthur Young (agriculture), and William Cobbett (the political and economic state of the countryside)[7]—as did artists, who stocked the walls of watercolor exhibitions and the pages of books with views developed from their travel sketchbooks. Finally, architects and scholars of architecture traveled, bringing back images both evocative and precise of buildings from around the world.

Asking why architects took to travel is a little like asking whether the chicken preceded the egg. Travel offered the only way to find out about the vast majority of the world's buildings, which were neither within sight nor already represented in books. Research naturally therefore took the form of travel, even of voyages of discovery, and the language of scholars reflected this. So the great early-nineteenth-century Norman antiquary Arcisse de Caumont liked to refer to his research as "*exploration*."[8] And as late as 1879 the leading Oxford historian E. A. Freeman could still claim that his chapter on Norman architecture was "less the result of reading than of travelling"[9]—a claim he would not have made for the more purely historical chapters of his book.

At the same time, travel and topographical study appealed to intellects in many fields because they provided not only a means of research but a concept for structuring knowledge. So John Britton claimed (quoting the poet Wharton) that even studies of county topography could "be made the vehicles of much general intelligence," providing a key to science, art, literature, and history;[10] while for Thomas Arnold

> a real knowledge of Geography embraces at once a knowledge of the earth and
> of the dwellings of man upon it; it stretches out one hand to history, and the
> other to geology and physiology: it is just that part of knowledge where the
> students of physical and of moral science meet together.[11]

Travelers and travel writers approached the world in just this broad and inclusive spirit: so Jacob Spon, the famous late-seventeenth-century traveler to Athens, while assuring his readers that "my biggest researches had the goal of knowledge of the ancient Monuments of the countries I saw in my Voyage,"[12] nevertheless commented liberally on topography, politics, trade, religion, history, costume, flora and fauna, the protocols of the local official-dom, and so forth. The architectural travelers of a later day, though more professional in their investigative techniques, inherited this inclusive and non-specialist view of travel as a way to apprehend the basic structure of the world.

The books that came out of architectural voyages during the century or so following 1750 enlarged the horizons of the architectural world and fundamentally altered the practice of architecture. This chapter aims to illu-minate the contribution of travel to this reconstruction of architectural knowledge. Broadly, it is about architectural representation; more narrowly, about the architectural exploration historiography of two regions—Greece and the Levant on the one hand, Normandy on the other. These two levels of concern come together in the analysis of how architecture was represented in English architectural books from about 1750 until about 1840. Here, the emphasis is not on individual pictures but on larger units composed of groups of pictures, or of pictures and words, indeed of entire books. Beyond that, finally, this chapter is about how the eclectic architecture of this period, both pictured and built, emerged from and represented an understanding of the world based on the assumptions and experiences of travel.

THE MAJOR EXPEDITIONS

Though travel to Greece was not unheard of in the late seventeenth and early eighteenth centuries,[13] knowledge of Greek architecture was limited before the middle of the eighteenth century. The impetus to enlarge it was initially due to two young Englishmen, James Stuart and Nicholas Revett, who went to Rome in 1741 and 1742 to study painting. While there, they seem to have supported themselves as *ciceroni*, or guides to traveling Englishmen.[14] In 1748, they conceived the idea of mounting their own expedition to study the architecture of Athens and to bring back accurate information to the west. This was an expensive proposition, and they had first to find backers, includ-ing Robert Wood (about whom more later) and the Society of Dilettanti, a group of aristocrats founded in 1732 and dedicated to the joint pursuit of revelry, travel, and the improvement of taste.[15] Arriving in Athens in 1751, Stuart and Revett worked until they were forced to leave by a combination of plague and popular unrest in 1754. Back in London by 1755, they began work on their promised book, *The Antiquities of Athens*, whose first volume appeared in 1762, the second in 1789.[16]

By this time, the situation was substantially transformed. As early as 1750, a second party consisting of three monied and well-traveled Englishmen—James Dawkins, John Bouverie, and Robert Wood—had left Naples, together with the Italian architect G. B. Borra. The spring of 1751 found all but Bouverie, who had died *en route*, at the magnificent ruins of Palmyra and Baalbek. On their return to London, Dawkins and Wood passed through Athens, where they found Stuart and Revett at work. Wood's *Ruins of Palmyra, Otherwise Tedmor, in the Desart* appeared in 1753, its sequel, the *Ruins of Balbec*, in 1757.

In 1764 the Society of Dilettanti decided to send a party to study the classic monuments of Ionia, which became the third great English expedition to the eastern Mediterranean. They chose the Oxford classicist Richard Chandler and the artist William Pars, along with the veteran Revett. On their return to London, the party stopped in Athens, where Revett completed his studies of the Propylaeum, interrupted a decade earlier. Back in England by 1766, their *Ionian Antiquities* (with a few drawings supplied by Robert Wood), was published by the Society in 1769.

The "exploration" of Normandy began almost simultaneously with that of Greece and the Levant. In 1752, the well-known antiquarian Andrew Coltee Ducarel[17] became troubled by controversy over the relative chronology of Norman and Saxon architecture: a veteran of numerous antiquarian expeditions, he "went into Normandy on purpose to view and examine such buildings of duke William"—that is, William the Conqueror—"as were remaining."[18] Ducarel's voyage, sponsored by the Society of Antiquaries, took him from Calais through Dieppe to Rouen, Lisieux, Caen, and Bayeux. He published it in 1754, and again, with illustrations, as *Anglo-Norman Antiquities, Considered in a Tour Through Part of Normandy*, in 1767.

There followed a hiatus lasting until after the cessation of Napoleonic hostilities in 1815. Then English artists and travelers rushed to the continent, among them the Norwich watercolorist and etcher John Sell Cotman, who went to Normandy three times, in the summers of 1817, 1818, and 1820.[19] His *Architectural Antiquities of Normandy*, a sumptuous collection of etchings, appeared in 1822 with "Historical and Descriptive Notices" by Dawson Turner, the Yarmouth banker and antiquarian who had helped to support Cotman's travels. In fact, the text contained extensive quotations from Turner's own *Account of a Tour in Normandy, Undertaken Chiefly for the Purpose of Investigating the Architectural Antiquities of the Duchy*, published in 1820.

That year was a momentous one for the study of Norman architecture, for in 1820 Arcisse de Caumont began his architectural *"explorations."* At this time, he was preparing geological maps, and he decided to combine the *"géographie des roches"* with *"géographie monumentale."*[20] The year 1820 also marked the publication of the first volume, *Normandie*, of Baron Taylor's *Voyages pittoresques et romantiques dans l'ancienne France*, an immense and magnificent endeavor in antiquarian topography that would accomplish for the dissemination of Gothic imagery in France what Britton's many books were accomplishing in England.

John Britton was in fact the next significant English scholar of Norman architecture. His autobiography describes how he began to travel at an early age, and the urge never left him. Like so many topographers from Tudor times onwards, his interests were engaged by the new as well as the old, and his books ranged all the way from volumes of picturesque views through guides to the new railway lines; he even wrote a "how-to" book on topographical research. But Britton's supreme interest was medieval architecture, and a protégé later wrote to him in terms that suggest his fusion of travel and architectural study: "I have a vivid . . . recollection," said artist W. H. Bartlett,

> of the awakening of the antiquarian spirit within me under your tuition; of drives and walks about the Wiltshire downs, and of the great gig-umbrella swaying to and fro, and the danger of all being capsized, of cromlechs, stone temples, old churches, and old gateways.[21]

Britton's energy bore fruit in a remarkable series of publications, including the *Beauties of England and Wales* (1801–1816), the *Architectural Antiquities of Great Britain* (1807–1826), and the *Cathedral Antiquities of England* (1814–1835). These richly illustrated volumes had a profound impact on the appreciation of Gothic architecture among professionals and public alike. Britton also collaborated with the architectural draftsman Augustus Charles Pugin on a more professional volume, the *Specimens of Gothic Architecture* (1820–1825)—the first collection of accurately measured orthographic plates of Gothic architecture—and an equally rigorous sequel, the *Antiquities of Normandy* (1825–1828).[22] For the latter, Britton planned a whirlwind trip with his draftsmen to study and measure the sites; but, falling ill, he sent Pugin off to Normandy with a team of draftsmen, including Pugin's thirteen-year-old son, Augustus Welby Northmore Pugin, who would later become the age's most passionate proponent of the Gothic.

A very different sort of enterprise, finally, was Henry Gally Knight's. Like Britton, Gally Knight was a great traveler: in 1810–11 he had done the Grand Tour through Spain, Sicily, Greece, Egypt, and Palestine; later, he would travel extensively again in the Mediterranean. But in 1831 Gally Knight's national pride was offended by the implausibly early dates proposed for certain monuments by the Norman Society of Antiquaries, and he "determined to cross the water for the sake of inspecting and examining the architectural miracles in question."[23] He engaged the architect Richard Hussey as his companion, and the pair left Brighton by steamer in May of 1831. Their itinerary, much more extensive than Ducarel's, included a detour through the Loire Valley and a meeting with the famous Norman antiquary Gerville. Knight then published their findings in *An Architectural Tour in Normandy; with Some Remarks on Norman Architecture* (1836).

PATTERNS AND MODELS FOR ARCHITECTURAL TRAVEL

Some significant patterns emerge from these facts. In both Greece and Normandy, an engagement with travel and topography tended to precede a dedication to architectural research. The conditions of architectural travel in Normandy and Greece differed in significant ways, however. In Normandy, scholars could make short expeditions in a relatively impromptu manner. Antiquarian travelers had been doing this since the sixteenth century, and the travels of Ducarel, Britton, Cotman, and Caumont were all shaped by this tradition—not only in their practical details but also in their focus on such traditional antiquarian staples as charters, deeds, seals, manorial rolls, monumental inscriptions, local chronicles, and lists of bishops, deans, and vicars. Travel in the eastern Mediterranean, by contrast, was not only far more dangerous, but also demanded far more time and money than most English architects or antiquarians could contribute. For Stuart and Revett, the planning stages alone (largely centered on finding funds) consumed two years, and they were away from western Europe for a further five. In the eastern Mediterranean, then, the antiquarian model of travel could not be applied. Instead, architects adapted two modes of travel: the Voyage of Exploration and the Grand Tour.

The voyage to Palmyra and Baalbek introduces us to the former. Financed by Dawkins's fortune, Wood and his companions spent an entire winter studying in Rome. Meanwhile, their own ship was being fitted out in London with "everything we could think might be useful" for the voyage, including a library of the Greek historians and poets, works on antiquities, and "the best voyage writers," as well as mathematical instruments and "presents for the Turkish Grandees, or others."[24] Except for the specifically classical part of the library, such preparations closely mimicked those of the great voyages of exploration—Captain Cook's, for example. When Wood and his companions were ready, the ship embarked from London, picked them up at Naples, and sailed for the Levant.

The Society of Dilettanti's Ionian expedition also resembled a voyage of exploration. It began with the Society's resolution to send a qualified party to Ionia, "to collect informations relative to the former state of those countries, and particularly to procure exact descriptions of the ruins of such monuments of antiquity as are yet to be seen in those parts."[25] The Society then "selected" its three explorers and proceeded to "fix their Salaries, and draw up their Instructions," so that "the different Objects of their respective Departments were distinctly pointed out": classical lore (Chandler), architecture (Revett), views and records of the sculpture (Pars). In this exercise of direction by the Society, achieved in part through financial control and in part through a written brief or "Instructions," the Ionian voyage closely resembled those directed by the Admiralty or by large trading organizations. The three travelers were also "strictly enjoined to keep a regular Journal, and hold a constant Correspondence with the Society,"[26] in a clause similar to one contained in the instructions for Captain Cook's third voyage, in 1776:

> You are, by all opportunities, to send to our Secretary, for our information, accounts of your proceedings, and copies of the surveys and drawings you shall have made; and upon your arrival in England, you are immediately to repair to this office, in order to lay before us a full account of your proceedings in the whole course of your voyage.[27]

For the sponsors of architectural as well as exploratory voyages, the critical issue was control, not merely over the expedition's conduct but also over its findings. The *Antiquities of Ionia*, published "with permission of the Society of Dilettanti," was not so much an architectural monograph (though it was this, too) as the official record of the Society's expedition.

Unlike the Admiralty model, the Grand Tour had a long tradition in the Mediterranean; devoted to the classics, antiquities, art, and architecture, it furnished the leading model for cultivated British travel in the region. It was essentially an upper-class experience, available only to those of wealth and leisure. Yet it was made possible by an infrastructure of support personnel, including not only hoteliers and coachmen but also tutors, guides, and paid companions. These could be highly trained professionals, and it was in this role that something like Grand Tour travel was typically available to architects. In this situation, the architect was the employee of a wealthy patron and, even if he had no cause to bewail his patron's impatience or lack of interest in architectural study (as the architect John Soane did in a letter to John Britton[28]), he did not control his own actions.

From this perspective, Stuart and Revett's proposal for an Athenian expedition, which enfranchised two lowly members of the support personnel to carry out their own expedition, violated the social norms of Grand Tour travel even while extending its geographical range. Perhaps this could only have been done by moving well outside the normal geographical limits of Grand Tour operations, either to Greece or, as Robert Adam did a few years later, across the Adriatic to Spalato. Adam's *Ruins of the Palace of the Emperor Diocletian, at Spalatro, in Dalmatia* (1764), at any rate, was published as an explicit gesture of professional accomplishment, serving symbolically to mark the enfranchisement of the professionally trained expert as an architectural traveler.

Because architects were coopting, rather than rejecting, upper-class travel habits, the Grand Tour shaped their views. One index of this was the role Mediterranean travel played in their lives. "Foreign travel completes the education of an English gentleman," said Gibbon[29]—a statement that accurately situated the Grand Tour as a sort of finishing school or initiation rite for young aristocrats. Grand Tourists were generally young: the Earl of Sandwich, a founder member of the Society of Dilettanti, was nineteen when he set out for the eastern Mediterranean in 1737. So were architectural travelers. Stuart was all of thirty-five when he began planning his expedition in 1748, but his better-born companion Revett was only twenty-eight. Wood was twenty-eight when he left on his first trip for the Levant in 1742; so was Dawkins when he accompanied Wood on his second in 1750. Even well into the nineteenth century, architectural travelers to Greece tended to be young men, frequently traveling in convivial groups: Willey Reveley was twenty-five when he left in 1785; Smirke, twenty-one (1801); Wilkins, twenty-three (1801); Cockerell, twenty-two (1810); Taylor and Cresy, thirty-seven and twenty-five respectively (1817); Barry, twenty-three (1817); Inwood, twenty-five (1819); Railton, twenty-four (1825). Though Cockerell was a dignified seventy-two when he finally published the rather cool and measured account of his trip to Ægina and Bassae,[30] the adolescent excitement of architectural forays into the Greek hinterlands—of campfires, bandits, revels, and manly camaraderie—comes through unmistakably in his diaries.[31]

In Wood's account of the Palmyra expedition, he notes the qualities he sought in his traveling companions, and they are consistent with the Grand Tour attitude to travel: "strict friendship for one another," love of art and antiquities, taste, leisure, wealth, "being well accustomed for several years to travelling," and physical stamina.[32] Knowledge of the terrain through previous travel experience was also valued. What no one looked for was professional expertise in architecture, for these were gentlemanly amateurs, and, as their traveling library reveals, their intellectual preparations for the voyage were much like those of other educated Mediterranean travelers. Gibbon's "plan of study" for his "transalpine expedition" to Rome, for example, included readings in the Latin historians, antiquarian works, studies of medals and coins, books on ancient and modern travel, and tables of roads and distances.[33] Whether to Rome or Palmyra, and regardless of any special interest in architecture, travelers brought with them a general understanding of classical civilization, emphasizing written sources and movable objects (sculpture, coins, medals), coupled with an overview of the topography based on the existing travel literature.

Not surprisingly, this intellectual and social preparation helped shape the activities of architectural travelers *en route*. Thus despite danger and discomfort the Palmyrenes traveled as elegant gentlemen and connoisseurs, reading the classics, transcribing inscriptions, and collecting voraciously. It was not that they lacked respect for architectural expertise, but this was for others to provide. Before their departure, Wood and his companions accordingly invited the Italian "architect and draughtsman" G. B. Borra to join them, and to prepare all the measured drawings. They found Borra "fit for our purpose"; in Wood's phrase, they "fixed him for the voyage." The words were telling. They suggest the social gulf that sundered the three gentlemen from the architect whom they "employed."[34] Though Borra's name appears at the bottom of every plan, elevation, and section in *The Ruins of Palmyra*, Gavin Hamilton's epic painting of Wood and Dawkins discovering those ruins does not even include him.

The tendency to separate general culture from professional expertise, and to relegate the latter to a technical and supporting role, was common to both the Admiralty and the Grand Tour models. The main difference was that in the former the directorate stayed home, whereas in the latter it came along. Either way, the division tended to fall along class lines. Even where these were not strongly drawn, hierarchies could still assert themselves. Stuart and Revett fit the pattern. The gregarious and unbusinesslike Stuart—responsible for the interpretative text and the picturesque views—played the role of aristocratic leader, claiming the honors of authorship and of election to the Royal Society of Arts and the Society of Antiquaries,[35] while the more retiring Revett—like Borra responsible for the technical work of the measured drawings—took second place. Nor was this pattern strictly limited to the Mediterranean. For Gally Knight (a seasoned Mediterranean traveler), the role of an architectural companion in Normandy was essentially technical—"a practiced eye to examine the construction of the buildings, and a practiced hand to delineate their outline"[36]—and, if his book is to be believed, Gally Knight reserved authority over travel planning and architectural interpretation absolutely to himself. John Britton and Baron Taylor applied this pattern to the pursuit of architectural topography on a large and public scale. Both men directed large numbers of traveling artists and scholars, masterfully organizing their inflowing material into a steady stream of books. Britton's rule seems to have been rather benign, but Taylor's letters to one of his artists, Adrien Dauzats, are detailed and peremptory. On one occasion, Taylor was furious to find that Dauzats had locked up his drawings and forgotten to leave the key:

> I have told you twenty times that all the drawings that you have made for me in Spain belong to me, you have answered that you understand it very well and that you were so much in agreement on this point that you had put in your will that all the drawings of the Orient, Sicily, France, and Spain that were at your home were my property.[37]

ATTESTATIONS OF AUTHORITY

Throughout this period, then, architectural research was carried out within the framework of intellectual and social assumptions developed in the traditional practices of travel. This meant that architectural scholars tended to define themselves as travelers and travel writers. They located their historiographical tradition in the travel literature, argued points of interpretation with earlier travel writers, framed their own research goals in terms of travel missions: they even adopted many of the forms of the traditional travel accounts, especially the attestations of authority with which they opened their accounts.

Attestations of authority are found in all scholarly literature. But they can reveal different ways of gathering and assessing information. Take that made by the great historian Edward Gibbon in the preface to his *History of the Decline and Fall of the Roman Empire*. Noting that "Diligence and accuracy are the only merits which an historical writer may ascribe to himself," Gibbon claims to have "carefully examined all the original materials that could illustrate the subject which I had undertaken to treat." He is evidently thinking in terms of textual sources and modes of analysis, and he promises to compile at some later date a "critical account of the authors consulted during the progress of the whole work."[38]

This is the claim of the historian. How different the opening of Robert Wood's *Ruins of Palmyra*: Wood, too, asserts that "the principal merit of works of this kind is truth"; he, too, promises to give "such an account of the manner in which it was undertaken, and executed, as will give the publick an opportunity of judging what credit it deserves."[39] But what follows is an account of Wood's travels. Wood's claim to "truth" is, in fact, a variant on the travel writer's habitual claim to have actually visited the places, and seen the sites described. It also plays upon the apologia for blunt, unvarnished prose with which the travel writer habitually distinguished his work from the imaginative compositions of more learned or polished writers. Wood's "truth" is not the historian's but the travel writer's.

The attestation of presence was another way in which architectural scholars emphasized their identity as travelers. Thus *The Antiquities of Athens* included not one but two pictures of Stuart and Revett drawing in front of the ruins (Figure 4.1). *I was there*, they say, staking a public claim to the reality of the authors' travel experiences and grounding their architectural authority in them.

Beyond attestations of presence, architectural travelers liked to dwell upon the hardships of getting there. Henry Gally Knight emphasized the "difficulties which beset his path" through Normandy;[40] and, although he identifies himself in this context as an antiquarian, the difficulties he instances are not the inaccessibility of documents but bad roads, carriages stuck in the mud, and so forth. John Britton also liked to recall the "rain, snow, cold, and other unpleasantries" of his journeys,[41] while Thomas Hope believed that the "fatigues, hardships, and even dangers" that he had "willingly encountered" in his travels lent a unique authority to his architectural opinions[42]—a bold and indeed tactless extrapolation of Lodoli's Vitruvian critique.

Even their safe arrival at the site did not stem the complaints of architectural travelers, who found that the difficulties of examining the ruins they had come to see not only lent their accounts a further authority but could even excuse their shortcomings. Soane told his Royal Academy audiences

Figure 4.1   James Stuart: View of the Erechtheion in Athens with Stuart sketching, from Stuart and Revett's *Antiquities of Athens*, vol. II (1789).

how he had groped about in the dark in order to measure the ruins of Pompeii,[43] while Ruskin wrote of the perils endured on scaffold and ledge to bring back drawings of the architectural sculpture of Venice. A related and popular category of complaint, one with direct parallels to the literature of exploration,[44] focused on the obstructions presented by unruly natives. This was particularly exploited by architectural travelers to the eastern Mediterranean.[45]

The recounting of hardship and ingenuity located architectural authors within the fraternity of travel initiates and thereby lent their accounts a very particular authority; but it also shaped those accounts, casting the representation of observable fact into the framework of the traveler's perceptions and validating it through intense experience. Such attestations are therefore profoundly subjective. One thinks of romantic stories like that of Turner lashing himself to the mast of a storm-tossed ship in order to paint the scene (or of Horace Vernet's painting of himself in the same self-inflicted travel predicament).

For the architectural traveler, the crucial moment of heightened experience was typically the first encounter with the ruins. This was a standard theme of Mediterranean travel. Gibbon experienced such "strong emotions" when he "first approached and entered the *eternal City*" that he could not sleep at night; "several days of intoxication were lost or enjoyed before I could descend to a cool and minute investigation."[46] Architectural travelers to Greece and the Levant (and even to Normandy) played upon this pattern of response, first pitching their expectations very high, and then finding them surpassed. Wood's account of his first glimpse of Palmyra can stand for many similar encounters:

> the hills opening discovered to us, all at once, the greatest quantity of ruins
> we had ever seen, all of white marble, and beyond them towards the
> Euphrates a flat waste, as far as the eye could reach, without any object which
> shewed either life or motion. It is scarce possible to imagine any thing more
> striking than this view . . . things rather exceed than fall short of our
> expectations.[47]

At this moment in his account, Wood refers the reader to a magnificent fold-out panorama for a "juster idea" of the ruins' grandeur. This is a significant move, for it is now that Wood shifts from travel narrative to architectural description. In thus pivoting the text upon his first encounter, Wood enframes the description (and illustration) of architecture in the exhilaration of the exhausted traveler. The reader catches his first glimpse of Palmyra, so to speak, from the back of Wood's camel, and it is in the playing out of this literary strategy that the importance of the expectation–response pattern is revealed. Without high expectations, the traveler's astonishment constitutes an incomplete claim for its object; but, at the same time, the traveler's high expectations constitute an equally flawed claim for their subject without the capacity to see them surpassed, to be swept away, overwhelmed by an as-yet-unencountered greatness.

THE TRAVELER'S VIEW OF ARCHITECTURE

Through attestations like these, architectural scholars established their credentials, which were those of travelers. But the texts themselves supply the strongest evidence that they saw themselves as travelers. Predecessors as diverse as Francis Bacon, Jacob Spon, and Samuel Johnson had advised the returning traveler to be prepared to answer a wide range of questions about the places he had visited, and architectural scholars took this responsibility seriously. The Normandy traveler Dr. Ducarel could not leave the architecture of Rouen without remarking on the city's situation on the Seine, its walls and ramparts, thirty-seven parishes, religious organizations, streets, houses, trade, population, water supply, quays, shipping, markets, and even the provisions available in them.[48] For Wood and Stuart, despite the latter's more intense professional interest in architecture, the situation was much the same: they reveled in ethnographic detail, lavishing attention on costume, folk customs, and (in Wood's case) ethnic entertainments such as singing, dancing, and mock fighting. Stuart even illustrated himself and his partner in Turkish garb, using these portrait-views to introduce their scholarly accounts of the ruins in the background. For Ducarel and Stuart as returned travelers, the great subject was not Norman or Greek architecture but Normandy and Greece themselves: specialist observation was enframed in travel reportage.

Travel descriptions like Ducarel's or Stuart's implicitly claim to represent places in their totality, but this is misleading. Typically, they follow a stereotyped list of categories—antiquities, medals, landscape, flora and fauna, historical traditions, agriculture, local administration, costume, religious practices—so that what they actually describe is not so much the place visited as the practice of visiting them. In fact, many of the observations on custom and costume that garnished the early architectural accounts were lifted straight from standard travel accounts.

Beyond this debt, architectural scholars adapted the fundamental narrative strategies of travel writing to the new task of architectural reportage. From the ancient itineraries of the Romans through the exploration narratives of Columbus and Cook to Goethe's *Italian Journey*, the literary form of the itinerary had given travel writers a dependable structure upon which to hang all sorts of observations, and architectural writers eagerly adopted it as such. It would be hard indeed to overstate the importance of the itinerary, and of travel narration in general, to the architectural books of this period. Wood's account of his "Journey through the Desart," garnished with Arab scouts, swarms of camels, "mock fights" staged "for our entertainment," and finally a forced march across the burning sands, is a worthy counterpart to the expeditionary narratives of the great explorers. And though few reached Wood's level, a great many books on Greek architecture, from Stuart in 1762 through Cockerell almost a century later, prefaced their architectural matter with such a voyage narrative. As a literary device, this made the ruins the endpoint of a journey: they were the traveler's goal.

When Wood began his sequel, published four years later, with a narrative of his "Journey from Palmyra to Balbec," the ruins at the former site became an incident along the traveler's route. And this was the narrative mode followed in Normandy. Blending architectural description and travel narrative, Ducarel cast his entire book into the form of a travel account, so that the reader, in following his argument, also follows his itinerary:

> From Rouen I continued my route to Gisors. . . . At a small distance from Gisors is ANDELY. . . . Quitting Andely, I crossed the Seine at PONT DE L'ARCHE. . . . In my way from thence, turning out of the Paris road, I passed by the church of ST. STEPHEN DE VAUVREY.[49]

Gally Knight, writing almost ninety years later, was even more attentive to the details of high roads versus "traverses," of travel by cart, or carriage, or foot, of the depth of ruts and the height of hedges, of views from hilltops along the way. G. E. Street's influential study *Some Account of Gothic Architecture in Spain* (1865) varied the pattern by combining several journeys "in the form of one continuous tour,"[50] garnishing them with more hints on local restaurants and hotels than either Ducarel or Knight had offered. Goethe and Ruskin could elevate this kind of chronicle into the realm of poetry, acutely observant as well as vibrantly introspective; but Street's prose is closer to the sort of writing that could be found throughout the travel literature of the period. No wonder his early-twentieth-century editor called his account "the traveller's inseparable fellow," regarding it as superior even to Murray's or Baedeker's handbook.[51]

Itinerary narration served a number of purposes. At a time when such information was still very hard, or even impossible, to obtain, it offered the surest way to explain where something was: hence, when the renowned Norman antiquarian Gerville sent Knight and Hussey on their way, he gave his English visitors as a parting gift a "route" with sites and directions to find them—perhaps the most precious gift of local knowledge he could confer.[52]

The habit of prefacing description and analysis with locational information, which endured in scholarly monographs well into the nineteenth century,[53] points to another basic fact about the itinerary: it forms not only the record of a voyage but also directions for replicating it. This is how such travel accounts were normally used, and we frequently find architects retracing earlier itineraries, whether of heroic figures from the distant past (as when Soane followed Horace across southern Italy)[54] or other travel writers (as when Stuart and Revett, not yet arrived in Athens, proposed to follow Spon and Wheler's route across the Acropolis). Travel writers typically hoped their books would supplant the itineraries of earlier authors, and so did architectural scholars from Ducarel onwards. As late as 1865, R. P. Pullan's scholarly essay on architecture in Asia Minor provided "detailed accounts" of the routes he and his colleagues had followed, "in the hope that the itineraries thus furnished may be useful to other travellers."[55]

Beyond any practical function of aid or enlightenment, the itinerary stood for a shared experience. The pursuit of travel formed a bond which the relation of an itinerary both memorialized and perpetuated. Going over the old ground allowed the traveler to bond with his predecessors; and so, even in an age of tremendous exploratory energy, the impulse to retrace well-traveled routes always counterbalanced the urge to discover new ones. Thus, too, sites worn bare by the footsteps of travelers, like the Acropolis or Chartres Cathedral, retained their extraordinary attraction for architects long after precise architectural information was readily available in print—as witness the travels of Street, Waterhouse, or Le Corbusier. And on a popular level, firms like Brogi could (and still can) sell tourist views of the same much-photographed sites, taken from the same much-photographed angles.

Perhaps the most remarkable demonstration of the authority of travel tradition is the "discovery" of Palmyra, so grandiloquently proclaimed in Gavin Hamilton's painting of 1785, *Dawkins and Wood Discovering Palmyra*. We have already seen how dramatically Wood's account sets up his first encounter with the ruins. Yet, far from claiming credit for their discovery, Wood actually attributes it to a group of English merchants from Aleppo who had reached the site in 1699. For his own expedition, he reserves only the "merit of a more inquisitive examination"[56] (which, incidentally, is more or less what Captain Cook said about his South Sea voyages). This is not false modesty; it is Wood's attempt to specify his own place in a still-unfolding travel tradition. That place is revealed more suggestively by Wood's great panorama. Though introduced to illustrate his first encounter with the ruins, it displays them not from the southwest—his own angle of approach—but from roughly north-northeast—that is, from the vantage point adopted in the Aleppo merchants' panorama, published some fifty years earlier.[57] Text and picture thus seek to balance Wood's own first impression with his place within travel tradition.

At times, the habit of wrapping architectural analysis in itinerary narration constrained architectural scholars. Ducarel, for example, who had gone to Normandy to settle a dispute over style and chronology, found that the itinerary form of argument made it difficult for him to present his conclusions. He therefore placed them *after* the tour: "As I am now leaving Normandy," he wrote, "I shall close my account with some GENERAL OBSERVATIONS."[58] Gally Knight resorted to the same formula: "Having concluded the history of my excursion, and stated the facts which I collected on my way, I must now be permitted to draw from these facts a few inferences."[59] George Edmund Street did the same.[60] Each attempted, through the fiction of the author's return from his travels, to open up a space outside the itinerary for stylistic or chronological argument. Yet these stratagems actually reinforce the power of the itinerary, for they leave such argumentation dependent upon it: they imply that authorial command over what Street calls "history" and "style" is attainable only through travel.

In any event, such chronological or stylistic afterthoughts do not really undercut the preponderant effect of the itinerary itself, which is to fix the monuments within a conceptual framework that is not chronological but rather spatial and narrative in a specifically touristic sense. Even the illustrations frequently reinforce this effect. In the *Ionian Antiquities*, for example, the tailpiece of the chapter on the temple at Priene shows a view of distant

Miletus; the next chapter, on the Temple of Apollo Didymaeus near Miletus, opens with a "View from the latter City toward the Sea," thereby encouraging the reader to conceive of the two temples as standing in a relationship not primarily stylistic, chronological, or even typological, but rather topographical, one to be apprehended by the traveler's feet and gaze. At the other end of Europe, Joseph Halfpenny's *Fragmenta Vetusta* (1807)[61] treats the medieval gates and towers of York in essentially the same way. So strong, indeed, was this tendency to imagine antiquities through the itinerant eye of the traveler that it was sometimes applied not merely to the spaces between the buildings but to the buildings themselves, especially in the north, where the buildings had interiors. Thus Gally Knight begins his description of Saint-Etienne at Caen with the traveler's initial encounter ("the eye is first caught by its spires"), then moves through the west portal into the interior ("but enter it, and you perceive that . . . the effect is noble and imposing"). Once within, he pauses to survey the structure, his eye traveling methodically upward where his feet cannot go. Again he pauses for a framed vista ("As you look up the nave, the half pillars . . . produce the effect of a long colonnade") before proceeding finally to the east end.[62] Street's description of Burgos Cathedral differs only in that he ends up on the roof where, he says, "it is quite worth while to ascend . . . if only to see what is, perhaps, the most charming view in the whole church."[63]

TRAVEL AND THE "HISTORY" OF ARCHITECTURE

From such accounts, the spatial and narrative relationships of the itinerary stand out quite clearly. Relationships of style, type, or chronology, on the other hand, have to be inferred. To the question of how architectural phenomena were related to one another (and to the questioner), then, these accounts suggested a primarily topographical answer, one quite different from the essentially chronological abstraction of architectural historians later in the nineteenth century. Not that the earlier authors lacked any concept of architectural "history"; theirs was simply a different history, a different project. They tended to construct a world of places, not of times, a world whose essential structures were topographical, not temporal. As travelers and topographers, in short, they imagined a "history" that would explain the world as they knew it.

The distinctive characteristics of this history were clear at the outset. The mid-eighteenth century saw the beginning of a search for archetypes, which led some thinkers to look to the very distant past—Marc-Antoine Laugier to the theoretical first hut, others to the Greek Doric temples of Paestum and elsewhere. The terms were being set for an energetic debate between those who held the traditional view that history was a process of ascent and those who argued that the earliest forms were the best. This debate was already in progress when Stuart and Revett were in Rome, and it is hard to avoid the inference that their advocacy of Greek architecture was motivated by the latter view of history. Yet in *The Antiquities of Athens*, Stuart was noncommittal on this question: "It is as useful," he wrote, "to attend the progress of an Art while it is improving; as to trace it back towards its first perfection, when it has declined. In one of these lights, therefore, the Performance which we now offer to the Public, will, it is hoped, be well received."[64]

Perhaps Stuart's lack of interest in the question reflects the caution of an author launching an expensive book; but in light of his announcement that the *Antiquities* would "illustrate the history of Architecture,"[65] we may assume that there was more to it than that. Stuart's engagement with "history" is curiously untouched by any sense of time or temporal change. Revealingly, the predicates he supplies for "Athens" are spatial rather than temporal; indeed he explains that he selected ancient Greece as a field of study not from among all historical epochs but from "all the Countries which were embellished by the Ancients."[66] The best orders and dispositions of columns were invented *there* (not then), the most celebrated buildings erected *there* (not then). Within Greece, the "City . . . most renowned" for architecture "was Athens. We therefore resolved to examine that Spot rather than any other."[67] If Stuart's sense of historical relationships is ambivalent, his awareness of geographical ones is quite precise, and we shall see that Robert Wood adopted a very similar attitude.

Stuart's conception of post-Roman history, by contrast, is firmly based on the notion of development. As Stuart explains it, the excellence of Rome was followed by a decline into barbarism, which led in turn to an artistic rebirth. This rebirth was indeed in progress as Stuart wrote, though it was as yet "reduced and restrained" "for want of a greater number of ancient Examples than have hitherto been published." It was this sense of historical actuality that gave Stuart a rationale for his own work: might he not assist the cause of regeneration by adding Greece to the existing stock of Roman examples? Yet even here Stuart's thinking is essentially the traveler's. For, as he remarks, "every such Example of beautiful form or proportion, wherever it may be found, is a valuable addition to the former Stock; and does, when published, become a material acquisition to the Art."[68] Stuart thus firmly situates the entire enterprise of discovery and publication within the arena of collecting, a central preoccupation of Mediterranean travel as he knew it. Each of Stuart's examples exists, then, in two dimensions: first in the spatial ("wherever it may be found"), and only later in the temporal ("when published"). That is because its existence, until published, is contained within the spatial experience of travel (of locating it, "wherever it may be found"). It is only later that it can be released into a temporal framework, which is not that of "history" but of Stuart's readers and fellow-travelers—the present.

Such images of wandering, choosing, and collecting—so foreign to later notions of coherent historical exposition—mark an alliance between travel account and pattern book that would endure well into the nineteenth century, finding characteristic expression in the rough typologies, constructed over even sketchier itineraries, of A. C. Pugin's *Examples of Gothic Architecture* (1831–1836) or in Britton's *Architectural Antiquities of Normandy*. In fact, Britton's conception of architectural history is very close to Stuart's. Britton, too, made gestures towards historical analysis, vowing in Normandy to "investigate history," seek the "origin of the pointed style," and show when and by whom stylistic change was effected.[69] Yet these gestures were counterbalanced by his desire to "characterize the architecture" of Normandy, to "point out what is really indigenous and what is exotic"[70]— that is, to characterize the place itself by distinguishing what properly pertains to it. In effect, Britton was using architectural analysis as a method of topographical description: that is, as a way of describing places. And it was wholly characteristic that he took pride not in assembling a wide range of chronological evidence (which one might have thought his "complete history" would require) but rather in collecting "examples from all the different parts of the province."[71]

Because of this fundamental orientation toward travel and topography, architectural history writing tended to be understood not as a developmental stream linking buildings across time but as an essentially descriptive process pertaining to specific places and their relationships. Questions of crucial import (like the origin of the pointed arch or of Gothic architecture) were framed not as "when" but as "where first"—which lent them a slightly different emphasis. That emphasis on *where* things happened first was indeed one reason why Normandy was such a magnet for architectural travelers: research there promised to reveal whether Norman was really the architecture of northern France or of England. Because this question involved much larger issues of national identity in the years around the Napoleonic Wars, a broadly significant description of England, France, and their relationship could be framed around the answer.

Quite apart from such obvious—and important—political issues, the pervasive attention to places helped shape the central scholarly issues of stylistic discrimination and ordering that were developing at this time, as in Thomas Rickman's very influential *Attempt to Discriminate the Styles of Architecture in England* (1817). Rickman opens with a synopsis of the classical orders, claiming that the nuances of "age and style" to be found in "English Architecture" could be distinguished "as easily as the distinctions of the Grecian and Roman orders."[72] He then proceeds to elucidate these distinctions, and it is here that the parallel with the classical orders becomes particularly significant. For though Rickman sets forth the English styles chronologically, following his new and hugely successful nomenclature (Norman, Early English, Decorated, and Perpendicular), he describes them synchronically, as if they were coexistent and comparable—element by element, like the classical orders. Vitruvius, it should be remembered, had similarly placed the origins of the Doric, Ionic, and Corinthian in chronological order, even while describing them synchronically and comparatively. Vitruvius had also set the origin of each order in a specific *place*, so that its forms became emblematic of that place, and this underlying topography of architectural origins became the real basis of Rickman's history. Locating the origins of the classical orders generally in the south of Europe, of Gothic in the north, Rickman could interpret the latter as a sort of North European meta-order, England's indigenous parallel to the classical system of the south.

For Rickman, the discrimination of "age and style" in Gothic architecture served therefore to express an underlying notion of topography—of the relationship of architecture to place, and of places to one another—and of nationality. So it is symptomatic that the largest part of Rickman's book is not the chronological review but a gazetteer—a list of sites arranged alphabetically, not according to style or date but to location.

The gazetteer was in fact a favorite form for presenting architectural information in the early nineteenth century, a counterpart to the itinerary used by authors as diverse as Joseph Gwilt (*Notitia Architectonica*, 1818), Arcisse de Caumont (the enormously influential *Statistique Monumentale*, begun in 1820), and the Ecclesiological Society (*Handbook of English Ecclesiology*, 1847). At first glance, its fractured spatial relationships seem antithetical to the spatial and narrative structure of the itinerary, but in fact the gazetteer was a powerful adjunct to the topographical outlook, since it made all architectural information accessible according to place, and referable to a map. More than that, the gazetteer furthered just the sort of ahistorical synchronicity favored by the topographical approach, displaying all monuments as if coexistent in the traveler's world, equally accessible, and equally deserving of his notice, without regard to age or style. The gazetteer implies that the very act of travel is a form of collecting: it is the ultimate traveler's pattern book, a pattern book of itineraries. The underlying image is of a cornucopia of historical wonders, all crowded into the traveler's present and awaiting his choice.

The traveler's viewpoint tended to flatten the contours of historical time into a single, uniformly accessible plane. Yet the fascination of the distant past furnished a central justification for topographical study. This is beautifully suggested by the frontispiece to the *Auvergne* volume of the *Voyages pittoresques et romantiques dans l'ancienne France* (Figure 4.2). Here a Romanesque portal composed of representative fragments invites the reader to enter the splendidly dramatic landscape of the Auvergne, making the act of turning the page a metaphor for travel or discovery but also for entry into the past. Britton also made this clear when, quoting the famous antiquarian Richard Gough, he defended the "Science of Topography" as a reflection upon men and manners "through all the changes and revolutions of time,"[73] as a mirror that "carries the mind back to remote ages," becoming "the most positive and incontrovertible data for historical deduction."[74] The very act of being in a place could call forth historical reflection. And writing about it could elicit historical recitation. Thus when Spon and Wheler, *en route* to Constantinople and Athens, had to wait in Venice for a ship, Wheler used the time to write the city's history.[75] The historian Edward Gibbon furnishes an even more significant example. In 1764, having cast about unsuccessfully for a great historical theme,[76] Gibbon went to Rome; there, one evening as he "sat musing in the Church of the Zoccolanti or Franciscan friars, while they were singing Vespers in the Temple of Jupiter on the ruins of the Capitol,"[77] the idea came to him to write the history of the decline and fall of Rome.

Figure 4.2   Baron Isidore-Justin Taylor: frontispiece to the *Auvergne* volume of the *Voyages pittoresques et romantiques dans l'ancienne France* (1829).

Significantly, Gibbon at first intended to chronicle only the "decay of the City"—that is, of the specific place that had so touched him—"rather than of the Empire."[78] His project, of course, expanded vastly beyond his initial aspirations. Yet, even in its final form, Gibbon's *History of the Decline and Fall of the Roman Empire* never lost touch with its travel origins. Its final word-picture is of a modern Rome thronged with tourists, as if the sweep of history had finally deposited its author in the present-day world of travelers, all seeking through travel to understand or at least to savor the "changes and revolutions of time." Last of all, in a brief postscript Gibbon recalled his epiphany of 1764 when, "among the ruins of the Capitol," he "first conceived the idea of a work which has amused and exercised near twenty years of my life."[79]

Gibbon's experience of the integrity of history and place is paralleled in many architectural accounts of the late eighteenth century. Standing at the Temple of Bacchus at Teos, Chandler invited the "classical reader" to "recollect" Livy's story of a Roman naval engagement whose "relation" was "too minutely connected with the View not to be inserted."[80] In an especially fervid exercise of "poetical geography," Wood and Dawkins paced the Scamandrian plain for two weeks, "Homer in our hands." There was a dimension of understanding that only a visit to the site could bring: as Wood put it, "the particular pleasure . . . which an imagination warmed upon the spot receives from those scenes of heroick actions, the traveller only can feel."[81]

For Wood, as for most writers on travel and history, the mechanism linking history and place was the late-eighteenth-century theory of the association of ideas. Place names in particular became meaningful through association with historical figures and deeds, and a great many popular historical stories were essentially etymological. Even the most trivial circumstances of climate, said Wood, could "become interesting from that connection with great men, and great actions, which history and poetry have given them."[82] But the essential point is that historicity, in the modern sense of the word, was less important to the traveling historian than poetic resonance. Travelers looked to place for a sense of narrative plenitude; and in the absence of history, a recollected story, particularly a pathetic one, would suffice. So the traveling narrator of Lawrence Sterne's *Sentimental Journey* collects the life-stories of characters met in passing and sets them down in his own travels. And so a great many travel writers included affecting stories or legends in their accounts, thereby inscribing them onto the places they described, until ultimately they merged into the lore of popular tourism.[83]

History, then, was a fund of stories called up through a process of recollection and association, set in motion by the traveler's experience of place, and enframed by it. Place called up history; history completed place. Robert Wood might assume that the contemplation of the "present remains" of Palmyra would excite the reader's curiosity as to how they got there,[84] and that curiosity might prompt historical research and recitation; but it was not even remotely likely to lead to the construction of a larger, transtopographical history of architecture—a history in the later, nineteenth-century sense. Historical story-telling was a form of topographical description, equivalent and complementary to architectural analysis. The Reverend John Milner, in his important *History Civil and Ecclesiastical & Survey of the Antiquities of Winchester* (1798–1801)—a work especially lauded by Britton—brings out the implications of this partnership. Explaining that his aim was at once "to draw up [Winchester's] genuine history, and to display its existing antiquities,"[85] Milner divides the work into two volumes, a "Historical Part" and a "Survey of the Antiquities." History and architecture are thus paired, yet with a distinction: the antiquities are "existing" and are thus "displayed" in a "Survey," a descriptive process that spreads them out synchronically before the reader. The implication is that, though old, they do not belong to the sequence of times that make up Winchester's "history" but rather to its present space. Like the marvels of Languedoc or the Auvergne, these antiquities are accessible to research not into time but into place: to travel. This is what Arcisse de Caumont meant by *géographie monumentale*.

DISPLAYING ARCHITECTURE: PICTURES BETWEEN
TRAVEL AND PRACTICE

The historical project imagined by Stuart or Britton was so different from that described by Riegl that calling their work history can cause misunderstanding. Though they themselves used the word, it is perhaps better to think of their work by analogy with another prominent field of research around 1800: natural history. Although increasingly evolutionary in its approach, natural history was still concerned less with time in the later sense than with describing and ordering the natural phenomena found on, under, or above the surface of the earth. Thus natural and architectural history both concerned themselves fundamentally with objects, whether artifacts of man or nature.

The analogy helps refocus our minds from travel practices and historical theories to the artifacts, illustrations, and theories that architectural scholars brought forth from them, especially their recommendations of certain buildings or styles as models for emulation. Both Britton and Baron Taylor propagandized effectively for the Gothic; Stuart's support for a notion of architectural rebirth has already been noted. The propagandists attributed qualities like purity, simplicity, beauty, grandeur, variety, imagination, warmth, or enthusiasm to their chosen exemplars. But they also had to present them in attractive and intelligible ways that could encourage emulation. It was in doing this that the early scholars of Greek architecture departed from travel traditions, for to encourage emulation they introduced a new type of illustration to the travel literature: the orthographic projection. Adopted directly from architectural practice, this rigorously measured and abstracted way of presenting plans, elevations, and sections allowed Stuart and his colleagues to give professional architects information beyond the haphazard mixture of panoramic profiles, cavalier perspectives, and rough plans and elevations typical of travel accounts. Looking at their plates, one can understand why Stuart rudely dismissed the illustrations of Spon and Wheler with the remark that they had had "very little practice in the Arts of Design":[86] here, at least, technical expertise could proclaim superiority over the amateur tradition.

Thanks to Stuart and Wood, or to their draftsmen, Revett and Borra, orthographic representation became *de rigueur* in studies of Grecian architecture. In northern Europe, by contrast, modes of illustration associated with antiquarian topography lasted much longer; and it was only with James Murphy's famous monograph on the late Gothic church at Batalha in Portugal (1795), and with John Carter's series of cathedral monographs, also begun in 1795,[87] that orthographic representations of high quality began to appear for the Gothic. Even much later, many serious books continued to offer a mixture of perspectives with the odd plan or roughly measured elevation, while some (like Gally Knight's or Street's) were very scantily illustrated; even of those that were long on orthographic illustrations, most (like the *Architectural Antiquities of Normandy*) fell far below the publications on Greece in system and completeness.

The inspiration for the new, orthographic approach was the famous *Edifices Antiques de Rome* of Antoine Desgodetz, published in 1682. With his elegant and meticulous engravings, Desgodetz had introduced new rigor to the study of Roman architecture. Yet the essence of his innovation lay not so much in the use of orthographic projections, widespread in the architectural literature since the sixteenth century, as in their integration into well-ordered and comprehensive sequences (twenty-three illustrations of the Pantheon, for instance, as against Palladio's ten), and in their relentless empiricism of measurement. Unlike earlier architects, Desgodetz was interested not in the Pantheon's average or ideal diameter but in the actual distance between each pair of columns. And so he measured, and recorded on his ground plan, no fewer than twelve diameters of the rotunda and every intercolumniation in both rotunda and porch.

Stuart and Revett understood the implications of this method perfectly. Although their coverage of the Parthenon contained only seven plates, exclusive of sculpture, these were carefully arranged in a sequence of plans, elevations, sections, and details. (Wood's coverage of the temple at Baalbek contained thirty-six orthographic plates, plus ten perspectives). More important, Stuart eschewed the use of a system of "modules," which he called one of the "most dangerous enemies to accuracy and fidelity,"[88] emphasizing instead the minute precision of his measurements. These he took in feet, inches, and hundredths, even where the condition of two-thousand-year-old masonry could hardly have supported such a level of accuracy. Like Desgodetz, he contrasted his measurements with the less-precise figures of rival scholars, in one instance cataloguing no less than thirty errors in LeRoy's measurements.

Wood and Stuart were explicit in their intention to extend Desgodetz's method to Greece and aware of the break it represented with the traditions of travel illustration. Yet a remark by Wood reveals that the break was only with the conventions of illustration, not with their underlying topographical logic. He "imagined that by attempting to follow the same method in those countries where architecture had its origin, or at least arrived at the highest degree of perfection it has ever attained, we might do service."[89] Thus Wood saw himself as extending Desgodetz's work in a geographical way, not to new ages but to new countries. And like the most scientifically minded explorers of the era—Captain Cook or Darwin, for example—he thought of himself as a traveler who wished to bring back accurate representations of what he had seen. At times, indeed, Stuart sounds like a traveling naturalist, as when he emphasizes the accuracy not merely of his measurements but of his instruments. And when Stuart and Revett take their "brass scale of three feet, divided by that eminent Artist Mr. John Bird, whose works are known all over Europe,"[90] and laboriously apply it to the Parthenon to test the hypothesis that it was called the Hecatompedon because it was one hundred feet long[91]—then they are behaving like traveling naturalists, too.

Getting accurate measurements was sometimes a matter of applying an accurate instrument, but often it required first unearthing what was to be measured: books on Greek architecture rarely fail to mention excavations carried out at considerable cost in time and money. Here again, architectural scholars followed travel tradition, for travelers had long used excavation as a means of treasure-hunting, and this practice hardly ceased; on the contrary, as Chapter 5 suggests, architects and scholars amassed substantial collections of fragments. But excavation had another, specifically topographical, purpose, which was to facilitate an accurate description of the site. Scholars anchored these descriptions in travel tradition by recounting anecdotes that emphasized their interactions with hostile, avaricious, or merely picturesque natives.[92] Like measurement, therefore, digging served at once to support the rigors of the new orthographic illustration and to heighten the reader's engagement with the travel narrative.

The power of Desgodetz's plates lay partly in the intellectual rigor of their sequential unfolding. But here, the influence of travel practices led his Grecian followers to diverge from his example. Desgodetz's dedication to orthographic projection had been absolute: no views or perspectives were allowed to impede the steady march of plans, elevations, sections, and details. Both Stuart and Wood, by contrast, introduced their orthographic presentations, and indeed their books, with broad panoramic perspectives. Stemming from the traditions of travel illustration, these views indicate the complexity of the fusion these authors achieved; more specifically, through their position in the book, they made each sequence of plates into a bridge from the practice of travel to that of architectural investigation, and ultimately to that of practice.

Wood's choice of the panorama format for his grand opening plate was particularly revealing. It was the equivalent of the "coasting profile," or fold-out panorama, found in innumerable voyage accounts; deploying it at the outset made sense quite apart from its visual impact, because it provided not only a synopsis of the site but a well-understood pictorial equivalent for that all-important moment of heightened travel experience, the "first glance," that is, for the experience of arrival. Chandler and Stuart adopted similar procedures to enframe their technical illustrations; as late as 1860, indeed, Cockerell could still preface his scholarly monograph on the temple at Ægina with a "General View," accompanied by an invocation to the arriving traveler ("As the traveller looks over the plain of Athens from the foot of Mount Brilessus, he sees spread before him the whole extent . . .").[93]

Such devices must have triggered touristic expectations among readers, and scholars were quite willing to satisfy them. Following his arrival at the site, the reader-traveler would presumably wish to orient himself: Wood helpfully follows his panorama with a site map. The architectural plates follow, arranged in roughly the order in which the visitor might encounter the sites as he walked or rode from the left edge of the panorama to the right, and then back toward the center. In this way, Wood carries the propulsive power of itinerary narration into the site itself. Along the route, he inserts occasional perspective views that aid the reader's spatial comprehension; for the most part, however, the sequence consists of Borra's careful orthographic plates. The authorial "eye" of Wood's *Palmyra* is that of a traveler, but also that of an architect.

In the north, where literary traditions of itinerary narration were extremely strong (and antiquarian traditions of illustration almost equally so), this tendency to conceptualize buildings through the imaginary eye of a moving spectator was even more pronounced. But it was typically attained, as we have seen, through textual description, accompanied perhaps by a smattering of views and small plans. When Murphy and Carter introduced orthographic representation into the north, they respected this tradition, adapting it to the illustrative model provided by Stuart and Wood. Thus, whereas Wood had ordered a sequence of plans and elevations along the line of route, Murphy and Carter used their texts to describe a touristic route *through* each orthographic plate, so that the movement of eyes and feet through the building was projected onto the sheet of paper. Once again, the orthographic plate had become the point of contact between touristic perception and the professional need for accurate information.

Beyond itinerary narration, the illustrative sequences of Stuart and Wood drew upon that other central theme of architectural travel writing, the integration of architecture with a touristic sense of place. Stuart's perspectives, indeed, make a fascinating study in the tourist ethnography of architecture. The very first plate, for example—the panoramic "arrival" at Athens—introduces one of the standard *topoi* of travel accounts: a description of the local notables, arranged in their characteristic finery and centered upon the Vaiwode of Athens, shown (at his own request) as an archer. The Acropolis appears in the background, behind the figures, a spatial organization that suggests what travelers knew all too well: that the antiquities could be reached only by going through the local administration.

Stuart's view of the so-called Doric Portico (Figure 4.3) extends these travel themes and introduces new ones. Again, the monument is treated as little more than an incident in a picturesque travel view of modern Athens: like most of the monuments Stuart depicts, it is literally embedded in the accretions and accidents of a provincial Turkish town. Yet this is far from a casual view; a minaret prompts a disquisition on Moslem religious instruction, a church on the Turkish suppression of Christian religion. Significantly, Stuart admits to having warped the scene's true perspective in order to display a curious fountain in the foreground. This was built, we are told, by the French consul, whose house Stuart also points out, together with the consul himself, "here introduced sitting between two Gentlemen, one a Turk, the other a Greek, for the Sake of exhibiting the different habits of this Country." A view of an ancient ruin thus provides a pretext for a discourse on local customs. The same view also supports other typical travel themes: the fountain calls forth a paean to the consul's benevolence, the house an expression of thanks for the "disinterested Hospitality with which this Gentleman receives all Strangers"—including Stuart himself. Finally, in a move typical of eighteenth-century travel writing, Stuart turns the phrases back upon their author, remarking that "to pass in Silence" over the consul's hospitality "would argue a Want of Sensibility" in himself.[94] While no one would call Stuart's a "sentimental journey," for a moment we hear the voice

Figure 4.3 James Stuart: View of the Doric Portico, from Stuart and Revett's *Antiquities of Athens*, vol. I (1762).

of Yorick—of Sterne's Yorick—charting the ups and downs of his own emotional condition as his sensibility is refined through travel.

Though all of these themes are conveyed by Stuart's descriptive text, it is really the picture that carries them, and this is true of all of his perspectives. Devotional practices recur with particular frequency, but so do other aspects of tourist ethnography, like local customs of hospitality (including a digression on the use of napkins and the prevalence of Albanian servants in Athens). One has the impression that Stuart constructed his perspectives not so much to display the ancient monuments as to provide a pictorial summary of travel themes. On this level, the perspectives tell a coherent story from chapter to chapter. But each also introduces an individual monument, thereby embedding it in an entrancing display of local customs, costumes, and characters. The implication is that antiquities must first be appreciated in what Stuart calls their "Present State" (that is, after all, how the traveler apprehends them); and Stuart actually shows us two exemplary travelers, himself and Revett, doing just that. It is only afterward that they begin to extract the pure forms of the monument from its surroundings. Each monument follows the same pattern (Figure 4.4). Following the obligatory perspective, plans and elevations excise it from its touristic context, repair it, strip it of accretions, and right it into orthogonal projection. Then it is sectioned, and finally, in a series of details similar to an architect's working drawings, broken down into measured subsections suitable for close study and replication.

Figure 4.4   Nicholas Revett's elevation of the Tower of the Winds and details of the Erechtheion typify the sequences of drawings with which Stuart and Revett's *Antiquities of Athens* made it possible for architects to accurately reproduce Greek architecture in England.

In the end, Stuart and Revett have arrived at the same point reached by Desgodetz. But since their starting point was so different, the progression charted by their illustrations is also quite different. For the seventeenth-century classicist, the Pantheon already existed in the abstract realm of architectural example; it had only to be carefully measured to be translated into that of practice. For the late-eighteenth-century classicist, the monument existed first in the space of travel; before it could be moved into that of practice it had first to be shifted into the realm of example. One is tempted to say that it is "restored" in the process, but this would be misleading: each perspective shows the monument in its "Present State," as the traveler sees it; but no succeeding plate attempts to imagine it as the ancient Athenians might have seen it. Instead, it is abstracted into technical drawings, where it becomes available to architectural practice.

Seen in sequence, then, the illustrations of Stuart and Revett offer an extended metaphor for a new relationship between architectural travel and practice that was developing in England, one that they themselves did much to promote. It would be logical to regard the buildings that some of the architectural travelers designed on the basis of their detail drawings as the culminating illustrations in their sequences, and not merely because the drawings themselves seem to encourage this further step. Cornelis de Bruyn, the great Levantine traveler, had written at the end of the seventeenth century that the traveler who wished to "bring back some fruit from his voyage" needed, above all else, to know how to draw "in order by this means to imprint things more deeply upon the spirit, and to allow one to place them before the eyes at any time, as if they were still there, which is the surest way to prevent one from losing the memory of them."[95] De Bruyn's drawings are extraordinarily vivid, as if deeply imprinted upon the traveler's memory. By contrast, one could not use Revett's orthographic illustrations to preserve memory, for they do not represent things as they look. Attempts were made to enliven such orthographic plates: in the *Ionian Antiquities*, for example, each detail was presented first in outline with measurements, and then again shaded to simulate its actual appearance. But these shaded drawings remain diagrams. Their inadequacy as vessels of travel memory called for some restitution of vividness. Buildings fulfilled this need. Better than any orthographic diagram they could contain the vitality of travel memory, the "souvenir," and restore it to the architectural form.

Buildings modeled on plates from travel books staked a double claim on behalf of their architects: first to expertise rooted in travel, and second to membership in the aristocratic fraternity of travelers. Lesley Lawrence pointed out that most of Stuart and Revett's architectural patrons were members of the Society of Dilettanti, while Pierre du Prey has suggested that Soane, upon his return from Italy, developed a special style intended to play upon the architectural experiences he shared with patrons met in foreign travels—a "consciously affected Grand Tourist manner."[96] For these architects, and for their patrons, travel motifs stood for travel fraternity. Even clearer was the case of the Society of Dilettanti's project of 1753 to build a new headquarters in London. This was to be based on the temple of Pola in Istria, which Stuart and Revett had measured, under the Society's aegis, *en route* to Athens. To the Dilettanti, then, the temple at Pola was not just an exemplar of classical taste but a site visited; its recreation in London would symbolize not merely the Dilettanti's artistic ideals but also the shared experience of travel that defined its membership.

Quite literally, the design for the Society's headquarters was a souvenir. Closely based on something brought back from the site (the measured drawings), it would serve to remind the members of their own travels. It also drew on the collecting instincts of these travelers, an instinct that was leading to the formation of vast collections based upon travel expeditions—collections of paintings, manuscripts, sculpture, and architectural fragments of which the Elgin marbles are only the most famous example. These collections were displayed in museums and published in books, but they were also incorporated into architectural designs. Thus Lord Stuart de Rothesay bedecked his Neo-Gothic Highcliffe Castle (W. J. Donthorne, 1830–1834) with a collection of fragments picked up in Normandy[97] (Figure 5.3); and when R. C. Naylor of Kelmarsh Hall returned home bearing a load of marbles "from various ancient buildings in Rome," his architect, J. K. Colling, had to work them into his design for the chancel of the neighboring church (1874).[98] In each case, the architect's task was to incorporate evidence of his patron's travels. Conceptually it was only a small step from this to the solution adopted by the Society of Dilettanti, and by traveling architects like Stuart, Soane, or Wilkins: to incorporate purely formal qualities—pure travel knowledge—into their designs.

There are other reasons why three-dimensional buildings became a persuasive form of travel illustration. Once travel became the basis of professional authority, a contest began for control of travel knowledge, pitting architects and architectural experts not only against travel promoters or "admiralties" but against other experts. Sometimes architects claimed authority by publishing a book. Adam's *Ruins of the Palace of the Emperor Diocletian, at Spalatro, in Dalmatia* (1764) was such a declaration of competence. But Stuart's first volume did not appear until about seven years after his return, his second over thirty, Inwood's eight, Cockerell's almost fifty—so that, in these cases, publication did not launch careers. Instead these architects demonstrated their command of travel knowledge by building three-dimensional illustrations of it. From 1758, three years after his return, Stuart was busy designing small garden pavilions, first at Hagley, then at Shugborough (Figure 4.5). These were based on the Theseion, the Tower of the Winds, and other monuments seen and measured at Athens. At the time Stuart was one of a very few men who had the knowledge to do so. Revett based his church at Ayot St. Lawrence (1778) on the Temple of Apollo at

Figure 4.5 James Stuart: Tower of the Winds, Shugborough, UK (1764).

Delos, later to be published in Volume III of the *Antiquities of Athens* (1794). Later examples of the same pattern include William Wilkins, returning in 1804, hurrying forth the Grecian designs for Downing College, Cambridge (based on the Propylaeum), and Grange Park (based on the Theseion) in the same year, and publishing in 1807; Inwood, returning in 1819, basing his church of St. Pancras on the Erechtheion (among other Athenian models) in that year, and publishing his scholarly monograph in 1827; Cockerell, returning in 1817, adapting the unusual Ionic order from the temple at Bassae—one of his signal discoveries—to the new Dining Room at Grange Park in 1823 and again at the Ashmolean Museum, Oxford, in 1840, but not publishing the full account of his discoveries until 1860. Each architect embodied his special travel knowledge in erudite buildings whose forms made reference to the places he had visited; later, he might publish his find-ings in a book.

And so the landscape of Britain came to be dotted with buildings that were, like the Dilettanti's unrealized temple, not only exemplars of eclectic taste but also illustrations or souvenirs of travel. Their private significance might be accessible only to the patron, the architect, and their friends. Yet when Cockerell designed a splendid Parthenon upon Edinburgh's summit, or when Britton called the city "Modern Athens" and imaged its old cliffs as a frowning Acropolis[99]—for that matter, when English builders set down Grecian buildings in Madras or Calcutta—any educated citizen could under-stand the allusions that were being made and upon which arguments of political and cultural persuasion could be founded. It was not necessary to have gone to Greece to hold a conception of its place in the world, and that conception was sufficient to play the game of architectural reference and association.

In a sense, much of Britain's eclectic architecture from this period can be understood as an abstraction of architectural topography, a diagram of the architectural world as seen by travelers. The very practice of eclecticism—of the simultaneous adoption of many borrowed styles—was a logical extrap-olation from the topographical view of "history," in which all architectural styles coexisted in a gazetteer of places to be visited. It could be objected (as nineteenth-century critics did object) that most of those styles looked very foreign when they were replicated in England. Yet to the topographical view of history this was no objection at all. One would hardly expect the gather-ings of travel to look indigenous in England: England was *home*, the place where traveling architects returned with their travel notebooks and souvenirs. It was also where architects displayed the forms and styles they brought back.

Perhaps the most perfect demonstration of travel eclecticism in practice is to be found in the remarkable "experimental group" of buildings designed by John Foulston in Devonport in 1823–1824 (Figure 4.6). This consisted of buildings "exhibiting the various features of the architectural world": a Greek Doric town hall and column, an Oriental chapel, an Egyptian library. Though Foulston wished to avoid the "abomination of having exhibited a

Figure 4.6   John Foulston: Town Hall, Commemorative Column, Mount Zion Chapel, and Civil and Military Library, Devonport (UK), from his *The Public Buildings Erected in the West of England* (1838).

combination of styles in the same building,"[100] he nevertheless aimed to combine them "in one view," thereby emphasizing the simultaneity and spatial contiguity of styles. His group forms an apt image of the architectural world as imagined by the traveler.

A few years later, George Wightwick picked up the theme. A former pupil of Soane and successor to Foulston's West Country practice, Wightwick published *The Palace of Architecture* in 1840, though he claimed to have developed its ideas before 1830. The book describes an imaginary museum of architecture, an "epitome of the Architectural World" laid out as a landscape garden. Like Foulston's "experimental group," Wightwick's open-air museum juxtaposes buildings in a wide range of styles. Yet Wightwick goes beyond Foulston, for his exemplars are arranged sequentially along a looping garden path so that the process of architectural learning mimics the experience of travel (Figure 4.7). The museum's entrance gateway, by contrast, seems at first to contradict Foulston's argument. Wightwick describes the gateway as:

> a Portal of strangely compounded architecture. .. exhibiting a kind of monstrous combination, in which discordant features sought to harmonize themselves within a general outline of forced uniformity. The dark rock of India, the granite of Egypt, the marble of Greece, and the freestone of Italy and middle Europe, were here commingled.[101]

In fact, much more than that is thrown together: round and pointed arches; pinnacles and domes; Greek, Roman, Indian, and Gothic styles. Wightwick

Figure 4.7   George Wightwick: Plan of the Palace of Architecture, a hypothetical outdoor museum of architectural replicas, casts, and fragments; and the Palace Gate, from *The Palace of Architecture* (1840).

appears, and in the most blatant way, to commit Foulston's "abomination" of exhibiting different styles in the same building. Yet Wightwick explains that the gateway is not an exemplar but an exception to normal practice, one justified by its rich geographical evocation of what lies within the museum. He also calls the gateway "a returned traveler," a "picked man of countries": it is "crammed with observation."[102] Thus it is not intended to present an image of the world but rather of the world-traveler's mind, which synthesizes what it has learned through travel into universal knowledge. Like Foulston's "experimental group," then, Wightwick's portal reveals very clearly how the spatial simultaneity of the traveler's world view could sanction and inform an eclectic practice.

POSTSCRIPT

Wightwick's architectural garden reveals something else, for, though the buildings were to be experienced through travel, their order was not that of geography but of chronology: Egyptian, Greek, Roman, Romanesque, Gothic, and so forth. The museum may therefore be said to presage the rise of a new chronological or developmental conception of architectural history and, with it, of an equally new and exclusivist ideal of historical revivalism at odds with Wightwick's topographical eclecticism. For Gothicists of the new generation, like A. W. N. Pugin, all buildings had to be Gothic, for they referred to the world at a specific time and defined a relationship between that time and the present. Moreover, once the world came to be seen not as a spatial continuum but as an organism continuously replacing itself, then nothing but confusion could ensue from simultaneously depicting many styles: each time demanded its own.

Why the new historical view arose so rapidly is not the subject of this chapter. But a few factors deserve notice. Just as geographical exploration had dominated the late eighteenth century, the nineteenth saw an explosion of interest in the exploration of time: suddenly, the researches of paleontologists, fossil-hunters, archaeologists, and geologists revealed staggering new expanses of time. One might say that the structure of the world projected by architecture changed in parallel with that projected by science. At the same time, the travel mentality contained the seeds of its own decline. Every piece of travel information, every fragment that was published or exhibited, made future acts of travel less necessary. Moreover, as information was brought back and published, it became increasingly available to other, non-topographical schemata. The churches of Athens and Rouen, so distant on the ground, could be adjacent in the library; the Theseion and the Arch of Hadrian, so close on the ground, might be widely separated in the library. And, as Chapter 5 explains, the same disengagement from topography was being forwarded by museums, as objects brought back from travel were detached from their original *loci* and thrown into new contiguities.

Despite the dramatic rise of time, the old topographical world view survived in important ways. Even the new engagement with time was in some sense founded upon it, for, whereas earlier topographers had been primarily concerned to map horizontal relationships across the earth's surface, the new explorers simply redirected their attention, breaking through the crust, boring downwards, and mapping the vertical relationships that articulated time. Similarly, the new historical view did not so much replace the older one as displace or overlay it. It displaced it into the realm of ethnography and anthropology, where research and observation continued to be framed in terms of travel and architecture (and other artifacts) to be interpreted against a background of local culture.[103] It also displaced it into archaeology where, again, research continued to be based on massive expeditions, published in the form of official expedition reports, and centered on the description of particular sites.

Within architectural theory and practice, the travel view was not replaced but rather layered by other conceptions. Thus the standard mid-nineteenth-century arguments for the revival of Gothic as the historical architecture of England (or France, or Germany) were all based on Rickman's notion of indigenous style; and the theory of structural determinism advanced by Pugin, Scott, Ruskin, Viollet-le-Duc, and others—that construction with large stones had produced post-and-lintel architecture (the Greek temple) in the south; construction with small stones, the pointed arch (the Gothic cathedral) in the north—was just as firmly based on eighteenth-century notions of cultural geography. Structural determinism was really geographical determinism. Ultimately, therefore, Greek-style buildings lost acceptance in England not so much because Greece was less esteemed as because a new and more literal-minded concept of architectural truth required buildings to refer to or exemplify their own locales exclusively. Greek-style buildings could no longer be accepted as allusions to far-away places; instead they were condemned as false images of England. One might say that an element of topographical wit had been lost.

In the sphere of popular imagery, the traveler's view was neither layered nor displaced but firmly centered. A flood of popular guidebooks appeared, Murray's handbooks beginning in 1836, Baedeker's in 1839.[104] The marvelous illustrated books of Samuel Prout, Thomas Shotter Boys, Baron Taylor, and many others, as well as the portfolios of innumerable traveling photographers, continued to locate architecture in travel. Souvenir photograph albums, stereographs, and postcards made the experience broadly accessible. The railways, themselves engines of an expanding popular tourism, promoted view books that relentlessly emphasized the linear and narrative arrangement of sights along routes of travel. They also began to produce guidebooks, as later did the automobile interests, which went on to create two of the very best and most durable of architectural guidebook series, Michelin's *Guides Verts* and the little red volumes of the Touring Club Italiano. Even as historical scholarship was asserting dominance in the scholarly community, then, travel and topographical description was flooding the popular marketplace.

Nowadays, in an architectural world that has rediscovered a sense of history after the period of modernist amnesia, the claims of history to control the structure of architectural knowledge still seem rather tenuous. Through an immense apparatus of guidebooks, picture books, souvenirs, snapshots, postcards, and even the travel sections of the Sunday newspapers, the touristic view continues to be impressed upon architecture, and I would venture to guess that, for the general public, the touristic referents of architectural styles are still stronger than the historical ones. This might even be true for many architects and architectural historians. Architects still regard travel as a primary mode of architectural research, feeling that they do not fully understand a building unless they have experienced it personally and *in situ*: that is, as travelers. They also love to travel. And so architects and architectural scholars continue to move across the face of the planet, sketching, photographing, consuming some image of local culture. They are constructing their own version of a broadly public touristic ritual. At the same time, they are reenacting one of the fundamental patterns of their profession, a pattern that, established over two hundred years ago, gave rise to the very possibility of architectural scholarship as we have known it ever since, made possible the practice of stylistic eclecticism, and fixed its essential repertory of meanings.

NOTES

1. The words are those of Andrea Memmo, cited in Joseph Rykwert, *On Adam's House in Paradise* (New York, 1972), 50.

2. The French Académie Royale d'Architecture began offering the annual Prix de Rome in 1720; the English Royal Academy (founded in 1763) offered traveling studentships from the 1770s, the Architectural Association (founded in 1847) from 1881, Columbia University's School of Architecture (founded in 1881) from 1889; and so forth. See, *inter alia*, École Nationale Supérieure des Beaux-Arts, *Paris—Rome—Athens: Travels in Greece by French Architects in the Nineteenth and Twentieth Centuries* (exhibition catalogue; Paris, 1982); Donald Drew Egbert, *The Beaux-Arts Tradition in French Architecture*, ed. David Van Zanten (Princeton, NJ, 1980); Sidney C. Hutchinson, *The History of the Royal Academy 1768–1968*

(London, 1968); Richard Oliver (ed.), *The Making of an Architect 1881–1981: Columbia University in the City of New York* (New York, 1981); John Summerson, *The Architectural Association 1847–1947* (London, 1947).

3. Eugène Emmanuel Viollet-le-Duc, *On Restoration*, trans. Charles Wethered (London, 1875), 13.

4. William Morris, cited in E. P. Thompson, *William Morris* (New York, 1976), 236.

5. Alois Riegl, "The Modern Cult of Monuments: Its Character and Its Origin," trans. Kurt W. Forster and Diane Ghirardo, *Oppositions* 25 (1982): 21.

6. John Britton, *An Essay on Topographical Literature* (n.pl., [1849]), xi.

7. See, *inter alia*, John Howard, *State of the Prisons in England and Wales* (1777); Arthur Young, *A Six Weeks' Tour through the Southern Counties of England and Wales* (1768); and William Cobbett, *Rural Rides* (1830).

8. See, for example, his *Statistique Monumentale du Calvados* (Paris and Caen, 1846–1857), 1,1,3.

9. Edward Augustus Freeman, *History of the Norman Conquest of England*, 6 vols. (Oxford, 1869–1879), V, 598.

10. Britton, *Essay*, [v].

11. T. W. Freeman, *A Hundred Years of Geography* (London, 1961), 18.

12. Jacob Spon and George Wheler, *Voyage d'Italie, de Dalmatia, de Grèce, et du Levant, fait aux années 1675 & 1676* (Amsterdam, 1679), 1, "Préface," unpaginated.

13. Recent studies of British architectural travel in Greece and the Levant (all with further bibliography) include J. Mordaunt Crook, *The Greek Revival* (London, 1972); David Watkin, *Athenian Stuart* (London, 1982); Claire Pace, "Gavin Hamilton's *Wood and Dawkins Discovering Palmyra*: The Dilettante as Hero," *Art History* 4 (1981): 171–290; and Dora Wiebenson, *Sources of Greek Revival Architecture* (London, 1969).

14. Lesley Lawrence, "Stuart and Revett: Their Literary and Architectural Careers," *Journal of the Warburg and Courtauld Institutes* 2 (1938–1939): 130.

15. For the Dilettanti, see (in addition to the sources cited in note 13 above) Lionel Henry Cust (comp.) and Sidney Colvin (ed.), *History of the Society of Dilettanti* (London and New York, 1898).

16. Revett sold his interest in the work to Stuart after the publication of the first volume; by the time the second volume appeared, Stuart was dead. Later volumes appeared in 1794, 1816, and 1830, with increasingly little connection with Stuart and Revett's work.

17. For Ducarel, see J. P. Malcolm, *Lives of the Topographers and Antiquaries Who Have Written Concerning the Antiquities of England* (London, 1815), unpaginated; and Thompson Cooper, in *Dictionary of National Biography* (London, 1888), xvi, 84f.

18. Andrew Coltee Ducarel, *Anglo-Norman Antiquities, Considered in a Tour Through Part of Normandy* (London, 1767), iii.

19. Recent publications on Cotman's Norman work are: Andrew Hemingway, "Cotman's 'Architectural Antiquities of Normandy': Some Amendments to Kitson's Account," *Walpole Society* 46 (1976–1978), 164–185; Andrew Hemingway, "'The English Piranesi': Cotman's Architectural Prints," *Walpole Society* 48 (1980–1982), 210–244; Miklos Rajnai, *John Sell Cotman: Drawings of Normandy in Norwich Castle Museum* (Norwich, 1975); and Miklos Rajnai (ed.), *John Sell Cotman 1782–1812* (London, 1982).

20. Caumont, *Statistique*, I, i.

21. J. Mordaunt Crook, "John Britton and the Genesis of the Gothic Revival," in John Summerson (ed.), *Concerning Architecture* (London, 1968), 109.

22. John Britton (ed.), *Historical and Descriptive Essays Accompanying a Series of Engraved Specimens of the Antiquities of Normandy* (London, 1833). Plates and text were first published separately, the former (as *The Architectural Antiquities of Normandy, the Subjects Measured and Drawn by Augustus Pugin, Architect . . . and Engraved by John and Henry Le Keux*) in 1827, the latter in 1828.

23. Henry Gally Knight, *An Architectural Tour in Normandy; with Some Remarks on Norman Architecture*, 2nd ed. (London, 1841), 2. Knight's later works include: *The Normans in Sicily: Being a Sequel to "An Architectural Tour in Normandy"* (London, 1838); *Saracenic and Norman Remains, to Illustrate the Normans in Sicily* (London, 1840); and *The Ecclesiastical Architecture of Italy*, 2 vols. (London, 1843).

24. Robert Wood, *The Ruins of Palmyra, Otherwise Tedmor, in the Desert* (London, 1753), "Publisher to Reader," unpaginated.

25. Richard Chandler, Nicholas Revett, and William Pars, *Ionian Antiquities* (London, 1769), 11.

26. Ibid.

27. Captain James Cook and Captain James King, *A Voyage to the Pacific Ocean; for Making Discoveries in the Northern Pacific* (New York, 1796), I, xvii–xviii.

28. Pierre de la Ruffinière du Prey, *John Soane: The Making of an Architect* (Chicago and London, 1982), 141.

29. Edward Gibbon, *Memoirs of My Life*, ed. with intro. by Betty Radice (Harmondsworth, 1984), 134.

30. C. R. Cockerell, *The Temples of Jupiter Panhellenius at Ægina, and of Apollo Epicurus at Bassae near Phigaleia in Arcadia* (London, 1860).

31. C. R. Cockerell, *Travels in Southern Europe and the Levant, 1810–1817: The Journal of C. R. Cockerell, R.A. Edited by his Son Samuel Pepys Cockerell* (London, 1903).

32. Wood, *Palmyra*, "Publisher to Reader," unpaginated.

33. Gibbon, *Memoirs*, 140.

34. Wood, *Palmyra*, "Publisher to Reader," unpaginated.

35. Lawrence, "Stuart and Revett," 128, 133–134.

36. Knight, *An Architectural Tour*, 2.

37. Anita Louise Spadafore, "Baron Taylor's *Voyages Pittoresques*" (Ph.D. Dissertation, Northwestern University, 1973), 231–232. Original: "Je vous ai dit vingt fois que tous les dessins que vous avez faits en Espagne pour moi *étaient à moi*, vous m'avez répondu que vous le compreniez si bien et que vous étiez tellement d'accord sur ce point, que vous aviez mis dans votre testament que tous les dessins d'Orient, de Sicilie, de France et l'Espagne qui étaient chez vous étaient ma propriété."

38. Edward Gibbon, *The Decline and Fall of the Roman Empire*, ed. H. H. Milman (New York, n.d.), I, 22.

39. Wood, *Palmyra*, "Publisher to Reader," unpaginated.

40. Knight, *An Architectural Tour*, "Advertisement," viii.

41. John Britton, "The Late Samuel Prout," *The Builder* 10 (1852): 339.

42. This argument is advanced in the course of his withering attack upon James Wyatt's design for Downing College. Thomas Hope, *Observations on the Plans and Elevations Designed by James Wyatt, Architect, for Downing College, Cambridge; in a Letter to Francis Annesley* (London, 1804), 8–9.

43. Du Prey, *John Soane*, 137.

44. See, for example, the wonderful story of Captain Cook's traveling artist, forced to give away his buttons one by one to be allowed to draw the inside of a Nootka house. Cook and King, *Voyage to the Pacific Ocean*, ii, 257.

45. Thus, for example, Stuart's anecdotes of menacing Turkish guards and wild dervishes, and similar stories told by Henry William Inwood in his *The Erechtheion at Athens: Fragments of Athenian Architecture* (London, 1831).

46. Gibbon, *Memoirs*, 141–142.

47. Wood, *Palmyra*, 35, 37. See also James Stuart and Nicholas Revett, *The Antiquities of Athens*, I (London, 1762), vii; and Ducarel, *Anglo-Norman Antiquities*, unpaginated.

48. Ducarel, *Anglo-Norman Antiquities*, 11.

49. Ibid., 40f.

50. George Edmund Street, *Some Account of Gothic Architecture in Spain*, ed. Georgiana Goddard King (New York, 1914), I, xix.

51. Ibid., I, xi.

52. Knight, *An Architectural Tour*, 87.

53. Thus, for example, the architect William Butterfield prefaced his account of a Gothic church with the statement that it was "about three miles from the Twyford Station on the Great Western Railway." William Butterfield, *Elevations, Sections, and Details, of Saint John Baptist Church, at Shottesbrooke, Berkshire* (Oxford, 1844), [1].

54. Du Prey, *John Soane*, 135. For an interesting discussion of the authority of travel routes and travel books, see Chapter 7, 129–147.

55. Charles Texier and R. Popplewell Pullan, *The Principal Ruins of Asia Minor, Illustrated and Described* (London, 1865), vi.

56. Wood, *Palmyra*, 14.

57. In the *Philosophical Transactions of the Royal Society* of 1705. It was again published, with revisions, in Cornelis de Bruyn's *Voyage au Levant* (Paris, 1714).

58. Ducarel, *Anglo-Norman Antiquities*, 93.

59. Knight, *An Architectural Tour*, 191.

60. Street, *Some Account*, II, 221.

61. *Fragmenta Vetusta, or the Remains of Ancient Buildings in York.*

62. Knight, *Architectural Tour*, 57.

63. Street, *Some Account*, 32.

64. Stuart and Revett, *Antiquities of Athens*, I, v.

65. Ibid., I, Dedication, unpaginated.

66. Ibid., I, ii.

67. Ibid.

68. Ibid.

69. Britton, *Antiquities of Normandy*, viii.

70. Ibid.

71. Ibid., [5].

72. Thomas Rickman, *Attempt to Discriminate the Styles of Architecture in England*, 4th ed. (London, 1835), 37.

73. Britton, *Essay on Topographical Literature*, xii.

74. Ibid., v.

75. George Wheler, *A Journey into Greece; in Company of Dr. Spon of Lyons* (London, 1682), 2.

76. Gibbon, *Memoirs*, 130–133.

77. Ibid., 143.

78. Ibid.

79. Gibbon, *Decline and Fall*, V, 565.

80. Chandler et al., *Ionian Antiquities*, 1ff.

81. Wood, *Palmyra*, "Publisher to Reader," unpaginated.

82. Ibid.

83. See, for example, [Comte de Choiseul-Gouffier], *Voyage Pittoresque de la Grèce* (Paris, 1782–1822), I, 102ff.; and Thomas Roscoe, *The Tourist in Italy, Illustrated from Drawings by J. D. Harding* (London, 1832), 259ff. And see the marvelously funny parody in Mark Twain's *Innocents Abroad* (Hartford, 1869), 210ff.

84. Wood, *Palmyra*, 1.

85. Rev. John Milner, *The History Civil and Ecclesiastical & Survey of the Antiquities of Winchester*, 2nd ed. (Winchester, 1809), I, 6.

86. Stuart and Revett, *Antiquities of Athens*, I, 50–51.

87. James Murphy, *Plans Elevations Sections and Views of the Church of Batalha, in the Province of Estremadura in Portugal* (London, 1795). Carter's series begins with *Some Account of St. Stephen's Chapel, Westminster* (London, 1795). Subsequent titles follow the same format and include Bath Abbey (1798), the cathedrals at Exeter (1797), Durham (1801), and Gloucester (1807), and St. Alban's Abbey (1813).

88. Stuart and Revett, *Antiquities of Athens*, I, vii.

89. Wood, *Palmyra*, "Publisher to Reader," unpaginated.

90. Stuart and Revett, *Antiquities of Athens*, ii, 9.

91. Ibid.

92. See, for example, Stuart and Revett, *Antiquities of Athens*, 1, vii, 17; and Inwood, *Erechtheion at Athens*, 4.

93. Cockerell, *The Temples of Jupiter Panhellenius*, vii.

94. Stuart and Revett, *Antiquities of Athens*, 1, 3.

95. De Bruyn, *Voyage au Levant*, [1]. Original text: "il n'y a rien de plus nécessaire ni de plus utile à un voyageur qui veut retirer quelque fruit de ses voyages, que de sçavoir dessiner, afin de s'imprimer par *ce* moien plus profondément les choses dans l'Esprit, & de se les pouvoir remettre devant les yeux en tout temps, comme si elles étoient encore présentes, ce qui est le plus sur moien d'empecher qu'on n'en perde le souvenir."

96. Lawrence, "Stuart and Revett," 134; Du Prey, *John Soane*, 109–128.

97. For Highcliffe Castle, see Christopher Hussey, "Highcliffe Castle, Hants," *Country Life* (1942): 805–809, 854–857; and J. H. Powell, "Highcliffe Castle, near Christchurch, Hampshire," *Transactions of the Ancient Monuments Society* 15 (1967–1968): 83–94.

98. The quotation is from a memorial tablet in the vestry of Kelmarsh Church.

99. John Britton, *Modern Athens Displayed in a Series of Views: Or Edinburgh in the Nineteenth Century* (London, 1831).

100. John Foulston, *The Public Buildings Erected in the West of England, as Designed by John Foulston* (London, 1838), 2, 56.

101. George Wightwick, *The Palace of Architecture; A Romance of Architecture and History* (London, 1840), 2.

102. Ibid., 6.

103. On the role of travel in anthropology, see Mary Louise Pratt, "Fieldwork in Common Places," in James Clifford and George E. Marcus (eds.), *Writing Culture: The Poetics and Politics of Ethnography* (Berkeley and Los Angeles, 1986), 27–50; and, for a perceptive critique of the "participant-observer," Paul Rabinow, *Reflections on Fieldwork in Morocco* (Berkeley and Los Angeles, 1977).

104. For the development of guidebooks, see John Vaughan, *The English Guide Book c. 1780–1870* (London, Newton Abbot, Vancouver, and North Pomfret, VT, 1974).

CHAPTER 5

Collecting Architecture, from Napoleon Through Ford

Originally written to accompany a new installation of architectural frag-
ments at the Art Institute of Chicago, this chapter was published in two
versions, the first in Assemblage *in 1989 and the second in the Art Institute's*
own exhibition catalogue in 1990. The version here incorporates material
from both while omitting some of the original illustrations.

Collecting paintings and sculpture is a time-honored pastime. It is also a relatively straightforward one: in principle, one simply chooses the objects of
desire, acquires them, and arranges them according to taste. Collecting architecture is both a more recent and a more puzzling phenomenon. Of course,
the noble lords of Europe, with their two, three, or even more country
houses, can be said to have collected architecture since a very early age; even
the landowner with a single estate might be called a collector if, as many did
in the eighteenth century, he embellished his garden with miniature temples,
pergolas, and grottos. But this is not exactly what we mean by architectural
collecting. If what we do mean is the conscious assemblage of works of
architecture as specimens of their age or style, and if we further stipulate that
considerations of domestic comfort or real estate value must be at most
secondary, then we must wait until the mid- to late eighteenth century—the
age of eclecticism and of a growing consciousness of history—for the first
collectors and collections of architecture.

What makes the collecting of architecture a puzzling pursuit is that
buildings are so much more difficult than paintings or statues to take home.
Though surprisingly easy to remove, they are very difficult to move. And
once moved, they are extraordinarily difficult to arrange and display. To be
sure, attempts have been made, but, on the whole, collectors of architecture
since the late eighteenth century have found it easier to channel their acquisitive urges in the direction of more readily collectable substitutes such as
drawings and prints, and this displacement of the collecting urge underlies
the entire history of architectural collecting.

Architects have always collected drawings as sources of professional
instruction and inspiration: Palladio's, for example, descended through at
least six generations of such collections before ending up in public institutions. But drawings also afforded amateurs a means of possessing things and

experiences that would otherwise elude their grasp. The Englishman John Tweddell, writing from Tenos in 1798 on his way to Athens, eloquently revealed this displacement of the collector's hunger to drawings:

> My collection of Levantine Dresses (I mean drawings of them) is already considerable, amounting to nearly two hundred—and will soon be greatly augmented—so that I hope one day to show the richest portfolio perhaps that was ever carried out of Greece, Asia, and Turkey. But Athens especially is my great object. I promise you that those who come after me shall have nothing to glean. Not only every temple, and every archway, but every stone, and every inscription, shall be copied with the most scrupulous fidelity.[1]

As well as providing a surrogate for uncollectable objects, the sheet of paper could constitute the space for an entire museum of surrogate buildings. The most famous examples of this are to be found in the plates of Durand's *Receuil et parallèle des edifices de tout genre, anciens et modernes*, published in 1800, in which typologically similar but geographically dispersed buildings are brought together onto a single sheet. But Werner Szambien has shown that such plates originated in the middle of the eighteenth century.[2] During the nineteenth century, a similar but more pictorial technique was used to suggest landscapes out of widely disparate buildings brought together for the purpose: famous examples exist by the English architects C. R. Cockerell, Sir John Soane, and A. W. N. Pugin.

Mid-eighteenth-century architects like Robert Adam and Sir John Soane also supplemented their drawing collections with plaster casts, whose three-dimensional immediacy recommended them to many architects as vehicles of inspiration. Thus the Greek Revivalist Thomas Harrison wrote to Lord Elgin on the eve of his embassy to Constantinople in 1799, asking him to bring back some Grecian casts to fire the imagination of architects schooled in engravings.[3]

The hunger for three-dimensional things could lead to more daring exploits. Years later, Lord Elgin claimed that "it was no part of my original plan to bring away any thing but my models"[4]—by which he meant casts. The statement is significant because in 1804 shiploads of marble fragments prized from the temples of the Acropolis—including the famed Elgin Marbles—had begun to make their way back to England. Indeed, as early as 1801, Elgin was writing to his agent in Athens requesting "examples in the actual object, of each thing, and architectural ornament—of each cornice, each frieze, each capital—of the decorated ceilings, of the fluted columns—specimens of the different architectural orders and of the variant forms of the orders,—of metopes and the like, as much as possible."[5]

Elgin's importation of architectural drawings, casts, and fragments was part of an ambitious attempt to improve the state of English art. But, from the middle of the eighteenth century, architectural fragments had played a quite different role for English collectors. Sir Horace Walpole had scoured the English countryside for bits of old furniture and decorative fragments with which to furnish Strawberry Hill, the villa which he had begun to gothicize in

1748. His friends did the same on a smaller scale, and a fashion soon developed for "antique" furniture and interiors cobbled together out of architectural fragments. Perhaps the most remarkable expression of this taste for fragments was Plas Newydd (Figure 5.1), the cottage just outside Llangollen in Wales, where Sarah Ponsonby and Eleanor Butler set up house together after running away from their aristocratic Irish families in 1778.[6] All the world came to visit the famous Ladies of Llangollen—the Duke of Wellington, the Darwins, Wordsworth, Sir Walter Scott—and it was customary for visitors to bring a small tribute, a bit of paneling or oak carving, a newel post, or perhaps a piece of stained glass. In due course, these architectural fragments were pieced together and stuck up all over the house, inside and out, until it had been transformed into a sort of lived-in museum of architecture, whose specimens blended together into an enveloping romantic decor, infused with the histories of travel and tribute, and of personal devotion, which had brought them there.

Somewhat different from casts and fragments are models. Like casts, these have played an important role in the pedagogy of architecture, especially in

Figure 5.1   The Ladies of Llangollen incorporated hundreds of architectural fragments into the design of their house, Plas Newydd, in Llangollen, Wales.

late-eighteenth-century France. But like fragments, models also had a particular significance for amateur collectors, frequently being found in cabinet
collections, those flexible, yet often highly systematic, assemblages of scientific
specimens, instruments, freaks of nature, and expensive and marvelous works
of art. The famous Parisian cabinet of Joseph Bonnier de la Mosson, assembled
during the 1730s, exhibited models of buildings and building machinery
amidst an extensive collection of scientific instruments and specimens, faience
globes, shells, and other naturalistic specimens.[7] A little later, that of Richard
Greene of Lichfield displayed an enormous clock in the form of a Gothic tower
(made about 1748 and one of the incunabula of the Gothic Revival) in the
midst of a collection of South Sea curiosities presented by Captain Cook and
a wide assortment of what James Boswell, after visiting it with Dr. Johnson,
called "truely, a wonderful collection, both of antiquities and natural curiosities, and ingenious works of art."[8]

If a model is inflated to full scale, it becomes a replica, which is quite a
different sort of object. The distinction between replicas and originals is indeed
ambiguous, especially when the reproduction is not exact. As explained in
Chapter 4, many late-eighteenth-century garden temples were close copies
after the measured drawings published by James "Athenian" Stuart and
Nicholas Revett and others of the Tower of the Winds, the Monument of
Lysicrates, and other famous Greek buildings (Figures 4.4 and 4.5): the
landscape gardens that contained them might therefore be called informal
museums of Greek architecture, and indeed we shall see that such gardens
furnished an important prototype for the architectural museums of the late
nineteenth and twentieth centuries. But the desire to possess treasured buildings did not stop with their replication in the form of garden temples.
Lord Elgin, in the midst of his fragment collecting, considered bribing a local
abbot to allow him to carry off the Monument of Lysicrates. He even tried to
remove the entire caryatid porch of the Erechtheion, but in the end he had to
content himself with a single caryatid. The founders of outdoor museums a
century later, collections like Skansen or Greenfield Village, were more successful: they carried off houses, barns, and shops by the dozen and re-erected them
in their museum precincts. Yet in reality, the gap between what they wanted
and what they got was just as great, for they wanted not individual houses or
shops but whole towns. They wanted village life, tradition, the whole of the
national past. Far from attaining the object of their desire, they had merely
displaced it once more, this time into the realm of the immaterial, where it
hovered safely out of reach: they could refer to it, could represent it, and could
collect its material manifestations, but *it* they never could have.

THE POETRY OF THE ARCHITECTURAL MUSEUM

Architectural museums have used two rhetorical mechanisms to represent
the unattainable objects of desire: synecdoche and metonymy, the representation of things by their parts and by their neighbors. Both had already been
heavily exploited in the traditional cabinet collection (and in this regard
the influence of the cabinet was particularly important), but the rise of

architectural museums in the early nineteenth century was predicated upon a broad cultural recognition of their power. The associational aesthetics of the period, according to which architectural forms were valued for their power to suggest pleasurable thoughts or experiences, were based in part upon metonymy: a chimneystack represented the hearth attached to it, the hearth in turn the family seated around it, so that, by a series of linkages, a drift of smoke could signify happy family life. As for the representation of things by their parts, synecdoche stood behind the claim made by admirers of the Elgin Marbles that all the beauty and perfection of the entire frieze could be apprehended within its smallest fragment.

Such claims constituted a powerful endorsement of fragments: in their presence, the early-nineteenth-century artist or scientist did not regret the lack of completeness, for the significance of the whole was somehow fully contained in the part. But there was a poetic dimension, too, for the literary conventions of romanticism used metonymy and synecdoche to pack fragments with rich and soul-satisfying meaning. Thus Mark Twain, confronting an ancient tear-jug in Pisa, heard it speak to him "in a language of its own":

> with a pathos more tender than any words might bring, its mute eloquence swept down the long roll of the centuries with its tale of a vacant chair, a familiar footstep missed from the threshold, a pleasant voice gone from the chorus, a vanished form! . . . No shrewdly-worded history could have brought the myths and shadows of that old dreamy age before us clothed with human flesh and warmed with human sympathies so vividly as did this poor little unsentient vessel of pottery.[9]

Sir Walter Scott would have understood. Indeed, the impressive antiquarian collection that he assembled at Abbotsford, his Scottish country mansion, included such humble relics as an oatcake found on the body of a dead Highlander at Culloden, or a soldier's diary picked up on the field of Waterloo. Inside his desk was a yet more pathetic collection of objects, whose full impact was reserved for Scott's executors, searching for his testament on the evening after his death:

> On lifting up his desk, we found arranged in careful order a series of little objects which had obviously been placed there that his eye might rest on them every morning before he began his tasks. These were the old-fashioned boxes that had garnished his mother's toilette, when he, a sickly child, slept in her dressing-room—the silver taper-stand which the young advocate had bought for her with his first five-guinea fee—a row of small packets inscribed with her hand, and containing the hair of those of her offspring that had died before her—his father's snuff-box and etui case, and more things of the like sort, recalling "The old familiar faces."[10]

Scott's mementos of his youth and family became, on his death, mementos of the great author himself, and it is hardly surprising that a whole new category of previously innocuous furnishings, such as pipes, spectacles, and paper cutters, simultaneously made the transition to relic status.

What allowed these quite ordinary objects to achieve poetic resonance was not only their associations but also their fragmentary and incomplete quality. An environment dominated by large numbers of such fragments was in effect a breeding ground for anecdotes, reveries, and morals, which were generated almost spontaneously as adjacent fragments coupled in new and unpredictable ways. It was the same with the bits and pieces in the architectural museum. To be sure, odd juxtapositions were unintended, yet it was just this capacity of fragments to complete one another in unexpected ways that underlies their peculiar poetry and, as all the early collectors of architecture understood (Sir John Soane, in particular), that of the architectural museum.

It is important to specify the *early* collectors of architecture, for efforts were soon made to stem the illicit minglings of casts and fragments. The architectural museums of the late nineteenth century were far larger and more institutional than the earlier ones, and this tended to work against spontaneity, idiosyncrasy, and self-expression. Yet the poetry of the fragment could never be entirely purged from the architectural museum. For Scott and his descendants, the humble contents of a desk were treasured because they preserved the memory of things lost and regretted. Scott himself collected architecture in the same spirit he collected other fragments, and so, up to a point, did the most important of early architectural collectors, Alexandre Lenoir and Sir John Soane. Much later in the century, the development of the period room and outdoor museum would follow the same pattern, for the intimate odds and ends which composed them—chairs, beds, cooking pots, knitting needles, kerosene lamps, old newspapers—were infused with the lives of their original possessors, and often of their collectors. They spoke Scott's language of metonymy and synecdoche, and that is what made them worthy of preservation. This is an important point, for architectural preservation has been a recurrent and frequently misunderstood theme in the collecting of architecture. Lord Elgin thought he was saving the Parthenon from the Turks, Lenoir the Sainte-Chapelle from his own countrymen; the later history of the architectural museum provides plenty of dramatic rescues, and just as many protestations of preservationist intent. Yet the architectural museum's preservation initiatives have been accompanied by inevitable and often deliberate destruction. While architectural collectors have been motivated by a deep-seated sense of loss, that sense of loss has generally been focused not on architecture but on the objects of desire represented by it: youth, family, tradition. In short, while gestures of salvage and protection have frequently contributed to the architectural museum's poetry, historic preservation has never been its chief goal.

If the objects in the architectural museum have sung the gentle elegy of the tear-jug, they have also sung sprightlier airs. Sometimes they have been not mementos but souvenirs—essentially the same word but with a very different connotation. Souvenirs are what one brings back from a foreign place to remember it by. Sometimes architectural museums have commemorated travel, as in the fragments embedded in the walls at Plas Newydd; at other times they have simulated it, as in the national pavilions of the late-nineteenth-century world's fairs. Very frequently, too, they have encouraged it, as architectural museums have become tourist sites in their own right, with their own paraphernalia of guidebooks and souvenirs; and then, finally, the expansion of travel has spurred the growth of architectural museums, as the Director of the American Association of Museums realized in 1933, when, observing that "it is plainly not just a coincidence that motor cars and historic house museums have multiplied during the same decades and by closely similar stages of progression," he advised the directors of historic houses to exploit the potential of motorized tourism.[11]

The forms of travel are of course many. Chapter 4 showed how architects and historians in the late eighteenth century adapted the models of the voyage of exploration and the grand tour. In the context of architectural collecting, a third model became important: the military expedition, in which collecting becomes pillage, souvenirs booty, and the museum a trophy. The trophy was indeed a popular form of architectural ornamentation during the late eighteenth century, incorporated into sculpture and plasterwork by designers like Piranesi, Jacques Dumont, and Robert Adam. Originally an elaborate mound of spolia dragged home from a victorious expedition and displayed for the edification of victors and vanquished alike, the trophy strikingly exemplified the rhetorical power of fragments: its shields, spears, and other precious objects represented the conquered civilization, while their rearrangement made evident the conqueror's superior might. No wonder that the trophy formed one of the most powerful models for the architectural museum.

As John Tweddell contemplated the prospect of Athens, he clearly thought of himself, at least metaphorically, as gathering spoils, and the image of himself triumphantly bringing them home was already adding to their emotional appeal. Robert Adam had surveyed the ruins of Rome in a similarly acquisitive spirit when he arrived there as a student in 1755, proposing not only to have "models made of all the antique ornaments, of friezes, cornices, vases, etc., etc., in plaster," but also to hire "painters, drawers, etc., to do the fountains, the buildings, the statues," and, finally, to buy up "all the books of architecture, of altars, chapels, churches, views of Piranesi and of all gates, windows, doors and ornaments that can be of service to us. In short," he concluded, "I intend to send home a collection of drawings . . . which never was seen or heard of either in England or Scotland."[12] Finally, there is James Stuart himself, writing from Athens in 1761:

> A Load of Treasure is at Athens. I offer my shoulders to the Shafts, as if I were a Cart-Horse: & regardless of fatigue & danger, resolve to dragg it, where alass tis greatly wanted; even to this fair flourishing Isle. Oh—toilsome task—Ah, tedious way! how slow I move—what obstacles I meet!—from Athens to London, no road has yet been made for such conveyance.[13]

For eighteenth-century enthusiasts of the antique, the spoils were informational: drawings, memoranda, and plaster casts. Soon, travelers like Lord Elgin would begin to send home material spolia of the greatest value and in sufficient quantity to convince anyone of their countries' prowess. What prompted this shift from metaphorical to real spoliation and gave birth to the architectural museum was nothing other than the intervention of real warfare and political turmoil.

THE FIRST MUSEUMS

When the Revolutionary government of France confiscated clerical and aristocratic goods, a great part of France's artistic heritage lay exposed to the gravest dangers of depredation and destruction. One solution was to establish a depot for works of artistic merit on the site of the old Convent of the Petits Augustins in Paris and to appoint a young man named Alexandre Lenoir to administer it. Lenoir's mandate was quite restricted, but his ambitions soon led him beyond it, and he proposed to form a "special museum, historical and chronological, where one could rediscover the ages of French sculpture."[14] The Musée des Monuments Français opened to the public in 1795 and scored a tremendous popular success.

The main portion of Lenoir's museum was a sequence of galleries, each exemplifying a century from the thirteenth to the seventeenth (Figure 5.2). These rooms contained not only sculpture but also architectural fragments and decorative objects, and each room was decked out with glowing wall paintings and other contemporary accessories, so as to evoke an enchantingly authentic mood. Outside the museum, these rooms were supplemented by some very large architectural fragments, most notably the frontispiece of the château of Anet and the triumphal arch from that of Gaillon, and by a

Figure 5.2   The thirteenth century gallery of Alexandre Lenoir's Musée des Monuments Français.

picturesque garden, called the Jardin Elysée, in which the remains of great Frenchmen were inspiringly entombed.

Lenoir's museological success was based not simply on growing interest in the Middle Ages, nor even on patriotic fervor, but on his insight that centuries could be represented within the space of a museum, with each room having "the character, the exact physiognomy of the century which it represents."[15] This equation of time and space, however rudimentary, would prove enormously significant for the collecting of architecture, for it provided a straightforward equation between the most insignificant material fragments and the grandest conceptual schemes. By relying upon it, in conjunction with the rhetorical power of fragments, Lenoir was able to present his comprehensive historical panorama through a collage of fragments picked up as opportunity allowed.

Lenoir actually helped his specimens to combine into new and unprecedented configurations. For the centerpiece of his fourteenth-century room, for example, he placed an impressive tabernacle composed of statues of Charles V and Jeanne de Bourbon on top of a cenotaph made up of the "debris" of some ecclesiastical woodwork and ornamented with bas-reliefs from the Sainte-Chapelle; this he crowned with a canopy composed of fragments of "various monuments" of this period.[16] Objects like these were not genuine antiquities, however genuine their components, but rather impressive and exotic piles of spolia assembled by Lenoir.

To understand the significance of Lenoir's trophies, we must see them against the background of the international situation around 1800, and in particular of the vast movement of art works from all over Europe into Paris, and particularly the Louvre. Not that the traffic in art had only one destination: Lord Elgin's Parthenon marbles began to arrive in London in 1804. But the essential point is not where this or that object went, but the atmosphere in which they were collected. Elgin's position as British ambassador, charged specifically with countering French power, was in complete harmony with the conduct of his antiquarian collecting. At one point, attempting to obtain a warship for the purpose of removing the entire caryatid porch of the Erechtheion, he wrote to Lord Keith that "Bonaparte has not got such a thing from all his thefts in Italy."[17] The secret maneuvering that took place between Elgin's archaeological agents and those of his French counterpart were notorious and frequently ludicrous, but they could have been exactly matched in Egypt. After the French defeat, indeed, Elgin's personal secretary advised the English general of the importance of securing the Rosetta Stone, discovered by Napoleon's engineers in 1799 and kept under close guard in the French general's own house: in the event, a detachment of gunners was sent to take it away.[18]

Lenoir's trophies, however, also had a more personal significance. A proud and ambitious man, Lenoir identified with his museum to an extraordinary degree. His descriptions of the collection, in which he narrates his hairbreadth rescues of threatened treasures, leave no doubt about this. One story is particularly revealing. It appears that the "asiatic character" which

Lenoir sought to give to the room he called "my thirteenth century" (Figure 5.2) was

> so well grasped that First Consul Bonaparte, visiting the museum, said in entering this room: "Lenoir, you transport me to Syria. I am satisfied with your work. Continue your useful researches, and I will always look with pleasure at the results."[19]

A small personal triumph, no doubt, yet by including the incident in his catalogue of the collection, Lenoir inscribed it upon his objects, thereby entwining his own history with that of France.

In the end, Lenoir's phenomenal success deserted him. With the reestablishment of the church, the museum was ordered to return its art works to their former owners. The idea of moving art works from their original locations came under criticism, and in 1816 the museum was closed, its buildings turned over to the École des Beaux-Arts, and its collections made available to their former owners.

By this time, Napoleon's triumphs had also turned to bitterest defeat, and the trophies had begun to flow out again: it was now the turn of Englishmen to exult. That the Duke of Wellington should display Antonio Canova's nude statue of Napoleon in his stairhall was, under the circumstances, perfectly proper. But other collectors also used objects to stake out a personal relationship with the greatest events of the age. Sir Walter Scott was one: among the many objects that crowded his beloved Abbotsford were Napoleon's pen case and blotting book, pistols taken from Napoleon's carriage after the battle of Waterloo, a captured French flag, and a miscellaneous collection of armor and other memorabilia picked up from the battlefield by Scott.[20] Then there was Charles Stuart, Lord Stuart de Rothesay, ambassador to Portugal and an invaluable ally to Wellington during the Peninsular campaign. After the wars, Stuart became ambassador to the restored Bourbons and amassed an impressive collection of Napoleonic furnishings and memorabilia. Recalled at long last to England, he acquired his last trophy, the Manoir des Andelys, which was being demolished as he passed by on his way home. He had it shipped to England, where the best morsels—especially a beautiful Flamboyant Gothic oriel window—were incorporated into his new mansion, Highcliffe Castle (Figure 5.3).[21]

One who had no particular Napoleonic relationship to declare was Sir John Soane, the greatest English architect of the age. But Soane held strongly by the diplomatic value of antiquities and was fiercely alive to Britain's cultural prestige. He once concluded a lecture at the Royal Academy with this doggerel, celebrating the influx of cultural treasures into Britain:

The time not distant far shall come,
When England's tasteful youth no more
Shall wander to Italia's classic shore.—
No more to foreign climes shall roam
In search of models, better seen at home.

Figure 5.3   Highcliffe Castle (UK), boasting architectural trophies from the Napoleonic wars.

Soane's acquaintance, the antiquarian John Britton, quoted this verse and even expanded upon it in his published—and authorized—description of Soane's museum. The implication was that the entire museum was a sort of prospective trophy of emerging cultural triumph.[22]

Like Lenoir's trophies, Soane's also had a personal dimension. Yet whereas Lenoir's claims to greatness had been largely political, Soane's were essentially artistic: at Pitzhanger Manor, his country house, he embedded fragments in a facade modeled after a triumphal arch; later, at his town house in Lincoln's Inn Fields, Soane lofted his drafting room onto a balcony overlooking a panorama of casts and fragments, as if to root his own work in the debris of history.

Soane also had trophies of a more enigmatic and personal kind, but, as his museum was unquestionably the most complex and significant in England, it deserves a more detailed account (Figure 5.4).[23] Soane, like Adam, had first collected casts as a student in Rome, but he started to think

Figure 5.4   The rotunda at the core of Sir John Soane's house in London: the architect surveys
his collection of casts and fragments.

in terms of a museum when he bought Pitzhanger Manor in 1800. At this
point, the pedagogical impulse to collect was probably uppermost in Soane's
mind, for the collection was intended to form a sort of private architectural
academy for his son John.

Ultimately, the son disappointed the father, but Soane's pedagogical
ideals, far from being crushed, blossomed in the more public light of
London. There, in 1809, Soane was appointed professor of architecture at
the Royal Academy. Already, in the previous year, he had begun to expand
his house in Lincoln's Inn Fields to accommodate his ever-growing collection, which the *European Magazine* referred to as "the *Academy* for the
Study of *Architecture*."[24]

Soane's museum thus originated within the tradition of professional
collecting and teaching. Yet it was far more than an architectural academy.
For one thing, it was an extraordinarily diverse collection, containing not
only architectural books, drawings, casts, models, and fragments, but also
bronzes, gems and medals, Roman cinerary urns, Greek vases, Mexican pots,

Chinese ceramics, Indian miniatures, medieval manuscripts, and modern paintings and sculptures. There were also specimens of natural history, and even a few curiosities of the "Wunderkammer" type, like "the Mummies of two Cats, one found . . . with the Rat in its mouth."[25] Soane's museum, in short, drew heavily upon the tradition of the cabinet collection, as well as on that of the antiquarian interior. Unlike Lenoir, Soane lived in his museum, and whereas Lenoir had tended to complete his fragments artificially, forcing them into "tombs" or "shrines," Soane treated his more as decor, hanging them on pegs, bracketing them out from walls and parapets, setting them on shelves, cornices, and windowsills, until the walls, and even the very ceilings, were encrusted with them. At the center of this seeming chaos, he erected a very type of the whole museum, and indeed of all the early architectural museums, "a kind of trophy composed of a capital of an Hindoo column and of other architectural fragments."[26]

In thus uniting the principle of the trophy with the procedures of antiquarian decoration, Soane raised disorder to an unprecedentedly high level of aesthetic organization. And out of this organized chaos, a new ambiguity emerged. Viewed casually, his fragments tended to dissolve into an overall texture. Yet seen under the right conditions, they seemed to stir with a queer, incipient life, that quiet and dangerous life of fragments that was to be so poetically explored in paintings of casts and masks by Menzel, Corinth, and Ensor, but of which Soane appears to have been the discoverer. The many watercolors made by Soane's pupils Joseph Michael Gandy, George Bailey, and C. J. Richardson show his eccentric spaces mysteriously illuminated, their flickering shadows inhabited by tribes of disembodied fragments. The effect is always eerie and disquieting, and, though these watercolors seem to the modern eye exaggerated and implausible, Soane certainly wanted his museum to be perceived in this way: the early-nineteenth-century architect could call upon imagination to supply what his own hand could not.

If Lenoir's museum excelled Soane's in its dedication to public, political, and historical purposes, Soane's excelled Lenoir's in its exploration of the decorative and expressive possibilities of fragments. This was particularly true on the autobiographical level. As we have seen, both men used their collections to construct a certain kind of self-portrait. But in its eerie romanticism, Soane's was far more subtle and more intimate than Lenoir's. It was even, in places, ironic. John Britton's description avers that "the house of an Architect" is a better index to his character than either "phrenological bumps, or craniological organs."[27] Soane's character had a streak of introversion, of melancholy and frustration, even paranoia, which tinged his enjoyment of professional success with ambivalence.

In Soane's Picture Cabinet, for example, a pair of large folding panels hung with pictures hides a second pair, which in turn hides a third; folding back the last pair reveals a statue of Venus shyly clasping her robe in the golden glow of a stained glass window. Nature, or Greek perfection, stands disclosed behind the veils of art. Yet this undraped young lady hovers provocatively above a little chamber called the Monk's Parlor; while from the inner surface of the last shutter the portrait of a man seems to gaze at her with an interest neither religious nor artistic. The emblem that Soane constructs out of hitherto unrelated elements is richly ambiguous and disturbingly intimate—disturbingly because it seems to draw the viewer into an unwanted intimacy with Soane himself. Elsewhere, indeed, the collector puts himself directly into his emblematic collages, as in the dining room, where a large portrait of Soane gazes wistfully across the table at Sir Joshua Reynolds's voluptuous *Love and Beauty*.

The museums of Lenoir and Soane stand at the fountainhead of organized architectural collecting, and an entire generation of collectors and collections followed their examples: Scott at Abbotsford, Lord Stuart de Rothesay at Highcliffe, and Alexandre du Sommerard at the Musée de Cluny. Yet, as early as the 1820s, new ideas of architectural collecting were being advanced, and this from the most unlikely quarter, a young architect named George Wightwick, who was briefly Soane's assistant from 1826 to 1827 and who helped prepare the plates for Britton's description of the museum. After leaving Soane's office, Wightwick made his way to Plymouth, where he became the partner and soon the successor of the distinguished local architect John Foulston. He tells us that he began to write his best-known book, *The Palace of Architecture*, in the late 1820s, but it was not published until 1840.[28] Already introduced in Chapter 4 for its commentary on travel (Figure 4.7), it is a guidebook to his ideal museum of architecture.

In a sense, Wightwick's title is misleading. There is a palace, a grandly columnar classical affair, but the museum proper is a landscape garden, strewn with little buildings and ringed with a wall, through which the public can enter by a domed and spired gateway, weirdly concatenated out of the most discordant elements. The buildings inside the wall are of two kinds. The first are exhibit halls containing jumbles of fragments. The second, more novel and more numerous, are exhibits in themselves. There is a little group of Greek temples, some Indian stupas, a miniature segment of the Great Wall of China, and so forth, all disposed in such a way that a stroll through the garden is a voyage through the history of architecture.

Superficially, Wightwick's museum recalls the Jardin Elysée that Lenoir arranged behind his museum, but that is because both drew on the same source, the picturesque English landscape garden. Wightwick had another source of inspiration, too, a remarkable group of public buildings erected by John Foulston in Devonport, just outside Plymouth, in 1823–24 (Figure 4.6). Already described in Chapter 4, Foulston's town hall, commemorative column, chapel, and library were arranged to produce a "picturesque effect, by combining, in one view, the Grecian, Egyptian, and a variety of the Oriental" styles[29]—in short, a veritable museum. Foulston's example must have helped Wightwick to go beyond the conventions of landscape gardening as adopted by Lenoir; in any case, his museum offered perhaps the first demonstration that a landscape garden need not rely for organization upon character and association but could tell a chronological, historical, or even ethnographical story. This would prove an extraordinarily fertile insight.

Wightwick's outdoor museum advanced another significant concept, that such abstractions could best be represented through entire buildings. These little structures looked more complete than Soane's or Lenoir's splintered fragments, and thus less open to poetic allusion. In this they reveal a new and impersonal objectivity that becomes even clearer within the villa that forms the culmination of Wightwick's museum. From the tower attached to this villa, Wightwick tells us that one can survey the entire museum, "as the poet . . . can comprehensively estimate the heart of man."[30] The architectural museum is thus an intimate portrait, and one might expect Soanean revelations to follow. But the villa's program is a conventional allegory of life, leading from youth in the breakfast room to death in the chapel. Midway through this progression comes a significant juxtaposition: inside the library, a sculpture of "a boy rising from his completed studies, unconsciously to experience those pure emotions of the heart, which form the Episode betwixt youth and manhood," confronts the *Venus de' Medici*, standing just beyond the doorway to the tower room.[31] The pairing recalls those tense moments in Soane's museum where fragments call out to one another and men confront feminine beauty, but in the Palace of Architecture we understand no intimate revelation. The incident is quite without mystery or complications, smooth, blandly idealistic, and totally impersonal. It is public in just the way that those grand pictorial allegories of life made so popular at this time by John Martin, Francis Danby, or Thomas Cole are public. It is institutional in just the way that the great public collections of architecture in England and France were becoming institutional.

THE INSTITUTIONS

In 1820, the new buildings of the École des Beaux-Arts, designed by François Debret (and later completed to designs by Felix Duban), began to rise on the site of the old convent of the Petits Augustins, latterly the Musée des Monuments Français. Legally, the museum's collections had reverted to their original owners. But many pieces were never claimed and survived instead in inspiring disorder around the rooms and courtyards of the old museum. Duban featured the largest of them, the facades from Anet and Gaillon, in his design; others were incorporated in trophy-like arrangements in niches and archways. In many ways, the École des Beaux-Arts was the natural successor to Lenoir's museum; it even formed its own cast and fragment collection. Yet it conveyed a quite different mood from that of its predecessors. The bland lighting of its central court, roofed over with a magnificent skylight in 1863, was the very opposite of Lenoir's stained-glass effulgence, or of Soane's disquieting shadows; ranks of graceful statues seemed by their very orderliness to rebuke the passionate confusion of those earlier collections. In short, the École des Beaux-Arts had institutionalized the collecting and display of architectural fragments.

The process of institutionalization that led from Lenoir to the École can be traced even more clearly in one of England's most important cast collections, that of the architect Lewis Nockalls Cottingham. Cottingham, a leading scholar and restorer of medieval churches, had begun to collect casts and fragments of medieval and Elizabethan architecture by 1815, and in 1825 he installed them in a house specially designed for the purpose. To some extent, this was certainly done in emulation of Soane. Yet his collection differed significantly from Soane's in that it concentrated on medieval and Elizabethan architecture. In any case, the house and its collection soon became famous among architects, and, when Cottingham died in 1847, architects worried publicly about their future.

One reason for the widespread concern over the fate of Cottingham's collection is that it had become tied up with a larger issue, the rise of medievalism. The classicizing slant of most public institutions was becoming irksome to architects, and Cottingham's collection was seen as an essential counterweight. Already in 1838, Cottingham's former apprentice, the architect Edward Buckton Lamb, had advanced a proposal to turn underutilized cathedral naves into local museums of medieval architecture.[32] Four years later, he was calling upon the trustees of the British Museum to devote space to a "Classification of Gothic Architecture," a proposal which was met with polite indifference.[33] The museum establishment was not ready to place Gothic on an equal footing with classical. But the architectural profession was.

In 1851, the prominent architect Sir George Gilbert Scott spearheaded a move to establish an educational museum and school of art whose collections would consist of architectural models, plaster casts, and actual fragments of medieval architecture.[34] Scott raised funds for the museum, contributed his own collection of casts, persuaded Ruskin and others to do likewise, and secured the bulk of Cottingham's private museum. The Royal Architectural Museum opened in a loft on Cannon Row, Westminster, and remained there until 1857 when it had to seek new quarters. It accepted an offer from the South Kensington Museum, where the Architectural Museum's collections remained for twelve years, in the upper floor of one of the three iron galleries known as the "Brompton boilers."[35] The Architectural Museum returned its collections to Westminster and celebrated the opening of its own building, at 18 Tufton Street, in July 1869, containing "specimens not only of the remains of ancient architecture, and ancient casts, but specimens of modern art generously contributed by many of those who are foremost in the good work of renewing art-workmanship in our day."[36]

At first, the Royal Architectural Museum thrived, rapidly building up its cast collection, opening a drawing school, and generally carrying out its mission of educating the architectural and artisanal public. Then it fell upon hard times. In 1903 the trustees of the Architectural Museum made a free gift of the Tufton Street building and its contents to the Architectural Association, which, it seems, never grew accustomed to these quarters and sold its lease in 1916. The remaining collections were transferred to the Victoria and Albert Museum.[37] Some of them, portals, statuary, and segments of wall, can still be seen in the great Cast Court, though the smaller specimens lie hidden in dusty romantic heaps along the balconies high overhead. Some are still attached to the original specimen boards on which they were assembled.

From an architect's home through a professional teaching institution to a public museum, the trajectory of Cottingham's collection followed the development of architectural museums in the nineteenth century. But long before the final transformation, other institutions had arisen to serve a broad public. One was the Victoria and Albert Museum itself. Established in 1852, the V&A inherited a collection of casts of ornamental art assembled by the Government Schools of Design starting in 1841. After 1857, the V&A hoped that the Royal Architectural Museum's casts would become part of its own collection, and, although that did not happen, the V&A became an international leader in the collecting and display of plaster casts. Its director, Henry Cole, even enlisted the aid of the Foreign Office in promoting the international exchange of casts, and in Paris at the Universal Exposition of 1867 he was able to persuade fifteen European princes to sign an "International Convention for Promoting Universally Reproductions of Works of Art." After 1873, the V&A's collections of casts were magnificently housed in two enormous glass-roofed halls, either one of which would have been grander than the courtyard of the École, and which together were called the Architectural Courts.

Paris also developed its great cast collections. In addition to that of the École des Beaux-Arts, which seemed to many by the mid-nineteenth century too narrowly classical, there was the Musée de Sculpture Comparée, founded at the instigation of the great Gothicist Eugène Emmanuel Viollet-le-Duc. Now called the Musée National des Monuments Français, this museum opened in 1882, housed yet more grandly than the V&A in one wing of the Palais du Trocadéro, the vast exhibition palace left over from the International Exposition of 1878. A great many other cities, all across Europe and North America, also developed extensive cast collections of sculpture and architecture during the second half of the nineteenth century and even the first decade or so of the twentieth. In Pittsburgh, for example, the young Carnegie Institute—following the example of museums in Boston, New York, and Chicago—embarked on a massive campaign of cast collecting in 1903; its great glass-roofed Hall of Architecture opened to the public five years later and is now the finest such collection to survive in the United States (Figure 5.5).

Just as the trophy value of antique fragments during the early nineteenth century is difficult now to conceive, so is the prestige of plaster casts during the later part of the century. In 1887, Louis Courajod wrote a long article claiming François I and Louis XIV as the precursors of the Musée de Sculpture Comparée and providing the making of plaster casts with a distinguished history going back to the Renaissance.[38] Great interest was also shown in the technical refinements of plaster modeling. But most of all, the production and distribution of casts became an immense and well-organized industry. Firms of plaster modelers flourished commercially as they basked

Figure 5.5   The Carnegie Institute in Pittsburgh: a surviving example of the cast collections of the nineteenth century.

in the glow of academic approval: that of Alexandre de Sachy, established within the École des Beaux-Arts in 1848, had a stock of almost 3,000 models by about 1890, casts of which could be ordered from a handsome catalogue. In London, the leading modeler Brucciani ran a shop called the Galleria delle Belle Arti near the British Museum. His catalogue of Gothic ornaments included 425 items, mostly based on Cottingham's collection; his regular catalogue listed 195 classical architectural ornaments (some retailed from the École des Beaux-Arts), in addition to "Figures for Gas Lights, Lamps, etc.," vases, tazze, anatomical studies, and uncountable busts, torsos, statues, and statuettes, ancient and modern.[39]

Despite the differences in scale and arrangement, the purposes to which the great institutional engines of the late nineteenth century set themselves were not entirely different from those indicated by the smaller museums of the preceding period, although, with the loss of intimacy, those purposes tended to become more fixedly public. Essentially the goals were pedagogical: they focused on the elevation of taste. Sir George Gilbert Scott explained that the Royal Architectural Museum provided objects of study for "art-workmen" who could not afford to travel to the originals.[40] Like Soane, therefore, Scott used his museum as a machine to reverse the flow of tourism, the principal difference lying in the social class that was addressed. On a more broadly public level, the director of the Carnegie Institute's Department of Fine Arts was confident that his new casts were "silently but surely raising the standard of taste in the community."[41] The general intention was loftily vague: "to create by the supreme dignity of the groups an inspiring and uplifting sense of the beauty of art. . . . The average visitor may forget the historical data, but an enduring impression of beauty will remain."[42] The common premise shared by London and Pittsburgh (and by all institutional cast collections) was the same one espoused by collectors like Soane and Elgin, namely that the display of revered models would lead to an improvement in national taste.

The methods by which late-nineteenth-century curators sought to achieve these aims owed a great deal to the methods of Soane and Cottingham. James Van Trump has observed the "bland plaster banality" of the room housing the Carnegie Institute's Hall of Architecture.[43] The nineteenth-century cast court had generally little or no decor of its own (the École des Beaux-Arts was a striking exception), because the exhibits were its decor, indeed its architecture. Scott implied as much when he warned the visitor to the Royal Architectural Museum that "he will find within the structure no architectural beauty, but a stark and unambitious interior of naked brick and timber; but he will be startled at finding himself surrounded by innumerable models of architectural art workmanship."[44] These models were deployed with a profusion and disorder reminiscent of earlier private collections: Bedford Lemere's invaluable photographs of the Royal Architectural Museum bring its crowded specimen boards and its encrusted walls and columns hauntingly to life. Even the courtyard of the École des Beaux-Arts must have presented an initial appearance of ungraspable confusion. At the Carnegie Institute, visitors were actually discouraged from too readily picking out the individual specimens: as Dr. Beatty explained, "the great monuments, portals, and columns, and the groups of casts of sculpture have been arranged, not so much as individual examples, but as parts of consistent compositions, the position of each object having relation to the completed group."[45] In fact, the impression of collage was heightened by interspersing models among the casts, thus causing abrupt and disquieting shifts of scale. If the late-nineteenth-century cast collection could not quite equal the chaotic complexity of earlier collections, it nevertheless made up in sheer extent what it had lost in surface depth and richness. Above all, it offered a sensation of plenitude, and that sensation can still be experienced today, among the looming pillars and portals of the V&A's Cast Courts, in the gently spiraling galleries of the Trocadéro, or in the doorway to Pittsburgh's Hall of Architecture, where 15,000 square feet of fragments rise up to meet one in a single tremendous *coup d'oeil*.

The immensity of the vistas offered by the great cast collections was matched by the sheer scale of the objects they contained. By the second half of the century, a kind of competition had set in for bigger and more imposing casts. The Trocadéro had its succession of great portals—Moissac, Autun, Vézelay, Chartres, Bourges. The Carnegie Institute had the entire Romanesque porch of St. Gilles du Gard, seventy-five feet long and thirty-eight feet high (Figure 5.5).[46] The Cast Courts of the V&A are dominated by portals from Bologna and Santiago de Compostella, and by Trajan's column—so tall that it must be broken in half and exhibited in two pieces. Such gigantism was a response to the institutionalization of collecting. But it also reflected the impact of the International Exhibitions, vast exercises in competitive showmanship that had been held regularly in European and American cities since the first one was mounted in London's Crystal Palace in 1851. In fact, the World's Fairs were revolutionizing the collecting and display of architecture in far more significant ways. Before the Victoria and Albert's Cast Courts opened in 1873, indeed, as the very ink was drying on the princely signatures collected by Henry Cole in 1867, the seeds of the cast collection's demise were being sown. They were sprouting all about Cole, in the national pavilions, restaurants, and costume tableaux of the Paris Universal Exposition of 1867.

FROM WORLD'S FAIR TO ARCHITECTURAL MUSEUM

> We might perhaps, on former occasions, by viewing the products of various nations . . . [have conceived] some idea of their manners and customs, but never had we before such an opportunity of studying their every-day life in its most minute details. Without undertaking long and perilous journeys, without running the risk of being frozen in the North, or melted in the South; we have seen the Russian drive his *troika* drawn by Tartar steeds, the Arab smoke the *narghilê* or play the *darbouka* under his gilt cupolas, the fair daughters of the Celestial Empire sip their tea in their quaint painted houses; we have walked in a few minutes from the Temple of the Caciques to the Bardo of Tunis, from the American log-hut to the Kirghiz tent.[47]

The writer, Eugene Rimmel, leading perfume manufacturer and Assistant Commissioner of the Paris International Exposition of 1867, alludes here to what he, and indeed every commentator, regarded as the chief novelty of the 1867 Exposition: the proliferation of national pavilions (Figure 5.6). Though writing about buildings, his attention fixes only with difficulty upon architecture. Rimmel is entranced by the power of the fair's architecture to simulate the experience of travel, the object of which, however, lies less in the buildings than in the social customs they support. All of this is perfectly symptomatic of the dawning mood of the international expositions. These grandiose displays, launched in London's famous Crystal Palace in 1851, fostered intense concentration on national representation through architecture, food, and the display of all manner of agricultural, industrial, and even intellectual productions; they nurtured an insatiable curiosity about the life of foreign peoples; gave a tremendous boost to the study of ethnography; bestowed new allure on the art of travel; and, in the process, placed the collecting and exhibition of architecture on a new footing.

Alfred Normand, in his learned monograph on the foreign pavilions of the 1867 Exposition, claimed that this was the first exposition at which architecture had been represented other than by drawings and small models.[48] This was not strictly true: the various courts (Medieval, Grecian,

Figure 5.6   A new way of displaying architecture: the Austrian Village, from the International Exposition of 1867 in Paris.

Alhambra) built within the Crystal Palace for the Great Exhibition of 1851 had already contained large-scale mock-ups of architecture. But the 1867 Exposition was the first to include a significant number of buildings outside the main exhibition palace. Egypt, Tunisia, Morocco, Russia, Austria, Great Britain, Prussia, Holland, and Spain, all staked out parcels of the Champs de Mars; there one could also find a Romanian church, an American school-house, an Italian villa, a replica of the temple of Xochicalco, and many other exotic structures. In this motley collection of national pavilions, the 1867 Exposition mounted what was perhaps the first museum of architecture to present entire buildings. In doing so, it laid the groundwork for both the period room and the outdoor architectural museum of the twentieth century.

The magic of the Paris Exposition was not completely novel, however. The principle of arrangement adopted at the Champs de Mars was essentially that of the English landscape garden, as adopted by George Wightwick in his Palace of Architecture of 1840. Moreover, as Rimmel's rhapsodic travelogue suggests—and other commentators on other fairs return repeatedly to this theme—the success of the national pavilions was based upon their ability to capture and recapitulate the experience of travel. Finally, like the casts and fragments of earlier architectural museums, the national pavilions invoked the rhetorical power of fragments to suggest grand but invisible generalities, which were now sought in the abstract but emotionally laden sphere of nationhood and the march of civilization. In what broad terms these little pavilions could speak is suggested by the words of an American commentator who found in the tiny American schoolhouse "the great secret of the general intelligence of the American people, the source of their astonishing material progress," and who reported that "republican institutions have never had more eloquent advocates abroad than the two unassuming structures on the Champ de Mars."[49] Nor were the Americans alone in such rhetoric. The Commissioner General of the Egyptian exhibition remarked that the four buildings under his jurisdiction offered, "in miniature and as if condensed into a very small space, all of Egypt, brilliant, splendid, revealing the grandeurs of its past, the rich promises of its present, leaving to public opinion itself the responsibility of drawing conclusions about the future."[50] One might think that the net of representation could hardly be cast more broadly, yet Normand himself claimed that the same four buildings "summarized in a sense all of oriental life."[51]

We can, however, be a little more specific about how and what the national pavilions represented. Most obviously, they stood for national identity, and this function would be strengthened and regularized at later fairs: at those of 1878 and 1900, both in Paris, national pavilions were grouped to form impressive "Rues des Nations." Within these assemblages, the pavilions of rich western countries like Prussia and Great Britain also stood for modernity and progress. But the pavilions that interested Normand most were not those of prosperous modern countries, but rather those from what would later be called the Third World. In his text, he calls attention to two distinct categories among the foreign buildings: first, those of "oriental nations" like Egypt, Tunisia, and Morocco, which were "emerging from their isolation for the first time," and, second, those of northern countries like Russia, Norway, Sweden, and Austria, "where wood was the principal element of construction." True, there existed a third group, too, which included Great Britain, Spain, and Prussia, but it held little interest for Normand. And this is precisely the point: what the oriental and northern nations had in common was that both maintained traditional cultures untouched by modern Europe's inexorable march of progress. The architecture of the pavilions articulated this cultural difference quite clearly; they represented foreignness, ethnicity, difference.

In order to see the image of difference, architects and fair organizers had first to construct it. This they literally did in 1867, for a great many of the national pavilions were designed by Parisian architects. They also had to reach consensus on the boundaries of their own civilization. They articulated these boundaries in two ways: by drawing a spatial line around the perimeter of modern western culture, and by drawing a temporal line across its threshold. The first defined a realm of foreignness that included Egypt, the Far East, North Africa, Russia, Scandinavia, and the American West; the second created a realm of pastness that stretched backward from around 1800 into the furthest mists of time. What was left over, the residual area consisting of western Europe after 1800, was the realm of the fair organizers themselves and their public.

To understand how difference was constructed and displayed, it must be remembered that the fair goer of the late nineteenth century was not primarily interested in buildings but rather in the kind of experience suggested in

Normand's phrase, "all of oriental life." As Burton Benedict has pointed out, in the organization of the fairs from 1867, there was a rapid proliferation of categories relating to social life.[52] This development had a profound impact on the display of architecture. On the one hand, the official interest in social welfare prompted a rapid rise in the popularity of exhibits of workers' housing. These had already been introduced at the Great Exposition of 1851 but would culminate only much later in independent exhibitions such as the Weissenhof Siedlung in Stuttgart, begun by the Deutsche Werkbund in 1925. On the other hand, increasing attention was paid to the texture of popular life in the past. One of the great attractions of the Paris Exposition of 1867 was a History of Labor, which set forth the development of human skill in a display of well over 5,000 tools and craft objects dating from the Stone Age to about 1800. Even more entrancing were the exhibits of native costume. Rimmel particularly enjoyed the Swedish exhibit, which featured "figures of life-like expression engaged in all sorts of occupations." So anecdotally suggestive were these that around them one could "build a little story illustrating Swedish manners and customs": first, a "lightly clad" young maid mows hay in a field; she returns home, where her companion dresses her hair; her lover enters, leading to a tender scene of avowal; in due course, a baby arrives; and finally the happy family (whose father is an itinerant clock maker) departs on a business tour of Lapland.[53]

In exhibits such as these, an attempt was made to involve a broad range of artifacts in a total picture of human life; at the same time, the artifacts were animated by a warmly human presence. The house itself was the most complete and expressive of domestic artifacts—after all, as had been expressed by many, including the antiquarian John Britton in his description of Sir John Soane's museum, the house was a portrait of its owner[54]—and so the display of foreign, ethnic, or historic architecture came to be deeply affected by this preoccupation with social customs. Already at the 1867 Exposition, some of the national pavilions were peopled by characteristic figures: at the Egyptian *okel*, Rimmel noted that "real natives, varying in shade from light brown to ebony black, work at several trades," including turning, jewelry, and barbering.[55] In later expositions, the importance of native figures to the display of architecture increased significantly: at the Philadelphia Centennial Exposition of 1876, a hunter's cabin was not only equipped with "all the paraphernalia that a pushing and ingenious pioneer would be likely to provide" but also occupied by several real hunters who gave demonstrations of fishing and beaver hunting, "lounge on the rough log couch, smoke, dress skins, cook and eat, thereby illustrating their manner of living in the West" (Figure 5.7);[56] at the Paris Exposition of 1889, meticulously reproduced pavilions and villages housed over 400 Indochinese, Senegalese, and Tahitians;[57] and at the Chicago Exposition of 1893, such displays of native life proliferated as amusements of the most popular sort.

Another spectacular manifestation of this concentration on domestic architecture and domesticity was the "History of Human Habitation" presented at the Exposition of 1889. This was a series of twenty-three full-scale houses designed by Charles Garnier, the famed architect of the Paris

Figure 5.7 A hunter's cabin set up at the Philadelphia Centennial Exposition in 1876 provided an opportunity for visitors to observe not only the architecture but the habits of its occupants.

Opera. While few of Garnier's houses pretended to any great accuracy (a flaw noted apologetically by the architect himself), this hardly mattered: the differences they illustrated had more to do with popular life and culture than with architecture, and here Garnier's exhibit worked brilliantly. Like the histories of labor mounted in both 1867 and 1878, it demonstrated the steady rise of civilization, but it also told the story of human lives that differed from those of its viewers, and in such tableaux as the house of a Phoenician sea captain, with its canopied roof gallery from which (we are told) the proprietor might watch his ships sailing off across the blue Mediterranean, it told the story with anecdotal verve and imagination.[58]

If exhibits like these used architecture to invite the viewer's participation in alien forms of culture, other kinds of exhibits encouraged consumption of a more literal sort. Alongside the pavilions of 1867 sprang up a host of national restaurants and bars, which worked hand in hand with the national pavilions to provide an access to foreign modes of life. The Viennese brewer Dreher set up an immense beer hall in the midst of the Austrian Village, where the enjoyment of Austrian and Hungarian national dishes, wines, and beer was enhanced by the "blue-eyed *madchen* in national costume," who served fair goers and contributed to the "*couleur locale*."[59] Local color was evidently the main attraction: the Russian restaurant caused such a "great sensation" with its booted and pantalooned waiters that "many visitors, in order to have a nearer view of the denizens of the place, venture to dive into the horrors of Russian cooking. . . . Others less bold, or less wealthy, content themselves with staring in through the windows."[60]

In exploiting food as a medium of cultural consumption, the Paris Exposition of 1867 was not absolutely novel: across the Atlantic, theme restaurants had already formed a popular attraction in the local fairs mounted three years earlier by the United States Sanitary Commission.[61] Known as New England or Olde Tyme Kitchens, these restaurants were evocatively decorated to suggest the ambience of a colonial kitchen, and they were furnished with a bill of fare to match. The New England Kitchens differed from the national restaurants of the Paris fair in that the *couleur locale* they offered was that of the past, rather than of a foreign country; yet, as always, it was difference that was emphasized, and the techniques for the display of that difference remained essentially the same. And, indeed, in the late-nineteenth-century fairs, the increasingly elaborate presentation of foreign culture was paralleled by an ever more loving exaltation of the national past.

The chief vehicle for presenting national traditions was the historical theme village. Paris in 1867 had an Austrian Village, as well as Russian and Egyptian compounds, all obviously foreign, but native villages soon appeared as well. Two exhibitions held in 1886 featured historical recreations based on local topography: Old Edinburgh and Old London. For the Manchester Royal Jubilee Exhibition of 1887, Alfred Darbyshire and Frederick Bennett Smith designed another large theme village called Old Manchester and Salford, whose putative site was adjacent to the site of the exhibition itself. The exhibit's most prominent feature, the cathedral tower, replicated the existing tower of Manchester Cathedral, so that the connection between Manchester within and without the fair could hardly be missed. Yet the Manchester exhibited was Manchester of the past, and the traveler who entered it found himself caught up in a strange chronological collage. "It was a sort of dreamland," wrote Walter Tomlinson, the fair's official commentator, "a wonderfully delightful jumble of incongruities" where "nothing happened but the unexpected":

> The Roman gateway, guarded by Roman soldiers in full costume, led to Tudor houses. You had stocks and pillory, and hideous ancient crosses, and Chetham College, and the first Exchange, all in a heap; a fine old bridge, spanning a river of cobble stones; a cathedral tower ninety-three feet high, without any cathedral attached. Edward the Third's crossbowmen wandered about the streets; the terribly fierce and warlike bodyguard of the Young Pretender was for ever on parade; and anon you came full tilt upon the ghost of a Georgian watchman, bill-hook and all. There was a post-office where you didn't post; a coach-office from which no coaches started.[62]

From these impressions, three themes can be extracted: they would remain important in the architectural presentation of the national past, and in the outdoor architectural museum, right down to the present. First was the fracturing of time and space which prevented a coherent picture of Manchester at any given time from coming into focus, but only the ideal Manchester of all past epochs—Old Manchester. This synthesis was achieved by the same techniques of fracturing and recombining fragmentary specimens that had been perfected by Lenoir. Second was the mixing of heroic and quotidian elements in the tableaux: the cathedral tower and the coaching office, the intrigue of the Young Pretender and the daily life of the streets. Third was the populating of this generalized image of Old Manchester with the sort of ethnic figures and amusements that had become familiar in national pavilions, restaurants, and costume displays. You could watch "Master Caxton and his assistants, all correctly costumed," working an ancient wooden printing press.[63] You could also buy the books whose making you had watched, along with jewelry, umbrellas, and so forth. You could, in short, consume both the process and the product of traditional handicraft along with any number of old-time refreshments, served up in old-time decor.

The main themes and procedures of Old Manchester were soon developed at other fairs, especially at the Paris Exposition of 1900, where a great swath of land along the river was given over to a display of "Le Vieux Paris," whose fruitcake richness of effect exceeded even that of Old Manchester. But the Vienna Fair of 1873 helped to articulate a more explicitly ethnographic or folk-oriented view of national tradition. Part of the fairgrounds along the Danube was reserved for a display of rural houses from various Austro-Hungarian regions. As usual, the emphasis was on the demonstration of differences: traditional timber construction was marveled at, while one illustrated chronicle commented on a peasant house from Hungary: "The contemporary inhabitants of the province of Haudorf take no part in the great progress owing to the immense conquests of modern civilization."[64] Yet an attempt at national self-description was also at work, for these were not the peasants of some foreign country but of the homeland: they and their cottages represented a repository of fast-disappearing native traditions.

Within the same sector of the Vienna Fair was another noteworthy group of buildings. Though individually the timber houses and church that made up the Transylvanian Village hardly differed in principle from the Haudorf house, or for that matter from the Polish, Alsatian, or Russian farmhouses, their disposition did. For now they were grouped into a rough semblance of a village. This new emphasis on the entire settlement was carried further at the next great Austro-Hungarian fair, the Budapest Millennium Exposition of 1896. Here, the "Ethnographic Group" consisted of two segments, a "Hungarian Street" and a "Nationalities Street," both displaying rustic or peasant houses and both offering craft objects for sale.[65] The "Nationalities Street" represented Romania, Swabia, Bosnia, and other neighboring regions, so that the entire ethnographic group formed an open-air museum of Austro-Hungarian regional folklife and architecture.

A few years before the Budapest Exposition, in fact, the world's first permanent open-air architectural museum had opened in a capital city at the other end of Europe's great timber belt, Stockholm. In order to understand its genesis and its relationship to the international expositions, we must go back to 1872. In that year, a Stockholm philologist named Artur Hazelius had taken a holiday trip to the province of Delecarlia. There he became aware of the encroachment of industrialization on the traditional peasant culture, and, filled (like so many architectural collectors) with a sense of impending loss, he began to accumulate old costumes and implements. He exhibited his new collection in Stockholm, and the following year, 1873, he founded the Skandinavisk-etnografiska Samlingen. In 1876, helped by generous government subsidies, he was able to take his growing collection to the Philadelphia Centennial Exposition. There, his "admirable groups of costumed figures illustrating peasant life" won particular praise. Arranged in anecdotal tableaux like those of the 1867 Paris Exposition, Hazelius's groups were noted for their verisimilitude: instead of the usual wax mannequins, he had used plaster figures modeled by a well-known Stockholm sculptor, with hands and faces painted in an "exceedingly lifelike" manner. The costumes had all been purchased directly from their peasant wearers, and such great care had been taken to assure "absolute correctness in detail" that, when a hand was broken in shipping, it was replaced by another modeled from a Swedish girl.[66]

In 1878, Hazelius again took his collection on tour, this time to the Paris Exposition, where his tableaux scored a great success. But Hazelius had greater ambitions. In 1880, his ethnographical collections became the national property of Sweden, and a grand structure, the Nordiska Museet, was built to house them. Still Hazelius was dissatisfied, for he now wished to exhibit not just the costumes and artifacts of traditional farm life but that life itself, or at least whole farms, complete with buildings, animals, and people. And so, in 1891, he opened the world's first permanent outdoor architectural museum, Skansen. This was a seventy-five-acre park in Stockholm, furnished with a collection of Swedish village buildings, supplemented by traditional crafts, peopled by guides in traditional costume, and animated by demonstrations of folk song, dance, and crafts. It was at once a costume tableau and an ethnographic theme village.

Outdoor museums caught on rapidly in Scandinavia: Denmark's first, in Copenhagen, opened in 1897 (then moved to Sorgenfri in 1901); Norway's first, the Norwegian Folk Museum at Oslo, in 1902; its second, the Sandvig Collections near Lillehammer, in 1904; Finland's first, at Folis, in 1908. Yet others followed, all pursuing essentially the same ethnographic or folk-oriented lines laid down by the Nordiska Museet and Skansen: by 1928 it was estimated that approximately 150 such outdoor museums existed in Sweden alone.

If the outdoor architectural museum grew out of the international expositions of the late nineteenth century, changes in the indoor display of architecture were also bringing traditional art museums into line with the expositions. Throughout the nineteenth century, museums had grouped decorative art objects according to material—silver with silver, glass with glass, and so forth. This was equally true of the exhibits mounted by decorative arts manufacturers at the fairs. But during the 1890s this practice began to break down. At the Swiss National Museum in Zurich, for example, the collections were rearranged more naturalistically in sixty-two rooms designed to evoke period settings; the same procedure was followed in Munich, Nuremberg, and elsewhere. In Brussels, London, and Paris, avant-garde galleries of decorative arts adopted a parallel principle of quasi-domestic installations, and, at the Paris Exposition of 1900, Siegfried Bing's Pavillon de l'Art Nouveau presented the most up-to-date home furnishings in a convincing approximation of a house. And though the new methods were not immediately appropriated by English or French museums, the period room—the more or less authentic but always evocative architectural setting for the display of domestic furnishings—was well established in museums throughout the Germanic and Scandinavian lands by the turn of the century.

The other place where both period rooms and outdoor museums caught on and multiplied was in the United States. Until recently, it was generally believed that the first period rooms in America were the three installed by George Francis Dow at the Essex Institute in Salem, Massachusetts, in 1907 (Figure 5.8). Yet recent research has shown that Charles Presby Wilcomb anticipated him.[67] Born in 1868, Wilcomb grew up in the equivalent of Hazelius's Delecarlia, rural New Hampshire, surrounded by just the sort of relics that incited the Swede's desire. Some time in the 1880s he began to collect those relics, but it was his move to

Figure 5.8   An early period room: the seventeenth-century kitchen opened at the Essex Institute in Salem, MA, in 1907.

California in 1888 that gave him the requisite distance to see his collections in perspective. He was struck suddenly by a perception of cultural difference and, like Hazelius, by a sense that valued traditions were slipping away. Having convinced the commissioners of San Francisco's Midwinter Fair of 1894 to appoint him curator of the museum that would be the fair's permanent memorial, he opened his New England collections to the public in 1896, displayed in two period rooms, a colonial kitchen and a bedroom.

Wilcomb's association with the Golden Gate Park Memorial Museum was unhappy, and in 1905 he resigned. But three years later, after a brief stint in the East during which he furnished more period rooms in private houses, he returned to California as curator of the Oakland Public Museum, where he built up yet another colonial collection and, in 1910, opened yet another pair of period rooms.

By this time, however, George Francis Dow had opened his rooms at Salem. Dow himself would later claim that his were the first period rooms in America;[68] yet whether or not he actually knew of Wilcomb's work, his assertion was an interesting one. Dow was certainly not averse to acknowledging precedents; indeed, he referred liberally to those of Munich, Zurich, Nuremberg, and Stockholm, lauding in particular the outdoor museums of northern Europe. But as a cultivated easterner in one of America's oldest cities, Dow probably wished to be seen as an importer of European fashions. He may simply have been blind to native precedents.

Dow's rooms—a bedroom, a parlor and, as always, a kitchen—were constructed in the typical exposition manner out of a mix of original elements, reproductions, and approximations (Figure 5.8). In the parlor, for example, a genuine mantel by Samuel McIntire consorted with wainscot, cornice, and other woodwork "reproduced from the finish of a house known to have been designed by him."[69] The emphasis was not on the authenticity or historical integrity of the rooms but on the texture of life that was lived in them, and the "illusion of actual human occupancy" achieved by old newspapers, spectacles, and a knitting basket, all disposed with artful casualness.[70] The scenes lacked only figures in old-fashioned dress, and these were soon provided. In 1908 Dow spotted an important late-seventeenth-century house about to be demolished; he had it moved to the back of the Essex Institute, furnished "as though occupied," and peopled with caretakers in seventeenth-century costume. He then dug a well (dry but equipped for operation), planted an old-fashioned garden, set up a "fully equipped shoe-maker's shop," attached the porch of Hawthorne's famed House of Seven Gables to the rear of the institute (as well as a porch by McIntire), and planted a cupola from the roof of a Salem merchant's house in the garden.[71] The resulting ensemble must have been rather bizarre and was doubtless amateurish compared to Skansen. Yet it had a better claim to priority than Dow's period rooms: it was almost certainly the first permanent outdoor museum in the United States.

The importance of Dow's work, however, lies in the fact that at the Essex Institute the two new methods of architectural display, period room and outdoor museum, were introduced into the mainstream of American museology at the same time. Together they would take root and proliferate during the 1920s, though the period room caught on more quickly. Professional interest in period-room installations began very rapidly indeed, particularly at the Metropolitan Museum of Art, where significantly there was a European connection in the person of W. R. Valentiner, who had been named curator of the new Department of Decorative Arts in 1907. Before coming to America, Valentiner had assisted Wilhelm Bode, Director General of the Royal Museums of Berlin and a leader in the movement toward period installations, and, in arranging the Metropolitan's new collection of French decorative arts in 1908, he naturally followed the latest European fashion.

Though Valentiner returned to Germany during World War I, his impact on American museums was just beginning. After the war, he became Director of the Detroit Institute of Art, where period settings were introduced in 1923. In the meantime, his former assistant, Joseph Breck, had become Curator of Decorative Arts and Assistant Director of the Metropolitan Museum. Valentiner and Breck would wield considerable power at the museum throughout the formation of what were arguably the most important period-room installations in America, the American Wing and the Cloisters; and, after Breck's death in 1933, it was his close associate, James J. Rorimer, who guided the Cloisters to completion.

The story of the American Wing began two years after Valentiner's arrival, with a major exhibition of American decorative arts mounted by the Metropolitan in connection with the Hudson–Fulton Celebration of 1909. At the same time, the museum purchased a collection of over 400 objects— a daring move, for received opinion held that American craft objects had no place in a serious art museum. The exhibition's success proved otherwise, and demand grew for a permanent display of the museum's new collection. This was to be at once a "complete exemplification" of the "Zurich method" and a vindication of Dow's work at Salem.[72] Accordingly, the museum began to purchase rooms from old houses to serve as period settings, and in 1919 Grosvenor Atterbury was hired to design a new wing to contain them.

The Metropolitan's American Wing opened in 1924, complete with seventeen period rooms. It was a great success. Its evocative settings captured public and professional imagination and had immediate repercussions. At the Metropolitan itself, Edward Robinson's Roman Court, a large Pompeian atrium stocked with Greek and Roman sculpture, followed within two years. Far more important, though, were the Cloisters, the celebrated collection of medieval architecture and sculpture amassed by George Gray Barnard, bought for the museum with a gift from John D. Rockefeller, Jr., in 1925 and magnificently housed a few years later in a romantic compote of genuine and reproduction medieval settings, poised high above the Hudson River. But by now museums in Detroit, Brooklyn, and other cities were also following the Metropolitan's lead. Nor was the triumph of the period room restricted to museums. Even shops now sold luxury goods in period-room settings (indeed, Neil Harris has shown that museums were strongly influenced by innovations in shop display).[73] More significant, private collectors had discovered the attraction of period settings for their collections: George Gray Barnard and George Blumenthal, much of whose collections went to the Metropolitan; William Randolph Hearst, who spent a lifetime and a fortune building San Simeon in California, itself now a museum; James Deering and John Ringling, who built splendid mansions in Florida, Villa Vizcaya and Ca d'Zan, both now museums; Electra Havemeyer Webb, whose collection of decorative arts and transplanted buildings is now the Shelburne Museum; and Henry Francis Du Pont, whose enormous collection of American period rooms and furnishings, begun in 1918 and inspired by the examples of Shelburne and the American Wing, opened to the public in 1951 as the Winterthur Museum. Nor should one overlook Mrs. James Ward Thorne, who in the late 1920s began to build period rooms in miniature: some of her marvelous rooms, after being shown at the Chicago World's Fair of 1933 and the New York and San Francisco World's Fairs of 1939–40, became part of the Art Institute of Chicago (Figure 5.9), whose curator called the thirty-seven American examples "a fully developed American Wing in miniature."[74]

By this time, the Cloisters had finally opened: it was perhaps a coincidence, but a significant one, that in 1938, the year of the opening, the skylit cast court of the old Metropolitan Museum was rebuilt and the entire collection of architectural casts and models swept away. The triumph of the "Zurich method" was complete.

Complete, too, was the triumph of the fairs, for the similarities between the twentieth-century period room and the nineteenth-century fairground exhibit are too striking to overlook. One was the tendency to treat "rooms" as three-sided stage spaces, or tableaux, a conception enforced in the Thorne Rooms by their miniature, peep-show presentation (Figure 5.9), but elsewhere by ropes and barriers (or even by the removal of whole walls), and always redolent of the fairground tableaux. Along with this reorientation of historical material to the exigencies of display came a willingness to alter original proportions, arrangement, and lighting; the results were frequently reminiscent of the Alhambra Court at London's Great Exposition of 1851, which was reduced in scale (but the ornaments reproduced at full size) and shorn of one story in the elevation. Then, too, period rooms were generally cobbled together out of the most disparate bits and pieces of decoration and furnishing—Hudson Valley portraits, Virginia paneling, London wallpaper— often genuine in themselves but historically incompatible. These assemblages, above all, recalled such fairground exhibits as the Tunisian palace of the 1867 Exposition, which closely resembled none of the Bey's three residences yet was somehow typical of all three. Of course, the collage effect of many period rooms also significantly recalled the architectural environments constructed out of fragments by Alexandre Lenoir well over a century before in his Musée des Monuments Français.

The reemergence of the outdoor museum in American museology paralleled the rise of the period room in the 1920s; again wealthy private collectors were in the vanguard. But here the emphasis differed slightly. The

Figure 5.9   Mrs. Thorne poses with the Thorne Rooms of the Art Institute of Chicago.

growth of interest in American decorative arts had played a central role in the development of the American period room; in the outdoor museum, the celebration of native tradition was all-important. It has been suggested that the first museum village in the United States was begun in 1925 when a group of log cabins were moved to Decorah, Iowa, and opened to the public.[75] Yet in 1923 Henry Ford had already purchased the famous Wayside Inn in South Sudbury, Massachusetts, along with over 2,000 acres of land, a church, schools, and houses, all of which he proceeded to restore as a showcase village.[76] More ambitious schemes followed rapidly. In 1924 the city of Williamsburg, Virginia, offered itself to Ford as a restoration project on the largest scale; and, though he turned down the proposal, two years later John D. Rockefeller, Jr., began to rebuild the town, providing it with all the accoutrements of an outdoor museum. In 1927 Ford began to construct his own outdoor museum, originally called the Early American Village (and now known as Greenfield Village), which would open in Dearborn, Michigan, in 1929, in conjunction with a vast indoor museum of American decorative and industrial artifacts (Figures 5.10 and 5.11). After 1929 the popularity of restoration villages climbed rapidly, so that by 1955 it was estimated that there were more than 30 east of the Mississippi alone; but then, the enthusiasm for American tradition had also increased phenomenally, so that by 1967 these restoration villages could take their place among "more than six hundred thirty museums, historical houses turned museum, and townlike enclaves—conserved, restored, or reproduced—that concentrate on the wherewithal of everyday living as our ancestors lived it."[77]

The outdoor museum, as well as the period room, represented a reaction against the traditional museum presentation of architecture through casts and fragments. Again, the debt to the nineteenth-century fairs is clear. Like the Champs de Mars at the Paris Exposition of 1867, American outdoor museums were frequently laid out along the lines of a romantic landscape garden (though often, as at Ford's Early American Village, with a touch of suburbia). And like the ethnic villages, they presented a varied array of costumed guides, craft demonstrations, and traditional foods, while, like the fairs in general, providing a sophisticated range of tourist services. Finally, as did most of the national exhibits, they focused attention not on architecture but on the details of "old-fashioned" life contained within the buildings' frame, and in doing so encouraged anecdotal interpretation. "Of houses, Vermont House is conceived as the retirement dwelling of a much-voyaged sea captain," remarked *House Beautiful* of an exhibit at the Shelburne Museum, invoking a vein of narrative invention reminiscent of such fairground exhibits as the "History of Human Habitation," with its Phoenician sea captain's house, at the Paris Exposition of 1889.[78]

The debt to the world's fairs shared by period rooms and outdoor museums was as great on the ideological as on the technical level. In celebrating national traditions, these collections nevertheless created a sense of cultural difference similar to that fostered in the fairs. Their attempt to commemorate or retrieve vanishing traditions was fueled by an acute sense of loss, and this conjunction of loss and retrieval once again brings up the issue of architectural preservation, for both indoor and outdoor museums have repeatedly claimed to be motivated by its spirit. But, as with architectural collectors ever since the days of Lenoir and Lord Elgin, destruction was as central to their work as salvation: by 1955, for example, Colonial Williamsburg had restored 82 buildings, reconstructed 375, and destroyed 616.[79] If no one thought to criticize this ledger, it was not only because the buildings destroyed were less esteemed as architecture than those restored, but, more important, because, as with Hazelius and the other organizers of ethnic fairground displays, the preservation urge was rooted in a deeper sense of loss concentrated not on architecture but on a way of life. Henry Ford professed to despise history as taught in books and to value instead the stories of everyday life told by artifacts: his Early American Village was designed to expound that life, and visitors understand this quite clearly. A writer in *House Beautiful*, commenting as recently as 1967 on the proliferation of restoration villages and house museums, noted the "delightful preoccupation with domestic archeology" that "now pervades the land": "Great-great-grandmother's quilts never seemed more precious, and everyone is avid to learn how she cooked her griddle cakes, churned her butter, hung her curtains, entertained her friends, spent her vacations."[80] Abbott Lowell Cummings, too, could put architecture and preservation in the proper perspective: "For those many Americans who have been troubled successively by the vanishing of the Indian, the buffalo, and the familiar loco-motive, with its beloved steam whistle there can be added a new cry, 'lo the poor American village!' "[81]

As Cummings suggests, the way of life "preserved" by open-air museums was an idealized preindustrial culture that revolved around the traditional handcrafts. This was the ideology promoted at the fairs, institutionalized at Skansen, and quite universally followed in open-air museums throughout Europe (and in more recent decades in the former U.S.S.R.). In the United States, the hostility to industry was at times palpable, as at Old Deerfield, whose director in 1955 admiringly ticked off a list of stalwartly Anglo-Saxon names—Abercrombie, Allen, Ashley, Childs, Fuller, Hawks, Wells, Williams —who had "had the vision to keep industry off the quaint old Street."[82] But elsewhere, this nostalgia for a preindustrial culture subsisted in strange harmony with the symbols of industrialism. Thus when Henry Ford opened his Edison Institute, no conflict was perceived between the adulation of tra-ditional handcrafts and village ways of life, which dominated part of the complex, and the adulation of industrial pioneers such as Edison, the Wright brothers, and Ford himself, which dominated the rest. Indeed, so strongly held was the belief in an ideal preindustrial culture that the geniuses of industrialism were simply ruralized: even Ford's automobile factory was so reduced in scale that it appeared hardly out of context with the surrounding craft shops, the miniature town hall, and the old-fashioned inn (Figure 5.11).

All the same, this bucolic ideology of the village everyman was seriously complicated by other factors, and not only by the adulation of industrial heroes. There were also political heroes to commemorate. The saintly virtues of relics had always enlivened architectural museums, but in the United States the concept of the secular relic formed the very foundation of the architectural preservation movement. In 1850 Washington's revolutionary headquarters in Newburgh, New York, had become the first historic house museum in the United States. Ten years later, Mount Vernon—replete with such relics as the shaving stand presented to Washington by the first French minister and a chair that "stood in the room the night of his death"—also became a national shrine, soon followed by Washington's headquarters at Morristown and Valley Forge.[83] Not all of the ethnographic enthusiasm of the late-nineteenth-century fairs, nor all of Ford's agrarian populism, could dim this national cult. On the contrary, Ford went to great lengths to acquire a building dignified by association with Abraham Lincoln. Other collections, like Colonial Williamsburg, played this theme with flourishes, splashing bril-liant touches of fame and honor against the more subdued background of everyday life in a way closely reminiscent of nineteenth-century theme villages such as Old Manchester and Salford.

In the Americana collections, however, the two levels of representation shared a somewhat special significance that was not exactly prefigured by the nineteenth-century fairs. Those fairs had, of course, done a great deal to emphasize concepts of nationhood. But American craft collections had to expound not only a uniquely American tradition but one that was quite specifically independent of European values. Royal Cortissoz, commenting on the Metropolitan's new American Wing, drew the lesson that "these ancestors of ours" were "people of good breeding and consequent good taste."[84] Others, too, spoke of "taste and culture" and portrayed the past as an idyll. This sat poorly with the equally popular depiction of early Americans as rugged conquerors of a hostile land, but, relative to the construction of American traditions and the demonstration of their achievements, these contradictions must have seemed niggling. In consequence, the distinctions between the heroic and the quotidian, between high-style production and rustic craft, were not nearly so well articulated as in European folk museums.

One reason may be that the fear of losing native traditions, whether rustic or refined, had taken on a peculiar and paranoid intensity in the United States. "Traditions are one of the integral assets of a nation," intoned the official chroniclers of the American Wing in 1925:

> Much of the America of to-day has lost sight of its traditions. . . . Many of our people are not cognizant of our traditions and the principles for which our fathers struggled and died. The tremendous changes in the character of our nation, and the influx of foreign ideas utterly at variance with those held by the men who gave us the Republic, threaten us and, unless checked, may shake its foundations.[85]

The danger so darkly hinted at here was specifically the threat of immigration. The 1920s indeed witnessed strenuous attempts to stem the influx of immigrants, as well as elaborate programs to Americanize those who continued to arrive. Such programs as Greenwich House or the University Settlement in New York frequently relied upon colonial architecture and design as environmental influences.[86] And the American Wing, born in 1909 as an artistic adventure, came to maturity in 1924 as an abettor of this rootedly conservative political ideology. Nor did its promoters express their hostility to non-Anglo-Saxon peoples in mere generalities. In evoking a cozy family scene in the New England kitchen, its chroniclers quite gratuitously conjured up an image of "the war-painted ferocious face of an Indian, tomahawk in hand," who "may have leered in at the little family gathering around the fire."[87] Anti-Semitism was implicit in Old Deerfield's campaign against industrial encroachment. As for Henry Ford, he used patriotic symbols and public education to promote a positive program of Americanization at Greenfield Village, not only in the Early American Village, with its working schoolhouse and its exemplary New England town hall, but also in the museum, whose vast industrial spaces were entered through a full-scale replica of Independence Hall. Yet during the 1920s, he engaged in an ugly campaign of anti-Semitism.

Given their political ambitions and the scale of their funding and layout, enterprises such as the Early American Village might have become vast and impersonal ideological machines. Yet the many great American collections of the 1920s begun by private collectors—Greenfield, Shelburne, the Thorne Rooms, Winterthur—long preserved that quality of idiosyncrasy and personal vision peculiar to the private collection. This was true of other architecture and period room collections of the time as well. Indeed, Winterthur shares with San Simeon, Villa Vizcaya, Ca d'Zan, and even George Gray Barnard's original Cloisters the signally important fact that each was not just a museum but a home; and, if the Winterthur Museum seems distinctive by virtue of its well-articulated scholarly purposes, the arrangement of its interiors was no less influenced by Du Pont's domestic predilections, and the stories of how he imposed his imperious and refined taste upon them are legion.

Such collections clearly have little in common with the institutional cast collections of the preceding half-century. For Du Pont, Ford, Hearst, and Webb were all collectors in the grand manner, neither museum curators nor public servants, but individuals at once passionately acquisitive and opinionated. They became fiercely identified with their collections, living in them and shaping them to their own prejudices; and it was most decisively in this intimacy that they denied the heritage of the institutional cast collections, returning instead to the obsessive, egotistical brilliance of the very first architectural collections founded in England and France over a century earlier. If indeed they have a model, it is to be found in the house museums of the early nineteenth century: Sir Walter Scott's Abbotsford, Lord Stuart de Rothesay's Highcliffe, or Soane's house at Lincoln's Inn Fields. Only by returning to these earliest architectural museums can we discover a comparable fusion of decor and collection.

At the same time, it must be recalled that the ideal of domesticity was also heavily reinforced by the farmhouses, fishermen's cottages, and old-time kitchens of the world's fairs; and twentieth-century architectural museums continued to feed that "delightful preoccupation with domestic archeology" that we have already noted. The primary difference was that, whereas the fairground exhibits had been designed as mere stage sets for a simulation, or at best a transitory recreation, of bygone ways, the new museums were in many cases conceived as habitats for ongoing life. Thus Hearst and Du Pont ensconced themselves within their collections. Even more interesting, Henry Ford, though not himself living among his furniture and farm implements—they filled his office and overflowed into Ford Company warehouses—nevertheless tried to establish a fully functioning community of some 300 people within his Early American Village. The similar attempts at Old Deerfield and Colonial Williamsburg were rather more successful, since they were founded upon living communities that had only to be redesigned and redefined as outdoor museums.

In such villages, the nineteenth-century fascination with the past was transformed into a practical strategy to inhabit it: the theme village thereby became an open-air extension of the romantic house museum, complete with the entire romantic apparatus of self-revelation through objects. Of course, it was not the village's inhabitants whose tastes and beliefs were so depicted. They were mere surrogates for the absent collector, to whose personality the open-air museum could, in extreme cases, become just as intimately formed as any romantic house museum. Perhaps Henry Ford's combination of indoor and outdoor museum in Dearborn, Michigan, is the extreme case: certainly its history provides a remarkable illustration of how collecting on the grandest scale could be used to articulate an image of the self (Figures 5.10 and 5.11).[88]

Figure 5.10   Greenfield Village: the Martha–Mary Chapel is at upper left, the indoor museum, entered through a replica of Philadelphia's Independence Hall, at lower right.

Figure 5.11   A scaled-down replica of Henry Ford's automobile factory is moved into place at Greenfield Village.

Ford's first act as a collector can be dated precisely to 1904, when he repurchased his own Quadricycle of 1896 for sixty-five dollars. But the onset of collecting mania took place ten years later. A casual remark by his wife prompted a recollection of verses learned in childhood from McGuffey's

Eclectic Readers, and this, in turn, set off an intensive search for second-hand copies of the old books: in the end, Ford's collection would include not only over 450 volumes of the *Readers*, but also a "McGuffey School" built out of the timber from an eighteenth-century barn, and even McGuffey's Pennsylvania birthplace, transported to Greenfield and reerected in 1934.

By this time Ford was collecting architecture on an ambitious scale. His introduction to the field had come in 1919, when, in order to save the Ford family's old farm near Greenfield from the approach of a new road, he moved the house and reerected it some 200 feet from its original site. He then set out to restore it to its condition as remembered from 1876—a difficult task, as crucial items were out of production and not readily available through the antiques market. Next he commissioned a Ford Company draftsman to design a replica of the original windmill (the draftsman would soon become the architect of Ford's Early American Village). Finally, in a move prescient of the domestic archaeology that would become so important a part of Colonial Williamsburg, he began to sift the dirt for evocative fragments of his childhood—broken plates, hardware, rusty skates—which he shared with his brothers and sisters. At no time during this campaign of recollection and recreation did Ford intend to move back into the house, which was always conceived as a form of exhibition space. Yet he used it as a domestic background for certain aspects of his personality, donning old-time costume to dance there with family and friends to old-time melodies, and even threshing with old-time farm equipment.

Such were the origins of Ford's architectural collecting: essentially domestic, autobiographical, and intensely centered on childhood memories. Rarely indeed can the architectural collector's sense of loss have been more acute, more personal, or ultimately more productive than Ford's. For his need to discover and expose his own childhood could not be satisfied by the reconstruction of his house; on the contrary, this same autobiographical urge motivated the shaping of Ford's grandest architectural endeavor, the Edison Institute at Dearborn. We have already seen how the Early American Village's program of hero worship fit in with the political ideology of Americanization widely espoused in the 1920s, but its particular hagiography was shaped by personal enthusiasm. One hero was McGuffey. A second was Edison, Ford's boyhood idol and long-time friend. Ford had begun to collect Edison relics in 1905; and he commemorated Edison not only in the institution's name and in its dedication ceremonies, which lavishly dramatized "Light's Golden Jubilee," but also in a meticulous reconstruction of Edison's Menlo Park research complex, complete with truckloads of New Jersey soil. Ford even bought the little country station where Edison was once thrown off a train—an anecdotal touch that reminds us of the essential intimacy of history as told in the architectural museum.

Finally, a third hero was Ford himself, present in the scaled-down replica of his first assembly plant (Figure 5.11), and in a range of more intimate settings. The mill where Ford and his father had taken the wool from their farm was reerected in the Early American Village; so, too, was the Ford farmhouse itself. Even more interesting was the addition of a chapel dedicated to Martha and Mary—not, however, the biblical women, as might be supposed, but Ford's mother and mother-in-law. Moreover, though the chapel's design was very loosely based on a colonial church in Massachusetts, the building itself incorporated materials taken from the house in Greenfield where the Fords had been married. So in this central icon of American values, the visitor to Greenfield confronted neither a genuine historic building nor an abstract symbol, but rather a complex artifact in which history, country, and religion were inextricably mingled with personal mementos—relics, really, of Henry Ford's family life.

In its interweaving of private and public narrative, the Martha–Mary Chapel at once epitomizes the spirit of Ford's architectural collecting and reveals its kinship with that of the greatest early collectors of architecture, Sir John Soane and Alexandre Lenoir. They, too, had seen architectural collecting as a form of autobiography, and, if the intimacies that Ford proffered were essentially banal, he was nonetheless using his collections as Soane had used them, to articulate a self-portrait. More particularly, he used them to mediate a relationship between himself and the public and to claim a personal stake in the national history. Thus, like Lenoir, Ford treated his objects as trophies, public demonstrations of triumphs both personal and national; indeed, the distinction between the two realms seems especially obscure in Ford's case, since prominent among the incentives that the Early American Village offered to public belief was the illusion of a kind of camaraderie with Ford himself.

Most of all, however, the buildings in the Early American Village were mementos, material relics of lives lost and regretted, of self and family, of friends, heroes, everyman. They had the power to recall these things, and in some wordless way to hold their significance. This power was not magic: it was invested in fragmentary objects through the rhetorical conventions of metonymy and synecdoche, and it operated at McGuffey's birthplace or Edison's country train station just as it had throughout the history of architectural museums. But perhaps the best analogy to the fragments that made up Ford's museum, the rusty skates, the childhood books, the buildings with their anecdotes and associations, is a more recent and a very familiar one. At the beginning of Orson Welles's film *Citizen Kane* of 1939 based on the life of another great architectural collector, William Randolph Hearst, and set in a fantasy of San Simeon, the dying Kane drops a little glass globe filled with snowflakes, murmuring as he does so the enigmatic word "Rosebud." The globe prefigures the wintry scene, told later in flashback, when the young Kane is simultaneously informed of his inheritance and torn from his parents: in relinquishing this treasured fragment of the past, Kane relinquishes life itself. In the last moments of the film, as the servants toss the heaped remnants of Kane's life onto the fire, a reporter wonders—and it is the central question of the film—whether the meaning of that life might have been revealed by his enigmatic last word. As the film closes, the flames consume Kane's long-forgotten childhood sled, which bears the name ROSEBUD. It is the fragment that contains the key to Kane's life—and to the history of architectural collecting.

NOTES

1. Quoted in David Watkin, *Thomas Hope, 1769–1831, and the Neo-Classical Idea* (London, 1968), 67.

2. Werner Szambien, "Durand and the Continuity of Tradition," in Robin Middleton (ed.), *The Beaux-Arts and Nineteenth-Century French Architecture* (Cambridge, MA, 1982), 251–252, n. 33. Szambien notes that this information came in part from Robin Middleton.

3. William St. Clair, *Lord Elgin and the Marbles*, rev. ed. (Oxford and New York, 1988), 7.

4. Ibid., 97.

5. Ibid., 100.

6. Elizabeth Mayor, *The Ladies of Llangollen: A Study in Romantic Friendship* (London, 1971). See also the illustrations of Plas Newydd in Clive Wainwright, *The Romantic Interior: The British Collector at Home, 1750–1850* (New Haven, CT, and London, 1989), 272–273.

7. Marianne Roland Michel, "Le Cabinet de Bonnier de la Mosson, et la Participation de Lajoue a son Décor," *Bulletin de la Société de l'Histoire de l'Art Français* (1975): 211–221. See also Frank Bourdier, "L'extravagant Cabinet de Bonnier," *Connaissance des Arts* 90 (August 1959): 52–60.

8. *Life of Johnson* (London, 1970), 709, recording a day spent in Lichfield, March 23, 1776; Clive Wainwright, "The Romantic Interior in England," *National Art-Collections Fund Review* (1985): 83. See also J. Whiston, "The Lichfield Clock: A Musical Altar-Clock from Richard Greene's Museum, Lichfield," *Transactions, South Staffordshire Archaeological and Historical Society* 18 (1977): 73–82.

9. Mark Twain (Samuel Clemens), *The Innocents Abroad, or the New Pilgrims' Progress* (Hartford, 1869), 252.

10. Quoted in Mary Monica Maxwell Scott, *Abbotsford: The Personal Relics and Antiquarian Treasures of Sir Walter Scott* (London, 1893), 2.

11. Laurence Vail Coleman, *Historic House Museums* (Washington, DC, 1933), 99.

12. Quoted in John Fleming, *Robert Adam and His Circle in Edinburgh and Rome* (London, 1962), 152–153.

13. Quoted in David Watkin, *Athenian Stuart: Pioneer of the Greek Revival* (London, 1982), 47.

14. Quoted in Emmanuelle Hubert, "Alexandre Lenoir et le premier Musée des Monuments Français," *Archeologia* 39 (1971): 40.

15. Ibid.

16. Alexandre Lenoir, *Musée des Monuments Français, ou Description Historique et Chronologique des Statues en Marbre et en Bronze, Bas-Reliefs et Tombeaux des Hommes et des Femmes Célèbres, pour Servir à l'Histoire de France et à celle de l'Art*, vol. 2 (1801), 83ff., 136ff.

17. St. Clair, op. cit., 101.

18. Ibid., 116.

19. Lenoir, op. cit., vol. 3 (1802), 8.

20. Maxwell Scott, op. cit., 31–32, 27.

21. Christopher Hussey, "Highcliffe Castle, Hants," *Country Life* 91 (1942): 854ff.

22. John Britton, *The Union of Architecture, Sculpture, and Painting; Exemplified by a Series of Illustrations, with Descriptive Accounts of the House and Galleries of John Soane* (London, 1827), 47.

23. A thorough study of Soane's collections, both at Pitzhanger Manor and in London, is Susan Feinberg Millenson, *Sir John Soane's Museum* (Ann Arbor, 1987), a revision of her dissertation, "Sir John Soane's 'Museum': An Analysis of the Architect's House-Museum in Lincoln's Inn Fields, London" (Ph.D. diss., University of Michigan, 1979).

24. Millenson, 1979, op. cit., 76.

25. Ibid., 127.

26. Britton, op. cit., 27.

27. Ibid., vii.

28. George Wightwick, *The Palace of Architecture: A Romance of Art and History* (London, 1840).

29. John Foulston, *The Public Buildings Erected in the West of England as Designed by John Foulston* (London, 1838), 3. The group is illustrated in Plate 80.

30. Wightwick, op. cit., 206.

31. Ibid., 204–206.

32. Edward Buckton Lamb, "Brief Hints for the Preservation of the Architectural Remains of the Middle Ages," *Architectural Magazine* 5 (April 1838): 159–162.

33. Edward Buckton Lamb, letter of November 7, 1842, in British Museum, Original Letters and Papers, vol. 27, September 1842 – February 1843.

34. The story has been well told in John Summerson, *The Architectural Association, 1847–1947* (London, 1947), 35–41.

35. See photographs of the installation in John Physick, *The Victoria and Albert Museum: The History of its Building* (Oxford, 1982), 38.

36. "The Royal Architectural Museum," *Builder* 27 (July 24, 1869): 583.

37. Summerson, op. cit., 38–41.

38. Louis Courajod, "Le Moulage," *Revue des Arts Decoratifs* 8 (1887–88): 161–168, 250–255, 277–283, 311–315.

39. *Catalogue of Casts from Medieval Art, for Sale by D. Brucciani* (n.p., n.d.); *Catalogue of Reproductions of Antique and Modern Sculpture on Sale at D. Brucciani's Galleria delle Belle Arti . . .* (n.p., n.d.). I am grateful to Malcolm Baker for showing me the Victoria and Albert Museum's copies of these catalogues.

40. Sir George Gilbert Scott, *A Guide to the Royal Architectural Museum . . .* (London, 1876), 2.

41. Carnegie Institute, *Annual Report* 11–12 (1907–08, 1908–09): 13.

42. Ibid., 17.

43. James D. Van Trump, *An American Palace of Culture: The Carnegie Institute and Carnegie Library of Pittsburgh* (Pittsburgh, 1970), 30.

44. Scott, op. cit., 2.

45. Carnegie Institute, op. cit., 17.

46. Van Trump, op. cit., 31–32.

47. Eugene Rimmel, *Recollections of the Paris Exhibition of 1867* (London, [1868]), 1–2.

48. Alfred Normand, *L'Architecture des nations étrangères: Etude sur les principales constructions du parc à l'Exposition universelle de Paris (1867)* (Paris, 1870), 1.

49. Quoted in Ellen Weiss, "Americans in Paris: Two Buildings," *Journal of the Society of Architectural Historians* 45 (June 1986): 166.

50. Normand, op. cit., 3.

51. Ibid.

52. Burton Benedict, "The Anthropology of World's Fairs," in Burton Benedict et al., *The Anthropology of World's Fairs: San Francisco's Panama Pacific International Exposition of 1913* (Berkeley, CA, and London, 1983), 29ff.

53. Rimmel, op. cit., 205.

54. Britton, op. cit., vii.

55. Rimmel, op. cit., 238.

56. Frank Norton, *Illustrated Historical Register of the Centennial Exhibition, Philadelphia, 1876, and of the Exposition Universelle, Paris, 1878* (New York, 1879), 86–87.

57. Benedict, op. cit., 48.

58. Frantz Jourdain, *Exposition universelle de 1889: Constructions élevées au champs de Mars par M. Ch. Garnier. Pour servir à l'histoire de l'habitation humaine* (Paris, n.d.), 8–9.

59. Rimmel, op. cit., 41.

60. Ibid., 42.

61. See Rodris Roth, "The New England, or 'Olde Tyme,' Kitchen Exhibit at Nineteenth Century Fairs," in Alan Axelrod (ed.), *The Colonial Revival in America* (New York: Norton, 1985), 159–183.

62. Walter Tomlinson, *The Pictorial Record of the Royal Jubilee Exhibition, Manchester, 1887* (Manchester, 1888), 127–128.

63. Ibid., 129–131.

64. Edoardo Sonzogno (ed.), *L'esposizione universale di Vienna del 1873 illustrata* (Milan, 1873–74), 182.

65. Zoltan Balint, *Die Architecktur des Millenniums-Ausstellung* (Vienna, [1897]), 22ff.

66. Norton, op. cit., 87.

67. The following discussion is based on Melinda Young Frye, "The Beginnings of the Period Room in American Museums: Charles P. Wilcomb's Colonial Kitchens, 1896, 1906, 1910," in Axelrod, op. cit., 217–240.

68. George Francis Dow, "Museums and the Preservation of Early Houses," *Metropolitan Museum of Art Bulletin* 17, pt. 2 (1922): 16–20.

69. Ibid., 17–18.

70. Ibid., 18.

71. Ibid., 18–19.

72. H. W. K., "The American Wing in its Relation to the History of the Museum Development," *Metropolitan Museum of Art Bulletin* 17, pt. 2 (1922): 14–16.

73. Neil Harris, "Museums, Merchandising, and Popular Taste: The Struggle for Influence," in Ian M. G. Quimby (ed.), *Material Culture and the Study of American Life* (New York: Norton, 1978), 140–174.

74. Meyric R. Rodgers, preface to Mrs. James Ward Thorne, *American Rooms in Miniature*, 4th ed. (Chicago: Art Institute of Chicago, 1941), 3.

75. Abbott Lowell Cummings, "Restoration Villages," *Art in America* (May 1955): 12.

76. Geoffrey C. Upward, *A Home for Our Heritage: The Building and Growth of Greenfield Village and Henry Ford Museum, 1929–1979* (Greenfield, MI, 1979), 3–4, 15.

77. Marion Gough, "Little Journeys to the Way We Used to Live," *House Beautiful* 109 (1967): 148.

78. Ibid., 203.

79. Singleton P. Moorehead, "Problems in Architectural Restoration: Colonial Williamsburg," *Art in America* (May 1955): 64.

80. Gough, op. cit., 148.

81. Cummings, op. cit., 64.

82. Henry N. Flynt, "Old Deerfield: A Living Community," *Art in America* (May 1955): 41–42.

83. Paul Wilstack, *Mount Vernon: Washington's Home and the National Shrine* (Garden City, NY, 1916), 275.

84. Royal Cortissoz, "Appreciation," in R. T. H. Halsey and Elizabeth Tower, *The Homes of Our Ancestors as Shown in the American Wing of the Metropolitan Museum of Art* (Garden City, NY, 1925), viii.

85. Ibid., xxii.

86. See William B. Rhoads, "The Colonial Revival and the Americanization of Immigrants," in Axelrod, op. cit., 341–362.

87. Halsey and Tower, op. cit., 9.

88. The following discussion is based on facts provided in Upward, op. cit., and James S. Wamsley, *American Ingenuity: Henry Ford Museum and Greenfield Village* (New York, 1985).

PART III

Winning and Losing in New York City

INTRODUCTION: "CULTURAL LANDMARKS" AND THE CHALLENGES OF PLACE, RACE, AND STORY IN NEW YORK CITY

The preceding chapters were written in Chicago and Montreal. The final chapters range from Yorkshire to the Catskills. This part is about New York City. Chapter 6 considers the special challenges of preserving places that are important for their history or associations rather than their architecture. Chapter 7 reflects on the campaigns to save two of the most important of them, the African Burial Ground and the Audubon Ballroom. Chapter 8 looks at the continuing plight of the city's history, especially that of its immigrants, communities of color, and working people. It describes the threats to these communities' past, but also to their future, and shows that the solution to one problem must also be the solution to the other.

Racial issues erupted into the consciousness of New York's preservationists late in 1989, when it became known that the city of New York and Columbia University had agreed to demolish a striking yet decrepit building known as the Audubon Ballroom, located on Broadway in the Washington Heights neighborhood just north of Harlem. Designed in 1912 by the famous theater architect Thomas W. Lamb, the Audubon Ballroom contained a theater seating well over 2,000 in addition to a spacious ballroom. The building was notable as one of the first theaters built by William Fox, later of Twentieth Century Fox; as the synagogue Emez Wozedek; as the site of early efforts to organize the city's transport workers and as the long-time meeting place of the powerful Transport Workers Union; as the San Juan Theater; and as a masterpiece of terra cotta design. It was also the site where Malcolm X was assassinated while giving a speech on February 21, 1965, and it was this emotionally gripping connection with the civil rights movement which inspired a fierce grassroots preservation campaign to preserve it.

With the Audubon Ballroom fight raging, news emerged in 1991 that archaeologists clearing a site for a massive new federal office building just north of City Hall had found human remains. The existence at one time of an eighteenth-century African and African American burial ground on that site was known, but most experts assumed that any remnants of the burial ground had been cleared away by deep excavations made for construction during the nineteenth century. Now it became obvious that burials remained intact under the ground: how many it was impossible to say. It also became obvious that the federal government was determined to redevelop the site at any cost—including the removal of any remaining graves. New York now witnessed an unprecedented situation: the two biggest and most energetic grassroots preservation campaigns of recent decades, or perhaps of all time, were largely being fought by African Americans, and to protect sites of special importance to African Americans. These two campaigns and the differences between how they were fought and how the public, politicians, and preservationists responded are the subject of Chapter 7.

If the racial politics of the situation were challenging to New York's white preservation establishment, so too was the fact that neither campaign was fought primarily over architecture. Though the Audubon Ballroom's architectural quality was high, it was not the reason why most advocates fought for it; at the African Burial Ground, the significant cultural resource was the graves: they were invisible, and many advocates wanted them to remain that way. New York's preservation groups were not used to situations like these: they were accustomed to judging and advocating for sites largely on their architectural merits. There was nothing in law or history that required this— the city's landmarks law recognized many other reasons why buildings or sites might deserve protection—but for many years both the city's official preservation agency and the leading advocacy groups had emphasized architectural values. And so, confronted with the Audubon Ballroom and the African Burial Ground, many preservationists were unsure of how to proceed, or of what good or bad precedents they might set by doing so.

Controversies over other sites were igniting similar questions. One was a brick rowhouse on East 17th Street in Manhattan, an utterly ordinary building which had been the home and workplace of the great Czech composer Antonín Dvořák from 1892 through 1895. While living there, he had written some of his most famous works, including the *New World Symphony*, which received its premier in New York's Carnegie Hall. Moreover, it was there that Dvořák became familiar with the Negro spirituals which became an important influence on him, and there too that Dvořák consolidated an influence on American music that extended down to the generation of Aaron Copland, George Gershwin, and Duke Ellington. Now Beth Israel Hospital wanted to tear the house down.

Another site was the magnificent Pier 54 on the island's Hudson River waterfront (Figure 6.5). Unlike the Dvořák House, this was a real work of architecture, completed in 1910 by Warren and Wetmore, designers of Grand Central Terminal. But again, it was not mainly the building's architecture that moved supporters. Pier 54 was the last vestige of the Cunard Line piers and an imposing reminder of the huge steamships whose ponderous arrivals and departures used to be a New York ritual. Moreover, it was to Pier 54 that the survivors of the Titanic were brought in 1912, and from Pier 54 that the *Lusitania* set sail three years later: German torpedoes sank it, helping to throw the United States into World War I. Now the State of New York wanted to demolish Pier 54 for highway construction.

A third site was the long-abandoned and ruinous hospital complex on Ellis Island. Though never as imposing as the beautifully restored Great Hall, the hospital buildings were an integral part of the nation's most important immigration station and a monument in the history of public health. Now the National Park Service wanted to turn them over to a private developer who planned to demolish much of the complex and replace it with a luxury conference center.

As a group, these sites provoked a mixed response from the city's preservationists. On Ellis Island, preservation groups were unanimous and uncompromising: the buildings should be preserved. But on the Dvořák House preservationists split, some arguing for preservation, others for a plaque or statue. In general, what these sites revealed was the lack of consensus on the importance of non-architectural values like historical association, local tradition, and place affection. Moreover, even where advocates fought for preservation, it was proving to be exceptionally difficult to make the case to politicians and editorial boards. In a city where preservationists were used to hard fights, these seemed even harder.

Faced with these challenges, the Municipal Art Society of New York, where I served as director of historic preservation, convened a committee to advise on a report and recommendations. Some of the initiative's backers hoped the study would reaffirm the prevailing emphasis on architectural values and justify the status quo. But the advisory group formed to assist with the study was not interested in defending the status quo. In addition to preservationists, the committee included historians, oral historians, urban geographers, environmental psychologists, folklorists, public artists, educators, clerics, and writers. It also included spokespersons for the cultural heritage of some of New York's distinct racial, ethnic, religious, and neighborhood communities. Bringing new perspectives, the committee saw new opportunities and urged expansion rather than retrenchment. The report, called *History Happened Here* and reprinted in this book as Chapter 6, urged New York's preservationists to pay more attention to history, tradition, and local culture, and to embrace a broader understanding of what made places important to people. It did not argue that the old kind of preservation was wrong, but it did show that it failed to capture the full range of heritage values that mattered to New York's residents. It did not argue for overthrowing architecture, but it did call for recognizing community sentiment, memories, traditions, and feelings of attachment as valid dimensions of heritage. True, these factors might be hard to evaluate, but, for heritage stewardship to become effective, the effort would have to be made.

History Happened Here was controversial. All forty members of the advisory committee endorsed its recommendations; so did the Municipal Art Society's standing preservation committee, which was charged by its board of directors with formulating preservation policy for the organization. Yet the report so alarmed some trustees and senior officials that the words "Discussion Draft" had to be added to the title before they allowed it to be printed and distributed. There was irony in this, for, as Society officials hesitated to endorse the conclusions of its own study, opinions outside the Society were swinging strongly towards them. When the project began in 1993, many professionals and community leaders had found it hard to understand or accept its general drift. Yet the same ideas which struck them then as contrarian, even perverse, were received enthusiastically in 1996 when the report was released to a broader public in a symposium held at the Museum of the City of New York. *History Happened Here* appeared to strike a chord: ideas which had recently seemed perplexing now seemed intuitively obvious to many observers: *of course* some places were important for their history or their community associations; *of course* such considerations should motivate preservationists. Naturally not everyone saw things this way. One respected figure walked out of the conference, muttering that preservation was doomed. He belonged to the gold-standard group that I described in the Prologue: those who believe that the way forward lies in refining professional standards. But at that moment he was in the minority.

The generally enthusiastic reception given to *History Happened Here* persuaded me that, although the report anticipated a broad shift in attitude, it did not cause it. In other ways, though, the document did have some influence on the city's preservation movement. Place Matters, a non-profit program which I and others founded in 1998, represented a direct and concrete effort to put its ideas into practice. With the help of the Joyce Mertz-Gilmore Foundation and the New York Community Trust, Place Matters set out to find and celebrate places of local attachment and to fight for their preservation.

Other responses have been less direct. During the later 1990s, a distinctive habit of speech took root among the city's preservationists, a tendency to divide potential landmark sites into three categories—architectural, historical, or cultural landmarks—according to their preeminent values. Architectural landmarks, obviously, were the kind with which everyone was familiar. Historical landmarks referred to sites valued for their history. This concept too was easy to accept, for, even if it was not strongly emphasized within the city, the National and State Registers gave it ample recognition. The third category, cultural landmarks, essentially stood for everything of value that was left over after history and architecture had been accounted for: local affection, social memory, tradition, and so forth. Of the three, this was the one that represented—depending on how one looked at it—the biggest challenge to, or the biggest opportunity to expand on, existing policies.

History Happened Here did not invent these phrases, but it did put them into wide circulation. In fact, the advisory group was named the Historical and Cultural Landmarks Committee. Actually, the terms are problematic, for they reinforce hard distinctions among categories which are fluid, continuous, and overlapping. Still, they do have the value of concision, which has made it easier to debate policies and programs. This is especially true of the third category, cultural landmarks, which is most in need of further research but also of convenient labels. There have been some efforts to promote thinking along these lines. In 2004, the Historic Districts Council, a leading preservation group, dedicated its annual conference to "Cultural Landmarks: Controversy, Practice and Prospects." In 2008, the organizers of a conference at the Museum of the City of New York structured a discussion of landmark policies around the same three categories: architectural, historical, and cultural landmarks.

During the last decade or so there has been much discussion of cultural landmarks, much talk of loosening up the old rules. There have also been some failed efforts to put these ideas into practice, like Van Wagner Communications' 2004 bid (for which I served as consultant) to place "storyboards"—panels presenting stories drawn from local history or tradition—in the city's roughly 3,300 bus stop shelters. But there has not been a lot of action. The city's preservation community remains more focused on architectural values than those of many other cities, and certainly than the National Park Service and most state preservation agencies. Perhaps it is time to recognize this odd distinction as a local tradition of sorts: perhaps it should even be nurtured as such. But perhaps not. The failure to seize the opportunities presented by the Audubon Ballroom and African Burial Ground campaigns—the opportunities to nurture alliances with environmental justice advocates, to serve new constituencies, to broaden and diversify the preservation movement—has left preservationists with narrower, rather than wider, options.

And there have been costs to inaction. The real estate boom which took off at the end of the 1990s did not merely threaten a few historic sites, as happened earlier in the decade: it has transformed entire neighborhoods, including some of the city's most historic working-class and industrial zones and communities of color. Historic preservation organizations were slow to recognize the threat to the city's heritage. And they had no better policy tools to combat it in 2004 than they had in 1994. As a result, large areas of the city have been remade with little regard for preservation: in the process, much of its working-class and immigrant history has been erased without strong opposition from preservationists.

In 2008 the National Trust for Historic Preservation placed the entire Lower East Side on its annual list of the country's "Eleven Most Endangered" historic sites. If the Lower East Side, Harlem, and the industrial waterfronts of Manhattan, Brooklyn, and Queens are allowed to become unrecognizable, then key episodes in the city's history will have been lost. This is the problem set forth in Chapter 8. It is one of the basic problems that confront New York's preservationists as they struggle to update long-established preservation conventions in response to the challenges of place, race, and story.

CHAPTER 6

A Plan to Save New York's Places of History and Tradition

This chapter originated as a policy study carried out in 1993–95 for the Municipal Art Society of New York, where I served as director of preservation, and was published by the Society in 1996 as History Happened Here: A Plan for Saving New York City's Historically and Culturally Significant Sites. *Excerpts were republished by the New York Council for the Humanities in* Culturefront *the following year, with responses from Mahasti Afshar, Thomas Bender, Nathan Glazer, and Douglas Greenberg. Because it is in some sense a historical document, the full text is reprinted here with only minor changes intended to clarify the meaning. No attempt has been made to update it.*

PREFACE

This report aims to set forth a general plan for the preservation of New York's historically significant sites. In part it is a call to action, in part a call to further thought about issues which do not lend themselves to easy solutions. The Municipal Art Society became committed to this project as a result of the long and bitter fight to save the Audubon Ballroom at Broadway and 165th Street (Figures 7.4 to 7.6). This was a historically significant site by any measure: notorious as the scene of Malcolm X's assassination in February 1965, it is also where William Fox started his movie empire, and where early meetings of the Transport Workers Union were held in the 1930s. The partial destruction of the Audubon Ballroom was followed by the loss of the Dvořák House and of Pier 54, the last of the great Cunard piers (Figure 6.5). The destruction of portions of the African Burial Ground (Figures 7.1 to 7.3), and the controversies over the retention of the Naumburg Bandshell in Central Park and, more recently, of the Children's Zoo made it clear that a great many people were responding with passion to the claims of historic sites. The movements to save the Audubon Ballroom and the African Burial Ground, indeed, generated a level of popular mobilization that had not been seen in preservation issues in a long time.

It was becoming clear that historical sites had a great power to arouse controversy. In some cases, indeed, there was no consensus on whether they were of value at all. Did they matter? How could one distinguish important sites from less important ones? What should be done to preserve them, how should they be preserved, and who should do it? The question of historical sites, their value, and their preservation needed a fresh look.

A particular focus of this study from the beginning was the Landmarks Preservation Commission, whose declared public purpose is to "safeguard the city's historic, aesthetic and cultural heritage" by preserving the places which "represent or reflect elements of the city's cultural, social, economic, political and architectural history." It appeared that these phrases gave the Commission the authority, or even the mandate, to designate sites for historical reasons. If so, was the Commission fulfilling that mandate? If not, how could it do so?

To address these and other questions, the Municipal Art Society convened a study group. The group began as a subcommittee of the Society's standing Preservation Committee, a group of over thirty architects, preservationists, historians, and neighborhood activists. It was the committee—and particularly its chair, Charles Platt—which pressed for this study. The participants quickly recognized the need to open it to experts in a wide range of subject areas. A loose structure was evolved in which people were brought into the discussion as the need and opportunity arose, so that in the end well over fifty individuals contributed in some way to drafting, reading, and redrafting this report, taking part in more than twenty formal meetings in addition to less formal working lunches and site visits.

Those who participated in the Society's Committee on Historical and Cultural Landmarks included architectural historians; urban historians; oral historians; public historians; social historians; labor historians; literary historians; urban planners; clerics; architects; public artists; museum curators, administrators, and consultants; educators; arts administrators; folklorists; archaeologists; archivists; professional preservationists specializing in the care of religious properties; environmental psychologists; cultural anthropologists; journalists; current and former landmarks staff and commissioners; staff members from the State Office of Parks, Recreation and Historic Preservation and the National Park Service; City Council members; labor activists; professional tour guides; travel administrators and consultants; community development experts; and neighborhood advocates from the South Bronx, Harlem, the Lower East Side, Chinatown, Corona, College Point, Coney Island, Crown Heights, and elsewhere.

The committee held its meetings at various locations around the city, some of them historic sites: the Weeksville Society in Brooklyn, the Lower East Side Tenement Museum, the Museum of Chinese in the Americas, the Brooklyn Historical Society, Kingsland House in Flushing, and the "Alcove Lounge" in Corona. Committee members toured historic sites in Chinatown and Corona, synagogues in the Bronx, rehabilitated tenements in the Lower East Side, and sign markers in Lower Manhattan; they assembled a library of printed material from all over the country. In the meantime, the committee was redefining its mandate. From an initial focus on the work of a single governmental agency, its scope expanded to encompass just about anything that anyone might do to protect a historic place or keep its story alive.

This is not, finally, a report about "landmarking"; rather, it is a report about the value of our historic sites and what people can do to safeguard, mark, interpret, and celebrate them. Landmark designation and regulation play a part (as do federal and state preservation programs), but only within a much broader context of options and actions. "Broader" is indeed the key word of this report. It urges those who love the city and care about preserving what is best and most important in its fabric to broaden their sense of mission: to recognize traces of history in all its many wonderful (and often unexpected) guises, and to care for them with the same solicitude that they extend to the beautiful cornice or the rare fanlight.

The committee found history in neighborhoods all over the city: we wish others the same joy of discovery and recognition that we experienced. The report also urges lovers of the city to broaden their definition of "preservation": to throw themselves into the challenge of interpreting with the same zeal that they have long applied to saving. For in interpretation lies the saving of the stories, associations, memories, and lessons that make historic sites valuable to people.

The report finally urges lovers of the city fabric to broaden the alliance of its stewards and interpreters. Just as history is the birthright of each of New York's residents—and the shared inheritance of all—the preservation of history is a civic responsibility that can be discharged only if it is shared. Preservationists will need to build partnerships—with folklorists, geographers, historians, artists, museum curators, and no doubt other professionals as well—to get the job done. And professionals will need to work with amateurs, because communities will always have to be involved in discovering, writing, saving, and telling their own stories.

In the end the committee was ambitious in its goals: We chose to lay out a vision of what the city might look like, perhaps ten years hence, if it were genuinely dedicated to preserving historic sites and if its various public and not-for-profit agencies were able to express that dedication in comprehensively effective programs. The goals are lofty, but we believe that each of the specific recommendations is practical and achievable.

A VENERABLE VISION FOR NEW TIMES

It is difficult to imagine that anyone could find the goals set out in this report—to preserve and protect New York's historically and culturally significant sites, and to promote understanding of them through interpretation and appropriate use—revolutionary in any way. This paper is, in fact, based on a venerable tradition. Americans have been working together to save their most beloved historic places ever since a group of women banded together to preserve Mount Vernon in 1858. Sites associated with the Founding Fathers were favorites, as were Civil War battlefields a little later. Thus was America's historic preservation movement born. The effort to protect culturally and historically significant places was, in fact, one of the preservation movement's earliest goals.

Eventually, though, the emphasis shifted and architectural quality became the touchstone, especially in New York. With the city's Landmarks

Preservation Commission in the vanguard, this movement has given vitality to our cities and neighborhoods. Now, however, many preservationists are looking back to their roots and rediscovering history—not the same old history, but one fortified by a new appreciation of the richness of our urban society and its many interlinked strands. When we say "history happened here," we mean the history of how we became the city we are. We mean the aspirations and accomplishments—and the sufferings and disappointments, too—of each of our communities. We mean the prologue to our future as a city. And, of course, we mean the historic places that can help us remember and understand this history.

What is a historic place? It is a place where something happened—an event, a pattern of events, a movement, a way of life, a traditional ceremony or activity. But it is more. It is a place where that something can be understood, remembered, or retold especially well because of the physical survival of a structure or landscape. It may also be a place where vital traditions, carried over from the past, are still being enacted: places some people call "cultural sites" or even "living landmarks." Such living landmarks remind us that history not only happened but is still happening here, and that the past is connected with the present. Both historical sites and living landmarks enrich our lives as urban citizens. A visit to New York's African Burial Ground brings a long-lost chapter of American history to life as no book can do; a walk through the tenements of the Lower East Side (Figure 8.2) provides a visceral understanding of immigrant life beyond any verbal description. These are examples of survivors—places that can still communicate to us if we know how to look at them and respond. Sadly, when a place is destroyed, very often an important chunk of history dies with it. When the lobby of the Biltmore Hotel was demolished, for example, and its famous clock removed, the unique and cherished New York social tradition of "meeting under the clock" vanished with it, living on only in literary references.

As this committee considered the value of historical and cultural sites and met with people around the city, a shared vision came to motivate our work: a vision of a city whose buildings and spaces proudly display the history of its people, and whose people cherish their historical and cultural sites and use them to understand their past and chart their future. We found that preservationists are sharing this vision in growing numbers; without renouncing the movement's great achievements they are forging new partnerships with schools and museums, with artists, historians, and folklorists, and above all with communities to save the city's past. Yet we also came to realize there were obstacles to be overcome to fully achieve our vision. Not only were cultural and historical sites threatened with demolition, defacement, or decay, but they faced a special threat: the threat of neglect, of forgetfulness. For this reason the task force articulated the double goal stated above: to protect and to interpret.

This report presents the recommendations of the Municipal Art Society's Committee on Historical and Cultural Landmarks. It is our hope that this report will inspire thought and spirited discussion that may eventually lead to both a change in thinking and a change in the way we do things. We address both in the report that follows. In the first section, "Premises for Preserving New York's History," we propose new ways of thinking about preservation, ways that preserve sites and buildings not solely for their architectural merit, but also for their historical importance. In it, we invite preservationists to take up a wide-angle lens and begin looking not just at extraordinary buildings, but at typical ones; not just at single structures or small units, but at communities; not just at one moment in time, but at the layers of history that exist in aging structures and sites. It is an approach that emphasizes inclusion; encourages different—even conflicting—views of history; and calls for the involvement of many disciplines, communities, and institutions in the process. We also explore—and invite the readers of this report to reflect on—the need for interpretation of sites and buildings that may not yield up meaning as readily as buildings of more obvious "importance."

The second section of the report explores the value of partnerships in identifying and protecting historical and cultural sites. The report's final two sections address the roles of the New York City Landmarks Commission and the state and federal agencies that administer preservation programs. These sections of the report make specific recommendations designed to improve the way these agencies deal with historical and cultural sites.

PREMISES FOR PRESERVING NEW YORK'S HISTORY

For many New Yorkers, historic preservation is—and should be—based on architectural beauty and significance and is focused on saving structures and places possessing those qualities. These values are not wrong, but they are too narrow. What we are suggesting could be characterized as a new way of thinking about buildings and locales—not merely as bricks and mortar, or as aesthetically pleasing landscapes, but as living "texts" that have much to teach us about New York's past and the people who have lived here and contributed to the city's development. And because the stories associated with a historical site are often hidden from the eye, we must also take every opportunity not only to save buildings that contain important stories, but to tease out, tell, and explain those stories. In short, we must become interpreters as well as preservers.

Saving our history will require a broader understanding and appreciation of our city's built forms. In fact, many people already appreciate buildings for reasons beyond those considered valid by the majority of professional architectural historians or preservationists: Association with historical events, tradition, symbolism, communal identity, and the fondness that comes with long familiarity and use all can make a building or urban place significant in people's lives. These meanings are all part of our cultural inheritance; they constitute what has been called the "social value" of our built environment. One of the themes of this report is to encourage preservationists to protect the social value of place by understanding and finding ways to support the feelings of attachment that their history engenders.

In fact, this way of thinking is not new at all. For a generation or more historians have been exploring ways of telling history in more dynamic and representative ways. Sociologists, environmental psychologists, and geographers have documented the phenomenon of "place attachment." And folklorists have demonstrated the cultural value of urban rituals and traditions of place. What this committee found is that, by applying this thinking—most especially that of historians—to preservation issues, certain basic premises emerged, which in turn suggested new preservation strategies.

Our first observation is that history is everywhere and is constructed—both literally and figuratively—out of the day-to-day experiences of New Yorkers from all walks of life. Anyone who has ever worked in an office or factory, taken public transportation, attended a public or private school, celebrated in a neighborhood house of worship, belonged to the PTA, visited a museum, or lived in the confines of a family has taken part in history. For personal and communal experiences like those—and the places in which they happened—are the fragments that make up the grand sweep of New York's long and varied history. This committee concluded that looking at everyday experiences over time as they are embodied in the city's buildings, parks, and pavements is an important way of getting at the intricate mosaic that is New York's history.

Second, we assert that diversity is not, as some would believe, a "politically correct" remedy but a central and cherished part of New York's history which must be reflected in the city's preservation policies. Since the mid-seventeenth century, when visitors to New Amsterdam were already commenting on the presence of an astonishing variety of languages, ethnic groups, and religions, our city has been known for its diversity. The surges of immigration in the mid- and late nineteenth century ensured that New York would remain diverse, but immigration was only one factor. Again and again, New York has provided a home for distinctive forms of art and cultural expression, religious belief, intellectual endeavor, commercial and financial innovation, and lifestyle. No public presentation that fails to convey this diversity—or to convey the diversity of opinions about history that is its inevitable result—can be deemed fully adequate.

Third, we concluded that communities are the city's essential building blocks and must be at the center of any historical preservation effort. A community can be defined as a group of people who live in face-to-face association or who share a distinctive lifestyle. A community supports a distinctive pattern of social relationships, values, and knowledge which distinguish it from other communities. In New York City, communities have been defined not only by neighborhood—like Greenwich Village, Harlem, Park Slope, Astoria—but also by race and ethnicity or by shared values and lifestyle—for example, Wall Streeters, Christian conservatives, gays and lesbians. Considering community when making preservation choices provides a framework that recognizes not only the history of geographic neighborhoods and their dominant ethnic and affinity groups, but also larger narratives about New York's historical appeal to diverse groups, its history of tolerance for diverse cultural expressions, and its extraordinary fertility in nourishing innovation.

There is a fourth premise for our recommendations. It is that the enterprise of preserving our history should be a collective one, involving folklorists, geographers, historians, museum curators, and artists as well as preservationists; and citizens—community leaders, elders, schoolchildren—as well as professionals. Preservationists can't do it alone. Even assuming they could, the preservation and telling of our history by a small group of experts would defeat the purpose. Through partnership with communities and collaboration with other disciplines, however, preservationists can make an enormous contribution to preserving New York's cultural and historical legacy.

Toward a New Way of Thinking

New York City is filled with buildings, neighborhoods, and sites that have important historical associations to millions of New Yorkers and visitors to the city. Seen through the lens of conventional preservation criteria, many of them may not appear significant or worthy of preservation. The challenge is often to look past the architecturally oriented criteria of value that many of us bring with us, and to recognize historical significance in its many guises.

In New York the range of building types in which historical significance may be found is broad indeed: in Chinatown, barbershops (Figure 6.1), general stores, the headquarters of political and community organizations, the sites of important advances for garment and restaurant workers; on the Lower East Side, synagogues (Figure 6.2), buildings that once housed

Figure 6.1   Barbershops along Doyers Street in Chinatown are important markers of the history of New York's Chinese community.

Figure 6.2   Kehila Kedosha Janina is unusual for being a Romaniote synagogue but is otherwise typical of many small synagogues squeezed between the tenements of New York's Lower East Side. First Corinthian Baptist Church in Harlem was designed by Thomas W. Lamb as the Regent Theater, a year after the Audubon Ballroom. Though not designed as a church, its history as such is an important part of its community significance.

landsmanschaften and *schteeble*; in East Harlem and the South Bronx, *casitas*, storefront churches, markets, salsa clubs and record shops, and the sites of political rallies; in Greenwich Village, coffee houses, restaurants, and piers; in Harlem, nightclubs, public libraries, churches, and sites of streetcorner oratory; in the Financial District, skyscrapers, clubs, and countinghouses; along the waterfront, warehouses, docks, grain elevators, sugar refineries, oil storage tanks, and the Coney Island Boardwalk; in the Garment District, lofts and the site of famous political rallies; in mid-Manhattan, mansions, corporate headquarters, and Central Park; and, almost everywhere, apartment buildings, rowhouses, union locals and health clinics, factories, bars, and storefront community organizations.

By pointing to such humble structures, we are not suggesting that we have stopped needing the Mount Vernons, Carnegie Halls, gentlemen's clubs, and mansions that dignify our cities. But, if we are to represent the full texture and richness of our history, we must also learn to recognize the factories, workplaces, and tenements in which ordinary people passed their lives; the union halls and drinking establishments where they gathered; the streetcorners where day laborers endured the daily "shape-up," and the clubs where distinctly new—and distinctly New York—forms of popular music were born.

This committee did not arrive at these recommendations lightly. We do not believe that architectural and historical values are mutually exclusive or in opposition—though we have found that proponents of both have helped to enforce a misleading tension between the two. In fact, many architecturally important buildings are historically significant above and beyond their aesthetic quality (though all too often this goes unremarked). Conversely, many historical sites have great aesthetic power: witness City Hall, or the Art Deco lofts of Manhattan's Garment District. Yet some sites of undoubted importance lack aesthetic distinction, such as the famous and much-discussed examples of the Garibaldi–Meucci house on Staten Island and the Louis Armstrong House in Queens (Figure 2.3). These are both designated landmarks; it should be an easy step to move from them to, say, the quite ordinary house in Corona, Queens, where Malcolm X and his family lived at the time of his assassination (Figure 2.3). It is more challenging, yet ultimately essential, to move to a greater appreciation of the cityscape and its historical content.

A particular challenge has long been and continues to be preservation of archaeological resources that often lie undetected beneath the ground until uncovered in surveys preceding new construction. The rediscovery of the African Burial Ground near Manhattan's Civic Center in 1991 (Figures 7.1 to 7.3) has made New Yorkers particularly aware of these hidden resources. Its designation as part of a New York City Historic District has established a valuable precedent for such sites' protection under local law. But we don't know how many important resources of industrial archaeology still lie unprotected.

Yet another important challenge lies in the preservation of open-air sites, such as the Lower East Side's "Pig-Market," where laborers once congregated in search of day work, or Union Square and Seventh Avenue, which both hosted historic labor rallies and parades. Stock market panics, the Draft Riots, Jacob Leisler's execution, and the trading of slaves all took place out of doors (Figure 6.3). Marcus Garvey first preached his gospel of African nationalism at the corner of Lenox Avenue and 135th Street. Vito Marcantonio addressed a rally for Puerto Rican independence on East 113th Street between Madison and Fifth Avenues. Orville Wright flew the first four flights over American waters from an open field on Governors Island.

Typical, Extraordinary, and Exemplary

Landmarks have most often been used to present exceptional individuals and achievements, and that is wholly appropriate, especially in a city where so many local individuals and events have had a national and even international impact. But New York is also a city that was inhabited by millions of individuals and groups who, though unsung, are as much a part of the city's development as its more celebrated citizens. In recognizing the exceptional individual, we must not lose sight of these collective stories. Historic sites can help to tell those stories, as the National Park Service (NPS) has shown.

In 1993–94, the NPS, with the help of the Organization of American Historians, National Coordinating Committee for the Promotion of History, and American Historical Association, revised the thematic framework which governs its approach to history in the National Historic Landmarks, National Register, and other programs. The result is a series of preservation criteria set in a broad framework that includes social forces and sweeping historical themes that could provide a useful basis for thinking about New York's history.

Figure 6.3 This sign on Water Street in Lower Manhattan, designed by the public art
collaborative RepoHistory, marks the site of New York's slave market.

A few examples will suggest what we mean. While homes associated with
famous immigrants present the high points of the immigration story—its most
exceptional successes—the synagogues and burial societies of the Lower East
Side recall the lives of the great masses of immigrants at the turn of the century
(Figure 6.2). While the handsome apartment building at 555 Edgecombe
Avenue, in which Paul Robeson and Count Basie lived (a designated landmark), represents the development of Harlem through its most notable cultural
achievements, the more modest apartment building at 31 West 133rd Street—
had it survived—would have presented tangible evidence of a great population
movement which soon made Harlem the capital of black America. For it was
here, in 1905, that realtor Philip A. Payton moved Harlem's first African
American families. The home of Alice Paul, outside Philadelphia, speaks to the
heroic determination of the Women's Suffrage movement through the courageous efforts of one of its leaders. But women have displayed courage and
tenacity on smaller stages: as workers in department stores, garment factories,
offices, and homes. Their stories need telling, too.

To recognize and attempt to preserve the "typical" does not require us to turn our backs on the extraordinary. It does require us to open our minds to what is significant, remarkable, occasionally even marvelous in the lives of "ordinary" people. And it demands that we seek ways of presenting the "typical," not just for its own sake, but as the "epitome" of the most sweeping and dramatic episodes in our history.

The Centrality of Communities

New York, it is often said, is a city of neighborhoods. This task force prefers to think of it as a city of communities, a word that suggests groupings that sometimes transcend the geographic. While it is true that New York City residents often identify with their immediate neighborhood, whether that is Morrisania, Bedford Stuyvesant, or SoHo, it is equally true that many New Yorkers belong to communities based on professions, religious beliefs, or lifestyle. As our committee explored what we meant by history and examined ways to recognize that history in terms of the built environment, we concluded that community was an invaluable concept. The community is smaller than the city but larger than the individual. The distinctive life experiences of its members stand out more clearly than that of the city's residents as a group or individually. The history of communities thus mediates between the awesome scale of New York and the minutiae of individual experience.

Identifying the significant historical sites in a community's history calls for special survey techniques. Whereas a typical preservation survey might start by identifying a building type or architectural style, then cataloguing and comparing existing examples, a historical site survey typically starts with an understanding of how the community functioned—where people lived and worked, how they interacted socially, educated their children, worshipped, and entertained themselves—and then moves on to a listing of the buildings or places important in the life of the community, and finally to a survey of surviving examples.

The State of California's Ethnic Sites Survey showed how a community-oriented survey method can lead to an inventory of historically significant sites that speaks to community and universal values. The authors' recognition that the religious confraternities known as Sociedades Guadalupanas were central to California's Mexican communities led them to buildings which architectural historians might have overlooked. A barbershop was an important landmark to African American history; a canning factory, a ruined borax plant, a laundry, and a general store to the Chinese story; and a labor camp and a grammar school to the Japanese story. Each historical experience generated its own particular range of significant building types.

As an example, in New York it would be possible to apply this kind of community-oriented survey to the history of Mohawk steel workers who participated in the construction of the city's skyscrapers and bridges. The Verrazano Bridge is one of their great monuments and memorials. But their history as a community could perhaps better be told by sites in their downtown Brooklyn neighborhood, like the building occupied by the Wigwam

Bar on Nevins Street (Figure 2.1), a place not only of male drinking and companionship but also of weddings and other community celebrations; the Cuyler Church on Pacific Street (where a young Anglo came to minister to their community and published a Mohawk translation of the Bible); and Local 361 of the Association of Iron Workers on Atlantic Avenue. Similarly, the history of New York's rise to ascendancy in abstract art after World War II could be remembered through the most significant studios, galleries, and other gathering places where Abstract Expressionism was nurtured through interaction among artists and between artists and the public.

As these examples suggest, the places where communities gathered, where information was exchanged and bonds forged, can be particularly valuable in telling their stories. Because they are not always monumental in appearance, such sites may be easy to overlook and can be identified only through a survey process that is firmly rooted in the written, and sometimes in the oral, history of the community.

Interpreting Change Over Time

Buildings are not static. Often their appearance and configuration change with changing inhabitants and uses. Preservationists have long wrestled with the problem of how to restore a building that has undergone significant changes; practice has generally favored restoration to the original appearance. Even in the exceptional cases where a later "period of significance" is chosen, the interpretation remains static: the building is presented as an object which existed in a certain state at that moment and is revered for its associations with that particular moment. Yet buildings and places pick up significant associations along the way. A preservation practice that is sensitive to historical narrative will treasure and protect those associations wherever possible.

If the typical preservation approach presents the historic site reverently as if it were the cave of a famous hermit, our approach is to see historic sites as the shells of hermit crabs, used and reused by generations of occupants. By presenting sites dynamically, rather than statically, preservationists can provide imaginative access to the rich, confusing swirl of urban life that has passed through them.

Some of New York's "shells" bear the distinctive markings of their first occupants or constructors; the dissonance between those marks and their current appearance allows us to measure historical change. On the Lower East Side, buildings marked with the Jewish star of David today burst with immigrants from China and Vietnam; in Tribeca, dry goods warehouses— some still bearing their original occupants' company names—are now home to upper-middle-class professionals and successful artists; a once-great cinema in Harlem is now a Baptist church (Figure 6.2), while another in the South Bronx is a furniture store. But change to some of New York's most richly historic shells have not been so marked. A rowhouse in Brooklyn Heights, Cobble Hill, or Gowanus may have started as home to an upper-middle-class family, then been subdivided into single rooms for the elderly poor, and may now once again house a single well-to-do urban professional family, all with little exterior change other than in the style of the window blinds and the grime on the glass. The challenge for preservationists is not merely to save the building but to provide access to the sweep of its historical associations. This may mean retaining accretions or alterations even where they compromise the building's original design integrity. Or it may mean simply acknowledging its later history—including the events and forces that led to its preservation or rehabilitation—in its interpretation.

City of Layers

What is true of individual buildings is even truer of New York's neighborhoods. Dig down into the past of most neighborhoods and you will find a multi-layered story of immigration, settlement, social and geographic mobility, and ethnic succession—processes which are central to much larger American stories of migration, ethnic aspiration, and sometimes discrimination.

Visitors to New York have been especially aware of this ceaseless change and instability. Learning that Harlem (Figure 8.2) hadn't always been an African American community—that it had successively harbored Dutch, German, Irish, Italian, and Jewish immigrants—was one of Malcolm X's "biggest surprises" on moving there. "Each group left its deposits, as in geology," wrote Michael Gold in *Jews Without Money*, describing the Lower East Side's successive habitation by Native Americans, the Dutch, English, Irish, German, Italians, and Jews. One of the special opportunities of a historical and cultural preservation is to illuminate the processes of history that laid down those layers.

Some institutions have been successful at interpreting this layering. The Museum of Chinese in the Americas, for instance, has done an excellent job of presenting Chinatown's dual nature as a living Chinese community and as a neighborhood that was at various times home to large numbers of Irish, Italian, Jewish, and African American settlers. But marking the presence of former inhabitants within the actual spaces of a neighborhood can be much more difficult than doing so in museums, because such marking may be perceived as a challenge to the current inhabitants' legitimacy. Whether the site is a street in Brownsville once occupied by Jews and now by African Americans, or one in Corona once occupied by African Americans and now by Koreans, such enterprises will require diplomacy and efforts at mutual understanding.

There are, however, some relatively simple techniques that can recognize this layering. One is through the identification and interpretation of sites that trace a community's migration. Linking such sites could trace the African American community's trail from Lower Manhattan northward, that of the East European Jewish community from the Lower East Side to the Bronx and then on to the suburbs and Queens, and that of successive waves of Chinese immigrants from a localized Chinatown in Lower Manhattan into the former Little Italy and on to Flushing, Queens, and Brooklyn's Sunset Park.

Using birthplaces of well-known figures can demonstrate how one individual's rise represents not just his or her own upward mobility, but the aspirations of the group to which he or she belonged.

A particular challenge is to reveal historical layers whose traces have been erased by time or were never meant to be visible. Little Africa, the neighborhood just north of Manhattan's civic center where so many important African American institutions were founded in the early nineteenth century, has left few if any visible traces. Yet to allow it to vanish is to erase an important part of the city's history. A related challenge is to unmask important themes which by their very nature were invisible: In New York, for example, the earliest gay and lesbian bars of Greenwich Village were intentionally hard to identify—they had to be in order to protect their clientele. Yet even when physical traces of their presence have disappeared, such stories can lend richness to a neighborhood when they are brought to life through plaques, guidebooks, and walking tours. Not to do so serves no cause but the distortion of history.

Representing Diversity

New York has always been a culturally diverse city. This diversity, upon which visitors have always commented, offers a good foundation for a program of historical and cultural landmarks preservation. But it also poses a daunting challenge: how to present New York's many separate histories while also linking them into larger narratives of the city. This committee does not call for a single, overarching narrative (who, after all, would have the authority to prescribe it?), any more than we want to see the city's history splintered into countless "specific" narratives, each to all appearances unconnected to the others and speaking only to its adherents. We do urge preservationists and their partners to support multiple narratives than can bring the special insights of an ethnically or culturally specific point of view to bear on the city's history as a whole. We believe that supporting this kind of diversity—a diversity of opinion—can enrich our practice of protecting and interpreting historic sites. The following sections provide some suggestions for achieving this goal.

The Contribution of Culturally Specific History

Culturally specific histories have made a valuable contribution to our understanding of the past, and to our practice as preservationists. In California, the Office of Historic Preservation surveyed the state's five largest ethnic minority groups present between 1848 and 1898. Compared to the state's official roster of historical landmarks, the resulting list not only illuminated specific ethnic histories but also dramatically enriched the overall presentation of California history in ways that all citizens, visitors, and armchair travelers can appreciate.

Governmental powers have been used to do more than simply survey culturally specific histories. In 1990, Congress passed the Maine Acadian Culture Preservation Act, aimed at identifying and preserving sites, artifacts, and even cultural traditions associated with the Acadian community that settled in Maine after 1775. The act authorized a comprehensive study of Acadian culture; established an advisory commission; and gave the Department of the Interior authority to make agreements with private property owners for land purchases and the preservation and interpretation of Acadian culture, and to operate historic sites.

In 1992, the Pennsylvania Humanities Council initiated an innovative three-year project, "Raising Our Sites," which aimed to strengthen the presentation of women's history at fourteen historic sites throughout the state. At each site a team comprising board and staff members, volunteer docents, and local historians worked with outside consultants to develop programs and work plans aimed at improving exhibits, programs, archival collections, and the dissemination of information.

Even in the absence of official surveys or commissions, published guidebooks are helping to draw public and official attention to neglected cultural heritages and to increase the perceived value of sites associated with them. There are well-known national guidebooks to African American and women's history sites but few such efforts within New York City. A recent one is a brochure on gay and lesbian sites recently published by the Organization of Lesbian + Gay Architects and Designers.

These projects all share a dedication to restore their subject group to a historical record from which it has been omitted. "We were there," say advocates; "our presence should be reflected in the historical record." Many speakers at the public hearing concerning New York's eighteenth-century African Burial Ground spoke with great emotion about the site's role in restoring the community's past and placing it back in the historical picture. But what needs to be emphasized is that efforts to correct the historical picture benefit everyone—not just those newly restored to it, but all those who are part of it.

It should be noted that compensatory history—what historian and preservationist Daniel Bluestone has called the effort to "crowd more groups and histories, individually told, under preservation's existing tent"—is not the goal. We need narratives that bind the parts, explore their interrelationships, and speak across the gaps—narratives of shared experiences told from different points of view.

Describing an Elephant

History is interpretation, and the history of any place, event, or group is as much a product of the "facts" as of who is doing the telling. As we learn to interpret sites and events in ways that respect and encourage different versions of the same stories, conflicting accounts are inevitable. They should be welcomed. Two examples illustrate the way this encouragement of different points of view can enrich history for everyone.

According to a popular guidebook, the Downieville (California) of Gold Rush days was

> known for its spontaneous sense of justice. One collective citizen action earned
> national headlines. In 1851, a local dance hall girl fatally stabbed a Scottish

miner—in self-defense, she claimed, since he "pressed his attentions" on her. She was summarily convicted of her crime and lynched from a bridge over the Yuba River, the first woman in California executed by hanging.

In contrast to the guidebook's breezy dismissal of the woman involved, California's Ethnic Sites Survey gives her a name (Juanita), a place of origin (Mazatlán), and a nationality (Mexican). It adds that she had a good reputation in the community. It tells us that the drunken miner broke down her door and called her a whore in front of a crowd, and that his fellow miners rushed to hang her even though she may have been pregnant. This account places the incident within the context of the hostility toward Mexicans prevalent in California at the time, giving it greater resonance for all visitors.

In Seattle, an official plaque on the waterfront commemorates the American warships that "bravely repulsed" a group of Native Americans intent on attacking the settlement. A second plaque nearby, recently erected by two local artists, adds another point of view by telling visitors that the Native Americans had not come to attack the city but to protest the federal government's seizure of their lands. In both cases, choosing a different viewpoint resulted in a markedly different narrative from the accepted one.

In New York, broad historical themes such as the impact of public works and real estate development, of municipal services, of immigration, and of deindustrialization and community displacement offer numerous opportunities to explore the viewpoints and historical experiences of different groups within our society. Preservationists can contribute to this enrichment of history through their selection of sites as well as their interpretations.

Binding Us Together

As these examples illustrate, groups—even very different groups—and events do not exist in isolation. One reason many will find the "Ethnic Sites" interpretation of the Downieville lynching more satisfying than the popular guidebook's is that it links a dramatic incident to larger historical themes. It gives us insights into the relationships between very different groups of people occupying the same spaces. Interpreting relationships between disparate groups opens a window onto a larger and more meaningful narrative about American history. Illuminating the complex forces of acceptance and rejection that have shaped the history of many communities offers preservationists an opportunity to transcend simplistic views of cultural diversity or "multiculturalism." By recreating these links, preservationists can close in on the shared history that binds us together.

Another way to build a larger narrative is by focusing on historical experiences that have affected the lives of disparate groups within society. The experience of work, for example, is central to New York's development into an economic powerhouse. Work is an experience shared by almost all New Yorkers, regardless of occupation or economic status—from salsa musicians to stock brokers, Puerto Rican cigar makers to Native American steel workers, Jewish garment workers to Philippine nurses, teachers to tap dancers.

The history of work is woefully underrepresented in New York City, compared to many other places. In Lowell, Massachusetts, a National Historical Park and a Heritage State Park tell the story of mill workers. There, the National Park Service has preserved mill buildings, workers' dormitories, and industrial artifacts; mounted ambitious exhibitions; established a visitors' center with an excellent bookstore; published a guidebook; and developed a program of trolley and canal boat tours in order to preserve and present Lowell's industrial heritage.

In New York State's Capital District the Hudson-Mohawk State Heritage Area, also known as RiverSpark, tells the story of American labor and industry through a twenty-eight-mile heritage trail linking over sixty sites scattered across Watervliet, Troy, Green Island, Lansingburgh, Cohoes, and Waterford. In southwest Pennsylvania, the America's Industrial Heritage Project, funded with over half a million dollars of congressional appropriations, has empowered a Heritage Preservation Commission to develop a broad range of strategies for preserving the industrial heritage of nine counties. On the western shores of the Hudson River, Senator Frank Lautenberg of New Jersey has obtained federal funding to preserve, reuse, and interpret industrial sites in Perth Amboy, Trenton, and Paterson.

Yet in New York City, site of one of the world's great ports, of significant industries ranging from oil refining to dressmaking, of major labor unions including the ILGWU and Transport Workers Union, of Samuel Gompers and the American Federation of Labor, of the country's first Labor Day parade, of the Triangle Shirtwaist fire, of Susan B. Anthony's Working Women's Association, of A. Philip Randolph, and of dozens, if not hundreds, of working-class immigrant communities, there are few historic sites where visitors can learn about this heritage. Moreover, its survival is anything but assured: New York's most famous working-class neighborhoods, such as Chinatown, the Lower East Side (Figure 8.2), Little Italy, Hell's Kitchen, Red Hook, Gowanus, and Harlem as well as neighborhoods like Steinway, Sandy Ground, Ridgewood, and Belmont, remain almost entirely unprotected. So do the workplaces associated with the city's greatest industries, including garment manufacturing, maritime trade, printing and publishing, and public transit (Figures 6.5 and 8.7).

A program for preserving the history of work in New York might be symbolically anchored in Union Square, recently designated a National Historic Landmark. Union Square hosted the first Labor Day parade in 1882 and was headquarters for several major labor unions, including the ILGWU and the Amalgamated Clothing Workers. The square represents a chunk of New York's labor history and the many ethnic groups that participated in that history.

A program of tours and public art could be developed to interpret the rich labor history of Union Square itself as well as the surrounding neighborhood. At the same time, a committee of preservationists, historians, and labor leaders could work to identify other significant sites throughout the city. The selected sites could cover a wide range of building types, including workplaces, homes, popular gathering spots, union halls, streetcorner hiring sites, the routes of political marches, and the sites of important strikes. These sites could reflect the diversity of work experiences in New York—of taba-queros, garment workers, dock workers, restaurant workers, office and transit workers, railroad porters and domestics, nurses, and homemakers.

In addition to proposing sites for landmark designation, such a "labor history" committee could also develop interpretive programs. These could include posters on bus shelters or in subway cars (a format already used by Local 1199's Bread and Roses project); a permanent or semi-permanent public exhibition in building lobbies and subway stations; public service tele-vision and radio spots; and banners and/or commemorative observances along Seventh Avenue in the Garment District.

In addition, new interpretations could be developed for historic resources which have already been protected and celebrated for reasons other than their links to labor: for example, the SoHo Cast Iron Historic District, generally celebrated for its architectural richness and innovative construction techniques, could be interpreted to tell the story of workers who filled its factory and loft building. Interpretive programs in some of New York's elegant residential historic districts could be developed to tell the history of domestic work.

Finally, the program could include a major initiative by New York's history museums to tell the history of work and working people. The South Street Seaport Museum has ambitious plans for a permanent exhibition on the theme of work; the Brooklyn Historical Society is also developing exhibits on the subject. These are worthwhile efforts that should be studied and used as models by other institutions. The theme of work is universal; its development at historic sites and in institutions devoted to history can only enrich the general understanding and appreciation of a vital force that contributed to New York's greatness.

Crossing Lines, Healing Fractures

Our society is fractured in many directions, and the current emphasis on the separateness of different cultural groups is sometimes cynically misused to drive people further apart. While it is important to recognize and cherish the diversity of historical experience, preservationists should also seek opportu-nities to tell history in ways that reach across cultural lines. After the Crown Heights riots of 1991, three Brooklyn institutions—the Brooklyn Historical Society, the Society for the Preservation of Weeksville and Bedford Stuyvesant History, and the Brooklyn Children's Museum—showed the way to do this by joining forces to develop a series of exhibits and programs focusing on interactions between the Hasidic and African American commu-nities of Crown Heights. Preservationists can participate actively in this process through site selection and interpretation that respect the shared yet divergent experiences of people who may have inhabited and used the same spaces, but who have experienced them very differently. This does not mean trying to convince disparate groups to embrace a single viewpoint; it does mean presenting important issues in ways that promote understanding. It means choosing and interpreting landmarks in ways that not only reinforce community identity but speak to the outside world as well. It means sharing one another's histories.

Preserving Living History

Early preservationists recognized the importance of protecting places "where history happened." But how do you approach and evaluate a site where history—in the form of living traditions—is still happening? Do preservationists have a responsibility to protect aspects of the city's cultural legacy that may indeed be still part of a community's everyday experience? The concept of "social value," developed by heritage agencies in Australia and elsewhere, provides one of the best ways of approaching the knotty issues raised by such "living landmarks." The Burra Charter, developed by ICOMOS Australia, defines social value as embracing the "qualities for which a place has become a focus of spiritual, political, national or other cultural sentiment to a majority or minority group." The Australian Register of the National Estate, the equivalent of our National Register, explains further that places possessing social value are significant "because of strong or special associations with a community for social, cultural and spiritual reasons." An important paper by Chris Johnson, "What is Social Value?," was published by the Australian Government Publishing Service in 1992 and develops the idea further.

The concept of social value posits that feelings of attachment to places are fundamental to our identity as individuals and as community members. They anchor us to the world. Take the places away and our sense of security is weakened. Places that possess great social value may be public areas (Times Square, Brooklyn Heights Esplanade); informal meeting spots (the clock at the old Hotel Biltmore); entertainment venues (theaters, ball fields, community halls, beaches, piers, parks, restaurants, or bars); favorite shopping places (open-air markets, department stores, neighborhood shops); communities with special ethnic or occupational character (Little Italy, Sheepshead Bay); places associated with significant events (Stonewall Inn); commemorative places (cemeteries); or places with longstanding spiritual or religious attachments. They can provide links between past and present, help give disempowered groups back their history, anchor a community's identity, play a prominent role in a community's daily life, provide a distinctive feature within the cityscape, or provide a habitual community meeting place for public ritual or informal gatherings.

If we accept the importance of places like these—their "social value"— then we may conclude that heritage professionals "have lost touch with sentiments that inspire community love of a place and therefore action for its protection." We may also want to acknowledge that an understandable desire to be "rigorous and scientific," coupled with increasing pressure to create specialist roles in heritage conservation, may actually be endangering aspects of cultural heritage by further "distancing its conservation from its traditional guardians." To be fair, few if any guidelines exist to help preservationists define their engagement with concepts of social value, or with sites that embody living aspects of our history. Some indeed may wish to dismiss the entire issue as irrelevant or unprofessional; others may wish to pursue a more traditionally defined "historical" agenda by distinguishing between historic places and those of contemporary cultural significance. Yet, apart from the difficulty of drawing a clean line between the two, closer attention to the social value of places and their content of living history can enrich the practice of preservation and enlarge its constituency.

One needn't go around the world to find precedents for cultural preservation; much has already been done in this country. The United States Congress addressed the importance of our living cultural heritage through passage of the American Folklife Preservation Act of 1976. The act defined folklife as "the traditional expressive culture shared within the various groups in the United States: familial, ethnic, occupational, religious, regional." In 1980 Congress requested the Department of the Interior and the Library of Congress's American Folklife Center (created under the terms of the Folklife Preservation Act) to study the conservation of "intangible cultural resources." The result was an influential study, *Cultural Conservation: The Protection of Cultural Heritage in the United States* (Library of Congress, 1983). This called for an expanded program of "cultural conservation" focusing on heritage issues which affected "community cultural life." Ormond Loomis, its author, emphasized both preservation and encouragement and placed significant emphasis on documentation as a form of protection.

In 1992, the National Register of Historic Places issued *Guidelines for Evaluating and Documenting Traditional Cultural Properties*, which it defined as properties eligible for inclusion in the Register because of their "association with cultural practices or beliefs of a living community that (a) are rooted in that community's history, and (b) are important in maintaining the continuing cultural identity of the community." In issuing these guidelines, the National Park Service stated that "any comprehensive effort to identify historic properties in an area . . . should include a reasonable effort to identify traditional cultural properties." Though the National Register cannot list "purely intangible" cultural values, the guidelines called on preservationists to consider them together with the tangible sites, properties, or objects they inform.

Locally, City Lore, the New York Center for Urban Folk Culture, initiated a program called "Endangered Spaces" in 1988. In his description of the program, City Lore's director, Steve Zeitlin, wrote: "While historic preservationists have fought to preserve landmark buildings," the Endangered Spaces program is "concerned with the culture that brings those building to life." But City Lore also cares, far more than many folklife programs, for buildings themselves, places like the Essex Street Market, Brighton Beach Baths, Shapiro's Winery in the Lower East Side, Philip's candy store in Coney Island, fishing piers at Sheepshead Bay, and *casitas* in the South Bronx. Local establishments like these are valuable both as traditional gathering places and as supports for the memories and associations they evoke. Beyond their immediate communities, Zeitlin notes, they "play a vital role in the city's fragile human ecology, contributing to the integrity of neighborhoods and to the sense of continuity between past and present that renders urban environments habitable." City Lore seeks not only to save "living landmarks" like these, but to create a greater appreciation for the intangible values that make them important.

Mechanisms to protect socially valuable spaces are very limited at present; further study is urgently needed to develop policies that could help in such efforts. One area worth exploring is zoning, which offers some promise of help for both historical and cultural sites. The protection accorded to the world-famous views from the Brooklyn Heights Esplanade provides one precedent for protecting cherished public places. In a similar vein, a report recently published by the Parks Council recommends zoning regulations limiting building heights along the margins of public parks. Special Districts provide another precedent. New York's Zoning Resolution includes a number of Special Purpose Districts, many of which, like the Little Italy Special District, are intended to "preserve and strengthen the historical and cultural character" of particular neighborhoods. In general, they adopt a two-pronged strategy, one that stipulates acceptable uses while regulating aspects of bulk and appearance such as height and setback, street-level wall treatment, signage, and off-street parking. The Little Italy District attempts to encourage rehabilitation of existing housing, the Special Garment Center District to preserve industrial space and employment, the Special Midtown District to encourage retention of theaters through transfers of development rights. The Little Italy District regulations also list eighteen individual buildings whose demolition is discouraged, either because they are "socially or traditionally significant or because they are important physical influences in the life of the community." (The eighteen buildings appear to have been chosen primarily on the basis of their architectural qualities, but this is no reason why neighborhood historical and cultural factors could not form the basis for this or other such efforts.)

The success of Special Purpose Districts as a cultural conservation tool has been limited by their strategy of mitigating against the impact of projects rather than of taking positive action to preserve or enhance neighborhood character. Yet Special Districts have had some success. In Little Italy, for example, the public campaign to accord recognition to the neighborhood's special character—even more than ensuing regulations themselves—is widely credited with breathing new life into the district. Some would argue that the steady influx of Asians into the neighborhood is proof that zoning regulations are powerless to preserve a neighborhood's character in the face of demographic change, but this misses the point: the Little Italy Special District has succeeded insofar as it has helped to preserve the neighborhood's social value to the city and region at large as a venue for Italian dining and shopping, regardless of who lives upstairs. Special District zoning thus remains a promising, if limited, tool for cultural conservation.

The environmental review process provides other opportunities for preserving culturally significant sites, simply by providing another level of oversight. The State Environmental Quality Review Act's (SEQRA) definition of "environment" includes "existing patterns of population concentration, distribution, or growth, and existing community or neighborhood character." The City Environmental Quality Review (CEQR), which implements SEQRA within New York City, includes "the character or quality of . . . existing community or neighborhood character" in its definition of environment. These laws, like the National Environmental Policy Act, prescribe few effective remedies for harmful actions, but they do provide a forum for public review and debate of the impact of development projects on traditional aspects of neighborhood culture. Such reviews, even if not immediately productive, could, over time, be highly educational. State and federal review processes could also help to protect publicly owned places of "social value," like piers and boardwalks, from certain kinds of threats.

Beyond these limited protective tools, it is clear that mechanisms of encouragement are needed. The Mayor's Lower Manhattan Plan, adopted in 1995, provides subsidies for rehabilitation in the form of reduced property assessment and utility payments; the Citizens Housing and Planning Commission has recently recommended making similar support more broadly available to property owners, and the potential impact of measures like these on culturally valuable businesses is well worth study.

It is clear that places with social and cultural value, "living landmarks," are at risk in New York. Until more tools to protect them are available, preservationists can begin to make a difference by following the lead of the National Park Service's guidelines on traditional cultural properties and documenting living traditions, rituals of place, and relevant oral lore as part of every community survey. Such efforts to survey, list, document, and interpret socially valuable places will contribute in the long run to their preservation by increasing public understanding of their value and by creating an inventory of knowledge about their characteristics.

PARTNERSHIPS FOR PRESERVATION
Because historical and cultural sites don't necessarily release their meaning to the casual spectator, meaning needs to be teased out and explained. Preservationists, therefore, must be willing, indeed eager, to use every available resource to tell the stories that make places significant, and to tell them in a compelling fashion. The opportunities for interpretation are many and call on a wide range of skills and knowledge. Possibilities include plaques and markers, sculpture and mural paintings, lectures and sermons, museum exhibits and public programs, walking tours, guidebooks and leaflets, inserts in local newspapers, videos, public access television programming, commemorative observances, local newspaper articles, school projects, essay contests, storefront or bank lobby exhibits, posters, public service announcements, advertisements, block parties, street fairs, and house tours.

Many preservation groups are already devoting resources to interpretation. The Friends of the Upper East Side Historic Districts recently developed an exhibition of endangered sites which highlighted the stories of immigrant groups in those neighborhoods. The Greenwich Village Society for Historic Preservation has taken a special interest in that area's rich social history, developing children's walking tours that focus on the lives of young immigrants; an oral history project to collect the stories of the Village's preservation pioneers; and a series of meetings and tours to compare the historical experiences of Greenwich Village and Harlem. The Organization of Lesbian + Gay Architects and Designers has produced a leaflet map and guide to historic sites around the city. Under the banner of the National Historic Landmarks program, the Women's Landmark Project has not only carried out a nation-wide search for sites associated with women's history but has helped to reinterpret many popular sites.

The key to successful interpretation by preservationists may lie in finding partners who can contribute knowledge, production skills, and access to audiences. Such partners may include community boards, council members, borough presidents, community centers, neighborhood literacy programs, public libraries, nursing homes, artists and arts groups, local businesses, unions, newspapers, local bookstores, stationery stores, craft stores and neighborhood art centers, local development corporations, business improvement districts, merchants associations, banks, office building owners, historical societies, and museums. New York City's schools represent an enormously valuable resource for stimulating interest in historic sites. By devoting resources to interpreting historic sites, preservationists can not only bring history to public attention but can also increase the perceived value of landmarks. And by engaging in activities that increase their own usefulness and visibility within communities, preservation professionals can enhance their leadership role in the ongoing and important work of identifying and protecting historic sites.

The next section explores some of the ways in which partnerships can foster more effective interpretation.

Working With Communities

Some of preservation's greatest successes have come when preservationists have been in touch with and have advanced community interests. Building alliances with communities need not mean passively waiting for others to discover the value of preservation. Although our committee disagreed about many things, we all concurred that preservation decisions must be based not only on professional expertise but also on the feelings and ideas of communities and affinity groups. It would have been possible, indeed relatively easy, for this task force to propose a set of public history programs and policies that could be carried out by a small number of experts, but this would have flown in the face of the very kind of historical interpretation we are seeking. Our belief is that civic participation is essential if preservation is to be representative of all New Yorkers and of the broad sweep of the city's history.

Many models exist for developing history at the community level. One of the most interesting is represented by Centerprise, one of a number of community-based cultural centers established in London in the early 1970s and partly supported by public funds. Centerprise is located in a dense shopping street in the heart of working-class Hackney. Its activities are rooted in the specific culture and history of the neighborhood. When Centerprise's bookstore opened in 1971 it was the only one in Hackney; in addition to standard books it carries pamphlets and books on local history as well as books of particular relevance to the neighborhood's immigrant populations, such as bilingual children's books, Asian-language and Turkish books, and health and educational aids. An adjoining coffee bar serves inexpensive meals and provides a space for exhibitions, performances, and readings of work by local artists. A Reading Centre provides free literacy and basic math classes as well as referrals for other kinds of adult education. An Advice Centre helps residents with immigration, welfare, housing, employment, consumer, and debt problems, dispensing free advice in Urdu, Punjabi, Turkish, and sign language. A Publishing Project instigates and publishes autobiographies, oral histories, and studies of local history, organizes writers' groups, workshops, and readings, and provides a manuscript-reading service. Finally, Centerprise makes its meeting rooms available to community groups. In the historical works it has published, Centerprise, arguably, pays too little heed to the shaping influence and historical value of the built environment: it has not embraced preservation as an important goal. Yet Centerprise shows how an organization can nurture local history by rooting it in a community's day-to-day needs and by providing much-needed community services. Just as preservationists have found it possible to leap from "quality of life" issues like street paving and storefront design to concern for the preservation of a neighborhood's building stock, so Centerprise has bridged the gap from a neighborhood's need for basic cultural services to an interest in knowing—and telling—its history.

Institutions modeled on Centerprise could make a valuable contribution to New York. At the very least, preservationists and local historians can learn from it. Many existing New York City organizations already embody some aspects of Centerprise's mission. Some public libraries, for example, run language and literacy programs; the Brooklyn Children's Museum runs an after-school "latchkey" program; museums like the Museum of Chinese in the Americas, Caribbean Cultural Center, and the Jewish Museum offer their communities a focal point for cultural identity, provide important cultural services, and instill strong feelings of loyalty in return. Preservationists can assist such institutions—which already enjoy support and credibility in their communities—by offering expertise in the areas of identifying, protecting, and interpreting historical sites.

New York's schools, public, private, and parochial, offer extensive opportunities for meaningful collaboration based on neighborhood history. Yet working with schools seems daunting to many preservationists, who lack a dependable road map to working with the public school system. The Historic Districts Council has carried out a useful survey of elementary school programs focusing on the historic architecture of neighborhoods. At present there is no comparable resource for programs that deal with local history, nor is there a single obvious curricular route to instigating such programs. Success appears to depend primarily on developing a good relationship with a receptive school and an energetic, imaginative teacher.

One such program that has produced important results was undertaken at Louis Armstrong Middle School, IS 227Q, in Corona, Queens. As part of a collaborative agreement with the Board of Education, the Center for the Improvement of Education at Queens College augmented the school's staff with college faculty, graduate students, and consultants. One consultant was public historian Arthur Tobier, who developed a program in which students interviewed neighborhood residents. They discovered that a building they had passed numerous times without thinking much about it was a garment factory; through interviews they learned about the lives of workers there. The program's emphasis was on the discovery of such stories throughout the neighborhood. Parents as well as students and teachers became interested, and out of this school program grew an ongoing community history workshop dedicated to collecting, understanding, and passing on the neighborhood's history. Were preservationists to participate in such a project, they could not only contribute their skills but, in so doing, reshape the project to include greater attention to the preservation and marking of the built environment.

For Tobier, such projects exemplify what schools should be doing. He sees schools, ideally, as "community-based institutions" which draw curriculum from their communities: "With schools at their best," he writes,

> our curricular activities would need to bring into the school the narratives of
> the people who live and work in the community. Our children's sense of
> history would be brushed with an understanding of those strangers with whom
> they grow. . . . The school would endeavor, as a legitimate part of its work, to
> bring those who live in obscurity in the community out from the shadows.

Tobier has shown how to turn these ideals into a workable and successful program. Preservationists who believe in the value of historical sites and are willing to work with schools can use the same resources to great effect.

Involving Museums

History museums can and should play a larger and more active role in the preservation of historically significant sites. Even if every historic site in the city were preserved and marked, we would still need history museums to help us think and talk about them. In fact, history museums should be leaders in promoting discourse about our city's history and its implications for our future. By promoting such discussions, history museums can help provide the framework for preserving our historic sites.

New York has dozens of history museums, including institutions with a broad, city-wide mandate, such as the New-York Historical Society and the Museum of the City of New York; borough historical societies in Brooklyn, Queens, the Bronx and Staten Island; institutions with a community or culturally specific focus, such as the Museum of Chinese in the Americas, the Lower East Side Tenement Museum, and the Society for the Preservation of Weeksville and Bedford Stuyvesant History; museums devoted to a specialized subject area, like the Ellis Island Museum of Immigration, the South Street Seaport Museum, and the Transit Museum; and house museums like the Jumel Mansion, Rufus King Manor, and Bartow-Pell Mansion.

These museums could be contributing more than they currently do to the preservation and interpretation of historic sites that are not part of their actual physical plant. The vision of this committee is of a network of history museums that would actively lead the public in an ongoing discussion of New York's many histories and their relationship to our city's future and which would take part in identifying, preserving, and interpreting its historic sites. Some of the specific ways in which museums can do so include:

- *Exhibitions and programs on historical themes of broad contemporary relevance.* The histories of capitalism, finance, deindustrialization, neighborhood development and disinvestment, popular culture and religion, public education, and public services are examples of themes that have shaped and continue to shape the lives of every New Yorker. Compelling exhibits on topics like these at New York's leading history museums would engage broad interest and spark vital public discussion. They would also provide a context for the work of New York's smaller museums and for the interpretation of historical sites.
- *Provision of a centrally located showcase for the city's local history museums.* New York's city-wide history museums could provide a much-needed showcase for smaller institutions by holding regular exhibits and events highlighting the work of local history museums. (The community gallery run by the Museum of the City of New York offers a useful model.) Additionally, they could serve as distribution points for information about the activities of local history museums and provide technical assistance to smaller museums. (The Historic House Trust offers a valuable model, as does the Smithsonian Institution's museum internship program, in which interns are shared by a major Washington museum and by a smaller institution in another city.) Were the New-York Historical Society or the Museum of the City of New York to take such steps, those institutions could not only bring the work of New York's lively local museums to the attention of visitors, but could also build up their own constituency among the city's residents.
- *Taking a leadership role in preserving community history outside their walls.* Community-based museums like the Schomburg Center, the Museum of Chinese in the Americas, and the Weeksville Society, as well as some house museums, are already demonstrating how museums can make history a vibrant part of a community's cultural life. Community-based institutions could also use their influence and resources to help spur public involvement in the process of identifying, celebrating, interpreting, and preserving significant places within their communities.

They can contribute further by participating in neighborhood surveys, working with schools and community groups, organizing local landmark committees, sponsoring oral history research, presenting lectures and walking tours, contributing to plaque and marker programs, and publishing booklets and maps. And they can work with local libraries, schools, and businesses to present exhibitions that focus on significant sites and the memories and traditions associated with them.

Local history museums and societies possess essential skills for preserving community history; working with preservation groups, they can play a leadership role in protecting New York's historical and cultural sites. To assume that role, museums will need increased public support for building upkeep and utilities, as well as line-item funding in the city budget. This aid could be delivered by giving certain institutions the kind of assistance currently reserved for the thirty-one premiere institutions housed in city-owned buildings and known as the "Cultural Institutions Group." The Society for the Preservation of Weeksville and Bedford Stuyvesant History, whose buildings are a resource of city-wide significance, could qualify, as could the Louis Armstrong House if it is reorganized as a vital public museum.

Neighborhood-based history museums, which cannot match the private fundraising capability of large and well-connected central institutions, might be able to stretch scarce resources by sharing them more intensively. The Historic House Trust currently provides a vehicle for communal fundraising and public relations for sixteen house museums located in city parks, as well as a mechanism for apportioning Parks Department services, such as the use of a skilled restoration crew. The model of the Historic House Trust could conceivably be extended to neighborhood history museums and to areas such as public relations, fundraising, and advocacy.

Developing Tourism

Tourism to New York is growing, particularly among international visitors. Increasingly, sophisticated visitors want to learn more about the history of New York and its communities, yet the tools for helping them find their way are strikingly inadequate. New York's history museums and its historic communities have not done enough to reach out to these visitors, quite possibly because the task of reaching the market exceeds the resources of all but the largest institutions.

A good starting point might be joint publication of a brochure featuring a number of smaller institutions, which could be distributed at the city's major visitor centers and hotels. Ultimately, however, a more aggressive and interactive approach will prove more effective. A tourism coordinator, working for a coalition of historic museums and sites, could help local history museums develop programs comprising an exhibit, a walking or bus tour of historic sites, and possibly neighborhood shopping and dining. The coordinator could also be responsible for the logistics of bus charters, parking arrangements, and so forth. She or he could not only provide information to tour operators and guides but organize visits. A tourism coordinator could be based at one of the city-wide history museums or at a not-for-profit such as the Municipal Art Society.

Preservation and Public Art

For many people, the phrase "public art" conjures up an image of grandiose and somewhat irrelevant monuments standing in splendid isolation. But unlike the celebratory statuary of another era or the abstract art of recent decades, some of the liveliest new public art draws deeply on the history of urban communities. In short, public art can be, in Gail Dubrow's words, a "magnet attracting public interest to historic places." Its power to galvanize public attention depends in part on its imagery, but begins, long before the art work materializes, in the process of selecting sites, shaping themes, and developing the appropriate form. Public art may take shape as a sculpture, but it could also be a bench, a manhole cover, placards, postcards, signs on buses, advertisements in newspapers, audiocassettes, television broadcasts, children's photography, or an oral history project. Artists are often eager to work with local historians as well as urban designers; they and the agencies that hire them may also be willing to work closely with communities.

Four ambitious public art projects, in Los Angeles, Seattle, Charleston, and Boston, illustrate the power of public art to interpret historic sites and themes. Seattle's deep commitment to public art centers on its Percent For Art ordinance. Passed in 1973, the program was responsible by the early 1990s for generating approximately thirty art projects per year. Seattle has taken a strongly site-specific approach to its public art and has emphasized community participation, inclusion of culturally diverse groups at all levels of decision-making, and the involvement of underserved audiences and artists. Installations have included street paving, street furniture, and electrical substations, as well as figural art works based on the history of communities, like Richard Beyer's *People Waiting for the Interurban* (1979), which recalls the rail line (now closed) whose arrival sparked the neighborhood's founding and shaped its working-class character.

In 1991, the Seattle Art Commission created a series of temporary works at sites chosen by artists. The Commission provided a talented historian as consultant to the artists, and many of the resulting works drew deeply upon the collaboration. Working with the Port of Seattle, artists Gloria Bornstein and Donald Fels designed a series of markers, placed next to the official historical plaques lining the waterfront, which presented an alternative history of the waterfront. These were so successful that the Port of Seattle is considering making them permanent. An accompanying "interactive voice library" provided further information to visitors and allowed them to record their own comments. Martha Rosier produced a series of public-service television announcements called "Seattle: Hidden Histories," which told stories about Seattle history from the perspective of various ethnic groups.

In 1991, the Spoleto Festival used Charleston, South Carolina, as a site for an ambitious outdoor sculpture exhibition modeled on similar shows in Europe. In the curator's words, each of the festival's eighteen works, almost all temporary, "addressed a location, not just from a design and physical point of view, but also in relation to a social and cultural past." The installations became like chapters in a book that together told a larger, more complete, and alternative story of Charleston. Some were located within historic houses open to the public, others in the city's streets and public spaces. They included powerful meditations on slavery, the Civil War, and the history of industry in Charleston. Because the project was conceived of more as an international art exhibit than a civic art program like Seattle's, community involvement was not as extensive as it could have been, and many visitors criticized the exhibition's sense of detachment.

A 1983 project in Boston provides yet another model. In that year, the Massachusetts Bay Transportation Authority retained a not-for-profit agency, UrbanArts, Inc., to manage its Southwest Corridor public art project, part of a massive building campaign affecting a number of diverse neighborhoods. Residents saw the project as a way to represent their communities to themselves and to the outside world and to enhance the sense of place within their neighborhoods. Their goals for community participation and expression went beyond traditional public art.

For each station, a community-based site committee was responsible for developing a community profile, participating in the artist selection process, and contributing to the project's mission and direction. In addition, a series of educational programs eventually involved theatrical productions, off-site exhibitions, the collection of oral histories, photographic documentation of communities in transition by students and professionals, poetry readings in local libraries, and the permanent installation of a unique "anthology" of poetry and prose by local urban writers. The photography project, focusing on the effects of relocation within communities, was carried out by teams of high school students working with professionals. The Southwest Corridor project's most distinctive contribution may lie less in the permanent works of art produced than in the process which shaped them. The consultant Pamela Worden believes that the participatory nature of the project "generated a sense of ownership of place, the right on the part of residents to define and redefine themselves, and, most especially, to project their existence into the future."

The projects described above have all been government sponsored, but perhaps the most remarkable public art project to explore historical themes was developed apart from any official sponsorship by a small not-for-profit organization in Los Angeles, The Power of Place. Founded by UCLA professor Dolores Hayden in 1982, The Power of Place set out to identify and celebrate landmarks of ethnic, women's, and labor history, and to provide witness to some of the ways in which Angelenos had earned their livings—a profoundly important but largely unrecognized historical theme. In 1985, a guidebook to over thirty such downtown sites was published: some had recognized historic buildings that needed new interpretation and marking; others had buildings whose historic value had not yet been recognized; still other sites had no historic buildings at all. Public art was to be a key interpretive component at many of these locations.

A parking lot where Biddy Mason's home once stood became the site of two related art installations. Biddy Mason was an African American who gained her freedom from slavery, became a midwife, and founded the first predominantly African American church in Los Angeles. With the collaboration of the Community Redevelopment Agency, a sculptural assemblage recalling Mason's life and house was placed in the elevator lobby of a new development at the site. Outside the building, an eighty-foot-long poured concrete wall was ornamented with granite panels telling Biddy Mason's story through a portrait, a midwife's bag and scissors, Mason's freedom papers and homestead deed, and historical texts. A timeline of Mason's life was juxtaposed with maps showing the city's growth.

Hayden and her colleagues understood that the creation of site-specific art was just one part of a larger strategy for restoring Biddy Mason's story to the consciousness and cityscape of Angelenos. They augmented the art works with a limited-edition artist's book, an inexpensive poster, and a series of articles about Mason. Here and in other projects, they also used the art installations to generate and sustain community involvement in ways that ranged from picking sites that would generate high pedestrian counts to arranging community workshops and dedicatory ceremonies. Biddy Mason's descendants participated in the dedication of the wall, which has become a favorite place for snapshots.

The opportunities to achieve comparable results in New York are enormous, as are the resources for creating public art: Arts for Transit and the city's Percent for Art program have already been responsible for sponsoring art in the subways, schools, and elsewhere. The Public Art Fund, a not-for-profit organization, has also sponsored major public art projects. RepoHistory, an artists' collaborative, has produced temporary sign projects in Lower Manhattan and Greenwich Village and is developing projects elsewhere in which community input is an important part of the process (Figure 6.3). A new foundation called Minetta Brook is dedicated to producing public art based on collaborations between artists and local historians and is considering several possible themes for a major project.

Preservationists can look at New York's abundant public art possibilities on two levels: while the finished works enhance the cityscape and aid in a greater appreciation of history, the process of developing the art has the potential to foster creative collaborations between communities and professional historians, artists, preservationists, and funders.

Plaques and Markers—Pros and Cons

Far less expensive than most other forms of public art, plaques can be visually powerful and thought provoking. They offer a direct and attainable way for communities to mark sites, and they provide practical and affordable opportunities for collaboration between preservationists, artists, historians, and communities. In our conversations with community leaders and historians, we found broad support for historical plaques and markers. Some preservationists, however, view plaques with suspicion, fearing they will deface landmark buildings or be employed in lieu of true preservation. These are legitimate concerns. Yet, properly used, plaques are the allies of preservation, and campaigns to erect them can foster pride in local history and support the growth of new constituencies for historic sites and their preservation.

Unlike cities such as London, Dublin, or Charleston, New York has never had a sustained, institutionalized plaque program. This committee considered the merits of such programs—official recognition, broad coverage, and graphic consistency—but does not recommend such a plan for New York. We are in entire support of the Landmarks Preservation Foundation's recently initiated historical plaque program, but would prefer to see it as one component of a broader interpretive scheme rather than as a model for a single, official city-wide plaque program. The reason is simple. If plaques are to be effective vehicles for community organizing—or for conveying diverse historical viewpoints—then local campaigns are preferable to a single, city-wide program.

Local site-marking campaigns can be spearheaded by historical societies and museums, or by cultural centers and community organizations. Schools have initiated significant local history projects which could form the basis for public art and marker programs. The Bronx Landmarks Task Force, perhaps in combination with the Bronx Council for the Arts, could turn its accumulated knowledge of Bronx history and sites into an ambitious marker program. Local religious and political organizations can also make important contributions, as can senior residences. And of course community-based preservation organizations can play a leading role in public art and marker projects, as Landmarks Harlem! has done with its Harlem Landmarks Trail. The Friends of the Upper East Side Historic Districts' recent exhibition on the "other East Side," or the Organization of Lesbian + Gay Architects and Designers' guide to historic sites could form the basis for significant marker or public art programs.

Most city-wide public art agencies have the capacity to help initiate or lend significant support to community-based historical plaque programs. Both the Department of Cultural Affairs and the New York State Council on the Arts have supported plaque programs. Another promising basis for historical marker programs exists in the City Council's street renaming program, which has renamed dozens of streets—often to celebrate local figures. Community involvement in renaming is the rule, and the signs are frequently inaugurated with festivals or observances which unite community members in commemorative rituals. Were the new street signs augmented with historical plaques or other site markers telling the story behind the new name—or for that matter explaining existing names that reflect local history—street namings and renamings could become a catalyst for community-based historic interpretation.

Plaques are an old idea for marking sites, but they need not be simple ceramic or metal shields imprinted with information. Some recent projects demonstrate how the old idea of plaques and site markers can be made new again through the use of new technologies or the adaptation of older marking devices. In the spring of 1994, for example, a historic preservation studio at Columbia University proposed mounting a series of viewing machines along Manhattan's 57th Street. Resembling the familiar binocular telescopes found on the Staten Island ferries and at other popular lookout points, the Columbia versions would offer visitors historical video images of a site. Visitors would be able to contribute their own thoughts or memories to a computerized database.

Computers can also be used in lieu of plaques to provide information in an interactive way, as do the two computer screens installed in information kiosks at City Hall. The use of advanced audio headsets is currently being studied for Lower Manhattan's Heritage Trail. The dynamic and interactive marking of sites through sophisticated audio and video technology is a welcome development, but these systems are expensive and require intensive maintenance if they are not to become broken toys. If site markers are to be a useful vehicle for stimulating community participation and projecting community voices, then more traditional markers, employing relatively simple, accessible, and inexpensive media and technologies, will remain a logical choice.

Regardless of technology, good historical markers share a few important characteristics:

- *A good marker combines a good story and a good location.* It communicates that there is something special about the place— something happened not just anywhere, but right here—and it links that something to larger historical themes. Because a plaque has to speak to a community that may be familiar with the site as well as to strangers, the plaque's content, both visual and literary, must attract and reward their attention. A good plaque should be serious, but can also be fun.
- *Effective markers stand at appropriate and prominent locations.* Where will the largest number of passersby be exposed to the plaque? Where will current site conditions be most conducive to explaining the plaque's historical theme? Of various historically plausible sites, which is symbolically the most appropriate at which to discuss the theme?
- *Effective markers attract and hold attention.* Whatever the context, a plaque should catch and hold the eye of the maximum number of visitors. It need not be attached to a building to do this. In Seattle, artists have used banners and tablets attached to railings to commemorate the neighborhood's musical and theatrical past. Sometimes an unusual choice of location, like the tablets set into the sidewalks in front of the Second Avenue Deli and on West 52nd Street, can draw attention to a small, reticent plaque.
- *Effective markers present information in generous, yet not overwhelming, amounts.* Plaques with too little information—which announce that so-and-so was born on the spot without explaining why it matters—fail to tell history: they appear to exist solely for the benefit

of those already "in the know." Plaques with too much information leave the visitor equally frustrated and uninformed. The right amount of information is whatever gives the reader a clear understanding of why the site and its history are worth commemorating.

- *Effective markers link history with current concerns.* Plaques that interpret the city's streets and buildings for the people who live there are most effective when they engage people's current concerns. A site may be timeless, but a timeless plaque will likely be a lifeless one.

- *Effective markers present or invite different points of view.* Historical markers acknowledging diversity of outlook engage visitors' imaginations by prompting active choices. This can be accomplished by erecting a new plaque as a commentary on an existing plaque; by erecting two or more new plaques as commentaries on each other; by presenting contrary statements within a single plaque; by posing a direct question to the visitor; or by presenting a deliberately provocative visual image.

- *Effective markers balance text with compelling visual images.* Images that capture some essential aspect of the story attract attention and make information memorable. RepoHistory's Lower Manhattan signs juxtaposed images on one side with text on the other. Each seemed to comment on the other. Though modest in scale and materials, the signs became public art works.

- *Effective markers engage curiosity and prompt thought.* Historical markers are not there merely "for the record"; their perusal should be a positive pleasure. If it is, they will live on in memory.

- *Effective markers direct the visitor to related sites.* Historic sites rarely exist in isolation. Plaques directing visitors to thematically related sites magnify their impact. Plaques placed in groups, as part of walking tours or trails, can do this with special effectiveness.

Spreading the Word

Researching, designing, fabricating, and installing a good plaque is only half the job of marking a site because, in a sense, a plaque is a pretext for involving people in a site's preservation, a source of talking points about its meaning and future. The next step is to let people know the marked sites exist. Many cities do this by including mention of marked historic sites in walking tours or trails. Many such trails exist outside New York: for example, Boston's Freedom Trail, Florida's Black Heritage Trail, and the Women's History Trail in upstate New York. Interest in trails is growing in New York City. RepoHistory's Lower Manhattan Sign Project constituted an exciting temporary trail in Lower Manhattan in 1995. Lower Manhattan's Heritage Trail is up and running; color-coded street markers and a keyed booklet now guide visitors on several walks through the district. In 1994, Landmarks Harlem joined with the City College Architectural Center and the West Harlem Community Organization to inaugurate a Harlem Landmark Trail along Adam Clayton Powell, Jr., Boulevard.

Opportunities for additional trails are almost unlimited. An African American heritage trail could extend from Lower Manhattan to Harlem, allowing visitors to trace the growth and movement of Manhattan's African American community over more than 350 years. (A grant from the Municipal Art Society is helping by providing funds for research on churches along the trail.) A labor history trail could be anchored in Union Square, and could wind through Chinatown, where sweatshops still operate, and on to the Garment District. Or it could focus on the history of maritime labor and labor unions with a trail that starts at the South Street Seaport Museum, with its views of the Brooklyn docks, and then wends its way to the Hudson River piers. An immigration trail could be anchored at Castle Clinton, a Jewish heritage trail (possibly extending into Brooklyn and the Bronx) on the Lower East Side, a Gay and Lesbian liberation trail in Greenwich Village, and an American literature and journalism trail in Lower Manhattan. A women's history trail would fill a real void in New York and would be widely visited.

The value of a marker can also be amplified through a descriptive leaflet or brochure that visitors can take away with them. Producing leaflets need not be expensive, and banks, businesses, or local newspapers may be willing to underwrite them, thereby initiating partnerships upon which preservationists can build. Distributing the leaflets is the challenge. Not only must appropriate spots be identified and secured but they must be kept stocked and maintained throughout the project's life. Distribution opportunities will depend on the neighborhood. In Philadelphia, Bicentennial brochures were widely distributed in public buildings throughout the center city area, an approach which would work well in Downtown Brooklyn or Manhattan's Civic Center (where a guidebook produced by the Municipal Art Society, the *Juror's Guide*, is already distributed in courthouses). Banks, office lobbies, restaurants, bars, newsstands, local businesses, public libraries, cultural and social centers, history museums, and bus shelters may also provide opportunities to reach neighborhood residents or workers.

Mechanisms for disseminating local history information to out-of-town visitors are currently very limited. However, a tourism marketing consortium, like the one proposed above, could provide access to the display racks at the visitors centers at Columbus Circle and the World Trade Center, which few local history or preservation societies can currently afford. And were the New-York Historical Society and the Museum of the City of New York to act as showcases for the city's local history museums, they too could serve as excellent distribution points for information about historical trails around the city.

THE LANDMARKS PRESERVATION COMMISSION: A KEY PLAYER IN CONSERVING NEW YORK'S HERITAGE

This committee was initially charged with answering a single question: Should the Landmarks Preservation Commission use its power to protect New York's historical and cultural sites? The committee's answer was a resounding yes, and it concluded that in many cases a great public benefit would be served by protecting historic sites from unregulated change or destruction. More eloquent and compelling than the committee's views, however, are the words of the 1965 Landmarks Law itself. Its statement of public purpose speaks of the power of landmarks to stir civic pride. It never refers to architectural value alone, but speaks of "cultural, social, economic, political and architectural history," and calls upon the Commission to "safeguard the city's historic, aesthetic and cultural heritage, as embodied and reflected in" sites of "special historical or aesthetic interest or value."

Those words recall the earliest days of this country's preservation movement. In 1850, for example, New York State purchased the Hasbrouck House, General Washington's headquarters in Newburgh. A State Assembly committee explained at the time that:

> if our love of country is excited when we read the biography of our revolutionary heroes, or the history of revolutionary events, how much more will the flame of patriotism burn in our bosoms when we tread the ground where was shed the blood of our fathers, or when we move among the scenes where were conceived and consummated their noble achievements.

High-flown rhetoric, perhaps, but the preservers of Hasbrouck House well understood the power of historic places to stir the imagination, a power that has not diminished with time. For our committee, then, the question moved from *whether* to preserve historical and cultural sites, to *which* and *how*. How, specifically, can deserving sites be rationally selected and, once selected, how can they be equitably and intelligibly regulated?

The Landmarks Commission has never entirely neglected its broader historical and cultural mandate. Over the years it has designated many sites of great historical import from colonial and Revolutionary-era wood frame houses to Broadway theaters and skyscrapers, all of which tell important stories of the city's development. But, despite these worthy efforts and the law's clear intent with respect to historically important structures and sites, the Commission has tended to favor architectural criteria in its decision-making. It was a tendency fostered by the climate of the 1960s with its tragic architectural losses, coupled with the fierce assault on neighborhoods by urban renewal and highway programs. It was a tendency, moreover, that was largely in harmony with the wishes of professional and community-based preservationists. The challenge now facing the Landmarks Commission is to address the preservation of New York's historically and culturally important sites in a more determined, systematic, and thorough way.

In making this recommendation, the committee considered several ways of proceeding. One was to advance a list of, say, fifty or one hundred potential landmarks for designation. We rejected that approach because it would contradict our belief in the value of civic participation and of an ongoing process of discussion and action that would embrace many different voices. Another possibility was to urge the Landmarks Commission to undertake a comprehensive survey of the city's history, like the "theme studies" carried out by the National Historic Landmarks program. This, too, was rejected, because any such massive, top-down survey would likely fall short of encompassing the histories of New York's many and diverse communities, and could impede the Commission's efforts to build the partnerships it must foster with those communities. We also felt it could hamper the Commission's ability to act quickly if rapid action were needed to protect a site not included on the list.

The approach we detail below will take longer to carry out. It will be harder to control; its results are less predictable. Yet it will draw many more people into the landmark process, will help foster a civic dialogue about history, and will evolve as the city's history—and future—evolves.

Though we are proposing a long-range plan, we would urge the Commission to begin filling the gaps in the record immediately by designating important historical sites that have already been considered: for example, the remnants of the nineteenth-century African American oystering town of Sandy Ground, the remaining undesignated portions of the brickmaking town of Kreischerville (both in Staten Island), the Steinway workers' houses (Queens), the heart of Tin Pan Alley, represented by the Brill Building in Times Square. It could additionally designate a group of landmarks that exemplify profoundly important and relatively underrepresented and unprotected aspects of our history such as immigration (Chinatown and the Lower East Side, Figure 8.2), labor struggles (the Union Square area), and the Harlem Renaissance.

More important, ultimately, than a list of such immediately achievable landmark designations will be the creation and nurturing of a public process that supports the protection of our history and culture as an ongoing—and never ending—project. That means, first of all, a survey process that is attuned to historical and cultural sites and that fosters partnership with communities and collaboration with a variety of disciplines. It also means a clear yet flexible understanding of what qualities make a historic site a potential landmark. It means, finally, an understanding of how historic sites can be regulated and, even more fundamentally, a level of confidence that they can be successfully regulated. Each of these areas is dealt with in turn in the following sections.

Toward a New Surveying Process

Because historical and cultural landmarks elude traditional surveying methodology, with its bias toward architectural connoisseurship, they pose challenging problems for Landmarks Commission staff. A historical and cultural site survey typically begins with an analysis of the historical themes, communities, or lifeways under consideration, rather than with a search for buildings. This analysis leads to identification of representative sites and building types. This, in turn, can be amplified with a condition survey which identifies the types of resource that are the rarest and most threatened. To achieve maximum effectiveness the survey process should be flexible, open-ended, and very public. Its success will depend on building effective partnerships. Experts in oral history, folklore, urban history, geography, and other fields, as appropriate, should be involved early in the process.

Even more important is community participation from the outset, when the basic approach to historical themes or lifeways is being established. This will ensure that preservationists understand the community's history as told from within. Community participation can then be maintained throughout the survey process, as sites are identified, weighed, and documented. Later in the process, public forums at local historical societies or other civic organizations can be used to discuss potential designations long before formal designation hearings are held. Surveys like these can not only lead to good preservation planning; they can also enrich a community's civic life and indeed that of the entire city.

One consequence of carrying out a survey in this way is that preservationists may at times feel pressed to include sites whose significance they would not ordinarily have recognized on their own. Though this may be perceived by some as a threat to professional standards, it may equally be an expansion of vision. The guidelines outlined below will help ensure a rigorous process of assessment, but the key question to ask at this point in the survey is whether the site in question has a significant story to tell about the historical theme or community under review, regardless of preconceptions about aesthetic merit or architectural significance.

Surveys like this could conceivably be funded with grants from the New York State Humanities Council or from the National Endowment for the Humanities. Universities with strong community-oriented history or archives programs, such as the American Social History Project at Hunter College, the archives and public history programs at New York University, and the LaGuardia and Wagner Archives at LaGuardia Community College, could assist in organizing and carrying out such surveys. However these surveys are funded and organized, they can best be understood as collaborative processes in which community memories and values are drawn out, shaped, tested, and refined with the help of historians, folklorists, urban geographers, and preservation planners—and vice versa.

Standards for Designation

The challenge of distinguishing historical sites that merit landmark designation from others which do not has caused considerable anxiety. Some have called for written rules which could set a clear and unchanging standard. Others have argued that, by contrast with architectural excellence, there is simply no objective standard for historical significance. Both attitudes miss the point. The Landmarks Commission has never judged architectural significance according to written rules. Had such rules been drafted at the Commission's founding in 1965, neither the Chrysler Building nor the Jackson Heights Historic District could have been designated. Had they been drafted ten years earlier, neither could Carnegie Hall, the Woolworth Building, the Upper West Side, SoHo, or Ladies' Mile. The architectural taste of the times would not have recognized these buildings as worthy of preservation. Yet all have become cherished parts of our cityscape, landmarks of unquestioned worth.

Neither architectural nor historical significance can be reduced to a formula. Both are based upon generally acknowledged standards that evolve over time. The Landmarks Commission's ability to make appropriate choices has never stemmed from rigid rules but rather from a strong social consensus in favor of preserving important architecture, coupled with high standards of professional staff work, a strong and independent Commission, and an effective public process for reviewing designations. The thirty-year rule—that a building (or the historical events associated with it) must be at least thirty years old to qualify for designation—has effectively protected the process from faddism. The same combination of factors—and not a rigid set of rules—will provide the best underpinnings for a program of historical and cultural designations and will lead most reliably to sound designation decisions.

The following guidelines offer a framework for evaluating nominations for landmark designation:

- *Designate sites whose existence or appearance significantly aids our ability to understand or remember important historical or cultural values associated with them, or to continue a historically important cultural activity associated with them, and whose alteration or disappearance would diminish those abilities.* It is easy to think of buildings that help us retell and understand some chapter of the past. The small synagogues of the Lower East Side (Figure 6.2), touching in their modest simplicity, help us understand the lives and aspirations of their congregations, and of the immigrant communities they represented. Without the continued presence of these buildings, it would be much harder to understand this chapter in New York's history. The African Burial Ground (Figures 7.1 to 7.3) has proved to be a remarkable resource not only for understanding the lives of eighteenth-century black New Yorkers but actually for remembering them, since before the Burial Ground's discovery they had been virtually forgotten. Now the Burial Ground has become a touchstone of historical memory for all New Yorkers.

  Two tests can be useful in assessing a site's value as a spur to memory. One is to ask whether there is a connection between some aspect of its appearance and the historical theme in question. In the case of the synagogues described above, it is the very modestness of their scale and design that speaks to us. At Jarmulowsky's Bank, also on the Lower East Side, it is the opposite: the structure's overweening height and grandeur help explain Jarmulowsky's hold on the imaginations (and money) of his immigrant community—and the impact of the bank's collapse. Another test is to ask how our ability to remember would be affected if the site were destroyed or altered. Although there is almost nothing about the African Burial Ground today that suggests its eighteenth-century appearance, it is clear that unregulated digging could destroy both its historical evidence and its emotional resonance. The changes approved by the Landmarks Preservation Commission to the Eighth Street Playhouse are regrettable for a similar reason. The odd, guitar-shaped brick bulge which had marked its facade since 1970 was a feature added by Jimi Hendrix to accommodate his Electric Lady recording studios; its removal diminishes our ability to recall that aspect of the building's (and the city's) history.

The National Register applies a test, known as the "integrity" criterion, which requires that a historic site retain the "essential physical features that made up its character or appearance during the period of its association" with an important historic event. We prefer, for New York City landmarks, the concept of "intelligibility": does the site's appearance help significantly to illuminate its historical associations?

- *Designate sites whose appearance contributes significantly to the symbolism, imagery, mythology, or folklore of New York and its communities, and whose alteration or disappearance would diminish that contribution.* The famous Times Square ball drop, the ball whose descent has marked the New Year for millions of people around the world since just after the turn of the century, is the centerpiece of an important urban ritual. The space of Times Square, essential for the assembly of crowds, is as integral to this culturally significant site as the great pop art neon spectaculars that visually define it. Both the Empire State Building and the Brooklyn Bridge form so essential a part of New York's mythology, folklore, and image that their disappearance is almost unthinkable. Both are designated landmarks. So is the marvelous ensemble of buildings that helps define the experience of swimming and socializing at Orchard Beach. Yet, the towers and canyons of Lower Manhattan, forming one of the city's iconic images, are still imperfectly protected, despite significant recent gains. If they were to be replaced by boxy buildings in open plazas an essential image of New York would be lost.

- *Designate sites with regard to their historical and cultural significance alone, where appropriate.* This may seem self-evident, yet the suggestion that sites of historical and cultural merit must also possess architectural distinction in order to warrant landmark designation is still often made. The Landmarks Law itself gives no support to this requirement, which would impose a narrow view indeed of our history. In fact, many of our more powerful historic sites (including some landmarks) are not aesthetically distinguished: the houses of Kreischerville and Sandy Ground, the Stonewall Inn, Louis Armstrong's House (Figure 2.3), the African Burial Ground, or the Lower East Side's "Pig-Market."

In arguing that historic sites can merit protection for their historical values we are not asking for a redrafting of the accepted professional definition of what makes buildings and places visually and experientially meaningful; rather we are asking for an expansion of that definition to one that embraces the far broader range of values that the interested public applies to such sites. Only by doing this can the public record begin to match the richness of our history and the places where it happened.

- *Designate landmarks with community significance where they help illuminate larger themes.* New York is a city of some eight million people, five boroughs, well over one hundred distinct ethnic groups, numerous languages and religions, and a myriad of professions, trades, and occupations. The histories of this complex organism are entrusted to a single, city-wide Landmarks Commission. How can this Commission pick and choose among the thousands of worthwhile stories locked inside New York's buildings, streets, and landscapes, some of which may be cherished locally, but may be little known outside the community's boundaries?

  The question of how far the Landmarks Commission's city-wide mandate extends to the protection of community heritage is a vexing one, and one that could arise frequently should this committee's recommendations be adopted. This committee believes that, in order to protect the history of the city as a whole, it is necessary to protect sites of significance to its communities. At the same time, the Landmarks Commission must be able to hold up such sites to a city-wide standard; we recommend a test that allows the Commission to do so without becoming mired in invidious comparisons between superficially similar sites—or between profoundly different communities. A former Woolworth's store on Northern Boulevard in Corona, Queens, shows how a two-part test might work (Figure 2.1). The Woolworth's is important to Corona's history because it was here that popular protest first broke the color barrier in hiring in this African American community. Though this event may have had little direct impact elsewhere, the theme it symbolizes—the achievement of equal opportunity in hiring—is important to the entire city's history. The Woolworth's is the best site for marking, interpreting, and remembering how one community, that of Corona, experienced this historical theme.

- *Protect sites that represent the full range of our historically significant cityscape.* New York's history has taken place in factories, warehouses, tenements, bars and restaurants, laundries, bodegas, markets, and storefront churches and synagogues, and on streetcorners, piers, parks, and squares. Preserving that history requires receptivity to these and many other kinds of sites. Over time, New York's officially designated landmarks should include sites representative of the full diversity of historically significant places.

- *Seek, to the greatest possible extent, to protect historic resources in their entirety.* The nail or scrap of wood that is reverently enshrined in a reliquary is understood to be but a tiny fragment of something larger, now long gone. Its purpose is to inspire. If our historic sites are to instruct as well as inspire, we must make them whole enough to contain the event in imagination. Drawing the boundaries around historic resources can be a contentious exercise. Debate raged after Columbia University and the City of New York proposed to demolish and redevelop the Audubon Ballroom, scene of Malcolm X's assassination (Figures 7.4 to 7.6). Certain proponents of redevelopment argued that the historic site worthy of preservation was the bloodstained square of floorboards on which Malcolm X had stood at the fatal moment. They then proposed, as an alternative, the preservation of the entire stage. These admittedly political proposals missed the point. Malcolm X was not the sole actor in the drama of his assassination; his killers were there, of course, and so were throngs of people who had come to hear him speak and who ended up watching him die. The floorboards might have served as a relic, but nothing less than the entire room, or better yet the entire building, could possibly convey the enormity of the event.

Many historic interiors—those of most houses and apartments, for example—are closed to the public. They cannot be regulated as landmarks. Yet many historic interiors meet the criterion of public access and are eligible for designation. Similarly, many historic resources are larger in scope than an individual building. In such cases, it may be appropriate to designate a group of individual landmarks or historic district.

- *Designate groups of thematically related landmarks that convey the many facets of a historical theme or community.* Two landmarks often tell more than twice the story of one. Often, therefore, there will be much to gain from supplementing existing landmarks with new ones. On the Lower East Side, for example, the *Jewish Daily Forward* Building tells a wonderful story of Jewish immigrants' aspirations to literacy and political involvement. A few blocks away, Jarmulowsky's Bank tells the equally important story of their aspirations to economic success. The *Forward* building is protected; the bank is not. Designating the two buildings, each literally rising above the community and representing complementary aspects of its aspirations, would give shape to a historical narrative larger than that suggested by either structure alone. Likewise, a richer, more nuanced story of Jewish religious life would be told if one or more of the Lower East Side's most modest and unpretentious synagogues (Figure 6.2) could achieve the landmark designation already bestowed on the magnificent—and architecturally distinguished—Eldridge Street Synagogue.

In fact, the Landmarks Commission already adopted this policy in another part of the city when it designated the church and workers' houses at Kreischerville, Staten Island, thereby amplifying the significance of the already designated Kreischer mansion nearby.

There are many opportunities for other such groups that record multiple facets of a community's life, mark successive stages of a social movement, or chart the migrations of an ethnic group through the city. Wherever such group designations can support a larger historical narrative than a single site, multiple designation will be an appropriate strategy.

• *Designate historic districts that represent the historical and cultural dimensions of New York's neighborhoods.* New York City currently has sixty-eight historic districts. Most have been designated largely for their architectural character. Yet the Landmarks Law clearly empowers the Commission to designate districts, as well as individual landmarks, on the basis of historical or cultural significance.

The law defines a historic district as "any area" that "contains improvements" that: "(a) have a special character or special historical or aesthetic interest or value"; and "(b) represent one or more periods or styles of architecture typical of one or more eras in the history of the city"; and "(c) cause such area, by reason of such factors, to constitute a distinct section of the city." Although the law requires a district to "represent one or more periods or styles of architecture," it does not require it to manifest architectural unity. It is our view that the characteristics that cause a district to "constitute a distinct section of the city" could be historical or cultural, as well as aesthetic.

One could argue that drawing district boundaries on the basis of architectural style alone yields a misleading historical picture by selectively preserving only the aspects of a neighborhood that most appeal to contemporary taste. Certainly, a historic district—even one largely distinguished by its "architectural" character—will provide a far more meaningful record of the city's history if the many facets of its social, physical, economic, and cultural development are taken into account when it is mapped. Sometimes this means being sure to include not only the most attractive rowhouses (or apartment buildings), but a mix of housing and other building types that represent the neighborhood's overall development, as was done in the Greenwich Village Historic District or in the National Register's Sunset Park Historic District in Brooklyn. Many historic neighborhoods present a close relationship between homes and workplaces: these too need to be included in historic districts. In Carroll Gardens, South Brooklyn, a small enclave of unusual rowhouses has been preserved as a historic district, but nearby workers' housing, factories, and docks have been excluded. Extending the district eastward and westward would incorporate a fascinating cross-section of nineteenth-century history, from the warehouses and factories of the Gowanus Canal through the tiny brick rowhouses occupied by the workers, up the slope through ever larger rowhouses to the grand mansions cresting the ridge, down the western slope through houses of diminishing scale, and finally to the docks of the East River. Such a district would convey a rich picture of the life and work of a nineteenth-century neighborhood, with all its social and architectural gradations—a far richer picture than that presented by the historic district as jewel box.

Beyond contributing to a historic district's definition, historical and cultural factors may sometimes be the main factors that create the requisite sense of place.

The following guidelines are intended to provide a framework for deciding when historic district designation is merited.

Designate historic districts where:

○ a historical or cultural theme is associated with a neighborhood as a whole;
○ significant sites are relatively numerous and close together;
○ the relationships among significant sites are part of, or add to, their meaning or value;
○ the place's character as a distinctive neighborhood contributes to the significance of sites within it;
○ the concept or image of the neighborhood at a particular moment was part of its historical significance or its image in folklore;
○ the neighborhood's historic character is the basis for the continuance of culturally significant traditional activities;
○ historic district designation will protect historical and cultural values more effectively than individual landmark designations.

The historic cores of Chinatown, the Lower East Side, and Harlem (Figure 8.2) are examples of neighborhoods whose identity as communities—places shaped by work, domestic arrangements, worship, ethnicity, and culture—is integral to their history and folklore, and where historic sites are numerous and densely packed. District designation could provide better protection than individual landmark designation here. Perhaps even better would be a combination of both approaches in which a core district was supplemented by individual landmarks outside the historic core.

Though some tenements have already been designated as part of the Greenwich Village Historic District, proposals to include tenements in historic districts continue to raise urban planning and housing questions. Would such designations perpetuate sub-standard housing and hamper community development? After speaking with experts in affordable housing and community development, this committee does not believe so. Many tenements in New York remain essentially sound, and numerous community housing groups are busy rehabilitating them for low- and moderate-income housing. Where they are partially occupied, rehabilitation allows the possibility of providing improved housing without displacing residents. Rehabilitated tenements can not only provide good housing but also help stabilize communities. Some experts in the rehabilitation of tenements believe they can be made into good, up-to-date housing without major structural alterations. Others favor drastic interior alterations such as enlargement of air shafts or removal of rear-lot extensions. Though such alterations could conceivably pose regulatory challenges, the Landmarks Commission has already demonstrated that it can successfully accommodate rear-yard alterations within the rowhouse neighborhoods of Brooklyn or in the factory and loft buildings now being converted to residences in Tribeca. We believe, in short, that the designation of tenements can be compatible with good housing policy, and good housing policy need not be antithetical to good landmarks regulation.

Goals for Regulation

All too often, the question of how to regulate historical or cultural landmarks becomes a sterile debate over whether such regulation should be "more strict" or "less strict" than that accorded architectural landmarks. Both views miss the point: landmark regulation proceeds from the rationale for preserving a site and the values perceived in it. If a building has historical or cultural values, then regulation should protect the features associated with those values. This may require differing degrees of "strictness" in different circumstances. Since, in practice, few landmarks are exclusively "historical" or "architectural," regulation will often have to recognize and arbitrate among potentially conflicting values. The important point is that, wherever present, historical and cultural values should be recognized and their protection advanced as a regulatory goal. Significant differences can then be clearly articulated and submitted to public hearings. The committee therefore proposes the following simple, predictable, yet flexible, guidelines for regulation:

- *Regulation should aim to protect those physical aspects or features of a site that convey its historical or cultural values. When significant conflicts arise between this and other regulatory goals, they should be submitted to public hearings.* In applying these guidelines, it is useful to remember that though the values represented by historical sites are associational, rather than aesthetic, they are conveyed by qualities of form and matter—height, color, texture, roof pitch, window shapes—that are just as visible and tangible as those of "architectural" landmarks. There is no meaningful distinction to be made on a regulatory level between the protection of such elements for their associational or their aesthetic value.

  However, because elements sometimes considered undesirable from an architectural viewpoint may possess great historical significance, their protection may lead to results substantively different from those produced by a purely aesthetic approach to regulation. Fire escapes, for example, are often thought to detract from the architectural qualities of buildings. Yet photographs and written accounts of life in the Lower East Side (and in tenements elsewhere) stress their importance as social spaces, sleeping balconies, and outdoor linen closets. Landmark regulation should protect them. Alterations may also be historically significant even while detracting from the host building's architectural purity, as the example of the Eighth Street Playhouse in Greenwich Village, discussed above, makes clear.

Signs, though often considered an architecturally unfortunate (albeit at times necessary) intrusion, may preserve the most telling evidence of a building's or a neighborhood's history. Though the building housing the famous Minton's Playhouse in Harlem has been rehabilitated, the removal of its sign has rendered its history unreadable. Small's Paradise, though for some years an empty shell, still fortunately retains its neon sign, which offers an authentic and (quite literally) legible element of continuity with the building's history [note: as of 2008, the building has been rehabilitated and the sign removed: Figure 6.4].

Though signage is often thought of as ephemeral, historically significant signage has not always given way to changing use of occupancy, nor need it do so. Though the Kletzker Brotherly Aid Association on the Lower East Side is now an Italian funeral home with its own new sign, its original inscribed cornice remains unaltered. Such layerings can be part of the richness of New York's historic fabric, and the eradication of historically significant signage is a tragedy that frequently need not happen. When the Garden Cafeteria, a famous Lower East Side institution, became a Chinese restaurant, all traces of its former identity were removed. This did not need to happen; intelligent landmarks regulation would have provided a framework for preserving some of the signage without

Figure 6.4   Small's Paradise was one of Harlem's great night spots. Its neon sign survived years of vacancy and decay—but not conversion into a public school, the Thurgood Marshall Academy for Learning and Change.

impeding a change in use. Even where full preservation is impossible, landmarks regulation could mitigate such losses by requiring or persuading an owner to incorporate all or part of an old sign in a new design, make less severe modifications than originally proposed, maintain historical continuity through installation of a plaque or marker, or donate the historic sign to a museum. Solutions like these, though falling far short of preservation, may be preferable to the complete loss of historical elements and can be achieved only if the Landmarks Commission uses its regulatory authority to protect historical and cultural values.

- *Use landmark protection as one part of a larger, coordinated strategy to preserve cultural and historical resources.* Protecting cultural and historical resources often demands more than simply preserving a physical object or space, however important it may be. At some sites, the challenge is to mark and interpret; elsewhere it may be to protect a pattern of social activity, a view, or a sense of context. These challenges admittedly often go beyond the power of landmark regulation, and this committee debated whether landmark regulation was appropriate in such instances. Our conclusion was strongly affirmative: landmark designation should never be rejected because it does not provide the whole answer to protecting a resource; it should rather be adopted wherever it provides an essential part of the answer.

This committee believes there is great potential in combining landmark regulation with other policies of protection or encouragement, such as Special District zoning, tax incentives, state or national Heritage Area designation, not-for-profit management, and public art programs. At Kreischerville, Staten Island, for example, historic district designation, coupled with sympathetic zoning and existing individual landmark designations, could protect the surviving architectural elements of the village—workers' housing, church, hotels, school, and mansion. The remains of the vast Kreischer brickworks and docks, surviving buried under the ground, could be included within Harbor Park, New York City's State Heritage Area. This would help guide investment in rehabilitation and interpretation within the community. The clay pits upon which the factory depended still exist within Clay Pit Ponds State Park Preserve, whose management plan and interpretive activities should ensure their preservation and appreciation.

With certain "living landmarks," physical preservation could be accompanied by zoning regulations or carefully constructed tax incentives to maintain traditional uses. A combination of landmark and zoning regulation could also help prevent the introduction of inappropriate new uses where that might be highly destructive of a cultural site's benefit to the public. Where the public's use and enjoyment of a cultural site depends on preservation of its visual context, zoning overlays could be adopted, as has been done to protect the view from the Brooklyn Heights Esplanade. In each case, landmark protection can be an important part of the solution, even if not the entire solution. The committee believes there is an urgent need to debate and develop these and similar ideas to the point where coordinated policies of cultural resource protection can be adopted.

Beyond Regulation: Landmarks and Public Education

As an agency with expanding regulatory responsibilities, the Landmarks Commission must leave the task of interpreting its sites largely to others. Yet the Commission can and should do much to bolster its historical and cultural designations and explain their importance. One of the obstacles to historical landmark designation is said to be the difficulty of explaining their value to City Council members who must ratify them. To address this over the long run the Commission might consider including historical and cultural factors in all designation reports—even those for "architectural" landmarks— thereby giving the Commission opportunities to talk about historical significance where it is not a factor of contention.

The Commission has other opportunities to support its preservation mandate. Guidebooks, brochures, leaflets, and regulatory guidelines produced by the Commission (or with its cooperation) can stress historical and cultural significance. So can plaques erected under its aegis, as the Landmarks Preservation Foundation's new historical plaque program promises.

To bring its historical and cultural preservation efforts to the public, the Landmarks Commission should consider appointing a public historian and educator to work with local history museums and societies, schools, and community groups throughout the city to develop educational and interpretive programs that would exploit the huge and underutilized public history resource represented by historical and cultural landmarks. Such a program would support the Landmarks Commission's legislative mandate to "promote the use of historic districts, landmarks, interior landmarks and scenic landmarks for the education, pleasure and welfare of the people of the city" while building new constituencies for landmarks.

Toward a More Diverse Landmarks Commission Staff

Landmarks Commission survey, research, and preservation staff are drawn largely from graduate programs in architecture, architectural history, and historic preservation. Such heavy emphasis on expert architectural knowledge inevitably predisposes the staff toward architectural considerations and away from historical and cultural landmarks preservation. We are fully aware of the severe burdens that budget cuts have placed upon the Commission's regulatory staff. Under more favorable fiscal conditions, the Commission could amplify and diversify its professional staff, hiring experts in urban anthropology and folklore, for example: areas that could also be valuable additions to the Commission itself. In the meantime, the Commission could supplement its internal resources by drawing on outside consultants for specific projects.

Often community groups can provide appropriate partners. Foundation support could help pay the bill. The issue of ethnic diversity is a touchy one. The Commission staff did superb work on the African Burial Ground, though not one member was African American. (African American representation on the Commission itself, on the other hand, undoubtedly helped gain the issue the attention it deserved.) We do not believe that membership in an ethnic or racial group is a precondition to an informed understanding of that group's history. Over time, however, increasing ethnic diversity tends to foster a greater breadth of historical investigation and openness to exploring new themes. The Landmarks Commission and historic preservation in general can only gain from such a development.

STATE AND FEDERAL PRESERVATION PROGRAMS

Federal and state preservation programs fall into three areas: listing programs with limited regulatory power (National and State Registers, National Historic Landmarks); site ownership and management (national and state parks and historic sites); and programs of public/private property management (state and federal heritage areas). In addition, the Department of the Interior publishes a broad array of technical assistance and educational publications that set the tone for historic preservation nationally. State and federal government programs already make an important contribution to preserving New York's historical and cultural landmarks, but it is the sense of the committee that more could be done. The following recommendations address each of the three major program areas in turn.

The National Register: Bringing Down the Barriers to History and Culture

Three federal and state programs list and provide limited protection for historically and culturally significant sites. The National Historic Landmarks program was initiated in 1935 to identify sites of great importance to the nation's history. The National Register of Historic Places was created in 1966 to include sites of local and state significance, as well as a broader listing of national sites. The State Register essentially duplicates the National Register's listings for New York State. As of 1995, there were about 2,100 National Historic Landmarks throughout the country, while approximately 61,000 properties throughout the United States were listed on the National Register. As of 1992, New York City boasted about 100 National Historic Landmarks and about 550 National Register sites.

Though the criteria for evaluating properties are clear and reasonably inclusive, the list of New York City sites tells a disappointingly narrow history, emphasizing Manhattan, official institutions, Founding Fathers, finance, upper-class culture, and fine architecture. African American cultural achievements are represented by a group of sites designated during the mid-1970s. Yet the histories of other ethnic communities, of industry, of working people, neighborhoods, business, and the arts are sparsely represented, while "living landmarks" with rich cultural traditions—La Marqueta in East

Harlem, the fishing piers at Sheepshead Bay, the Esplanade in Brooklyn Heights, Chinatown, the Lower East Side, Little Italy—are virtually absent.

What concerns us is the effectiveness of the criteria and listing process. Do the criteria support or impede the listing of significant sites? Does the process encourage or discourage applicants? The Register's limited regulatory powers have led many New York City preservationists to ask another question: is the prize of listing worth the struggle? There are indeed solid reasons for seeking listing—and for seeking to extend and correct the historical picture it presents. National and State Registers are frequently used as the basis for "official" histories and guidebooks. Perhaps more important, Register listing can instill pride in owners and communities, change the nature of public debate over a threatened site, and bolster community preservation efforts. The cachet of national recognition makes Register listing a valued prize. "This makes us feel terrific!" said an advocate for a just-listed armory in Brooklyn. Register listing had conferred validity on his arguments in favor of preserving the building; it also gave his group a "win" which might help build institutional strength and credibility.

But the National Register should do more than provide pats on the back for deserving sites. As a preservation planning tool, Register listing could help provide recognition and protection for New York's "living landmarks," the socially valuable spaces which contribute so much to the city's cultural richness and sense of historical tradition. Register listing can also help protect historic piers and other industrial structures exposed to the threat of federal or state-sponsored demolition. Finally, the tax credits triggered by Register listing can help to encourage the rehabilitation of historic commercial or industrial buildings. An active strategy is needed to achieve these goals, one that aims not only at listing more sites but also at removing the obstacles which hinder the registers from achieving their full potential. The following recommendations would advance these goals and would be relatively easy to achieve:

- *Lower the "integrity" barrier to listing living landmarks and significant industrial sites on the National Register.* Many historic sites owe their significance not to a discrete event but to a long association with a pattern of events or activities, one that may even continue today. Such sites are often altered, sometimes more than once, during their useful life. These alterations may contribute to, indeed enhance, their historical associations. Yet sometimes they cause important sites to be ruled ineligible for Register listing or National Historic Landmark status. The main office of the Amalgamated Bank on Union Square is such a building. Founded by the Amalgamated Clothing and Textile Workers Union, this was the country's first union bank, and today it remains the country's only union bank. The banking hall itself is a nondescript modern intrusion into a dignified stone building. Nevertheless, it remains an important landmark of labor history. Yet the building was ruled ineligible for landmark status because of the ground-floor alteration.

Pier 54 in the Hudson River—the last surviving Cunard pier, home berth to the *Lusitania*, point of arrival for the Titanic's survivors, and of embarkation for thousands of World War II soldiers— furnishes a more complex example (Figure 6.5). Pier 54 was in very poor condition by about 1990. Its survival would have required the replacement of many original elements. Yet its value as one of New York's most powerfully evocative monuments to the age of steam navigation would not thereby have been lessened, because these elements were originally fabricated to be replaceable, and because the structure's value lay in its overall form, rather than in the authenticity of its individual components. Nevertheless, the state declared it ineligible, paving the way for its demolition. The same reasoning would spell danger for many "living landmarks" that manifest their longstanding community importance through repeated changes or renewals of material. The original wooden planks and pilings of the fishing piers at Sheepshead Bay may long since have been replaced, yet the piers' historical and cultural significance are not thereby diminished: they stem from a tradition of use rather than from a precise architectural form.

As these examples demonstrate, when a site's period of significance is too narrowly defined, its architectural and formal qualities are over-emphasized, or its original appearance is inappropriately prized over later historical associations, the integrity criterion can become a barrier to designating some of our most cherished and meaningful historic sites, particularly "living

Figure 6.5   Pier 54 in its heyday. It survived as the last of New York's Cunard Line piers until the State of New York demolished it in the 1990s.

landmarks," industrial buildings, and sites whose historical associations do not depend on the authenticity of replaceable materials.

To remedy this situation would require no substantive change to the National Register's Criteria for Evaluation, but merely clarification of their application to historically and culturally significant sites. Amendments to the National Register's informational bulletins spelling out how living landmarks, industrial buildings, sites with long periods of historical significance and a history of frequent alteration, and structures built of replaceable materials can meet the integrity criterion would give applicants, consultants, and preservation staff a sense of certainty in the application of this important criterion.

• *Clarify the fifty-year rule with regard to "living landmarks."* Properties that have achieved significance only within the fifty years preceding their evaluation are not eligible for inclusion in the National Register," with certain exceptions, according to the Register Bulletin. This exclusion seems to present an insuperable barrier to the listing of many of New York's culturally significant and socially valuable spaces. It is not, in fact, as insuperable as it seems, if the rule is correctly interpreted. The question concerns sites which owe their significance to an ongoing pattern of use. Must that pattern of use have been so well established fifty years ago that the site was already historically significant for its association with it? Or must the pattern merely have begun at least fifty years ago? The Register's *Guidelines for Evaluating and Documenting Traditional Cultural Properties* favor the less restrictive standard. They state that a mountain peak used by an Indian tribe for religious purposes is "probably not eligible" "if its use has begun only within the last 50 years," implying that it would be eligible had its use begun at least fifty years ago. It is possible that some newer sites could also qualify under the exception alluded to above: namely that "sufficient historical perspective exists to determine that the property is exceptionally important and will continue to retain that distinction in the future." Some of New York's popular public gathering places, such as the Esplanade in Brooklyn Heights, would probably meet that criterion, in that sufficient historical perspective exists to recognize their traditional social value, and that value is likely to be altered only by the sort of catastrophic alteration which Register listing could help prevent.

• *Ensure that standards of documentation and evaluation are appropriate for historical sites and attainable by applicants.* As a preservation planning tool, Register listing should be available to communities and concerned citizen groups; in practice, this ideal is not always attained. One reason is that most Register nominations nowadays are carried out by professional consultants at a cost of several thousand dollars (a district could cost as much as $15,000). The state office sometimes demands a level of historical research and documentation that can be burdensome even for consultants. When this happens, Register listing is effectively placed out of reach of communities, frustrating the Register's preservation goals.

The demand for highly academic forms of data gathering and analysis is in part a consequence of the professionalization of historic preservation, compounded by a requirement that nomination forms accepted by state preservation officials be reviewed by Department of Interior preservation officials. Because the state is graded on how closely its Register listings conform to DOI standards—and funding formulas are based on the grade—there is an understandable tendency to bend over backward to ensure correctness. The result can be stifling to preservation.

The Register's requirement that properties be "evaluated against other examples of the property type" can be particularly burdensome. This appears to be founded on the Register's reliance on the concept of historic context, or "broad pattern of historical development in a community or its region," as a basic planning tool. Contexts are generally historical themes or categories within which a property's significance can be evaluated. Where this sensible system breaks down is where historical contexts become too closely identified with particular building types. To evaluate historic sites by reference to building types—often, in practice, by how closely they typify those building types—is to judge them by an architectural standard that can eclipse their associational content. It may also miss the very individuality, even idiosyncrasy, that makes them valuable. And finally it may miss the social role that has lent significance to popular gathering places, religious institutions, workplaces, and other sites.

Establishing reasonable standards for documentation and analysis is a matter both of seeking the right information and of setting an appropriate level of effort. The need to screen out frivolous or meritless nominations must be balanced by the need to encourage deserving nominations, so that planning for the long-term preservation of significant sites can take place. Register listing can be made more accessible without lowering standards. Where sites owe their significance to their role within a community, they should be evaluated in that framework—not by reference to a building type. At the same time, state and federal preservationists must be reassured that their reputation for professionalism—and their agency's funding—will not be jeopardized by accepting nominations for properties whose historical importance within a community has been demonstrated without a full-scale academic defense.

- *Speed up the listing process by increasing the frequency of state board meetings.* The state board must review all State and National

Register nominations. Yet it meets so infrequently that little time is available to review nominations submitted by communities. The resulting delays in reviewing and approving nominations become discouraging to communities and chilling to preservation. Scheduling more frequent meetings would help; so would a more supportive attitude to reviewing such nominations.

• *Increase the size and diversity of OPRHP staff in order to respond to communities.* Low staffing levels have forced the State Office of Parks and Historic Preservation (OPRHP) to concentrate its resources on a relatively small number of identified preservation priorities, placing long-range planning and pro-active Register listing campaigns on the back burner and making it difficult for staff to support preservation projects initiated by communities. An increase in both central and field office staffing would help promote a prompt and supportive response to applicants seeking Register listing. This would serve the goals of historic preservation while also serving constituents and increasing the popularity of the state's preservation programs.

In addition to increasing in size, state preservation staff, heavily dominated by architectural historians and preservationists, could benefit by becoming more professionally and culturally diverse. Adding anthropologists, urban historians, and folklorists would help the agency to fulfill its role in the area of historical and cultural landmarks protection. Increasing ethnic and racial diversity would encourage a broader receptivity to historical themes.

• *Launch a series of aggressive Register campaigns to list historical sites, beginning with New York's most beloved "living landmarks"—the sites still in active use by New York's communities.* The National and State Register programs can provide more than passive support to preservation efforts. State Historic Preservation offices can mount pro-active campaigns to identify, call attention to, and protect historic resources. Some states, such as New Jersey and Vermont, have already done this with great success. Working with preservation groups, history museums, and community groups, the SHPO should compile a list of the city's most beloved living landmarks—sites like the Sheepshead Bay fishing piers, Corona's Big Rock, East Harlem's La Marqueta, Philip's candy store in Coney Island, Katz's Deli in the Lower East Side, the Alcove Lounge in Corona, Farrell's Bar in Windsor Terrace, the Brooklyn Heights Esplanade, the Staten Island Ferry, the Coney Island beach and boardwalk, Times Square. The SHPO should then schedule a series of public hearings around the city to discuss these sites and their preservation, followed by a rapid and determined effort to enter them into the National and State Registers.

Sites which do not yet meet the "fifty-year rule" could be listed in an informal "pending" category. Throughout this process, the SHPO should do everything possible to celebrate, as well as study, these cherished places. At the conclusion of the campaign, a series of commemorative festivals should be held throughout the city. The program outlined above would do much to advance the cause of New York's "living landmarks." It would also expand the constituency for historic preservation throughout the city.

The SHPO need not stop there. Subsequent campaigns could focus on New York's industrial heritage, particularly along the waterfront, where Register listing provides important safeguards against government actions and valuable aid in long-range planning, or on New York's extraordinarily diverse history of popular musical expressions, ranging from the cantorial traditions of the Lower East Side synagogue through Tin Pan Alley to the famous night spots of the Tenderloin and Harlem and on to the development of salsa in East Harlem and the Bronx. The principles in each case would be the same: to choose a theme of city-wide importance which can engage broad participation and use that theme to expand the recognition and protection of New York City's most characteristic historical and cultural sites.

National Historic Landmarks: Putting New York in the Picture

Unlike the National and State Register programs, the National Historic Landmarks program is guided by a "thematic framework" which is intended to cover all of American history and prehistory. Until 1994 there were thirty-four themes, divided into sub-themes, which were further divided into facets. A new thematic framework, adopted in 1994, promises to be more streamlined, but is unlikely to cure the NHL program's inherent anti-urban bias. Over the years, the NHL program has tackled a wide range of subjects, but the pre-1994 list reveals a preference for patriotic themes like major American wars and westward expansion at the expense of some of New York City's most important themes, including classical and popular music, dance, journalism, labor, and business. This committee believes that, as a first step toward correcting these deficiencies, the NHL program should launch a series of theme studies on finance, banking, insurance, and commerce—fields in which New York City, and particularly Lower Manhattan, have had a worldwide impact.

Though the National Park Service may undertake such theme studies at any time, many result from specific Congressional appropriations, spear-headed by elected representatives whose regions stand to gain recognition from the studies. We believe New York's elected officials could obtain a Congressional appropriation for carrying out the requisite studies; preservationists, local elected officials, and downtown business and real estate leaders could then form a local steering committee to monitor and advise on the study and ensure that it receives the press and public attention it deserves.

Such recognition would provide federal funds for survey work of importance to New York. And National Historic Landmark designations—indeed the entire study process—would help celebrate the historical significance of Lower Manhattan's spires and canyons at a time when public policy and private investment are spurring their rehabilitation. The NHL process would increase public appreciation, shore up Lower Manhattan's image, and assist in the area's revitalization. In addition to NHL designations, the process would likely include research which could lead to a larger number of National Register nominations. This would allow more building owners to take advantage of the Rehabilitation Tax Credit without the delays and uncertainties of seeking determinations of eligibility.

In short, working together, downtown business interests and preservationists could use the project to generate favorable public and press attention not only for preservation but also for Lower Manhattan in general.

Harbor Park: A Sleeping Giant

Harbor Park, New York's State Heritage Area, is a tremendous resource for preserving our waterfront and maritime heritage. As yet, its potential has hardly been tapped. By expanding its boundaries, it can become a leading force in saving important sites along the Brooklyn, Queens, and Staten Island waterfronts; by expanding its interpretive programs, it can become a powerful engine for increasing public awareness of these sites and the maritime, industrial, and immigration heritage they represent. Harbor Park has the potential to unlock state funds to support much-needed preservation, rehabilitation, interpretation, marking, and public visitation to these sites. Passage of the 1996 Clean Water/Clean Air Bond Act, which sets aside $50 million in grant fund for municipal preservation, park, and State Heritage Area projects, makes this an especially attractive possibility.

Harbor Park is not a park in the traditional sense but rather a hybrid kind of "heritage area" which includes both private and public lands and which is founded on the principle of public–private partnerships. Distantly rooted in the founding of New York State's Adirondack Park around 1890, the "heritage area" concept was first fully developed at Lowell National Historical Park, founded in the 1970s. It has been further developed at the federal level at Ebey's Landing National Historical Reserve, at congressionally designated national heritage corridors (Illinois and Michigan Canal, Blackstone River, Delaware and Lehigh Navigational Canal), in the America's Industrial Heritage Project (a nine-county partnership effort in Pennsylvania), and elsewhere. New York State initiated its own heritage areas, the urban cultural park system, in 1982; recent legislation has expanded the system and changed its name to the New York State Heritage Areas System, which currently includes fourteen urban cultural parks plus the newly designated Mohawk Valley State Heritage Corridor. Each of the urban cultural parks has a specific historical theme: Harbor Park's is "maritime trade" and "immigration."

As a state heritage area, Harbor Park aims to identify, interpret, develop, and use its historical resources for public education and recreation. In the words of a consultant, Richard Rabinowitz, Harbor Park:

> appropriates New York's harbor with all of its history, its life, its people and the evidence of their trade and traffics for fun—and learning. The park is a

place for recreation and relaxation, and it is also an outdoor history museum—without walls or boundaries. Its collection is the sites that cluster at the water's edge; and its story is about the port and its people and how they shaped the peculiar and unique city of New York.

The State Office of Parks (OPRHP) provides general oversight for Harbor Park, but the New York City Department of Parks manages it. Within this system, Heritage Area designation provides mechanisms for directing state financial assistance to local government or "other appropriate entities" to acquire or develop sites, design projects, plan and carry out interpretive exhibits, and mount public programs. Heritage Area designation also empowers OPRHP to award grants to "encourage urban revitalization of, and reinvestment in, urban cultural park resources," and to contract with other state agencies for services and programs, including planning and transportation. Finally, the Parks Commissioner is directed to provide technical assistance in areas such as recreation and preservation planning. In addition to providing valuable state aid for preservation and interpretation, Heritage Area designation triggers a few important regulatory provisions. All state agencies must carry out actions affecting the park in a manner consistent, as far as possible, with the park's approved management plan, and must consult with state parks. In the words of Title G, "appropriate local action" must be taken "to protect and safeguard the defined resources," and interagency agreements must ensure that local regulatory powers are used in ways consistent with the plan's goals; regulatory power over privately owned property remains in the hands of the local Landmarks Commission.

Harbor Park currently includes six sites: Ellis Island, the Statue of Liberty, Battery Park, South Street Seaport, Fulton Ferry/Empire Stores (Brooklyn), and Snug Harbor (Staten Island). All six are publicly owned and, with one exception, already operated as historical or cultural sites or parks. The exception is Empire Stores, a group of nineteenth-century warehouses slated to be rehabilitated and to include an industrial history exhibition. In addition to these sites, the state is also in the process of developing a visitors' center in Pier A at Battery Park.

In the few years since its founding, Harbor Park has taken important steps forward, and the Empire Stores and Pier A projects will take it yet further toward its central goal of increasing public use and appreciation of New York's waterfront and harbor. Yet Harbor Park will not fulfill its potential until it incorporates significant sites not already owned and operated as historical or cultural sites:

- *Expand Harbor Park to incorporate privately owned waterfront industrial sites in Brooklyn, Queens, and Staten Island.* An expanded Harbor Park could facilitate public investment in the rehabilitation of historic waterfront industrial sites and in related infrastructure improvements, provide grant funding and technical support for recreational programs, signage, public art, interpretive exhibits, and bus and walking tours, contract with private operators to provide boat tours, and create financial incentives for private investment in rehabilitation and revitalization. The beneficiaries would be local government, preservation groups, history museums and historical societies, property owners, and private enterprise. Administratively it is relatively easy to expand a state Heritage Area. The State Parks Commissioner can do so with local legislative approval. Harbor Park's master plan, in fact, envisions expansion along the Queens, Bronx, and South Brooklyn waterfronts. A preliminary site survey, carried out in 1988–90, recommended that the Park "continue searching for suitable sites in other boroughs, including the western Queens riverfront, the South Brooklyn waterfront and other areas." OPRHP and the City Parks Department should work with community leaders, union and industrial representatives, preservationists, and experts on the history of maritime trade and industry to identify and assess significant sites. One good candidate for inclusion would be Kreischerville on Staten Island's west shore. The aging industrial waterfronts of South Brooklyn (Figure 8.7), western Queens, and Staten Island, including Sunset Park, Red Hook, the Gowanus Canal, Newtown Creek, Long Island City, St. George, and Staten Island's western shore, furnish an impressive array of factories, warehouses, docks, refineries, grain elevators, float bridges, and other monuments to maritime trade which would also make excellent additions to Harbor Park's "museum without walls." Many of these sites are decaying and in need of reinvestment and new uses. Others are still operating and could form the basis for innovative interpretive programs. Harbor Park could fill both needs, funneling much-needed resources for interpretation and reinvestment and providing coordination among regulatory policies such as landmark, zoning, and coastal zone management. Harbor Park, in short, can help preserve New York's priceless industrial heritage while making it accessible to visitors.

• *Expand Harbor Park's interpretive programs to include New York's waterfront industrial heritage.* In the view of consultant Richard Rabinowitz:

the most important program Harbor Park can offer its visitors is the special point of view they command when they are out on the water on New York harbor. Afloat, they see the city as they never have before, and they get a look at port operations that are seldom seen, even by people who live near the docks.

Harbor Park should offer boat tours of the harbor, providing access to newly designated waterfront industrial sites: half-hour stops could provide opportunities for visiting historical exhibitions, taking harborside walking tours, viewing public art, or simply enjoying the outdoors. And Harbor Park interpretive material need not be limited to the park's own boats but could be made available to passengers on the harbor's growing number of excursion and commuter ferries. In this way, without owning or managing any sites, Harbor Park could become known as the leading interpreter and historical "tour guide" to New York harbor. Benefits would accrue not only to the agency but also to the many historic industrial sites which would be exposed to visitors.

Federal Historic Sites: Toward a Stewardship Model

The National Park Service operates seven federally owned historic sites in New York City and has recently assumed partial jurisdiction over an eighth. These include some of our most significant historical landmarks. These sites should set the standard for the preservation and operation of historic sites. Ellis Island illustrates the problems which bedevil federal site management. Though the Museum of Immigration, housed in the restored main building, is visited by well over one million people each year, many of the island's historic buildings lie derelict and decaying, their deplorable condition hidden from visitors by fences and foliage. The National Park Service cannot fund their stabilization, much less restoration, out of its annual budget. Congress has not yet chosen to provide a special allocation for them but has preferred to wait for a private investor to rehabilitate them. It did, however, appropriate $15,000,000 to build a permanent bridge connecting Ellis Island to Jersey City. This bridge would have had the capacity to carry vehicular traffic onto the island, would have been visually out of character, and would have deprived many visitors of the opportunity to experience Ellis Island in the most meaningful and appropriate way. After public outcry, the plan was rescinded. The episode illustrates one problem that frequently confronts federal historic site managers: no money for maintenance, but large sums available for high-profile construction projects.

Hamilton Grange, the country house built by Alexander Hamilton, provides another illustration. The Grange had to be closed to the public because of long-uncorrected structural problems. A commendable plan to move it into a historically appropriate park setting around the corner from its current site and thoroughly restore it is now moving forward thanks to Congressman Rangel's initiative. Yet it took a state of severe deterioration to prompt a remedy.

The Park Service can provide stewardship of a high caliber, but only if our legislators provide the necessary funding. For this to happen, the public needs to help lawmakers understand the importance of genuine stewardship: that is, stewardship which forestalls drastic restoration—and huge expense—by emphasizing ongoing preservation, maintenance, and repair. Ellis Island could be the site of a demonstration project. For the same sum allotted to the proposed bridge, most, if not all, of the island's unrestored buildings could be stabilized and protected from further deterioration.

EPILOGUE (2008)

History Happened Here was released to the public at a conference sponsored by the Municipal Art Society and City Lore and held at the Museum of the City of New York on November 22–23, 1996. Many of the participants expressed hopes for a revitalized form of historic preservation, one characterized not only by greater attention to the history in historic preservation but also by a new humanism and a willingness to connect with people. These hopes are summarized in two pairs of excerpts from the conference.

In the first pair, two historians express complementary yet divergent views of history's role in preservation. The second of these includes what may have been the first use of the word "storyscape" in public.

Historians should ask big questions, fashion large stories from their research, and present them to the public with all the art they can muster. So much the better if these narratives provoke thought about how we got to where we are today and where we might be going tomorrow.

The broadest view sets New York in a national and global context, tracing a trajectory from the edge to the center of the world, leading us to ask what happens if and when the city is no longer the center, or when centers in the older sense might no longer even exist. A host of sites could help make this story tangible: a Dutch farmstead, the Morris-Jumel Mansion, the Erie Basin, the Red Hook warehouses, a sea-captain's house in Staten Island, the World Financial Center, or the headquarters of Morgan Bank, Standard Oil, or Chase Manhattan.

Another big story traces New York's economic transformation from mercantile port to the largest manufacturing center in the nation, and then to an administration and financial headquarters. And there are many broadly encompassing stories of immigrant cultures, civic struggles for justice, technological innovation, crime, and so on.

The major benefit of grounding the preservation and presentation of artifacts in big-picture themes like these is the expansion of our sense of what is important to preserve. Traditionally, preservation started with an endangered space and worked back from there to build a narrative. I am suggesting that it is more useful to start with a narrative sequence and ask what kind of spaces we must protect in order to tell that story.

The challenge of this approach is that the artifacts that illustrate broad narratives are rarely side by side. To project a historical narrative out of them, we need tools that go beyond the usual site-specific interpretations. Imagine a program of interactive historical markers, touch screens that would link each site to a broader historical continuum and to other sites round the city. A history website could make this information available to people without constraints of place or time. A history center, a place where visitors, residents, and schoolchildren can get a sweeping overview of New York's past, would provide a physical anchor for these programs.

The key to making these and other ideas work is collaboration. A history consortium would include people working in historic houses and history museums as well as preservationists, neighborhood activists, artists, tourism promoters, historians, and government officials. It's time we got better organized.

Mike Wallace (co-author, *Gotham: A History of New York City to 1898*)

Nowadays, I think, we are entering a new period in preservation, one of storyscape. The landscapes of conquest and of treasure house are giving way to those of memories and associations. Many social movements that stem from the sixties have played a part here: ethnic pride, feminism, massive immigration and the demographic changes that flow from it, a growing concern for the city's natural habitat and environmental health, have all provided powerful ways of understanding the city as storyscapes. Yet each of us also has a personal storyscape. Let me mention a few of the historic landmarks I would include in mine.

First is Seward Park on the Lower East Side, where my grandfather shaped up for day work on construction crews on the winter mornings in the 1920s when he couldn't find work as a "presser by clothes." It's right next door to Seward Park Library, where my father as a small child learned to speak and read English and then had to hide that fact from his friends and family. Essex Street is where my father was born in 1914. The "Forvärts," or *Jewish Daily Forward*, Building on East Broadway was a source of great contention in my parents' household, half of which read the *Forward* and half the *Freiheit*, the Communist paper. And the median on Delancey Street, because my grandmother came home one day and said, "This is a miraculous country: they put parks in the middle of the street." The Third Avenue El is how my grandfather got to work as a presser in the Garment District. He had to walk across town from Third Avenue, and I realize now that he must have passed the Empire State Building as it was being built. So in a small way my grandfather is part of the history of the Empire State Building. The Brooklyn Navy Yard is where my father worked when I was born. And 502 Alabama Avenue in Brownsville, Brooklyn, is the first place I lived in New York. It happens to be around the corner from where Fortunoff's got started. Then there are the house we moved to, where I spent my childhood, and the stoop where we played stoop ball endlessly, and the backyards.

Is this a personal scrapbook or a public collection? If we are willing to link the physical evidence of places like these with oral histories and family stories, with images of the great photographers of New York, and with broader social history narratives, they can become a way of creating history that reaches beyond personal experiences to conditions of life that are shared among many groups. They can illuminate issues about immigration, acculturation, the Depression and World War II, suburbanization and urban renewal, preservation and revitalization of communities. Though I have put myself at its center, my collection has as much to do with what went before me as with my own life: with how a landscape was made and modified, changing from wetland to agricultural and industrial terrain, to real estate venture, to religious and social community, and with how this community finally came apart and was reconstructed. This is as much a Dutch, Anglo-Dutch, African American, or Caribbean story as it is an Eastern European Jewish story.

Public presentation and interpretation of our community history can make a vital contribution to the richness of our lives, to economic development, to our cultural expressiveness, and to achieving our social and political ideals. We need a heritage program in the city that reduces isolation, explores our common roots, confirms us as a city of connectedness rather than segregation, makes room for constantly evolving understanding and modes of expression, presents the layers of history and stories about each site, and shows us that no one and no one generation has an exclusive claim on the history of any site in the city.

How do we apportion the shared responsibility to preserve, renew, and create? It is certainly up to designers, architects, and landscape architects to shape the way a site connects to its previous incarnations, the way a building has been adapted to retain a patina of the urban experience. History museums are important too: we need exhibits that move assertively beyond the wall into the public environment, that are dialogues with the contemporary community. Educators should find ways to bring children into the streets. Public officials and developers have a responsibility to create new developments that embody the experience of New Yorkers. Public artists have a role too, as do inventors and designers of electronic media that can encourage a dialogue between sites and experiences. Libraries and cultural institutions are important too. Preservationists are key: one thing that I hope will come out of this conference is a shift in the rhetoric of preservation from inhibiting the exercise of private property to expressing the positive value of community identification. And finally, every property owner in New York has a responsibility, because if you own a piece of land in New York, you are the custodian of its history.

Richard Rabinowitz (President, American History Workshop)

In the second pair of excerpts, the founder of one of New York's leading landmarks of African American history describes what preservation can do for communities, and a former Landmarks commissioner lays out a role for the city's official preservation agency.

I am here because of the children, children of the Weeksville community, who in the late 1960s decided that the tiny little houses of this nineteenth-century free Black settlement were something special. African American people had lived there in the nineteenth century. It was the children who said, "Let's fix up these old beat-up houses and make a Black history museum." They had not heard the words preservation or restoration. They said this from their hearts. They asked for these houses to be preserved as a place where they could learn who they are.

The children of our community did not wake up one morning and say, "Let's do this great thing." They were growing up at the end of the civil rights movement in this country. Many of their teachers, parents and friends had been on the freedom rides and sit-ins. And children were asking questions. That was the environment into which these children were born and that inspired them to say, "Let's fix up these old houses and make a Black history museum."

When I got into historic preservation almost thirty years ago, people wondered why a black New York woman was involved in this. Historic preservation was something for rich white people. I have come to the conclusion that historic preservation is an incredibly powerful tool in the preservation of people. Everything we've done in our organization has been to further that vision. I really believe in that. Otherwise, I would be doing something else with my life.

> Joan Maynard (Founder and Executive Director, Society for the Preservation of Weeksville and Bedford Stuyvesant History, Brooklyn)

The Landmarks Preservation Commission's name understates the breadth of its mandate. The Landmarks Law mandates the Commission to preserve the city's "cultural, social, economic, political and architectural history," a mission substantially broader than that which "landmarks preservation" connotes. This disparity becomes apparent when considering how to protect and interpret a culturally significant site. Clearly, there are a lot of ways to do this other than physical preservation. Designation and regulation, while important, may be inadequate to accomplish the task.

Even with traditional architectural landmarks, designation and regulation are not always adequate tools of preservation. Though designated, such buildings may continue to deteriorate and lose architectural features unless their owners are required to put a preservation plan into effect. The Commission itself cannot do this. Designation is a public recognition that the building has a reason for existence beyond its value to the owner, that it contributes something to all of us. Landmark designation can leverage investment and public interest. The private sector, which often originally opposed landmarks protection, has found that such designation can actually enhance real estate value, and this may prove equally true of historical and cultural landmarks as well. It is our hope that the designation of cultural sites will help ensure their survival through adaptive reuse. However, protecting our "cultural, social, economic, political and architectural history" will require much more than designation and regulation.

Most significantly, the Commission must promote public education, not narrowly as it relates to landmark buildings, but in a way that engages all of us as citizens in a dialogue about the preservation and maintenance of New York City itself. New York, historically, was an extraordinary engine of transformation. Millions of people came from all over the world, bringing their ideas and their energy. They changed New York and in the process transformed themselves and families and their fortunes. New York flourished as a result. Today, many of these engines of transformation have decayed. New York no longer has the vast array of entry jobs that allowed people with rudimentary skills and a desire to work to improve themselves. Yet New York is again becoming a city of immigrants as it was 75 years ago. The need to integrate our new New Yorkers and to give them an intellectual and physical stake in our city is urgent. Preservation of our history should foster an appreciation of the common enterprise that has bound New Yorkers together in a shared belief in our civic destiny.

> Stephen M. Raphael, Esq. (Former Commissioner, New York City Landmarks Preservation Commission)

APPENDIX: MEMBERS OF THE ADVISORY COMMITTEE
(Affiliations are for identification purposes only and are given as of 1996.)

Bill Aguado (Bronx Council for the Arts)
Stanley Aronowitz (Graduate School and University Center, City University of New York, Department of Sociology)
Petra Barreras (formerly El Museo del Barrio)
Debra Bernhardt (Robert F. Wagner Labor Archives, Bobst Library, New York University)
Daniel Bluestone (University of Virginia, School of Architecture)
Francis Booth (Architect; Member, Municipal Art Society Preservation Committee)
Susan Brustman (Poppenhusen Institute)
Fay Chew (formerly Chinatown History Museum)
Stanley Cogan (Queens Historical Society)
Howard Dodson (Schomburg Center for Research in Black Culture)
Andrew Dolkart (Columbia University, School of Architecture, Planning and Preservation; Member, Municipal Art Society Preservation Committee)
Joe Doyle (New York Labor History Association)
Deborah Gardner (former Managing Editor, *The Encyclopedia of New York City*; Member, Municipal Art Society Preservation Committee)
Joan Geismar (Professional Archaeologists of New York City [PANYC]; Member, Municipal Art Society Preservation Committee)
Michael George (Columbia Broadcasting System; Member, Municipal Art Society Preservation Committee)
Sam Gruber (World Monuments Fund)
Betti-Sue Hertz (Bronx Council for the Arts/Longwood Gallery; RepoHistory)
Evelyn Kalibala (New York City Board of Education)
Connie Kopelov (New York Labor History Association)
Jeff Kroessler (Queensborough Preservation League; Member, Municipal Art Society Preservation Committee)
Conrad Levenson (Phoenix House)
Setha Low (Graduate School and University Center, City University of New York, Department of Environmental Psychology)
Ken Lustbader (New York Landmarks Conservancy; Organization of Lesbian + Gay Architects and Designers)
Kevin McGruder (Abyssinian Development Corporation)
John Manbeck (Brooklyn Borough Historian; Kingsborough Community College)
Joan Maynard (Society for the Preservation of Weeksville and Bedford Stuyvesant History)
Ed Mohylowski (New York Botanical Garden; formerly New York Landmarks Conservancy; Member, Municipal Art Society Preservation Committee)
Christopher Moore (Member, Landmarks Preservation Commission)
Evelyn Ortner (Member, Municipal Art Society Preservation Committee)

Charles Platt (Principal, Platt Byard Dovell; Chair, Municipal Art Society Preservation Committee; former Member, Landmarks Preservation Commission)
Edward Quinn (New York City)
Richard Rabinowitz (American History Workshop)
Donald Shriver (Union Theological Seminary)
Arthur Tobier (Public Historian; formerly Community History Workshop, St. Marks-in-the-Bowery)
Sally Yerkovich (New York City)
Steve Zeitlin (City Lore)

The following also shared their expertise with the Committee, in meetings or telephone calls, or through their careful reading of the manuscript at various stages:

Ruth Abram (Lower East Side Tenement Museum)
Leslie Agard-Jones (Board of Education)
Robert Baron (New York State Council on the Arts; Folk Arts Program)
Rina Ben Maior (Center for Puerto Rican Studies, Hunter College)
Rachel Bernstein (New York University, Department of History)
Jon Bloom (Workers Defense League)
Steve Brier (American Social History Project, Hunter College)
Jim Clarke (formerly Public Art Fund)
Honorable Una Clarke (New York City Council)
José Colon (Local Development Corporation Del Barrio)
Bill Conklin (Conklin and Rossant; Member, Municipal Art Society Preservation Committee; former Member, Landmarks Preservation Commission)
Nestor Danyluk (Department of City Planning, Bronx office)
Bill Davis (Fleming Corporation; former Member, New York City Landmarks Preservation Commission)
Gail Dubrow (University of Washington, School of Architecture and Urban Design)
Laurily Epstein (formerly Municipal Art Society)
Justin Ferate (Gray Line Tours)
Phyllis Franklin (Modern Language Association)
Susan Freedman (Public Art Fund; Trustee, Municipal Art Society)
Ann Gibson (Yale University, Department of Art History)
Paul Glassman (Pratt Institute; formerly Morris-Jumel Mansion)
Larry Gobrecht (formerly New York State Office of Parks, Recreation and Historic Preservation)
Lois Godwin (Staff Member, New York City Councilmember Mary Pinkett)
Jeff Gottlieb (Central Queens Historical Association)
Roberta Gratz (Journalist, Author of *The Living City*)
Mary Ellen Hearn (formerly New York City Historic House Trust)
Merrill Hesch (New York State Office of Parks, Recreation and Historic Preservation)

Joe Jamison (New York State A.F.L.–C.I.O.)

David Kahn (Connecticut Historical Society; formerly Brooklyn Historical Society)

Lisa Knauer (RepoHistory)

Michael Kwartler (Environmental Simulation Center, New School for Social Research)

Peter Kwong (Author, *The New Chinatown*)

Charlie Lai (Office of Manhattan Borough President Ruth Messinger)

Frank Lang (Asian Americans for Equality)

Paul Lauter (Trinity University, Department of English Literature)

Bill Lenahan (Italian American Labor Council)

Jill Levey (formerly Brooklyn Historical Society)

Ben Levy (Department of the Interior, National Historic Landmarks Program)

George Lopez (District Leader, 35th Assembly District, Queens)

Paul Luskin (New York Guides Association)

Honorable Helen Marshall (New York City Council)

Gene Norman (Trustee, Municipal Art Society; former Chair, Landmarks Preservation Commission)

Mark O'Brien (RepoHistory)

Bob Ohlerking (New York City)

Jayne Pagnucco (RepoHistory)

Marjorie Pearson (Landmarks Preservation Commission)

Karen Phillips (Abyssinian Development Corporation)

Reverend Thomas F. Pike (St. George's Church, Stuyvesant Square; Member, Landmarks Preservation Commission)

Donald Presa (Greater Ridgewood Restoration; Landmarks Preservation Commission)

Reverend John Redic (Bronx Landmarks Task Force; Longwood Historic District Community Association)

Tony Robins (Landmarks Preservation Commission)

Honorable Annette Robinson (New York City Council)

Charles Sachs (South Street Seaport Museum)

Eric Sandeen (University of Wyoming, Department of American Studies)

Vincent Seyfried (Queens Historical Society)

Peter D. Shaver (New York State Office of Parks, Recreation and Historic Preservation)

Robert Singleton (Bowne House)

Jane Stanicki (Co-chair, Municipal Art Society Planning Committee)

Jim Steere (New York City)

Clark Strickland (formerly Preservation League of New York State)

Karen Tabern (Landmarks Harlem)

Vernon Takeshita (Museum of Chinese in the Americas)

David F. M. Todd (former Chair, Landmarks Preservation Commission; Member Municipal Art Society Planning Committee)

Anthony Max Tung (former Member, Landmarks Preservation Commission)

Debbie Van Cura (Astoria Historical Society)

Anne Van Ingen (New York State Council on the Arts, Architecture, Planning and Design Program)

Marta Vega (Caribbean Cultural Center)

Danny Walkowitz (New York University, Department of History)

Sherrill Wilson (African Burial Ground Project; Reclaim the Memories: Black History Tours of Old New York)

Anthony C. Wood (Ittleson Foundation; formerly J. M. Kaplan Fund)

John Young (Department of City Planning)

CHAPTER 7

Heritage and the Cultural Politics of Preservation: The African Burial Ground and the Audubon Ballroom

This chapter is based on an article written for Places *magazine in 1996, first published there in 1998, and reprinted in* Designer/Builder *the following year. It has been updated to reflect more recent developments at both sites.*

HERITAGE AND THE PROBLEM OF DISCORD

Heritage is a slippery word. Throughout much of the world, heritage conservation is the phrase people use for what we in the United States call historic preservation. It seems admirably clear. It tells us that we are conserving something: that thing is heritage. What is heritage? *Tangible heritage* refers to objects, including buildings, *intangible heritage* to other cultural products such as music, language, or dance. So far so good. But connotations intrude. Does heritage conservation mean something different from historic preservation when a practitioner in the US uses the phrase? Perhaps. Because of heritage conservation's acceptance outside the United States, it may connote awareness or even approval of international trends. Because of its breadth, it may also connote a more expansive attitude to the business of preserving things.

These connotations have a vaguely progressive ring. And yet the core ideas behind the word *heritage* are entirely illiberal. *Heritage* is what one inherits: it is a form of inheritance. At its root, the word suggests generational connectedness, family solidarity, goods, and ownership—all time-honored conservative values. This is even more true of a related word, *patrimony*. Patrimony has many of the same connotations as heritage, but its root (and that of the widely used French and Spanish equivalents, *patrimoine* and *patrimonio*) stems from the Latin "pater," for father, thus adding the notion of patriarchy to that of family.

Herein lies a problem: when patrimony or heritage is invoked, one cannot be sure whether the argument points toward expansion of consciousness or retrenchment in possessions, change or status quo. The murkiness hurts everyone who is interested in an open discussion of the values of conservation. But it particularly impedes those who see heritage conservation as part of progressive movements towards social, economic, or environmental justice, because the conservative connotations are "hard-wired" into the words and, being almost never explicitly stated, are difficult to extirpate. Conservative notions of kinship sometimes resonate even through apparently progressive declarations of global solidarity. When preservation groups appeal, for example, to a "national" or "world" cultural heritage, they imply that all Americans, or even all people, belong to a single family and share a single cultural inheritance. Although this sounds broad-minded, within this metaphorical construct "family" members who disagree about how to evaluate or divide up the inheritance—or who challenge the testator's fairness—may be accused of being ungrateful, or of unseemly squabbling. Thus the notion of *heritage* can help to suppress or stigmatize dissent: it denies the legitimacy of conflicting claims for recognition and attempts to hide the turmoil of politics behind a mask of unity.

At its root, then, *heritage* helps to prop up an essentially conservative ideology of cultural harmony: we are all in this together, and, if there is a problem, the elders will solve it for you. Even when the explicit argument is for social change, the hidden argument tugs the other way. Unfortunately, heritage conservation itself sometimes displays the same tendency: even when they do not explicitly appeal to *heritage*, many historic preservation policies and programs quietly adopt the "status quo" image of cultural harmony and stasis implied by the word.

One symptom of this is the class bias which is built into many preservation programs. For example, the lists of important heritage sites issued by organizations like the World Monuments Fund have typically emphasized royal or princely palaces or major religious complexes. When sites of special relevance to working-class history have been included, it is often by virtue of assimilation to other values: association with a war of national liberation (a flour mill near Dover that was used to feed the troops fighting Napoleon) or a movement of national expansion (a frontier mining town), exemplification of upper-class ideals of charity or paternalism (model housing complexes and settlement complexes), aesthetic or technological merit (Victorian loft buildings), or conversion into luxury condominiums or marinas (dockside warehouses in Liverpool).

A similar bias is reflected in official interpretations. When New York City's Landmarks Preservation Commission declared SoHo, the city's largest surviving ensemble of nineteenth-century cast-iron loft buildings, a historic district, the Commission's official report emphasized the buildings' owners, architects, styles, and materials. Hardly a word was said about the work that went on in them, and nothing about the economic and class relations that defined that work. A tremendous resource for interpreting New York's labor history and class relations was redefined as a monument to entrepreneurship, technical innovation, and aesthetic skill. Nowadays these magnificently gloomy lofts have been reborn as fashionable apartments, art galleries, and shops. Their future as architecture has never looked brighter, yet their value as carriers of working-class history has been deeply compromised.

Can a non-traditional preservation practice evade or subvert the underlying ideology of heritage and present a more genuinely inclusive, or even oppositional, cultural inheritance? Two strategies suggest themselves. One is to focus on episodes of injustice in history. This is something that public history programs must sometimes do, and sites associated with such episodes can be very helpful at correcting popular misconceptions about slavery, labor relations, and so on. But to hold something up to opprobrium successfully the offense must be very grave and widely understood. Otherwise, the mechanics of public exhibition may subvert the message. This is because objects placed on exhibit tend to elicit admiration. People understand that work hanging in a museum is there to be admired, and this expectation carries over to work placed on display in the streets. It is very hard to counteract this effect of enframement. The Nazis tried it but encountered difficulties: they exhibited examples of "degenerate art" in hopes that these would attract scorn, but they found that many people liked the works. Heavy indoctrination was needed to defeat this tendency. More recently, the Nazis' own genocidal legacy has been placed on display at Auschwitz and elsewhere. This appears to be more successful, yet again this success depends in part upon maintaining a level of negative interpretation so pervasive that it fixes visitors' attitudes before they arrive. In everyday public spaces like streets, this is much harder to do: critical commentary on sites and sights cannot compete with the ideological weight of the urban environment.

This problem is compounded by the preservation movement's success in linking historic preservation with civic celebration. Politicians, editorial boards, and citizens feel comfortable preserving fine things, not only because this fits with their civic image but, I suspect, because it also fits with their understanding of what preservation does. By contrast, it is much harder to make the case for preserving places of dubious moral value, places where celebration is inappropriate. Many New Yorkers, for example, will oppose overt attempts to preserve tenement buildings because they sense instinctively that this would be tantamount to signifying admiration of poverty and overcrowding. (On the other hand, some will enthusiastically support the preservation of tenements where they are part of an architecturally admired streetscape).

The National Trust for Historic Preservation manages Kykuit, a Rockefeller family country estate; tour guides celebrate the Rockefellers' taste, philanthropy, and family life. Would the Trust change its tours to emphasize the Rockefellers' accumulation of wealth, their violent and deplorable relationship with labor unions, and the impact of their real estate dealings on working-class New York? Certainly not. Would the Trust permit outside groups—radical history or labor history groups—to offer such tours? Again, probably not. When powerful groups like the Trust (or New York's preservation movement) organize to celebrate heritage, critical commentary inevitably gets pushed to the margins. Radically critical interpretations may simply be beyond the reach of historic preservation. Still, it would be worth asking the Trust for permission to run such tours.

A second strategy for side-stepping the ideological burden of *heritage* is to coopt preservation's celebratory tendencies by extending them to new subjects that expand society's cultural inheritance. This is quietly happening in many places. "Quietly" is the important word here: as long as the historical themes in question do not challenge majoritarian views of what deserves celebration (Duke Ellington, the Underground Railroad), upset the balance of the historical record, or threaten important political or economic interests, these activities can gain the support of preservationists and the public.

What happens when these conditions are not met? During the 1990s, New York witnessed two simultaneous preservation campaigns: though superficially similar, one site met these conditions, the other did not. Comparing them allows us to gauge the limits of preservation's ability to escape the limitations of *heritage*.

THE AFRICAN BURIAL GROUND AND THE AUDUBON BALLROOM

New York's eighteenth-century African Burial Ground (Figures 7.1 to 7.3), located just north of City Hall, originally covered about five acres and held perhaps 20,000 burials, mostly of slave and free blacks. In 1989, planners for a new thirty-four-story federal office tower first came across the historical evidence of its existence. That the Burial Ground had been there during the eighteenth century was beyond dispute: the question was whether any of it survived under Lower Manhattan's heavily disturbed surface. If so, it would be a unique archaeological and cultural find.

The federal government made a less than painstaking investigation and found nothing. Site work proceeded. In summer 1991, excavators began to uncover well-preserved skeletons: by December, almost 100 had been removed,

Figure 7.1   New York's eighteenth-century African Burial Ground, seen here in 1992, was located just north of City Hall, in what later became a bustling and heavily developed part of Manhattan.

Figure 7.2   The foundations are laid for the federal building in 1992. All burials have been
cleared from this portion of the African Burial Ground, while archaeological
excavation proceeds on the adjacent annex site under the tent visible at the left.

and opposition to the construction project was mounting. The government
persisted, removing more and more human remains. Against this juggernaut,
protest seemed futile.

The coalition to save the Burial Ground began with a few local
politicians, archaeologists, and black activists. It also attracted civic and professional organizations dedicated to minority issues, the Landmarks Preservation
Commission, a few celebrities and a small number of prominent civic organizations like the Municipal Art Society of New York, where I served as director of
historic preservation. Eventually it expanded to include virtually every local
politician from Mayor David N. Dinkins on down (most of the major national
politicians stayed away until very late in the game) and much of New York's
civic establishment.

This broad coalition voiced several consistent themes, most notably the
desire of the African American community to be included in the picture of
history. Public hearings and meetings provided many opportunities for black
community leaders to speak eloquently on this subject, and they regularly cited
the rightness of inclusion as well as its beneficial effect on disaffected young
people and society as a whole. White liberals and progressives had no difficulty
accepting these arguments or the undertones of guilt that frequently accompanied them. Yet the federal government continued digging and building.

Help finally came from an unexpected quarter. A lame-duck black
congressman from Illinois, Gus Savage, headed the committee that oversaw
the federal agency responsible for the project. On July 27, 1992, he held a
hearing in New York and told the General Services Administration that its

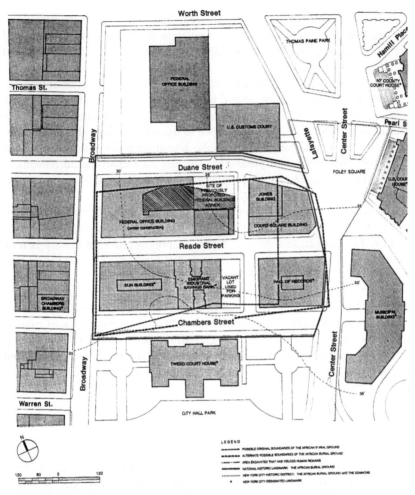

The African Burial Ground and Vicinity
site plan showing current conditions

Figure 7.3   A map of the African Burial Ground prepared in 1993 shows both National Historic Landmark and New York City Historic District boundaries, as well as the approximate outlines of the original burial ground and the two lots within the burial ground which were then vacant. That intended for the federal building annex is now landscaped and contains the official memorial.

funding would be in jeopardy if the agency persisted in violating the Burial Ground. Work stopped three days later.

By this time, a large part of the site had already been cleared, and the tower was on its way up. Only the adjacent annex site, slated for a two-story extension to the tower, remained incompletely excavated. The government had no definite plan for using this wing and now, in a face-saving compromise, the GSA traded it away. The annex site was filled and leveled with clean soil, planted in grass, and fenced; the remaining skeletons were left under-ground. The federal government promised to install an interpretive center and art work in the adjacent office building and to build a permanent memorial on the annex site.

After construction stopped, the site—indeed the entire precinct of the orig-inal Burial Ground, covering several blocks—was declared both a city historic district and a National Historic Landmark. The excavated human remains, as well as associated artifacts, were shipped to the anthropological research labo-ratories at Howard University. A public education office was established in New York and began interpreting the site and its archaeological remains. It quickly became a place of study, pilgrimage, and the observance of various traditional religious and cultural rituals.[1]

Lifted as it was by the urgency of struggle, the Burial Ground's rediscov-ery had a profound impact on the way people think about New York's history. The African and African American presence in that history is now both bigger and clearer, among white as well as black people, than before. The African contribution to Dutch New York has been described and discussed, as have African–Indian relations. The existence of slavery and slave trading in New York has been publicly acknowledged. The bones and artifacts have yielded archaeological information of national interest about African cultural traditions and living conditions in eighteenth-century America. The fact that this part of Manhattan, so close to the city's centers of government and finance, was once known as Little Africa has been incorporated into many people's mental maps in a poignant way.

Preservation's celebratory power has worked well at the African Burial Ground to reinsert a forgotten piece of history in the canon. But the lessons can be more complex, as the case of the Audubon Ballroom shows (Figures 7.4 to 7.6). The Audubon Ballroom and Theater, located in Washington Heights, a poor neighborhood north of Harlem, would have qualified for an all-out preservation effort on almost any grounds. Designed in 1912 by leading theater architect Thomas W. Lamb, the build-ing's Broadway facade was a masterpiece of early terra cotta decoration. Though vacant and derelict, all the important architectural elements survived. The vast, ornate theater was one of the earliest designed expressly for film. The ballroom was once the largest dance floor in New York and was a powerful social magnet for decades; it was where Mike Quill organ-ized the Transit Workers Union, and it was where the Organization of Afro-American Unity, founded by civil rights leader Malcolm X in 1964, held its weekly meetings. But the historical event that galvanized people was the assassination of Malcolm X, which took place in the ballroom on February 21, 1965.

The fate of the ballroom became a public issue in 1989, when New York City, which owned the building, announced an agreement with Columbia University to demolish it and replace it with a center for commercial biotech research. Both the city and the politically powerful Port Authority of New York and New Jersey would contribute public funds to the project, which

Figure 7.4   By the early 1990s, the Audubon Ballroom and Theater on New York's upper Broadway was vacant and decrepit, awaiting removal by the City of New York and Columbia University and replacement by a commercial biotech research facility. This view shows the terra cotta facade wrapping around the corner of ballroom, with the theater to the right.

was heralded as essential for New York to retain its leadership in this field. Even if the center failed, this would be a marvelous deal for Columbia, which would gain five square blocks of free and upzoned land adjacent to its vast, overcrowded medical complex.

The strategic issues raised by the campaign to save the Audubon were complex. Washington Heights was in the process of becoming a Dominican neighborhood, and some Dominican groups, feeling no direct connection with Malcolm X, saw the project as a source of jobs and economic development. On the other hand, many residents of Washington Heights and Harlem opposed the biotech project not only because it would destroy the building but also because it would add a new load of toxic emissions to an already badly polluted neighborhood. They also resented what they saw as Columbia's imperialistic attitude, remembering earlier notorious attempts to encroach on the surrounding communities. Finally, some African American preservationists, as well as political groups connected to the movements of the 1960s, strenuously opposed the demolition of the ballroom because of its connection with Malcolm X.

The latter factions favored a strategy of uncompromising opposition. Yet others counseled political pragmatism, believing that such opposition would be futile and that winning something would be better than losing all. My organization, the Municipal Art Society, was in this group, as were some

Figure 7.5   Public protest focused both on the demolition of the Audubon Ballroom and on the toxic emissions to which, according to the environmental impact statement, the new biotech facility would subject the low-income neighborhood of Washington Heights.

Harlem politicians and preservation groups. This loose coalition accepted (some with great reluctance) the inevitability of the biotech project yet opposed the demolition of the ballroom to accommodate it.

Problems soon developed within the latter group. The Municipal Art Society assembled a pro-bono architectural team and put forth a proposal to restore the ballroom and the terra cotta facades while allowing the theater to be demolished. The group showed how a combination of adaptive reuse and new construction could accommodate both the biotech project and some promised public services, perhaps even more economically than Columbia's own proposal. Architecturally this was an intelligent scheme, yet politically it failed to factor in the opposition of much of the community to biotech research, and to Columbia.

Another problem with the scheme was that it sacrificed the theater. Though Malcolm X had never been associated with this portion of the build-ing, it was architecturally valuable, and it became difficult to hold the moral high ground while allowing its destruction. Some supporters backed away from the proposal. "They want to carve it up like a Thanksgiving turkey," remarked Harlem preservationist Michael Henry Adam as he left (and publicly denounced) the coalition.

Figure 7.6   Part of the Audubon Ballroom was ultimately saved and awkwardly incorporated into the new biotech building designed by Davis Brody Bond.

Valuable support for the proposal came from one of New York's most consistently progressive politicians, Manhattan Borough President Ruth Messinger, who endorsed the scheme and fought hard for it. She incurred bitter attacks from the mainstream press, which supported development in general and Columbia in particular. In the end, she and the coalition were overpowered and out-maneuvered by the formidable bureaucratic powers available to the mayor, the university, and the city and state development agencies. Nevertheless, Messinger was able to negotiate a compromise: to save and incorporate some 60 per cent of the terra cotta facades and 40 per cent of the ballroom into a redesigned biotech facility. A community health clinic and Malcolm X exhibit would also be installed in the building.[2]

At the time, Messinger's solution pleased few people. It did violence to the building. It mocked history. It reeked of political compromise. And it offered nothing to biotech opponents. Yet, in the real world, it was all that a courageous politician could win. Looking at the result some years later, it is possible to feel that this partial victory is far preferable to the complete loss that would otherwise have occurred.

TWO CAMPAIGNS FOR BLACK HISTORY

No two preservation campaigns are alike. But these two display striking similarities. They took place simultaneously in the same city, focused on important sites of African American history, prompted widespread popular concern and support among African Americans, and were fought in opposition to government plans and agencies. Even their outcomes were remarkably similar: partial destruction of the historic site, partial restoration, and the installation of public art memorials and interpretive exhibits. Yet there were also important differences in how they were fought, how the public reacted, and how they were resolved. The civic establishment and local governmental hierarchy enthusiastically joined the movement for the African Burial Ground. Reporters covered it avidly. It became virtually impossible to be against it. By contrast, the civic establishment largely stayed away from the Audubon Ballroom, Mayor Dinkins (along with much of the political establishment) sided with Columbia, the press was unfavorable, no savior rose up from Illinois, and even some prominent African American voices opposed the ballroom's preservation. Afterwards, many advocates of the Burial Ground left that battle with a feeling of uplift and accomplishment, while advocates of the ballroom left feeling bitter and defeated. These differences continued long after the struggles were over. The African Burial Ground was accepted into the canon of preservation sites and stories, becoming both a New York City and a National Historic Landmark. Once its preservation was assured, government officials at all levels rushed to embrace the site, providing public art work, exhibitions, and substantial public funding. By contrast, the preservation establishment continued to reject or ignore the Audubon Ballroom. It enjoys no official status as a historic site, either at local or at national level, and has received little if any public funding. Efforts to mark the site and to generate exhibits and other interpretive programs have been slow and halting.

What explains these differences? The contrast in the line-up of opponents may have played a role. At the Burial Ground, the federal government—a distant, faceless bureaucracy that inspired little love locally—offered an excellent target for attack, one that could unify New Yorkers of many different stripes. At the Audubon, by contrast, the mayor, Columbia University, and the Port Authority commanded extensive networks of local allegiances within the power elite; they were much more difficult to attack. Also, they had substantial political and economic interests at stake, while the communities of Washington Heights and Harlem were relatively weak. Conversely, after the outcome was decided, it became possible to pressure the federal government into becoming a partner in commemoration and interpretation, with the National Park Service playing an important role, while at the Audubon the city and Columbia University offered more elusive targets.

More important though was the symbolism of the two campaigns and how it resonated with the cultural politics of preservation. Twenty years after his assassination, Malcolm X remained a troubling figure to many white New Yorkers, and to some black ones as well. Even some of his admirers questioned whether he could best be remembered at the site of his martyrdom. These were challenging issues that split the community. The African Burial Ground, by contrast, was rather unproblematic. The eighteenth century was a long time ago, and, more than any particular political stance, the Burial Ground stood for the simple "thereness" of black people. One could concede this without calling into question the fairness of current political and economic arrangements, and in the 1990s a great many white New Yorkers were prepared to admit African Americans to the historical picture on these terms. Moreover, while the Burial Ground stirred up potentially troubling themes of guilt and recompense, it also offered a relatively painless way to address them. These themes thus served on a sentimental level to unify, rather than divide. In the end, the preservation canon opened up to recognize a site that did not threaten the appearance of social or family harmony represented by *heritage*. In contrast, it remained closed to the Audubon Ballroom, because to recognize Malcolm X was to raise still-unanswered questions that would disturb that harmony. To commemorate the legacy of Malcolm X was to admit the existence of social conflict, not merely as a historical fact but as a present reality.

The comparison between the two sites is instructive for what it says not only about the politics of preservation but also about the relationship between preservation battles and broader campaigns for social change. Many participants in both battles were motivated at least partly by the belief that they were participating in such a broader campaign. It is worth asking to what extent this belief was justified. The 1990s were a time when real progress on important economic and social issues seemed extraordinarily difficult to achieve, and, for some, heritage battles may have provided an outlet for energy that might otherwise have gone to waste. Yet the cases of the Audubon Ballroom and African Burial Ground suggest the limits of heritage campaigns as a tool of genuine empowerment. Heritage victories, unless accompanied by significant gains in economic justice or political power, are likely to remain essentially symbolic: inclusion does not necessarily lead to empowerment, nor do heritage politics offer a direct route to social, economic, or political change.

This does not mean that efforts to improve preservation's representation of history are not worth undertaking. On the contrary, they are valuable in their own terms and need no outside justification. Nor does it mean that such efforts are irrelevant to achieving social change. But, at least in the context of the United States, it does suggest that they may be incapable of stimulating social change by themselves. As Chapter 3 shows, significant change in the heritage arena is more likely to reflect than to stimulate larger political and social change; similarly, economic and political empowerment is more likely to produce heritage changes than vice versa.

What heritage inclusion can do is to consolidate, support, and represent social change. This is not trivial: it forms the necessary basis for social progress in the future. This may be true even of efforts that fail or, like the Audubon Ballroom, achieve limited success. Moreover, there is no way to measure how far change has actually progressed except to push the limits. Whether they succeed or fail, then, campaigns to correct the heritage canon will continue to be useful, both to social reformers and to preservationists.

NOTES

1. The subsequent history of the African Burial Ground site may be briefly told. Commemorative art works began to be installed in the federal office building, now named the Ted Weiss Federal Building, starting in 1994 with Houston Conwill's *New Ring Shout*. In the fall of 2003 the human remains were brought back from Howard University in a three-day cycle of observances that began in Washington, DC, and ended with their reinterment in the Burial Ground in New York. In 2006, the site became a National Monument and was incorporated into the National Park system; the visitor center, located within the Ted Weiss Federal Building, was provided with extensive interpretive exhibits. In the fall of 2007 the promised outdoor memorial, designed by Rodney Léon and called *The Door of Return*, was dedicated. In addition to federal involvement at the federal office building and former annex site, in 2000 the City of New York dedicated its own monument to the African Burial Ground at Foley Square, a few blocks away. Called *Triumph of the Human Spirit*, by Lorenzo Pace, this was described by the city's Department of Parks at the time of its dedication as "the world's largest site-specific installation venerating the experience of African American enslavement."

2. The subsequent history of the Audubon Ballroom is here summarized. By 1997, the Audubon Business and Technology Center had opened in a building designed by Davis Brody Bond and incorporating the ballroom and restored portions of the original facade. The community health clinic was operating, and commemorative art works had been installed, including a mural by David Galvez in the ballroom and a statue of Malcolm X in the lobby. Following the preservation campaign, Malcolm X's widow, Dr. Betty Shabazz, led efforts to start a research center. Following her death in 1997, Mayor Rudoph Giuliani announced that this would soon be opened, but there was no further action. In 2005, Columbia University announced the creation of the Malcolm X and Dr. Betty Shabazz Memorial and Educational Center in the ballroom space. By the following year the space was equipped with multimedia kiosks and was hosting exhibitions and performances. As of 2008, however, the lobby and ballroom remain closed to the public most of the time; no public plaque, marker, or exhibit identifies the site, nor does the Audubon Business and Technology Center's official website mention its historical and architectural significance. Unlike the African Burial Ground, the Audubon Ballroom has not been given National Historic Landmark, National Register, or New York City landmark status.

CHAPTER 8

Historical Memory, Social Equity, and the Disappearance of New York's Working-Class Neighborhoods

This chapter has been recast and updated from a talk given at the biennial conference of CICOP, the Centro para la Conservación del Patrimonio, in Buenos Aires in 2006.

I had occasion to reassess the progress of preservation in New York when I was asked to lecture in Buenos Aires in September 2006. The previous decade had not been a very good one for preservation in New York. In the opinion of many supporters, the city's Landmarks Preservation Commission had become underfunded, understaffed, and overly eager to accommodate real estate interests. It was a fact that the agency had sat out one of the most interesting preservation battles of these years, refusing even to hold a public hearing to consider protecting Edward Durrell Stone's distinctive Gallery of Modern Art at 2 Columbus Circle—and this despite pressure from the National Trust for Historic Preservation, the World Monuments Fund, most city and state preservation organizations, and a long roster of famous New Yorkers. The malaise was not limited to government: some major civic organizations, once known for their hard-hitting preservation advocacy, appeared to have become cautious in their old age. Frustration simmered.

But it was one particular aspect of this discouraging picture which interested me, because it touched on an issue I had been much involved in: the fate of historic sites, that is, places valued for their historical associations rather than their architectural merit. During the early 1990s the city's preservation establishment had become alarmed over the fate of these sites. Yet, more than a decade later, little had really changed: the city's historic sites were still under attack, indeed more so than ever. Preservation was still being done in pretty much the same ways, and, though many people now espoused a broader view of what made places preservation-worthy, official standards had not changed much. No major surveys had been undertaken to identify the city's most indispensable historic places; no far-reaching policy initiatives had been mounted to protect places of neighborhood tradition or affection. Nor had the preservation community capitalized on the tremendous upsurge of public interest prompted by the Audubon Ballroom and African Burial

Ground campaigns. A wake-up call had been sounded, but the city's preservation movement had not woken up.

The situation in 2006 did, however, differ in one important way from that of 1996. Then, the places which goaded preservationists into concern were discrete and precisely bounded sites: the Dvořák House, Pier 54 (Figure 6.5), the Audubon Ballroom (Figures 7.4 to 7.6), Dorothy Day's seaside cottage, the hospital complex at Ellis Island, the African Burial Ground (Figures 7.1 to 7.3). Now, entire neighborhoods were disappearing. A boom in high-end real estate development was sweeping the city, transforming both its physical and its social fabric, and preservationists appeared to be doing little to stop it. The city was well on its way to losing essential chapters of its history.

The neighborhoods under threat were not those which had traditionally attracted the interest of preservationists. They were not the fine residential enclaves of Manhattan, brownstone Brooklyn, or semi-suburban Queens: the Upper East Side, Brooklyn Heights, Park Slope, or Douglas Manor. Nor were they the magnificently showy nineteenth-century industrial ensembles of SoHo, NoHo, or Tribeca. Instead, they were immigrant and working-class neighborhoods, communities of color, and still-functional industrial areas (Figure 8.1). One was the Lower East Side, legendary home to generations of poor migrants from Germany, Ireland, Italy, eastern Europe, Russia, China, and Latin America (Figure 8.2). Another was Harlem, the nation's premier African American urban community for half a century or more, site of grinding poverty but also of remarkable cultural achievement. The waterfront of Manhattan's Lower West Side was a third: a zone of docks, warehouses, and former sailors' hotels, this was once—in the days when New York was truly a port city—a major point of connection to the rest of the world. Across the East River, much of Brooklyn's once mighty waterfront was also being transformed, including neighborhoods like Williamsburg and Greenpoint, home to established Polish and Latino working-class communities and, farther down the shoreline, Red Hook and Gowanus.

Most of these neighborhoods were not exactly beautiful. Much of the housing stock looked beat up. Blocks of old rowhouses and small tenements in Greenpoint were covered with vinyl or aluminum siding; paint was peeling and cornices falling off the tenements of the Lower East Side. Many of Harlem's streets were marred by vacant buildings and empty lots, remnants of the devastation that had swept the area during the 1960s and 1970s as landlords burned buildings for insurance payments, the moderately well-to-do left for the suburbs, and the social fabric of the community collapsed. These neighborhoods, then, challenged preservationists in some of the same ways as had the threatened historic sites of the 1990s: they too were places whose historical importance outweighed their architectural value. But now these historic sites were writ large across the cityscape.

Their historical importance was fundamental. New York was once a port city; it was also a great industrial center, and well into the twentieth century its character was largely that of a working-class city. Now that much

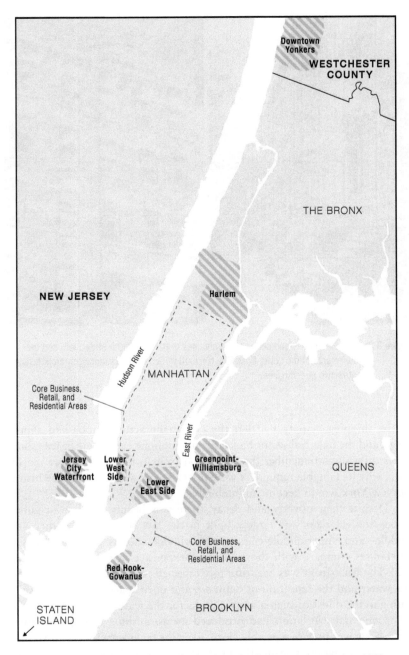

Figure 8.1 The historic working-class and industrial areas threatened since the late 1990s are located in a loose ring around the city's business and residential core, defined here as the area that takes in the city's major retail areas, its two leading business districts, Midtown and Lower Manhattan or the Financial District, and the majority of its most fashionable residential neighborhoods, including the Upper East and West Sides, Greenwich Village, SoHo, and Brooklyn Heights. This area also includes a large majority of the city's designated landmarks and historic districts.

Figure 8.2   Despite poverty and decay, the rowhouses of Harlem (130th Street: left) and the tenements of the Lower East Side (Orchard Street: right) present many architecturally attractive streetscapes.

of the shipping activity had left the city, manufacturing jobs had slipped away, and the financial sector had come to dominate everything, it was sometimes difficult to remember that historical New York. All the more reason, then, why its tangible reminders were priceless, for without them the history of New York would become unintelligible.

Despite their poverty and decay, there was beauty in these neighborhoods too. Harlem was largely built in the late nineteenth century as a middle- and upper-middle-class neighborhood, and its elegant blocks of rowhouses compare with those of more expensive neighborhoods (Figure 8.2). The waterfront was beautiful too, especially the spectacular views over the water and the sensation of light, air, and open space which was exhilarating in the midst of such a great city. As for the water itself, forty years of environmental legislation had produced an astonishing change: the once-toxic brew was now remarkably clean. Even the tenements of the Lower East Side were not without beauty (Figure 8.2): substandard living conditions had been well hidden behind masonry facades graced with lavish helpings of ornament.

For decades, investment largely passed these neighborhoods by. Owners and residents were pretty much left to their own devices, with the help of some government housing and social service programs. Some areas held on; others declined. The Lower East Side, despite severe overcrowding, continued to provide much-needed housing to immigrant communities, including an expanding Chinatown and a large influx of Latinos who renamed it "Loisaida." Along the Brooklyn waterfront, even as major industries were leaving New York, smaller industries actually enjoyed a revival—for example, manufacturers of picture frames, lamps, jewelry, and other expensive design and household goods in Greenpoint–Williamsburg. But now, private capital, backed by city policy, had rediscovered these areas and was transforming them.

To understand what was happening, it helps to go back in time. The 1970s had been a low point in the city's history. The Bronx was burning—literally. By the end of the decade, as many as 30,000 housing units were being abandoned each year. Entire neighborhoods went up in smoke. Photographs from those days look like Matthew Brady's images of Richmond after the Civil War, or newsreels of Dresden after the firebombing of World War II. The city's subway system, long a source of urban pride as well as economic vitality, had deteriorated disastrously. Middle-class white people were fleeing to the suburbs. The city government teetered on the brink of default. The federal government turned its back.

By the 1990s, the trend lines had reversed. Vast public investments had rebuilt the city's transit system and brought abandoned neighborhoods back to life. The city's population, which had bottomed out in 1980, was rising. Wall Street was booming. Living in New York had become chic once again. It all seemed like good news, and in many ways it was.

But, at the same time, changes in the national economy guaranteed that the new city would not be the one that had been almost lost: instead, it would be decisively reshaped by new social and economic forces. The period from the Great Depression of the 1930s up to the 1970s had seen the growth of a vast American middle class. Teachers, policemen, secretaries, and union workers in basic industries achieved a comfortable standard of living. The gap between rich and poor narrowed dramatically: between 1947 and 1973, real wages rose by 81 percent, while the incomes of the richest 1 percent of the population increased by only 38 percent. Yet, in the 1980s, as the city began to recover, these trend lines reversed. Between 1980 and 2004, real wages in manufacturing flattened and actually fell by 1 percent, while the incomes of the richest 1 percent of the population rose by an incredible 135 percent. The gap between rich and poor was expanding again, and at an alarming rate. Today, in fact, the United States boasts the widest gap between rich and poor of any post-industrial nation, and it is continuing to widen. Despite working more hours and taking fewer vacations, the poor and the middle classes are becoming poorer while the rich become richer, the very rich fabulously so. In 1964, the chief executive officers of major corporations earned, on average, 24 times the average American worker; in 1979, 35 times; in 2006, 364 times, though by some counts the gap is actually much wider. The average American worker now earns a little less than $42,000 per year; the average CEO earns just under $11 million per year, or 821 times the minimum wage set by federal law.

These trends have been especially severe in New York. In 1980, New York City ranked eleventh among US cities in income disparity; by 2000, it had climbed to fourth place. The Bronx had become the poorest urban county in the nation. Within Manhattan, the disparities were even more exaggerated. In 1980, Manhattan was placed seventeenth among the nation's counties in income disparity: the top fifth of Manhattan earners made twenty-one times what the lowest fifth made. By 2000, the top fifth was making fifty-two times what the lowest fifth was, and Manhattan boasted the nation's most severe income disparities, with statistics comparable to those of the African country of Namibia. Today these shocking gaps continue to widen. Wages are stagnant: "The gains are all going to the top," explained one sociologist. "Manhattan dwellers top US in salary," announced a *New York Post* headline in 2007, citing new federal statistics.[1] The average Manhattan salary was now $147,000 per year, while financial workers were earning an average of $528,000; meanwhile, at the other end of the scale, Manhattan had some of the country's lowest earnings, while the city's other four boroughs, containing more than three-fourths of the city's population, remained stuck below the national average: Bronx and Brooklyn residents earned $40,000 or less per year. And once more the disparities were growing. While average earnings in Manhattan were increasing at a rate of 16.7 percent per year—more than five times the national average—the city's next highest growth rate, in the Bronx, was only 5.1 percent, just one-tenth of 1 percent above the national average. The remaining three boroughs scored below it, Queens and Staten Island each at 3.5 percent per annum. This meant that, with incomes already below the national average, most of the city was falling further behind.

New York has been stunningly rebuilt since its near-collapse in the mid-1970s. Yet it is not at all the same city as it was. It has become a city of gross inequities, in which a relatively small number of residents command enormous financial resources and use them to cultivate the most expensive tastes, whether in food, clothing, cars—or housing. To be sure, this is not merely the result of national trends. In a book published in 2007, Kim Moody spelled out in painstaking detail how, starting with the financial crisis of 1975, a succession of mayors worked with the city's financiers, business leaders, and real estate developers to impose a neo-liberal economic program on the city.[2] Public services essential to the poor, such as hospitals, schools, homeless services, and the city's public university system, have faced repeated budget cuts while the city has given away literally billions of dollars each year in tax breaks for midtown office buildings and luxury apartments. Despite phenomenal increases in property value, the city has lowered property assessments on office and luxury buildings so that property tax revenues actually contribute a smaller percentage to the city's budget than they did thirty years ago. Meanwhile, the city's public sector unions have had to accept contracts that do not keep up with inflation. As national and global trends have encouraged the growth of an economy in which large numbers of poor migrants subsist alongside and serve the interests of wealthy entrepreneurs and financial technicians, the city's elites have ridden the tide, meanwhile dismantling the network of social services that used to soften the hard edges of poverty.

These trends were bound to have an effect on the city's physical fabric, and so they have. There have been times in New York's history when the construction of housing was largely driven by the needs of middle- and working-class people: mile after mile of apartment buildings in the Bronx, Brooklyn, Queens, and Upper Manhattan attest to this, as do the tenements of the Lower East Side and nearly 200,000 units of city-owned public housing. But this is not one of those times. New construction today is heavily oriented to the luxury market. Meanwhile, landlords are upgrading older affordable housing to luxury rents in order to take advantage of the increasing concentration of wealth at the high end.

The case of Stuyvesant Town and Peter Cooper Village provides a striking example. Built by Metropolitan Life Insurance Company between 1943 and 1946 with state subsidies to provide affordable housing, these adjoining complexes contain 11,232 apartments in 110 buildings; described in 2006 by the *New York Times* as "a refuge for generations of firefighters, nurses and civil servants,"[3] they constituted the city's single largest reservoir of middle-income housing. By 2001, Metropolitan Life was trying hard to raise rents to market level, even incurring charges that the company was harassing long-time tenants to vacate apartments. Tenants protested. Five years later, Metropolitan Life sold the entire complex in a single transaction—the biggest in the history of US real estate. Though the new owners moved quickly to reassure tenants that no dramatic changes were planned, at a purchase price of $5.4 billion it seemed clear that they would have no choice but to raise rents as fast and as high as the market would bear.

Meanwhile, many other middle-income complexes built with public subsidies during the 1960s and 1970s were being privatized as their rent restrictions expired. And, across much of the city, private owners were making individual decisions to upgrade apartment buildings and houses, meanwhile raising rents to high-end levels. And no wonder: driven by the same economic forces that were lifting high-end earnings—"record Wall Street bonus income," as one real estate newsletter put it in 2006—the luxury housing market offered the possibility of enormous profits. A weak dollar helped too, subsidizing the purchase of luxury Manhattan apartments by wealthy foreigners. In Manhattan, housing prices set all-time records in the second quarter of 2006, when the average sales price for an apartment reached almost $1.4 million. In 2008, prices of $48 million and $52 million were recorded for Manhattan apartments. Even outside Manhattan, the expansion of the luxury market has put economic pressure on many middle- and working-class neighborhoods: one symptom is the cost of vacant land, which in 2004 rose by 24 percent in Manhattan, but by 40 percent in the rest of the city.

What all of this has meant is that, even as the city's population is growing—even as its total housing stock is growing—the stock of so-called affordable units has actually shrunk. Since the mid-1970s, government has been, with few exceptions, unable or unwilling to step in. Construction of public housing as well as major subsidy programs for affordable housing stopped or petered out even as subsidies for luxury housing ballooned. An aggressive program of affordable housing construction and reconstruction, launched in 1986 by Mayor Ed Koch, ended ten years later. From 2000, a Republican administration in Washington and, until 2006, a Republican Congress cut federal housing budgets and programs every year. Not only have new units not been built; existing units have been lost. Out of about 121,000 units built under the major subsidy programs of the 1960s and 1970s, 23 percent stopped being affordable sometime between 1990 and 2005, and a further 13 percent were considered threatened as of the latter date.[4] It was a record year in 2005, as more than 5,500 apartments— 80 percent of them in Harlem and the South Bronx—left the subsidy system.[5] Overall, the stock of affordable units has declined by over 200,000 since the 1990s. This has not only produced overcrowding but further pushed up rents and exacerbated poverty: the percentage of rent-burdened households, defined as those paying more than 30 percent of their gross income on housing, rose from under 25 percent in 1960 to about 45 percent in 1985 and is now over 50 percent.

With this background, we can understand what started happening to old working-class and industrial neighborhoods like Harlem, the Lower East Side, and Greenpoint–Williamsburg around the end of the 1990s. A growing number of New Yorkers with unprecedented amounts of disposable income were looking for housing at a very high level of luxury. Because their incomes were soaring ever higher above the rest of society, they easily bid up the market. And because they themselves were becoming more numerous as well as demanding larger living quarters, they put pressure on areas beyond the traditionally desirable neighborhoods. Looking at the city's working-class and industrial neighborhoods through their eyes, one saw some highly desir-able assets: fine housing stock, stunning waterfront views, vacant land, loca-tions close to the heart of the city, good transit access. Best of all, years of neglect had left these assets undervalued. Now the wealthy were competing for them, with predictable results. In Harlem in 2002, a price of $400,000 for a rowhouse was considered astonishing. In 2006, Harlem rowhouses requiring complete rehabilitation from cellar to roof sold for an average of $1.1 million, and one could spend as much as $2 million for an apartment there—this in a neighborhood where the 2000 Census reported a median household income of under $20,000, or enough to afford a monthly housing payment of about $550. Overall, apartments in Harlem had quintupled in price since 1995.

These trends were reshaping both the physical and the social fabric of neighborhoods like Harlem. The new or renovated dwellings there were clearly not intended for the neighborhood's long-time residents (Figure 8.3), and the billboards that advertised them frequently underlined the point, sometimes causing resentment and public controversy. Another dramatic example of physical and social transformation came in the form of a pair of

Figure 8.3   By 2006, huge banners advertised new luxury apartment buildings in poor and working-class neighborhoods like Harlem (seen here), Greenpoint–Williamsburg, and the Lower East Side.

apartment towers completed in 2001 on the Lower West Side waterfront. In an area where five stories is the norm, they reached fifteen. Designed by world-famous architect Richard Meier, they were obviously intended to call attention to themselves, to distinguish themselves from the old neighborhood around them. They accomplished this not only through height but also through an aesthetic based on hard-edged white metal and large expanses of glass, which contrasted glaringly with the area's prevailing character of red brick walls punctuated by sash windows. Most decisive, though, was their unmistakable impression of luxury. The towers were evidently meant for people as different from their neighbors as the buildings themselves, and indeed early purchasers included celebrities Nicole Kidman, Calvin Klein, and Martha Stewart. Social and physical transformation were proceeding hand in hand.

Similar processes have been reshaping the Lower East Side. There, amidst the tenements, a luxury apartment tower by star architect Bernard Tschumi was completed in 2007 (Figure 8.4). Its bid to be different from its neighbors started with its provocative name—Blue—but otherwise mimicked that of the West

Figure 8.4 The shape of an expensive future rises above the Lower East's Essex Street Market, built during the Great Depression by Mayor LaGuardia to house pushcart peddlers. In this and similar neighborhoods, resources are not trickling downward from rich to poor: rather, they are flowing upward from poor to rich.

Street towers, relying on obtrusive height, shiny glass (blue in this case), a distinctive sculptural shape (bulgy) and, above all, heavily marketed luxury touches: a doorman, concierge, roof deck, top-of-the line kitchen cabinetry, and so forth. In the summer of 2008 it was reported that actor Justin Long, best known for starring in commercials for Macintosh computers, had bought a nearly 2,000-square-foot apartment for a price of $2.4 million. To put this in context, consider that the Lower East Side was a neighborhood where (according to the 2000 Census) almost 165,000 people squeezed themselves into 1.7 square miles; where 88 percent of housing units were occupied by renters; where 63 percent of housing units contained fewer than four rooms; where the median family income was $28,505; and where 36 percent of families with children lived below the federal poverty threshold. Mr. Long joined a mere 967 non-Hispanic white people living among the more than 10,000 residents of his census tract.

Astonishing changes were also taking place in Greenpoint–Williamsburg, a low-rise district of tenements, nondescript industrial buildings, and modest rowhouses, many sheathed in unfashionable vinyl or aluminum siding. According to the 2000 Census, the median family income for Brooklyn's Community District 1, which included both neighborhoods, was $27,285; over 40 percent of families with children lived below the federal poverty threshold; and 85 percent of the housing units had been built before 1970. Yet, by 2006, new luxury apartment buildings were rising in every direction (Figure 8.5). Architecturally, these slabs and towers rejected the nineteenth-century urban vernacular that remained intact all around them; economically, they brought residents with unprecedented wealth to the neighborhood. The most sweeping transformations could be seen on the waterfront itself, where the city's planning authorities were actively encouraging the construction of the biggest and tallest towers. There was no mistaking the air of luxury projected by these alien buildings: it was hammered home in the advertisements and billboards designed to lure new residents. As in Harlem or the Lower East Side, it was perfectly clear that these new buildings were not intended for the neighborhood's current residents: eventually the old-timers would have to move out, displaced by rising rents and taxes, if not by actual eviction. In fact, this is already happening. Noting that growth in Greenpoint–Williamsburg was continuing "at a rapid clip," New York University's Furman Center for Real Estate and Urban Policy reported in 2007 that, while housing prices had more than doubled since 2000, the area had "become significantly less racially diverse" as the proportion of white residents had increased, while those of blacks and Hispanics had decreased.[6]

The old-time residents of Greenpoint–Williamsburg were an interesting mixture, for at least three distinct groups intersected there. There was, first of all, a long-established Polish working- and middle-class community, signaled by the many travel agencies and food shops whose signs were entirely in Polish; according to the 2000 Census, over 21,000 residents of Polish ancestry lived in the district, of whom more than 17,000 spoke Polish at home. Then there was a large Hispanic working-class community, traditionally with roots in Puerto Rico but now also from the Dominican Republic, Mexico, and Colombia. Finally, there was a newer community of upwardly mobile young people who were mostly though not entirely white and English-speaking. This latter group began to move in during the 1990s. Its members did not necessarily have a great deal of money, but they had prospects. And they had a sense of style, often self-consciously so. If you stood on any corner of the neighborhood's main shopping street you could see crowds of them flowing by, talking on cellphones or perhaps listening to music on headphones. Though quite distinct from the older working-class residents, they were drawn to the neighborhood for some of the same reasons, especially inexpensive housing. At times indeed it seemed as if the streets were crowded with young people looking for apartments. Yet, by 2006, although new apartments were advertised everywhere, they were clearly not intended for them, any more than for their Polish or Puerto Rican neighbors: the new apartments were far too expensive. The older housing stock was moving out of reach too, as owners renovated and raised rents to

Figure 8.5 New luxury apartment towers dwarf the low-rise, working-class streets of Greenpoint and Williamsburg. Just as they introduce new residents, they also introduce a new architectural language based on metal and glass, in stark contrast with the neighborhood's brick and wood-frame houses, shops, and industrial facilities.

unprecedented levels. Absent an abrupt reversal, the end was in sight for all three communities.

The question of displacement has received much discussion, particularly in relation to gentrification, the process by which wealthier in-migrants to many neighborhoods gradually replace their existing residents. Gentrification has gone on for a long time in New York, long enough for it to seem natural. But a 2005 study by Kathe Newman and Elvin Wyly, of Rutgers University and the University of British Columbia, found that the wave of gentrification which began in the late 1990s was "of a scale and pace that is unmatched historically." Their findings also cast doubt on the oft-repeated and politically popular assertion that everyone benefits from gentrification. Not only did the authors find evidence of higher levels of displacement than previously suspected, and of overcrowding caused by rising housing costs, but they also found that many poor residents viewed gentrification not as a "benevolent market force that gives them a reason to stay" but as a looming threat to their ability to stay: "Residents who remain in gentrifying neighborhoods," they report, "fear that it is just a matter of time until they are displaced." Gentrification, they conclude, is "not a minor phenomenon that affects a few communities" but rather "evidence of vast urban restructuring."[7] As is so often the case, the process has a racial dimension: a report published the following year found that, as indicators of gentrification like housing values, education, and income rise, "minority populations generally decrease."[8] Clearly gentrification was not benefiting everyone.

At first glance, the sweeping changes reported by Newman and Wyly, and by others, appear to be market-driven, the natural results of free-market capitalism allowed to take its course. But this is not really the case: government policy and public money are behind them. An unusually clear example can be seen in an area of central Brooklyn which is slated for complete redevelopment as a gigantic multi-use project called Atlantic Yards. Like the other neighborhoods in question, the area around Atlantic Yards contains a mixture of working-class communities and decaying industry, along with some artists and professionals who belong culturally to the upper middle class but, unable to compete in the housing market elsewhere, have rehabilitated old houses. As of 2006, the 21-acre development was slated to include a sports arena, hotel, 6.8 million square feet of housing, 606,000 square feet of office space, and a quarter of a million square feet of retail space. As then proposed, the tallest tower would have reached 620 feet or fifty-eight stories, overtopping everything in Brooklyn, including the Williamsburgh Savings Bank tower, a local icon and the tallest building in Brooklyn since its construction in 1927. By 2007, the proposed new tower had been cut down to 511 feet—exactly one foot shorter than the Williamsburgh Savings Bank—and other quantities had also been somewhat reduced. But naming the tallest tower Miss Brooklyn will not make it any less incongruous. If completed, the development will be completely alien to the neighborhoods around it, and, as elsewhere, the disjunction is intentional. The architect is Frank Gehry and, like Meier or Tschumi, he has employed a hefty sampling of his now-stereotyped architectural tricks—funny-shaped buildings, walls that lean out, and so forth—to make everyone understand that Atlantic Yards is different, more modern, more cosmopolitan, more luxurious, more expensive than anything around it. And, as elsewhere, the impacts of this intrusion will spread far beyond the margins of the site itself. The buildings will loom over tree-lined streets of nineteenth-century rowhouses (Figure 8.6). Their high rental values will also gradually overwhelm those streets.

At Atlantic Yards, these changes are largely government-driven. There are developers, and they stand to make a substantial return, but the public is underwriting the risks, absorbing the negative consequences, and subsidizing the profits. City and state governments have provided political support, exemption from city and state rules, and massive infusions of taxpayer dollars. In exchange, the developers have promised to include a significant number of apartments at below-market rents, as well as jobs for Brooklyn residents, but opponents have pointed out that the rents would still be high for many area residents and that the promises are much less definite than they sound. What has particularly disturbed many opponents is a government ruling that the neighborhood was "blighted." This determination could not be contested because it was not based on any objective criteria. But it was extremely valuable to the developers because it allowed the government to condemn people's houses and turn them over to the developers.

Atlantic Yards is the latest in a string of exceptionally large, government-driven projects that includes Battery Park City, the redevelopment of Times

Figure 8.6   The towers of Atlantic Terminal reject the architectural vocabulary of the surrounding neighborhoods and will tower over them. These before-and-after views were created for a neighborhood organization which opposes the project.

Square, and Metrotech in Brooklyn. In this sense, it represents the extreme rather than the norm. But government has encouraged and subsidized the redevelopment of all of the neighborhoods we are considering. A common strategy has been to provide expensive and visually appealing infrastructure improvements as a loss leader to attract private luxury development. In decaying industrial waterfronts in nearby Yonkers and Jersey City, as well as in New York, this has meant claiming a narrow strip of land along the water as a public promenade and furnishing it with benches, railings, and lights. The model for all these amenities is the Esplanade in Brooklyn Heights, built in 1950 as a terrace to cover the new Brooklyn–Queens Expressway, at once insulating the neighborhood from noise and fumes and providing a platform for enjoying spectacular views of the Manhattan skyline. Later, a waterfront promenade was included as a key feature of government planning for Battery Park City. More recently, promenades have been adopted in official plans for redeveloping the old industrial and working-class neighborhood of Paulus Hook, in Jersey City, with upscale apartments and financial offices, and for bringing upscale Manhattan commuters to the decaying downtown area of Yonkers.

These waterfront promenades are good for strolling and sitting, and they provide an attractive setting for new buildings. But they do not fulfill everyone's ideal of public access to the water. For old-timers in Jersey City, accustomed to picking their way through chain link fences and rubble to fish or harvest crabs, the old waterfront offered better access than the new one, where such informal activities are strictly forbidden. The barriers are not only physical: the obvious spatial and visual unity between the new promenades and the expensive new buildings immediately behind them makes the waterfront seem less inviting to people who don't live or work in them than its legally public status might imply. In both Jersey City and Yonkers, moreover, large new buildings have visually walled off the river from the old neighborhoods and downtown public spaces; as elsewhere, the high rents and luxury character of these buildings make them intentionally alien to their surroundings.

Far more expensive than these promenades are the publicly funded improvements to Manhattan's Lower West Side. This section of the Hudson River waterfront, once devoted to shipping and commerce, was ringed by an elevated highway from about 1930 until it partially collapsed in 1973. Then the waterfront was staked out as the route for a much bigger highway, a federally funded interstate called Westway. This was defeated in 1985, after which the city and state agreed to build a handsomely landscaped boulevard with planted medians, special light fixtures, a promenade, a bikeway, and mini-parks with attractive seating areas. This has transformed the waterfront into a site of fashionable leisure, a place to see and be seen, and this in turn has helped open up the adjoining neighborhoods for luxury development. Meier's two towers, which look out on the park and boulevard, were an early result. The Regional Plan Association found that the publicly funded amenities of the so-called Hudson River Park had substantially raised property values not only along the waterfront but also a block or more behind it.[9]

Infrastructure investment has also been important in Greenpoint–Williamsburg. But there the city has brought an even more potent city policy tool to bear, namely zoning. The waterfront was formerly zoned for industry: residential construction was actually illegal. But the city rezoned the area to permit, and indeed encourage, large-scale residential development. The planning agency has actively pushed for construction of very tall towers along the water. In Central Harlem too, though luxury housing was springing up without the assistance of special zoning, sweeping zoning changes promise to accelerate the pace of change. A rezoning approved in 2008 will, according to the development-friendly *New York Times*, "remake 125th Street, one of the city's liveliest streets—and home to many small businesses like clothing stores, pawn shops and hair salons—into a regional business hub with office towers and more than 2,000 new market-rate condominiums."[10] As part of a political compromise, the city agreed to reduce a proposed twenty-nine-story height limit to nineteen stories, still far above the neighborhood's low-rise horizon. The city envisions such heavily capitalized development projects as two shopping malls, hotels, and a headquarters building for Major League Baseball's cable television network, this latter exempted from the height limit.

Zoning and infrastructure are but two of the powers government wields for channeling the development of real estate. Another is historic preservation. By designating individual buildings as landmarks, and larger areas as historic districts, the city's Landmarks Preservation Commission can not only block demolition but also guide investment and shape its architectural form. The National and State Registers of Historic Places can do the same: though it lacks coercive power to prevent demolition, Register listing can bring tax advantages for rehabilitation. But historic preservation has been almost entirely absent from these conflicted zones. Had these neighborhoods been declared historic districts, their social fabric might still have been transformed, but some portion of their physical fabric would have been protected. There would have been a public debate about their history and its importance to the city. But this did not happen. As some of the city's most historic neighborhoods faced transforming change, the city's preservation agency remained notably quiet, as did the major civic groups which advocate for preservation in New York.

To be fair, this absence has not been entirely the fault of preservationists. Some had hoped the Greenpoint Terminal Market, a complex of fifteen buildings covering six square blocks, would receive landmarks protection (Figure 8.7). But, in May 2006, arson destroyed the entire complex in a blaze that required nine million gallons of water to extinguish. The Landmarks Preservation Commission did declare the Austin Nichols warehouse a landmark, but the City Council exercised a rarely used prerogative and overturned the designation. The mayor vetoed the Council, but the Council overrode the veto. On another occasion, in 2003, the LPC was more successful, designating several blocks of the Lower West Side, adjacent to the

Figure 8.7 Before it was destroyed in a devastating fire, the Greenpoint Terminal Market presented a historically important reminder of Brooklyn's industrial and maritime history, as well as abundant possibilities for reuse.

long-established Greenwich Village Historic District, as the Gansevoort Market Historic District.

In recent years the city's preservation establishment has shown signs of waking up to the crisis. At the end of 2005, the Municipal Art Society of New York presented an exhibition on the heritage of Brooklyn's industrial waterfront and, in 2007, helped persuade the National Trust for Historic Preservation to include the area on their annual list of the nation's eleven most endangered places. In 2008, the National Trust added the Lower East Side to the list. The city's Landmarks Preservation Commission has also become more active on the industrial waterfront, designating a small historic district within the industrial sector of Greenpoint and opening discussion of a second waterfront district not far to the south. And in October 2007 the Commission moved to protect one of Williamsburg's most prominent and historic industrial buildings, the Domino Sugar refinery.

These developments are welcome. But they come very late. At Domino, the refinery had closed and developers had bought the complex years earlier: plans to develop the site with new housing were far advanced and indeed had received extensive public discussion before the Landmarks Preservation Commission stepped in. In other neighborhoods too, processes of transformation were well underway, and the chance to guide area-wide changes had been lost before preservationists arrived on the scene.

How had this unfortunate situation come about? One explanation lies in the preservation community's slow response to the crisis of historical and cultural sites in the early 1990s. Though the problem was widely discussed, site surveys were not undertaken, standards were not revised, and new coalitions were not built. And so, when real estate development began to transform neighborhoods like Greenpoint–Williamsburg, the city's preservation establishment remained largely unprepared to recognize the crucially important historical values they contained or, if they recognized them, to create compelling plans and strategies to protect them.

A second explanation lies in the difference between the threats to history and heritage that emerged around 2000 and those of the previous decade. In fact, had the new challenges been identical to the old, the outcome might well have been more positive. But the shift from discrete sites to entire areas introduced new complexities of preservation planning, assessment, and regulation. More significant, it pointed to a profound change in the social and political context in which preservation decisions were made. Just as the historic sites of the early 1990s were tightly bounded, so were the implications of the decisions made there. No important dimension of the city's future hinged on the preservation of the Dvořák House, apart from how the composer would be remembered and how big the hospital's proposed clinic would be. But now, crucial decisions about the city's future were being made in historic neighborhoods like Harlem, the Lower East Side, and Greenpoint–Williamsburg. Would the entire island of Manhattan be turned into a preserve for tourists and the rich, like Aspen or Jackson? Would working people, immigrants, and people of color be pushed deeper into poverty, chased from one neighborhood to another by the forces of money and policy? Would the gap between rich and poor keep expanding until New York became a radically divided society? Or, conversely, would the city be a place of opportunity for everyone, where working people as well as investment bankers could live decently and without fear of the future?

By 2000, then, the goal of preserving an equitable history had converged with that of assuring an equitable future. Historical memory shared common ground with social justice. And neither was doing well. Answers to these critical questions were emerging, and they were not encouraging. Although Mayor Michael Bloomberg expressed concern over growing inequity and housing scarcity, his policies promised to exacerbate the problems. In 2007 the mayor's office released an impressive long-range plan for the city, called *PlaNYC*. It envisioned a city of nine million by 2030 and called for housing an additional 700,000 residents between 2010 and 2030. *PlaNYC* framed the affordability issue very clearly. Recalling the catastrophic housing abandonment of the 1970s, it praised former Mayor Ed Koch for his efforts to rehabilitate and build new affordable housing yet concluded that the city's challenge had "shifted from abandonment to affordability." It illustrated the point with the story of a long-time Harlem resident who had been driven out by arson and housing abandonment, had moved back as soon as conditions permitted, yet now faced the threat of a second displacement as rents rose in response to high-end demand.

PlaNYC called for preserving the city's stock of affordable housing and proposed various strategies for building new units. But affordable housing was far from the plan's paramount goal, and policy conflicts were sometimes resolved in favor of others. For example, the plan lauded the Greenpoint–Williamsburg rezoning for encouraging new housing development—even though this same rezoning was transforming an existing reservoir of affordable housing into a luxury enclave. While the city sought to ensure that some new units would be "affordable," the definition of affordability made them too expensive for many neighborhood residents. Worse than this flaw in the policy for new housing was its effect on existing housing. For in combination these two conflicting policies—new affordable units on the one hand, luxury upgrades of existing units on the other—could only diminish the total stock of affordable housing. It would also dissolve community bonds and rupture long-established ties to place. Whether the goal was to create livable communities for working people or to preserve the city's history, these policies could only fail.

New Yorkers typically blame housing scarcity and rising rents on the real estate market. But the real estate market is a symptom of a larger problem, which is not the lack of affordable housing but the lack of economic justice. When economic conditions combine with political choices to enrich the wealthy, the real estate market naturally responds by building luxury housing and raising rents. Conversely, if the same conditions depress many of the city's residents into a marginal or sub-marginal economic status, then many of those residents will not be able to afford decent housing. When faced with luxury conversions, rising rents, and escalating property taxes, they will flee the neighborhood.

To see the affordable housing problem as a real estate problem, then, is to treat the symptom rather than the cause. It would be better to reduce the economic imbalance that caused the housing shortage. That would promote community stability *and* protect historical memory. Failing that (for no one can believe that this will happen very soon), the best hope is to stop writing off existing neighborhoods as undervalued real estate ready to be exploited and, instead, start nurturing them as reservoirs of affordable housing. That would mean shielding them from luxury development—not opening them up with rezonings, attractive promenades, and subsidies. A policy which does the latter—which subsidizes the construction of luxury apartments, bends planning and zoning rules to shoehorn them into low- and moderate-income neighborhoods, and then fails to control their impact on nearby rents—will inevitably produce less, not more, affordable housing. It will also destroy historically valuable buildings, networks of social connections, local traditions, and patterns of place affection—all vital dimensions of the city's heritage.

And so the interests of preserving history and of building an equitable future run together, and will continue to run together, as long as rising incomes at the top and growing demand for luxury housing put pressure on both. Under these conditions, the best policy will be the one that protects affordable housing *and* the character of affordable neighborhoods; that stabilizes the physical fabric of neighborhoods *and* sustains the economic chances of people who live in them; and that shows a decent regard for people's lifeways *and* for their history. A policy that meets these goals will serve the ends of both social justice and historical memory.

Some will probably object that such a policy interferes with the free market and with the city's natural evolution. But there is little free about the market and nothing natural about the tax breaks and planning measures that lie behind these problems. These reflect political decisions. Out of $617 million given away by the government in tax breaks for housing development in fiscal year 2005, only 4 percent, or $25 million, went for low-income housing.[11] Yet, in the summer of 2008, apartments subsidized with tax breaks were being advertised in the *New York Times* for sale prices of $13 million. Simply put, the long-time residents of Harlem and the Lower East Side were helping the super-rich to pay for their luxury apartments even as they were being driven out by them.

However easy to describe, the conjunction of interests between history and equity has been harder to recognize, especially for those in the thick of things. Few community planners and affordable housing advocates found it natural to seek common ground with preservationists. Few preservationists found it natural to make common cause with advocates for communities like Greenpoint or Harlem. There are plenty of reasons for the disconnection. But both sides stood—and still stand—to gain by overcoming them.

What might New York City accomplish if it stopped subsidizing its richest residents and used its abundant resources instead to protect the affordable housing and historical memory contained in its older working-class neighborhoods? That is a question all New Yorkers have a right to ask. Preservationists in particular have a stake in answering.

NOTES

1. Andrew Beveridge, quoted in Sam Roberts, "In Manhattan, Poor Make 2 Cents for Each Dollar to the Rich," *New York Times* (September 4, 2005); *New York Post* (November 20, 2007). The statistics were from the US Department of Labor.

2. Kim Moody, *From Welfare State to Real Estate: Regime Change in New York City, 1974 to the Present* (New York and London: New Press, 2007).

3. Charles Bagli, "Sale of Stuyvesant Town and Peter Cooper Village Goes Through Despite Some Tenants' Efforts," *New York Times* (November 18, 2006).

4. Tom Walters and Victor Bach, *Closing the Door: Accelerating Losses of New York City Subsidized Housing* (New York: Community Service Society, May 2006).

5. David R. Jones, "Subsidized Housing," *Gotham Gazette* (March 2006).

6. Amy Armstrong, Vicki Been, Carolin K. Bhalla, Kitty Kay Chan, Ingrid Gould Ellen, Johanna Lacoe, Josiah Madar, and Stephen Roberts, *State of New York City's Housing and Neighborhoods 2007* (New York: Furman Center for Real Estate and Urban Policy, 2008), 66.

7. Kathe Newman and Elvin Wyly, "Gentrification and Resistance in New York City," *Shelterforce Online* 142 (July–August 2005); and Kathe Newman and Elvin K. Wyly, *Gentrification and Displacement Revisited: A Fresh Look at the New York Experience*, Research Bulletin No. 31 (Toronto: University of Toronto, Centre for Urban and Community Studies, July 2006).

8. *The Cost of Good Intentions: Gentrification and Homelessness in Upper Manhattan: A Report of the Institute for Children and Poverty* (New York: Institute for Children and Poverty, March 2006).

9. Information provided by Rob Pirani of the Regional Plan Association.

10. Timothy Williams, "Compromise Is Reached on Harlem Rezoning," *New York Times* (April 16, 2008).

11. Moody, op. cit., 171.

PART IV

Choosing a
Different Future

INTRODUCTION: YESTERDAY'S AND TOMORROW'S FUTURES

I

In the concluding part, we return to the themes laid out at the book's opening. But here the balance shifts from analysis to proposals, present to future. Since these proposals were developed in specific contexts and for distinct purposes, it is worth explaining them.

"Sugar Songs" was the keynote address for a conference organized by InterCulture, an English not-for-profit, and held at Harewood House, a grand aristocratic mansion in a magnificent estate just outside the city of Leeds. Harewood's location is relevant for two reasons: first because Leeds houses one of England's largest concentrations of Caribbean immigrants; and second because the family that built Harewood more than two centuries ago made its fortune in the Caribbean, in part by trading and owning slaves. The Lascelles family still owns Harewood, so that today the descendants of some of those slaves are the Earl of Harewood's neighbors, though they do not see much of one another. These facts formed the background to the conference, which brought together historians, museum professionals, artists, activists from Leeds, and the next earl to discuss how Harewood might publicly acknowledge and address its own history. It was thus an occasion for honesty, but also for tact, for these were sensitive questions. The Lascelles family had never previously admitted its debt to slavery and the slave trade: doing so now was deemed particularly touchy because the earl was first cousin to the queen. Yet there were solid reasons for taking the risk. Revenues from visitation fees and heritage grants were important to the Lascelles family and, in a country becoming steadily more racially and culturally diverse, there was political and economic pressure to adjust the estate's image. Moreover, the timing was not accidental: both InterCulture and Harewood were anticipating the year 2007, when Britain would mark the bicentennial of the Act abolishing the transatlantic slave trade. "Sugar Songs" set the old-world house in the context of new-world plantation slavery in order to frame the challenge of interpreting a racially troubled past for a racially mixed public.

Chapter 9 began as a policy study for a foundation which had a notable record of environmental giving and was interested in better understanding the linkages between environments and human cultures. The Nathan Cummings Foundation was active in Hawai'i, and its officers were struck by the intense bonds that Native Hawaiians had developed not merely with the environment in general but with specific places. These bonds were fragile. If the U.S. Army blocked off an entire valley, people would be separated from sites of traditional reverence; if the Army heaved artillery shells at them, archaeological sites holding the record of Native Hawaiians' past might fall victim to fire or accidental damage. Again, if a hotel or resort complex developed a section of shoreline, then Native people might be blocked from performing traditional activities, from salt-gathering to surfing (Figure 9.1). On a handful of tiny islands in the midst of the world's vastest ocean, these problems had become intense: the stock of potential replacements for lost places was strictly limited, and, under intense development pressure, the end of the road could be glimpsed.

Still, Native Hawaiians' ties to the land occasioned admiration as well as sympathy, for the same pressures that were eating away the islands' ecological health and cultural heritage were also provoking intense efforts at stewardship (Figure 9.2). These included both Native Hawaiian grassroots efforts and innovative legal tools, and they inspired foundation officers to inquire more deeply into how land use rules and practices affected traditional ways of life when the survival of those lifeways depended on particular places. With Hawai'i as a point of departure, then, Chapter 9 takes a national look at this question. Moving from Native peoples to the inhabitants of towns, suburbs, and cities everywhere, it documents some of the ways in which the laws of land and property—even those designed to protect heritage—can work against people's efforts to maintain traditional ways of life. It also offers some suggestions about how to redesign the tangled web of regulations governing zoning, preservation, environmental conservation, archaeology, public land management, and the ownership of private property in order to better sustain those efforts.

"Moving Forward" first appeared as the final chapter of an anthology on the history of preservation. But it looks to the future, drawing the themes of race, place, and story into an explicitly political platform for preservation's further development. This platform is also explicitly progressive in that it describes a preservation policy consistent with, and supportive of, progressive policies on other social questions. This raises the general question of whether politics and political ideology, of any stripe, are appropriate in heritage conservation. I believe they are: moreover, appropriate or not, they are present anyway, not least of all when their existence is being denied. There are many reasons for this. Because cultural identity supports social status, and because heritage supports cultural identity, it is impossible to insulate the treatment of heritage from fundamental questions of social justice. One can try to do so by defining heritage narrowly—for example, as fine architecture and attractive neighborhoods—and by ignoring association and intangible heritage. But rather than solve the problem, this frequently puts the profession in the position of defending the prerogatives of the society's most entitled members and propping up a conservative social order. There are other reasons why historic preservation both is and should be the focus of an open and vigorous ideological debate. From local landmarks commissions through federal land policies, preservation is a political process which sets public priorities and commits public funds. These decisions inevitably favor some people's interests and harm others', and deciding who will end up in each category is the core of the political process. Why, then, is there so little ideological debate about historic preservation? Perhaps because many people have written off preservation as unimportant, or perhaps as unsalvageable from a stodgy and reflexive conservatism. "Moving Forward" rejects both views.

II

The following chapters were written between 2001 and 2004, and so it may be appropriate to conclude by reflecting on a few important developments that have happened since then, especially the beginnings of what may prove to be a momentous shift in the climate of public opinion. Though these chapters were written in a hopeful spirit, and with a belief that change was possible, there was little in the American political scene at the time to encourage that belief. Different as they often seemed in other ways, the causes of preservation and of social progress were both trapped in an atmosphere of repressive stagnation. Advocates fought not to lose ground and hardly had the luxury to dream about a better future. But the future has a habit of looking different depending on where one looks at it from. And already it looks a little different.

In 2007, Harewood House opened an exhibition commemorating the end of the slave trade and outlining the Lascelles family's involvement in that trade. This was a direct and positive outcome of the 2003 conference. Other institutions also responded. At the conference, an official from the English Museums Association was moved to promise a major initiative to place the history of slavery on center stage at museums across England by 2007. That commitment was met with substantial exhibitions at the British Empire and Commonwealth Museum in Bristol and the Museum in Docklands (London), and by the expansion of the already impressive exhibition at Liverpool's Merseyside Maritime Museum into an International Slavery Museum. These and similar measures help make the public fact of heritage more racially diverse, honest, and interesting. Once one has grasped the connection between the splendors of Harewood House, or Liverpool's historic docks, and Europe's centuries-long sponsorship of African slavery, one can never again see them in quite the same way: their beauty is not diminished, but their meaning is changed, infused with the complexities of human history and experience. This is what the interpretation of historic sites can do at its best.

Outside the UK, UNESCO marked the 2007 anniversary with exhibitions, conferences, teacher training programs, oral history projects, and even a documentary film award—initiatives which touched Central America, North Africa, Ghana, the Caribbean, and the Indian Ocean. By contrast, the anniversary passed with little attention in the United States. This did not necessarily point to racism or even indifference to race issues on the part of North American heritage managers. In some ways the public debate on race and history in the United States, for all its flaws, was already more open than that in the UK. Moreover, the parliamentary Act of 1807 had less impact in the United States than in the British Empire or Africa and therefore offered a less compelling subject for commemoration. However, the oversight may also reflect a real problem of isolation from international currents in heritage conservation. As Russell Keune has shown, this isolation has afflicted American preservation for decades.[1] In the 1960s, the United States played an important role in developing the UNESCO World Heritage Convention, and it was the first nation to ratify the Convention after its adoption in 1972. Yet, in 1984, President Ronald Reagan led the country out of UNESCO; under his successor, the first President Bush, the US became the world's largest United Nations debtor state. And, although the US rejoined UNESCO in 2003, the second President Bush led a broad-based withdrawal from international treaties, laws, and negotiations.

This constriction of contact with the rest of the world has been especially unfortunate for preservation, because, as the Prologue suggests, there is much to gain from studying international ideas about place and heritage. One of the most interesting developments is the growth of interest in intangible heritage. In 1999, UNESCO launched its Programme for Masterpieces of the Oral and Intangible Heritage of Humanity, which was superseded in 2003 by the UNESCO Convention for the Safeguarding of the Intangible Cultural Heritage. This is an international accord which binds signatory states to respect and care for intangible heritage within their borders and establishes both a "representative" and an endangered list. The Convention and the lists represent an effort to counterbalance the emphasis on monumental heritage enshrined in the earlier World Heritage Convention, and they were particularly favored by representatives of African, Latin American, and Asian countries who believed the existing system unfairly favored a European definition of heritage.

The Convention is far from perfect. Though it calls for safeguarding, it fails to define the term. And though it commits the signatory nations (which as of 2008 did not include the United States) to safeguard intangible heritage, it does not provide any way to evaluate their efforts. Nor, finally, does it do much to reweave the connections between the tangible heritage, intangible heritage, and places that were broken when (as described in the Introduction to Part II) the narratives of architectural history and folklife diverged. It is symptomatic of the Convention's disregard for place that it uses the word only once, in a rather unspecific call to protect "places of memory." Few in the heritage fields will object to paying attention to places of memory. Yet what about places of performance—of socializing, shopping, coffee-drinking, vegetable-buying, and all the other rituals of community life? Here are no masterpieces of intangible heritage but only lives lived, memories nurtured, and traditions passed on in particular places. On these place-based dimensions of heritage the Convention has little to say.

Others, however, are exploring the linkages between intangible heritage and place. In 2003 the International Council on Monuments and Sites (ICOMOS) devoted its symposium to the theme of "Place, Memory, Meaning: Preserving Intangible Values in Monuments and Sites"; a subsequent symposium in 2008 focused on "Finding the Spirit of the Place." In Argentina, the Centro para la Conservación del Patrimonio organized its 2006 conference around "The Social Dimension of Patrimony." In Belgium, the Ename Center for Public Archaeology and Heritage Presentation called its 2008 colloquium "Between Objects and Ideas: Rethinking the Role of Intangible Heritage." Within UNESCO itself, there are signs that the World Heritage Committee too is becoming more receptive to the intangible values of place. This is significant because the committee administers the World Heritage Convention and the World Heritage List—the very instruments criticized by framers of the Convention on Intangible Heritage as being too monument-oriented. One indication of this changing attitude is the 2005 nomination by Argentina of a large area of Buenos Aires to the World Heritage List under the category of "cultural landscape." The nomination was novel, first of all, for the sheer size and character of the area proposed, which was not the historic core of a well-preserved specimen town but the working heart of a huge, vibrant, and changing metropolis, and, second, for the arguments advanced in its favor, which made reference not only to architecture and urban form but also to the city's intangible heritage, especially its immigrant history and the uniquely place-based phenomenon of the tango.[2]

As this is written, it is still not known whether the center of Buenos Aires will be accepted as a World Heritage Site. But, in 2007, another innovative nomination was approved: the 160,000-hectare Richtersveld Cultural and Botanical Landscape in the far northwest corner of South Africa. As the name suggests, Richtersveld is important both environmentally and culturally, and it is this conjunction which makes it notable. Richtersveld is still inhabited by the indigenous Nama people. Their historically significant forms of building still survive as living traditions. So do their traditional patterns of settlement and methods of land management. These differ widely from the science-based practices favored by modern environmental managers, yet after long and difficult discussions the South African authorities decided to adopt them as the basis for environmental conservation at Richtersveld. The World Heritage Committee in turn accepted this determination. It also displayed a new flexibility in understanding tradition and change. Previously, it had been assumed that, although western cultures change constantly, native cultures had to resist change in order to be judged authentic. Thus the residents of a medieval town in Europe might fit up their ancient houses with the most modern kitchens and bathrooms without endangering their World Heritage status, yet natives had to stick to old ways and traditional materials. Yet Richtersveld was inscribed on the list even though the Nama people now travel with pick-up trucks instead of oxen and built their portable buildings out of modern materials. As Andrew Hall, a senior heritage manager in South Africa's Northern Cape province, put it, the World Heritage Committee accepted that "indigenous people can modernise and yet retain the fundamental values of their cultures in the same way that the rest of us have been doing for eons."[3]

Different as they are, Richtersveld and Buenos Aires both signal a confluence of living tradition with long-accepted UNESCO site values like architectural significance and biodiversity. Other international currents are leading toward a similar fusion. One is human rights law. After World War II, the idea that people had a fundamental right to enjoy the benefits of culture began to appear in international treaties and conventions. But the right to culture was understood in an essentially modernist way as the right to benefit from scientific knowledge and to profit from intellectual or artistic activity. Since then, definitions of culture have changed: now, as a UNESCO report puts it, culture is more likely to be understood as "deeply internalized and identity-creating ways of thinking, feeling, perceiving, and being in the world." What was once seen as abstract and universal has become "a particularistic experience with a specific, identity-forming content."[4] One result of these shifts has been to encourage the world-wide development of multiculturalism as a political tenet. Another has been to move the definition of culture closer to that of heritage—not, however, the old monument-oriented heritage but one that increasingly recognizes social and intangible values. The phrase "intangible cultural heritage" is one index of this confluence.

As noted in the Prologue, Native peoples around the world have pushed especially hard for this realignment. And, when the Inuit Circumpolar Conference used international human rights law to take the United States to court in 2005 for the devastation caused by global warming, it demonstrated the fusion of cultural heritage and place in an unexpectedly compelling way. As global warming changed the physical characteristics of the Arctic—its snow, ice sheets, weather patterns, and so forth—those changes in turn threatened cultural traditions like igloo building and seal hunting. The simultaneous breakdown of the physical environment and of cultural heritage was the breakdown of exactly that fusion of place and culture whose success was being demonstrated in Buenos Aires and Richtersveld.

III

Since these chapters were written, new heritage challenges have risen to claim our attention. One is the tide of vacancy and property abandonment which, as noted in the Prologue, is sweeping over urban neighborhoods in the United States. A second is global warming. The threats to heritage posed by climate change have not become as obvious within the lower forty-eight states as in the Arctic, but they are appearing in many regions, from Missouri, where duck hunting is suffering from an absence of ducks, to the northeast, where cross-country ski areas are closing for lack of snow. The

prospect of what rising sea levels will do to New York is almost too fright-
ening to contemplate. New Orleans has already been devastated by a hurri-
cane whose severity may be linked to climate change.

The challenges of global warming are not the subject of this book, but
the dramatic shift in public response to the problem is highly relevant. As
recently as 2006—despite abundant scientific evidence—climate change
remained, politically speaking, a hypothetical problem. Official U.S. policy
ignored it, and those who called attention to it were attacked as unpatriotic
naysayers. Yet, by 2008, climate change was on everyone's lips: citizens, politicians, even corporate spokespersons. Former Vice President Al Gore, his film
on climate change, and his Nobel prize did much to stimulate this change of
heart. Yet it was also part of a broad-based shift in public opinion about the
relationships between individuals, government, and community—a shift with
significant implications for preservation.

Just a few years ago, the idea of mounting a concerted public response—of
acting together as a community—to solve *any* pressing problem was widely
derided as socialistic. Instead of supporting new laws, politicians and pundits
advised people to change their personal buying habits. Citizens were reduced to
consumers, and the highest form of public engagement was to pick one's
purchases carefully. The political atmosphere was permeated by an exaggerated
faith in the ability of markets to fix all problems, and by unreasoning hostility to
government. The solution to every kind of dilemma—environmental collapse,
economic inequality, racism—was to privatize public property and services.

It was against this background that the concluding chapters of this book
were written. Within the preservation profession, political stagnation seemed
in danger of producing a paralysis of ideas, as retrenchment—a not unreasonable tactical response—discouraged long-range thinking and creative
risk-taking. In opposition to this trend, the final chapter, "Moving Forward,"
asked preservationists to think and dream beyond the political limits of that
moment, to get beyond reflexive reliance on private actions as the cure for
overwhelming public problems, and to consider government as a legitimate
instrument of public will. In a similar spirit, Chapter 9 urged readers to reex-
amine the institutions of private property and public action. Though it was
perfectly obvious that many of the proposals in these chapters could not be
implemented immediately, the stasis might end someday. It seemed important
to lay out options and ideas for the future.

Now, there are signs that the long freeze may be thawing. The appearance
in 2004 of the liberal talk radio network Air America and the Democratic
victories of 2006 were symptoms of a shifting political climate. Activism is
returning to college campuses. Ideals of social and economic justice are
staging a political comeback. Criticism of market thinking is becoming
socially acceptable. So is the idea of public action to solve public problems.
By 2008, these shifts in attitude had made it possible for a serious debate on
combating climate change to take hold: they were well advanced before the
financial crisis of fall 2008 dramatically reshaped the relationship between
government and the marketplace.

Early in 2007, a seventh-grader submitted a question to an internet teach-in on the environment: what could he, personally, do to help avert global warming? This was almost exactly the question which had been asked at that earlier conference described in Chapter 11. But the answer could not have been more different. Then, panelists urged the questioner to wash his car more carefully. Now, climate scientist James Hansen argued that changes in personal habits would not and *could not* solve the problem. Instead, he called for political engagement: new laws, regulations, and mandated standards. Today, such calls are increasingly frequent. This is not simply a shift to more government regulation: rather, it marks the return of collective action, of thinking as citizens, and of faith in the law as an instrument for solving problems. It marks the breakup of a rigidly conservative ideology and creates an opening for new ideas, including new ideas about conserving heritage. It is too soon to say, but it appears that a long era of political stagnation and reaction may be drawing to a close. If so, no one will be happier than the author of these chapters to discover that they have become dated and irrelevant.

NOTES

1. See Russell V. Keune, "Historic Preservation in a Global Context: An International Perspective," in Robert E. Stipe (ed.), *A Richer Heritage: Historic Preservation in the Twenty-First Century* (Chapel Hill and London: University of North Carolina Press, 2003), 353–384.

2. *Cultural Landscape of Buenos Aires: The River, the Pampa, the Ravine and the Immigration* (Buenos Aires: Gobierno de la Ciudad de Buenos Aires, 2007).

3. Email to author, October 2008.

4. UNESCO, Division of Cultural Policies and Intercultural Dialogue, "UNESCO and the Issue of Cultural Diversity: Review and Strategy, 1946–2004," Revised version, September 2004, pp. 3, 5 (on-line at http:www.unesco.org/culture/culturaldiversity/docs_pre_2007/unesco_diversity_review_strategy_1946_2004_en.pdf; consulted April 2008).

CHAPTER 9

Sustaining the Living Heritage of Places: Some Suggestions for Using and Owning Land

This chapter originated as a study commissioned by the Nathan Cummings Foundation in 2001. The conclusions in the original paper were addressed to a relatively narrow circle of readers within the philanthropic profession; they have been lightly rewritten to interest a broader readership, and a few points have been selectively updated.

When the Taliban destroyed ancient statues of Buddha, the world wept in outrage. Surely killing culture is not worse than killing people, but, if it seems to entail a special barbarity, that may be because it exacts a special price. As a species, people regenerate; culture, once killed, stays dead.

Modern warfare has exacted a terrible price from culture. Let us remember that in the holocaust died not only six million Jews but also the Jewish culture of Europe; that in the Balkans succumbed not only Bosnian people but also Bosnian mosques and libraries; and that the libraries, museums, and archaeological sites destroyed or looted during the United States' invasion of Iraq can never be made whole.

Most attacks on culture are quieter, less dramatic, but more pervasive. They seem almost to be byproducts of something else. Assaults against the environment, for example, are often assaults on culture too. When General Motors allowed PCBs to leach into the St. Lawrence River, the water, the land, and the fish became poisoned. Eventually, the Mohawk people of the Akwesasne reservation, a fish-eating people, could no longer eat fish: now they eat spaghetti. So devastating has the pollution been that Akwesasne environmentalist Ken Jock says, "Industry has pretty much taken the entire traditional lifestyle away from the community here."[1]

Culture suffers every day, in thousands of smaller ways. People make speeches, sign petitions, file lawsuits, but eventually leave when an urban expressway destroys an established working-class community. People cry when a new mall shutters the traditional shops of Main Street. They throw their cellphones into ponds when ranks of new towers mar the vistas of home. That's what Mark Nelson did when cellular phone companies applied for permits to build thirty-six towers along New York State's Taconic Parkway. "I like Stanford the way it is," he said. "There was no more avid cellphone user than me, but this is a different world up here. What makes this place so valuable, and so attractive, is not what's here—it's what's not here."[2]

Winona LaDuke estimates that 2,000 indigenous cultures have gone extinct in the western hemisphere alone.[3] Compared to this rollcall of death, a cellular tower is a trifling annoyance. Yet it would be difficult to know just where to draw the line between them because, though vastly different in severity, they are on the same spectrum of violence to culture, habit, tradition, custom, and established ways of life. It is tempting to dismiss the complaints of Stanford's cell tower opponents as just another case of NIMBY—"Not In My Back Yard." But let us, just once, resist that temptation and listen to the real message of those marching phone towers: that the citizens of Stanford are only a little less helpless than the Buddha statues of Afghanistan to protect their traditions, their special sense of place, against incursions momentous or minuscule.

This chapter is not concerned with the ends of the spectrum but with the middle: what might be called average threats against average culture, the sorts of culture that are all around us in the United States and the sorts of threats that overshadow them every day. Specifically, it is about those aspects of culture that are most directly rooted in particular places: neighborhood customs and traditions, memories, affection for place, and the perception of being at home that underlies the sense of place felt by residents. It is about threats to these aspects of culture. And it is about how to protect them better.

Though I will propose some practical steps, this chapter is not a prescription. What I hope to do is raise to consciousness some of the decisions that society routinely makes, often unconsciously, about the survival of places and cultures. Those decisions are usually framed in terms of quite other issues: where to site a new power plant or mall, for example. Were people to debate and ultimately to make these decisions with full awareness of the impacts on place and culture, I believe that communities would ask for, and ultimately gain, greater control over their own places. And many of those decisions would be made quite differently.

Though this chapter describes the present and refers to the past, it is really about the future, or about several possible futures. In this spirit it offers two sets of recommendations. The first includes concrete, practical ways of creating a tomorrow that is better than today. The second mediates between today's reality and a more distant one. They are tentative first steps towards a possible future reality in which the rights of people to maintain their places and ways of life are recognized in ways that are hard to imagine now. I believe our society *will* eventually move towards such a future (though how far no one can say), because the broadly felt needs and desires of a great many people will slowly, gradually push us towards better ways of living. If we are willing to take a chance on this future, on our intuition that this (in Wayne Gretszky's beautiful phrase) is where the puck is flying, then these suggestions will help us to skate to it and speed it along.

A LESSON FROM HAWAI'I

Traditions and the intangible culture of places are under threat in communities throughout the United States. Some of the casualties are well known because they concern groups with some degree of public recognition and sympathy: New England dairy farming, Pittsburgh steel working, or Chesapeake Bay crabbing. These are the poster children for cultural loss. This chapter focuses on loss of place and culture that is happening more or less out of sight, whether in unremarkable urban neighborhoods, ordinary towns and suburbs, or great regions of countryside that our national media do not cover. It opens, however, with a very special case: the Native culture of Hawai'i. Hawaii's Native culture is not only remarkable; its relationship to land, and the measures that have been adopted to protect that relationship, have much to teach us.

Hawaii's Native culture is typical of indigenous cultures throughout what is now the United States in that it is deeply rooted in place. It is not simply a matter of people loving places; it is a matter of places supporting the traditions and rituals that constitute a way of life (Figures 9.1 and 9.2). The state of Hawaii has instituted a unique form of legal protection to ensure that that relationship has a fair chance of surviving. Hawaii's state constitution binds the state to protect the rights of descendants of Native Hawaiians to continue using traditional lands for "subsistence, cultural and

Figure 9.1 A stretch of ocean frontage at Kohanaiki, near Kona, on the Big Island of Hawai'i serves multiple purposes for residents, including Native Hawaiians, ranging from age-old traditions like salt-gathering and surfing to picnicking. Behind the beach are environmentally important anchialine ponds as well as archaeological remains. Local efforts to protect access to Kohanaiki led to important legal victories. However, resources like these are threatened by resort development throughout the Hawaiian islands.

Figure 9.2   Near Waiahole, on the island of Oahu, the revival of traditional taro cultivation by Native Hawaiian activists is helping not only to preserve Native Hawaiian culture but also to restore the environment, especially water quality. Classes are offered in an open-air shed in the fields: poi, the traditional food made from taro, is sold in a roadside store.

religious purposes."[4] Other laws spell this out, specifically guaranteeing Native peoples the right to take materials such as firewood, certain kinds of leaves, and drinking water for subsistence use (but not to sell for profit), and to retain the right of way across lands used for these purposes.[5] As has long been recognized, these guarantees clash with the European-based notions of property ownership prevalent in mainland America, which give owners the right to exclude other persons from their property at will. Precisely where to draw the line between the (European-based) rights of landowners to exclude neighbors, and even to develop their land in ways incompatible with the interests of those neighbors, and the (distinctively Hawaiian) rights of Native people to continue using land in traditional ways has not been settled. On the one hand, the courts have held that Native rights do not extend so far as to block all development, nor do they guarantee continued access to land once it has been fully developed. On the other (referring to the traditional Hawaiian unit of land), they have warned that "the State does not have the unfettered discretion to regulate the rights of ahupua'a tenants out of existence."[6]

Hawaii's unique constitutional provisions are further embodied in land use measures that seek to protect historic or prehistoric cultural resources "significant in Hawaiian . . . history and culture"[7] and in some cases direct government officials not to issue land use or development permits if they would produce a "significant adverse environmental . . . effect" on cultural and historic values, such as the "loss or destruction of any natural or cultural resource, including but not limited to, historic sites and view planes," or a negative effect upon the "economic or social welfare and activities of the community, County or State."[8] In 2000, Hawaii's state legislature amended the state environmental rules to require that environmental impact statements consider the impacts of proposed developments on "cultural practices" as well as economic and social welfare and other environmental factors. Though the requirement applies to all cultures equally, the legislature stated clearly that its motivation was to stem the "loss and destruction" of Native Hawaiian cultural resources and to mitigate the interference of new developments with the "exercise of native Hawaiian culture," and that the rule's central purpose was to "ensure the continued existence, development, and exercise of native Hawaiian culture."[9]

It is important to be clear about why Native Hawaiians receive the specific protection of the state constitution. This is not (as some may think) a special privilege given to some Hawaiians by virtue of race or ethnicity. It is a right stemming from the Native Hawaiians' prior sovereignty over the land, and the courts have spoken clearly on this point. In 1893 agents of the United States government participated, illegally and without authorization, in a conspiracy to depose the Hawaiian monarchy, which the US had recognized since 1826. As a result, the formal annexation of Hawaii five years later lacked the legitimacy of a transfer of authority from one properly constituted government to another. Article XII, section 7, is a reminder that Hawaiian sovereignty was never fully or properly extinguished. In 1993, in fact, the U.S. Congress issued an official acknowledgment and apology for helping to suppress the "inherent sovereignty" of the Hawaiian people.[10] The protections accorded by the state constitution, then, are not special rights "given" to Hawaiians but the remnants of long-held rights that were never formally taken away. Native Americans on the mainland also exercised prior sovereignty over the land, and this fact continues to be expressed not only in the existence of reservations and of laws which apply specifically to Indians and Indian land (such as the Native American Graves Protection and Repatriation Act) but most saliently in the legal principle that the relationship between the government in Washington and the tribes is that of one government to another. Washington does not deal with Italian Americans or African Americans as if they had their own governments, because they do not: the Native tribes, however, do have their own governments and retain some of the prerogatives of sovereignty. Native Hawaiians lack federal recognition at this level, but they too retain elements of prior sovereignty, and the Native Hawaiian Government Reorganization Act introduced by Senator Akaka could begin a movement towards formal recognition like that of the tribes. Legalities aside, many other Americans recognize that Native Hawaiians and Native Americans have been here longer than anyone else and have a special relationship to the land.

What of the large remainder of Americans whose forebears migrated to this continent within the last half-millennium? They cannot claim prior sovereignty. Yet they too have traditions worth conserving, traditions rooted in land and place. And these traditions, like those of Native Hawaiians, frequently depend on land which they use and inhabit but do not own. Country people, whether in the Catskills or the Rockies, hunt, ride, and fish on their neighbors' property. City people depend on the transit system, schools, churches, parks, and shops, a network of neighbors, and of course the factories, offices, or stores where they work. City and country people, and suburbanites too, expect their neighborhood to maintain a certain "feel"—a mix of roughly the same number of more or less similar people, traffic at roughly the same level, a favorite view, or even a pleasant patch of sun or shade on the walk home from school or work. They do not own, and cannot hope to buy, most of the places on which the security of their sense of neighborhood and place depends.

All of this sounds mundane, and it is. But it has great cultural value nonetheless. And what makes it particularly important is the fact that many of these Americans are facing threats to the continuity of their lives and traditions. As in Hawai'i, the *users* of land are frequently finding their activities disrupted by its *owners*, who may decide to develop or redevelop it, stop maintaining it, or simply block access to it. This happens because modern American law distinguishes sharply between owning and using land: it grants sweeping rights to landowners but only very restricted ones to land users. It is just this problem which Hawaii's state constitution attempts to mitigate. And in so doing, it encourages us to consider the problem afresh. Are we comfortable with the level of stress that European-based concepts of landownership place on traditional ways of life? Do our ideas of private property serve our desire for a richly satisfying community life as well as they might? Or could we do better?

To answer these questions, it is helpful to begin by surveying the laws and procedures which already exist to protect place-based traditions or ways of life in the United States. The review which follows focuses first on those which apply specifically to Native cultures and lands and then to those of general applicability. Having grasped the general contours of the situation, we may then consider some practical ways to improve the existing tools and, finally, speculate on a more distant future in which the entire nation might be able to benefit from the lesson of Hawai'i.

PROTECTING PLACE-BASED TRADITIONS IN NATIVE AMERICA

> We want to be in the way of development if they are going to disturb our grandmothers. We *must* be in the way if they are going to disturb our grandmothers.[11]

Once upon a time, Native Americans held sway over North America. The most obvious reminders of this fact on the ground are the reservations. But Indian rights to practice certain traditions such as fishing, gathering, and religious observances outside the reservations are substantial, and they are protected by treaties and laws. Today Indians of many tribes are making strong efforts to preserve threatened cultural traditions: many see this endeavor as not only important in its own right but as an essential step towards achieving economic and legal equity.

The laws which safeguard Indian culture basically fall into two categories: those which protect traditional patterns of life and those, more numerous, which protect the cultural properties created by those traditions. The two frequently overlap: it becomes difficult to honor traditions involving death, for example, if graves are desecrated and grave goods plundered. But protecting sites and artifacts does not necessarily support tradition, so the distinction is an important one.

Safeguarding the Cultural Products of Native American Traditions

The spectrum of laws designed to protect cultural properties—the artifacts that embody the heritage of Native American traditions—is broad. First are national laws of general applicability: the National Environmental Policy Act (NEPA) and National Historic Preservation Act (NHPA). These are essentially disclosure requirements: they direct government to study and, in some circumstances, require mitigation for the impacts of government-sponsored, funded, or permitted projects on environmental or cultural resources. In addition to NEPA and NHPA, each state has a state-level preservation law, and many have enacted counterparts to NEPA. Finally, on top of this structure are laws that apply specifically or primarily to Indian cultural sites and resources.

The nation's first historic preservation law focused on Native American heritage. The Antiquities Act of 1906 authorized the president to declare historic landmarks on federal property and to reserve the land necessary to protect them: the lawmakers wanted to protect ancient Indian ruins, such as those at Mesa Verde, from vandals and pothunters. In doing so, unfortunately, the federal government frequently severed the living connections that Indians had with the ruins. The Act assumed that the ruins and artifacts belonged to the United States, and Indians were often forbidden to frequent or take care of them. The purpose of protecting cultural resources from depredation has rarely been to ensure their continuing use by Native Americans.

Other major archaeological protection laws followed the Antiquities Act, so that today an archaeological site may be covered not only by NEPA, NHPA, and the Antiquities Act, but also by the Reservoir Salvage and Archeological Protection Act of 1960 and the Archeological Resources Protection Act of 1979; some artifacts may additionally be covered by the American Indian Religious Freedom Act.

The Reservoir Salvage Act, despite its name, applies to "any alteration of terrain caused as a result of any Federal construction project or federally licensed activity or program."[12] Like NEPA and NHPA, it is a disclosure law. It requires federal agencies engaged in such activities to notify the Secretary of the Interior if its activities may "cause irreparable loss or destruction of significant scientific, prehistoric, historic, or archeological data."[13] Although it imposes some responsibility for preserving threatened resources, it does nothing to protect the *places* where such resources were found, which in most cases are destined to become reservoirs.

The Archeological Protection Act, by contrast, sets up a system for obtaining permits to excavate and remove archaeological material from public and Indian lands and imposes criminal penalties and fines for unauthorized "excavation, removal, damage, alteration or defacement of archeological resources" and for illegally trafficking in such resources.[14] It thus belongs among a larger family of state laws that attempt to deter vandalism, particularly of burials, and subject archaeological excavation to professional standards. Arizona's archaeological discoveries law, for example, requires persons in charge of construction or other work on state or federal land to report discoveries of any archaeological, paleontological, or historical material to the Arizona State Museum and then subjects further excavation and preservation to the standards of the Museum. In the case of Indian burials, the law establishes a process for notifying related tribes and for reburying the remains after the conclusion of scientific study.[15]

Protecting Traditional Indian Customs and Access to Land

Subsistence hunting, fishing, and gathering, as well as religious and spiritual practices, continue on as well as outside the reservations, and the rights to maintain specific activities on public land are guaranteed in numerous treaties. Alaska also provides an example of a federal law that broadly protects subsistence hunting and fishing. Unlike Hawai'i, Alaska is dominated by public land. The Alaska National Interest Lands Conservation Act (ANILCA), passed by the United States Congress in 1980, requires the Secretary of the Interior to manage the wildlife on that land "for purposes of preserving and enhancing the opportunity for native and non-native rural residents of Alaska to engage in subsistence uses of such lands."[16] ANILCA defines subsistence uses as:

> customary and traditional uses by rural Alaskan residents of wild, renewable resources for direct personal or family consumption . . . for the making and selling of handicraft articles . . . for barter, or sharing for personal and family consumption; and for customary trade.[17]

Importantly, ANILCA assigns such subsistence uses priority over sport hunting and fishing and requires federal agencies both to weigh the impacts of any proposed land disposition on subsistence uses and to take substantive steps to avoid harming them. All is not quite well for the future of subsistence in Alaska, however, for the courts have found that Alaska's state-level counterpart to the federal ANILCA conflicts with the state constitution's prohibition of special privileges in the taking of fish and wildlife.[18]

Explicit federal protection of subsistence hunting, fishing, and gathering may be unique to Alaska's public lands. But ANILCA provides for the required impact analysis to be carried out within the framework of a national law of general applicability, the National Environmental Policy Act of 1969. This enormously important law requires the federal government to analyze the environmental impact of its actions. It will be discussed in greater detail below. For now it is important to note that NEPA provides a national framework within which protections like ANILCA's could be applied beyond Alaska.

Joining Tradition and Artifacts

During the 1990s important progress was made in recognizing the connection between artifacts and living traditions. The Native American Graves Protection and Repatriation Act (NAGPRA) was enacted in 1990. Ostensibly it is concerned with objects: it protects Native American graves on public and tribal land and directs museums to return human remains and associated grave goods to the appropriate tribe, if asked to do so. But it has also helped to support traditional observances, not only by returning ritual objects to Native custody but also by giving the tribes some voice in the care of objects which remain in museums. Instead of being disassembled, for example, a medicine bundle might be left intact. Or a ritual object might be made available to the tribe for religious purposes.

Another area that saw progress was the federal historic preservation system. The National Register of Historic Places, a nation-wide listing of historically, culturally, or architecturally significant sites, is the key to protection under federal preservation law. Unfortunately, the criteria for listing were developed with European architectural values and European notions of history—written sources and clear, linear chronologies—in mind. Many important Indian sites didn't fit those criteria very well. Their significance came not from architectural distinction or a famous occupant or event but from a long and continuing tradition of use for vision quests, ceremonies, or gatherings. The problem was compounded by the discomfort of professional staff and political officials with historical narratives based on oral testimony, and by the reticence of many Indians in disclosing the location of sacred sites. Some of these problems were addressed in 1992 by a pathbreaking publication: *Guidelines for Evaluating and Documenting Traditional Cultural Properties*, often referred to as Bulletin 38. These guidelines show how "traditional cultural significance" can qualify a site for listing on the Register: "traditional" being used to describe "beliefs, customs, and practices of a living community of people that have been passed down through the generations, usually orally or through practice," and "significance" to refer to "the role the property plays in a community's historically rooted beliefs, customs, and practices." In sum, then, a traditional cultural property is defined as a site that merits inclusion in the National Register "because of its association with cultural practices or beliefs of a living community that a) are rooted in that community's history, and b) are important in maintaining the continuing cultural identity of the community."[19] Bulletin 38 describes how to research and document such sites and, importantly, how to present them in ways that satisfy the underlying Register criteria. As a result, the National Register's protection of artifacts has begun to support the continuation of living traditions.

Unlike the National Register, the American Indian Religious Freedom Act (AIRFA), passed in 1978, was designed to address specifically Indian issues. However, it did not effectively embody Indian concepts of sacred spaces within the landscape and so proved incapable of protecting Indian sacred sites from desecration by federally constructed, funded, or permitted projects. The situation improved dramatically in 1996 when President Clinton issued Executive Order 13007.[20] This directs all federal agencies to "accommodate access to and ceremonial use of Indian sacred sites by Indian religious practitioners" and to "avoid adversely affecting the physical integrity of such sacred sites."[21] Importantly, Executive Order 13007 does not attempt to define sacred sites: in essence, a site is sacred if Indian testimony authoritatively states that it is so.[22] Moreover, the Order builds in a process of direct consultation with Indian tribes, and it promises confidentiality regarding the location of sacred sites.

Federal Land Management

The federal government's managerial engagement with Indian sites is far-reaching, as are the complexities of that engagement. Every unit of the National Park Service's land in Alaska, for example, is associated with a Native group and contains Native cultural remains. In addition to its own property, the Alaska National Interest Lands Conservation Act requires the Park Service to manage certain cultural sites to be conveyed to Native corporations established under the Alaska Native Claims Settlement Act.[23] And the Park Service cooperates with Native groups in managing conservation easements in which it has an interest, which in 1990 amounted to about 6,000 acres of Alaskan Native land.[24] Nationally, as of 1990, the Park Service's responsibilities were far larger: 133 tribes were culturally or historically associated with 101 of the Park Service's 355 units.[25]

The National Park Service is not the only federal agency to manage Indian cultural sites. The Bureau of Indian Affairs manages Indian schools and other culturally significant sites on federal lands. The National Forest Service and Bureau of Land Management (BLM) are even more active in this regard. Though (unlike the Park Service) their activities are confined to land under their control, both agencies manage many areas valued by Indians for both food gathering and religion. The BLM has been particularly organized in its approach to traditional lifeways on its land. It attempts to accommodate both forms of traditional activity within its management practices and defines "cultural resources" to include both historical properties and "traditional lifeway values."[26]

Federal land managers operate under numerous mandates: to provide opportunities for hiking, fishing, and the contemplative enjoyment of nature; to supply timber, irrigation water, and hydro-power; to help those who wish to produce oil, gas, and uranium; to pump dollars into local economies; to cooperate with development interests that wish to build ski areas; to protect endangered species and prehistoric ruins; and to respect Indian sacred sites. There is certainly room for improvement in the protection of Indian cultural sites on public land.

Protecting Artifacts Does Not Necessarily Protect Tradition

Though entwined, protecting the artifacts of tradition and protecting the tradition itself are not the same. They diverge, for example, whenever conservation initiatives shift control of the artifacts away from Indians and towards a white public of connoisseurs and collectors. During the 1930s and 1940s, commented one member of the Seneca tribe, many musicologists came to the reservation to tape their music. "The recordings have since disappeared into the Library of Congress, Smithsonian Institution, Folklife Museum, Folklore Library at the University of Indiana. . . ."[27] Those recordings helped preserve a knowledge of Indian music for white scholars and connoisseurs but not (at least at that time) for those who might carry on the tradition. Archaeology has been particularly criticized for its impacts on Native American culture. First, many of the laws that should protect Native sites have been criticized as inadequate: though legal provisions exist against vandalism and grave robbing, the state must generally prove that damage was inflicted "knowingly and willingly," and so many clever grave robbers continue to escape punishment.[28] More fundamentally, archaeology can trigger a far-reaching transfer of control. Starting with the Antiquities Act of 1906, government protection has brought with it an assumption of government authority over archaeological sites: authority to remove, catalogue, research, describe, interpret, store, and generally dispose of the contents. Arizona's state law, discussed above, is typical in insisting that, once discovered, sites and artifacts be treated strictly according to the State Museum's professional standards. The problem is that Indians with a living cultural connection to the objects often have different standards for their care. For them, meticulous cataloguing and research, and display in glass museum cases (or storage in locked drawers or cabinets) may be antithetical to tradition because they offend against the nature and spirit of the objects and interfere with their traditional use. "In the mid-1970s," says a member of the Zuni tribe,

> the tribal council noticed that with every project on the reservation, archeologists came in from the outside and did projects, took the materials away and studied them, and that was the last that was heard of the project.[29]

Results like this are not aberrations, produced when the system functions poorly: they are what one would expect from the established system of archaeology when it is functioning as intended.

Protecting the Environment Does Not Necessarily Protect Tradition

Thanks in part to NAGPRA, archaeology is changing,[30] and some archaeologists oppose the law for just this reason. It interferes with their freedom to pursue their own dedication to scientific research, which many perceive as selfless. Their responsibility, as these archaeologists see it, is to artifacts and knowledge, rather than to people and lifeways. Something similar is true of many well-meaning environmentalists and preservation professionals. Until recently, neither group was very interested in the people who inhabit their idealized worlds. Thus conflicts developed between protecting artifacts and supporting traditional lifeways. The fact that artifacts and lifeways often share common enemies sometimes obscures these conflicts. But opposition to vandalism or development does not automatically translate into support for traditional lifeways. Moreover, both historic preservation and environmental protection can sometimes create their own problems.

Outdoor recreation is one flashpoint for conflicts between land conservation and protection of tradition. At Devil's Tower, Wyoming, the National Park Service was forced to adjudicate between the claims of Indians, for whom it was a sacred and ceremonial site, and rock-climbing guides, for whom it was both an intriguing challenge and an income source. Climbers were interfering with Indians' traditional observances; when the Park Service asked for a month-long voluntary ban on climbing out of respect for Indian religious observances, a climbing guide sued. The courts have sustained the Park Service's right to request the voluntary closure (they have also supported a *mandatory* springtime ban on climbing to protect nesting falcons), but the solution is obviously not an ideal one from a Native American point of view.[31]

Is recreation really the enemy here? Not exactly. Nor is environmental conservation *per se* (though in other examples it may be). The problem is that environmental protection itself can become a form of development, and a threatening one. By law and common understanding, national parks are places not only of environmental protection but also of public recreation, and so, within limits, they are open to recreational forms of development. Indeed the National Park Service itself has at times been severely criticized for promoting an inappropriately high level of development in its parks. Putting land into a national park or monument then does not hang a "Do Not Disturb" sign over it. It may be more like putting out the welcome mat for a wide variety of development proposals. Another way of saying this is to observe that, as Americans, we are not very good at simply letting things be: if they interest us at all, our system of land and artifact protection encourages us to develop them for *something*, even if not for profit. And, as with other forms of development, this can cause conflict with established ways. Archaeology again provides an illustration: protection often brings with it a train of interpretation, display, and so forth, all of which can dramatically change the site; excavation, of course, can literally destroy the artifacts that make the site important.[32]

PROTECTING PLACE-BASED TRADITIONS AMONG NON-NATIVE AMERICANS

If there is a salient difference between Native and non-Native Americans, it is not the presence of tradition, or even attachment to place. Many Native people may feel these emotions more deeply than many non-Native people. Perhaps more pertinently, Native-ness supports a philosophical framework in which place attachment is central and can be widely accepted as a virtue, not least of all by some who do not necessarily espouse it for themselves. Yet non-Native Americans too have traditions, and many feel deeply attached to the places where they live. Throughout the country, traditional lifeways have created stores of cultural artifacts and place-based traditions which continue to add to society's stock of cultural capital. Yet many of these lifeways are threatened, and customs rooted in place are everywhere maintained in the face of threats and opposition. The paradox is that, while few other groups in American society have faced deprivations of place comparable to those experienced by Native people, non-Natives lack even the few legal protections accorded to Native people. As immigrants, non-Native Americans cannot claim the status of prior sovereignty.

Threatened American lifeways and communities are many and varied: family farms, ranches, country towns, urban working-class neighborhoods, even middle-class suburbs. The forces threatening them are also varied, but many are directly connected to land use. They are similar to those that work against the survival of Indian and Native Hawaiian traditions:

- *Intensification of land values*, manifested in development or "growth." Development replaces traditional activities with new ones: ranching with skiing, dairy farming with suburban houses, theater or down-market retail with corporate offices, warehousing with artists' live/work spaces. It also replaces traditional communities with new and frequently richer ones: working-class black or ethnic families with young professionals in finance, art, or e-commerce. Gentrification, of course, can be as much a cause as a result of development: as relatively wealthy home seekers, who may have been economically zoned out of their preferred neighborhood, flow into a less expensive neighborhood, capital and (if they are lucky) rising land values flow with them. Rising land values lead to higher property taxes, accelerating the displacement of traditional communities. Meanwhile, newcomers who find traditional activities unpleasant may seek to legislate, litigate, or harass them out of existence: thus farm operations give way to suburbanites, factories and sweatshops to art patrons, peepshows to corporate executives and office workers. Finally, intensification of land values may cause intensification of use, with all of its attendant side effects—traffic, noise, the hardening of surfaces, a feeling of hurry or loss of privacy that may diminish the quality of life enjoyed by communities at some distance from the center of investment.
- *Disinvestment, or declining land values*, manifested in the withdrawal of capital and credit and leading to the decay of building stock, the collapse of essential businesses (branch banks, groceries, dealers in farm machinery), and the decline of public infrastructure and services (roads, schools, parks, libraries, fire and police protection)—in short, to an inability to sustain community life. By the mid-twentieth century, older neighborhoods in most American cities faced disinvestment as capital and credit migrated to the developing suburbs, speeded by bank and government redlining policies. Within cities, certain neighborhoods have suffered from disinvestment as others attracted favorable attention. Recently,

however, the problem of disinvestment and abandonment of property has reached almost epidemic proportions throughout the United States, affecting not merely neighborhoods but vast areas of literally dozens of cities (Buffalo, Philadelphia, Pittsburgh, Cleveland, Detroit). In a separate phenomenon, smaller towns throughout the entire Great Plains region of the country (the Dakotas, Nebraska, Kansas, Colorado, Wyoming) are emptying out.

- *Siting decisions* that destroy nearby community resources, as regional malls or big-box stores draw the life out of nearby Main Street businesses and diminish the attractiveness of streams and woods, or as a highway may destroy the heart of a cohesive neighborhood or separate its homes from its shopping and recreation. Siting decisions especially threaten poor communities and communities of color, as nuclear power plants, chemical factories, hazardous waste incinerators, garbage transfer stations, diesel bus depots, and mines poison air, soil, and water, destroy homes and businesses, and make communities literally uninhabitable.

- *Diminishing access to land* due to development or privatization. Maintaining traditional lifeways would be relatively easy if those who followed them owned all of the land needed to sustain them: if, that is, they needed nothing from, and were unaffected by, anyone else's property. In practice, however, this is almost never the case and, for most Americans, is an utter impossibility. Many Americans do not own the houses or apartments in which they live, much less the streams where they fish, the field they cross to get there, the rangeland their cattle graze, the forest where they hunt, the botánica or Kosher winery where they shop, the homes of their friends, their union hall, or the bar or schoolyard where they socialize. Nor do they own the sites of memory—the cemetery where their grandparents are buried or the playground in the neighborhood where they grew up. The maintenance of community lifeways and memories typically depends on residents having access to property owned by others. And changing patterns of property ownership and development appear to be diminishing or threatening that access. It is true that home ownership rates have generally risen over time, yet for many Americans access to land owned by others has diminished. Adirondackers in the early nineteenth century were accustomed to take timber from wherever was most convenient; as the land became the property of big lumber companies, private preserves, and ultimately New York State's Forest Preserve, such resource use became redefined as punishable trespass.[33] Landscape historian John Stilgoe has seen evidence of a special quality of childhood experience in many memoirs of small-town life a century ago: that quality stemmed from the ability to roam across a large, informal commons: train tracks, fields, bogs, other people's front yards, and so forth.[34] Perceptions of public safety, increasing automobile traffic (and automobile dependence), ongoing development, and tightening controls on access have constricted this spatial freedom. And, in many big-city neighborhoods, the empty lots where people socialized have been developed, while working waterfronts, where formerly people braved pollution and commerce to swim and sunbathe, have been walled off behind razor wire and cargo containers. More recently, the explosive growth of electronic communication and entertainment have dramatically altered the traditional meaning of public or even of shared space. Yet anecdotal evidence suggests that the use of streets, sidewalks, front steps, and porches for socializing and children's games was already on the decline: air conditioning, perceptions of urban crime, and diminishing leisure time are presumably among the causes.

Land continues to be locked up, by private and public owners, for many reasons. Sometimes new owners from outside the community, ignorant or uncaring of local traditions, want exclusive use of their land: they do not want to participate in the local culture of sharing, and so urbanites who purchase ranches in the west or woodlands in the Catskills may build fences, post land, and close off traditional access for hunting, fishing, gathering, and passage. Similarly a business may buy a building in a residential neighborhood, fence in the forecourt for parking, and deprive neighbors of access to a particularly beautiful flowering tree; or the new owners may simply cut down the tree. In other cases, new uses make it literally impossible to carry on the old ones: thus suburban subdivisions replace not only the formal practices of farming or orchard care but also the informal activities associated with farms or orchards.

An apparent exception to this pattern of declining access to shared land is the increase in recreational access to National Parks and other public lands that urbanites and suburbanites now enjoy. Yet public landownership *in itself* has not been a guarantee of support for traditional lifeways. In the 1930s the State of Virginia bought up land along the Blue Ridge and, after shutting down the working farms, donated the land to the federal government to create Shenandoah National Park. These actions left a legacy of bitterness. More recently the National Park Service evicted Native Hawaiians from an area near Kona harbor on the Big Island in order to create a park dedicated to Native Hawaiian culture.[35] Indians, ranchers, and country dwellers in many parts of the country still resent the reservoirs built decades ago by the federal Bureau of Reclamation and by major cities like Los Angeles and New York.

The public land picture today is complex. On the one hand, the maintenance of large blocks of public lands in the west, upstate New York, and elsewhere is vital to the maintenance of traditional rural and small-town lifestyles. Still, the imperatives of environmental conservation and public recreation sometimes work against those same lifestyles. Thus hunters in a National Forest find themselves unable to rebuild a gravel road after it is washed out, Indians at Devil's Tower are disturbed by rock climbers, New York City's last eel fisherman was shut down by Gateway National Recreation Area[36] and, in the Escalante/Grand Staircase region of Utah, or on Steens Mountain in Oregon, ranchers fear that protective designation will bring more outsiders and activity, threatening local ways of life and the character of the place as they know it. This is not an indictment of national parks but simply a reminder that, though parks do keep land from being privatized and closed off to traditional users, they do not necessarily protect rural lifeways: at times, indeed, they do just the opposite.

As these and other forces continue to batter many traditional lifeways, a small corps of laws and regulations seek to defend them. They are rarely strong enough to win, but they do help to fend off or forestall defeat. They include historic preservation laws, zoning ordinances, planning regulations, building codes, environmental laws, special environmental justice policies, banking laws, and rent control regulations. We now survey a few of the tools and techniques which directly address the use and development of land:

- *Right-to-farm laws.* Among all of the nation's many traditional (non-Native) ways of life, only one, farming, has prompted widespread adoption of laws to protect it. The debate over the loss of farmland in the United States is confusing: on the one hand, while the total loss of farmland is alleged to be very small, the loss of good-quality farmland near large, urban markets is significant.[37] The debate over the demise of the family farm, a revered social institution as well as an economic unit, is even more confusing: some urge us to campaign for its salvation as if the nation's future depended on it, while others pronounce it already dead.[38] The family farm has an exalted status in the nation's mythology, and this, as much as any accepted facts about farms or farming, has helped build the political power necessary to enact "right-to-farm" laws.

  Right-to-farm laws are designed to protect farms and farmers from the resentment of suburban newcomers who may have been attracted by the rural ambience but are dismayed by the reality of farming, which includes noise, smells, chemicals, and dust.[39] Such newcomers often invoke the police power to declare farming operations a public nuisance and shut them down or harass them out of business. Right-to-farm laws protect farmers from such attacks. All fifty states have them: most were passed in the late 1970s or early 1980s. Today, though, the increased mechanization of corporate agriculture has meant that right-to-farm laws are protecting not only small farms but also industrial-sized plants processing 40,000 hogs at a time. Right-to-farm laws are increasingly criticized: it is one thing to put up with pollution on behalf of the local farmer, quite another to suffer for the sake of a shamelessly polluting corporate giant.[40]

Like farming, ranching inspires a warm glow of nostalgia; and, as with farming, ranching's endangered future has generated a lively and confusing debate. Measured in terms of food production, or of the overall economy, ranching is insignificant. Yet the ranching life is central to the mythology (at least the non-Native mythology) of the American west. Like farming, ranching is threatened in many locales, by economics as well as changing land use and land values. Yet there are no "right-to-ranch" laws. Where they exist, right-to-farm laws cover the situations where ranching and suburban development collide (an increasing number of places). But, unlike farming, ranching depends heavily on public lands: millions of acres of federal land which are open to grazing, often at subsidized rates. These federal subsidies could fairly be called a government ranching-support program. But the system of grazing permits, together with the environmental degradation inflicted by cows, has with good reason been under attack by environmentalists, and new National Monument designations as well as revised grazing permits have begun locally to constrict traditional grazing rights.

- *Development agreements.* In contrast to farming, threatened urban lifeways have inspired few protective measures. One, roughly comparable to right-to-farm laws, is the development agreement. Development agreements are crafted to protect industrial activities—an important but declining source of blue-collar employment—from being eliminated as public nuisances. Zoning and financial techniques are sometimes adapted to help owners continue in business.[41] A related tool is the special zoning district, discussed below. And, as in rural settings, voluntary efforts supplement official, legal measures: in this case, the leading actors are community development corporations and not-for-profit organizations dedicated to producing affordable housing; in addition, some business improvement districts could be thought of as helping to maintain place-based traditions.

- *Zoning.* Many people are lulled into a false sense of security by the belief that "it can't happen here—we have zoning." In fact, it generally *can* happen, because zoning typically permits more growth, and less attractive forms of growth, than citizens realize. (Real estate developers, however, understand this very well.)

Zoning was developed early in the twentieth century to protect residential neighborhoods from industry, and exclusive residential neighborhoods from apartment buildings. It also established a level playing field on which real estate developers could make investments with some confidence about the risks. Zoning regulations assured a developer that his Class A office building would not be rendered valueless by a waste dump next door. Today, developers continue to rely on zoning to lay out the ground rules by which they play and to protect their investments. Both they and most municipal planning officials see it primarily as a tool of development rather than of preservation policy. Though admittedly it works by setting limits on factors like height, bulk, or number of dwelling units, these are often higher than existing conditions. Moreover, like those written into nuclear weapons treaties, the limits tend to become goals, at least in a rising market. This happens because a robust market values property according to its highest economic potential rather than its existing use. Sales prices and taxes are set accordingly. Thus zoning, by setting ceilings above existing conditions, may actually encourage property to move towards higher levels of development.

Two other almost ubiquitous aspects of zoning inflict further harm on many communities. One is the preference for separating different activities into distinct areas: separate zones for living, shopping, working in offices, manufacturing, and so forth. Such segregation of activities is almost never found in traditional urban or even suburban neighborhoods, where homes and places for working, dining, buying things, or worshipping are typically intermingled. Yet single-use zoning has not only shaped the development of new communities but has been widely imposed on existing communities, making the land uses on which their lifeways depend literally illegal. The other is the favoritism with which most zoning codes treat automobiles. By generously providing all of the space which drivers might conceivably want for highway ramps, interchanges, and even local access streets—with little regard for competing demands—zoning and engineering standards end by creating dead zones which are largely devoid of human contact and which disrupt established pedestrian patterns. This too has been harmful to many long-established neighborhoods.

Despite these failings, zoning has furnished a few helpful tools to protect traditional ways of life. Techniques such as exclusive-use zoning, farmland zoning, cluster zoning, overlay zones, and performance standards have been developed for or applied to the problem of saving farms and ranches.[42] None of these erects an invincible palisade around the farm: rather, some help farmers hold out against the pressure of rising land values while others permit them to profit from development without eliminating farming. They do this essentially by concentrating the full permissible quantity of new development within small areas, thus leaving open space for farming or recreation. Another tool, the transfer of development rights, shifts the farm's development potential *outside* its borders,[43] allowing the farmer to sell the right to build additional structures to a neighbor, or to a government "bank," which may in turn sell them or simply retire them from the marketplace. Once stripped of its development potential, the farm will no longer be a target for development in the future and will be taxed at a lower rate reflecting its value as a farm, rather than as condominiums, second homes, or a mall.

Another useful tool is the special zoning district. This is simply a set of place-specific zoning regulations designed to recognize and sustain the character of a particular neighborhood, rather than generically to regulate development. As noted in Chapter 6, New York City has been particularly creative in this regard, establishing regulations tailor-made to protect the special character of Little Italy, Chinatown, Sheepshead Bay (especially its tradition of ocean fishing), the working-class community of Clinton, the garment manufacturing and theater districts in Manhattan, and other neighborhoods. They have been modestly successful: at the very least, they give local activists the ability to argue against projects that would harm the traditional character of their district and can constrain city officials against approving them. But they can do no more than what zoning does—regulate development—and cannot keep traditional activities such as garment manufacturing or fishing economically viable.

Special zoning districts long ago fell out of favor with New York's City Planning Commission but have made a limited comeback since about 2000. More important, the city has begun to design zoning districts which appear to be generic yet are intended to maintain neighborhood character in specific places. This trend began as early as the 1980s with the Quality Housing Program, which offered developers the option of a contextually appropriate building envelope instead of the standard modernist tower or slab zoning. At first the option was available only in a few high-density residential districts, but at community insistence it has gradually been extended to ever larger parts of the city. Most recently it has even been applied to low-density residential districts. For example, the R2A classification was established in 2005: its size, height, and setback requirements differ subtly from those of other low-density residential districts and were crafted, according to the city's planning department, "to preserve the low-rise context" of certain specific neighborhoods in Bayside, Whitestone and Cambria Heights in Queens.[44] The zoning rules will obviously permit development but are designed to ensure that new buildings fit closely with the existing character of the neighborhood.

The movement known as New Urbanism has offered other valuable corrections to the established norms for zoning. Codified in 1991 in the Ahwahnee Principles, the goal of New Urbanism is actually to foster traditional urbanism through plans, regulations, and developments that integrate housing, shops, and workplaces, support pedestrian activity and public transit, and create mixed-income communities. Though the movement has focused on applying these ideas to the design of new real estate developments rather than to the improvement of existing communities, the principles are strikingly similar to what community advocates have been trying to achieve in many long-established neighborhoods, without necessarily calling their efforts New Urbanism.[45]

- *Easements and taxes.* Landowners themselves may be able to act on behalf of tradition, thanks to government measures that reward conservation efforts with lower taxes. One such measure is the easement, a device which splits off a specific ownership right from the bundle of rights held by the owner and places it in other hands. Conservation easements essentially work by allowing a landowner to transfer the right to do that which is not desired—to build condominiums on the farm, for example—to someone who pledges not to do it—the government or a non-profit organization. The sale may diminish the property's value, but this may actually be attractive to the owner because it will also reduce the tax burden. Donating rather than selling the easement may bring yet other tax advantages. Farmers and ranchers in states as distant from each other as Arizona and Vermont are increasingly turning to conservation easements as a way to continue farming.

Just as property taxes sometimes drive change, forcing long-time occupants off the land, they can be adjusted to aid stability. In some jurisdictions landmark properties are assessed at a lower valuation reflecting their reduced development potential; a similar device is to base the valuation on an existing use, such as farming, rather than on the property's "highest and best use."[46] A small sect of economists known as the Georgists, after the nineteenth-century economist and social reformer Henry George, has long advocated more fundamental change. They propose that buildings should not be taxed at all, only land. Depending on how rates are adjusted, there may be little or no net impact on the tax revenue of particular jurisdictions, but the burden on individual taxpayers may shift dramatically, with those who are sitting on undeveloped land paying much more than previously, those with valuable buildings much less. In general, the Georgist "single tax" seems designed to spur growth and investment, but some environmentalists are interested in its premises, such as the idea that socially created value, including the increased value of land due to infrastructure, should be recaptured by society. And in some Pennsylvania towns and cities where it has been applied, it seems to have had some success in stemming urban disinvestment and suburban sprawl. Since the problem of property abandonment is emerging as a major threat against long-settled urban neighborhoods throughout the country, the Georgist land value tax may prove to be, at least in this context, a valuable tool for protecting placeways.[47] The problem deserves further study.

In general, the possibilities for using tax policy to reward conservation have hardly begun to be explored. Ecological economists like Herman Daly and Robert Costanza are reassessing basic economic concepts like gross national product in light of environmental systems and the fundamentally important services which they provide. And they and others are proposing new forms of taxation such as pollution taxes or throughput taxes. In Canada, an experiment called Alternative Land Use Services (ALUS) is being tried: under this concept, farmers are actually compensated for their stewardship, receiving payments for maintaining existing natural assets. Conceived partly as a way to offset the additional costs imposed by environmental regulation, ALUS also constitutes, in effect, a sort of reverse tax payment.

- *Heritage areas and special districts.* Special districts can combine tax, easement, and other government policies in defense of a traditional activity. Pennsylvania, for example, allows groups of farmers to petition for creation of an Agricultural Security Area within which right-to-farm measures protect farming operations from attack as public nuisances and farmers may sell agricultural conservation easements to the state.[48]

A heritage area is an area with distinctive history, folklife, culture, or local traditions that are worthy and capable of preservation. Unlike a national park, which is federally owned and managed and is largely if not entirely uninhabited, a heritage area consists mainly of private land and may contain villages, towns, farms, businesses, and other kinds of habitation and economic activity. Congress has been designating heritage areas since 1984; as of 2001, there were twenty-three, and they were concentrated (unlike the great national parks) east of the Mississippi. Some states have heritage area programs: New York State's, initially called the Urban Cultural Park System, was launched in 1982. Whether federal or state, heritage area designation typically signals the creation of resource studies, management plans, and public–private partnerships intended to conserve the area's heritage, develop tourism, and support the region's economy.

The idea of the heritage area has many antecedents. It is similar to the English national parks, in that much if not all of the land is and remains in private ownership, while government provides special regulations, services, and funding to preserve and promote the area's heritage. Within the United States, New York's Adirondack Park (created in a succession of legislative acts between 1885 and 1895) mixes private and public land. Within the national park system, Cape Cod National Seashore (1961) was the first park to include living communities with the explicit intention of allowing them to continue; it was followed by Fire Island National Seashore (1964) and Lowell National Historical Park (1979). Internationally, the heritage area concept echoes UNESCO's World Heritage List, launched in 1972.

Federal guidelines recognize folklife and local customs as important factors contributing to the value of heritage areas. It is harder to know how successful these areas have been in protecting them. The emphasis frequently is on developing tourism, which is at best a mixed blessing for traditional ways of life and land. On the other hand, heritage areas can provide a vehicle for coordinating special agricultural districts, local taxing schemes, and preservation efforts, and for funneling tourism income into depressed local economies in ways which sustain communities.

- *Non-profit programs.* Not-for-profit organizations in historic preservation, planning, housing, community development, and other fields are helping to protect traditional land uses through a variety of programs, indeed far too many even to name here. The greatest attention has been given to farming, ranching, and related rural activities. The Sonoran Institute helps ranchers to adapt to new economic pressures, while the Nature Conservancy and the Trust for Public Land are participating in collaborations designed to keep ranches operating while improving the environmental quality of rangeland. The National Trust's Barn Again! program promotes the continuing use of old barns. Greenmarket programs, such as the one launched by the Council on the Environment of New York City in 1976, aim to support family farms by giving farmers direct access to urban consumers in attractive and popular open-air market settings. Towns have also attracted considerable attention from non-profits. The Glynwood Center (Cold Spring, NY) and the Orton Family Foundation (Middlebury, VT) have developed new planning tools to strengthen small towns, and the Glynwood Center is working to support traditional agriculture. The National Trust for Historic Preservation's Main Street Program promotes the revitalization of shopping streets.[49] Nowadays, larger cities are also adopting the National Trust's approach to commercial revitalization. In addition, urban housing non-profits are helping to keep low-income communities viable by developing or rehabilitating affordable housing, while community development corporations sponsor programs to support local businesses and provide community services.

A special category of non-profit is the land trust, an organization that exists to protect property from development by owning land or easements. It was estimated in 1993 that over 1,100 land trusts were operating in the United States, with new ones forming at the rate of over one per week.[50] Community land trusts are a little different: developed in the late 1960s, they can hold land for the purpose of developing it in the community's interest, for example for affordable housing or a community center. They may also own and lease residential or business property at below-market rents.

There are probably under one hundred community land trusts in the United States.

- *Folklore.* Folklore programs may be either government-sponsored or non-profit. They are in a separate category because they work differently from the programs discussed above. Folklore began to emerge as a significant force around 1930, with the establishment of the Archive of American Folk Song in the Library of Congress (1928), followed by the first National Folk Festival (1934). A big step came in 1976 with the passage of the American Folklife Preservation Act, which established the American Folklife Center at the Library of Congress and charged it to "preserve and present" American folklore through research, documentation, archives, training, live presentation, exhibitions, and publications.[51] Today the National Endowment for the Humanities as well as many state arts and humanities councils support folklore.

    Most folklore programs have focused on documenting rural traditions and collecting their artifacts; only a few, like New York's non-profit City Lore, have concentrated on urban folklore. To some extent folklore programs can encourage the continuance of tradition, but, just as preserving artifacts doesn't always preserve tradition, so documenting and presenting tradition don't necessarily ensure its continuing vitality.

- *Historic preservation.* Historic preservation programs work either to ensure preservation through regulation or to encourage it through financial incentives. Most local preservation ordinances fall into the former category: the Department of the Interior's Rehabilitation Tax Credit program falls into the latter. Both have been enormously helpful in protecting fine buildings and architecturally distinguished neighborhoods, an accomplishment that should not be underestimated: when urban renewal, highway construction, and downtown redevelopment were bulldozing viable urban neighborhoods as well as such emblems of downtown public and commercial culture as department stores, town halls, and banks, historic preservation was an important bulwark of tradition. Yet historic preservation did little in those years to preserve the fabric of working-class urban residential neighborhoods. Where they survived, it was because of the care that their owners, often African American or white ethnic workers, put into maintaining their homes. Sometimes they did so because, unlike their richer fellow citizens, they lacked the resources to abandon their old neighborhoods and move to the suburbs. As former Massachusetts State Senator Byron Rushing remarked, the poor have been the real preservers of America's urban neighborhoods, though they have received little thanks for it.[52]

    In contrast to their success at preserving buildings, many historic preservation programs have had at best a neutral impact on the preservation of tradition. Two hypothetical examples of preservation at work may help to explain why. In the first, a group of decaying loft buildings is threatened with demolition for a highway or mall. Preservationists and neighborhood advocates defeat the proposal and save the buildings, which are beautifully rehabilitated as artists' lofts and boutiques. In the second, a working-class neighborhood of nineteenth-century rowhouses is declining: absent intervention, it faces a slow but continuous erosion of architectural features. Preservationists do intervene, urging owners to restore their houses with impeccable period details and, where existing owners cannot do so, encouraging new and more affluent owners to move into the neighborhood and do so. These examples are obviously oversimplified, but they do throw into clear relief some of the typical impacts which preservation can have on existing communities and traditional lifeways. In the first example, preservation has no net impact on traditional lifeways, which were either defunct or facing obliteration anyway. In the second, preservation is associated with the displacement of an existing community, together with the loss of its place-based customs and traditions.

The process at work in the second example is often called gentrification. There is much debate over whether historic preservation causes, results from, or simply accompanies gentrification. What is clear is that preservation *in itself* does not bring about the death or displacement of traditional communities. The movement of capital does that, as the pressures of the real estate market encourage relatively affluent people to see certain underpriced neighborhoods as good investment opportunities. The impact of their disproportionate investment power on the property values and population of those neighborhoods would be roughly the same whether the newcomers built grand new houses or restored the existing ones. It is the openness of neighborhoods to the flows of capital which exposes them to gentrification, not the specific form taken by those flows. Historic preservation is just one of the forms that they may assume.

The preservation movement is changing. Appreciation of vernacular folk artifacts has been growing, and so too respect for traditional lifeways. Though not the same, the first can lead to and encourage the second. Some preservationists began taking a more active interest in folklore, or "intangible cultural resources," as long ago as the 1980s, led by the National Park Service and the American Folklore Center of the Library of Congress: as Thomas Carter and Carl Fleischhauer put it, there was "a gradual coming together of approaches to cultural preservation that once seemed disparate."[53] More recently, international influences like Australia's Burra Charter have encouraged this movement; these are discussed further in the Prologue. The approaches to preservation taken by Native peoples around the world have provided yet another powerful impetus, in this country most obviously through NAGPRA and the National Register's Bulletin 38, *Guidelines for Evaluating and Documenting Traditional Cultural Properties.*[54] While success in applying the traditional cultural significance criteria to non-Native sites has been mixed, it remains a promising avenue for further exploration.[55] Two other influential initiatives which preserve traditions along with artifacts are the National Trust's Main Street and Barn Again! programs (launched respectively in the 1970s and in 1987). The Trust's ongoing campaigns against suburban sprawl and big-box stores are also aimed equally at protecting communities' traditional lifeways and at protecting their physical character.

- *Environmental conservation legislation.* Established professional and bureaucratic structures enforce a distinction which is not always helpful between the conservation of natural and man-made environments. Structures and man-made spaces belong to "the built environment" and thus to historic preservation; spaces without buildings belong to the "natural environment" and thus to environmental conservation. But environmentalists increasingly recognize that human beings are part of nature, and that many worthy environments include human features and even human habitation.[56]

The law provides significant support for this view. As described in Chapter 3, the National Environmental Policy Act makes it national policy to "preserve important historic, cultural, and natural aspects of our national heritage."[57] To trigger preparation of an environmental impact statement (EIS) under NEPA, a proposed federal action must significantly affect some aspect of the physical world, including air, water, land, cities, and historical and cultural resources. But what makes NEPA a potential ally of traditional lifeways is that, once triggered, the EIS may document harmful impacts beyond the mere physical changes, including harm to health (psychological as well as physical), social welfare, and aesthetic values.[58] Whereas the protections afforded by NHPA are narrowly focused on physical structures (and moreover on structures over fifty years old), the provisions of NEPA may extend to less tangible aspects of culture as long as they are connected to physical conditions. The environmental policy sketched out by NEPA, in short, also provides the outlines of a policy to recognize the value of traditional lifeways. In Alaska it is doing just that, providing the procedural framework for the required impact analyses on subsistence uses of fish and wildlife.

NEPA has given rise to a series of state laws, known as "little NEPAs," that apply similar provisions to the actions of state governments. One of them, New York's State Environmental Quality Review Act (SEQRA), is considered in greater detail in Chapter 2. In some instances, these laws are an improvement on NEPA. For, whereas NEPA merely requires the government to disclose the environmental consequences of its proposals, some little NEPAs require the avoidance or mitigation of certain harmful impacts. Some of these laws (such as those of New York and California) apply to virtually all government projects throughout the state, others (such as those of New Jersey, Michigan, and Mississippi) only to specific kinds of projects. In at least one instance, in Michigan, a little NEPA has been used to analyze the impacts of a proposal on traditional culture.

In 1987 Michigan passed a law requiring environmental assessments for new radioactive waste facilities, and as part of this process a team of folklorists soon thereafter analyzed the impacts of a proposed facility on folk traditions in the region. They focused on occupation-related, recreation-related, and community (i.e. ethnic and religious) traditions, emphasizing "foodways, special events and festivals, vernacular architecture, and other material culture," and noting "traditional uses of environmental resources, the relationship of residents and nonresidents to community cultural resources, and evidence of community cohesiveness and stability through traditional activities and structures."[59]

This may have been the first time an environmental assessment included a folklore study. It need not be the last.[60] As we shall see, environmental laws have considerable potential for recognizing and protecting tradition.

GETTING BETTER PERFORMANCE FROM EXISTING TOOLS

Those who seek to defend place-based traditions and lifeways can call on a wide range of laws, procedures, and programs. Yet the erosion continues. Could the existing tools produce more torque? Yes: with some redesign, many existing tools could yield broader and more substantial protection for place-based traditions. The proposals that follow point out how some of them could be redesigned or used more effectively:

- *Reform the tax system.* The tax system right now favors replacement over retention of existing buildings, abandonment over investment in inner-city property, and suburban sprawl over conservation of farmland and "unused" wildland around the perimeter. The system is well designed if the goal is to produce a more or less constant state of churning, disruption of places, and waste of natural resources. However, if we prefer the opposite— stability of places and conservation of resources—then we need to reform the tax system. The goal is not to increase the tax burden but rather to shift it so that it no longer penalizes socially constructive behaviors like conservation of resources or affection for places and becomes a support, rather than an insuperable obstacle, to nurturing place-based traditions.

This is a substantial and complex undertaking. Ecological economists are developing proposals for new forms of taxation designed to encourage conservation of resources, and these should be closely studied. Meanwhile, the existing property tax provides a good place to start. Property tax is usually assessed on the basis of "highest and best use"—that is, the dollar value that the property might fetch if put to the most economically rewarding use. This means that, in a rising market, owners are forced to pay the costs of growth even if they are not reaping the profits and do not wish to do so. Property taxes push land towards development and population towards turnover. Assessing property tax on the basis of current use, as is already done in limited contexts (special districts established to protect farming, for example, or landmark structures), would help stabilize many communities and their traditional activities. There are other problems associated with assessments based on current use: they may encourage speculators to warehouse properties in hopes of future gains, and they may encourage leapfrogging, development which jumps over warehoused properties and exacerbates problems of suburban sprawl. As noted earlier, the Georgists propose a quite different kind of tax reform. The point is that how property is taxed—not only at a specific location but throughout a region—has an enormous impact on how it is developed or not developed. Taxes may provide the tipping force in large numbers of individual decisions about whether to maintain buildings or let them deteriorate, cultivate fields or replace them with houses, retain land or sell it. And the cumulative force of these individual decisions can dramatically and quite quickly alter the character of places which have appeared stable over long periods of time. Property tax solutions must be context-sensitive: the goal is to alleviate the pressure towards the redevelopment or abandonment of property exerted by them. The subject deserves much more attention than it has received.

- *Relieve the pressure of zoning.* By setting limits that are higher than the existing sizes of buildings and intensities of use, most zoning regulations describe an imagined future that can only be reached through growth. In a strong market, growth ensues. Were zoning instead to describe our communities *as they are,* many traditional communities would find it easier to survive. This is what New York City has begun to do, at least within limited areas. Growth advocates will point out that such a policy, if universally applied, would stifle the creation of needed housing and economic opportunities, while conservationists will correctly argue that controls applied in some places may simply direct unwanted growth to other places. These are fair objections. But there are places where protecting the existing configuration of a community may be as important as other social needs and should not automatically be sacrificed. The point is simply that zoning should not provide a blueprint for automatic growth.

• *Where appropriate, manage public lands in ways that respect traditional uses.* Public demand for open space and outdoor recreation has risen dramatically in recent decades. Meanwhile, suburban expansion and the development of resorts and second-home communities continue to put pressure on land used for farming, grazing, or forestry. Both trends generate demands on governments and land trusts to purchase land (or conservation easements) and to manage land for recreational purposes including hiking, rock climbing, or family picnicking. Conflicts with traditional uses, whether Native or non-Native, will not soon disappear. While conservation efforts should not be stymied by demands for unsustainable levels of resource use, however sanctioned by tradition, flexible management policies can often accommodate traditional hunting, ranching, or plant gathering. More can probably be done too to shield such activities from conflicts with newer recreational uses.

• *Change the focus of the siting debate from "where" to "whether."* Where to put highways, power plants, waste dumps, malls, and other neighborhood-destroying land uses remains an enormous problem for all communities, but especially for poor ones. For, despite a good deal of hand-wringing from developers and politicians about the difficulties of getting such things built, the truth is that it is actually extremely difficult to stop them. Even when a community does ward off a threat, the likelihood is that the project will simply move to another location. The permitting process (an apt name) turns out to be more about *where* than about *whether*: in this elaborate and highly political game for determining who will bear the burden, all participants apparently assume that *someone* will eventually do so.

This is a bad premise. There are many things that should not be built anywhere. Instead of prompting fights over whose back yard to put them in, the public process should be redesigned to encourage citizens to ask, first, whether the project ought to be built at all: not *where* but *whether*. Some environmental justice groups are doing this, replacing "Not In My Back Yard" with "Not In Anyone's Back Yard."

• *Nurture the art of doing less.* Humans, specifically American humans, bring a restless energy to the business of life. Whether that business is leveraging a buyout or preserving a neighborhood, the motto is "Don't just sit there; do something." Sometimes we might be better advised to heed the meditator's mantra: "Don't just do something; sit there." At present, most ways of protecting things end by subjecting them to new pressures. National Monument designation may bring fears of additional visitors and more intensive use as well as prohibitions against grazing. Landmark designation may prompt fears that exacting standards of restoration may be applied. We need to perfect ways of leaving things alone: not ignoring them but consciously, intentionally, keeping our hands off them except when intervention is needed. The federal government has at times reserved land: that is, taken it out of play. Perhaps this idea could be extended to land and buildings in towns and cities. I imagine new forms of protective designation that could shelter buildings and sites from destructive change without imposing (or seeming to impose) higher standards of care, standards which may encourage other changes which end by transforming the neighborhood. I imagine, too (see Chapter 11), preservationists declaring independence from the growth machine.

- *Require cultural impact statements everywhere, along the model of Hawai'i.* Thirteen words were all it took to amend Hawaii's environmental law. In many states little more would be required. Neighborhood groups threatened by development projects would no longer have to argue for the need to consider cultural factors: it would be required. How effectively cultural impact statements met the needs of traditional place-based lifeways would depend on how the implementing regulations were written. The writing of them would surely prompt an energetic public discussion, and that in itself would be beneficial. Once regulations were implemented, advocates would find themselves in a much strengthened position.
- *Carry out a demonstration project to show how existing environmental laws can protect community lifeways.* The National Environmental Policy Act (NEPA), as already noted, acknowledges the importance of place and culture, and environmental law offers a number of intriguing options for protective efforts. Some of these come from the area of environmental justice. For example, the Clean Water Act protects "existing uses" as of 1975, and it has been argued that:

> to the extent that minority or low-income populations are, or at any time since 1975 have been, using the waters for recreational or subsistence fishing, EPA could reinterpret the current regulations to require that such uses, if actually attained, must be maintained and protected.[61]

The little NEPAs also offer great promise, and New York State's Environmental Quality Review Act provides an excellent starting point. It provides powerful hooks for considering complex factors like "community or neighborhood character," including non-physical characteristics of the environment. The bounds of "community or neighborhood character" under SEQRA are not precisely delineated; persuasive argumentation backed up by solid research could surely establish precedents for including a wide range of factors important to the survival of traditional place-based activities. In fact, an environmental impact statement prepared under SEQRA could probably resemble the cultural impact analysis which Hawaiian law specifically requires.

SEQRA, in short, is a tool that could do much more to protect community traditions, as could many other state environmental laws. The problem is that, when an environmental threat becomes known and an EIS is produced, it is usually already too late to use it for this purpose. The consulting firms which specialize in carrying out impact statements are not particularly interested in exploring new terrain or in trying out experimental methodologies, nor are the government agencies which employ them, and even less so the private developers, if they are involved. As for the affected neighborhood groups, understaffed and underfunded as they typically are, they are instantly thrown into crisis mode. At this point in the process, they lack the time and resources needed to identify, document, and advocate for the importance of neighborhood traditions and the places which support them. Unlike the agency officials, consultants, and developers, they are rarely experts in environmental law: confronted with an EIS they may not automatically think of the appropriate methodologies by which to document community traditions; indeed they may not recognize the opening offered by the law. Working against unforgiving deadlines and, frequently, intense official pressure, they must stick to familiar ways of working and concentrate on a few key issues.

This problem could be alleviated if a cultural impact statement were required, as it now is in Hawai'i. But, even when cultural impact statements are required, as I believe they will eventually be, neighborhood residents will frequently find it difficult to identify important cultural resources under the stress and deadlines of an imminent threat. Within a complex community, there may well be differences of opinion over which places, activities, or local memories are important. Some residents will not speak out at all, because they are unaware of the public process, afraid of government authorities, or reluctant to subject traditional activities to public attention and, possibly, disapproval. Opponents of protection will exploit all such disagreements or uncertainties as evidence of the community's flawed understanding. But there is something that community residents can do to prevent this from happening: they can identify and document important local places and traditions ahead of time. The concept of storyscape outlined in Chapter 2 offers a way to do so. Story sites provide essential anchors for many traditional place-based activities, and a storyscape survey is a sensible and methodologically defensible extension of the standard environmental and preservation survey techniques which are already in widespread and uncontroversial use.

SEQRA, moreover, provides a way to ensure, in advance, that impacts to story sites are considered during the environmental review process: by including them in an official community plan, such as the 197(a) plans prepared within New York City. SEQRA declares that any proposal that would create a "material conflict" with such a plan automatically constitutes a "significant adverse impact," requiring an environmental impact statement. Thus neighborhood sites or characteristics which a community plan identifies as important for their value to community character or traditions are automatically recognized under SEQRA. And were community plans to explicitly study and make policy statements regarding the protection of traditional life patterns, SEQRA would give them force at the level of state environmental review. Ensuring that 197(a) plans or the equivalent take account of story sites and local traditions is a practical step that advocates can take right now.

Even without the vehicle of an approved local plan, the important principle is, as much as possible, to carry out the research *ahead of time*, interviewing neighborhood residents, documenting important traditions and the places that sustain them, and creating a dossier of solid information against future need. A demonstration project can show communities across the state and country how to do this and, at the same time, provide an opportunity to test and refine methodologies and to amass experience that will prove useful some day in writing cultural impact assessment regulations. To have the widest methodological validity, such a project should be organized across several communities, all with strong locally based organizations yet with contrasting physical and demographic characteristics, and perhaps in states with substantively different environmental laws. Within each neighborhood, a community-based organization should carry out a survey of traditional lifeways and associated sites, assisted by experts in history, folklore, oral history, and related fields. The final product should include not only the surveys themselves but also a template for a sound, defensible, and widely replicable methodology. To bolster the results against future legal challenges, a separate panel of experts could serve as a jury, vetting the survey results for methodological rigor and significance.

Beyond helping the participating neighborhoods, a project of this kind will demonstrate the potential of environmental law to protect the traditional character of neighborhoods and will create a model for broader adoption. Not least of its benefits is that it will help the environmental assessment process, first mandated over forty years ago, to achieve its full potential as a forum for genuine public discourse about the environment, shifting the focus of debate from scientific experts to citizens, and from hard data to the profound knowledge and feelings of residents for the places they inhabit.

- *Carry out a second demonstration project to show how existing preservation law can protect community lifeways.* Some of the story sites identified through the model project described above will surely qualify as traditional cultural properties (TCPs), and advocates should work to get them listed on the National Register. One reason for doing so is that some state environmental laws explicitly recognize National Register sites: under SEQRA, for example, impacts on National Register properties automatically trigger an environmental impact statement. But national preservation law deserves its own initiative. And, while this could be coordinated with an environmental law initiative, it should be organized along its own lines. One reason is a structural difference between the kinds of law. State environmental laws differ widely, and some offer broader potential than NEPA. By contrast, state preservation laws and the core programs of many state preservation agencies are closely bound to the national framework provided by the National Historic Preservation Act, federal regulations governing eligibility for National Register listing, rehabilitation tax credits, and so forth. Below the state level, one finds a myriad of local preservation ordinances. This is the level at which the law's regulatory authority bites into private property: ultimately therefore it is the level at which reform must aim. Yet local demonstration projects are likely to be perceived as lacking national relevance. A demonstration project should be organized at the state and federal level.

Historic preservation law is focused on the protection of tangible things, and this is specifically true of the National Register, which the law defines as listing "districts, sites, buildings, structures, and objects. . . ." However, the reasons for protecting these physical things may lie outside themselves: for example, Register properties may be significant to American "history" or "culture."[62] More broadly, the stated purpose of preserving Register properties is to maintain and enrich their "vital legacy" of "cultural" and other benefit for future generations.[63] This language is open to the recognition that places which support local customs or traditions embody important aspects of cultural heritage as well as significant benefits for future generations and that, as such, they deserve to be protected. The goal should now be to demonstrate the truth of these assertions.

Again, the concepts of storyscape and story sites provide a workable framework. The National Register program itself has created an opening in this direction through Bulletin 38 and the concept of traditional cultural properties. These provide a sound basis for further work. The TCP idea recognizes the vital connection between living cultural traditions and place, and it provides a framework for considering oral testimony and direct observation of social customs along with written history as valid evidence of significance. The widespread listing of traditional cultural properties would help place-based communities to maintain valued traditions.

There are, however, substantial obstacles to this. Some are bureaucratic: many federal and state preservation officers have been trained to place a high value on architectural significance and written history while distrusting oral evidence and doubting the historical significance of living community traditions. These habits of thought are hard to change, and resistance to the entire notion of TCPs can give exaggerated importance to other difficulties, definitional and theoretical, which are challenging enough. For example, Bulletin 38 relates traditional significance to communities, but what is a community? In twenty-first-century America, communities may be fluid, redefining themselves continuously; cultural identities may be multiple. Some communities organize themselves around affiliation or values rather than neighborhood, and people may belong to several. Defining community in ways that preserve the cultural benefits of places for today's society and that of the future presents interesting challenges, but clearly a narrow definition based on the past would not serve the intent of the law.

TCPs present other definitional challenges as well. So do the basic National Register regulations. For example, fundamental concepts like significance and integrity (discussed in Chapters 2 and 3) continue to require reinterpretation to fit society's evolving needs. A demonstration project could help work out these questions, build awareness of how TCPs can help support local traditions, and promote clarity about the criteria for listing. While a fifty-state project is clearly unfeasible, these goals could be reached by carrying out coordinated surveys in several states within different regions: they could share a thematic focus, such as traditional gathering places or places that symbolize local identity, interpreted according to the region. The surveys could be carried out by local coalitions including not-for-profit groups as well as state preservation agencies, assisted by academic experts in local history, geography, folklore, and so forth. Coordination and information sharing could be provided by an overall steering committee, which could include or be led by one or more regional offices of the National Trust for Historic Preservation. The project should conclude with two final products: a series of new National Register listings and a conference, accompanied by a publication, to share the experiences of participants and develop a set of best practices for working with TCPs.

We must be realistic about what an improved National Register can do: the Register provides limited protection, and only against federal aggression. Thus it is extremely important where federal land is plentiful and the federal presence prominent, less so where these conditions do not obtain. Beyond its protective role, the Register also provides access to federal Rehabilitation Tax Credits, so its extension to traditional cultural properties could bring some benefit to those that are in commercial use. Finally, the Register is widely accepted as a sort of coin of the realm, the only national standard for preservation that we have, the tool that is in every preservationist's toolkit. It *should* serve our evolving understanding of tradition and traditional properties. And a National Register program that embraces traditional cultural properties *should*, and will, encourage preservationists everywhere to do the same.

- *Talk, talk, talk about the value of neighborhood traditions and the places that support them.* At landmarks hearings in New York City, community advocates sometimes try to explain how the construction of a new building (or the demolition of an old one) will harm the character of their neighborhood. They must be careful to frame their concerns in the specific terms laid out by the landmarks law, for otherwise they will be told their testimony is not germane. That is because the landmarks law does not recognize affection for place as a relevant factor in making decisions. Nevertheless, members of the public continue to try to put "inappropriate" comments on the record, because to non-specialists it seems almost self-evident that attachment to place must be connected to heritage. Moreover, people facing unwanted changes to places they care about often feel driven to talk about them, and the Landmarks Preservation Commission is perceived as a sympathetic body. For all these reasons, then, neighborhood residents frequently assume that landmarks hearings are the logical place to express their feelings of place attachment and injury, and they are sometimes surprised to learn otherwise.

To get better protection for place-based traditions, it is essential to open up space in the public discourse in which to explain the social value of nurturing them. The hearings held by local landmarks commissions are merely one kind of venue: others include the hearings held by legislatures and by boards of city and regional planning, subdivision, environmental compliance, and zoning. Public meetings organized by community groups, political clubs, and community development corporations offer yet more. Local newspapers and community radio stations also provide important opportunities for discussing place affection, community traditions, and their value to neighborhoods, towns, cities, and regions.

The point is not merely to talk but, by doing so, to develop and legitimize a public language for expressing attachment to place. This will not be the environmental language of chemicals and parts per million, nor will it be the historical language of names and dates. It must be a counterpart to both, affective enough to express feelings of place attachment yet precise enough to sustain public decision-making. Only when we have such a language, and an energized debate in which to exercise it, will our public institutions protect the heritage of place-based traditions and the use values of home and neighborhood as they deserve.

GOING BEYOND EXISTING TOOLS: SOLVING THE PROPERTY PROBLEM

Getting more mileage out of the existing tools can lead to real improvement. But it will not dramatically expand the ability of most Americans to preserve community traditions from the pressures of changing land use. Is it possible to imagine a future in which the value of community traditions are recognized as they are in Hawai'i, in which the basic assumptions of land use law and practice support, rather than frustrate, the perpetuation of local traditions? How might we take the first steps towards such a future?

Native Hawaiians' land rights are based on prior sovereignty, and one of the ways in which that sovereignty was manifested and made real was through the act of inhabiting the land, of living in the place. Though sovereignty and inhabitation are not identical, long inhabitation can eventually confer something like sovereignty, a concept which survives in the law of adverse possession, or in the English custom according to which a right of way across private land remains open to the public as long as it continues to be used. Yet, despite these considerations, our legal system accords very few rights to people simply because they inhabit a place. Community planning boards and environmental review processes grant limited powers of expression to residents, while rent control and other tenant protection laws grant some protections to tenants. But in general the hard legal rights all go to the owners, whether they are residents or absentee landlords. This is one of the central reasons why place-based traditions are liable to disruption.

Extending legal rights in places to their inhabitants is one obvious way to correct the problem. Doing so would recognize the fact that title deeds do not represent the sum total of investment in place. The value of a piece of property—even defined in the narrowest terms—is never created entirely by its owner. If it were, location would not be the most important factor in real estate. The public sector creates much of any property's value by investing in infrastructure and public services. Community residents also create value by investing, financially and emotionally, in the life of the neighborhood. If residents want to stay (and others want to come in), that may be in part because the local customs, the neighborhood way of life, the community's indefinable feel, make it attractive. These factors, nourished by the affection and commitment of residents, create value. Given the depth and breadth of the commitment which countless residents make to their neighborhoods, it is actually surprising how little control they have over property decisions which can make or break them—and how little profit they stand to gain from their investment.

Should we wish for legal recognition of rights based on inhabitation? Not everyone thinks so. Real estate developers want to maintain their relatively untrammeled ability to exchange and develop property. The managers of transit systems and public parks (not to mention shops) want to make decisions about how to run their operations without more interference from the public than they already have. These are solid practical considerations. There are ideological objections too, like the widespread image of America as a place perennially open to change and personal advancement. In fact, many people do not want to be bound by tradition, and America has historically held out the possibility of emancipating oneself from the past. It has not offered this possibility equally to everyone: constraints of race, class, and economics make it almost unattainable to many. And yet to those who have benefited from it, the gift of social mobility, of choosing *not* to be what one's ancestors were, is priceless. It should not be traded away. However, that does not mean we must automatically accept the continuous destruction of cultural traditions as a price to be paid: what it means is that we should fight for people's right to *choose* change. This in turn implies that they must also have the right to choose tradition, for without meaningful options the right to choose becomes hollow. Currently our laws and customs of property do not always support meaningful choices. Recognizing legal rights based on inhabitation, rather than solely on ownership, offers one way to improve them.

There are other weighty concerns which must be understood if such a proposal is brought forward, and addressed if it is to succeed. The laws and customs of property ownership are deeply grounded in core American values, wrapped up in cherished ideals of democracy. It would not be inappropriate to regard these laws and customs as themselves constituting a dimension of cultural heritage worth fighting for. Certainly they are not to be lightly tampered with, any more than notions of social mobility are to be discarded. A genuine improvement, one which does not simply substitute one set of problems for another, must uphold the parts of our inherited notions of property ownership which we wish to keep, even as it modifies the ones which impede the rights of communities to protect traditions. To understand both the difficulties and the ways of doing so, we must look more closely at three basic American concepts of property ownership: first, that land is a commodity; second, that the ownership of this commodity confers the right to trade it with the greatest possible ease and the least interference; third, that wherever this commodity of land is not being developed to the highest possible intensity it is being misused or even wasted.

Emphasis on the right to own property runs deep in American history. An early draft of the Declaration of Independence had the phrase "pursuit of property" where we now have "pursuit of happiness." For statesmen like Thomas Jefferson, the ability of ordinary people to own land—real property—was both a sign and a guarantor of freedom because, at least in theory, a man who owned his own farm was resistant to tyranny and oppression.

It should be noted that in this context property meant individual or private property—an important qualification, because the North American continent largely consisted of communal property, land used by Native tribes or bands without formal title. The problem which faced European settlers, long before Jefferson, was not simply how to turn other people's property into their own but also how to turn communal property (which from their perspective was not really property at all) into private property. The important thing was to create a clear chain of title, something that proved the owner's legitimacy, for it was only with this assurance that owners could securely buy, sell, and develop property. An excellent way to establish a clear title was to buy the land from someone who already owned it, but what if no one owned it? Land that was not owned—communal land, for example—was difficult to buy and, from the seventeenth century onwards, immigrants were ingenious in finding ways to convert communal land into private land suitable for purchase. Dummy owners were sometimes set up for the purpose, Natives who might (at least to the satisfaction of the colonists) pose as private owners of land which was only ambiguously theirs. Of course the settlers also managed to obtain land in other ways than through purchase. But the important thing was to get land out of communal control and into individual ownership in order to create a legal title, for only thus could it be developed and traded.

The process of shifting land from communal to individual ownership continued well into the nineteenth century. Perhaps the most grotesque episode was the General Allotment Act, known as the Dawes Act, of 1887. This apportioned the communally held Indian reservations into privately owned parcels according to a formula: 160 acres per family. Indian families were allowed under certain conditions to sell their allotments to white people, while "excess" land (the difference between the allotted acreage and the total area of the reservation) was compulsorily sold to the government and opened to white homesteading. Though the law was an attack against Indian tribes, tribal identity, and hegemony, it was not necessarily an attack against individual Indians; as one government agent put it, "The common field is the seat of barbarism . . . the separate farm [is] the door to civilization."[64] The Dawes Act was meant to civilize the Natives, as another official explained, by giving them the right to say " 'This is mine' instead of 'This is ours.' " It was also meant to transfer Indian land to whites, and in this it succeeded: within the first five years, the Indian reservations were diminished by thirty million acres, including much of the best crop and grazing land. By the 1920s, the allotment system had cast more than half the population of the affected tribes into landless poverty.[65] In 1934, with the Indian land base severely diminished and age-old traditions of common ownership ruptured, the allotment system was terminated.

The Dawes Act suggests the lengths to which Americans have gone to transform land into private property capable of being traded and developed. This tendency to see landscapes as aggregates of privately owned and exchangeable parcels, so different from the Native outlook, has also deeply affected the way non-Native Americans view their own communities, and indeed their own homes. The sociologists John R. Logan and Harvey L. Molotch explain that, both "in legal statutes and in ordinary people's imaginations," the home is not merely a place for "making a life" but also a commodity, "a special sort of commodity: a place to be bought and sold, rented and leased. . . . Places can (and should) be the basis not only for carrying on a life but also for exchange in a market."[66] In the United States, they argue, place has been more thoroughly subjected to the impulses of capitalism than anywhere else, and they show that "this extreme commodification of place touches the lives of all and influences virtually every cultural, economic, and political institution that operates on the urban scene."[67]

One consequence explored by Logan and Molotch is that urban places become locked in an ongoing contest between "exchange" value and "use" value. Exchange value is land's worth as a commodity, to be bought, sold, leased, rented, or developed. Use value is its worth as a place to live, work, or play. Whereas use value is broadly spread among people who for the most part do not own land, exchange value is concentrated in the hands of owners and entrepreneurs. The interests of the two groups frequently fail to align, for maximizing a place's exchange value does not necessarily maximize its use value and may indeed diminish or even eliminate it. Though the conflict continues, it is an unequal one, for law and politics combine to give owners and entrepreneurs vastly more power than residents. And so, with few restraints on those who would maximize exchange value, and few protections for those who would maximize use value, the worth of places as home is frequently at the mercy of their value as property.

Use value suffers further in this unequal contest because of the last of the triad of fundamental American beliefs about land: that owners or users who do not develop their land to its full economic potential do not really deserve to keep it. Early in the nineteenth century, John Quincy Adams asked rhetorically:

> What is the right of a huntsman to the forest of a thousand miles over which he has accidentally ranged in quest of prey? . . . Shall the fields and valleys, which a beneficent God has formed to teem with the life of innumerable multitudes, be condemned to everlasting barrenness?[68]

Adams thought not: the huntsman had no right to the forest if others were prepared to put it to more economically productive use. Views like this were used to justify forced transfers of land, such as the Dawes Act, from Indians to Europeans and from shared to private ownership. If the laws of human progress and divine will demanded ever-increasing intensities of development as a basis for advancement, then it was only right to place land in the hands of those who would fulfill these demands.

Today few people would make such statements in public, yet similar ideas continue to guide our zoning laws, planning boards, politicians, civic leaders, and shapers of public opinion. The idea that the ownership of land and land-based resources is justified by putting them to economic use is found throughout society. Western water law provides a well-known example. Water is scarce in the west, and western water law exists to apportion it among many claimants. Its basis is the idea that the would-be owner of water must be willing to use it for some economic purpose. Admiring its coolness and purity is not an economic purpose, nor is maintaining an attractive habitat for fish or elk. The claimant who intends to leave the water in the stream—who wants precisely *not* to use it—will therefore lose his claim to another who is willing to irrigate a field, power a mill, operate a mine, or provide drinking water to a city.

A similar notion fuels the dynamics of urban redevelopment: aging buildings, having outlived their economic usefulness, should be replaced by new ones which boost the economic return yielded by the land. Widespread today, this idea was even more ubiquitous in 1974 when the New York Landmarks Conservancy was founded. This highly successful group set out to prove that old buildings could be profitably rehabilitated and returned to service. The Conservancy challenged the assumption that old buildings had outlived their economic usefulness, but not the underlying premise that buildings had to justify their existence through economic performance. Today one school of preservationists argues that the case for historic preservation should be based on non-economic values, such as historical interest, architectural quality, urbanistic character, or the contribution a building makes to the social fabric of a community. Yet the position staked out by the Landmarks Conservancy in 1974 continues to be an important one, and it is probably fair to say that most practicing preservationists have felt pressure at some point to demonstrate the investment potential of old buildings as part of the case for preserving them.[69] Preservationists, in short, share with real estate developers and western water lawyers the assumption that owners should use their assets to the fullest, increasing their economic value if they can.

Society's impetus towards growth has long had its critics. Environmentalists have pointed to limitless growth as a menace which threatens the very sustainability of natural systems. Other critics have attacked the pervasive emphasis of American society on individualism, personal expression, autonomy, and gain, arguing that these traits endanger fundamental bonds of community as well as important dimensions of self-realization.[70] The laws of property have contributed to both problems. Designed to protect the individual's (or the corporation's) right to own, develop, and sell land, the law provides few opportunities for people to express their common interest in place. And though the safeguards erected to protect use value—zoning, preservation and environmental laws, the police power, the law of nuisances, and so forth—do offer a vehicle for expressing community preferences, their power is largely negative: they block harm but do little affirmatively to foster community tradition.

The problem of private property cannot be solved by creating more public land. We already have an extensive public land network, including places as diverse as the sidewalks of New York City and the Presidio of San Francisco, the Neversink Gorge State Unique Area and the Arctic National Wildlife Refuge. But public lands by themselves cannot meet society's need to nurture community traditions. They belong to the *public* in a broad sense: to the city, the state, the nation. Place-sharing at the community level is more local, more intimate. So while there may be good reasons to expand our public land system, we will still need *private* land solutions to nurture place-based traditions and the use values of home and neighborhood.

The suggestions which follow represent practical steps which could be taken in this direction. They neither assume nor require far-reaching changes to our existing concepts of property but seek to accomplish more modest goals: to facilitate the informal sharing of "private" property on which all healthy communities depend; and to better shield communities from the relentless operation of the growth machine.

• *Encourage community management of land.* Informal sharing of
property takes place all the time: in the country, for example,
neighbors assume they will cross each others' fields and woods
(though they don't necessarily welcome strangers doing so). Granting
legal recognition to such customary activities and enabling
communities to create rules for them could help protect them from
the disruption caused by new owners or new land uses. In a limited
sense, this could be seen as reversing the course of history by putting
private property back into communal forms of management. Yet it
does not mean relinquishing the essential values of private property,
or turning it over to public ownership. It simply means finding ways
to recognize the value of sharing to a healthy community life. The
kinds of sharing allowed under a community management regime
may be quite restricted: walking but not driving all-terrain vehicles or
snowmobiles, for example. And the essence of such an agreement is
that it applies only to neighbors: an agreement might allow neighbors
to hunt, for example, while excluding strangers from any use at all.
Thus one of the central features of property ownership—the right to
exclude non-owners—is retained, albeit in a slightly modified form.
   A variety of legal structures could be used to enable such local
sharing arrangements. Neighboring landowners could write
agreements or covenants which would run with the land, creating a
communal right of access amongst themselves, while retaining the
right to exclude outsiders. Community land trusts offer another
model. These trusts are empowered to buy and manage property for
a wide range of community purposes, including recreation, farming,
public health, child care, education, and housing. They can hold
land in fee simple or easements and can lease property at rates that
reflect the value of the land in actual use, rather than its full market
value. Creating community land trusts and donating easements to
them could help many communities keep control over their places.
• *Create ownership rights based on habitual use or attachment.* Under
existing law, landownership is not a single right but rather a bundle
of rights. Thus residents of Wyoming or Pennsylvania sometimes
discover, when their house slumps into a tunnel dug by a coal
company, that they do not own the ground under their own cellar:
the coal company owns it. In Boulder, CO, homeowners cannot
collect and conserve the rain that falls on their property because it
belongs to the owners of downstream water rights. Elsewhere, the
surface of the ground, the building upon it, and the air above it may
have separate owners. Or a single person may own both the land
and the building but not the right to develop either. A neighbor may
own the right to walk or drive across a piece of property; the
telephone or electric company may own the right to build and
maintain a utility line across it. As these examples suggest, the
ownership rights pertaining to a single piece of land may be divided

in all kinds of ways. By the same token, new rights may be defined and assigned to new owners without fundamentally distorting the shape of the bundle. This is what Hawaii's state constitution does: it creates a limited right of access and use and assigns it to a certain class of neighborhood residents. This does not make them full owners, nor does it endanger the fundamental concept of ownership conveyed by the title deed. Most ownership rights remain firmly in the hands of the person or corporation that holds the deed.

Creating or assigning new rights is not a radical idea: society does it almost continuously. In the past, most African Americans had no rights: as slaves, they were considered a form of property. White women also lacked most of the rights accorded to white men. Later, society recognized both African Americans and white women as holders of rights. Today, heated discussions focus on reproductive rights, and the rights of children, political refugees, and prisoners. Even the question of whether nature has legal rights has been raised.[71] These debates frequently focus on who holds the rights in question. But new kinds of rights, or rights in new kinds of things, are also constantly being created and contested: property rights in the genetic formulae for corn, for example, or rights to digitally distributed intellectual property. The creation and assignment of rights are fluid, constrained by legal precedent yet guided by changing social needs.

One does not need to look to Hawai'i to find legal precedents for the idea that people should have rights in the places they live, even though they don't hold the title deeds. Burial places have a special and universally acknowledged emotional status for many cultural groups, and so it is not surprising to find that the American Indian Religious Freedom Act and some state archaeological statutes give Native Americans some control over burial sites even though they are not located on tribal property. For most cultures the home is another locus of heightened emotional bonds, and here too the attachment of residents has received some protection. This is notable because homes, far more than cemeteries, are subject to the play of real estate markets. Yet, despite the importance of exchange values in connection with housing, rent control and other tenant protection laws give residents important rights which they can and do exercise in opposition to those of the owners. Sometimes these rights may even be expanded: thus on March 13, 2008, the tenants of apartments in New York City gained the legal right to sue their landlords for certain types of harassment including repeatedly turning off the heat or hot water, changing door locks, or making physical threats.

In contrast to the home, residency in a neighborhood has conferred much more limited rights in property. Yet, even here, rights do exist. Planning and environmental laws give neighborhood residents and organizations the ability to voice their opinions within the public planning process; sometimes governmental authorities even set up organizations with the specific purpose of doing so, like New York's community planning boards. Though more limited in scope than tenant rights, these entitlements are distributed to a much wider circle of people.

The kind of rights I have in mind, representing the stake held by neighborhood residents in property, might be stronger than the mere ability to be heard yet weaker than the right to resist eviction; they might apply most intensely to the home but in a more diluted way to the rest of the neighborhood. They should include the right to affect the disposition of property, that is, its retention or redevelopment. They might also include mechanisms through which to share in the appreciation of property values which are due in part to the stewardship of residents.

Some will undoubtedly object to any such proposal as an infringement on the rights and powers of ownership as conveyed by the title deed. They will argue that such a distribution of rights would stifle progress by making development more difficult. But, in fact, it may be doubted whether a well-considered plan would necessarily impede development more than the maze of legal requirements and regulations that already exist. What such a proposal would do is help level the playing field in the unequal struggle of use values against exchange values. It could help residents to formulate and work for positive visions of community placeways instead of the largely negative power—the power to block things—encouraged by existing mechanisms. It would surely create a much-needed public forum for discussing and assessing the social value of community traditions and placeways.

To create and assign a new class of property rights to people who live in places is not something that will be lightly undertaken. It will require intensive study and public debate. What is certain is that, without such rights, the lifeways and bonds of affection which link people to specific places will remain at risk. Other measures can help protect them, but most will be defensive. Ultimately an ownership stake will be the best way to recognize the social value of place-based traditions. And that, surely, is consistent with the most hallowed American traditions of property.

NOTES

1. Quoted in Winona LaDuke, *All Our Relations: Native Struggles for Land and Life* (Cambridge, MA: South End Press, 1999), 18.
2. Winnie Hu, "Clash of Cellular Towers and Hudson Valley Vistas," *New York Times* (April 9, 2001).
3. LaDuke, op. cit., 1.
4. Hawai'i State Constitution, 1978, Article XII, section 7, as quoted in Public Access Shoreline Hawai'i. Certiorari to the Intermediate Court of Appeals (CIV. NO. 90-293-K), August 31, 1995. IV.B.
5. HRS s 7–1, quoted in Public Access Shoreline Hawai'i FN 22.

6. "Although access is only guaranteed in connection with undeveloped lands, and article XII, section 7 does not require the preservation of such lands, the State does not have the unfettered discretion to regulate the rights of ahupua'a tenants out of existence." Public Access Shoreline Hawai'i IV.B.5.d. For a review of Hawaiian court decisions, see ibid., IV.B.

7. HRS s 205A-2(b)(2), quoted in Public Access Shoreline Hawai'i IV.A.

8. Hawai'i County Planning Commission Rule 9–11(C), which specifies the conditions that must be met for a Special Management Area permit (as quoted in Public Access Shoreline Hawai'i IV.A), and 9–10(H)(1) and (10).

9. State of Hawaii, House of Representatives, Twentieth Legislature, 2000, H.B. No. 2895 (A Bill for an Act Relating to Environmental Impact Statements), Sec. 1, 2. See Hawaii Revised Statutes, Chap. 343–2. In 2007 the state legislature considered a further measure to amend the historic preservation law to require the state's historic preservation division to carry out a "comprehensive cultural impact study" whenever an environmental impact statement is required under the environmental law (24th Legislature, 2007, H.B. No. 610, Sec. 1).

10. U.S. Public Law 103–150, 103d Congress Joint Resolution 19, November 23, 1993.

11. Bob Christjohn, a member of the Oneida tribe, quoted in *Keepers of the Treasures: Protecting Historic Properties and Cultural Traditions on Indian Lands. A Report on Tribal Preservation Funding Needs Submitted to Congress by the National Park Service* (Washington, DC: U.S. Department of the Interior, National Park Service, May 1990), 43.

12. Reservoir Salvage and Archeological Protection Act, 16 U.S.C. §469, quoted in Michael B. Gerrard (general ed.), *Environmental Law Practice Guide: State and Federal Law* (Albany, NY: Lexis Publishing, 2000), v. I §2.06[1].

13. Ibid.

14. Archeological Resources Protection Act, quoted in ibid., v. I, §2.06[2].

15. Arizona Rev. Stat. Ann. §41–841 et seq., and Arizona Administrative Code R12-6-503, summarized in ibid., v. VI §43.16[2].

16. Alaska National Interest Lands Conservation Act, §804, 16 U.S.C. §3114, quoted in ibid., v. VI, §43.11.

17. ANILCA §803, 16 U.S.C. §3113, quoted in ibid.

18. Ibid., v. VI, §43.11.

19. Patricia Parker and Thomas F. King, *Guidelines for Evaluating and Documenting Traditional Cultural Properties*, National Register Bulletin 38 (Washington, DC: U.S. Department of the Interior, National Park Service, 1992), 1.

20. For the inadequacies of AIRFA as well as the impact of Executive Order 13007, see Andrew Gulliford, *Sacred Objects and Sacred Places: Preserving Tribal Traditions* (Boulder: University Press of Colorado, 2000), 101–102, 119–120.

21. William J. Clinton, *Executive Order #13007: Indian Sacred Sites*, May 4, 1996, published in *Federal Register*, May 29, 1996.

22. " 'Sacred site' means any specific, discrete, narrowly delineated location on Federal land that is identified by an Indian tribe, or Indian individual determined to be an appropriately authoritative representative of an Indian religion, as sacred by virtue of its established religious significance to, or ceremonial use by, an Indian religion." Ibid., I (b) iii.

23. *Keepers of the Treasures*, op. cit., 77; and Gerrard (gen. ed.), op. cit., v. I §43.15.

24. *Keepers of the Treasures*, op. cit., 77.

25. Ibid., 75.

26. Bureau of Land Management Manual 8100, quoted in *Keepers of the Treasures*, op. cit., 88.

27. Pete Jemison, quoted in ibid., 55–56.

28. Ibid., 70.

29. Roger Anyon, quoted in ibid., 48.

30. For issues of repatriation and recent changes in museums' treatment of Indian artifacts, see Gulliford, op. cit., 13–65.

31. For the conflict, see Gulliford, op. cit., 162–167. The Supreme Court's decision in 2000 not to review the lower court's ruling sustaining the Park Service's management plan is reported on the National Park Service's website. For the cultural conflicts surrounding Devil's Tower, see also John D. Dorst, *Looking West* (Philadelphia: University of Pennsylvania Press, 1999), 192–197.

32. See *Keepers of the Treasures*, op. cit., 74–75, for a discussion of the Chacoan sites in New Mexico.

33. See Barbara McMartin, *The Great Forest of the Adirondacks* (Utica, NY: North Country Books, 1994), for a detailed history of landownership and use in the Adirondacks.

34. John R. Stilgoe, "Boyhood Landscape and Repetition," in George F. Thompson (ed.), *Landscape in America* (Austin: University of Texas Press, 1995), 183–204, and esp. 193ff.

35. LaDuke, op. cit., 167ff.

36. Charlie LeDuff, "Despite a Warning, Reeling in the Eels," *New York Times* (November 12, 2000).

37. See, for example, John R. Logan and Harvey L. Molotch, *Urban Fortunes: The Political Economy of Place* (Berkeley: University of California Press, 1987), 225–226.

38. See, for example (Save the Family Farm!), Wendell Berry, *The Unsettling of America: Culture and Agriculture* (San Francisco: University of California Press, 1976); (The Family Farm is Dead!) John Fraser Hart, *The Land That Feeds Use* (New York and London: W. W. Norton, 1991); and (The Family Farm Is Dead: Save It!) Victor Davis Hanson, *Fields Without Dreams: Defending the Agrarian Idea* (New York: Simon & Schuster, 1996). Brian Donohue argues for community-based farms as a way of maintaining farming in rapidly suburbanizing areas: *Reclaiming the Commons: Community Farms and Forests in a New England Town* (New Haven, CT and London: Yale University Press, 1999).

39. Gerrard, op. cit., v. I, §3.02A.

40. Judicial conservatism may take its toll on right-to-farm laws as well: the Iowa Supreme Court struck down its right-to-farm law, ruling that the right to sue over nuisances was a property right and that, by preventing such a suit, the state had effected an unconstitutional taking of property.

41. Siemon, Larsen & Purdy (Attorneys at Law), "Land Use Techniques for Industrial Preservation: A Report to the National Trust for Historic Preservation," n.d. [*ca.*1988].

42. Gerrard, op. cit., v. I, §3.02[2].

43. Transfers of development rights were pioneered in center-city contexts as a way to save landmark structures whose size and income potential fell far short of the values possible with intensive, high-density development. See John Costonis, *Space Adrift: Landmark Preservation and the Marketplace* (Urbana: University of Illinois Press, 1974).

44. New York City Department of City Planning, *Zoning Handbook*, 2006, 13.

45. "The Ahwahnee Principles," available at www.lgc.org/ahwahnee/principles.html (consulted in April 2008). See also the website of the Congress for the New Urbanism at www.cnu.org.

46. As a result of California's Proposition 13, property taxes are essentially frozen except when the property is sold or transferred. This helps current owners but does not promote the intergenerational continuity of communities.

47. For Pennsylvania, see various publications available through the website of the Center for the Study of Economics in Philadelphia, at www.urbantools.org.

48. Agricultural Security Area Law, passed in 1981 and amended in 1988. See *Management Action Plan: The Schuylkill Heritage Corridor*, March 1995, 24.

49. Elaine Freed, *Preserving the Great Plains and Rocky Mountains* (Albuquerque: University of New Mexico Press, 1992), 227ff., chronicles the impact of the National Trust's Main Street Program on western towns.

50. Gerrard, op. cit., v. I, §3.05. See also Samuel N. Stokes with Elizabeth Watson et al., *Saving America's Countryside: A Guide to Rural Conservation* (Baltimore, MD and London: Johns Hopkins Press, 1989), esp. Chapter 5; Edward Thompson, Jr., "Preserving Farmland: The American Farmland Trust and Its Partners," in Eve Endicott (ed.), *Land Conservation Through Public/Private Partnerships* (Washington, DC and Covelo, CA: Island Press, 1993), 43–60; and Sally K. Fairfax and Darla Guenzler, *Conservation Trusts* (Lawrence: University Press of Kansas, 2001). As of 2007, the number of land trusts nation-wide was estimated at 1,600 (website of the Land Trust Alliance, at www.lta.org/faq, consulted in December 2007).

51. Quoted in Ormond Loomis, *Cultural Conservation: The Protection of Cultural Heritage in the United States. A Study by the American Folklife Center, Library of Congress, Carried Out in Cooperation with the National Park Service* (Washington, DC: U.S. Department of the Interior and Library of Congress, 1983), 106. Loomis provides a classic definition of cultural conservation from the folklorist's point of view. For a critique of folklore's relationship to the preservation of family farms, see J. Sanford Rikoon, William D. Heffernan, and Judith Bortner Heffernan, "Cultural Conservation and the Family Farm Movement: Integrating

Visions and Actions," in Mary Hufford (ed.), *Conserving Culture: A New Discourse on Heritage* (Urbana and Chicago: University of Illinois Press, 1994), 184–197.

52. Speech at the National Trust for Historic Preservation's annual conference, Boston, 1994.

53. Thomas Carter and Carl Fleischhauer, *The Grouse Creek Cultural Survey: Integrating Folklife and Historic Preservation Field Research* (Washington, DC: Library of Congress, 1988), 1. See also Loomis, op. cit.

54. For Native influences, see also Gulliford, op. cit.

55. Within New York City, a traditional beer garden (Bohemian Hall, Astoria, Queens) and a religious grotto (Our Lady of Mount Carmel Grotto) were entered on the State Register under this guideline in 2000. More recently, cottages on Cape Cod have also been listed as traditional cultural properties; however, fishing shacks in Florida failed on the grounds that they were no longer used for their traditional purpose, while a record shop in the Bronx, central to the evolution of salsa and Latin jazz in New York, was turned down because practitioners and devotees of salsa did not meet the definition of a traditional cultural group.

56. See, for example, "Towards a Common Method for Assessing Mixed Cultural and Natural Resources: A Case Study Approach, A Cross Disciplinary Conference" (report of conference jointly sponsored by the Howard Gilman Foundation and the World Monuments Fund, June 25, 1998).

57. Gerrard, op. cit., v. I, §1.08[10].

58. Ibid., §1.04[2][e].

59. Laurie Kay Sommers, Yvonne R. Lockwood, Marsha MacDowell, and Richard W. Stoffle, "Folklife Assessment in the Michigan Low-Level Radioactive Waste Siting Process," in Hufford (ed.), op. cit., 198–214, esp. 201.

60. The claim is made in ibid.

61. Memorandum, "EPA Statutory and Regulatory Authorities Under Which Environmental Justice Issues May Be Addressed in Permitting," from Gary S. Guzy, General Counsel to the Environmental Protection Agency, December 1, 2000. I am grateful to Michael Gerrard for providing this memorandum.

62. 16 U.S.C. 470a(a).

63. 16 U.S.C. 470(b).

64. Peter Nabokov, "Long Threads," in Betty Ballantine and Ian Ballantine (eds.), *The Native Americans* (North Dighton, MA: World Publications Group, 2001), 367.

65. See Paula Mitchell Marks, *In a Barren Land: American Indian Dispossession and Survival* (New York: William Morrow and Company, 1998), 252 and *passim*.

66. Logan and Molotch, op. cit., 1.

67. Ibid., 2.

68. Quoted in E. N. Feltskog, "The Range of Vision: Landscape and the Far West, 1803 to 1850," in Thompson (ed.), op. cit., 76.

69. See, for example, Raynor M. Warner, Sibyl McCormac Groff, and Ranne P. Warner, with Sandi Weiss, *Business and Preservation: A Survey of Business Conservation of Buildings and Neighborhoods* (New York: INFORM, 1978); and Donovan D. Rypkema, *The Economics of Historic Preservation: A Community Leader's Guide* (Washington, DC: National Trust for Historic Preservation, 1994).

70. For environmental critiques of growth, see, *inter alia*, Donella H. Meadows et al., *The Limits to Growth* (New York: Universe Books, 1972); Donella H. Meadows, Dennis L. Meadows, and Jorgen Randers, *Beyond the Limits: Confronting Global Collapse, Envisioning a Sustainable Future* (Post Mills, VT: Chelsea Green Publishing Co., 1992); and Herman E. Daly and John B. Cobb, Jr., *For the Common Good: Redirecting the Economy Toward Community, the Environment, and a Sustainable Future* (Boston, MA: Beacon Press, 1989). For threats to community, see Robert D. Putnam, *Bowling Alone: The Collapse and Revival of American Community* (New York: Simon & Schuster, 2000); Robert N. Bellah, Richard Madsen, William M. Sullivan, Ann Swidler, and Steven M. Tipton, *Habits of the Heart: Individualism and Commitment in American Life* (Berkeley: University of California Press, 1985); and the extensive literature of the communitarian movement, for example Amitai Etzioni, *The Spirit of Community: Rights, Responsibilities, and the Communitarian Agenda* (New York: Crown Publishers, 1993).

71. As for example in Christopher D. Stone, *Should Trees Have Standing? Toward Legal Rights for Natural Objects* (New York: Avon Books, 1975).

CHAPTER 10

Sugar Songs: A Modest Proposal
Delivered to the Earl of Harewood

This chapter was written as the keynote address for a conference organized by the English not-for-profit InterCulture and held at Harewood House in 2003. The subject was the complex relationships between the house, the West Indian sugar plantations and slaves who financed its construction, and the Caribbean immigrant community in nearby Leeds.

> Sugar, and the men I sing—and women, too—who, forc'd by greed,
> And haughty England's unrelenting might,
> Defiled and captured, left the Afric shore.
> Long labors, in Caribbean fields, they bore,
> And over millhouse fires, before they broke
> Enslavement's bonds, and won their human rights;
> But sugar's wealth not theirs but Harewood's house
> Did build, and too a stately park dispose,
> And settled sure succession on *his* line,
> From whence the race of Harewood earls comes,
> And Yorkshire's glorious mansion artfully bedecked.[1]

So might Virgil have written, had he been a Barbadian poet and Aeneas an English sugar planter. At any rate, it is sugar that *I* sing this morning, specifically the sugar that forms the foundations of Harewood House and of this conference. There are many songs of sugar, and I can hope to do no more than suggest the broad outlines of the extraordinary story that lies behind Harewood, as well as the difficulties and rewards of engaging it here.

But first, you may have noticed that a lump of sugar has been placed on each of your chairs. Pick it up; unwrap it; savor it. It is the taste of Harewood, for it was upon a fortune derived three centuries ago from Caribbean trade and sugar plantations that this great house was built (Figure 10.1). It has a sweet taste, just as we might expect. How puzzling, then, to find the library shelves lined with books like *The Bitter Memory of Sugar*, or *White and Deadly*. Why bitter? Why deadly? A few more well-known titles will get us closer to an answer: *Sugar and Work; Sweetness and Power; Sugar and Colonialism*. Work, power, colonialism—there you have the sugar story.

Figure 10.1   Harewood House, designed by Robert Adam and John Carr of York in 1759 for Edwin Lascelles and financed by profits from Caribbean sugar and slavery.

Deceptively sweet, sugar turns out to be one of the strongmen in British history. It created everything that you see around you today, birthed the English habit of tea drinking, devastated the societies of Africa, and spearheaded Europe's colonial adventure in the Caribbean. Auguste Cochin was right to remark that "the story of a grain of sugar is a whole lesson in political economy, in politics, and also in morality."

It is to the Caribbean that we are sailing this morning, and, to help us on our way, here is another sugar song. James Grainger, an *émigré* to St. Kitts, published his book-length poem, *Sugar-Cane*, in 1764. In it he evokes the "cheerful toil" of the "laughing, labouring, singing throng" of enslaved plantation workers at sugar-boiling time.

> How blithe, how jocund, the plantation smiles!
> By day, by night, resounds the choral song
> Of glad barbarity . . . .[2]

And so forth. Others, however, sang a different tune. Much later, an emancipated North American slave was astonished that anyone could think of slave songs as "evidence of . . . contentment and happiness." That former slave was Frederick Douglass, and he recalled the "ineffable sadness" of those songs: "they were tones loud, long, and deep; they breathed the prayer and complaint of souls boiling over with the bitterest anguish. Every tone was a testimony against slavery, and a prayer to God for deliverance from chains."[3]

Even in Grainger's time, other stories were being told. The Rev. James Ramsay documented days of backbreaking work on British sugar plantations that lasted from four in the morning until midnight. Sometimes indeed the slaves were kept at work around the clock, particularly at sugar-boiling time when, remarked Ramsay, "the mill every now-and-then grinds off an hand, or an arm, of those drowsy worn down creatures that feed it."[4]

By this period, sugar—which would have been virtually unknown to Virgil—had become a staple of European cuisine and was becoming ever cheaper and more widely distributed, thanks to the explosive expansion of European power in the Caribbean which Grainger, Ramsay, and Harewood House itself all document in their own way. Columbus had planted sugar cane on Hispaniola on his second expedition in 1493. By the sixteenth century it had conquered northern Brazil; next it spread over the Caribbean islands; and, when the Haitian plantation slaves revolted, it marched on into Louisiana. Its triumph involved three distinct factors: the plant itself, the plantation system, and slavery. I shall look briefly at all three.

First, the plantation system. The word refers to plants, obviously, and to planting them. But by the late sixteenth century it also signified the planting of colonies. It was in this sense that England established *plantations* in Virginia and also in Ireland. From the beginning, the sugar plantations of the Caribbean were plantations in this double sense: colonial as well as agricultural enterprises.

In North America, the plantation has taken on overtones of elegance and leisure, but nothing could be more misleading. Geographer Sam Hilliard explains that plantations were not country estates, nor yet family farms, but agricultural machines, designed "to make a profit for plantation owners or investors through the large-scale cultivation of agricultural products."[5] The overwhelming majority of plantation residents were not, of course, the owners, but field workers, and during the period under discussion these were slaves. Nowhere was this more uniformly true than on the sugar plantations. And so we turn next to sugar.

No ordinary grass, sugar cane grows to a height of over fifteen feet. Its fibrous canes contain a sweet sap that can be boiled down to produce brown sugar, and further refined into white sugar. Along the way, one can extract molasses and rum. Cane is picky about how and where it will grow, and the plantation catered to its demands, particularly for labor. Harvest time is an exhausting race to get the cane cut, a task Puerto Rican cane workers still refer to as "doing battle" with the cane. Next, it must be quickly milled before its quality and sugar content start to decline. So the harvesters may be cutting cane twelve hours a day or more, the roads will be choked with carts burdened high with cane, and the mills may run around the clock.

> The mills . . .
> See! there, what mills, like giants raise their arms,
> . . . What smoke ascends
> from every boiling house! . . .[6]

Grainger again. From an early period, the cane plantation was an industrial as much as an agricultural landscape. The early mills did not look much like the massive factories which today dot the landscape of southern Louisiana or other sugar-producing regions: they were little more than a crushing contraption, some basins and tubes to collect the juice, and a row of kettles in which to boil it down. But the important point was the intensive organization of labor and capital that all of this required. Slavery exactly met the planters' needs for labor, and they tried first to enslave the Native peoples. But the Natives disobliged by dying in great numbers, so the planters turned to Africa. "Legions of slaves," remarks Uruguayan author Eduardo Galeano, "came from Africa to provide King Sugar with the prodigal, wageless labor force he required: human fuel for the burning."[7] No one knows how many Africans were kidnapped and sold into slavery: at least twelve million, perhaps many more.

And the form of slavery that Europeans developed to serve the plantations was exceptionally severe. Workers were often subjected to degradation, generally forced to perform exhausting work, and always treated as a form of property. Much later, a leading Hawaiian sugar merchant could assert that there was no ethical difference "between the importation of foreign laborers and the importation of jute bags from India."[8] Perhaps he was speaking figuratively. But in eighteenth-century Barbados he would have been literally correct: the enslaved worker and the jute bag had about the same status.

Of the twelve million or more Africans shipped into slavery, about 70 percent would work in sugar cane. England became the leading slave trader, the Caribbean the largest consumer. Considering the islands' small size the numbers are staggering: 387,000 slaves to Barbados, 747,000 to Jamaica.[9] These figures reflect not only the size of the sugar industry but also an extremely high mortality rate: planters frequently found it more economical to replenish than to maintain their stock of slaves. Well might the protagonist of *The Negro's Complaint*, William Cowper's abolitionist poem of 1788, cry out:

> Why did all-creating nature
> Make the plant for which we toil?
> Think, ye masters iron-hearted,
> Lolling at your jovial boards,
> Think how many backs have smarted
> For the sweets your cane affords.[10]

Harewood House was, of course, both a beneficiary and a product of Caribbean sugar. So it may be helpful to situate Harewood within the range of products sugar brought forth—the material culture of sugar, so to speak. What a broad range these objects span! Most familiar are probably the articles associated with the pleasures of consuming sugar—tea sets, pastries, jars of treacle, and the like. The production side looks very different: agricultural implements such as machetes, hoes, ox yokes, and carts, as well as the human yokes, whips, and punishment collars that speak of enslavement in its most brutal aspect.

Among the most moving of sugar's artifacts are the slave cabins. At Evergreen Plantation in Louisiana (Figure 10.2), visitors are asked to walk by them in respectful silence, but the admonition is almost unnecessary, for

Figure 10.2   Twenty-two slave cabins survive at Evergreen Plantation in Louisiana and form a major focus of site interpretation.

visitors naturally fall silent: the place compels respect. It isn't so much the cabins themselves: in their small size and lack of comfort these resemble the housing occupied by very poor rural people the world over and in all times, whether eighteenth-century Irish peasants, nineteenth-century Montana homesteaders, or contemporary farm workers. It is rather an upwelling of empathy with the experience of the unfree people who lived here.

Beyond the slave quarters of the typical plantation lie the canefields and mills. Though little today remains of the early mills, newer ones continue to dominate the landscape of cane growing areas. This landscape could be called monotonous—little but cane as far as the eye can see—and in this it resembles other crops that are grown in bulk for trade and profit rather than local consumption, such as tobacco, sugar beets, cotton, or rice. These are all essentially extractive landscapes, and the contrast between their hard monotony and the gently rolling landscape of Harewood's park could hardly be more pronounced.

The last element of the plantation landscape is the big house. There is no recognizable style of plantation house architecture. Houses responded to local conditions and changing styles, so that a plantation house in Barbados might look very different from one in Louisiana, or for that matter in Hawai'i. Then, too, some owners were absentee landlords, living quite far from their plantations: their home might be a mansion in Memphis or New York—or a country house in Yorkshire. Yet each of these was still a plantation house in the sense that plantation profits flowed into them, and commands flowed back out. In this sense, Harewood too is a plantation house.

With Harewood we circle back to the consumption of sugar, and to the plantation mystique. Recall *Gone With the Wind*, the famous movie: beautiful ladies and dashing young men (all white, of course), honor and bravery, hooped skirts—and hardly a mention of slavery, or indeed of work. This image continues to fuel tourism and to provide an appealing imagery for upmarket country clubs and suburban houses in many parts of the United States and indeed in Latin America as well. Harewood, though it does not adopt the visual vocabulary of the typical plantation, sustains a similar illusion: what visitor, admiring its tasteful interiors, its fine silver and magnificent paintings, its lush flower gardens, its rolling meadows and coyly beckoning lake, can picture enslaved workers sweating and dying in cane fields under a broiling tropical sun? In such a perfect picture of leisure even the necessary work of mowing lawns tends to become invisible. How easy it is, then, amidst Robert Adam's subtle colors, to forget the stark black and white of the plantation story. Harewood, it seems, has completely consumed its legacy of sugar, leaving us staring at an empty plate.

Is sugar then but a mirage? Does its bitter taste signify nothing more than indulgence in post-modern guilt? I think not. Harewood's historical connections with the Caribbean, with sugar and slavery, are real enough. And, rather than seeing them as occasions for indulging in guilt, I would suggest that they present Harewood House with a unique opportunity to play a role entirely new in its history: to become a historical presenter, guide, or seer—in the sense of a see-er into the past. The story of Harewood's roots in the Caribbean is gripping, and the decision to acknowledge it creates an opening to do something of great social value, simultaneously forging significant international connections and building relationships with a new public here in the vicinity of Leeds. This will not be entirely easy, of course. Two difficulties, in particular, call for ingenuity and determination.

Let me illustrate the first by reference to a North American monument, the San Jacinto Museum in Houston, Texas (Figure 10.3). Built in the 1930s, this bathetic erection memorializes the United States' victory over Mexico and the capture of roughly half of Mexico's territory. All well and good if you are an Anglo, but perhaps not so good if you are a Mexican or Mexican American, as a great many Houston residents and visitors are. In fact, it is hard to tell what Mexican American visitors make of the place, but the pages of the visitors book suggest that some may feel uneasy or discontented. The Museum has made attempts to acknowledge a Mexican point of view, including renaming the access road after an important Mexican historical figure. But the form of the monument so relentlessly enforces a single, triumphalist meaning that efforts to shade it seem doomed to triviality.

Harewood presents a similar problem because it is so perfectly successful at being a splendid English country house. It would be folly to compromise its taste and grandeur with half-hearted footnotes on Caribbean sugar. What then to do? One obvious solution might be to install some historical galleries in the basement. But the symbolism of putting slavery below stairs would throw the entire song off key. Harewood will have to find a more

Figure 10.3 Fifteen feet taller than the Washington Monument, the monument to the Battle of San Jacinto, in Houston, Texas, was begun in 1936 to commemorate the battle's centennial. The San Jacinto Museum of History occupies the base.

creative, more self-assured way to present the story: one that neither competes with nor detracts from the house itself.

The second problem is that, in contrast to eating sugar, talking about it turns out to be rather disagreeable: so painful indeed is the sugar story that many might prefer to leave it untold. I think this would be a mistake.

I once met a man who opened a window into these issues for me. He told me he had been reading some old family diaries and had discovered a most disturbing fact: his family, back in the eighteenth century, had owned slaves! This shocking revelation had caused him to ponder his legacy and even reassess his own identity and beliefs. As we were parting, I asked his name: it was Knickerbocker! This man, who ran a canoe livery business in Vermont, bore one of the most fabled names in New York history. In effect, I had been talking to the descendant of a legend! Yet he seemed real enough, and so, I am sure, were his ancestors' slaves. As I thought about the incident later, what surprised me most, however, was not Mr. Knickerbocker's discovery of slaves but his surprise at discovering them. *Of course* his family had owned slaves:

what else would they have done as rich New Yorkers two hundred years ago? For this knowledge to have vanished from the Knickerbocker family memory amounted to an erasure of history worth pondering.

It is safe to assume that the descendants of those long-forgotten slaves would not have been as surprised as Mr. Knickerbocker by their rediscovery. I say this because of what was observed when the New-York Historical Society recently brought black and white New Yorkers together to discuss an exhibition on lynching. Many white New Yorkers said they had no idea this sort of thing had gone on: it had not appeared in their schoolbooks. But black New Yorkers knew all about it—not from books but from family stories. For them, lynching was no shameful secret but rather community memory. The fact that these discussions took place shortly after the terrorist attacks of 9–11 added another layer of meaning. While most white New Yorkers viewed terrorism as an unprecedented assault on American life, many black New Yorkers saw it differently: their family histories contained episodes of terrorism perpetrated against them. Some white New Yorkers were mystified by the difference in how 9–11 was viewed, but those who had taken part in the lynching discussions understood why.

I shall resist the temptation to draw easy lessons from these stories. But they do show that discussing painful racial histories can lead to enlightenment. And there is a great hunger for these discussions. I asked the curator of Evergreen Plantation in Louisiana why she focused a full half of the public tour on the slave quarters rather than on the elegant mansion which I assumed most visitors had come to see. "Because it's just fascinating to the public," she replied—African American as well as white.

Still, many people shy away from such discussions. Some African Americans would prefer to forget slavery, or at least not discuss it with white people. Some white people are inhibited by guilt and a presentiment that the issues, once raised, will be difficult to resolve. But it is not the Seventh Earl of Harewood's fault that his ancestors owned slaves, any more than it was Mr. Knickerbocker's. And while it is undeniably true that no amount of conversation will settle the five-hundred-year legacy of plantation slavery, it is also true that there will be no resolution without conversation. And, as Rabbi Hillel so eloquently asked: "If not now, when?"

The 1990s saw a spate of public efforts to promote racial reconciliation. The U.S. government apologized to the state of Hawaii. Within Hawaii, the Asian American churches apologized to the Native Hawaiian churches and even provided reparations. In South Africa the Truth and Reconciliation Commission worked to reconcile the opposing forces of apartheid and black liberation. More recently, the U.S. has apologized to African Americans for slavery and subsequent decades of legally enforced inequality.

Eric Yamamoto has studied efforts at racial reconciliation and believes that, to succeed, they must also bring racial justice. Towards this end he outlines a four-step process, starting with *recognition*, which he defines as acknowledging, empathetically, the woundedness of the other group.[11] This leads to *responsibility*, accepting agency for wrongs committed, which in turn opens the way to *reconstruction*, "reaching out in concrete ways to heal."[12] The final stage is *reparation*: social transformation by repairing not only the economic and physical conditions of life but also "injured human psyches—enabling those harmed to live with, but not in, history."[13]

Recognition, responsibility, reconstruction, reparation: a daunting challenge. Can Harewood achieve racial reconciliation and justice in Yamamoto's terms? Of course not. Can it contribute to a better understanding of the historical experience of black and white in the UK? Yes, absolutely. And I think we may fairly expect it to do so, not out of a sense of guilt but as a positive expression of citizenship.

Let me close, then, by offering a few suggestions to Harewood House as it considers whether to set out on this difficult but ultimately rewarding path—my own five-point plan, as it were, for launching Yamamoto's four-point plan:

- First, dare to speak truth. But speak it simply, without hand-wringing, finger-pointing, or rhetorical flourishes. And do not put it in the basement.
- Second, dare to be unoriginal. Draw widely on the experience and insights of other museums and historic sites that have taken on similar challenges.
- Third, dare to be original. Focus on the facts about Harewood's story, not generalities about race relations. This is how other sites have avoided stereotypical postures of blame, shame, or defensive guilt and succeeded in both educating and moving visitors.
- Fourth, dare to connect the dots. Draw the connections between past and present, Barbados and England, Harewood's story and the people and issues of our own time. Fling the historical net as broadly as you can, catching cultural phenomena as far from the archive room and library as music and sports.
- Finally, do not attempt to sing all the solos. The Harewood story belongs to many people with many voices, many songs to sing. Think of this as a choral performance. Recall that white and black New Yorkers had not merely different perspectives but different knowledge of lynching. In a similar way, those who bear the names of Lascelles or Harewood will have different historical knowledge depending on whether they are white or black, descended from earls or slaves, whether they sleep at Harewood House or in Barbados or Leeds. Each has a line in the song that no one else knows. And it is only by weaving them together, indeed by jointly composing the song, that those whose song it is can advance together to deeper understanding.
- And finally (for there is actually a sixth step to this five-step plan): *just dare*. Dare to get started; dare to get the job done, as Malcolm X advised, "by any means necessary."

To which Rabbi Hillel might have added: "If not now, when?"

NOTES

1. Here I offer my own version of the famous opening lines of Virgil's *Aeneid*, based on John Dryden's translation but altered to suit the facts of Harewood House.

2. James Grainger, *The Sugar-Cane: A Poem in Four Books: with Notes* (London, 1766), Book I, lines 146, 101, 414–416.

3. Frederick Douglass, "Narrative of the Life of Frederick Douglass, an American Slave," in Frederick Douglass, *Autobiographies*, ed. Henry Louis Gates, Jr. (New York: Library of America, 1994), 24.

4. Rev. James Ramsay, *An Essay on the Treatment and Conversion of African Slaves in the British Sugar Colonies* (London, 1784), 75.

5. Sam B. Hilliard, "Plantations and the Molding of the Southern Landscape," in Michael Conzen (ed.), *The Making of the American Landscape* (New York and London: Routledge, 1990), 105.

6. Grainger, op. cit., Book III, lines 526–528.

7. Eduardo Galeano, *Open Veins of Latin America: Five Centuries of the Pillage of a Continent*, trans. Cedric Belfrage (New York: Monthly Review Press, 1973), 72.

8. Gavan Daws, *Shoals of Time: A History of the Hawaiian Islands* (Honolulu: University of Hawai'i Press, 1968), 314.

9. The figures were provided by James Walvin and Thomas Eubanks.

10. William Cowper, "The Negro's Complaint," in *The Poems of William Cowper* (London: Methuen, 1905), 454.

11. Eric Yamamoto, *Interracial Justice: Conflict and Reconciliation in Post-Civil-Rights America* (New York: New York University Press, 1999), 178.

12. Ibid., 191.

13. Ibid., 203.

CHAPTER 11

Moving Forward: Futures for a Preservation Movement

The following was written in 2004 as the final chapter of Giving Preservation a History, *an anthology of articles on the history of preservation.*

PRESERVATION PROFESSION PICKS PRUDENCE OVER PASSION. Or so one might summarize Antoinette Lee's account of preservation's last forty years.[1] Once upon a time, historic preservation was a passionate protest. Now it's a prudent profession. The question is: could this careful, practical, well-organized profession of historic preservation once again give rise to a *movement*: a committed effort to change the way society imagines, preserves, and inhabits its heritage?

To raise this question is not to indict the preservation profession. On the contrary, hundreds of landmarks commissions, of state and federal and local laws, of government offices to implement them, of cultural resource studies and of consultants to carry them out—all these are signs of health, not sickness. It is good that preservation is buttressed by laws and procedures and implemented by well-trained professionals.

And there is more to celebrate. Because of the preservation movement, we have an active network of citizen groups who know how to mobilize and are prepared to do so. Even more valuable, we have a language in which to oppose the destruction of place and heritage.

Still, it is hard to avoid the conclusion that we are losing ground. Listen to Ronald F. Lee, a senior official of the National Park Service, addressing a conference of planners in 1964, just before passage of the New York City Landmarks Law and the National Historic Preservation Act. Calling for a "major new effort to preserve our 'total environment,'" Lee draws on some of the most eloquent voices of his time, describing the condition of the American environment as a "quiet crisis" (Secretary of the Interior Udall), "God's Own Junkyard" (Peter Blake), "the most affluent slum on earth" (network news anchor Eric Sevareid), and "Silent Spring" (Rachel Carson).[2] One could hardly argue with this dire assessment—except that, in the intervening forty years, things have gotten so much worse, *despite* the great successes of the preservation and environmental movements. How many millions of acres of farm and forest have given way to suburban sprawl since 1964; how many sturdy old industrial cities gutted and abandoned; how many villages overrun; how many miles of rural roadway turned into strip malls; how many Grecian rowhouses, Gothic churches, Moorish movie palaces bulldozed for parking; how many wetlands paved over, old-growth forests cut, streams polluted; how much acid rain dropped and how many tons of greenhouse gases lofted into the ozone layer? Surely things would have gotten much worse without the environmental and historic preservation movements; but does anyone really believe we are *better* off? That we no longer need a movement?

Despite its successes, in short, the movement has not stopped the destruction of the environment and the obliteration of history. It is as if a forest fire had simply leapt over the preservation movement's lines. While we are busy pouring buckets of water on this or that outbreak, the fire's front lines have swept far beyond us: so far that it is doubtful whether we can catch up.

It is worth asking whether the reasons for this failure lie in some shortcoming of preservation's message. Perhaps people don't care all that much about history, heritage, architecture, urbanism? I do not believe this is so. People of all kinds, in places all across America, are deeply troubled by the loss of places they love: loss of character, access, enjoyment, historical memory. Preservationists have spoken well for their constituents. All the same, amateurs and professionals do not always worry about the same things. While preservationists debate problems of authenticity, integrity, architectural quality, stylistic purity, and significance, citizens seem to worry more about the loss of character, pleasure, or usefulness in the places they inhabit and love, of the ability to recall the past in them, of being forced to leave them. Many worry also about the loss of cultural identity associated with them.

Preservationists could legitimately claim all of these concerns as central themes. The difficulty is that the field increasingly defines professional competence in rather narrow terms which do not easily accommodate such big, emotional, and socially complex issues. It may be comforting to note that preservationists are hardly alone in missing the brass ring here: both the environmental movement and the historical museums *could have* addressed the cultural dimensions of the environment but, until recently, largely haven't. Still, these big issues are really preservation's turf, and preservationists must decide whether to defend or concede it.

To concede it will be the cautious, professionally prudent course. To fight for it will require preservationists to move beyond the profession's internal discourse and acknowledge the full scope of popular concern over the loss of places and heritage. To fight for it opens up the possibility of an invigorated movement.

There are grounds for hope. In the last few years, a broad, humane language of place has taken hold in many quarters, a language subtly yet significantly distinct from the first language of the preservation movement. When people speak in this new language, they are able to take in historical landmarks, species habitat, favorite views or picnic spots, people's feelings about places—sometimes in a single sentence. This language lacks the precision of preservationists' professional discourse, but it expresses how human communities experience places, and how they feel about them.[3]

Adopting this language of place can help preservationists rebuild a movement out of what risks becoming a profession pure and simple. In the essay that follows I suggest a few other prescriptions: a new dedication to the power of history; courage to stand up to sacred cows like economic growth and the real estate market; vision to imagine an order of things different from the current one; boldness to make seemingly impractical proposals; and patience to see them through.

GROWTH IS NOT GOOD FOR US

Let us begin boldly, then, by contesting the ideology of growth. American society is dominated by what sociologists John Logan and Harvey Molotch, among others, have called the "growth machine," an alliance of real estate developers, business interests, government, and news media that promote the belief that progress equals growth[4]—meaning more people, more economic activity, new and bigger buildings. The preservation profession has adopted an awkward posture towards the growth machine, at once fearful and flattering. Preservationists fear, and with good reason, that opposing growth will result in their being marginalized: they will lose their seat at the table. Better to be seen as loyal supporters, even when it is painful: "I am wholeheartedly for growth—just not this *particular* growth, threatening this *particular* building."

This stance has worked well, enabling preservationists to negotiate the retention of thousands of buildings. But an underlying problem must be confronted. Ultimately, growth is not the ally but the enemy of historic preservation. How could it be otherwise? The ideology of growth prescribes constant change, disruption, ratcheting up of economic activity, density, people, production, and consumption. It has provided a rationale for the theft of Indian lands and the destruction of Indian communities over three centuries, the smashing of African American neighborhoods after World War II, and the smothering of towns, fields, and forests under a spreading mat of suburbs in our own time. Not that all of the symptoms of growth are experienced equally everywhere. On the contrary, while growth happens in one place, shrinkage may be taking place in another. That is because, in the capitalist system, money is supposed to flow freely towards profit. So, while one neighborhood of nineteenth-century rowhouses confronts developers' visions of thirty-story towers, a similar one suffers from deterioration, abandonment, declining real estate values, and the disappearance of mortgage financing and insurance coverage—all caused by the migration of capital towards growth opportunities in the first neighborhood. This is not a flaw in the growth machinery. This is how it is designed to operate.

Growth is a wonderful thing. It has brought us (or many of us) great blessings. It is hard to see how the social mobility and individual opportunities that so many Americans have enjoyed could have happened without growth. Yet, while the machinery continues to clank away, some fear that social mobility is declining. Apparently growth does not guarantee opportunity, at least not for everyone. On the other hand, growth *as we know it* does guarantee that the social fabric of many communities will be continuously threatened with disruption, their physical fabric by destruction—either the sudden death of development or the slow sickening of disinvestment and deterioration.

Growth has other consequences: the steady exhaustion of resources (including old buildings) and the fouling of the environment with ever-broadening waste streams. Those who maintain that growth on the planet can continue indefinitely base their belief on little more than faith: since fixes have emerged unexpectedly for past problems, they will conveniently appear for the problems of growth. Perhaps. But the problems are real. There are currently many ingenious efforts to solve or mitigate some of them, from hybrid cars to wind farms, and these efforts deserve support. But we should be looking beyond them, to the larger question of whether growth (and the imbalances that it seems to produce) can continue indefinitely. The answer we seek will probably not be a simple "yes" or "no." Rather, it will emerge from a thoughtful exploration of whether a society, or a network of global societies, could provide and broadly distribute social benefits without cranking up the engine of growth—without relying on constant increases in economic activity, intensity of land use, desire for products, consumption of resources, generation of waste, and increase of population—or, alternatively, whether growth *in some form*, perhaps quite different from what we are familiar with, could provide and broadly distribute social benefits without constantly threatening the stability and heritage of communities.

These are among the fundamental questions of our time, and the answers we propose will determine the success of the preservation venture in important ways. Preservationists must grapple with them if they intend to win more than a skirmish in a steadily retreating line of battle. They should contribute their special knowledge and ways of looking at the world towards solving them. This can only happen if they dare to take the first and most difficult step: to publicly question the ideology of growth.

THE MARKET WILL NOT SOLVE OUR PROBLEMS

Closely linked to growth is the ideology of the market: the faith that market forces will solve all problems and resolve all questions of value or policy. This is absurd on its face: the market, quite evidently, has not solved all problems, certainly not those having to do with the preservation of buildings, communities, and cities, though it has undeniably dominated the development of policy. Like belief in growth, faith in the market is an ideology that preservationists have not sufficiently questioned. Yet they must if they are serious about turning the tide of destruction.

Preservation's market posture mirrors its stance on growth: "I support the free and unfettered operation of the market—just not in this particular instance." *Here* we need a little regulation, a little subsidy, but only to help out the market: in fact, to increase its profits. The preservationist sees herself as David with a black belt, harnessing Goliath's immense market strength to achieve preservation victories in the form of National Register listings or rehabilitated buildings. The tactic has worked well. The problem is that Goliath gets up from each encounter unweakened. Real estate judo is a good way to manage a tactical retreat: the problem is that the market will continue to move capital around at will, disinvesting here and overdeveloping there, following instincts rooted in profit rather than in community character, social equity, quality of life, historical memory, architectural connoisseurship, or any of the other values in which historic preservation trades.

There are other problems with the preservationist stance. It forces preservationists to play the capitalist's game, with rules that capitalists understand better. This can be a shaky position, with preservationists defending profit when the important values at stake are in fact non-monetary; and it can be a weak one, when their arguments fail.[5] None of this is to deny the real estate accomplishments of preservationists, to question the value of the professional skills that have been built up in the course of achieving them, or to suggest that preservationists should abandon the real estate arena any time soon. However, while preservationists elect for tactical reasons to play the market game, they should never forget that their most enduring strategic strengths are cultural, historical, aesthetic, and communitarian, and that broad, lasting success can come only from them.

Unfortunately, loyalty to the market makes the effective deployment of these powerful assets less likely because it constrains preservationists from asking the strategic question of whether a better alternative to the market might be devised—one whose rules might be more favorable to preservation's broad goals, the conservation of historic architecture, neighborhoods, and cultural heritage. Casting preservation as the handmaiden to capital anchors the imagination in the here-and-now of a familiar battlefield on which we are almost as comfortable losing as winning, foreclosing many interesting possibilities for cultural action. And it dims the prospects for an energetic campaign that could push back the lines of engagement and perhaps even transform its rules.

WE CAN CHANGE THE RULES OF THE GAME

At an environmental conference in Westchester County a few years ago, an audience member asked what he could do to solve the region's burgeoning environmental problems. The speaker suggested he buy soap instead of detergent and clean up after washing the car. I found this an appalling answer. Was it truly the best that the environmental movement had to offer? Was this indeed the same environmental movement that brought us the Clean Air Act, the Clean Water Act, the Wilderness Act? That took the lead out of the air and the PCBs out of the water? That achieved these huge advances not by appeals to voluntarism but by laws and regulations—democratically enacted rules that are backed up by the full force of society's legal machinery?

I said something of the sort. In reply, the speaker advised me to consider the current political climate: did I not think this was a bad time to be talking about new laws and regulations?

It was indeed a bad time for environmentalists, and for the environment. But it was *precisely* the time to be talking about new laws and regulations, and not only laws and regulations but a broad program to advance preservationist values. Not timid tactical gestures but grand programmatic sweeps, bold assertions of value, improbable visions, laws, regulations, and perhaps even taxes that cannot possibly be enacted in today's climate: that is what we need now.

Our society's antipathy to law is truly tragic. We seem to have been remolded from citizens into consumers: to have accepted the lie that consumer choice constitutes the fullest expression of our values as individuals and as a society. But we are not only consumers. We are also friends, colleagues, family members, neighbors, volunteers, and citizens. In each of these roles we make choices. Laws, binding expectations, rules, and regulations can be profound expressions of the values that we, as citizens, choose to live by. Though not perfect, they are among the best instruments we have to mold the society that, as citizens, we want. Preservationists should not fear legislation as an expression of community values.

Of course, no ambitious program of new preservation legislation can be enacted in 2003. But that is no reason to defer thinking, designing, advocating, and preparing for the time when it may become possible. That time may be ten, twenty, or thirty years in the future. But, without preparation now, it will never come; or, if it does, the opportunity will be missed. What is needed is a beginning, a bold imagining of things that many will dismiss as impossible simply because they are impossible *today*.

There are many good legislative ideas within the preservation profession today, in stages ranging from energetic advocacy to wishful thinking. Many preservationists, including National Trust president Richard Moe, have pointed out that current tax laws tip the economic scales in favor of demolishing rather than rehabilitating old buildings: why not level the playing field by changing them?[6] Back in the fuel shortage of the 1970s, important studies were done on the energy embodied in the materials of old buildings—energy that is wasted and must be duplicated when they are torn down rather than reused:[7] why not anticipate the next spike in energy prices by preparing measures to encourage the conservation of embodied energy? The National Trust has launched an important campaign against suburban sprawl: there are dozens if not hundreds of measures that could control sprawl. In New York State, organizations including the New York Landmarks Conservancy and the Preservation League of New York State have taken the lead in advancing a legislative proposal for a homeowner's tax credit that would encourage the homeowners to invest in maintaining their houses. The problem is not that preservationists have abandoned the legislative arena, for they have not. But what is needed now is ideas that are bigger than single pieces of legislation, ideas that paint bold pictures of a better society founded on preservationist values. Legislative proposals on their own are good: coupled with big ideas they can be even better.

What might big ideas for a preservationist society look like? In a preservationist society, pieces of property would be treated first as places where people live, work, or play, and only secondarily as a real estate commodity to be traded for profit. People would have not only a language but also legal tools with which to express their intentions for their own places. In a preservationist society, communities settled in places would be able to determine their own destinies. People would still be able to choose change, but they would be able to choose it on their terms, and they could *also* choose stability. They would no longer be at the mercy of free-flowing capital and the market. In a preservationist society, communities would be able to provide and protect the shared resources through which their members express their cohabitation in place— public libraries, subways, favorite fishing holes, informal routes through fields or forests. In a preservationist society, resources would be cherished, reused, maintained, and kept in service—not thrown away like gnawed bones. A preservationist society would recognize the tremendous investments that communities make in their places—investments of memory, tradition, and hard work—as a form of wealth to be carefully increased, not an obstacle to gain. In a preservationist society, finally, historic sites, markers, and museums would present the experience of all groups in the land—of immigrant farm workers, African American slaves, homemakers, great musicians, and former presidents.

There is no dearth of ideas, no shortage of goals to be met. What is needed is the courage to propose, and the patience to pursue, them.

THINKING, TALKING, ORGANIZING

Enacting big ideas will also demand immense inputs of energy and organization. Unfortunately, it is not easy to see where these will come from, given the chronically under-funded and under-staffed condition of most preservation agencies, plus their tendency to focus on short-term goals (putting out fires and raising funds). Their organizational structure is problematic too, for it generally entrusts policy development to wealthy and well-placed trustees whose interests are typically better served by the status quo than by most alternatives to it. Nevertheless, a way forward must be found.

One way or another, the preservation movement must devote a larger share of its resources to thinking and planning on a ten-, twenty-, or thirty-year horizon. That means putting resources into undertakings which have no immediate application. It also means thinking expansively, abstractly, and politically; researching, writing, publishing, debating; and always relentlessly enlarging the public space onto which big preservation ideas can be projected. In twenty years, it is possible that ideas dismissed as politically absurd today may be debated and even enacted—but only if preservationists are willing to devote current resources to future returns that could be substantial but are far from certain.

One mechanism for doing this would be a preservation policy institute or think-tank—or several. Professional schools could also play an important role. In the United States, as of 2003, there are twenty-six professional degree programs in historic preservation. Mostly they teach the tools of the trade, and appropriately so. They train students to deal effectively with questions of mortar analysis, architectural design, and historical interpretation. But in the "real world," by the time these decisions need to be made, the most important issues have already been settled, many of them at the level of assumption or underlying policy. In short, the schools are training professionals to act competently within the confines of a game whose rules others have already established. They are not training leaders to grasp the full complexities of the game, much less to rewrite its rules.

This is not a failure of the curriculum so much as it is the loss of an opportunity to go beyond the curriculum, to use the schools' tremendous thinking, convening, organizing, and fundraising power to float the preservation enterprise far beyond where the curriculum could take it. Why teach only preservation professionals? The schools could also teach lawyers, journalists, real estate developers, and government officials—all people with a capacity to influence outcomes. They could supplement the professional discourse with proposals that engage policy and values at a profound level. They could convene working groups to debate and advance these proposals. They could publish them. They could form partnerships with foundations or other research institutes to create hatcheries for big preservation ideas.

Unfortunately, in the wake of the stolen presidential election of 2000, many people feel understandably cynical about national politics. It is indeed hard to believe that our corrupted system of national politics could once again become the engine for progress towards a more democratic and preservation-minded society, one in which greed is curbed, scarce resources are conserved, and communities of place have some control over their destinies. Some faith in this possibility would seem to be a prerequisite for action. Fortunately, however, there are other arenas in which to work. National elections, after all, are not so much the content of democracy as its most formal expression. In a vibrant democracy they would stand atop a robust foundation of civic activism. America has a tradition of such activism, and the preservation movement has been a vital part of it. While there is some evidence that America's tradition of citizen engagement is ailing, it is far from dead,[8] and the sickness of our national politics should not discourage preservationists from working at the local level.

There could not be a better time to do so. There is a ferment of ideas and energy in community planning: new planning techniques, a growing field of community economic development, creative ventures in community cultural development.[9] To participate in this unfolding movement, preservation will not have to do anything dramatically new, but it may have to do things a little differently. For, while preservation can point to a history of great campaigns pursued at the community level, these campaigns have sometimes merited the accusation of being elitist or narrow in scope. Not that preservation groups have refused to embrace racially, ethnically, or economically diverse citizens. But it is one thing to welcome diverse adherents to your cause, another to craft a cause that is broadly inclusive of diverse needs and values. The former requires only good will; the latter also demands willingness to bend and enlarge one's thinking, to move beyond professional discourse and embrace the full scope of what communities enjoy and expect in places. How fortunate would communities be if the insights of preservation could be merged with those of community economic and cultural development in a single coherent movement for the nurturing of place and community. And how great the gain for preservation!

HISTORY IS IMPORTANT, AND IT IS NOT OVER

One would think that the oldness of places would be one of preservation's proudest arguments. Yet how timid preservationists are, how apologetic, in standing up for oldness! How readily they concede this crucially important territory. You are right, they say to the apostles of growth, newness is better than oldness, but please make an allowance for *this* old building, for there is something special about it, something exceptional. Yet perhaps this special old building is not such an exception; perhaps there are positive values that are inherent in oldness and are to be found only in old buildings.

Societies have long recognized that old people have certain forms of wisdom that come from living a long time. Relationships with them take on a distinct character by virtue of their duration, another manifestation of age. People recognize intrinsic value in the oldness of plants too. A mature stand of trees has environmental qualities that younger trees lack. And even in the oldness of rocks: it takes a long time to make coal or oil. For that matter, it takes a long time to make rock. The very soil we stand in, and which nourishes our trees, corn, rice, and flowers, is old, and nothing can substitute for time in the making of good soil. Though the scales by which we certify the quality of oldness vary tremendously—three-score-and-ten with people, ten-to-the-ninth with rocks—we live in a world in which oldness carries special qualities. Are buildings, then, valuable only when new, or unless they possess some special, exceptional quality that redeems their oldness?

Though one should not push analogies too far, oldness in buildings does have distinct cultural value: it preserves evidence of past skills (or sometimes lack thereof), anchors sense of place, provides testimony to past events. Oldness also has practical value. As Donovan Rypkema explains, "you cannot build old buildings, and the cost of constructing new buildings is such that they provide only a narrow range of rental options."[10] A thriving local economy will include "small businesses, non-profit organizations, start-up firms, bootstrap entrepreneurs" who cannot pay the high rents commanded by new construction. Old buildings provide ecological niches for essential activities. Without them, settled communities cannot thrive.

One often hears the argument that we are a young society and therefore prone to overlook the values of oldness and indeed of history. This is an excuse, and it is time to debunk it. If we choose to see the United States as an offshoot of European civilization, its roots are old indeed. If we prefer to focus on its debt to Indian lands and cultures, its roots are yet older. Even if we pretend that American history started with the arrival of the first Europeans, we can now look back at 500 years or so of history, which is surely enough to claim a past. Americans of many kinds are trying to do just that: from many quarters the desire to delineate and belong to a history is being heard. And not just an abstract history but a vital and immediate one that can anchor people in communities and communities in places. A revitalized preservation movement can provide these histories.

Preservationists have never ignored history. On the contrary, while academic historians have largely ignored place, preservationists have nurtured the insight that the character and spatial relationships of places are the very stuff of historical experience and sometimes of causation. But preservationists' energy has occasionally been diverted into side streams. While it is good to know the construction chronology of each house in a historic district, good to chart the stylistic evolution of each of its architectural components, it is better to understand how the relationships between people and places have evolved. Though many preservationists appreciate this line of thinking, its power as an organizing tool has hardly begun to be explored. The history of communities in place, of the habitation of places, can be the foundation for preservation as a movement aimed at broad social change. It offers a robust intellectual lever for lifting up an inclusive, humane conception of place and heritage.

Many Americans can afford to take their heritage, or history, more or less for granted. An increasing number cannot and will not. African Americans, for example, whether descendants of southern plantation slaves or of free blacks in seventeenth-century New York, have a stake in the accurate presentation of American history, one that records both their sufferings and their contributions, and sometimes that simply acknowledges their presence. Many other groups in American society have a similar interest, not in order to complain (or boast) but because history offers a way to establish a presence within the public space of political and cultural discourse—and without presence one can hardly hope for leverage. History can't provide adequate housing, end discrimination, or prevent redevelopment, but it can contribute to the debate that is necessary to achieving these goals. It must be said, too, that the history of suffering as well as achievement, of the presence of society's most overlooked as well as its most celebrated actors, is also likely to be far more interesting than the narrow technical reports that preservationists must often write, or the flat and declaratory statements that pass for history at many historic sites.

There is no more important surface on which to project this history than the physical places of American society, which constitute not only historical documents but also a critically important dimension within the space of public discourse. Because places are the physical space that Americans cohabit, they register history's impact in extraordinary ways: slavery on the southern landscape, Mexican and Filipino migrant farm workers on California's, Spanish land grants on the southwest, English colonists on New England, clashes with Native Americans, Hawaiians, and Alaskans everywhere, the garment trade and the international art market on New York, Hollywood on Hollywood. It is a mistake to think that the American landscape has been homogenized by fast food and strip malls: though it may be fast becoming so, American places still show their history in powerful ways. And because, again, they constitute the physical space which Americans cohabit—a sort of tablet that everyone can read—it is crucial that they preserve and present that history accurately, engagingly, passionately.

History is never mere declaration. It is an argument, and a revitalized preservation movement could do more to harness its persuasive power on behalf of communities and peoples—not by slanting but by presenting the full truth of profoundly complex and often painful relationships among people and between people and the land. In so doing, preservation can become a vital and progressive force in the struggle towards a more just society based on preservation values.

Preservationists, of all people, should be inclined to support the claims of historical presence that so many groups are eager to stake out through historical markers, sites, museums, and stabilized communities. True, they may differ in where they wish to place the emphasis: where their constituents may wish to assert, "*We* were here," preservation professionals may prefer the less assertive formulation, "We were *here*." But the concept of "here" is surely vital to a preservation outlook. And its companion, the equally modest "were," amplifies it in ways that go far beyond the implication of mere presence. Those who have been present in the American landscape the longest, American Indians, Native Hawaiians, and Native Alaskans, have also evolved the most profound understanding of what it means to be in place.[11] Their conceptions of the sacredness of places, of their power to instruct as well as sustain, of people's responsibilities towards them, of the consciousness that emerges with habitation in a place, may seem irrelevant to the experiences of more recent immigrants. Yet they are anything but. A deep reverence for the act of inhabitation, manifested in presence and history, is the most powerful corrective to the excesses of growth and the market. Against the view of places as commodities to be traded or thrown away in a pitiless game of growth, preservation can argue a view of place based on history: history of presence, struggle, inhabitation.

And preservationists can do more than argue it. Preservationists have more opportunities than historians to be actors as well as chroniclers of history. They take sides in the struggles over place and heritage, using every available means to advance their side's interests, from grassroots organizing to sophisticated legal maneuvering, financial deal making to legislative lobbying. This is as it should be, though not all historians would agree. Many academic historians, indeed, see history as something enacted by *other* people: according to this view, historians should stand aside and watch. Some go further, arguing that the only genuine historical actors are those who promote growth in some way. According to this view, almost everyone should stand aside and watch. To these historians, history is a chronicle of newness. To cheer on their relentless march to modernism, some paradoxically fall back on a tired notion: that each age possesses a mysterious spirit peculiar to itself, and that it is the responsibility of historical actors to manifest this spirit—a spirit, moreover, that resides only in new developments and new anxieties, never in love of place. These historians do not acknowledge the preservers of places and buildings as legitimate historical actors. They see them rather as trespassers on the stage; they accuse preservationists of obstructing history's rightful evolution.

Nothing, of course, could be more false. The custodians of place and heritage express the desires of millions to wrest some control over the places they inhabit, while nurturing a connection with tradition. Are these feelings not a crucially important facet of our age? Have these millions not as much right to act on history's stage as the builders, financiers, and publicists of growth?

Without preservationists, the evolving story of our places would be a sadly one-sided affair—not so much a history as one half of a telephone conversation. A revitalized preservation movement is needed to speak for the possibility of a society founded in values of place, habitation, history, citizenship, and equity. This is no revolutionary declaration but a call for return—return to the origins of the preservation movement, which lie in social commitment, not remedies for wood rot. I ask preservationists not to throw professionalism overboard but rather to put it in the service of passion—and by that I do not mean the kind of agitation that exhausts itself in looking busy, but rather a precise, prudent commitment to deep-rooted change in the world outside the profession. I do not ask preservationists to return to the social vision that guided the movement's pioneers—all white, all well-to-do, none either immigrant or native—for that would be intolerable. I do ask preservationists to commit themselves and their practice to a social ideal appropriate to the dawn of the twenty-first century: a revitalized notion of citizenship within an equitable society, a public policy based in values of place, an invigorated concept of history, and a healthy skepticism toward growth and market forces. In short, to a passionate struggle to change how society imagines, preserves, and inhabits its heritage—a preservation movement.

NOTES

1. Antoinette Lee, "From Tennis Shoes to Sensible Pumps: How Historic Preservation Went from a Passion to a Profession," *History News* (2002).

2. Speech by Ronald F. Lee, February 4, 1964, to the New Jersey State Planning Conference, Trenton, NJ: typescript, Records of the Northeast Field Office, National Park Service, General Correspondence 1952–66, entry 414B: National Archives, Philadelphia.

3. An eclectic, personal, and incomplete selection of sources for this nascent understanding of place would include, in addition to the works on community planning and Native American senses of place cited in notes 9 and 11 to this chapter, the following: Irwin Altman and Setha M. Low (eds.), *Place Attachment* (New York and London: Plenum Press, 1992); Robert R. Archibald, *A Place to Remember: Using History to Build Community* (Walnut Creek, CA: AltaMira Press, 1999); Robert N. Bellah, Richard Madsen, William M. Sullivan, Ann Swidler, and Steven M. Tipton, *Habits of the Heart: Individualism and Commitment in American Life* (Berkeley: University of California Press, 1985); Wendell Berry, *The Unsettling of America: Culture and Agriculture* (San Francisco: Sierra Club Books, 1977); Philip Brick, Donald Snow, and Sarah van de Wetering (eds.), *Across the Great Divide: Explorations in Collaborative Conservation and the American West* (Washington, DC: Island Press, 2001); Robert D. Bullard (ed.), *Confronting Environmental Racism: Voices from the Grassroots* (Boston, MA: South End Press, 1993); Denis Byrne and Maria Nugent, *Mapping Attachment: A Spatial Approach to Aboriginal Post-Contact Heritage* (Sydney: New South Wales Department of Environment and Conservation, 2004); Edward S. Casey, "How to Get from Space to Place in a Fairly Short Stretch of Time: Phenomenological Prolegomena," in Steven Feld and Keith H. Basso (eds.), *Senses of Place* (Santa Fe, NM: School of American Research Press, 1996), 13–52; Sue Clifford and Angela King (eds.), *Local Distinctiveness:*

Place, Particularity and Identity (London: Common Ground, 1993); Michael Conzen (ed.), *The Making of the American Landscape* (New York and London: Unwin Hyman, 1990); Anthony English, *The Sea and the Rock Gives Us a Feed: Mapping and Managing Gumbaingirr Wild Resource Use Places* (Sydney: New South Wales National Parks and Wildlife Service, 2002); Larry R. Ford, *Cities and Buildings: Skyscrapers, Skid Rows, and Suburbs* (Baltimore, MD and London: Johns Hopkins University Press, 1994); Paul Groth, "Frameworks for Cultural Landscape Study," in Paul Groth and Todd W. Bressi (eds.), *Understanding Ordinary Landscapes* (New Haven, CT: Yale University Press, 1997); Dolores Hayden, *The Power of Place: Urban Landscapes as Public History* (Cambridge, MA, and London: MIT Press, 1995); Tony Hiss, *The Experience of Place* (New York: Vintage Books, 1991); Mary Hufford (ed.), *Conserving Culture: A New Discourse on Heritage* (Urbana: University of Illinois Press, 1994); John Brinckerhoff Jackson, *Discovering the Vernacular Landscape* (New Haven, CT: Yale University Press, 1984); John Brinckerhoff Jackson, *Landscape in Sight: Looking at America*, ed. Helen Lefkowitz Horowitz (New Haven, CT: Yale University Press, 1997); Chris Johnson, *What Is Social Value? A Discussion Paper*, Australian Heritage Commission Technical Publications, Series No. 3 (Canberra: Australian Government Publishing Service, 1992); Daniel Kemmis, *Community and the Politics of Place* (Norman: University of Oklahoma Press, 1990); William Kittredge and Annick Smith (eds.), *The Last Best Place: A Montana Anthology* (Seattle: University of Washington Press, 1991); James Howard Kunstler, *The Geography of Nowhere: The Rise and Decline of America's Man-Made Landscape* (New York: Simon & Schuster, 1993); Aldo Leopold, *A Sand County Almanac* (Oxford and New York: Oxford University Press, 1949); John R. Logan and Harvey L. Molotch, *Urban Fortunes: The Political Economy of Place* (Berkeley: University of California Press, 1987); J. E. Lovelock, *Gaia: A New Look at Life on Earth* (Oxford and New York: Oxford University Press, 1987); Peter Marquis-Kyle and Meredith Walker, *The Illustrated Burra Charter: Making Good Decisions about the Care of Important Places* (Canberra: Australian Heritage Commission, 1992); John Hanson Mitchell, *Trespassing: An Inquiry into the Private Ownership of Land* (Reading, MA: Addison-Wesley, 1998); Richard Moe and Carter Wilkie, *Changing Places: Rebuilding Community in the Age of Sprawl* (New York: Henry Holt & Co., 1997); Bud Moore, *The Lochsa Story: Land Ethics in the Bitterroot Mountains* (Missoula, MT: Mountain Press Publishing, 1996); Myron Orfield, *Metropolitics: A Regional Agenda for Community and Stability* (Washington, DC and Cambridge, MA: Brookings Institution Press, Lincoln Institute of Land Policy, 1997); Orion Society, *Into the Field: A Guide to Locally Focused Teaching* (Great Barrington, MA: Orion Society, 1999); Patricia F. Parker and Thomas F. King, *Guidelines for Evaluating and Documenting Traditional Cultural Properties*, National Register Bulletin No. 38 (Washington, DC: U.S. Department of the Interior, National Park Service, 1992); Matthew Potteiger and Jamie Purinton, *Landscape Narratives: Design Practices for Telling Stories* (New York: J. Wiley, 1998); Michael H. Shuman, *Going Local: Creating Self-Reliant Communities in a Global Age* (New York: Routledge, 2000); Wallace Stegner, *Beyond the Hundredth Meridian: John Wesley Powell and the Second Opening of the West* (Boston, MA: Houghton Mifflin, 1954); Carter Thomas and Carl Fleischhauer, *The Grouse Creek Survey: Integrating Folklife and Historic Preservation Field Research* (Washington, DC: Library of Congress, 1988); "Towards a Common Method for Assessing Mixed Cultural and Natural Resources: A Case Study Approach, A Cross-Disciplinary Conference. Conference Report" (Howard Gilman Foundation and World Monuments Fund, White Oak, FL, n.d.); and Yi-Fu Tuan, *Topophilia: A Study of Environmental Perception, Attitudes, and Values* (Englewood Cliffs, NJ: Prentice-Hall, 1974).

4. John R. Logan and Harvey L. Molotch, *Urban Fortunes: The Political Economy of Place* (Berkeley: University of California Press, 1987).

5. I am influenced in this argument by the insights of Daniel Bluestone, expressed in conversation.

6. Richard Moe and Carter Wilkie, *Changing Places: Rebuilding Community in the Age of Sprawl* (New York: Henry Holt & Co., 1997).

7. Advisory Council on Historic Preservation, *Assessing the Energy Conservation Benefits of Historic Preservation: Methods and Examples* (Washington, DC: Advisory Council on Historic Preservation, 1979); National Trust for Historic Preservation, *New Energy from Old Buildings* (Washington, DC: Preservation Press, 1981).

8. Robert D. Putnam, *Bowling Alone: The Collapse and Revival of American Community* (New York: Simon & Schuster, 2000).

9. See, for example: John P. Kretzmann and John L. McKnight, *Building Communities from the Inside Out: A Path Toward Finding and Mobilizing a Community's Assets* (Chicago: ACTA Publications, 1993); Ted Jojola, "Indigenous Planning and Community Development," *Traditional Dwellings and Settlements Review* (forthcoming; paper read in manuscript); Edward J. Blakely and Ted K. Bradshaw, *Planning Local Economic Development: Theory and Practice* (Thousand Oaks, CA, London, and New Delhi: Sage, 2002); Don Adams and Arlene Goldbard, *Creative Community: The Art of Cultural Development* (New York: Rockefeller Foundation, 2001).

10. Donovan D. Rypkema, *The Economics of Historic Preservation: A Community Leader's Guide* (Washington, DC: National Trust for Historic Preservation, 1994), 61.

11. See, for example, Keith Basso, *Wisdom Sits in Places: Landscape and Language among the Western Apache* (Albuquerque: University of New Mexico Press, 1996); Andrew Gulliford, *Sacred Objects and Sacred Places: Preserving Tribal Traditions* (Niwot: University Press of Colorado, 2000); Klara Bonsack Kelly and Harris Francis, *Navajo Sacred Places* (Bloomington: Indiana University Press, 1994); *Keepers of the Treasures: Protecting Historic Properties and Cultural Traditions on Indian Lands. A Report on Tribal Preservation Funding Needs Submitted to Congress by the National Park Service* (Washington, DC: U.S. Department of the Interior, National Park Service, Interagency Resources Division, 1990); Patricia F. Parker and Thomas F. King, *Guidelines for Evaluating and Documenting Traditional Cultural Properties*, National Register Bulletin No. 38 (Washington, DC: U.S. Department of the Interior, National Park Service, 1992); Jan Becket and Joseph Singer, *Pana O'ahu: Sacred Stones, Sacred Land* (Honolulu: University of Hawaii Press, 1999); Thomas R. Berger, *Village Journey: The Report of the Alaska Native Review Commission* (New York: Hill & Wang, 1985); Ted Jojola, op. cit.

INDEX